The Economist
BUSINESS
TRAVELLER'S
GUIDES

UNITED STATES

The Economist BUSINESS *TRAVELLER'S* GUIDES

UNITED STATES

The Economist
PUBLICATIONS

PRENTICE HALL PRESS
NEW YORK

This edition published in the United States and Canada in 1987 by Prentice Hall Press
A division of Simon & Schuster, Inc.
Gulf + Western Building
One Gulf + Western Plaza
New York, New York 10023

Guidebook information is notoriously subject to being outdated by changes to telephone numbers and opening hours, and by fluctuating hotel and restaurant standards. While every care has been taken in the preparation of this guide, the publishers cannot accept any liability for any consequences arising from the use of information contained herein.

Where opinion is expressed it is that of the author, which does not necessarily coincide with the editorial views of The Economist newspaper.

The publishers welcome corrections and suggestions from business travellers; please write to The Editor, *The Economist Business Traveller's Guides*, 40 Duke Street, London W1A 1DW, United Kingdom.

Series Editor Stephen Brough
Editors Lisa Cussans, John Farndon, Iain Redpath
Designers Mel Petersen, Alistair Plumb

Contributors Steve O'Connor, Lynn Feldman, Michael Frenchman, Robert Heller, Herbert Livesey, Jack Stephenson, John Whelan
City research Michelle Beardon-Mason, Michael Berryhill, Suzanne Stone Burke, Bob Case, Tom Derr, Nadine Epstein, Eileen Evans, Rick Eyerdam, Laura Garner, Teresa Sullivan Gubbins, Steve Higginbottom, Joanna Hoffman, Caryl Jaeggli, Elizabeth Jewell, Iris Jones, Susan Kaye, Mary Lance, Katherine Larkin, Catherine Lynch, Virginia McLean, Pat Maloney, Chris Michie, Jilian Mincer, Joe Poliforni, Paul Siegel, Tittle Gottlieb and Associates, Leslie Tweeton, Carla Waldemar, Tina Winn, Deborah Wise

Library of Congress Cataloging in Publication Data

The Economist business traveller's guide. United States.

Includes index.
1. United States – Description and travel – 1981- – Guide-books.
2. Business travel – United States – Guide-books. 3. United States – Commerce – Handbooks, manuals, etc.
I. Economist (London, England)
E158.E24 1987 917.3'04927
87–2264
ISBN 0–13–234881–0

Maps and diagrams by Eugene Fleury
Typeset by SB Datagraphics, Colchester, England
Printed in Italy by Arnoldo Mondadori, Verona

Contents

Glossary 6
Using the guide 7
Introduction 8

The Economic Scene
Natural resources 10
Human resources 12
International trade 14
The nation's finances 17

The Industrial Scene
Industry and investment 20
The top ten US companies 22
Oil and chemicals 24
Pharmaceuticals & biotechnology 26
The motor industry 28
Defense and aerospace 30
Computers and software 32
Telecommunications 34
Utilities 35
Retailing 36
The food industry 37
Media and entertainment 38

The Political Scene
The government of the nation 40
The reins of power 43
Party politics 47
National security 48
International alignments 50

The Business Scene
Government and business 52
Power in business 54
Business framework 56
Employment 64
Financial institutions 68
Commercial banks 69
Investment banks 71
Financial markets 72
Insurance 74
Accountants 75
Law 77
Advertising and PR 79
Importing and exporting 80
Distribution 81

Business Awareness
Working hours and attitudes 82
Corporate hierarchies 84
The business method 86
The business media 91

Cultural Awareness
A historical perspective 92
Beliefs, attitudes and lifestyles 95
Education 97
Living standards 98

City by City
Introduction and US map 100
Atlanta 102
Boston 110
Chicago 122
Cleveland 141
Dallas 149
Fort Worth 158
Denver 162
Detroit 169
Houston 177
Kansas City 186
Los Angeles 192
Memphis 208
Miami 214
Minneapolis/St Paul 222
New Orleans 230
New York 238
Philadelphia 278
Phoenix 288
Pittsburgh 294
St Louis 300
San Antonio 307
San Diego 313
San Francisco 319
Silicon Valley 334
Seattle 337
Washington 343
Baltimore 359

Planning and Reference
Entry details 366
Climate 366
Information sources 367
Holidays 368
Money 368
Getting there 369
Getting around 369
Hotels 371
Vintage chart 373
Restaurants 373
Bars 374
Shopping 374
Crime 375
Embassies 375
Health care 376
Communications 376
Dialing codes 378
Conversion charts 379
Index 380

Glossary

ABA American Bankers' Association.
ABM systems Anti-Ballistic Missile systems. Their development was banned under a 1972 treaty with the USSR.
Affirmative action Reducing racial inequalities by positively discriminating in favor of blacks and other minorities.
Arbitrage Trade in shares of companies involved in takeover struggles.
Bretton Woods US location of meeting in 1944 between 45 non-communist nations, leading to the creation of the International Monetary Fund (IMF) and World Bank.
CEO Chief Executive Officer. The effective head of a corporation.
CIA Central Intelligence Agency. Responsible for gathering intelligence from overseas.
DIA Defense Intelligence Agency. Responsible for military evaluation of allies and potential enemies.
EC European Community, also known as the EEC or Common Market. European free trade organization with 12 member states.
EEP Export enhancement program. A form of export subsidy.
FBI Federal Bureau of Investigation. Responsible for investigation of federal crimes and for some domestic counter-intelligence.
Fed, the The US Federal Reserve. An independent government agency which controls interest rates and the money supply.
FTC Federal Trade Commission. An independent commission set up to regulate competition and fight unfair business practices.
GATT General Agreement on Tariffs and Trade. Instituted in 1947 to liberalize trade and prevent discrimination. Nearly 100 countries are signatories.
Gramm-Rudman targets Statutory annual limits to the US federal budget deficit. If the deficit exceeds the target, the Comptroller-General makes automatic cuts in spending across the board.
Hispanics Spanish-speaking US residents and citizens from Mexico, Puerto Rico, Cuba and the rest of Latin America.
Junk bonds High-yield investment bonds in heavily-borrowed companies. Often used to finance takeover bids.
NATO North Atlantic Treaty Organization. An organization for collective security and defense set up in 1949. Its members include the USA, Canada and most of Western Europe, with the notable exception of France.
NSC National Security Council. An agency of the President's Executive Office which makes policy recommendations on domestic and foreign matters involving national security.
OAS Organization of American States. A political organization embracing the USA and 26 Latin American and Caribbean states.
OECD Organization for Economic Cooperation and Development. A forum for discussion and action on the world economy.
SALT Strategic Arms Limitation Talks. A series of negotiations between the USA and the USSR on nuclear weapons. SALT I lasted from 1969 to 1972; SALT II was negotiated by Carter but rejected by Reagan.
SDI Strategic Defense Initiative. Also known as Star Wars, it is a proposed ABM system based on satellites and laser weaponry.
SEATO South-East Asia Treaty Organization. Southeast Asian equivalent of NATO, dissolved in 1977.
SEC Securities and Exchange Commission. An independent body regulating the buying and selling of stocks and bonds.
START Strategic Arms Reduction Talks. The successor to SALT II. It was suspended in 1983.
USTTA United States Travel and Tourism Administration.
WASP White Anglo-Saxon Protestant.

Using the guide

The Economist Business Traveller's Guide to the United States is an encyclopedia of business and travel information. If in doubt about where to look for specific information, consult either the Contents list or the Index.

City guides

Each city guide follows a standard format: information and advice on arriving, getting around, city areas, hotels, clubs, restaurants, bars, entertainment, shopping, sightseeing, sports and fitness, and a directory of local business and other facilities such as secretarial and translation agencies, couriers, hospitals with 24-hour accident and emergency departments, and telephone-order florists. There is also a map of the city center locating recommended hotels, restaurants and other important addresses.

For easy reference, all main entries for hotels, restaurants and sights are listed alphabetically.

Abbreviations

Credit and charge cards
AE American Express; CB Carte Blanche; DC Diners Club; MC MasterCard (Access); V Visa.
Figures Millions are abbreviated to m; billions (meaning one thousand million) to bn. Trillions are used to mean one thousand billion.

Publisher's note

The Economist Business Traveller's Guides have been prepared for the international marketplace. This particular volume provides, first and foremost, practical information for any business person travelling in the United States. The general background information on customs and etiquette may seem obvious to an American, but it adds an important dimension to the book. Remember, it often pays to know and understand how others see us.

Price bands

Price bands are denoted by symbols (see below). These correspond approximately to the following actual prices at the time of going to press. (Although the actual prices will inevitably go up, the relative price category is likely to remain the same.)

Restaurants
(three-course meal with a half bottle of house wine, coffee, tax and service at 15%)

$	up to $15
$$	$16 to $30
$$$	$31 to $45
$$$$	$46 to $60
$$$$$	over $60
$$$$$	well over $60

Hotels
(one person occupying a standard room, including taxes and service)

$	up to $50
$$	$51 to $80
$$$	$81 to $110
$$$$	$111 to $150
$$$$$	over $150
$$$$$	well over $150

INTRODUCTION

After dominating the world economy for decades, the USA is both justifiably confident and justifiably anxious. The rush of national optimism during President Reagan's first term has left a legacy of faith in the future and an "America-first" enthusiasm. At the same time, the increasingly strong challenge to US industry from abroad has raised doubts – shared widely in American society – about how well the USA can compete in world markets.

At the end of World War II, the economies of Europe and Japan were in tatters, and the USA was able to make the most of the opportunity, powering its way to a position of world economic supremacy. For some time in the 1950s and 1960s, US industry cornered more than a quarter of the international market in manufactured goods, and Americans enjoyed a standard of living higher than any in the world. But since then the crown has slipped.

The USA is still the world's leading economy by a long way. But, for over a decade, it has lost ground to dynamic nations like Japan and West Germany. The US share of the international manufactures market has dropped to 11%, and Americans have slipped to fifth place in the standard of living league, behind Switzerland, Denmark, West Germany and Sweden. More worrying are the USA's yawning trade gap, which reached a record $165bn in 1986, and the nation's overseas debt – now about $700bn.

Years of recession

Economic performance first became a pressing public issue in the 1970s, when, for the first time since the war, the underlying growth of the US economy began to slow. The Carter administration tried to help US exports by allowing the dollar to slide, but succeeded only in accelerating inflation and bringing growth almost to a standstill. At this time, too, imports from Japan began to make deep inroads into the US domestic market. In 1980, for the first time ever, Japan manufactured more cars and trucks and produced more crude steel than the USA.

As the recession deepened and the USA faced embarrassment over the failure to retrieve US hostages held in Iran, Americans elected as president the robustly patriotic Ronald Reagan to restore their ailing fortunes. Reagan came to power in 1981 promising to recapture an earlier sense of security, revive progress and restore national self-confidence. President Reagan's solutions to the nation's malaise were partly a dose of traditional republican nostrums – greater defense expenditures, reduced government spending on social programs and increased reliance on the marketplace – and partly something entirely novel. A sharp reduction in personal taxation, he argued, would transform the supply-side of the economy by providing much greater incentives to work and succeed. A wave of entrepreneurialism would lead to faster growth, raising government revenues enough to offset the impact of the tax cuts.

The Reagan years

The verdict on the Reagan years is mixed. Supporters of "Reaganomics" can point to some notable successes. Thanks largely to the tight monetary policies of the Federal Reserve, inflation, running at 13.4% in 1980, has been brought under control and by 1986 was ticking along at little over 3%. Bank interest rates fell from 22% in the final quarter of 1980 to under 7% in 1986. Manufacturing has shown some dramatic improvements in productivity; millions of new jobs have been created in the burgeoning service sector. And exports, after falling in the early 1980s, are beginning to climb once more. To cap it all, the economy is growing steadily again, at around 3% per year.

Reagan's supporters contend that these successes are a clear indication that the corner has been turned, and that the USA is well on the road to economic health. His critics paint a rather different picture. They point out that a strong dollar in the early 1980s coincided with rising consumer demand to generate a surge in imports that has shown little signs of abating. The deliberate weakening of the dollar since 1985 – to allow US industry to compete more effectively abroad – has yet to demonstrably reduce the trade deficit, and the dollar has continued to fall. The federal budget deficit remains stubbornly high. The obverse of the USA's surge in job creation has been the low wages of the newly-hired service workers. And there is a widespread feeling that the living standards of those Americans now reaching maturity will not exceed those of their parents by a handsome margin.

The prospects for growth

As the Reagan administration moves into its last years, the revelations of the arms-dealing with Iran have once again created public unease about the effectiveness and direction of US leadership. Moreover, the administration has come under increasing pressure to erect barriers to protect US trade – something Americans have shunned for over a generation – and to knock down barriers erected by other nations. However, the years of pressure on manufacturing industry have left its surviving elements strong and combative, and US executives seem eager to match the Japanese, Germans and Koreans in the international market. Politicians of every stripe focus on "competitiveness" and set up think-tanks to promote it.

The climate for business in the USA is benign, many argue. Capital is freely available. Unions are weak and cooperative. Government control of business is less of an encumbrance than before. And cuts in top personal tax rates let those who make money keep it. A sturdy, if unspectacular, growth rate is projected through the rest of the decade, and the formidable American business machine will continue to rise to new challenges. As always, Americans put their trust in the future, and focus their attention on the present. The past they consign to historians.

The Economic Scene

Natural resources

Endowed with a wealth of commercially-exploitable natural resources matched by few other nations, the USA is among the top four world producers for a vast number of primary products, ranging from corn to aluminum. It also remains among the leading exporters of many basic food and mineral products. But the US resource base is not without its problems, and many sectors – notably farm products and oil – are facing real difficulties as a fluctuating world situation undermines economic viability; while the need to guarantee supplies of vital oils and minerals remains a key factor in American foreign policy.

Agriculture

US farms account for barely 2.5% of GNP and employ little over 3% of the work force, but their output is vast, and US farm production is rivaled only by that of the Soviet Union. More than enough of most basic commodities is produced to satisfy home need, and the USA is able to export 40% more agricultural produce than it imports. Exports of American grain continue to dominate the world market, and in the mid 1980s the US cornered four fifths of the world corn and soybean export trade, and not far short of 40% of the wheat trade.

US farm production and the world (1983): principal crops

	US as % of world	
	Prod'n	Exports
Wheat	13.5	37.8
Corn for grain	30.7	77.8
Soybeans	54.1	77.4
Rice	1.0	18.1
Tobacco	10.7	17.2
Vegetable oil	14.2	10.8
Cotton	11.5	35.2

Source: *Statistical Abstract of the United States, 1986.*

Cattle remain the most valuable of all agricultural products, and on the great ranches of the western USA and the smaller farms of the South and Midwest, millions of beef cattle are raised, while the Northeast has thousands of dairy farms.

The corn and soybean industry is centered in the Midwest, where many hogs are also raised, while the vast prairies of central USA are covered by acre upon acre of wheat. The Southeast is the focus of tobacco farming, and cotton is grown mainly in the South and Southwest. The other main crops are hay, sorghum (the Great Plains), oats, potatoes, barley, rice and sugar beet.

The demise of the small farmer In the years since World War II, US agriculture has become increasingly capital-intensive, and rising production costs have driven more and more small farmers out of business. The number of farms has more than halved since 1950 – in 1985 there were fewer than 2.3m – while average farm size has more than doubled to over 450 acres, although the total area of farmland has contracted slightly. Large agribusiness units dominate the US farming scene, and in the early 1980s farms with annual sales of over $500,000 accounted for a third of all farm sales.

Farm crisis After a boom in the early 1980s, which saw farm production and profits hit new records, US farms have now run into trouble. Falling world grain prices and over-production have devastated many small farmers in the Midwest, while the rapid decline in agricultural land values since 1982 has hit all farmers. Those who bought land on credit at higher prices at the beginning of the decade are now facing huge repayments on land that has dropped in value by 20% or more, and many US banks have been placed in real difficulties by the spiralling losses on agricultural debt, estimated at $212.5bn in 1984.

Forestry

Almost a third of the land surface of the USA is still covered by forests, although the total forest area is shrinking steadily. The last survey dates from 1977, when there were 737 acres of forest, of which 482m were commercially exploitable. More than 60% of US timber production is concentrated in the states of the Pacific Northwest, notably Oregon, Washington, Alaska and northern California, while the forests of the South produce wood pulp and nearly all US turpentine, pitch, resin and wood tar. In 1977 the USA was producing more than 2.5 trillion board feet of sawn timber, yet it still had to import almost $2bn worth.

Fishing

Despite the thousands of miles of coast, the USA is not a major fishing nation, and it now imports almost as much fish as is caught by its fishermen. In the mid 1980s, the US catch was worth some $2.5bn a year, of which about a third was caught in the Gulf of Mexico – notably in the form of menhaden, oysters and shrimps – a quarter in the Pacific (anchovies, crab, salmon, tuna) and about a sixth in the Atlantic (cod, flounder, haddock, hake and herring).

Minerals

The USA is blessed with commercially-exploitable reserves of virtually every major mineral, and it leads the world in the production of lead, while only the Soviet Union exceeds the US output of copper. The USA is also a major producer of iron ore, gold, molybdenum, silver and zinc. The main zinc deposits lie in the Appalachians and the interior plains, while most other mineral ores are mined in the Rocky Mountains. Although it imports more than 90% of its manganese, bauxite, alumina and cobalt, and a majority of its tin, nickel, potash, tungsten and zinc, the USA is less reliant on foreign sources than most leading industrial nations, and the Federal Emergency Management Agency (FEMA) makes sure there is always an adequate strategic stockpile of vital minerals. The proximity of Canada, the country's major supplier of minerals, further reduces the USA's vulnerability to disruption of supplies.

Energy

Extensive deposits of coal, natural gas, petroleum and uranium make the USA less dependent than most industrialized nations on imported energy. In fact, its oil and natural gas output is exceeded only by the Soviet Union, and its coal output only by China. The USA is essentially self-sufficient in coal, which provides well over half its electricity, and all but self-sufficient in natural gas, which generates a further 11% of US electricity. The high cost of exploiting some of the domestic oil reserves means that 40% of the country's oil must be imported, but US crude oil production is still enormous. In the mid 1980s crude oil production in the USA brought in revenues of more than $80bn – twice the value of US natural gas output and four times the value of the nation's coal output. The nation's great rivers, such as the Colorado and the Columbia, further increase its energy resources, in the form of hydro-electric power. It is the USA's rich energy base, combined with the abundant mineral supplies, that has underpinned the nation's industrial success.

Human resources

There are some 250m people living in the USA today, making it the fourth most populous country in the world, after China (1.03bn), India (746m) and the Soviet Union (275m). But the 1980s have seen a slackening of the vigorous growth – fueled by high birth rates and wave upon wave of immigration – that has trebled the population this century. Now the expansion of the American population is settling down to a steady 1% a year, compared to 1.8% in the 1950s.

An aging nation

Americans are getting older; two significant changes in the nature of US society – the decline in birth rate and the increase in life expectancy – have raised the average age of the US population to over 30. And demographers predict that it may reach 36 by the year 2000.

Fewer children As the birth rate has declined steadily over the last 25 years or so, from a peak of almost 25 per 1,000 population in the 1950s to less than 16, so the number of children has also dropped. Now only 25% or so of the population is under 18 – compared to 35.7% in 1960.

More elderly people
Improvements in health care and lifestyle are helping Americans live longer. The average American man now expects to live to be well over 70, while women expect to live almost to 80. The number of people over 65 has almost doubled (to about 30m) over the last 30 years, and it is estimated that by the end of the century more than 35m Americans – more than 13% of the population – will be over 65.

Observers have expressed considerable doubts about how the country will be able to support such large numbers of economically inactive people and provide all the extra care elderly people need. Even under the budget-cutting Reagan administration, expenditure on health, social security and Medicare has had to increase at almost twice the rate of inflation. But there are a number of positive spin-offs – booming sales of pharmaceuticals and "eventide" homes for the prosperous.

Shifting population

The USA is a vast country, and more than 98% of the land area is classified as rural. Yet 75% of Americans now live in towns, and the current plight of many farmers has renewed the steady drift from country to city and city suburb that has characterized this century.

The most densely populated area remains the Northeast, where vast conurbations and suburbs sprawl into one another to form an almost continuous belt of urban development. But the American population has always been unusually mobile, and as the traditional manufacturing industries in the Northeast and Midwest have declined, more and more Americans have moved West and South, homing in on the high technology industries in the sunbelt states of the South, and the Mountain West. The populations of western states like Nevada, Utah, Arizona and Wyoming have shot up over the past decade, while Texas has become the third most populous state after California and New York. Los Angeles, meanwhile, is set to take over from New York by the year 2000 as the USA's largest city.

It is Florida, though, that is showing the most dynamic growth as more and more people respond to its excellent location for business and travel to Latin America and as many of the growing population of elderly Americans decide to live out their last years in the sun. In the first half of the decade, the population of Florida soared by more than 1.5m.

Immigration

All but a few (6%) of the American population were born in the USA, yet this is a land of immigrants, and there are few Americans who cannot trace their family back to foreign settlers within half a dozen generations or so. Throughout its history the USA has received refugees, fleeing from poverty, war or political persecution – from the poor farmers and peasants who came in their millions from northwest Europe (especially England, Ireland and Germany) during the 19th century, to the well-publicized Soviet defectors of recent years. Not all came voluntarily: half a million Africans were brought here as slaves during the 18th and 19th centuries to work on the plantations. But each group has added its own particular culture and outlook to the American scene.

Today immigration is estimated officially at about 500,000 a year and contributes around 20% of the annual growth in population (twice as much as in the 1950s). Among the most recent arrivals are the Vietnamese "boat people," and it is believed that there are now more than 750,000 people from Vietnam, Cambodia and Laos living in the USA. Each year, many arrive from other parts of Asia, too, notably the Philippines and Korea, swelling the Asian-American population, at latest count, to well over 3.5m. But by far the largest influx comes from Latin America, notably from Mexico, and every year 250,000 "Hispanics" enter the USA legally; many thousands more enter illegally. Most of them head for the West Coast and Texas.

Illegal immigrants Until 1965, the USA barred entry to Asians, but allowed a certain quota of immigrants from most European and American nations. The 1965 Immigration Act, however, abandoned quotas and cut the annual limit to 170,000. Although the Refugee Act of 1980 raised the limit to 320,000, there are still many people who are prepared to risk the consequences of entering the country illegally. Illegal immigrants from Cuba arriving in Florida make headline news, but it is the millions of Hispanics who slip undetected across the southern border of the USA who make up the largest "fugitive" population group. Conservative estimates put the illegal Mexican population alone at more than 5m.

Americans abroad Only during one period have Americans emigrated to any extent. That was during the Depression years of the 1930s, when more people left the country than entered it. Today, the largest group of Americans overseas are the 2.1m military personnel.

Race and work

White people make up about 85% of the population while 12% are black – mainly descendants of slaves from Africa – and 3% other races. The black population is much younger (only 8% are over 65, compared with 13% of the white population) and is growing almost twice as fast as the white population. It is expected that the black population will reach 37.6m by the end of the century. The two other fastest growing racial groups are the 17.6m Hispanics and the 3.6m Asians. Experts predict that Hispanics, who now form 6.5% of the population, will become the largest minority group by the year 2000.

Discrimination continues to be a big issue, and blacks are still at a considerable disadvantage in the job market. Nonetheless, more and more are finding jobs and moving away from the ghettoes into more affluent areas of the big cities. Black-owned businesses have risen since 1970 from 185,000 to more than 235,000. In many ways, it is now Hispanics who are suffering the most acute discrimination, and it is they who provide the cheap, exploited labor in California and Florida as well as New York, not only on the fruit farms but also in the semiconductor industry.

International trade

The sheer size of the US economy means that the USA remains by far the world's largest trading nation and dominates the international trade scene, exporting to and importing from almost 180 different countries. Even though the impact of trade on the economy is proportionally smaller than for virtually any other developed nation – accounting for about 10% of the US GNP compared with 20–25% for Japan and the Western European nations – American trade in the mid 1980s was worth $361.6bn in imports and over $213bn in exports. The strength of the dollar in the early 1980s combined with soaring domestic demand to generate a remarkable surge in imports that shows little sign of abating, even though in the mid 1980s the dollar has declined in value. Exports have been left standing, and the gaping trade deficit created is now a major cause for concern in US financial circles.

Spiralling deficit

The rapid escalation in the trade deficit dates back to the middle of President Reagan's first term in 1982, and many commentators have laid the blame squarely at the door of "Reaganomics," a fiscal policy that, through tax cuts, boosted personal income at the expense of capital investment and generated a huge federal deficit. With domestic interest rates and the exchange rate both high, American exporters lost their competitive edge, while rising levels of personal spending encouraged a massive growth in imports. In the early 1980s, imports to the USA were worth around $270bn, and the trade deficit hovered above the $40bn mark. By 1986, imports had soared by over a third, and the trade deficit had reached $165bn. Exports actually dropped in the years 1982–86 by over $20bn. They have since begun to expand once more, and the growth in imports is expected to shrink to under 5% per annum. But the gap opened up in the mid 1980s is so vast that the trade deficit will dominate US economic thinking for years to come.

Manufacturing exports tumble Americans are acutely sensitive to the fact that it is in manufacturing that the turnaround in trade is most marked. From 1981 to 1985, the US's manufacturing exports actually dropped by 14%, while imports climbed more than 70%, and the USA swallows up more than a quarter of the world's manufacturing exports. After an $11bn surplus in manufacturing trade at the outset of the 1980s, the USA now confronts a deficit in manufactured goods of well over $100bn. In cars and trucks alone the USA runs a trade deficit of over $40bn, while there were negative balances of over $10bn in each of clothing, audio and video equipment, consumer goods, and iron and steel.

The Japanese invasion It is the Japanese who have made the most dramatic inroads into the US market. Japan is closing the gap with Canada as the USA's major trading partner, exporting well over $70bn of goods and services to the USA per year. Yet it imports only around $20bn worth of American produce. The USA's trade deficit with Japan is over $50bn – more than double the next biggest deficit ($22bn with Canada) – continues to rise by billions of dollars each month.

Protectionist pressure As the rising tide of imports begins to lap at the feet of American economic credibility, the administration has been faced by increasing demands in Congress for measures to protect US domestic producers, and President Reagan has deployed his veto on several occasions to block protectionist trade laws. A whole range of tariff barriers and "voluntary quotas" are already in action (see *Importing and exporting*). The administration meanwhile is focusing its attention on knocking down barriers to US exporters, negotiating deals within the General Agreement on Tariffs and Trade (GATT), the Group of Five and other supporters of free trade.

Dollar depreciation To increase American competitiveness abroad, the Reagan administration has attempted to hold down the value of the dollar, and in September 1985 Treasury Secretary James Baker negotiated an agreement with the Group of Five to orchestrate a decline in the value of the dollar. But the ensuing depreciation proved, initially at least, less of a boost to America's trade performance than hoped – essentially because the dollar exchange rate fell primarily against the yen and the deutsche mark and other European currencies. Its value remained high against the currencies of the developing nations of Southeast Asia, such as Taiwan and South Korea, whose exports to the USA soared.

Trading partners

The 1980s have seen the focus of America's trade shift radically away from the traditional European base toward the Pacific Ocean. Remarkably, Japan has all but taken over from Canada as the USA's major supplier, capturing a better than 20% share of US imports, and despite voluntary quotas it seems likely that imports from Japan will continue to rise. At the same time, South Korea, Hong Kong, and Taiwan, especially, have consolidated their status as trading partners at the expense of the Western European nations. Taiwan now ranks as the USA's fifth most important supplier, only a little way behind West Germany and Mexico. Nevertheless, the EC remains an important factor in US trade, just as trade with the USA is of central concern to the EC – a US Commerce Department report estimated that the increase in exports to the USA was responsible for half the EC's growth in 1984 and a quarter in 1985. US exports to Latin America, another traditional focus of trade, have been devastated by the political and economic instabilities there in the 1980s. Small wonder, then, that many American businesses are thrusting their way into new export markets, such as China, South Korea and the Comecon nations.

Main US trading partners (1985)

Exports to	%	Imports from	%
Canada	22.2	Canada	20.4
Japan	10.6	Japan	19.9
Mexico	6.4	W Germany	5.8
UK	5.3	Mexico	5.6
W Germany	4.2	Taiwan	4.6
N'lands	3.4	UK	4.3
France	2.9	S Korea	2.9
S Korea	2.7	Italy	2.8
Belgium	2.3	France	2.6
Italy	2.1	Hong Kong	2.4

Source: *Survey of Current Business*

Key exports

Despite the vast increase in manfacturing imports into the USA in the 1980s, manufacturing remains the dominant sector in the US export trade. Machinery, manufactured goods and transport equipment together made up almost 70% of US exports by value in 1985, and the USA was the origin of 20% of the world's manufactured exports – compared with 18% for West Germany and 16% for Japan. Moreover, the USA is strikingly successful in certain fields – notably the aircraft and defense industries, where the main challenge comes from Europe, not Japan. Boeing and McDonnell Douglas have spearheaded an American aviation export drive so effective that the USA now has a trade surplus of more than $11bn in the aircraft business. But in sectors where the Japanese competition is most intense, US successes are counterbalanced by even more striking Japanese success. US computer exports increased by 77% between 1980 and 1985, but imports rose even faster to cut the US trade surplus in computers by a third. And in sectors such as clothing, where low labor costs are paramount, the continuing high value of the dollar against Third World currencies means that the USA is finding it all but impossible to compete.

But it is the decline of farm product exports from the USA that is perhaps the most significant trend, for as world food import markets shrink and world food production continues to rise, the USA is fast running out of lucrative destinations for its food exports. US food exports are still worth almost $20bn, but their share of US export trade is now well below 10% and dropping every year. Already, competition from Europe, Argentina, Australia and New Zealand for access to the massive Soviet market has hit American grain exports. And soon South Korea, Thailand and Indonesia may try to knock the USA from its perch as top supplier to Japan, the only substantial food importer in the non-communist world.

Key imports

In a nation as dependent upon personal mobility as the USA, it is perhaps hardly surprising that transport dominates the import scene. Car and truck imports have soared over the last decade to become the largest single sector and now account for almost a fifth of all US imports by value at over $80bn, while the fuel needed to run them is the second largest import, making up a further 10% of the import total. These two categories alone accounted for well over half the trade deficit, and the Reagan administration for a time encouraged Japan to limit voluntarily car exports to the USA to prevent the deficit from rising still higher. Officially, however, voluntary restraints no longer exist.

The other major imports are machinery, clothing and footwear, and agricultural products. Significantly, the mid 1980s saw food imports exceed food exports for the first time ever.

Trade in services

Throughout the 1980s, healthy sales of services abroad have helped offset the massive deficits created by the swelling imports of merchandise into the USA. Imports of services have increased steadily throughout the decade and are approaching $125bn a year, but in 1985 there was still a services surplus of $16.6bn. Exports of services now account for more than 40% of the USA's foreign earnings.

Business services are particularly lucrative, and fees and royalties paid on goods made overseas earn the US billions of dollars a year. Insurance, banking and financial institutions are also major money-spinners for the USA, along with construction and engineering services. But the success of the business services sector has been partially offset by the slump in profits in travel and transportation, and the USA has come to rely more and more for its services trade surplus on money brought in by net gains in interest, dividends and profits from the US multinationals' massive overseas assets. Even here, though, there is some cause for concern in US financial circles, for the rapid growth in the stock of foreign-owned assets within the USA itself has been gnawing away at the overall surplus.

The nation's finances

The mid 1980s saw spiralling imports, a high dollar exchange rate and high interest rates wipe away a surplus of $6.4bn on the USA's balance of payments and transform it into a deficit of more than $120bn. For the first time since before World War I, the USA became a debtor nation – in fact, the largest debtor in the world, further into the red even than Brazil and Mexico. Henry Kaufmann of Salomon Brothers estimated that the total debt of the nation has climbed from $1.6 trillion in 1970 to over $8 trillion. The huge debts of the USA are set to become the major influence on the direction of the global economy.

Capital pressures

Throughout the 1980s, the swelling US trade, payments and federal deficits have transformed the economy into a financial "black hole," sucking in money from all over the world. It is now heavily dependent upon foreign capital and maintains high interest rates to obtain a steady flow of money into the country, aided in recent years by increasingly liberal financial laws (such as the repeal of withholding tax in 1984). Japan now has almost twice as much capital invested in the USA as the USA has invested in Japan.

For financial observers in the USA, one of the most worrying factors has been not the rise of capital inflows into the country but the collapse of capital outflows, which have plummeted from $121bn in 1982 to less than $30bn. The high interest rates at home are partly to blame, for they provide little incentive to invest abroad, while cuts in personal taxation have boosted after-tax return on investment. But many banks have been scared off putting their money overseas by Third World countries unable to service the interest on loans. In fact, bank failures have become a real concern in the USA, and the Federal Deposit Insurance Corporation (FDIC) estimates that a tenth of the USA's 14,000 commercial banks are facing difficulties.

Macroeconomic indicators

	1981	1985
GNP at market prices ($bn)	3,053	3,998
Real GNP growth (%)	2.2	2.7
Consumer price inflation (%)	10.4	3.6
Exports *fob* ($bn)	233.7	213.1
Imports *cif* ($bn)	273.4	316.6
Balance of payments ($bn)	6.4	-117.7
Public external debt ($bn)	136.6	214.6

Source: Economist Intelligence Unit

The dollar

Since the Bretton Woods Conference of 1944, the US dollar has been the world's major reserve currency, and it continues to be the reference point for most international financial deals. Japan, for example, holds nearly all its huge foreign investments in dollars – 640bn of them – and refuses to make the yen an international trading currency. Even without its vast economy, the pervasiveness of the dollar would enable the USA to wield influence over the world financial scene.

When the Reagan administration first came to power, it seemed determined to learn from the mistakes of the Carter administration. The Carter approach, by allowing the dollar to slide, stimulated exports but helped to create "stagflation" – a depressed economy combined with accelerated inflation. Under Reagan, the dollar's ailing fortunes were revived by high interest rates and a less strictly regulated financial

Origins of GNP 1985

market prices	% of total
Agriculture, forestry & fishing	2.2
Mining	3.0
Construction	4.6
Manufacturing	20.2
Transport & utilities	9.3
Distributive trades	16.5
Finance, insurance, etc	15.4
Government	11.9
Other services	15.9
Rest of the world	1.0
	100.0

Components of GNP 1985

market prices	% of total
Personal consumption	65.0
Non-residential investment	11.5
Residential investment	4.8
Federal expenditure	8.9
State & local expenditure	11.5
Exports: goods & services	9.2
Imports: goods & services	-11.2
Final sales	99.7
Stockbuilding	0.3
	100.0

Source: Economist Intelligence Unit

climate, and by 1984 its International Monetary Fund (IMF) trade-weighted index had climbed to over 150. But since 1985, the administration has been keen to see the dollar's value falling again, perhaps encouraging the foreign exchange markets with veiled hints.

Expanding economy Despite its debt and export problems, the US economy continues to expand, driven by rising personal consumption. At well over $4 trillion, the USA's GNP is already huge – three times the size of Japan's, six times the size of West Germany's and eight times the size of the UK's. But it is still growing at just under 3% a year in real terms, and most commentators expect this expansion to continue until the end of the decade, though at a reduced rate. Forecasting GNP growth, however, generates enormous contention, for the credibility of the administration's budget plans, among other things, depends on the GNP forecast. The administration's forecast of GNP growth is habitually more optimistic than independent forecasts.

Federal financing

President Reagan first came to power pledging to cut the deficit on government finances. But the Reagan years have seen the US federal deficit escalating to unprecedented levels, as tax cuts slice millions of dollars off receipts while the administration continues to spend heavily on defense. Standing at $57.9bn in the fiscal year 1981, the federal deficit has swelled to more than $170bn and the national debt has now surged to over $2 trillion – double the 1981 figure. Interest payments on the debt alone were expected to swallow up a fifth of the federal budget in 1988.

Beating Congress The budget for the following year (the fiscal year starts on October 1) is prepared by the Office of Management and Budget (using expenditure estimates prepared by each government department) and is submitted to Congress in January. As a result of President Nixon's attempts to sidestep congressional control of finance, Congress has acquired considerable power over the budget, and the budget committees in both House and Senate are now the most important in the legislature.

With the Democrats in control in Congress, the Republican administration has to exert all its powers of persuasion to push its budget proposals through the committees, and its success rate is low. Intense pressure from "special interest" lobbies ensures that the final budget will look very different from the initial proposals.

Gramm-Rudman targets In December 1985, in an attempt to halt the spiralling federal debt, the administration agreed to the Gramm-Rudman-Hollings budget plan. This is designed to balance the budget by 1991 by enforcing mandatory, automatic cuts in expenditure across the board if deficit targets for each year are not met to within $10bn. The scale of the spending cuts needed to achieve the Gramm-Rudman targets is so large, some in Congress believe the administration will never be able to push them through the House, and that President Reagan will eventually be forced to raise taxes instead.

Where the money comes from The bulk of US government money (around 80%) comes from personal taxes and social insurance, while most of the rest comes from corporation income tax (around 10%) and Customs duty (about 4%). But the Reagan administration has tried to reduce the overall burden of taxation on both individuals and corporations, in the belief that tax cuts will stimulate the economy. In its first term, corporate taxes were cut to the point where they contributed only just over 8% of the federal budget. Now the emphasis is more on cuts in personal tax, particularly for high earners. In 1987 sweeping changes in the tax structure were introduced to "simplify" income tax and shift the burden back onto the corporations, mainly through the removal of investment subsidies. To finance these cuts, the administration is attempting to raise money by asset sales, such as the privatization of government oil fields and utilities, and the sale of Amtrak, the nationalized passenger railroad.

Where the money goes The USA spends more money on weapons and the armed forces than any other country in the world (about $300bn) and defense swallows up almost 30% of the entire federal budget. The Reagan administration virtually doubled defense expenditure in its first term, and only persistent opposition in Congress has thwarted plans to boost it still further.

To finance tax cuts and defense spending the welfare budget has been heavily pruned. Income security has now been pared down to 12% of the budget (compared to 14% in 1980) – even though, at over 7%, unemployment is running at double the 1980 rate. Social security spending, the remaining large item of expenditure in the budget (apart from interest payments on the debt), is static at around 20%, despite the steady growth in the elderly population. Education, too, has suffered particularly savage cuts, with 1987 spending expected to be $27.4bn – roughly half the share of the budget it received in 1980.

Federal Budget receipts %

	1980	1987 (est)
Individual tax	47.0	45.4
Corporation tax	12.5	10.2
Soc insurance tax	30.5	35.6
Excise taxes	4.7	4.1
Estate & gift tax	1.3	0.7
Customs duties	1.4	1.5
Misc receipts	2.6	2.5
	100.0	100.0

Federal Budget expenditure %

	1980	1987 (est)
National defense	22.7	28.4
Social security	20.0	21.3
Income security	14.6	11.9
Health & Medicare	9.4	10.6
Education	5.4	2.8
Transportation	3.6	4.3
Veterans' benefits	3.6	2.7
Others	15.2	7.0
Interest	8.9	14.8
Offsetting receipts	-3.4	-3.8
	100.0	100.0

Source: Office of Management and Budget.

The Industrial Scene

Industry and investment

The single most salient fact about American industry is that it no longer enjoys the uncontested world economic hegemony that it maintained during the 1950s and early 1960s, peaking in 1966, the height of the nation's postwar boom. This fall from glory continues to color everything from national politics to the attitude of Americans toward visiting foreign executives.

Decline in manufacturing

Still the world's leading industrial nation, the United States remains a dominant force in the global economy. Its gross national product, at almost $4 trillion, is nearly three times that of Japan, its nearest rival. And, although the heady days when the USA held a 25% share of the world market for manufactured goods are gone, it retains around 11%, compared to Japan's 8%. Yet for more than a decade America has gradually lost ground in comparison to virtually every other industrialized country. The American standard of living, once the highest in the world, is now only fifth, behind that of Switzerland, Denmark, West Germany and Sweden. More significantly, the 1980s have seen the States afflicted with a swelling trade deficit, which reached a record of $148bn in 1985 despite efforts to lower the value of the dollar.

The real significance of America's trade deficits, however, lies not in their size but in their composition. In 1980, when the United States had a $10bn trade deficit with Japan, its largest imports in dollar value from that country were cars, iron and steel plates, truck and tractor chassis, radios, motorbikes, and audio and video tape recorders. Its major exports to Japan were soybeans, corn, fir logs, hemlock logs, coal, wheat and cotton. In other words, from the perspective of its main competitor, the USA seemed little more than a source of agricultural products.

Readjustment In many ways what has been happening to the USA has been less a decline than a reaction to an artificial situation. At the end of World War II the United States, with a huge and intact industrial base and IOUs from most of the industrialized world, found itself in a position of world economic supremacy; in a sense, however, it had only been set up for a fall. It was simply a matter of time before America's rapidly rebuilding European and Asian debtors became vigorous competitors – with the stiffest competition coming from the nations that had had to do the most rebuilding.

What went wrong

A measure of the complexity of America's industrial problems is the wide divergence of opinion among scholars, analysts and politicians as to their causes.

Going soft Many on the right blame excessive government intervention. Welfare payments have sapped the Puritan virtues of Americans, they say, while high taxes have undermined incentives for managers and entrepreneurs. Unions, too, are blamed, for making America's basic smokestack industries uncompetitive by forcing through huge concessions in pay and conditions in the early 1960s. Others look for more complex causes, attributing the decline to the inevitable waning of the technological revolution that radically transformed the world during the middle part of this century.

Quick fix American management, too, has been criticized for adopting a shortsighted, "quick-fix" approach to declining profits. Faced with growing competition from the re-emergent economies of Europe and Japan, it is argued, the managers of America's basic industries have panicked and backed out of the contest. Instead of funding R&D and plant modernization – which might have allowed their industries to retain a competitive edge – managers diverted their declining profits into mergers, takeovers and other kinds of non-productive, but stock market-pleasing, investments. In this way the managers saved their own jobs, but consigned the industries in which their companies had made their name to impoverishment and decline.

Diversification Countless American corporations have followed a similar path away from the product for which they are best known. Singer no longer makes sewing machines, Exxon owns microchip and real estate companies and General Tire has moved into television, radio, cable televison, rocket-propulsion equipment, plastics, bottling and aviation. Diversification has tipped the balance of the US economy away from the production of goods towards the provision of services.

Growth industries

Ever since the turn of the century, the focus of the American economy has been shifting away from manufacturing toward the service industries. But after World War II, the pace of this shift accelerated rapidly. In 1948 the goods-producing industries (agriculture, mining, manufacturing and construction) produced 46% of America's GNP; the service industries (including trade, communications, banking, entertainment, social services) accounted for the other 54%. Now, the service sector's share is more than 66%. The "post-industrial society" may be said to have finally arrived in 1981, when, for the first time, there were more Americans employed in services than in manufacturing.

High technology Clean, sophisticated and expensive, the "high-tech" industries are seen as one of the great hopes for America's industrial future. Between 1982 and 1985, when all other exports fell 10% in volume, the export of high-tech goods such as computers, telecommunications equipment, chemicals, aircraft, plastics and drugs rose by 30%. Indeed, America's high-tech industries have never had a negative balance of trade, and are the group most likely to benefit from the decline of the dollar from its highs in the 1970s.

Productivity While America's fall may have dented its ego and standard of living, there is reason to believe that the US economy will emerge, not weaker, but stronger, leaner and hungrier. For example, while American productivity may not be increasing as rapidly as that of other industrialized countries, its advance is not insignificant. Manufacturing productivity has risen by 4.7% a year during the 1980s, as compared to 1.7% in the rest of the non-farm economy, with the biggest rise coming in the oldest and hardest-hit industries. America's Big Three automakers – GM, Ford and Chrysler – boosted productivity 24% between 1983 and 1984 and had another 16% gain in the following year. It now takes workers in American integrated steel mills 7.5 man-hours to make a ton of steel, as opposed to 10.5 in 1982.

Vast resources The most efficient American industries may never be able to undersell foreign competitors whose labor costs are a tenth or a twentieth of their own, but the USA still has the world's largest economy and has vast human, technological and natural resources. The USA will probably never regain the uncontested industrial hegemony it enjoyed after the war, but it is a long way from becoming a decadent, depressed and ineffectual has-been.

The top ten US companies

International Business Machines

Perhaps America's most admired company, IBM makes everything from typewriters to photocopiers. But its most important product is still the computer, and it retains 70% of the mainframe market and 35% of the personal computer market. In the mid 1980s, however, a slowdown in business capital expenditure and ferocious competition from low-cost imitators ("clones") of its PCs sliced into IBM's growth so much that it was forced to lay off staff through early retirement programs. Now it is even prepared to consider a partial withdrawal from the PC market.

Exxon

Formerly Standard Oil of New Jersey, Exxon is the most substantial fragment of the oil empire founded by John D. Rockefeller in 1870 and split up by the Supreme Court in 1911. Exxon is the world's largest driller, refiner and distributor of petroleum products; it has more than 40 refineries in over 20 nations and subsidiaries or affiliates in another 58. Altogether, Exxon derives 65% of its oil and 75% of its sales from abroad. The company also has important chemicals, minerals, electrical equipment, telecommunications, computer and even real estate subsidiaries. But when oil prices began to fall in 1986, Exxon reacted by cutting its world capital and exploration spending by 26% and streamlining its domestic operations.

General Electric

GE is perhaps best known as a manufacturer of lightbulbs and appliances. But when it took over RCA in 1985, the century-old company took a big step away from manufacturing. Now, 80% of its earnings come from high technology and services, and although GE still makes washing machines, it pumped $11.4bn into its aerospace, factory automation and other high-tech businesses in the early 1980s – nearly six times the amount that went to traditional manufacturing. GE's acquisition of RCA brought it NBC, one of the big three television and radio networks, and GE is also the only non-bank among the nation's top ten business-to-business financers.

General Motors

In 1985, GM had larger revenues than any company in the world and made three out of every five cars sold in the United States. To combat increasingly strong competition from Japan, however, even in the home market, GM has been forced to modernize its plans to boost productivity. GM has also built itself up through alliances and now manufactures a subcompact car in a joint venture with Toyota. In the mid 1980s, it made two important acquisitions: Electronic Data Systems, a computer sevices company that is helping integrate GM's plant automation, and Hughes Aircraft, a major defense contractor.

American Telephone & Telegraph

When AT&T's monopoly over the US telephone service was curtailed in 1984 and the company was ordered to divest its local telephone subsidiaries it lost about two-thirds of its $80bn assets. But in exchange the company was allowed to move into new products and services, including computers. Divestiture was intended to encourage competition for the long distance telephone service, but AT&T managed to maintain more than 80% of this market. It has also held on to its famous Bell research laboratories.

E.I. Du Pont de Nemours

Du Pont is generally known as the developer of such chemical and fiber products as Teflon, Dacron and Lucite. But now more than a third of the company's after tax operating income comes from its oil businesses, especially the recently acquired Conoco. Du Pont is one of the nation's largest suppliers to the electronics industry and has embarked on joint ventures with Philips and British Telecom to develop optical electronic components. The company has also spent billions on biotechnology experiments to develop pesticide resistant crop strains and an AIDS cure.

Sears, Roebuck

Sears is a venerable institution, employing one out of every 200 Americans at more than 3,500 catalogue offices, department stores and other outlets. In recent decades, however, the retail giant has been unsure in which part of a volatile market its fortunes lie, first raising its prices to compete with high-class department stores like Bloomingdale's, then slashing them to compete with the discounters. It now seems to have accepted its middle-of-the-road image, and is expanding its market by opening smaller stores specializing in apparel and home decoration, and business systems. Sears also has major insurance (Allstate), financial services (Dean Witter) and real estate (Coldwell Banker) operations.

BellSouth

BellSouth, an amalgamation of two former Bell System local telephone service subsidiaries, South Central Bell and Southern Bell, came into being on January 1, 1984, as a part of the court-ordered break up of AT&T. Since then the young company's chief struggle has been with federal and state regulators over the precise limits of its operations. BellSouth is bidding against AT&T and other companies for a $4bn contract to provide telephone service to mainland China. In association with FiberLAN, BellSouth also provides fiber optic networks to corporate complexes and office buildings.

Amoco

Amoco is the third largest oil company in the world, behind Exxon and Royal Dutch/Shell. Like the rest of the industry, Amoco was hard hit by the declining crude oil prices of the late 1980s and had to reduce its capital and exploration budget by a third – despite selling off of an unprofitable minerals division, buying back 11.3% of its shares and eliminating 3,200 jobs. Although Amoco's downstream oil operations (refining and distribution) still dominate its business, Amoco derives 11% of its revenues and 7% of its profits from chemical companies, and it has significant interests in biotechnology and solar energy firms.

Ford Motor

Ford's 19% share of the domestic automobile market falls far short of General Motors' nearly 60% share, but Ford has much stronger foreign sales than GM, maintaining market leadership in Britain, Norway and Ireland. The company has been responding to Japanese competition in two main ways: first, by boosting productivity through plant closings and modernization; and second, by an all out effort ("The Alpha Project") to develop a new line of small, competitively-priced cars. However, Ford also plans to import low-cost cars from Taiwan, Mexico and South Korea.

	Market capital* $bn	1985 Sales $bn
IBM	92	50
Exxon	40	87
General Electric	35	28
General Motors	26	96
AT&T	24	35
E.I. du Pont	17	29
Sears, Roebuck	17	41
BellSouth	16	11
Amoco	16	27
Ford Motor	15	53

* Source: *Business Week*, June 26, 1986

Oil and chemicals

The fortunes of the US oil and chemical industries are deeply intertwined, and Du Pont, the nation's premier chemical producer, owns a major oil company, Conoco, while Exxon, the giant of oil firms, owns chemical subsidiaries that collectively rival Du Pont's output. But the effects on each industry of the collapse of world oil prices in the mid 1980s has been markedly different. While cheap oil has plunged some sectors of the US oil industry into deep trouble, many chemical companies have found their production costs slashed, boosting expectations for the immediate future.

Oil

The United States oil industry is big business. More than half the top 20 US companies in the Fortune 500 list are in oil, and the biggest oil company, Exxon, has yearly sales dwarfing the GNP of many countries. But the see-sawing world oil prices of the last decade have had a traumatic effect on the US oil business, exacerbated by the decline in domestic demand in the early 1980s.

Domestic crisis Companies reliant on US production have been devastated by the sharp downturn in oil prices since 1985. Many US fields developed in the 1970s, when the Arab oil embargo pushed the price as high as $40 a barrel, are now proving uneconomic. US wells lift on average only about 14 barrels a day, compared to 5,000 barrels a day for Arabian Gulf wells. For "stripper" wells, which lift under ten barrels a day and make up about 11% of total US production, costs can run up to $15 a barrel, more than the price a barrel was fetching at certain times in 1986. Large numbers of stripper wells and heavy oil-producing properties have already been shut down, and many US producers are going under, or being absorbed by stronger firms. With continued low prices, US output could decline by as much as 3m barrels a day by 1990, and oil imports could climb even higher than the peak import year of 1979. Meanwhile, cheap fuel may encourage both economic expansion and the abandonment of energy-saving measures – both of which will ultimately increase demand for oil.

Scraping the barrel The downturn in home production and the 1986 collapse of oil prices have accelerated the cuts in capital expenditure by US oil companies started when oil prices first began to fall in the early 1980s. Since 1982, partly through the inspiration and intimidation of T. Boone Pickens (chairman and president of Mesa Petroleum), the oil companies have been redirecting tens of billions of dollars away from exploration and development into the pockets of shareholders. They have achieved this in two principal ways: by large-scale buy-outs of other oil companies (Chevron bought Gulf and Texaco bought Getty); and by repurchasing shares (as with Atlantic Richfield and Exxon). The debt thus incurred is often reduced by sales of assets. The oil companies are also reversing the largely disastrous 1970s trend towards diversification and abandoning other operations such as hard minerals, petrochemicals, coal, synthetic fuels and insurance.

Downstream boom In contrast, the downstream end of the petroleum business, refining and marketing, is still buoyant. Lower prices and the reluctance of US tourists to go abroad because of terrorism have boosted domestic demand for gasoline, helping integrated companies that both produce and distribute to ride out the crisis better than those that only produce.

Chemicals

Throughout the 1970s, the chemical industry, like the oil industry, anticipated a future of surging demand and profits. Like the oil industry, it was disappointed. Chemical companies coped with falling demand in the early 1980s by slowing down production to keep pace. But by the mid 1980s the overcapacity the industry built up during the previous decade began to drag on profits. Now, however, as the oil companies tighten their belts, the chemical business is starting to ride high again, benefiting from the crash in oil prices. Even though 90% of all organic chemicals are petrochemicals, the declining oil prices are depressing only the prices of those olefins and aromatics (benzene, for example) that are derived at early stages of the refining process.

The prices of intermediate derivatives and plastic resins may also eventually be pulled down, but not before low production costs and growing demand, both fostered by cheaper oil, have swollen profit margins. High-value-added specialty chemicals, including top-of-the-line polymers, resins, pharmaceuticals, synthetic fibers and pesticides, are already beginning to thrive. International demand for chemicals is expected to grow at a compound rate of 5% a year for the remainder of the decade, and operating profits for the industry should climb substantially.

Cutting back The ground has been prepared for the expected upturn in the fortunes of the industry by a series of massive cutbacks and restructurings. In 1985, Delaware-based E.I. Du Pont de Nemours, the industry leader, retired 11,000 of its domestic employees, while Michigan's Dow Chemical has sold off over $1bn in assets and abandoned plans to develop a polyethylene complex in Saudi Arabia. Connecticut's Union Carbide, which has shed $1bn worth of businesses since 1978, took a $1bn charge for the write-down of assets, including petrochemical facilities, in 1985.

Saudi competiton Although falling oil prices are a temporary boon for the industry, the major chemical firms recognize that they are at a long-term disadvantage compared to the hydrocarbon-rich countries of the Arabian Gulf. Saudi Arabia, for example, has given high priority to the completion of 12 large plants which will enable it to meet 5% of the world's petrochemical demand. The result is that to avoid competing directly, the American chemical industry is moving increasingly in the direction of specialty chemicals and away from basic petrochemical production.

The environmental lobby The US public is extremely ambivalent toward the chemical companies. On the one hand, household products such as Dow's Saran Wrap (plastic wrap) and American Cyanamid's Simonize car wax, are familiar and widely used. On the other hand, chemical companies have been widely criticized for causing air pollution, for improperly dumping toxic wastes (such as dioxin) and for manufacturing war chemicals (Agent Orange, napalm). Nearly all the chemical companies – notably Union Carbide – have had confrontations with environmental groups and federal regulators. At home, Union Carbide's plant in West Virginia has been much in the headlines, while overseas, it was their plant at Bhopal in India that suffered a disastrous leak of methyl isocyanate gas in 1985. Although not always strictly enforced, the laws designed to curb environmental pollution have considerable public support, and chemical companies are sure to fall under increasingly stringent restrictions on the manufacture and transportation of their products, at least within US boundaries.

Pharmaceuticals and biotechnology

By far the world's largest drug-seller, the USA still holds almost a quarter of the world's pharmaceuticals market. But the increasingly lengthy and costly routine of obtaining government approval for new drugs – plus a generally buoyant dollar – has blunted the innovative edge of the US drug industry. New, more flexible laws and new fields of activity, especially biotechnology, may breathe new life into the industry.

Pharmaceuticals

For more than a decade the US pharmaceutical industry's profits have been rising at least 50% faster than those of all other industries. Drug companies' after-tax profits per dollar of sale stand at 13%, compared to 4% for all manufacturers. The steady increase in the number of Americans 65 years old and older has already been a big boost to the pharmaceutical industry; senior citizens make up only 11% of the population, but account for 25% of all prescription drug sales. The population of elderly Americans is expected to rise by 13% during the last half of the 1980s, driving the US per-capita drug expenditure in real terms from $110 in 1984 to $170 in 1990. The number of physicians is also expected to increase by 30% by the end of the decade, with the greatest growth coming in such specialties as family practice in which a large proportion of prescriptions are written.

Soaring development costs In the past, drug prices lagged behind the general inflation rate, but in the 1980s they have soared, increasing by as much as six times the Consumer Price Index. This rapid rise in prices has provoked congressional criticism of the industry for – in the words of Representative Henry A. Waxman, of California – "increasing its profits at the expense of the sick, the poor and the elderly." The drug-makers protest that they are forced to raise prices because of the increasing time and cost of new product development.

Counting failures, it now takes an average of eight years and $97m to bring a new drug successfully onto the market. Much of the added time and expense is the inevitable result of the increasing complexity of new drugs. But the stringent requirements of the US Food and Drug Administration have also contributed. The FDA requires drug-makers to test their products first on animals, then on healthy human volunteers, and then on large samples of the population the drug is intended to treat. The process has grown longer and longer. Drug companies claim that testing now eats up half of their products' 17-year patents, and so half the time when they have the exclusive right to market the drug, free of competition – the "useful life" of the drug. The declining useful life of drugs, maufacturers claim, is a direct cause of the decline in the number of new drugs introduced by US companies each year. Congress, fearing that the United States is losing its long-standing competitive edge over Japan and Western Europe, has recently come to the aid of the drug companies by enacting a law that will extend the patent life for new drugs for an additional five years.

Generic drugs – drugs no longer in patent – are now seen as the future money-spinners of the pharmaceuticals industry. Since the original version of the drug has already been thoroughly tested, it is comparatively easy for generic manufacturers to get FDA approval. Unencumbered by the developer's massive R&D, approval and advertising expenses, the generic manufacturer can market its copy for a tenth of the price of the original. Although generic drugs currently hold only an 18% market share, sales are growing rapidly at 20% a year, ten times as fast as brand-name drugs. Moreover, while the prices of patented drugs have been rocketing, generic drug prices have been holding steady and even falling. This has made them attractive both to consumers, who have seen their medical expenses quintuple since the 1960s, and to insurers, who shoulder some 14% of US drug expenditures. Insurance companies, and employers who provide medical coverage for their employees, are now encouraging patients to ask their doctors to write prescriptions for generic drugs. The Blue Cross and Blue Shield health insurance plans in California, Florida, Iowa and Michigan are offering incentives to choose generics.

The drug companies have been fighting competition from generics partly by pricing their patented drugs higher to maximize profits during the patent life and partly by entering the market themselves. Major brand-name manufacturers such as Parke-Davis, Pfizer, Smith Kline and French and Wyeth Laboratories have all moved into the generic business. With a declining number of new drugs coming onto the market and the ever-growing share of old standards coming off their patents (Valium, for example, came off in 1985) the average cost of medication should start coming down by the 1990s.

Biotechnology

Slower to take off than initially anticipated, biotechnology remains the most exciting and potentially profitable division of the pharmaceuticals industry. From a base of virtually zero in 1980 the market for genetically engineered drugs and chemicals had expanded to $200m by 1985 and could go to $5bn by the end of the decade.

At present there are some 300 US firms involved in commercial biotechnology, about half of them in just four states: California, Massachusetts, New Jersey and New York. By far the majority of these firms are small and were established after 1975, with a flurry of new starts between 1979 and 1983. But about 100 of the firms are older, more established pharmaceutical and chemical companies, such as Bristol-Myers, Eli Lilly and Hoffman-LaRoche, which have slid into the field by establishing in-house research groups, or by funding research and engaging in joint ventures with smaller firms. Alliances with large corporations have recently become the dominant mode of financing for small biotech firms, which often have difficulties meeting their huge R&D costs on their own.

Monoclonal The industry's biggest commercial success to date is monoclonal antibodies. Sales of monoclonal products bring in more than $130m and are expected to earn $2.5bn by 1990.

Farms and arms Biotechnology has considerable potential too in less publicized fields than drugs. Breeds of drought, disease and herbicide-resistant farm plants as well as toxic waste-eaters for the chemical industry are all being developed. So too, controversially, are biological weapons, reversing previous US government policy. Under the Reagan administration, Pentagon spending on germ warfare increased tenfold to $42 million in 1986. More than 20 university, commercial and military labs are developing new and virulent strains of everything from anthrax to snake venom. Molecular Genetics Inc, for example, has a $1.7m contract with the Army to develop a fast-breeding hybrid of the Rift Valley fever virus, a fierce bug normally found only in Africa. The Pentagon's claim is that these weapons will only be used defensively and that the Russians have already violated the treaty by developing such germ weapons as the yellow rain mycotoxin. But the growing weight of public opposition may eventually put a halt to this new research.

The motor industry

Intense competition, both at home and abroad, has forced the US car industry onto the defensive. Already more than one in three cars sold in the United States is imported, and the Japanese share of the US domestic market has climbed to over 24%; without a self-imposed limit of 2.3m units, it could climb even higher. The American launch of the South Korean Hyundai, and the Yugoslavian Yugo, both ultra-low-priced "sub-compacts," only underscored the pressure on the home producers. Extensive automation and a range of cost-cutting schemes have restored the earnings of US car manufacturers to healthy levels – although they have failed to stem the flood of imports. But the leveling out of population growth has curtailed expansion of the market, and the future may see competition fiercer than ever.

Modernization

The mid 1980s saw US automobile manufacturers energetically modernizing and automating plants to bring down unit costs to a level at which they can compete with the Japanese. With $84bn already invested in plant update between 1978 and 1985, they planned to spend a further $100bn by the end of the decade – but there is now doubt about the wisdom of this investment.

General Motors, with revenues larger than the GNP of many countries, spearheaded the drive to automate. By 1986, it had about 5,000 robots in operation, and planned to double this number by 1990. The company also purchased Electronic Data Systems to help it integrate its automation schemes, and it obtained small interests in several machine vision systems companies. But the company's most celebrated modernization venture, its Saturn Project, is being scaled down. This project encompasses every aspect of production in the development of a new family of sub-compact cars incorporating such innovations as modular assembly and Japanese-style "just-in-time" (JIT) parts delivery. Yet the early stages have run into trouble and the project is now considerably less ambitious than first envisaged.

Ford and Chrysler, too, joined the race to modernize, and they have also launched special development projects, christened Alpha and Liberty, respectively. And they too are now having second thoughts.

Besides rationalizing their plants, US car-makers are making cuts right across the board. They are buying an increasing proportion of their parts abroad, and now they are importing and selling vehicles made by minority-owned affiliates in low-wage countries. As part of its Saturn Project, GM is also conducting a labor experiment by paying workers slightly lower wages and offering production bonuses. Chrysler's cost-cutting exercises have been so effective that whereas in 1979 they needed to sell 2.4m cars to break even, now 1.2m is enough.

Car-makers are also by diversifying. GM has always had a big finance subsidiary, but now Chrysler has moved into finance to become one of the nation's largest money companies by purchasing EF Hutton Credit Corp and Bank of America's Finance America Corp. It has also cashed in on the defense boom by buying Gulfstream Aerospace Corp, while GM holds Hughes Aircraft Co, the receiver of the largest private sector contracts of the Star Wars program. And Ford has bought First Nationwide Financial Corp, the holding company of the nation's ninth largest savings and loan association.

Saturated market

The US car industry made huge advances during the first half of the 1980s. Sales increased from 7m vehicles in 1982 to 11.2m in 1985, and productivity hit new record levels. But this buoyant situation may have made the car-makers, especially GM, overconfident; and the mid 1980s have seen GM plagued by overproduction and the need to offer sales incentives every few months to shift cars. In 1986, GM offered loans at steadily decreasing rates, until they reached the rock bottom rate of 2.9%. The incentives worked, but they were costly. GM lost about $1,000 a car at the 2.9% rate of financing. GM's 1986 action was particularly vexing for Ford and Chrysler, which had been enjoying strong sales, but were compelled to follow GM's lead, simply to compete; American Motors went so far as to offer interest-free financing.

The entire automotive industry, regardless of individual successes, is headed for a squeeze produced by forces beyond its control. The driving age population of the US will grow at only a 1% annual rate for the remainder of the decade, as opposed to 2% during the 1970s. This slackening trend, coupled with the slow growth of personal disposable income, means that car sales in the United States will probably hover around the present level of 10–12m a year. Projected production figures for all the companies who are vying for the US market suggests there would be up to 7m more vehicles produced in 1991 than could be sold.

Immigrant plants

To circumvent future import restrictions, the Japanese are beginning to build their own plants in the US. The Japanese produced 250,000 cars in the United States in 1985 and expect to make 900,000 in 1988. The immigrants' share of the US market (predominantly, but not exclusively, Japanese) is expected to rise from 2.5% to 6.5% in 1990. The Japanese are also beginning to collaborate with US companies. Mazda, which has built a plant in Michigan, has a joint marketing deal with Ford, while Toyota has successfully combined with GM to build the Chevrolet Nova in Fremont, California.

Prospects

The number of different models of cars and lightweight trucks on the American market has risen from 190 in the mid 1970s to over 250, and the prospects are for an even greater variety in future. As the competition between domestic and foreign producers intensifies, the consumer is likely to be assailed by a wide range of incentives to buy, and increasing choice. Low maintenance is also held out as a carrot to the consumer. The auto industry publicity mills are already talking about the 1990s as "the decade of the defect-free cars!" when cars, apparently, will become as reliable as televisions and computers. But the Big Three American companies – GM, Ford and Chrysler – may well find an increasing proportion of their profits stemming from their non-automobile businesses.

Trucking future

In the truck market, the prospect that may transform the industry is the "standardized truck". At present, buyers of medium and heavy trucks can customize their vehicles by specifying which components from a wide variety of manufacturers go into their assembly. The standardized truck would reduce the buyer's options but also lower the truck's price by 25%. It is a Japanese and European innovation, however, so if consumers like it, US truck-makers could suffer. The Japanese have the lion's share of the compact pickup truck market, but US manufacturers are maintaining their grip on the market for pickups and also for the van, which retains its popularity as both a work and a pleasure vehicle.

Defense and aerospace

After leaping 20% a year for almost a decade, the phenomenal growth in US government spending on defense procurement finally began to flatten out in the middle of President Reagan's second term. A massive federal deficit and huge escalations in the cost of the most sophisticated weapons, plus a public scandal over the cost of basic parts, were largely to blame. But with $250bn of orders already on the books, commercial airlines buying heavily and President Reagan's Strategic Defense Initiative promising a golden future, the American defense and aerospace industries are still looking fat and sleek.

Military spending

Since 1986, when Congress decided to call a halt to the defense bonanza, US government defense spending has been capped at the inflation rate. Capping has meant not simply a limit on the cash the Pentagon has to spend, but a change in spending patterns as well.

New for old In the past, the mainstay of the defense industry has been multi-billion dollar weapons systems – such as the B-1 bomber or the MX missile – that demand ever more technological sophistication to stay up-to-date. Such is the pace of innovation that the real cost of state-of-the-art fighter planes, for example, quadruples every decade. Faced with a limited budget, the Pentagon is directing spending away from major new systems and investing instead in updating old planes and missiles with the very latest technology. The result is a small boom in defense electronics. The Pentagon's expenditures are expected to rise by only 2.3% annually until the mid-1990s, but the amount spent on electronics should grow at 3.7%. However, the shift to small, highly sophisticated projects means a tightening of profit margins, and defense manufacturers have to win new contracts worth nearly twice the dollar value of former agreements just to keep their earnings level.

The Big Four

Boeing, the Seattle-based industry giant, has ridden out the defense cuts very comfortably by capitalizing on a major spending spree by commercial airlines, which seem to be carrying more passengers every year. A contract from United Airlines brought in a record $3 billion, and Boeing anticipates that commercial jets may soon account for nearly 80% of its sales (compared with little more than 50% in 1985). But the boom in commercial aircraft sales is already showing signs of fading. Declining oil prices have encouraged airlines to stick with their old, fuel-hungry planes for longer, while a spate of airline mergers in the mid 1980s allowed some of Boeing's biggest customers to acquire fleets at bargain prices.

McDonnell Douglas The mid-1980s have seen McDonnell Douglas making an impressive comeback in the commercial aviation business. The company presently holds roughly 20% of the market (second to Boeing's 50%), but as recently as 1982 was delivering only five planes a year and was thought by many analysts to be moving out of the business. The reversal was largely due to James Worsham, president of the firm's Douglas division. In 1984, Worsham took the risk of telling American Airlines that Douglas would build and lease to them 20 narrow-bodied MD-80s that the airline could return with just 30 days' notice if not satisfied. American leaped at the deal and ultimately bought 200 of the planes, making it one of the biggest jet purchases in history. About 85% of McDonnell

Douglas earnings still come from the sale of combat aircraft, however, and the company is in an unusually secure position. Its F-15 and F-18 fighters and its AV-8B Harrier jump jet should all be flying well into the 1990s. McDonnell Douglas has also acquired Hughes Helicopter, which manufactures the AH-64, the US Army's main attack helicopter.

Rockwell International, chief contractor for the ill-fated Space Shuttle, is facing a difficult period. The original four shuttles it built for NASA brought in about $3bn but the future of the shuttle program remains uncertain in the wake of the disaster in 1986 that claimed the lives of seven astronauts. In addition, Rockwell's bread-and-butter contract for the B-1 bomber ended in 1986. Rockwell hopes to limit the damage in part by cashing in on the electronics boom and is designing a navigational system for an Air Force satellite. It is also buffered by its strong commercial business in car and truck parts, factory automation equipment and printing presses.

Lockheed After the complete failure of its L-1011 wide body jet persuaded Lockheed to quit the commercial aviation business in the early 1980s, the company slimmed itself down and poured its resources into a few carefully chosen operations. Now Lockheed specializes in such advanced technology projects as the Trident II ballistic missile, the Milstar satellite communications system and, it is suspected, the top-secret stealth fighter, a plane that is nearly impossible to detect on radar. The company now spends $900m annually on R&D and modernization, focusing its attention on sophisticated electronics to fit existing systems.

Star Wars

The Strategic Defense Initiative, popularly known as "Star Wars," has attracted a great deal of attention. But reaction to the scheme within the defense industry has been mixed. Few people now dismiss it as science fiction, as they once did, but its future is far from assured; for numerous scientific and political doubts as to its viability have yet to be dispelled. If the President's "Peace Shield" does prove viable, the implications for the defense and aerospace industry are enormous, for there could be $500bn worth of contracts available. So far, however, the SDI has been budgeted only at a modest $2–3bn annually for scientific research, although nearly every major defense contractor seems to have at least a small stake. The bulk of this money has gone to the Lawrence Livermore National Laboratory, for the design of a super-laser.

Helicopters

US helicopter manufacturers have been hard hit by a downturn in civilian demand, particularly from abroad. The greatest decline has been in purchases from debt-ridden developing countries. The manufacturers have been saved from a debt crisis of their own, mainly by their military projects. Bell Helicopter and Boeing, for example, have jointly contracted with the US military to produce the tilt-rotor V-22 "Osprey," which is slated to go into service in the early 1990s. Bell has also joined with Dornier of West Germany to promote sales of military helicopters abroad. Sikorsky is involved in a similar project with Short Brothers of Northern Ireland.

The Navy

US shipbuilders have suffered an even worse decline in civilian demand than the helicopter business. In 1986, only eight deep-draft commercial vessels of 1,000 gross tons or over were contracted for, compared with 77 a decade earlier. The slack has been taken up partly by the Navy's accelerated shipbuilding program. The Navy has more than 75 ships on order, including three nuclear aircraft carriers and 22 nuclear submarines.

Computers and software

In the managerial intelligence of the giant IBM or the plucky individualism of Steven Jobs and Stephen Wozniack, founders of Apple, the US computer industry provided the nation with its most inspiring and flattering image of itself for many years. But since 1985 that image has become tarnished. Foreign competition and declining corporate spending have cut the industry's 19% average annual growth by more than half, Steven Jobs has been ousted from Apple, and IBM has had to realize that it can keep its huge profit margins or its market share, but not both.

Computers

The US computer industry is dominated by the International Business Machines Corporation of Armonk, New York. IBM's success has forced most competitors to either copy its best products or find niches where it does not yet dominate. In the mid 1980s IBM's sales were five times as large as its closest competitor, Unisys, and six or seven times those of the Digital Equipment Corporation (DEC).

Big Blue, as IBM is called, is one of the world's most profitable businesses and has set its sights on becoming the world's biggest. Its stated goal has been to maintain at least a 14% annual growth rate, which would make it a $100bn corporation by 1990 and a $200bn corporation by the turn of the century. However, the mid 1980s have seen IBM experiencing its first-ever significant fall-off in growth – apart from a hiccup in the late 1970s. John Akers, IBM's chairman, has attributed the fall-off to the poor corporate spending that has slowed down expansion across the computer industry. But IBM also suffered from problems uniquely its own.

In the mainframe market, IBM's past success has been so marked that now many of its customers have more computing capacity than they know how to use. Sales in this market (of which IBM commands 70%) may not pick up again until businesses can think of new uses for their machines.

In the minicomputer market, however, in order better to compete in what were then widely separated market sectors, IBM decentralized in the early 1970s, giving each division responsibility for its own product. The result is that now few of its machines can easily be interconnected, something that has become an increasing liability. As more and more businesses computerize, they insist that their machines be able to exchange information. IBM has made the creation of specialized software a high priority, but the delay may cause the company to lose ground to DEC.

DEC, whose computers have always been able to "talk" to each other, has been stealing more and more of the market. The signs are that it will soon overtake Unisys and start encroaching on IBM's territory. Digital's biggest threat to IBM is a hardware and software package that allows its VAX minicomputers to invade offices already dominated by IBM products. The package makes communication between IBM (and compatible) PCs and Digital minis as effortless as if they were one system.

IBM clones IBM's extraordinary success with its microcomputers has created a different problem: the flattery of imitation. From Texas to Tokyo, in big factories and in garages, IBM's top-of-the-line PCs are copied, improved upon and undersold. During 1986 alone, the $35bn world market was flooded by 3.6m "clones" – 1m more PCs than IBM sold itself. Clone competition has cut IBM's market share dramatically and forced it to slash the selling price of its machines.

Far and away the most successful of the clones has been Compaq. Formed in 1982, Compaq had, by 1985, achieved sales of more than $500m despite the slump in the market, by pricing machines at the same level as IBM's, and adding a few flashy extras. But since 1985 a new generation of Asian clones has offered all the same extras and more, at a much lower price, biting deep into Compaq's share of the retail market. In 1986, Compaq took the daring step of launching a new top-of-the-line PC, the 386, before IBM had defined the standard for this class of machine.

To combat clone competition IBM has tried to bolster its relationship with dealers, develop new machines selling at more competitive prices, and perhaps move towards PCs that contain hardware and software that competitors cannot imitate. Eventually, however, IBM may have to slim down its 40% profit margins to retain its stake in the market. Chairman Akers has said that if price competition in the PC market becomes too fierce, IBM may partially withdraw.

Apple shines After a bad spell in 1985, when the company suffered its first quarterly loss ever and founder Steven P Jobs was forced out of power in a bitter struggle with John Sculley, the new chairman, Apple has seen a surge of growth. One of the main reasons for Apple's recovery has been the way its once-disappointing Macintosh has finally caught on with business customers, partly for "desktop publishing" of brochures, newsletters and reports. But Apple has also benefited from what had once seemed a mistake – its incompatibility with IBM – which has sheltered it from competition and marked it out as a clear alternative to IBM and clones.

Software

As the price war sparked off by the "clone invasion" pares profit margins on computers to the bone, software has emerged as the prime means of adding value to a computer system, and the industry's growth prospects are good.

In software, as in every other aspect of this business, IBM stands out as a giant. For example, although software accounted for just 7% of its total 1984 revenues, IBM sold $3.2bn worth of programs, more than ten times as much as any other software company. In the future, though, as much as 50% of IBM's software revenue may come from the publishing or distribution of products developed by independent companies. IBM already has agreements with BPI Systems and with Software Publishing.

Microcomputer software The microcomputer software industry consists of a thousand or so small firms dotted mainly around San Francisco Bay and along Route 128 outside of Boston. Not quite so dependent on corporate customers, they have not been as hard hit by the slump in capital spending as the developers of software for mainframes and minis. But even so, the micro software houses face a challenging future. Apart from Microsoft, the company that provides the operating system for IBM-compatible PCs, most are still only one-product companies. Like Micropro International, which achieved enormous sales with "Wordstar," their word-processing program, they have found that success in one field does not guarantee success in another. Faced with a similar problem after its triumph with its 1-2-3 spreadsheet programs, Lotus Development introduced a slew of new products, including Signal, which broadcasts stock quotes to home computers via FM radio frequencies. Many software companies are now following Lotus down a similar road to diversification, but it remains to be seen if they can break their dependence on a single product.

Telecommunications

Radical new departures were expected in the US telecommunications business after the courts brought to an end the giant American Telephone and Telegraph Company's 70-year monopoly of the telephone service in 1984. Yet AT&T is still a large and powerful company and retains its stranglehold over the profitable long-distance market. Indeed, with the end of the monopoly AT&T has broadened its operations into the potentially lucrative markets opened up by new technology. Here, though, it may face stiff competition from some of its former susidiaries, the "Baby Bells," and many of the new independents – who already offer integrated communication and data-processing services.

The monopoly is broken

After battling the Justice Department for close to a decade to protect its monopoly, AT&T finally succumbed in 1983. But the blow struck by the trustbusters was far from fatal. AT&T lost the 24 regional subsidiaries that provided the cheap local telephone service but retained its most profitable division – its long-distance service – and was freed to move into new spheres of activity such as making computers.

Baby Bells Consolidated into seven regional companies ("Baby Bells") providing local telephone service, the subsidiaries cast off by AT&T have also profited from the deal. Local rates formerly pegged artificially low are now allowed to float gradually upward and AT&T and other long-distance providers pay the Baby Bells fees for connecting local users to long-distance lines.

Despite government concern that the Baby Bells may exploit their protected status to subsidize other lines of business and undercut competition, they are already beginning to compete directly with their former parent in long-distance service and equipment manufacturing. Wall Street is smiling very favorably upon the Baby Bells. As a group their stocks rose 124% in the 18 months after independence, and their fortunes continue to look bright.

The independents

AT&T's monopoly on long-distance telephone calls was brought to an end as long ago as 1969, and there are now more than 50 independent companies providing a long-distance service. Most, however, only buy large amounts of discounted service from other carriers and resell it, for they can make few inroads on AT&T's territory. The independents charge up to 30% less than AT&T, but they have been plagued by technical problems, including poor line quality and difficulty gaining access to Baby Bell customers. As a result, AT&T has been able to maintain 83% of the long-distance business. MCI, with a 9% market share, and US Sprint, with 4%, are the only independents that can credibly challenge AT&T.

Partnerships The mid 1980s saw the computer giant IBM folding its own loss-making telephone subsidiary into MCI, the largest independent. As a result, IBM now owns 16.6% of MCI. So far, the two companies' sole joint venture has been the marketing of data, voice and video transmission systems to business. But there is speculation that the alliance took IBM one step closer to its long-anticipated showdown with AT&T. Another combination, US Sprint, formed by the merger of United Telecom and GTE, has made great progress in eliminating its transmission quality problems by laying a 23,000-mile fiber optic network which transmits calls by pulses of light. Fiber optics seem certain to play an increasingly significant role in the US telecommunications business.

Utilities

The USA still consumes a vast amount of energy – twice as much per head as West Germany and three times as much as Japan. But the 1980s have seen expectation of continually rising demand confounded by re-adjustments in patterns of energy use. Now both electricity and natural gas capacity far outstrip demand, and these utilities have been forced to re-examine their operations. Because the electric utilities can already meet the nation's power needs until the mid 1990s, they are cutting back on new construction and using the capital released for diversification. The recently deregulated natural gas utilities, on the other hand, are facing a major crisis as prices tumble ever lower.

Electricity

Experiments with alternative energy sources such as wave and wind power have proved increasingly popular over the past decade or so. But they still contribute less than one twentieth of US electricity production. Coal-fired stations generate almost 60% of the USA's electric power, and the 1980s have seen coal increase its market share at the expense of oil and natural gas. Nuclear power – once viewed as the great hope for the future of the power industry – is only gradually making inroads on the market, and its share remains stubbornly below 16%.

Private generation By far the majority of US power stations (85% of generating capacity) are in private hands; federal and municipal authorities hold barely 15%. Most of the power utilities are relatively small and supply electricity only to the area immediately around the station. But because they have a local monopoly, their activities are circumscribed by stringent state and federal regulation.

Nuclear fall-off The nuclear power plant disasters at Three Mile Island in 1982 and Chernobyl, in the USSR, in 1986 have tarnished the safety image of the nuclear industry in the public eye. But it is cost, more than safety, that is bringing the authorities down heavily on the industry, and it has been unable to pass on to the consumer the soaring construction costs for nuclear power plants. This, combined with plant cancellations and poor operational performance, has held down the amount of electricity generated by nuclear power. The last of the nuclear plants now under construction will be completed by 1990, and no more are expected to be built before 1995, when the nation's current energy oversupply is likely to end. But the freeing-up of cash with the cutback in plant construction has enabled power utilities to venture into other fields, such as cable TV.

Gas utilities

Natural gas producers too have found their fortunes in the hands of the regulators. In fact, it is federal regulations that have turned the industry around from a severe shortage in the late 1970s to a huge glut, known ruefully as "the Bubble," which may last into 1990s. The massive growth in gas capacity began when the Natural Gas Policy Act of 1978 lifted the price controls which shut down wells in the 1960s and '70s. Deregulation stimulated a drilling boom which peaked in 1981, and although competition from cheap oil has since put many wells out of business, the potential gas supply still exceeds domestic demand by nearly 3 trillion cubic feet. Falling prices may boost demand, but the industry is also developing new markets for gas. More than 30,000 vehicles have already been converted to run on methane, for example. And there are hopes that the spread of gas air conditioning will fill out the summer dip in demand for gas.

Retailing

A substantial decline in real disposable income and an increase in the proportion of women who work have contributed to the strong growth of two diametrically opposed sectors of American retailing: the discount store and the expensive, small, European-style specialty shop. The big loser, however, has been that American classic: the department store.

The rise of the discounters

In real dollars the income of the average US worker has seen a significant decline since the early 1970s, and Americans have sustained their standard of living partly by floating it on a sea of credit and partly by living with their old purchases longer. The average age of US cars, for example, is still rising. Americans have become increasingly willing to give up the status, the service and often the quality of traditional retailers to hunt for bargains. The result is that discount stores, including such chains as Mervyn's and Consumer's Distributing, have seen sales soaring. As a group, discount store sales are growing up to 40% faster than department stores and retailing in general. Particularly successful are the deep-discounters, which, through massive volume, manage to thrive on profit margins that are far too narrow for other retailers.

Me-shopping

The big cities and suburbs account for two thirds of all sales, and it is here especially that the retail trade has been transformed by the changing habits of women purchasers. In the past, women did the bulk of the shopping, buying not for themselves but for the whole family – a practice that the retail industry has dubbed "we-shopping". These we-shoppers tended to shop in large department stores where everything the family needed was conveniently arranged, functional and bland. Now that most women work, they no longer have as much time to shop for the whole family. At the same time, they have more money to spend on themselves, especially as more couples decide not to have children. The result has been the emergence of the "me-shopper", and a boom in specialty shops. Some of these specialty shops, like the electronics chain Crazy Eddie's, or Toys 'R' Us, are also discounters. But most of the new shops, especially the clothing shops, cater for much more expensive tastes. What they offer their customers is a high level of service, a pleasant ambiance and the all-important ingredient of style.

Foreign invasion Many of the trend-setters in the specialty business are foreign-based chains. Laura Ashley began selling her Victorian country-style clothing and textiles in the USA in the early 1970s, but the company is now expanding aggressively. Since 1980, Benetton has opened more than 400 US outlets, often clustering them on neighboring streets to maximize recognition.

Stores within stores

Faced with competition from the discounters and the specialty shops, the department stores have moved onto the offensive. One of their main strategies is to mimic the specialty shops by displaying their merchandise in boutique-like subdivisions aimed at particular markets. The giant Sears chain has taken the step of opening almost 300 mini-department stores specializing in high turnover items such as household and sports goods.

Department stores are also dropping those areas where they face the stiffest competition from discounters, usually in heavy appliances and toys. But some analysts are predicting that up to a third of US department stores will disappear by the year 2000.

The food industry

Two underlying trends in American habits and tastes are currently channeling the food industry in new directions: a widespread reduction in the time available for cooking, which has stimulated demand for both convenience foods and restaurants; and an increasing consumer tendency to buy on quality and image – especially a healthy image – regardless of the price.

Fast food

The past decade or so has seen a boom in the convenience food and restaurant industries, caused in part by the rapid rise in the number of women working – at least 60% of women between the ages of 20 and 44 now have jobs. Between the mid 1970s and mid 1980s eating and drinking establishment sales shot up from $44.6bn to $124bn, growing on average over 16% a year. Fast food outlets have spread rapidly across the USA, and chains such as McDonald's, Kentucky Fried Chicken and Pizza Hut are thriving. At the same time, there has been a rise in restaurants offering individual attention and finely cooked or unusual food, reflecting the growing concern for quality and image. Gourmet restaurants specializing in *nouvelle cuisine* and "ethnic" restaurants, such as Mexican, Italian and Chinese, have proliferated. Although they make a virtue of their individuality and ephemeral nature, these restaurants have lifted industry sales significantly.

Convenience foods, too, have benefited from the general reduction in time devoted to cooking. Specialty frozen foods – especially low-calorie products – are enjoying surging sales. Stouffer's "Lean Cuisine" frozen dinners, which are aimed squarely at working women and moderate- to upper-income households, were introduced in 1980, and by 1986, Stouffer's and its low-calorie imitators had captured a full 33% of the frozen dinner market.

Health awareness The media have made much of the increasing concern of Americans with the effect of food upon their health, and the young urban middle class have come under particular scrutiny. Yet the nation's calorie intake actually went up 8% between 1965 and 1985, and more than half of the population remains overweight. Nevertheless, much-publicized scientific studies on the connection between heart disease and fatty foods contributed to a 17% decline in beef consumption from the mid 1970s to the mid 1980s. Faced with falling demand and increasing insistence on quality regardless of cost, the $30bn-a-year beef industry is turning more and more toward very lean, but also very expensive, "designer" cuts of meat. Meanwhile, makers of products such as coffee creamers and cakes often cite exhaustive scientific trials testifying to their health value.

Traditional virtues

American food sales are still dominated by a handful of giants, but small companies (or subsidiaries) selling high-priced, high-quality products on the basis of their traditional virtues are having an increasing impact on the market. And after decades of diversification, many major food processing companies are reverting to the specialty that made them famous. In 1986, Kraft Inc effectively undid its 1980 merger with Dart Industries by spinning off most of Dart's ailing consumer product lines as a new company called Premark International, while General Mills shed its volatile toy and fashion businesses. The big corporate marriages of the mid 1980s – Nestlé and Carnation, for example, or Beatrice and Esmark – have been between companies in the same or closely related businesses.

Media and entertainment

The media and entertainment industries have always played a high-profile role in America's image abroad, but at home they are remarkably diverse, for there are literally thousands of daily newspapers and television stations. Changes in technology and advertising patterns have put the industries in a state of flux, yet their earnings are still growing faster than those of any other US industry.

Newspapers

Newspapers still draw more money from advertising than any other medium in the USA – 27% of total US advertising expenditure, compared with 22% for television. Newspapers also lead all media in total sales, taking in about $25bn per year. These robust figures, however, disguise the uneven health of the industry.

The US newspaper industry has always been characterized by a vast number of individual newspapers, serving localities across the states; and in the mid 1980s there were still more than 1,700 daily newspapers in existence. But although circulation of the dailies has continued to rise – and the Sunday newspapers, with their high entertainment-to-news ratio, have grown rapidly – the newspapers' share of advertising revenue has been steadily eroded by television and by direct mail advertising.

Meanwhile, growing competition from radio has driven many local newspapers out of business, and the total number of newspapers is slowly declining. Hardest hit have been the evening papers. They still outnumber morning papers by three to one, but since 1982 their circulation has been shrinking steadily. This trend has been reinforced by the acquisition of local papers by large chains such as Knight-Ridder and Gannett, which has been going on for decades.

A significant new development has been the emergence of national newspapers. Until recently, the famous New York business and financial paper, *The Wall Street Journal*, which started publishing a West Coast edition in 1929, was virtually the only paper with a truly national circulation – apart from the *Christian Science Monitor*. It was only from 1983, when the Gannett chain launched its colorful and chatty *USA Today*, that a general interest paper could be readily purchased from coast to coast. The *New York Times*, the *Los Angeles Times* and the *Washington Post* are now publishing national editions, and it is expected that other major newspapers will follow suit.

Magazines

The slowdown of the economy has caused a slump in advertising expenditure which is affecting all media. But magazines, with their comparatively small and scattered circulations, have suffered most. Special interest magazines, which cater for identifiable markets, have retained more of their appeal to advertisers and have remained the industry's one big growth area. But publishers of news weeklies and general interest titles have been driven to ever more desperate remedies to draw advertisers. One ploy has been to keep ad rates low by shifting costs onto the consumer. As a result, single issue prices have risen 9.7% a year since the 1970s – which may be the reason newsstand sales have declined by a third, a loss made up only by the steady rise in subscription sales. Traditionally, magazine ad rates have risen 7% to 8% every year, but in the mid 1980s increases in the official rate have been abruptly curtailed. Moreover, some publishers have been selling advertising space at heavy discounts – something rarely heard of before. There is concern within the industry that this trend will force many magazines out of business.

Book publishing

Unaffected by the dearth of advertising dollars, book publishers have been experiencing a modest growth in sales, predicted to continue at a steady 4% annually well into the 1990s. The number of publishing houses also grew 77% in the ten years after 1972, especially outside New York, to reach a total of 2,130, despite a number of mergers among larger houses. But perhaps the most significant trend has been the growth of bookstore chains such as B Dalton and Waldenbooks, and bookstores now account for 30% of all book sales, 20% more than in the 1970s.

Cinema

Movies are one of the USA's most successful exports, making a $1.3bn annual contribution to the balance of payments. American films are seen in 100 countries, and the USA provides 60% of the world's pre-recorded video cassette programs. The early 1980s saw the industry booming, and in 1984 box office receipts reached a record $4.03bn, while the nine major studios (including Paramount, Warner Bros and Universal) made 130 movies, more than during any year for a decade. Since then, however, receipts have declined, though few people expect the recession to last. Moreover, industry profits are no longer entirely dependent on box office receipts. Significantly, an increasing number of studios are being bought up by outside interests such as Coca-Cola and Rupert Murdoch (see *Los Angeles*). The studios now use their film successes to generate profits in a multitude of media: books, games and, especially, home video cassettes. Home videos are the success story of the mid 1980s, with sales of pre-recorded cassettes already over 60m a year.

Television

The number of television stations competing for the viewer's attention in the USA is already remarkable, and with the rise of cable television, the American viewer can expect to be spoiled for choice in the late 1980s.

Conventional stations The mainstays of the TV system are the VHF stations, dominated by the three major networks, ABC, CBS and NBC. UHF stations are fairly small and offer mainly network reruns, syndicated programs and foreign-language programs. The broad network of public television stations, described as "educational" though showing a wide range of high-quality programs, are supported mainly by sponsorship, especially from the oil companies. The commercial stations depend on advertising, but the mid 1980s slump in advertising is seen only as a temporary setback. More worrying for the long term is the loss of millions of viewers to video and cable, compounded by the loss of daytime viewing as more women go out to work. The emergence of competition from new networks such as Fox TV, and from syndication companies poses a further threat. Although the number of stations continues to grow slowly, the lean prospects for the future – christened the "New Reality" – have persuaded the networks to cut back on staff and streamline programs. Despite their present hard times, or perhaps because of them, the networks have been the objects of some dramatic takeover struggles. General Electric grabbed RCA largely to gain control of its subsidiary NBC, while Ted Turner waged a fierce, but finally unsuccessful, effort to win CBS.

Cable TV is the boom sector of the US television industry, relying on subscriptions as well as advertising.

The first large-scale cable programming companies began operating in the late 1970s and gained 9m subscribers in a single year (1980). Since 1983, cable TV's growth has slowed down, largely due to competition from the video industry, which can get the latest movies into circulation faster, but prospects for the future are still bright.

The Political Scene

The government of the nation

With an electorate of more than 170m, the United States is the second largest democratic republic in the world. It is one of the oldest, too, and the modern American system of government is based on a constitution that is now 200 years old, having survived the growth of the nation from 18th century colony to modern superpower. Americans' pride in their political system has taken a battering in recent years, both from the Vietnam War and from a series of scandals that have touched the highest levels of government. But history has shown the nation's institutions to have a resilience and flexibility matched in few other countries.

The Constitution

The Constitution of 1787 is a concise document just a few thousand words long. Yet it provides the basis for a vast and complex political structure that directly employs 3m people and is lobbied, analyzed and reported by thousands more. Much of this complexity can be laid at the door of the Founding Fathers who, fearing the abuse of power by government, divided it between various branches and levels, each limited in power by the others. The result is that the US government is divided both horizontally: between lawmakers (the legislature), law enforcers (the executive) and law interpreters (the judiciary); and vertically: between national (federal), state and local governments. All of these play a part in the political life of the USA, but the center stage is dominated by the federal government.

Americans are justly proud of the Constitution and Bill of Rights, which protect fundamental freedoms such as freedom of speech. But it was less than 20 years ago that the last discriminatory restrictions on eligibility to vote were removed. And the steadily falling voting turnout suggests that there is considerable disillusion with politics; only 53.2% of the electorate bothered to vote in the 1984 presidential elections.

The president and the executive

As head of state and chief executive, the president of the United States has enormous symbolic significance – not least in presenting the public face of the US government to the outside world. Yet although the presidency has played an increasingly prominent role in US politics, its real power is caught up in a web of factions (see *The reins of power*).

The road to the White House The president is elected for a term of four years and can serve a maximum of two terms. He (there have been no women presidents) and the vice president are the only members of the US government elected by a nationwide constituency, and this direct link with the public is a key part of the office's significance.

The election process is long and complex, and in election years, the campaigns of the major candidates dominate the media from late winter, when candidacy is announced, to the final election in November. For the final stages of the election, there are normally just two candidates, one representing each of the major parties, Democratic and Republican. But spring and summer of election year are occupied by the battle for the party nominations, beginning in most states with the "primary" elections for delegates to the parties' national conventions, and culminating in the ballots at the convention which settle the issue.

With the candidate decided, the campaign for the election begins.

Campaigns costing millions of dollars focus on "pivotal" states, the eight most populous states, which among them have 225 of the 270 electors. At the ballot box, the public do not vote directly for their chosen candidate, but for electors to represent them in the electoral college. The electoral college vote is largely a formality; electors cast their vote as they pledged before the public elections.

The administration When the voters elect a president, they are, in effect, electing an entire administration. As soon as he takes office, the president makes a clean sweep of the higher echelons of the bureaucracy, clearing out 2,000 or more, right from the cabinet down to assistant secretaries and below, in order to fill these posts with appointments of his own choice. This is not compulsory, but it has become the established way for the president to make the administration his own. During the changeover, anyone with any claim on the incoming president's favor eagerly scans the "plum book," in which all the best jobs and salaries are listed.

Departments of the executive
The job revolution with each new presidency does not extend to the permanent civil service – 13 executive departments, each with responsibility for a particular sector, such as Defense or Education. And the enormous expansion of this bureaucracy over the last last 50 years has created what most presidents see as an intractable problem. The executive departments are there, in theory, to do the president's bidding. In practice, the president finds himself up against a sluggish, often resistant bureaucracy (see *The reins of power*). Most presidents distrust the federal bureaucracy, and many have come to power pledging to cut it down to size.

The cabinet contains all the heads, or secretaries, of the departments. Although appointed by the president, they work closely with officials from their respective departments. Some recent presidents have come to feel that the loyalty of cabinet members is undermined by their association with the bureaucracy and prefer to work with the executive office. The cabinet plays only a very limited role in overall policy making, although individually some of its members, such as the secretaries of defense and state, wield considerable power.

The Executive Office has become the principal instrument of presidential government, and each incoming president appoints a large proportion of its 5,000-odd staff. Its relatively small size, and its closeness to the president, have given it a special place in the executive. The president now relies on it to provide information, analysis and policy recommendation – tasks once the responsibility of the civil service and the cabinet. Certain departments within the executive office – notably the National Security Council (NSC) and the Office of Management and Budget (OMB) responsible for preparing the federal budget – have assumed a pivotal role in US government. The president's closest friends and advisers are the White House staff. In constant contact with the president, and controlling access to him, the White House staff have considerable power and often provide his main link with the outside world.

Congress

The US Congress consists of two houses, the Senate and the House of Representatives, which sit at opposite ends of the Capitol building in Washington DC. Congress is the lawmaking body of the US government, responsible for initiating bills as well as voting them through. But strong presidents have always given a lead by preparing legislation they want to see enacted and working with like-minded members of Congress to secure its introduction and passage. External pressure groups, also, can approach members of Congress to introduce bills on their behalf.

In addition to lawmaking, the two houses have certain responsibilities peculiarly their own. The Senate, for example, must confirm or deny the president's appointments and ratify any treaty with a foreign power; laws concerning the raising of revenue must originate in the House.

The electoral connection The House of Representatives has 435 members, or "congressmen," elected every two years. The number elected from each state depends on its population; the allocation is adjusted automatically every ten years, after the census. The Senate, with only 100 members (two from each state), is the senior house, and many congressmen aspire to be senators. Election to the Senate is for six years, and a third of the seats in the Senate are up for election every two years at the same time that voting is held for the entire House of Representatives.

Since two thirds of the Senators in each new Congress were also in the last, the Senate has always conveyed a greater sense of continuity than the House. Moreover, because they were elected on a statewide basis, senators were in the past less vulnerable to the vagaries of political life in local districts, which could unseat a congressman after two years. But the demographic changes of the past 30 years – migration to the suburbs and dispersion to the sun-belt – have helped erode the stability of constituencies, and even senators are no longer secure. Members of Congress must now, as always, cultivate the local interest groups and sources of funds they need to keep their political career afloat. But with the televising of congressional debates and the attention which pressure groups pay these days to their voting record, they are perhaps more aware than ever of the electoral reckoning two or six years down the line. Many critics believe that because this encourages members of Congress to place a higher priority on local than on national interests, Congress has become a somewhat ineffective body. In particular, they argue, the need for members to protect local interest has made it unable to deal with the massive federal budget; for while members of Congress are happy to vote for tax cuts, nobody is willing to be seen supporting measures that would cut expenditure back home in the constituency.

The rise of committees Congress's committees have grown both in stature and number over the last 15 years. Now nearly all proposed legislation is sent to the relevant standing committee, which commissions a sub-committee to make a thorough investigation. After examining the sub-committee's report, the standing committee introduces the bill to the full house for further debate, or proposes amendments, or ditches it altogether.

The Supreme Court

In a nation that places a great deal of emphasis on democracy, the power wielded by the nine unelected justices of the Supreme Court may seem paradoxical. In deciding cases brought before it, the Supreme Court is able to review all the activities of federal and state governments and to decide whether laws are constitutional. The president is as subject to the Court's rulings as any other official. During the Watergate scandal of the early 1970s, the Supreme Court overruled President Nixon's claim of "executive privilege" and forced him to yield incriminating tapes.

The Supreme Court, through its power to interpret the Constitution and federal law, has made some crucial decisions over the past 30 years – particularly over civil rights. It was the Supreme Court, for example, that not only brought to an end racial segregation but also initiated moves toward "affirmative action" – and the still controversial policy of busing children across town to achieve a more even racial mix in schools.

The reins of power

As the American political structure has grown in size, so has the complexity of its hierarchy. The president is the focus of attention and the head of government. But his real authority is circumscribed by politics and bureaucracy. So numerous now are the factions competing for power both within and without the official hierarchy that it is often hard to predict the outcome of any particular policy debate, no matter what the president's own electoral rhetoric may have prescribed. No wonder, then, that many observers have come to see the US government as a hydra.

The power of the president

The office of president has a special hold over the public imagination, and Americans have always expected the president to be not just an officer of government but leader of the nation. Presidents most admired are those considered "strong," such as Lincoln and Roosevelt, and those least admired are often criticized for being "weak," such as Jimmy Carter. Respect for strong presidents has always been tempered by fears of the abuse of power, and those deemed to have taken too much to themselves – most notoriously President Nixon – are usually brought to book. But there is no doubt that most Americans expect the President to play a decisive role in the political process.

Power under the Constitution The power granted to the president by the Constitution is, on the surface, very limited. The president is commander-in-chief of the armed forces and is vested with the authority to make treaties with foreign powers. As head of the executive, he is also expected to see that laws are faithfully executed. But he has no authority to make laws himself. And his power to control the finances of the nation is circumscribed by Congress, which controls taxation and government borrowing, and by the Federal Reserve Board, which controls interest rates and monetary policy. The president can veto legislation passed by Congress but a two-thirds majority in both houses of Congress overrides a presidential veto.

Accrued power The real scope of the president's power, however, is not to be judged by the duties assigned by the Constitution, but by what has accrued to the office over the years, either through custom or through delegation of responsibility by Congress and through initiatives taken by individual incumbents. Two factors in particular have immeasurably enhanced the importance of the presidency since World War II: the explosive growth in the size and range of government services and the increasing significance of foreign affairs. Ironically, although both these developments have added to the influence of the presidency, they have actually made it harder for the president himself to impose his personal will. Also, in the wake of the Watergate scandal in the early 1970s, Congress has made strenuous efforts to limit his options still further.

Growing government services As the scope of government activity has grown, so have the demands upon the federal government. Until recently, Congress had neither the resources nor the expertise to cope. Up until the mid-1970s it delegated more and more to the president, who could cope – with the aid of a greatly enlarged bureaucracy.

For some time now, it has been the president's task to draw up the budget, devise new programs of legislation and set the policy agenda. Congress may throw out many of the president's proposals, or amend them drastically – but it is still the president who often provides the initiatives. Moreover, as legislation is extended into highly complex, technical areas, Congress has tended to leave details to be filled in by the executive; the use of "executive orders" – rules issued by the president which have the force of law – is increasing steadily.

Foreign affairs The USA's prominence on the world scene, plus the increasing impact of international events on domestic issues, have put foreign affairs at the forefront of US politics. The frequent need for speed and secrecy in foreign affairs has enabled strong presidents to make much of the running in this field. But it is in this field, more than any other, that Congress is now trying to limit the president's options – both through congressional committees which examine his conduct of foreign affairs and by cutting the funds he needs to pursue his foreign policy objectives.

The president's men The president has the entire civil service at his disposal to help him in his work. But the customary presidential distrust of the bureaucracy has meant that most presidents rely on a small coterie of close associates, often not only for advice but also for carrying out policy. Yet the civil service still expects its share of power, and so there is considerable jockeying for power within the executive. In theory, the Secretary of State has the foreign affairs brief. But as the control of the National Security Council over foreign affairs has increased, so presidents have tended to turn to the National Security Adviser, who heads the NSC staff, not to the Secretary of State, for advice. In fact, many Secretaries of State have found themselves deliberately excluded from the president's inner sanctum. Shut out of the real decision-making process, most recent Secretaries of State have found themselves in an invidious position. Six resigned between 1973 and 1983, and there was speculation that Reagan's second Secretary of State George Shultz would also resign when the NSC's dealings with Iran were revealed late in 1986.

A strong national security adviser can play a key role in foreign policy making; but not every holder of the office is as influential as Nixon's adviser Henry Kissinger. Many important foreign policy issues under Reagan seem to have been hammered out between the President, the Secretary of Defense and the Director of the CIA, for example. On some occasions, a determined White House Chief of Staff can set the foreign policy agenda as effectively as the domestic one.

Political appointments One of the president's most effective ways of impressing his personality on the political scene is through political appointments. Not only are the appointments of Cabinet secretaries and many other top bureaucrats within his brief – so, too, are ambassadors and Supreme Court judges (when the posts fall vacant). However, most of these appointments require the approval of the Senate, which is occasionally withheld. Political appointments inevitably reflect political preferences, but at least in the Supreme Court, presidents can get nasty surprises from their appointees. Political appointments are often made for political expediency rather than suitability for the job. For example, President Nixon tried to reverse the reformist tendencies of the Supreme Court by appointing conservative Warren Burger as Chief Justice in 1969. In fact, Burger turned out to be considerably less conservative than Nixon expected. Ronald Reagan was more successful in his choice of Sandra Day O'Connor for the Supreme Court.

Congressional power

After allowing the balance of power within the US government to swing far toward the executive, Congress has made strenuous efforts to restore the balance over the last 15 years or so – most notably in foreign affairs. President Carter was embarrassed by Congress's rejection of the SALT II arms treaty, while President Reagan has found his plans for money for the Nicaraguan Contra rebels thwarted on several occasions. Congress's gradual surrender of influence to the "Imperial Presidency" in the years after World War II was partly due to its lack of expert staff, but since the mid 1970s, Congress has taken on more than 20,000 bureaucrats to provide the necessary expertise. Most significantly, it has set up its own Congressional Budget Office to give it the ability to scrutinize the president's budget proposals thoroughly.

The power of the committees
The real power of Congress lies in its many standing committees and subcommittees, for Congress only rarely rejects the recommendations of these panels of experts. Of course, there is considerable jockeying for posts on the committees; chairmanships are especially sought-after, for the chairman sets the agenda. The chairman of the committee is always a member of the majority party – in recent years, usually the Democrats – and the balance of the rest of the committee reflects the balance of the parties within the corresponding house. Traditionally committee appointments followed the seniority rule, which gave priority to right-wing Democrats from safe southern seats. Moves to democratize the process in favor of younger members and those from the more volatile northern states have had only a marginal effect.

The Rules Committee Because the House of Representatives simply does not have the time to consider all the bills presented by committees, it relies on the 15-member Rules Committee to control the flow of bills. This committee thus has enormous power to decide which bills are considered and which are not.

Watchdog committees The watchdog committee, in combination with special investigating committees set up to find out the facts in situations such as the Iran arms scandal in 1986–87, are Congress's means of watching the executive and making sure that it is not overstepping its prerogative. These committees have considerable power to call on members of the administration to explain their actions.

Bureaucratic power
Although presidents have tried to shut the federal bureaucracy out of the decision-making process, the sheer size and stability of the bureaucracy means that civil servants still have formidable power. Within the bureaucracy lie years of expertise and considerable resources; and civil servants have a range of contacts those close to the president cannot match. The pressure of large departments such as the Pentagon is especially difficult for the president to ignore. Moreover, although presidents may sometimes think they are making the decisions, the range of alternatives is actually established by the bureaucracy.

Additionally, bureaucrats can often use their foreign contacts, or contacts in influential lobbies at home, to put pressure on the president's men. It is hardly surprising then, that the US government can appear to be following several different policies at once. Over Nicaragua, for example, the CIA undertook a series of covert operations to undermine the Sandinista regime, while the State Department was negotiating with it.

Lobbying
One of the most striking features of the US political scene in recent years is the enormous growth in number and influence of lobbying groups. Such groups concentrate on a single issue, and single-issue politics is fast becoming the order of the day in

Washington. Between 1960 and 1980 the number of specialist pressure groups in the USA grew by 60%.

In Washington alone, there are thousands of pressure groups, applying pressure on members of Congress, on civil servants and even on other pressure groups to get their views heard. Increasingly, they are employing professional lobbyists to help them target the right person or agency – for the range of government agencies and departments, and private influential organizations, can make it almost impossible for an outsider to decide whom to lobby.

Major pressure groups The most influential of the pressure groups tend to be those representing commercial and business interests, such as the National Association of Manufacturers. Big corporations have their own lobbying staff: General Electric's office in Washington employs more than 100 people, for example. Corporations and pressure groups orchestrate financial support for politicians through political action committees, which disburse funds to suitable members of Congress. Such financial resources ensure access to Capitol Hill.

Also influential are the professional associations, such as the American Medical Association and the American Bar Association – and, to a lesser extent now, labor organzations such as the AFL-CIO (see *Employment*). The farmers' lobby remains among the most powerful of all.

In recent years, public interest lobbies have gained prominence. Few politicians can avoid taking note of the Sierra Club's line on environmental issues; Ralph Nader, founder of Public Citizen, is well known to Congress committees working on "conscience" issues.

Clientelism Many American politicians feel that the relationship between congressmen and bureaucrats and the organizations their work brings them into contact with is sometimes just a little too close. The "revolving door" which allows experts in a particular field to switch easily between the private sector and the bureaucracy is a well-known feature of American political life; accusations of "clientelism" are common. Such criticisms surface in colorful phrases: the Federal Reserve Board was described by one politician as a "wholly-owned subsidiary of the American Bankers' Association." There is no doubt that business interests play a major role in government policy-making. The immensely powerful defense interest is often referred to as the "iron triangle," a potent alliance in the Pentagon between the congressional defense committees and the multi-billion dollar defense industry.

State power

A mistake many foreign visitors to the USA make is to underestimate the power of state and local government. Within certain limitations, states set their own taxes on top of the federal taxes, their own laws in local commerce, education, driving, drinking and every sort of crime. Certainly much state authority was lost to the federal government following President Franklin D Roosevelt's New Deal in the 1930s. But recently, encouraged by the Reagan administration, "federalism" has been experiencing something of a renaissance. And state governors, like senators are natural candidates for the White House. Both Reagan and Carter were state governors immediately before becoming President.

Party politics

American politics is dominated by just two parties, the Republicans and the Democrats. Between them they hold every seat in Congress, every state governorship, and all but a few political posts at state and local level. Over the years, these two vast coalitions have accommodated a wide range of often conflicting attitudes and interests. But there are signs that the cohesion of the parties is weakening, and voters are increasingly crossing party lines to express their views on specific issues.

The Democrats

At least since President Roosevelt's New Deal in the 1930s, the Democrats have seemed a little to the left of the Republicans: the party in favor of high government spending, both to invigorate the economy and extend the welfare state. But few even of the more liberal leaders of the party would be considered anything but moderates in Europe, while some older members from the south, are far to the right.

Traditionally, the Democrats have drawn support from an uneasy coalition of right wing white southerners with northern city dwellers, union members and ethnic and religious minorities – while, among the party elite, financiers, lawyers, and academics are prominent. The southern vote, dating back to the Civil War, used to be the most stable element in Democratic support and it was this, as much as the vote of the "little man," that enabled the Democrats to maintain a majority in both houses of Congress for all but a few of the last 50 years while providing all but one president from 1933 to 1969. Recently, however, worries about law and order, pornography and school busing have lost the Democrats support. Nevertheless, they remain in the majority in Congress.

The Republicans

Despite its origins in the mid 19th century as the anti-slavery grouping, the Republican party is seen as the more conservative of the two parties, opposed to the welfare state and big government. Supporters include the more affluent sectors of society – notably big business and farming interests (except in the Deep South) and inhabitants of well-to-do suburbs. Their identification with the traditional values of small-town America has also earned them the backing of many older white people of all classes. The recent moral backlash has brought to prominence extreme right wing Republicans, such as Senator Jesse Helms.

The weakening of the parties

Over the past 30 years, voters' identification with a particular party has been steadily waning, and now as much as a third of the electorate are believed to be casting their vote not on the basis of party loyalty, but on personality and, more importantly, on issues. Increasingly, they are also voting for members of different parties for different offices.

One of the most important reasons for this has been the weakening of the party organizations. The almost universal adoption of primary elections for party nomination in place of selection by the old political machines means anyone can try for nomination, regardless of party service or standing, so the grass-roots party organization has begun to disintegrate. Elections now tend to be more about candidates than parties, and, lacking the backing of a party organization, candidates have to conduct their own campaigns for nomination – hence the rise of Political Action Committees which provide funds and run campaigns.

National security

Defending the national interest has been a top priority with all administrations since the war. Defense spending consumes 30% of the federal budget and a tenth of the entire working and pensioned population depends on military expenditure to some extent. Many different government agencies deal with defense matters, often with their own agendas and priorities. Much of the subject is meant to be shrouded in secrecy, but in the USA more than in most Western democracies, an active press and a keen congressional interest in defense creates a lively debate and a plentiful supply of revelations. Vigorous discussion and criticism of the activities of US security agencies has made the whole issue of security a highly controversial area.

The nuclear deterrent

Since shortly after the war, the nuclear deterrent has remained the centerpiece of the USA's defense against the perceived Soviet threat, and since the 1950s the USA has been involved in an almost continuous race with the USSR to maintain superiority in nuclear weapons deemed essential to balance the vast Soviet conventional force. The USA's nuclear force includes an array of ICBMs (intercontinental ballistic missiles) fitted with MIRVs (multiple independently targeted re-entry vehicles) and Pershing II, and cruise missiles stationed on US bases in Western Europe, nuclear submarines with multiple warhead Trident missiles, and a fleet of bombers.

Strategic Defense Initiative Popularly known as "Star Wars," and pushed heavily by President Reagan, SDI has attracted consistent controversy. Critics still attack the technical feasibility of this high-tech nuclear defense umbrella – based on satellites in space and high-powered lasers designed to knock out incoming nuclear missiles but controversy centers on whether it infringes the 1972 Anti-Ballistic Missile treaty with the USSR, which bans the testing or deployment of ABM systems. The administration favors a "broad" interpretation of the treaty, which would allow development of components of an ABM system; many in Congress do not.

Arms control Attempts to slow down the pace of nuclear arms-building by agreement with the Soviets began in the 1960s, and achieved some success with SALT I (Strategic Arms Limitation Talks) in 1969-72. Congress failed to ratify the SALT II treaty negotiated by President Carter, and President Reagan has rejected it. The 1983 breakdown of the START (Strategic Arms Reduction Talks) when the USA deployed cruise and Pershing II missiles in Western Europe led to a halt to arms control talks. They are now beginning once again, but the USA's attitude to arms control remains ambivalent; late in 1986, the USA exceeded the limits set by SALT II.

The armed forces

In the wake of the Vietnam War, selective service (conscription) in peacetime was ended, though young men are required to register. But the US armed forces are still well over 2m strong, with around 780,200 in the army, 570,000 in the navy, 600,000 in the air force and 200,000 in the marines. More than 500,000 are stationed abroad, mainly in Europe and the Far East.

Rivalry between the services is intense, especially over procurement budgets. But there are moves to achieve unity of command by strengthening the Joint Chiefs of Staff (JCS) – consisting of the heads of the army, navy and air force plus the chief of staff to the secretary of defense – and by increasing the power of the JCS chairman.

Only Congress can declare war, and its control was strengthened by the War Powers Act of 1973. But presidents have launched the armed forces on "policing" missions not requiring prior agreement from Congress. These include the 1983 invasion of Grenada and the 1986 bombing raid on Libya.

Intelligence

Intelligence is a key element in the USA's protection of its national security and there are at least 11 government agencies involved in the gathering and analysis of intelligence about threats to the national interest, both abroad and at home. Principal among these are the Central Intelligence Agency (CIA), the National Security Agency (NSA), the armed forces intelligence units, the Defense Intelligence Agency (DIA) and the Federal Bureau of Investigation (FBI).

The US Intelligence Board, headed by the director of the CIA, meets regularly to analyze the intelligence gathered by the various agencies. But critics believe the multiplicity of agencies leads to considerable confusion and duplication of activities. Moreover, the secrecy of many intelligence-gathering activities inevitably means that the scope of operations of each of the agencies is often obscure – even to the congressional intelligence committees which, in theory, are supposed to be thoroughly informed of their activities. Revelations such as the involvement of the NSC staff in arms deals with Iran – without the knowledge or consent of Congress – ensures that their activities remain highly controversial.

The CIA is the most famous of the agencies concerned with gathering intelligence from abroad. Nominally under the umbrella of the NSC, its budget is obscure, since many of its appropriations are hidden in the general defense budget. Much of its time is spent monitoring broadcasts and publications freely available. But it is the CIA's clandestine operations which receive most media attention. Among the more controversial of its activities in the 1980s have been its efforts to overthrow the Sandinista government in Nicaragua and its active support for the government in El Salvador. In the mid 1970s, a congressional investigation revealed that the CIA was carrying on surveillance of Americans within the USA in direct violation of its charter.

The FBI has domestic counterintelligence responsibilities, but its operations are mainly concerned with criminal investigation. With a budget of around $850m, and 20,000 plain-clothes agents, the FBI investigates crimes against federal law: kidnaps, bank robberies and murders, as well as anti-trust and some civil rights violations and corrupt practices. It publishes a list of the "Ten Most Wanted Fugitives" and backs up state police forces with data from the National Crime Information Center in Washington.

The police

The federal government has no authority to police the nation under the Constitution, and policing in the USA is organized on a state and local basis. There are some 450,000 police officers altogether, split among 40,000 separate police forces, more than half of which are one or two man units with no training. In addition, there are 75 federal law enforcement agencies, concerned with interstate crime.

The National Guard is the volunteer armed forces of the individual states. With a combined strength of 400,000, it comes under the command of the state governor. In peacetime, it is primarily an emergency unit dealing with floods and fires. In the 1960s and 1970s, however, it was called out to quell racial and student disorders.

International alignments

Opposition to communist expansion remains the keystone of US foreign policy, and is the dominating influence on the pattern of the USA's relationships with other nations. But the need to promote commercial interests adds another dimension to the USA's international alignments, and in recent years closer links have been forged with the rising economic powers of the Pacific Basin.

Security pacts

Until World War II, the USA traditionally kept itself free from permanent alliances, but has been the post-war leader in building up defensive alliances, seeing them as vital bulwarks against the expansion of communism.

NATO remains the most important of all the USA's strategic alliances, and provides the basic framework for the defense of the West against the Soviet Union. Formed in 1949, NATO includes the USA and Canada, and most Western European nations – with the notable exception of France, which withdrew from the alliance in 1966.

As part of the collective security arrangements, the USA has military bases in many Western European countries, notably Britain and West Germany. Since 1984, US nuclear missiles have been stationed in six NATO countries in Europe, though their presence is controversial.

ANZUS and Southeast Asia The ANZUS pact, between the USA, Australia and New Zealand, was formed in 1951 to forestall the communist threat in the Pacific. The relationship has been ruffled by New Zealand's anti-nuclear stance but remains formally intact.

In the mid 1950s, ANZUS was expanded into the Southeast Asia Treaty Organization (SEATO), an Asian equivalent to NATO. But SEATO was dissolved in 1977 and, although the associated Southeast Asia Collective Defense Treaty remains in force, it has little significance. More important are bilateral pacts with Japan, the Philippines and South Korea.

Latin America The USA is particularly sensitive to the threat of a communist takeover in any of its Latin American and Caribbean neighbors, and the Rio Treaty and the Organization of American States (OAS) – which unites 26 American nations – has assumed new importance in the 1980s. Unrest in Central American states such as Nicaragua deeply concerns the US administration, and the OAS is seen as a means of uniting opposition to communism in the region. Increasingly, the USA is turning to the OAS, rather than the UN, for settling problems in Central and South America.

The United Nations As the United Nations organization has grown (it now has more than 160 member nations) so US commitment to it has waned. UN policy on major issues is often made in the General Assembly, and here the huge Third World vote may thwart the USA. But the USA can still use its membership of the five nation Security Council to veto any resolution it disapproves of.

Israel and the Middle East Support for Israel is a central component of the US Middle Eastern policy, and powerful Jewish pressure groups at home, such as B'nai B'rith, make sure it will remain so – despite growing unease over Israel's Palestinian policy, its links with South Africa and its role in the US arms deal with Iran in 1986. Israel receives upward of $3.5bn a year in economic and military aid, and the benefit of US diplomatic backing in many disputes with the Arab states. But the USA is keen to retain friendship with some, at least, of the

Arab states. Egypt, for example, receives substantial military and economic aid. The whole pattern of US relationships in the Middle East, however, has been disturbed by the terrorism which is often directed against US citizens. Nations identified as supporting terrorism are strongly condemned, and the USA has threatened (and used) military force against them.

Revolutions

Successive administrations have adhered, in rhetoric and in practice, to the "domino" theory, the belief that if one country fell to communism, then all its neighbors would topple. This has sometimes led the USA to support right wing dictatorships – or, in some cases, oppose dictatorships which seem ineffective bulwarks against communism. In the 1950s and '60s, it was Southeast Asia and South America – plus Cuba – that were the focus of US opposition to the communist threat. Now it is Central America and the Caribbean and, to a lesser extent, Africa. The memory of failure in Vietnam has discouraged direct military intervention, but covert support for "counter-insurgency" groups is extensive.

Economic relationships

Trade and aid have increasingly shaped the pattern of US international alignments since World War II. Both trade and aid, for example, were behind the US drive to create the Organization for Economic Co-operation and Development (OECD) in 1961. Most Western European nations are OECD members, along with the USA, Canada, Australia, New Zealand and Japan; and the OECD is one of world's major forums for discussion and action on the international economy.

It is the General Agreement on Tariffs and Trade (GATT), however, which has become the principal forum for the USA to apply pressure on Europe and Japan not to erect barriers to US trade – and also for justifying US barriers to foreign trade.

Canada The USA's closest bond, both physically and economically, is with its northern neighbor, Canada. Every year, some $80bn worth of trade crosses over the US-Canadian border, the longest undefended border in the world. Attempts to strengthen the link with a free trade agreement are encountering problems, partly due to protectionist pressure from the US lumber lobby, but Canada retains its place as the USA's foremost partner.

The North Pacific The growing economic power of countries such as Japan, South Korea and Taiwan – combined with demographic shifts at home from east to west, and the rise of the Alaskan oilfield – have moved the focus of US interest toward the Northern Pacific Basin. In the early 1980s, the volume of US trade across the Pacific exceeded that across the Atlantic for the first time. Diplomatic relations with Taiwan are smoother, and US business has moved strongly into communist China.

Europe The traditional links with the UK and Ireland, and to a lesser extent West Germany, still figure strongly in the US world outlook, and the high proportion of US investment in the UK underlines the "special relationship." Although the USA is not on such intimate terms with other members of the EC, it retains close economic ties with all of Western Europe.

Latin America US investment in Latin America is enormous, and the huge debts to US banks built up by some South American countries, notably Brazil and Mexico, ensures that Latin American affairs stay at the forefront of US economic policy.

South Africa After resisting pressure to reduce its links with South Africa for some years, the USA now imposes limited economic sanctions, while an increasing number of major US corporations are pulling out altogether.

The Business Scene

Government and business

With former businessmen prominent in the cabinet, the Reagan administration has projected a strongly pro-business image. But efforts to lift restraints have generated conflict within and without government, and the initiatives have met with only limited success. Extensive government intervention in business remains a fact of life in the USA.

Regulatory authority

Over the years, the federal and state governments have awarded themselves sweeping powers to control and regulate the way business is done in the USA. The statute books, both federal and state, contain a host of rules and regulations for business, primarily designed to protect free enterprise and ensure fair competition. As far as federal regulations are concerned, some are overseen directly by the relevant department of the executive; international air passenger fares, for example, are regulated by the Department of Transport. But the federal government has delegated much of its regulatory power to a string of independent regulatory commissions operating outside the departments.

Independent agencies The idea of creating independent agencies was to remove their activities from partisan politics. Members of the boards (usually seven strong) which head the agencies are appointed by the president, with the Senate's consent. But to prevent any one president achieving control over the agency, terms are usually long and overlapping. Operating independently, these agencies can sometimes work against the policies of the administration, and they have become targets for those wanting to deregulate the economy. There has also been some criticism that because they work closely with certain businesses, they sometimes protect business interests before those of the public.

The following are among the most important federal agencies.

Interstate Commerce Commission (ICC) The oldest of all the regulatory agencies, the ICC's main task is to oversee the thousands of private railroad, express, bus and truck companies in the USA. Recent deregulation legislation, however, has cut away much of the ICC's authority.

Federal Trade Commission has a wide brief covering acquisitions and mergers, cartels and price fixing, fraudulent advertising and a range of other infringements of fair trading regulations. However, it leaves most antimonopoly work to the Antitrust Division, and concentrates on consumer protection. The FTC has limited power to enforce its codes and operates mostly by persuading business to adopt acceptable practice – though critics say it is often business that persuades the FTC.

Federal Communications Commission The FCC is the agency that licenses television and radio companies and regulates radio, television and telecommunication. But under Mark Fowler, its head until spring 1987, the FCC gave up many of its regulatory powers – abandoning everything from the "fairness doctrine" which stipulated that equal airtime must be given to different political opinions to anti-trafficking regulations which required broadcasters to operate three years before selling the licence.

Federal Reserve Board (see *Financial institutions*)

National Labor Relations Board The NLRB is sometimes charged with being unduly influenced by unions.

But it plays an important role in preventing unfair labor practices and overseeing union recognition and bargaining.

Securities and Exchange Commission Established in the wake of the stock market crash of 1929, the SEC is Wall Street's watchdog and plays a prominent role in policing the activities of America's financial wheelers and dealers and regulating public share offers and financial disclosures. Its powers to investigate infringements of the regulations are extensive, and it can close a brokerage firm by revoking its licence – though in practice it only resorts to this sanction against smaller companies. The SEC's policy is to maintain a high profile to deter would be wrong-doers – though in reality its 2,000 staff are badly stretched. Recently, its activities have made the headlines with the uncovering of widespread insider trading on Wall Street.

The Antitrust Division is not actually an independent agency, but the division of the Department of Justice which has responsibility for the enforcement of the USA's stringent antitrust laws. Its lack of independence may be one reason the Reagan administration has been for more successful in deregulating antitrust controls than in most other areas (see *Business framework*).

The public sector

Nationalization of major industries has never received much support in the USA, and direct government involvement in manufacturing and services remains very limited. One of the few major federally-owned corporations is the Tennessee Valley Authority (TVA), which is responsible for hydro-electric power and flood control in the Tennessee Valley. The government also runs the US Postal Service, one of the biggest business operations in the world, employing 680,000 people and handling 114bn pieces of mail each year.

Privatization Schemes for selling off government-owned businesses have become one of the hallmarks of the Reagan administration's budget proposals. The proposals for the 1988 budget include: a scheme for selling off government loans; plans to sell the government-owned power marketing administrations, which sell 6% of the nation's electricity; and plans for the privatization of Amtrak, the state-owned intercity rail passenger network. Such schemes receive little positive support in Congress.

Contracting out Along with the privatization schemes, the Reagan administration has encouraged state and local governments to contract out services to private enterprises.

In the early 1980s, 44% of US cities contracted out the collection of commercial refuse, 41% contracted out their street lighting and 28% their road repairs.

Subsidies While the Reagan administration has supported private industry's own initiatives, it has shied away from increasing subsidies for business. Such programs as the Small Business Administration and the Trade Adjustment Assistance payments (for workers displaced by foreign competition) have been cut back heavily. And indirect incentives, such as tax deductions for capital investment, are being curtailed.

State agencies All states have their own semi-independent agencies which can issue bonds, provide cheap loans and offer tax incentives to private corporations.

Pork-barrel legislation
Encouraged by the US political system to place a high priority on local constituency interests (see *The government of the nation*), representatives in the federal and state legislatures push for "pork" – expenditure on local projects, such as highways and bridges – from the "pork-barrel" (the treasury), and this may have tipped expenditure unfairly towards the sunbelt states.

Power in business

Until recently, power in US business was largely in the hands of the corporate managers, who were little influenced by outside shareholders. But in the last decade, changes in the direction of US business have eroded much of their independence. The wave of mergers and acquisitions and the rise of institutional investors and "corporate raiders" have created a liquid market for corporate control, depriving managers of unfettered stewardship of their companies.

Corporate power

The sheer size of the largest US corporations enables them to wield enormous clout, in both the business and political worlds. Commanding revenues equivalent to the GNP of many nations, they are able to negotiate with government officials almost as if they were a foreign country; and the corporate lobby is one of the most powerful in the country (see *The reins of power*).

Few of the big corporations are now run by the entrepreneurs who were the heroes of US business in the past. There are exceptions, such as Ken Olsen, who built the computer company DEC up from nothing to a company worth $7.6bn in 30 years, and H Ross Perot, the Dallas billionaire who sold his company EDS to General Motors for $2.5bn. But they are rare. Perot controlled his company by owning a majority of the shares; most heads of public corporations now find themselves answering to a dispersed and largely passive group of institutional shareholders. Without much shareholder influence, the chief executive officers of the big corporations are able to exercise an authority that reaches far beyond the bounds of the company. But increasingly the power of the corporate managers is offset by the rise of corporate raiders, who watch constantly for companies that are badly managed, or possess underexploited assets.

Investors, raiders and arbitrageurs

With more than $200bn changing hands in 1986 alone, the merger and acquisition boom of the 1980s has given the financial manipulators a new power and status in the US business world. Hostile bids now succeed at least 50% of the time, compared with 20% in the past, and takeover struggles seem to absorb almost all the stockmarket's attention.

Corporate raiders Capturing the headlines, though not the most fundamental power, are the "corporate raiders," the "sharks" whose opportunistic bids so worry corporations. Devices such as "junk bonds" (large issues of high-interest debt) have helped the boldest raiders raise enough money to make hostile takeover bids for large corporations, even when their own resources are limited. Corporations can be so unnerved by bids or threats of bids that they resort to drastic action to protect themselves. Some companies set up complex share structures to frustrate a potential raider; a few even end up selling off the "crown jewels" – the company's most valuable assets – to make it a less attractive target.

Arbitrageurs The merger boom has also brought to the fore the risk arbitrageurs who buy and sell shares in companies involved in takeover struggles – or those likely to be. Although their real power is limited, the star players can make huge sums of money for their backers. But revelations of extensive insider trading have eroded confidence in arbitrageurs, and some heroes of the arbitrage game, like Ivan Boesky, have been discredited.

Investment banks The linchpins of the merger and acquisition machine are the big investment banks, which have emerged as the most dynamic financial institutions in the USA. Their ability to raise huge sums of money quickly can swing a takeover contest. Drexel Burnham Lambert, for example, was able to raise $730m for Gillette's Ron Perelman in four days for one bid; Drexel's Michael Milken pioneered the junk-bond market, and the bank now corners half such issues. The top six investment banks underwrite 80–90% of all corporate debt or equity issued. Confidence in the investment banks should survive the insider trading scandals; their influence remains enormous.

Investors and money managers

Traders and brokers may steal the limelight, but the institutional investors hold the purse strings. The growth of corporate pension funds – usually managed by outside advisers, – has transformed the balance of power in the financial markets. In 1985 alone, assets managed by the USA's 100 largest institutions topped $1.5 trillion. With this kind of money to play with, the 1,500 or so leading money managers in the USA can swing stock prices dramatically as they move their investments. Short term movements of institutional money have become more common. Money managers' clients insist on short-term performance; in response, money managers trade their portfolios far more actively. Critics say they are driven by herd instinct as much as investment prudence. It has been the willingness of institutions to invest in junk bonds that has helped fuel the takeover boom. The sheer scale of these investments, though, has made institutional investors increasingly anxious about the performance of their managers. Most pension funds now rely upon a consultant to monitor the money managers, and consultants have usurped some of their power – sometimes even dictating which sector of the market the manager should play.

Federal Reserve

"The Fed" is the single most powerful financial institution in the USA. The key to the Fed's power is its control over interest rates and the money supply. It is a government agency, but completely independent of politicians, as the Reagan administration's disagreements with Fed chairman Paul Volcker testify. In the early 1980s Volcker and the Fed fought relentlessly against inflation, keeping interest rates high and turning a deaf ear to criticism from the White House and Congress. The Fed's squeeze on the money supply plunged the economy into the 1981-83 recession but successfully brought down inflation. Volcker's term expires in August 1987, but he is eligible for reappointment.

Business connections

The old boy network is far less pervasive and influential in the USA than in Europe, but, like the exclusive clubs in the big cities, the small towns still use their local Masons, Elks, Rotary and Moose clubs to exchange favors.

Round Table The Business Round Table is a young organization, founded in the early 1970s, but its membership includes CEOs of 194 top US corporations.

Organized crime

Organized crime is big business in the USA, and it is estimated that the "mob" controls $50bn of revenues – over 1% of the GNP. The Mafia's activities reach deep into the labor unions and construction industry, and their operations are said to cost the USA 400,000 jobs and put 0.3% on prices. The power of the mob seemed to be waning in the mid 1980s when a number of bosses were brought to trial. But in businesses the mobsters think of as their preserve they remain a force to be reckoned with.

Business framework

The sheer scale of US business is staggering. At the last count, in 1982, there were almost 3m corporations, 1.5m partnerships, and more than 10m proprietorships registered in the USA; since then the numbers may have expanded by 20% or more. The tradition is that business here flourishes in a climate of unrestricted free enterprise. There is some truth in this, and in many respects businesses are free to do as they like; on the whole, regulations are designed to promote competition, not stifle it. But Americans are highly litigious and the amount of legal documentation needed to do business in the USA is paralleled in few other major industrial nations.

Corporate America

The US business scene is dominated by the corporation and, in particular, the big corporation. In the 1930s, only 0.2% of US corporations had assets of more than $50m; today there are literally hundreds of corporations worth billions of dollars. Yet the top 50 corporations account for almost three-quarters of the entire annual receipts of US business. And in certain sectors, such as manufacturing and oil, the predominance of the giants is even more striking. The top 13 manufacturing corporations, for example, draw in nearly 90% of total manufacturing receipts. Only in the retail and service industries, and also in construction, do small and mid range corporations have any real impact on the overall figures.

Chastened conglomerates? In the 1960s and 1970s, vast conglomerates were in vogue. Led by innovative, efficient managers, they successfully combined a disparate array of businesses to make large, profitable organizations that became models for others to emulate. Conglomerates like ITT, headed by the charismatic Harold Geneen, and the United Aircraft Company, headed by Harry Gray, seemed ready to sweep all before them. But in recent years they have lost some of their appeal. The mid-to-late 1980s has seen a resurgence in corporate acquisitions and mergers, and at times Wall Street seems to have been gripped by merger mania (see *Mergers and acquisitions*). By and large, the mergers have not been to create new conglomerates; they have been the result of companies' renewed determination to strengthen their core businesses, and sell off fringe activities. The trend away from conglomerates has been heightened by the poor performance of the big names like ITT, whose profits slumped so badly in the 1980s that it has had to sell off its telecommunications equipment companies, and United Aircraft (now known as United Technologies).

Incorporation

The procedure for setting up a corporation in the USA is, in many ways, similar to that in other countries. The principal difference is that US corporations are organized in a particular state, and so are subject to that state's own, often idiosyncratic, incorporation laws (listed in the Martindale Hubbell Law Directory). In fact, there are no federal incorporation laws.

Most US firms do business in more than one state, but this is not a problem. Once a firm is incorporated in any one of the 50 states, it can set up operations right across the country. Frequently, even the firm's headquarters are outside the state of incorporation. All operations are subject to state corporation laws – and to local taxes – but the firm only has to incorporate once. To operate in a state other than that in which it is incorporated, a firm simply has to file with that state's secretary of state its Certificate of Incorporation, a "good standing" certificate and other routine documents, together with a fee paid annually.

Where to incorporate Picking the right state in which to incorporate can be crucial, and most businesses consult a good corporate lawyer before making their choice. Choosing the wrong state can lumber a corporation with a charter that hamstrings any future expansion or change of direction. Moreover, the state's incorporation laws may have a significant affect on shareholders' rights, attitudes to dividends and so on.

Generally, it pays a firm to incorporate in the state where it does most business. But the strictness of the incorporation laws, tax liabilities and other considerations may make another state more attractive. Many firms are drawn to the states with the most liberal incorporation laws and in this respect New York, Maryland and especially Delaware are renowned. In fact, Delaware corporations are almost as distinctive a feature of the US business scene as Liberian tankers were of the shipping world.

One of the attractions of incorporating in Delaware is that there is no need for one of the incorporators to be a US citizen. Neither is there any need for directors to meet formally for board meetings; they can simply talk over the telephone. Moreover, Delaware law gives great freedom over the payment of dividends and allows firms to keep the minute book, stock transfer ledger and other books outside the state – unlike New York law. For any individual firm, however, New York and other states may have advantages which outweigh the liberality of Delaware.

How to incorporate The basic procedure for incorporation is so simple that do-it-yourself incorporation kits are available from bookstores. These include a stock register, certificate book, minute book and, sometimes, local bylaws. Those who can afford it, however, hire a lawyer, for in the USA it is always as well to guard against future litigation.

The whole process usually takes about a week and can cost as little as $40, although it generally costs around $1,000, depending on the state and the complexity of the charter. All it really involves is filing with the local secretary of state those articles of incorporation detailing the corporation's name, its purpose, its life (usually perpetuity), its capital, its stock value (if any), its statutory office address and the number of directors. Once the charter is granted, the firm is generally required to add "Inc" or "Corp" to its name.

For manufacturing businesses no capital is needed beyond that essential to start operations. But for financial enterprises most states have a minimum capital stipulation. Usually, there must be at least three founders and three directors.

Foreign investors Foreigners find few unusual problems setting up a business in the USA. There are not many federal rules regarding foreign investment, although the government may impose restrictions on investment in industries central to the security of the nation, notably defense, shipping, airlines, communications and mining. Similarly, although some states do have certain restrictions, they tend to be minimal. Most states will not allow foreigners to set up deposit banks or insurance companies, and several ban foreign participation in the drinks industry.

Interestingly, foreign corporations wanting to do business in a particular state are regarded in exactly the same light as American firms from another state. This is because, legally, a corporation is considered domestic only in the state in which it is incorporated. In California, a Delaware firm and a Japanese firm are both equally foreign.

Despite the simplicity of setting up a local branch, most foreign corporations conduct their business through local subsidiaries for legal and, increasingly, tax reasons. One plus point for staying foreign is that a foreign corporation is allowed to use its own, rather than US, accounting practice. The advantage of this is that whereas US firms are obliged to regard property and preferred shares as debt, foreign firms may be able to present them as assets and equity. When in 1986 Rupert Murdoch purchased six US television stations, he raised $1.lbn in preferred shares on the strength of News Corp Ltd's $101m profit by using Australian accounting practices; under the US system the company would have shown a $263m loss.

Foreign corporations with shares in US firms are subject to the scrutiny of the SEC and must file details of: executives' and directors' pay, transactions conducted between executives, directors and shareholders, changes in management, major acquisitions and the financial status of the company and its main subsidiaries.

Going public

Many of the biggest corporations in the USA are publicly owned, and every year thousands of US companies go through the rigmarole of a public share offer. The procedure is, in many ways, similar to that in countries like the UK, with rules about disclosures, acquisition, shareholders, shares and so on. But the amount of documentation is vast and much of it is dictated by the federal securities laws; much is also caused by the desire to protect the company and its advisers against possible litigation in the future.

Filing an offer When a company, domestic or foreign, plans a share offer of more than $500,000, it must usually file a range of documents with the Securities and Exchange Commission (SEC – see *Government and business*) whose task it is to oversee all public share issues. Besides a registration statement and prospectus, the filing must give a clear idea of the company's financial prospects. Established corporations have to file fully audited accounts, while firms less than three years old must submit a "plan of operation" (a cashflow projection) and a statement confirming whether any more funding will be needed within the first six months of going public.

In the past, many financial details had to be revealed only to the SEC, but over the last decade or so, firms have been required to disclose their financial status to the public in considerably more detail. Exactly what is for the public, and what is for the SEC's eyes only, varies from state to state. Most states have "blue sky" laws designed to prevent smart operators selling "the clear blue sky" to unsuspecting investors, but the details may be substantially different. Shares can be either common or preferred; preferred shareholders in most states have certain extra voting rights as well as receiving fixed interest. Shares can also be bearer or registered, though the preference in the USA is for registered shares.

The tender offer In some countries, the company's merchant and investment banks publish the share offer. In the USA, the offerer must publish the offer, and the company usually appoints a depositary – typically a clearing bank – to handle all the money. Some share offers need a little prodding along, so most offerers write to the "street names" (bankers and brokers holding shares on their clients' behalf) to suggest they recommend the idea to their clients. They may also appoint an information agent to chase the street names along and monitor progress generally.

All the same, there is much less of the hectic last-day rush so typical of share offers elsewhere. Shareholders in the USA are allowed to withdraw an offer up to 15 business days from the commencement of the tender offer, and making a speculative tender is common practice. The offer period is one of fluctuating fortunes for the shares, as arbitrageurs and dealers buy and sell stock.

Short term profits Public companies may start out as an extension of the private business of the founder. But it is rarely long before the institutional investors – who tend to hold the majority of shares in companies of any size – start pushing for professional managers to be brought in. Institutional investors expect a steady growth in profits to justify their investment, and the longer time horizon emphasis on asset development that may have characterized the company's private days is typically soon abandoned. Many shareholders demand instant results, and there are widespread complaints that this is why US business often concentrates on short-term profits at the expense of long term growth.

Proprietorships

Unincorporated and owned by just one person, the sole proprietorship is the simplest form of US business organization. By far the majority are small businesses employing just a few people; 80% of non-farm proprietorships have annual receipts of less than $50,000. All but 10% of US farms are in the hands of farmers or their families, and farms are much the biggest category of proprietorship. Many shops, too, are run on this basis. But the range of one-owner businesses and professional practices in the USA is as wide and varied as the nation itself.

The real attraction of proprietorship is that the owner is in total control. He or she is also at liberty to draw income at will, and deduct a whole range of expenses from the tax bill. The snag is that if the business gets into trouble, the owner is liable for all the debts.

Partnerships

In the legal and financial world, partnerships are perhaps the most common popular form of business set-up. But there are two kinds of partnership – general and limited – both of which are relatively simple and inexpensive to establish. General partners are jointly and severally liable for all the organization's debts and obligations; if the partnership goes bankrupt, creditors can claim against any one of the partners. Limited partners, on the other hand, can only be held responsible for those areas laid out specifically in the partnership agreement. However, in any partnership, at least one must be a general partner who has unlimited liability. There is no need for the general partner to be an individual; it could be a corporation. One quite common arrangement in the USA is for a few individuals to go into partnership as limited partners; they may also own a corporation which acts as general partner.

Mergers and acquisitions

In the mid 1980s, circumstances combined to send a wave of acquisitions and mergers surging through the US business world. The emphasis among institutional investors on short-term portfolio profits – together with low stock market values for asset-rich enterprises – provided the incentive for opportunistic bids, while commercial banks, and a range of other sources, provided ready finance. The laissez-faire attitude of the Reagan administration towards mergers and acquisitions provided a hothouse climate in which the takeover boom flourished. 1985 alone saw $94.6bn change hands in US corporate marriages as Nestlé took over Carnation, and Allied merged with Signal.

A series of startling revelations of insider trading on Wall Street, along with the poor performance of many debt-laden acquirers and the rise in stock market prices which eliminated asset undervaluation, may together end the merger boom. The uncovering of the criminal activities of some arbitrageurs will certainly bring calls for stricter controls on at least the financial side of mergers and acquisitions. Nonetheless, the merger boom has brought into common parlance a colorful array of techniques used by or against a "corporate raider." Even if the techniques fall into temporary disuse, the vocabulary will live on: terms such as "shark repellents," "white knights" and "junk bonds" (high-yield bonds in raising money for heavily-borrowed bidders), and "greenmail" (a payment from a target corporation to persuade a "raider" to leave it alone).

The regulations The powerful impetus towards free and fair competition in the USA has led to the creation of a complex array of antitrust legislation at both federal and state levels, beginning with the Sherman Antitrust Act of 1890. This bans monopolies and outlaws any contract or agreement that restrains trade. The Justice Department's powers to apply these laws, through its Antitrust Dvision, are sweeping. So, too, are those of the Federal Trade Commission (FTC), which works closely with the Justice Department. But the regulations leave considerable scope for differing interpretations by administrations of differing political complexion.

In recent years, the authorities have made it clear that, in most cases, they will continue to prevent horizontal mergers or cartels between firms engaged in similar activities. But they have tended to take a much more lenient attitude towards vertical mergers, such as that between a manufacturer and its distributors. The threat from abroad, however, has led the antitrust agencies towards the view that horizontal combinations, too, may be acceptable in certain circumstances – notably in the case of international joint ventures. In 1984, for example, the FTC consented to GM's venture with Toyota of Japan to set up a plant in Fremont, California.

Under the US Securities Exchange Act of 1934, anyone wishing to acquire "beneficial ownership" of a public corporation has to notify within 10 days the SEC and the target company, disclosing the source of funds, and plans for control. Beneficial ownership means 5% or more. No substantial corporate marriage – that is, one involving 15% of the voting shares at $15m or more, or 10% at $25m or more – can be consummated until the specified periods have elapsed. These are 15 days for a cash tender offer and 30 days for any other. During this time, the authorities may intervene and halt the merger, but only a minority are actually reviewed.

Tax

In the wake of the Reagan administration's tax revolution, begun in January 1987, the entire corporate tax system of the USA is changing. The detailed implementation of the change will take several years to complete. But overall, even though the top corporate tax rate is to come down, taxes on corporations will generally climb, because of the elimination of a host of tax deductions and credits. This is a reversal of the situation in the early 1980s, which saw taxes on business steadily falling.

Because many of the abolished deductions and credits are on capital investment, critics of the legislation feel it may encourage the perceived emphasis in US business on short-term gains. The net effect, they say, will be to transfer after-tax income from business, especially capital intensive businesses, to individuals. But the outcome of the reforms, which will take five years to come into full effect, remains to be seen.

Tax regulations The present US tax system is the kind of complex mass of statutes, rulings and acronyms that provides accountants with endless business. One of the problems is that tax regulations come from a plethora of different sources and each one has a different status. The main statute is the Internal Revenue Code of 1954, known as "the Code," which is being replaced under the current reforms. Besides this, though, there are Treasury Regulations which have most of the force of law, and occasional updates transmitted as Treasury Decisions. Through the Internal Revenue Service (IRS), the Treasury also issues Revenue Rulings designed to clarify any gray areas in the Code. Further IRS announcements may follow an important court judgment. Finally, the IRS may deliver a private letter ruling to an individual taxpayer.

Corporations (and individuals) are not only taxed by the federal government, but by state and local governments.

Taxes on corporations The IRS has a reach that is virtually worldwide, and all US corporations and citizens, regardless of where they live or do business, can be taxed on all of their income, real estate and investments anywhere in the globe.

Businesses are liable to tax in three principal forms: federal corporate income tax; state income tax (which may be on a unitary basis in some states); and withholding tax.

Federal corporate income tax is levied at five different rates according to income. Before the reforms, the top corporate income tax rate was 46%, payable on all taxable income of over $100,000, but this is to come down to 34%. Other rates, graduated in four $29,000 steps in income, have also come down. The new reforms also impose a much tougher minimum rate to insure that every company pays at least some tax.

It is actually up to the corporation to assess its own income and estimate how much tax it should pay. Three months after the end of each year – which can be either calendar or fiscal – it must file a tax return on Form 1120 for the IRS.

State income taxes are payable in any state where a corporation operates as well as in the state in which it is incorporated. But the rate varies considerably from state to state. Mississippi and Utah may claim as little as 3–5%; New York, Connecticut and the District of Columbia levy tax at 10–11.5%.

Considerable controversy surrounds the issue of just how much of the income of a corporation which operates in many states each state should be allowed to claim. In June 1980, a Supreme Court judgment confirmed a state's right to calculate tax on a "unitary" basis – that is, on all a corporation's income, no matter where it is earned. This is naturally very unpopular with multi-state and multi-national corporations, and has been challenged in the courts on a number of occasions. Pressure from other countries, notably Japan and the Netherlands, has persuaded President Reagan to promise to work towards abolition of worldwide unitary tax. At present, only three states – Alaska, Montana and North Dakota – claim tax on worldwide profit, but 22 operate unitary tax on a "water's edge" basis, levying tax on all profits earned in the USA.

Local taxes The effect of the new tax reforms on local taxation remains to be seen, and different municipalities will levy their own rates. Although local tax rates are generally low, they may still add significantly to the overall tax burden in many states. In New York City, for example, corporations paid 9% local tax, 10% state tax and 46% federal tax if on the top rate. State and local taxes could be deducted from taxable income when assessing federal tax – which meant that New York City corporations paid an effective maximum of 46%. But when the top federal tax rate comes down state and local taxes will not be deductible.

Tax deductions Tax deductible expenses include entertainment (strictly for business purposes) and contributions to charity. In the past, some of the allowances on depreciation were generous. Corporations could claim considerable reductions on tax for depletion of natural resources and wear and tear on equipment (under the accelerated cost recovery system: ACRS). But the new tax reforms are imposing significantly tougher codes on depreciation. They are also abolishing the Investment Tax Credit, which was worth 10% of the cost of new machinery and equipment.

Anti-avoidance measures

According to the liberal group Citizens for Tax Justice, US corporations are adept at tax avoidance. The group claims that of 250 large firms examined, 130 paid no tax at all in at least one year between 1981 and 1985. But there is no lack of anti-avoidance measures in the USA, including the"sub-part F" legislation which has been used as a model by many European countries for regulations to prevent the accumulation of income abroad. Under sub-part F, tax can be levied on the income of any "controlled foreign corporation" (CFC). A CFC is defined as one in which more than 50% of the voting power of the corporation is owned by US residents, each of whom has at least a 10% share. The USA is also tough on transfer pricing within multinationals and the IRS has considerable powers under section 482 to adjust the prices different sectors of the corporation charge each other.

Tax on dividends and interest

Since 1984, no withholding tax has been payable on dividends, interest, royalties or fees paid in the USA; Congress abolished it in the belief that withholding tax made it harder for US corporations to raise capital on the Eurobond market. Moreover, although dividends are taxed as income, 85% of those generated in the USA are tax deductible.

Tax on foreign corporations

Taxes on branches of foreign corporations are as heavy in the USA as anywhere. This is because the USA operates the concept of taxable income "effectively connected" with the US branch, and taxes the income of any foreign corporation with income effectively connected with a business anywhere in the USA. In fact, until the current round of tax reforms, foreign firms also paid withholding tax on dividends if more than 50% of their gross income was effectively connected. This has been replaced by a new Branch Level Tax. This imposes tax at 30% on the remitted profits of US branches of foreign corporations, after other tax payable in the USA and elsewhere has been taken into account. However, tax treaties with more than 50 countries, however, reduce the effect of these levies considerably.

Business information and regulations

The US scene is well documented, with many specialist agencies providing basic data on corporations, their financial standing and shareholder structure. Published information is extensive, but more detailed inquiries can be commissioned from a wide range of suppliers. Many corporations also take advantage of the USA's freedom of information laws to obtain data on rival companies.

Official sources of information

For detailed and specific information on business at a local level, the 14,000 state-run local industrial development and institutions are generally very useful – although it is worth bearing in mind that their job is to attract business to their own area. They can be contacted directly or via intermediaries such as the *US and Foreign Commercial Service Office of the Department of Commerce*, 14th St and Constitution Ave, NW, Washington DC 20230 ☎ (202) 377-3641.

The Bureau of the Census in the Department of Commerce also produces extensive and up-to-date statistical information, summarized in the annual Statistical Abstract of the United States, which lists sources for an enormous range of other statistics. Contact: *US Government Printing Office* ☏ (202) 783-3238.

Statutory bodies The *Securities and Exchange Commission*, 450 5th St, NW, Washington DC 20549 ☏ (202) 272-2650 is the body to which all share offers and all acquisitions of more than 5% in any publicly-owned US corporation must be referred. But it is also a very useful source of information on competitors' accounts and on subjects such as corporate law.

Other important regulatory bodies are: the *Anti-trust Division of the Justice Department*, 10th St and Constitution Ave, NW, Washington DC 20530 ☏ (202) 633-2401 which oversees monopolies and mergers, together with the *Bureau of Competition of the Federal Trade Commission*, 6th St and Pennsylvania Ave, NW Washington DC 20580 ☏ (202) 523-3601.

Trade and industrial associations The *Chamber of Commerce of the USA* 1615 H St, NW, Washington DC 20062 ☏ (202) 659-6000 is an umbrella group for the thousands of local organizations in the USA. Besides these, there are national associations for virtually every individual type of business, such as the American Manufacturers' Association and the American Bankers' Association. Most of these are represented in Washington DC.

Private information sources on companies Information on companies is not so freely available from public sources in the USA as in some European countries. However, *Dun and Bradstreet International*, One World Trade Center, suite 9069, New York, New York 10048, provides precise accounts and prospects in every market for the 120,000 biggest businesses in the USA and can be commissioned for credit reports.

Other valuable sources of information on companies are the following publications: the *Directory of American Firms Operating in Foreign Countries*, Uniworld Business Publications Inc, 50 E 42nd St, New York, New York 10017; *Ward's Directory of the 55,000 Largest US Corporations*, Gale Research Corporation, Book Tower, Detroit, Michigan 48226. There are also the *Thomas Register of American Manufacturers & Thomas Register Catalog File* and the *American Export Register*, both published by Thomas International Publishing Company Inc, One Penn Plaza, 250 W 34th St, New York, New York 10119.

One of the leading credit rating agencies is the *Standard and Poors Corporation*, 25 Broadway, New York, New York 10004. Standard and Poors also publishes the definitive and invaluable *S & P Register of Corporations, Directors and Executives.*

Management consultancies Management consultancy is booming in the USA. According to the American Management Consulting Association (ACME), there are now some 35,000 management consultancy firms in the USA, and the number is growing every year. The problem for those interested in using a consultant's services is the sheer number of firms competing to offer advice – and the fact that they all seem to sell similar services. However, many consultancy divisions attached to big accountancy firms such as Peat Marwick/KMG are now specializing in particular sectors, making the choice a little easier. Among the largest and most respected of consultancy firms are *McKinsey & Company Inc*, 55 E 52nd St, New York, New York 10022 ☏ (212) 909-8400; *Arthur Andersen*, 33 W Munroe St, Chicago 606033 ☏ (312) 580-0033; and the *Boston Consulting Group*, 780 3rd Ave, New York, New York 10017 ☏ (617) 262-3846.

Employment

With employment in the USA running at over 110m, more Americans are working than ever before, and the labor force is expanding by almost 3% each year – faster than in almost any other industrialized nation. But with the population rising and an increasing number of women looking for jobs, there are still over 8m unemployed (about 7% of the workforce), and in many parts of the USA it is very much an employer's market.

Changing job base

Two trends are changing the US employment scene dramatically: the continuing contraction of traditional sectors such as manufacturing and the boom in the new service industries.

Factory jobs lost Before 1980, more Americans still worked in manufacturing than in any other single sector – although manufacturing's share of the job market had been shrinking for a decade or so. But the 1980s have seen a steady whittling away of jobs in manufacturing, and there are now fewer than 19m people working in this sector. In 1980, manufacturing slipped into second place behind wholesale and retail, and now employment in the service industries has shot past both to almost 23m. Despite staggering improvements in productivity in some industries, the loss of jobs has sapped the bargaining power of manufacturing employees, and their wages are falling further and further behind. Some have been forced to accept "givebacks" – that is, cuts in their wages and conditions.

New service jobs The lion's share of the 2m or so new jobs created each year is in services – notably office and administration and the restaurant/fast food business. In two months alone in 1986, almost half a million service jobs were created. But most are poorly paid jobs, such as secretarial work, which tend to be taken by women.

Fall in real incomes Behind the apparently healthy employment figures, with millions of new jobs created each year, lies considerable hardship. The jobs that have been lost are generally the well-paid skilled and semi-skilled manual jobs; those that have been created are part-time or poorly paid. Whereas only 20% of the new jobs created each year in the 1970s were in the lowest wage category, now 60% are; and in the period between 1979 and 1984, 97% of the new jobs gained by white men were worth $7,000 a year or less – well below the federally-recognized poverty level for a family with two children (estimated at $10,989). More than a third of the 8m or so new jobs created in the first half of the 1980s were part-time.

The current boom in consumer spending belies the fact that personal income growth in the USA is actually lagging behind inflation as wages in manufacturing fall and more and more people take up low-paid service jobs. Real disposable income is falling at more than 2% a year, and Americans are sustaining their personal spending partly on credit and partly by many couples having dual incomes.

Labor laws

US labor law is founded on the fundamental doctrine of "employment at will," a traditional right which enables employers to hire and fire at will. Enshrined in this doctrine is the important principle that employers can terminate an employee's job at any time, without necessarily any justification – although employers rarely abuse this right. Employment is therefore on the basis of a short-term contract negotiated between employer and employee or by collective bargaining. This contract has to be drawn up and agreed on afresh every two or three years.

Because the contract must spell out the terms and conditions of employment completely and is the employer's/employee's only form of security, contracts tend to be complex documents that are legally binding on both parties. Wildcat strikes are rare in the USA – for strikers would be in breach of contract. Instead, strikes tend to occur after the contract has run its course and is being renegotiated.

Playing straight Ever since the Wagner Act was passed in the 1930s, employers have been under a legal obligation to negotiate contracts in good faith. If a union, or employee, can prove that management is not playing it straight, they can take their claim to the National Labor Relations Board. The Taft-Hartley Act of 1947 placed a similar obligation on unions.

Fair work standards The federal government sets a minimum wage for most non-agricultural employees subject to the Fair Labor Standards Act of 1938. The act covers all employees of enterprises engaged in interstate commerce and requires that employees be paid at time and a half for every hour worked over 40 per week. The law provides a basic reference point, but there are numerous ways it can be sidestepped to make sure that an employee is not covered by the act, and in areas where jobs are hard to come by, the act is frequently abused.

At present, the minimum wage can be adjusted only by Act of Congress, and this is a cause of some concern among labor leaders and politicians on the left. Throughout the 1970s, when inflation climbed steeply, the minimum wage was upped almost every year. But since Ronald Reagan came to power in 1981, the rate has stayed frozen at $3.35 an hour. Even though inflation in the 1980s has been slow, this means that yearly earnings at this rate are far below the federal poverty level for a family of four and little more than a third of the national average wage.

Advocates of raising the minimum argue that an increase would not only alleviate the distress of some of the USA's poorest people but also address the "chump change" dilemma. This is the dilemma facing poor people who see little point in working for derisory wages when they can earn more on welfare or hustling in the streets, a dilemma particularly associated with inner-city black youths. Critics of an increase in the minimum wage believe it would drive up labor costs, leading to higher inflation and unemployment.

Equal opportunities Over the past 30 years or so, civil rights movements have put considerable pressure on employers to prevent them from discriminating against people on the grounds of sex, race, religion or age. But the prevalence of the doctrine of employment at will has meant that there is actually less federal legislation on the statute books than in many other Western industrialized nations. Instead, equal opportunities and rights are often protected by executive orders from the president and incorporated in the contract.

In theory, the combination of federal legislation, executive orders, favorable high court judgments and amendments to the doctrine of employment at will achieved by the civil rights movement should provide groups that suffer discrimination with a high degree of protection. In practice, many women and blacks still find it difficult to get well-paid jobs. Well over a third of the long-term unemployed are black, and more than two thirds of the jobs taken up by blacks in the 1980s are at wages below the official poverty level. Women are faring only a little better and Hispanics much worse.

Nevertheless, there is considerable variation from state to state. When in January 1987, for example, the

Supreme Court upheld a woman's right under California law to return to work after maternity leave, within weeks it denied the same right to a Missouri woman.

Protection for the elderly The 1980s have seen a number of congressional measures banning companies from forcing employees into payouts for active workers age 65 and up. Thirteen states, including populous California, Florida, New Jersey and New York, had already outlawed the mandatory retirement age. But from January 1, 1987, all private US companies were required to do the same, although the public sector has seven years to comply. Experts predict that ending mandatory retirement could mean at least an 18% increase in the numbers of over-70 workers by 2000. The average retirement age is now 63.

Labor relations

The USA's past is littered with industrial disputes as bitter and as violent as any in the world. But the 1980s have seen the workforce, if not necessarily happier with their lot, at least less willing to fight about it. Rancorous disputes have by no means disappeared, but they are fewer in number and duration than they were a decade ago. In the mid 1980s, 2,500-odd strikes caused 25m worker days to be lost a year, whereas in 1970, 5,716 strikes cost 66.5m days.

However, the pattern of industrial relations is perhaps more varied in the USA than in any other Western industrialized nation. There are enormous differences even within the same industry. Pay negotiations, for example, are almost invariably conducted on a plant-to-plant basis, or at most a state-to-state basis, rather than nationally, even within the strongly unionized industries. In the shiny new high-tech factories of the Sunbelt and California, wages are high, unionization is rare, the lifestyle is attractive and industrial relations are as good as anywhere. In the traditional industries in the old industrial areas, though, hard times have meant that management and workers are often at loggerheads – although the more determined employers have been able to weaken union power.

The right to strike is a fundamental American freedom, but it is hedged around with numerous legal restrictions – restrictions that vary considerably from state to state. Perhaps the most significant qualification is the "cooling-off" period laid down by the Taft-Hartley Act, which stipulates the time that must elapse before the next step in the escalation of a dispute. The idea is that the labor and management will have time to reach an amicable agreement. In practice, however, the "cooling-off" period is often when both sides draw up their battle lines.

Picketing is also a fundamental right, a form of free speech protected by the First Amendment to the US Constitution. But like the right to strike, it is hedged around with restrictions.

The unions Union membership in the USA is low – barely a fifth of the workforce – and interest in unionization is on the wane. The combined membership of the umbrella organization covering the trade unions – the American Federation of Labor and Congress of Industrial Organizations (AFL-CIO) – was 17.3m in 1986, though there were 7m or so workers in non-affiliated organizations. And in the mid 1980s, only two unions, the United Automobile Workers (UAW) and the United Food and Commercial Workers (UFCW), had more than 1m members each.

Unionism remains strong in the old traditional industries such as manufacturing and transport, but has hardly any influence in industries such as finance, services and the retail trade. And while the unions retain a powerful grip on the workforce in long-industrialized states such as New York, Michigan, West Virginia and Pennsylvania, their presence in Florida, Texas and Mississippi is weak.

Union recognition The sheer diversity of the American labor movement is striking; there are more than 175 national unions with 71,000 affiliated local unions, and 35 national employee associations with almost 14,000 local chapters. But only one union is recognized as having the right to negotiate contracts in each place of work. A minority of workplaces now have a recognized union, but when there is one, the management are legally obliged to negotiate with it. To gain recognition, a union must send a petition to the National Labor Relations Board, which then organizes elections to establish the views of the workforce. If another union gains a foothold in a place where there is already a recognized union, it can insist on new elections to determine which union may negotiate on behalf of the workforce.

Closed shops are outlawed in many states by right-to-work laws. Some states have enacted right-to-work laws to weaken unions and attract industry. But strong opposition from labor leaders has made sure that none of the major industrial states has such laws.

Executive salaries

While their employees' wages have been stagnating, the salaries of US executives have surged ahead, and they are now among the highest in the world. Earnings of $1m a year are not unusual. The gap between the European executive and his US counterpart is wide and getting wider.

Part of the explanation for this is that American executives get a larger proproportion of their pay in performance-related bonuses, and corporate profits have risen strongly. As many as 73% of directors of US companies have performance-related pay, compared with only 42% in Britain. Significantly, the total earnings of US executives rose by over 11% a year in the mid 1980s.

Personal taxation Until recently, the USA had a labyrinthine tax system with no fewer than 15 different rates of taxation, ranging from 11% of the earnings of the poorest-paid to 50% for those at the top of the pay scale. Critics attacked not only its complexity but its "punitive" top tax rate which, they felt, was holding back entrepreneurs. Others commented that few top executives paid their taxes anyway, since the system embodied all kinds of tax shelters.

But in 1987 the Reagan administration launched a package of sweeping tax reforms, designed to be implemented over five years. At the heart of the reforms is a plan to slice the top tax rate back to under 30%, so that the USA will have the lowest top tax rate in the industrial world. In fact, the package replaces 15 tax rates with just two, at 15% and 28%. Since four out of five people will be on the lower rate, the effect should be to cut taxes across the board.

A few cherished tax dodges are being sealed up – notably in real estate – and capital gains tax has been upped to the same level as wages and salaries.

Average Americans, meanwhile, may carp about the loss of tax relief on interest on credit card debt, car loans and installment plan purchases which they had before the reforms. But 80% are paying less tax as a result, and Americans, on average, now pay less tax than their counterparts in Europe or Japan. Some 6m people with incomes below the poverty line pay no tax at all.

State taxes Besides federal taxes, most Americans also pay tax to their own state, and state tax rates vary considerably within guidelines laid down by the federal government. New York, for example, is very heavily taxed, and New York Republicans have called for tax cuts, arguing that the tax rate impairs New York's ability to compete for industry and skilled workers.

Financial institutions: introduction

The combined forces of deregulation and volatile interest rates have set off intense competition in the world's most highly developed financial system, spawning esoteric new products and financial markets. As foreign intermediaries, borrowers and investors flock to the USA, American banks and securities firms are increasingly turning to overseas and global markets.

Recent developments

Securitization Bank loans are being replaced by credit in the form of securities, as large corporations – sometimes more creditworthy than the banks from which they borrow – turn to the less expensive commercial paper markets for short-term funds. Even companies with unimpressive credit ratings can now gain access to public markets by issuing junk bonds or pooling their own receivables and selling them to investors. Prohibited from underwriting these securities, commercial banks have had to make do writing guarantees and letters of credit to back the issues. But not all securitization has hurt the lenders: by securitizing and then selling off portions of their own loan portfolios, banks and savings and loans institutions have been able to reshape their balance sheets, create liquidity, and generate fee income.

Product boundaries blurred Over the past decade, financial institutions have sidestepped many of the legal and practical constraints stopping them from treading on one another's turf. Securities firms have invaded commercial banking territory, laying claim to short-term corporate lending markets and siphoning consumer deposits into high paying mutual funds (see *Investment banks and other institutions*). Banks have retaliated by buying discount brokerages and offering alternative forms of long-term finance to corporations. Even insurance companies have entered the fray, selling investment products and making residential mortgage loans.

More risk, fewer profits Intense competition from within and outside the financial sector has driven commercial banks to book riskier loans and pursue less desirable markets; meanwhile, investment banks have been forced to put ever larger amounts of capital at risk for their clients. Some financial products – such as large corporate lending and bond underwriting – have become overcrowded and unprofitable for many participants.

Technology Advances in computers and telecommunications have revolutionized the financial services industry. Widespread automation brings investors instantaneous market data and allows securities firms to handle record numbers of transactions in a fraction of the time possible a few years ago. Commercial banks now offer dozens of electronic services, such as home banking and point-of-sale retail payments systems. The number of automated tellers has risen dramatically, and there are now over 60,000 nationwide.

Emergence of financial conglomerates Deftly skirting banking regulations, retail and manufacturing firms have used their consumer credit operations as a springboard into the banking and insurance industries. Sears, Roebuck, one of the nation's foremost department stores, has over 60m credit card holders and through the acquisition of numerous subsidiaries now sells mortgages, insurance, real estate, banking products and securities alongside the vacuum cleaners, toasters and dishwashers. American Express has become a diversified financial corporation with revenues of $12bn per year. Its market capitalization outstrips the nation's largest banks.

Commercial banks

Much of the legislation imposed during the 1920s and '30s to ensure bank safety has been stripped away, spurring innovation, risk-taking and – in some cases – imprudence. Rapid asset growth during the 1970s, particularly in lending to Latin America and energy firms, left many banks with problem loans and questionable levels of capitalization. Bank failures are at their highest rate since the Depression. Nevertheless, there are still over 14,000 privately-owned commercial banks, most of them small, local institutions with assets under $200m.

Federal Reserve System

The Federal Reserve, composed of 12 District banks, acts as the nation's central bank and is responsible for carrying out national monetary policy, usually in tandem with the Treasury. The 1,500 privately-owned member banks, which control 70% of the country's banking assets, are required to maintain sizeable interest-free reserves with the Fed.

Open market operations are the primary tool the Fed uses to control the amount of money and credit in the banking system. The New York Federal Reserve Bank buys and sells huge blocks of government securities on the open market. By altering the balance between the supply and demand for credit in the economy, the Fed effectively influences the interest rates banks charge. The Federal Funds rate – the rate at which member banks borrow and lend money to one another – determines the rate banks charge their customers. The Fed can also intervene in foreign exchange markets, raise or lower reserve requirements and control the levels of bank lending – but these powers are rarely used.

Regulatory powers The Fed sets capital adequacy guidelines and monitors the activities of its members. Non-member banks are regulated by state authorities.

In addition, member and most state-chartered banks are supervised and insured by the Federal Deposit Insurance Corporation (FDIC).

Principal activities

Commercial banks have traditionally supplied industrial firms with short- and medium-term loans, but long-term lending has grown as banks have attracted time deposits and issued bonds. Electronic information management products, such as cash management services, are on the rise. Now there are no interest rate ceilings on checking and savings accounts, banks are having to pay market rates for consumer deposits. Even so, the relative stability of these funds and the high profit margins possible on consumer loans have led banks to invest more heavily in retail banking than ever before. Tight restrictions apply to non-banking activities, but commercial banks are free to operate in related businesses such as discount securities brokerage, credit cards and investment management.

Correspondent banking

To circumvent restrictions against interstate branch banking, banks have formed an elaborate network of correspondent relationships. Larger banks frequently provide data processing and other high fixed-cost services to smaller banks in exchange for fees or deposits. Correspondent relationships also enable banks to sell assets to other banks. But the interdependence of financial institutions has become a matter of public concern. The near collapse of Continental Illinois, the nation's 10th largest bank, was precipitated by faulty loans it had purchased from a small Oklahoma bank.

Payments systems Lacking a centralized giro system, the US relies largely on bank-owned clearing houses to handle funds transfers and check-clearing. The US generates twice the payments per capita of any other country and writes nearly two-thirds of the world's checks; and the average check must clear three banks before being returned. Despite efforts to promote electronic funds transfers, paper-based transactions still account for more than 90% of all non-cash settlements.

Money center banks

Money center banks are the largest and most influential of all American banks. Besides traditional lending, deposit-taking and trust activities, money centers are active participants in the money and international capital markets, and in US government securities underwriting and trading. For regulatory reasons, most big banks are now owned by bank holding companies.
Citibank, a subsidiary of the bank holding company Citicorp, has set its sights on becoming the world's first global bank, offering a huge array of financial products to consumers and businesses worldwide. Domestically, it has been the most successful money center in building its consumer banking operations, which now contribute one-third of earnings.
Morgan Guaranty, owned by J P Morgan the most prestigious American commercial bank, serves an elite clientele of blue-chip industrial and corporate clients. Consumer banking is limited to a few thousand wealthy individuals. It is the only money center with an AAA bond rating and is consistently one of the most profitable large US banks.
Bankers Trust decided in 1979 to eschew retail banking altogether to become a self-styled "merchant bank". It has made impressive inroads into investment banking territory, establishing a hotly contested commercial paper operation and aggressively selling its loans to other banks.
Bank of America was, in 1980, the world's largest bank in terms of assets. But since then, its fortunes have been assailed by everything from third-world debt to farm loan problems. By late 1986, it was ailing so badly that it had to fight off a bid from the smaller Californian bank, First Interstate Bancorporation.

Regional banks

The largest regional banks and bank holding companies now equal many money center banks in size, but typically rely more on consumer deposits than money market funding. In recent years, large regionals have been among the most profitable and fastest growing banks in the country. Following a 1985 Supreme Court ruling allowing interstate mergers approved by the states, a rash of mergers took place. Many states formed regional pacts to shut out the New York and California money centers, and the USA could soon see some of the concentration of banking power shift away from New York into the hands of a few "super-regionals".

Foreign banks

Growth of foreign banks has been dramatic. Roughly 23% of the country's corporate and industrial loans are now on the books of foreign banks, compared to 10% a decade ago. Japanese banks are the most aggressive, controlling 40% of foreign bank assets in the US. With their low cost of equity and willingness to forgo short-term profits for market dominance, they are known for cut-throat loan pricing.

Savings and Loans

Savings and Loans Associations account for about 40% of residential mortgages. High interest rates in the 1970s dealt a heavy blow to S&Ls dependent on fixed-rate portfolios. Most S&Ls have since securitized their assets and begun making floating rate loans.

Investment banks and other institutions

With a fraction of the staff and one-tenth the assets of commercial banks, securities firms provide American corporations with most of their external funding. Following the deregulation of fixed brokerage commissions in 1975, many securities firms went under, but low cost competitors soon emerged, and today there are 8,000 securities brokers and dealers in the USA. As investors and issuers become more sophisticated and global in reach, it is the New York investment banks – with their vast networks of issuer/investor contacts and massive capital bases – that are the dominant players.

Investment banks

The top New York investment banks are among the most aggressive, innovative, and profitable financial institutions in the USA. The top six underwrite 80–90% of all corporate debt and equity issued. As financial consultants, investment banks wield considerable power over corporate decision-making. While their basic business is acting as intermediary between investors and private or public concerns seeking medium- and long-term funds, investment banks have rapidly broadened their fields of activity. Commercial paper operations, advising on mergers and acquisitions, project and lease financing, private placements and Euromarket securities issues have all become much more significant contributors to earnings than in the past. As a group investment banks pay the highest salaries in the USA, allowing them the pick of top graduates from the country's best schools.

Merrill Lynch is the largest brokerage house in the USA and one of the nation's most broadly diversified financial services firms, with a major position in both retail and institutional investor markets.

Salomon Brothers is the world's leading underwriter of new securities and the world's most profitable publicly owned securities house. It underwrites 30% of the corporate equity and a quarter of the debt issued in the USA. Salomon is famous for its aggressive approach as well as the infighting of its employees.

Goldman Sachs is pre-eminent in commercial paper, mergers and acquisitions and equity trading. The firm is one of the last old-fashioned private partnerships left on Wall Street, although it has recently sought external sources of capital. In a good year, a partner makes as much as $5m.

Other financial institutions

Mutual funds sell shares directly to investors; the money raised is then pooled and invested in a variety of securities by professional managers. With over 1,500 different funds, 35m investors, and assets of $500bn, the industry has burgeoned into one of the nation's largest financial services providers. A specialized type of mutual fund, the money market fund, grew rapidly in the late 1970s. It allowed small investors to participate directly in the high-yielding short-term debt markets at a time when regulations kept bank interest rates artificially low. Although these regulations have gone, money market funds retain much of their popularity.

Venture capital firms provide over $2.5bn a year to promising young companies denied conventional financing. In return for investment capital, venture capitalists receive substantial equity ownership and stand to make large profits if their companies prosper and go public or are bought by other companies.

Commercial finance and factoring firms typically cater to small and medium-sized businesses, advancing them funds against accounts receivables, inventory, equipment or other assets. The tax benefits of equipment leasing have made it a hot financing technique. With corporate lending markets drying up, many commercial banks are acquiring finance and factoring firms.

Consumer finance companies are the largest providers of consumer instalment credit after commercial banks. A number of manufacturing and retail firms have finance subsidiaries, notably General Electric, IBM and the nation's big three auto manufacturers.

Financial markets

The United States has the largest, most diverse and highly developed financial markets in the world. There are no exchange controls and, with the removal of the US interest-equalization tax, foreigners are encouraged to participate both as issuers and investors. About 80% of all securities are not listed on public exchanges but are traded directly between dealers in the over-the-counter market. New York is the center of most trading activity; Chicago is the leader in commodities and options.

Debt markets

Credit markets in the USA have grown dramatically in recent years, as equity financing has become less popular. The largest borrower is the US government, which accounts for $2.5 trillion of outstanding debt. Most of the debt is traded directly in the over-the-counter market.

Government securities Treasury bills, notes and bonds are sold at weekly public auctions held by the Federal Reserve. The market is served by 35-40 primary dealers – 40% of them owned by commercial banks and one by the Japanese – that purchase and make markets in the securities. There is also a vast secondary market, served by a few hundred brokers and dealers. Daily trading in government securities exceeds $80bn; it is the largest and most efficient securities market in the world.

Government agency securities
Agencies of the US government have issued or guaranteed more than $600bn of debt held by private investors. Over half is composed of securities backed by pools of residential mortgages. These securities have had unusually high yields although there is a risk that mortgages may be paid off early. Markets in agency securities are maintained by the primary dealers. Turnover ranges from $10–15bn a day.

Corporate bonds and commercial paper
US corporations issue almost $150bn a year in bonds. Large issues are usually sold directly to investors by a syndicate of investment banks, who then make secondary markets in the securities. The emergence of the "junk" bond in the past five years has allowed hundreds of corporations with low bond ratings access to public markets. Commercial paper – short-term promissory notes used to raise working capital – is fast becoming a leading source of short-term funds for major corporations. Trading in commercial paper exceeds $14bn a day.

Equity Markets

There are 12 stock markets across the USA operating independently. Trading hours vary according to time zone but electronic communications systems allow certain issues to be traded simultaneously on several exchanges. All public trading is controlled and supervised by the

Securities and Exchange Commission.

The New York Stock Exchange is the largest organized securities exchange in the world, with more than 52bn shares listed and a market value in excess of $1.9 trillion. The value of securities traded exceeds $6bn a day. Registration procedures are strict; most of the 1,500 listed companies are prominent domestic and foreign firms.

The American Stock Exchange (Amex) in New York has less stringent listing requirements and tends to trade issues of companies still too small to be included on the NYSE. Over 600 companies are listed and the annual volume traded is over $20bn.

Regional exchanges account for only about 10% of US trading volume in listed securities. Typically they feature the issues of local firms. The largest regionals are the Midwest Stock Exchange, the Pacific Stock Exchange, and the Philadelphia Stock Exchange.

NASDAQ is the market where over-the-counter, rather than listed, stocks are traded. More than three times the size of the London Stock Exchange, the National Association of Securities Dealers' Automated Quotation system is a computerized network that connects 500 firms making markets in 4,700 over-the-counter securities. Subscribers to the system include thousands of securities dealers, pension funds, and other financial institutions. The value of shares traded exceeds $230bn a year. NASDAQ is the most international market, with three times as many foreign issues as the New York and American exchanges.

Other markets

Foreign exchange The global foreign exchange market has doubled in size in recent years and now has a daily trading volume exceeding $200bn. New York is second in size only to London, trading $50bn a day. Only 10% goes to finance international commerce and investment; the great majority is traded by banks and speculators betting on market movements and hedging foreign investments. About 80 commercial banks dominate the market, although investment banks and commodity firms have become increasingly visible.

Futures The USA has the largest and most active futures markets in the world. Contracts in anything from pork bellies to precious metals to financial and currency futures are bought and sold with ease. Contracts are highly standardized and markets are closely tied to the underlying commodities. As a result, most of the world's hedging is done in the USA. The Chicago Mercantile Exchange is the biggest futures and commodities exchange, followed by the New York Futures Exchange. Increasingly, financial futures outweigh old-fashioned agricultural commodities in volume and activity.

Investors and investments

Pension funds and insurance companies and other financial institutions hold 60% of all outstanding securities and account for at least 85% of the transaction volume in every major securities market. Individual participation in the markets has waned as investors have cut transaction costs by letting professionally managed mutual funds invest for them. Now, direct household ownership accounts for less than 40% of the $6-7 trillion worth of securities portfolios in the USA. Corporate equities and government debt constitute two-thirds of all American securities portfolios. The remainder is largely held in corporate and municipal bonds, and as mortgage-backed securities on the commercial paper market. Although total investment in foreign issues has risen sharply, foreign securities still account for less than 3% of the securities held.

Insurance

The US insurance industry writes 48% of the world's insurance business. Most life, property and casualty insurance is sold by private insurance companies, while government-sponsored and non-profit organizations fund 60% of health benefits. The industry is primarily regulated at the state level, with tight controls over both insurance and investment activities.

Life insurance

Americans buy more life insurance relative to the national income than anyone but the Japanese and Canadians. In 1985 there were 385m life policies in force, providing $5.5 trillion in total coverage, 43% being accounted for by group life insurance offered by employers.

Companies Over 90% of these are publicly owned; the remainder are mutual life companies, owned by policyholders. Mutual companies tend to be older and larger, controlling 55% of the industry's assets. The largest life company, Prudential, writes less than 8% of the nation's life insurance premiums.

Products With banks and securities firms competing for consumer investment dollars, life companies have had to design new products: universal life, the most popular, divides premium dollars between a high-yielding investment portfolio and a death benefit. And many companies now sell the same mutual funds and individual retirement accounts (IRAs) as banks and securities firms. Insurance companies manage two-thirds of US private pension fund assets.

Sources of income Over the past two decades life premium receipts have declined from 49% to 25% of total income, whereas investments of capital and reserves, spurred by higher interest rates, have grown to contribute nearly 30%, with annuities and health premiums each contributing about 20%. To maximize investment returns, companies have aggressively entered the real estate markets, both as developers and equity owners.

Prospects Proposed legislation which will eliminate the tax-deferred status of life products, coupled with lack of management experience in pricing and selling more complex products – increasingly indistinguishable from those offered by banks and securities firms – will put the future of many companies at risk.

Property and casualty

Roughly 3,500 companies insure 93% of all homeowners and virtually all businesses in the USA. Property and casualty underwriting has proven consistently unprofitable. Until recently, companies were able to achieve bottom line profits by aggressively investing reserves and capital, keeping insurance rates low to allow for the healthy returns companies could get on idle funds. Declining interest rates and net underwriting losses of over $45bn in 1984 and 1985, however, pushed the industry into the red and set off the steepest ever rise in insurance prices.

Premiums and losses Over half of the $120bn P&C premiums written annually come from individuals – most of them to insure automobiles. Claims paid and claims adjustments absorb 83 cents of every premium dollar earned. Auto accidents are the leading cause of losses ($70bn a year), followed by theft ($10bn).

Lobbying for law reform Companies are pressing for extensive tort reform to combat the steep rise in out-of-court settlements. Limits on liability, awards, punitive damages and attorneys' fees have already been imposed in some states. These gains may prove a mixed blessing if states also insist upon lowering the ceilings on rates companies can charge.

Accountants

Accountancy in the USA is dominated by the Big Eight firms, which between them control 90% of the profits, revenues, income tax and employment of the companies listed on the New York Stock Exchange. But with 350,000 accountants practising in the USA, competitive pressures have forced this traditionally staid and restrained profession to branch out aggressively in new directions.

The professions

An accounting career in the USA begins with the long and arduous study for the Uniform CPA (certified public accountant) exam. This qualification is essential because, under state law, only CPAs can carry out audits.

Most of the brightest CPA graduates head for the Big Eight, which between them manage to interview nearly 150,000 graduates a year, and take on some 10,000. Each has his or her eyes on a partnership, but to become a partner in one of these firms, the young accountants have to put in years of arduous work. A few bright accountants prefer the less demanding hours of a smaller practice. But the high potential earnings, and the increasing glamor of life at the top of the profession, ensures that most set their sights on the Big Eight. It may take as little as five years to achieve partnership. But most of the big firms have hundreds of partners, and there is a wide difference in status and rewards between the working junior partners and their seniors.

Changing roles

Preparing tax returns and auditing company books still provides accounting firms with the bulk of their income. But over the past decade or so they have been branching out into fields such as executive recruiting, public relations, and, especially, management consultancy. Consulting now accounts for 15–20% of the total revenues of the Big Eight; and some of them want to boost this to 50%.

The KMG merger with Peat Marwick created a huge consultancy section; Touche Ross bought out the consultancy firm Braxton, and a string of others; and it is sometimes rumored that Price Waterhouse may join forces with McKinsey, the second-largest management consultancy firm in the USA. Arthur Andersen is the largest.

Diversification has gone hand in hand with marketing, as staid accountants took advantage of rules relaxing advertising. Deloitte, Haskins & Sells was the first to go into consumer advertising with the slogan, "Beyond the Bottom Line." Arthur Young, the sixth largest firm, has hired marketing experts from consumer-goods companies like Uniroyal, the tire company, and Lipton Tea to improve the selling skills of their accountants.

Choosing an accountant

The large firms have the benefit of extensive resources and back-up facilities, and are clearly in a position to attract the best talent. But some businesses may prefer the more intimate relationship possible with smaller firms. There are still CPAs who sit at clients' desks doing their books between cups of coffee with the bookkeeper and boss. For them, conversation is consultancy at no extra cost.

The American Institute of Certified Public Accountants (AICPA) helps keep up standards through a voluntary peer review programme, which the institute is considering making mandatory for firms auditing public companies.

While this sets a lower limit on

competence, the choice of an accountant is best made with advice from another professional, either a lawyer or management consultant. Firms working in the same field may also choose the same accountant – while they would never share an advertising agency, picking the same accountant means picking one who knows the field well.

The letter of engagement

Typically, an accountant will give a client a letter of engagement at the outset. The terms of this letter have to be examined carefully for they outline the way the accountant will work. It is often important, for example, to specify just how many hours will be worked by the partners, who charge a great deal per hour, and how many by juniors. It is also important to establish just what is expected of the client's employees.

Accountants' letters of engagement are essentially intended to establish the business relationship. But part of the letter will be designed to protect them against possible future litigation.

Litigation

Increasingly, the law is holding accountants responsible for failure to detect fraud or advise their client properly. In the 1984 case, *The United States v. Arthur Young*, Supreme Court Chief Justice Warren Burger stated: "The independent auditor assumes a public responsibility transcending any employment relationship with the client." State courts are also upholding suits against accountants for negligence when the audit fails to reveal potential problems. And the Internal Revenue Service penalizes accountants for understating a client's liability, turning the professional adviser into an ally of the IRS, rather than the client.

Insurance for accountants against lawsuits is increasingly costly, and fees have risen accordingly.

The Big Eight

KMG Peat Marwick The 1986 merger of Peat Marwick and KMG Main Hurdman created the largest US accounting firm. KMG, the smaller of the firms, concentrates on rapidly growing medium-size companies, while Peat Marwick courts the larger, more established clients. Both are strong on audits.

Arthur Andersen Chicago-based, this firm projects a clean-cut, mid western image. It is the only international accounting firm that is really organized as a single homogeneous operation worldwide. It has also moved strongly into management consultancy.

Ernst & Whinney Aggressive consultancy activity is shaking the dust off the image of this staid, old-line Cleveland firm and it now operates a corporate deal-making department, much like an investment bank's corporate finance division.

Coopers & Lybrand was one of the oldest and most respected auditing concerns, with a high class Ivy League image. But in recent years, it is diversifying.

Price Waterhouse cultivates a gilt-edged image and pays its partners accordingly. It still earns most of its income from auditing, and has backpedaled on diversification. But its rumored interest in the consultancy firm McKinsey suggests it will not resist the trend for long.

Arthur Young & Company Rather old-fashioned still, Arthur Young is branching out abroad and introducing specialized consulting practices.

Deloitte, Haskins & Sells is considered an "auditor's auditor," with the highest respect for care and thoroughness, and now uses this as its major selling point.

Touche Ross The most adventurous of all the Big Eight, its recent acquisition of a string of consultancy firms, including Braxton, is typical of a young firm which detractors sometimes call "yuppie."

Law

While still chief justice of the US Supreme Court in the early 1980s, Warren E Burger observed how Americans were turning increasingly to litigation to solve all problems – and the scale of litigation in the USA is enormous. There are now almost four times as many cases clogging the federal courts as there were in 1960, and more than seven times as many appeals, while the number of lawyers has doubled in 25 years.

The professions

In the early 1980s, there were some 500,000 lawyers in the USA, ranging from store-front legal advisers in poor inner-city neighborhoods to top-line partners in firms handling corporate mergers. About 370,000 of them were in private practice: 180,000 working alone and 190,000 in law firms, the fastest expanding sector of the profession. There were also 55,000 lawyers employed as "in-house" counsels by business, a further 50,000 working for the government and 15,000 working for the judiciary or teaching.

Commercial lawyers dominate the profession, and in New York there are many large firms specializing in legal advice to big business. Work in these firms revolves around routine commercial transactions, not dramatic courtroom battles – expensive litigation may steal the headlines, but filing company registrations with the SEC and similar tasks brings in the money.

Commercial law firms have suffered from the growth of in-house legal departments in the major corporations. But they have made the most of the complex nature of financial law to carve out a new niche for themselves, specializing in mergers and acquisitions, bankruptcy and anti-trust disputes.

Training Lawyers begin their training with a three-year postgraduate course at one of the hundreds of law schools in the USA. Top of the list are Chicago, Columbia, Harvard, Michigan, Stanford and Yale, and the class finishing each year at schools like these provides an informal network that helps a lawyer along throughout his/her career. Many of the big firms have strong links with a particular school, and this may similarly help graduates in their careers.

Once a budding lawyer has the JD or LLB degree, he/she is employed by a law firm while studying for the state bar exam, one year later. Once past the bar exam, the lawyer progresses rapidly – though the rate of progress varies considerably from firm to firm. Most of the big firms blood their trainees by placing them directly on a client's team.

Choosing a firm

The top firms are as likely to choose their clients as be chosen by them. "New business committees" pore over multi-page submissions from partners asking to take on clients, and the clients have to explain why they are going to the firm now and what happened with their last firm. At the same time, law firms face increasingly transactional relationships, in which any big client will typically use several firms even for the same kind of work.

A comprehensive overview of the top 200 law firms is provided by *The American Lawyer Guide to Leading Law Firms*. Besides listing the firm's major clients, the guide gives its thumbnail history. The *National Law Journal Directory of the Legal Profession*, with 600 firms listed, provides a measure of firm profitability by counting the number of associates per partner. *Martindale Hubble* tries to be complete and authoritative, with entries provided by the firms themselves, and shows the hierarchy of lawyers within each.

Litigation

Litigation in the USA is a long, drawn-out process that starts with the filing of a suit and proceeds through a long period finding and bringing prospective witnesses to court – a process that may take a year or more from the first filing. Most suits are filed under state law, which covers property, crime and corporate regulations. But if the outcome is likely to be unsatisfactory in one court, lawyers may well recommend trying a different one, and going "judge-shopping" to find a well-disposed judge is common practice. Appeals, both to state and federal courts, are frequent, and accepted as a normal part of the litigation procedure. The US Supreme Court is the ultimate court of appeal, but only deals with cases that involve the constitution, an act of congress, a treaty or a right protected by federal law.

Arbitration The expense and duration of litigation have encouraged Americans to try arbitration. This is organized by the American Arbitration Association, using former judges and trained arbitrators.

Major firms

At one time, the major firms all practised on Wall Street and mirrored the New York dominance of American industry. Now many of the biggest law firms are far from New York, and their geographical spread is reflected in their diversity, as this selection shows.

Sullivan & Cromwell Once headed by Roosevelt's Secretary of State John Foster Dulles, Sullivan & Cromwell represents the "white shoe" exclusive Wall Street legal tradition. Employs more than 400 lawyers worldwide, and has vast experience in dealing with investment banks.

Shearman & Sterling are the lawyers for the giant Citibank and the firm has an upright, well-heeled image. Senior partners make a point of handling all work with major clients.

Cravath, Swaine & Moore Old-fashioned and strongly hierarchical, this firm has a high reputation for litigation.

Paul, Weiss, Rifkind, Wharton & Garrison Known for Democratic Party associations, this firm sports a progressive image and corporate clients like Coca-Cola.

Wachtell, Lipton, Rosen & Katz One of the new generation of specialist firms, it has an impressive track record with mergers and acquisitions, building on senior partner Martin Lipton's mergers reputation.

Covington & Burling Marking the rise of Washington as a law center, it has a reputation for handling regulatory affairs going back 40 years.

Arnold & Porter Washington firm with big business clients like Xerox and Philip Morris. Courts controversy because of efforts to show a *pro bono* side while wheeling and dealing in the best Washington tradition.

Williams & Connolly Built on the flamboyant and brilliant litigator, Edward Bennett Williams, this Washington firm has business clients like Anheuser-Busch but gets most publicity for Williams's courtroom confrontations.

Baker & McKenzie has merged with firms all round the world to build the USA's biggest law operation, with more than 750 lawyers.

Morgan, Lewis & Bockius Old-line, Philadelphia-based, now moving towards an aggressive modern approach with 400 lawyers.

Montgomery, McCracken, Walker & Rhodes Despite its London office, this is a good example of the top-flight regional firm. It is based in Philadelphia and gives Wall Street-style service for less cost.

Vinson & Elkins Houston-based firm, developed to over 400 lawyers during oil's heyday, marking the rise of Texas firms and practices that survived oil's decline.

Advertising and PR

On Madison Avenue, New York – the heart of the US advertising industry – it has often seemed as if the copywriters and creative directors of the big agencies could mould America's consumer culture at will. But as demand for advertising has shrunk and consumers have become more choosy, the agencies have had to hone their sales pitch, learn to exploit new media and accept a smaller fee to sustain business. The public relations industry, meanwhile, is helping big businesses polish their corporate images and special interest groups to learn the power of PR in pressing their case.

Advertising

For many years now, US advertising agencies have dominated the advertising industry worldwide – often working through local branches or subsidiaries – and in 1985, 18 out of 21 agencies billing more than $100m to foreign clients were based in the USA. They ranged from McCann-Erickson Worldwide, with $1.3bn of its non-US billings accounting for 68% of billings, to Kenyon and Eckhardt ($103m and 68%). Only very rarely did foreign advertising agencies break into the US market. But when the UK firm Saatchi and Saatchi took over Ted Bates in 1986 to create the world's largest agency – following hard on the heels of the merger of three major US agencies to form the Omnicom Group – doubts were expressed about the seemingly invincible robustness of the US ad industry. These doubts were compunded by a fall-off in commission rates, and a growing tendency of clients to pay straight fees unrelated to the advertising budget. Despite a spate of lay-offs, though, advertising revenues continue to rise, and there seems little chance of the industry running into real trouble.

New media The changing nature of the US market, reflecting demographic and economic changes, has forced the ad agencies to define their targets more closely. Specialist magazines are attracting a growing proportion of magazine advertising revenue, while the rise of cable television has created new opportunities for narrowly targeted ads – spending on cable TV advertising is growing at more than 20% a year. But the agencies are trying all kinds of outlets from bill board size video screens to stickers on parking meters. Significantly, direct mail advertising has soared and now attracts twice as much advertising revenue as network TV.

The power of TV Consumers in nearly 84m households from coast to coast watch, on average, seven hours of television a day, and it is estimated that by the time the average American youngster graduates from high school, he or she will have seen 50,000 30-second commercials and be familiar with most of the leading jingles. No wonder then that spending on TV advertising was worth approaching $20bn in the mid 1980s.

Public relations

Being seen, and being seen in the right light, are as important to the rapidly multiplying lobbying groups as to big business. More than 80% of the USA's top 500 companies use PR firms, and PR has become a key element in nearly all political campaigns.

Even before the big ad agencies began to merge, though, PR firms were being taken over by agencies keen to offer their clients a comprehensive package. Now even independent PR firms often reflect the wider services demanded by advertisers, including investor relations and takeover battles.

Importing and exporting

Americans have always been wedded to the concept of free trade. But the rising tide of imports into the USA, combined with the competitive pressures facing US exporters in the world market, have brought increasingly strident calls for protectionist measures.

Trade agreements

The USA has never been drawn into any particular trading bloc, but has negotiated numerous bilateral trade deals with individual nations and groups of nations. Some cover a broad spectrum of goods, such as the free trade deals with Israel, concluded in 1985, and Canada, which is still under negotiation. But most cover a specific sector. Typical of such agreements is the 1986 semiconductor deal with Japan. Under this agreement, the Japanese must sell chips at "fair" (higher) prices in the USA and help boost the US share of the Japanese market from 9 to 20%. In return, the USA drops its 120% levy on Japanese memory chips.

GATT The General Agreement on Tariffs and Trade (GATT) was set up in 1947 to liberalize trade and has since become the world's major forum for negotiating tariffs and trade, with 92 member nations. The USA makes the most of GATT to press for the removal of barriers to US exports. But it has been accused of side-stepping GATT with a range of non-tariff barriers.

The EEC At the current round of GATT talks in Geneva, the USA is pressing for the abolition of the EEC's Common Agricultural Policy, which the USA believes subsidizes Community farmers unfairly and undermines US grain exports. In the meantime, the USA is operating an "export enhancement program" (EEP) which offers free grain to exporters making big sales to certain countries, notably the USSR – much to the annoyance of the USA's main competitors, the EEC, Australia and Argentina. Grain also brought the USA into conflict with the Europeans recently over Spain's entry into the EEC. The USA believed it would lose $400m of feed-grain sales to Spain because of EEC tariffs, and threatened to impose 200% tariff on selected imports from the EEC until agreement was finally reached.

Import controls

Imports to the USA are subject to a wide range of controls and restrictions. Imports of drugs, obscure material, certain furs and a number of other goods are banned completely, while many goods, such as automobiles, are subject to quotas and "antidumping" duties designed to protect domestic industry. Altogether well over 40% of US imports are subject to these non-tariff barriers. Direct tariffs, however, are generally low, and the average tariff on industrial products is 5%; exporters from Third World countries eligible for the GATT Generalized System of Preferences pay no duty at all.

US customs duties are enforced at all points of entry to the country, except for the 120 or so foreign trade zones, used mainly for warehousing. Duties on imported goods held in these zones can be deferred.

Export controls

The USA imposes its most wide-ranging restrictions on exports for political, not economic reasons. Sales to Cuba, Democratic Kampuchea, N Korea and Vietnam are banned altogether, and export of high-technology goods to the communist bloc is only permitted under licence. The USA also bans the re-export from other countries of technology containing US parts – a policy which is rigorously enforced, despite objections from nations who feel it infringes their sovereignty.

Distribution

Continuing deregulation of all the major transport networks – along with cheap oil – is bringing down the cost of travel and distribution within the USA, and cut-throat competition on the more popular routes has improved the range of alternatives. But with ever more companies starting up – and collapsing – the US transportation scene may become increasingly confusing, and there are fears that distribution to remote regions could deteriorate.

Road or rail?

Although the value of air freight is slowly increasing, its high cost means that only a tiny fraction of US freight is shipped by air; the vast majority still goes by either road or rail (or if suitable, by pipeline). After a continuing decline in the 1970s, which saw the government move in to take over seven down and out freight networks in the northeast, the railroads are successfully holding on to their one-third share (by volume) of the freight market. Their cost-effectiveness for carrying bulk goods over long distances has ensured the railroads still handle two-thirds of the nation's coal, grain and new automobiles and trucks freight, and more than half the food and household goods. However, this success has only been at the expense of drastic reductions in manning.

The 1980 Staggers rail deregulation act gave the 26 major railroad companies a great deal of flexibility to set prices as they wished, and also close uneconomic branch-lines. But their pricing policy has upset some shippers, whose only alternative is the roads.

The problem is that deregulation has had little effect on competition between the railroad companies, simply because each company has a monopoly on a particular route. In contrast, deregulation of the truck industry under the Motor Carrier Act (1980) has unleashed ferocious competition. This has driven the cost of shipping by road down significantly, and enabled truckers to carry a slowly increasing share of the freight market – especially for short-haul traffic. But as prices are slashed, so an increasing number of trucking companies are forced out of business.

Intermodalism Rather than ship freight solely by road, or solely by rail, a growing number of shippers are sending freight by systems that combine the different modes of transport. "Piggybacking" for example, unites the low cost of long-haul rail transportation with the flexibility of road transportation to the final destination. Although the transfer from road to rail is economic only for journeys of more than 700 miles, the long distances in the USA give this system enormous advantages, and piggyback freight is expanding at more than 20% a year.

Responding to the popularity of intermodalism, many companies from different transportation media are forging closer links. Symptomatic of this trend was the Norfolk Southern railroad's takeover of North American Van Lines, the USA's largest household goods trucker.

Wholesale progress

Wholesale distribution in the USA is largely in the hands of individual company branches and independent merchant wholesalers. But the merchants have been taking an ever larger proportion. By the mid 1980s, the merchant wholesalers were handling more than two-thirds of all US wholesale goods.

Increasing automation combined with lower transportation costs have enabled merchant wholesalers to sustain healthy profits – despite the increasing demand for Japanese-style JIT (just-in-time) deliveries.

Business Awareness

In a country with no aristocracy but that of wealth, social status in the USA is conferred by success and, in particular, business success, and the values of the business world are openly endorsed across a broad spectrum of society. There is none of the distaste for the profit motive that colors attitudes to business in Europe – nor any envy of those who make money through business. Significantly, few Americans believe high-earners should be taxed heavily.

Of course, the dice are loaded in favor of certain sectors of society: those who earn the coveted MBA business degrees which provide the key to the best jobs are from predominantly affluent backgrounds. But the belief that anyone can succeed, given the talent and the will, plays a large part in American attitudes to business. The rags-to-riches self-made man is the hero of the American business world. Nevertheless, it is rarely the entrepreneur who heads the USA's biggest corporations; it is the loyal company man or woman who has worked his/her way up steadily through the ranks.

In such a vast and cosmopolitan country, the variety is considerable, but as a rule, American executives can be insular and limited in outlook, even more naive, than might be expected. Their huge home market cushions most executives who do not travel abroad on business from outside influences. This insularity is lessening, but it still colors the outlook of Americans working in the more secure sectors.

Working hours and attitudes

The US executive is, typically, a dedicated professional, prepared to work immensely hard to achieve personal and corporate goals. Social and family life are deeply cherished, and interests outside business are common. But no external activities and commitments detract from the basic concentration on business and, above all, on business success.

Working discipline

The traditional image of US working practice is the well-disciplined office, in which managers do as they are told, are neatly dressed and sober at all times, do not argue with their superiors or gossip in the office, and acquiesce in a system that includes rapid and harsh dismissal. Although this image has softened a little over the past decade, it remains a characteristic feature of American business life.

High turnover US companies are far more ready to dismiss executives, both individually and *en masse*, than their European counterparts. In one recent year, for example, 56% of all large American companies were reported to have slashed large numbers of middle management; and in the five years up to 1986, according to *Fortune*, big companies dismissed a total of half a million managers. US companies can often be ruthless both in the treatment of people whose employment has been "severed" or "terminated" (they may be escorted out of the building by security guards, with scant time even to clear out their desks) and in the swiftness with which employees past their prime often find their services dispensed with.

Professionalism Most Americans accept harsh discipline pragmatically, acknowledging that it is an inevitable counterpart to a system that offers generous rewards and allows the talented and hard-working to climb swiftly to the top. In fact, the very brusque dismissal of older staff is accepted because it helps open the way to new young talent. Americans pride themselves on their professionalism, and dismissal is seen as just one facet of professional discipline. They take their work very seriously, and this seriousness has been reinforced by the wave of conservatism that has characterized the years of the Reagan presidency. But the work ethic was strong even before Ronald Reagan came to power – although it varies in nature from the Puritanism of the Midwest to the frenetic rat race of New York City. As a rule, the US executive works as hard, and with as much concentration, as any in the world.

Working hours Normal working hours are 9am to 5pm, but there are innumerable exceptions. Regional variations are particularly marked. In manufacturing areas such as Detroit, for example, the hours are linked to plant operations; office work starts at 7am and ends officially at 3pm. In Chicago, executives generally start work around 8am and finish about 4pm. (Avoid, therefore, trying to catch a 4pm plane from Detroit or a 5pm flight from Chicago; the rush-hour traffic is horrific.) In Washington DC and other cities with severe traffic problems, working hours have been staggered in an effort to ease the rush-hour congestion. There is also considerable variation from industry to industry. Thus, brokers and other financial services people on the West Coast are at their desks by 7am, because that is when (10am) Wall Street opens on the other side of the country. Some may start even earlier, in time for the 8am nationwide conference call.

These hours are observed quite faithfully, but they are the minimum. Many US executives at all levels work very long hours. Such long hours are not compulsory, but they are essential for any executive who wants to succeed. As a rule, the higher an executive climbs up the tree, the longer hours he or she tends to work.

After hours While at the office, American executives tend to work hard, with the minimum interruptions. Lunches rarely last much more than an hour. The business breakfast provides a valuable extension to overfilled working days. Occasionally Saturdays will serve the same purpose. But there is usually a marked separation between working hours and leisure hours. Rather than staying in town to socialize with business colleagues after work, American executives generally go directly home. They also make a point of keeping weekends free for recreation; even if they play golf with business associates, the contact will be primarily social, not business.

Home calls

Despite their careful protection of leisure hours, US executives are also accustomed to interruption by business calls at home at weekends and in the evenings. Home telephone numbers will certainly be circulated to all managers' colleagues, and there is rarely any objection to relevant calls from outsiders.

Home computers Even if office hours do not spill over into the evenings, office work may, and many executives take work home. Over the past decade, ownership of personal computers has expanded enormously, and executives will often work at home on their PCs quite intensively. Familiarity with PCs is only one aspect of the American's deep knowledge of, and fascination with, the hardware and software involved in his or her job.

Vacations Vacations tend to be very short. Most executives get only two weeks a year, and only at the very top of the corporation do people take more. Even there, the maximum is four weeks. This is one of the reasons why Americans lay so much emphasis on their recreation at weekends and on public holidays – they simply do not have the long vacations enjoyed by executives elsewhere.

Regional variations

The USA is an enormous country with citizens of every national origin, and there is enormous variation in attitudes to business and business practices.

New York heat In Manhattan the drive for success and the pervasiveness of the business mentality is more marked than anywhere else in the USA. Life in Manhattan is fiercely competitive, and rivalry for everything, from multimillion-dollar merger fees to tables at fashionable restaurants is intense. Besides being supreme in financial services of all descriptions, Manhattan is the hub of corporate America, the capital of advertising, marketing and the media, the center of the legal world, the home of fashion, and much more besides.

Beyond the Big Apple Away from New York, business life tends to be less formal, less cosmopolitan and less obviously pressured. But the more relaxed ways in other regions should not deceive visitors into believing that achieving a successful deal will be any easier. American business is quite ruthless in its pursuit of profit, even in the small towns and state capitals where important headquarters may well be located. In the Old South, being a "good old boy" – sociable and expansive – is the keynote, and a handshake is much more than a casual greeting: it is a bond between friends. There is a deep sense of honor here, though, and people are taken at their word – flippancy might well be misplaced. The West Coast, on the other hand, is casual and modish, with the emphasis on youth and dynamism. Far from being frowned upon, unconventionality (within narrow limits) is often admired here – a strong contrast to the conservative Midwest, where tradition is strong and things are done by the book.

Corporate hierarchies

Informality is the hallmark of the US business manner. Even in institutions where the etiquette is most rigid, such as the big Wall Street banks, first names are used at every level. But this informality goes hand in hand with intense involvement in the affairs of the company – in its internal politics (which can be savage) as much as in its external sales.

The ladder of power

It is power, rather than status, on which US executives set their sights. Thus, membership of the executive committee, where power resides, is much more important than membership of the board, which has no executive role except to hire (and sometimes fire) the CEO, or chief executive officer.

Executive power The CEO is the most sought-after position in the US corporation. Whatever other titles the CEO may have – he could be either chairman or president – CEO is the title that indicates that it is he/she who makes the decisions, exercises the ultimate executive power and "calls the shots."

The board If the company has a chairman who is not the CEO, the chairman heads only the board, not the company or the management. But the board has fiduciary responsibilities to the shareholder and always reserves certain important decisions to itself – the appointment and rewards of the CEO, for example. In a large company, the board has several committees which exercise a number of key functions. A compensation committee, for example, may deliberate on senior salaries, bonuses and stock options, while the audit committee plays a central role in monitoring the integrity of the corporation's finances. The compensation committee is dominated by non-executives, who are drawn mostly from other large corporations. But like other committees, and the whole board, it seldom takes decisions that are not to the taste of the top executives – especially the CEO.

The president The COO, or chief operating officer, may also be called the president. As the title indicates, he is responsible for operations, reporting to the CEO, who has wider strategic responsibilities.

Vice president Below the COO there is often a collection of vice presidents. Although much coveted, the position of the vice president can be highly ambiguous. A vice president who sits on the executive committee is probably called an "executive vice president" and has considerable powers. A "senior executive vice president" is even more important, but a "senior vice president" is usually inferior. Some vice presidents are powerful and influential figures within the company – on a par with finance directors in Europe – while others are merely junior executives. In advertising agencies and banks the title "vice president" is often bestowed on a large number of executives, simply because clients want to feel that a senior executive is handling their affairs. The key to a vice president's real status within the corporation often lies in additions to the title. The title may well have "and treasurer," or "and general counsel," or "engineering," or "public affairs" attached. This shows whether the vice president is head of a function or a division. The head of an important manufacturing subsidiary is often corporate "vice president and general manager."

Women in business

In recent years women have been making a determined assault on the doggedly masculine world of US business and have achieved some success. Women today are much more noticeable in decision-making positions in the major corporations and professional service firms, and in some sectors the proportion of women employed in middle management has risen to 40%. But they still encounter considerable prejudice and resistance.

In particular, very few women have penetrated the highest levels of management, despite equal rights legislation which has been in effect for more than 20 years. One recent survey of 50 top US companies found only 2% of the executive positions held by women. Women, moreover, still feel disadvantaged and discriminated against: a recent Gallup Poll showed that 71% of them thought their chances of promotion were lower than those of men with equal ability.

Despite this, women are now much more conspicuous in US business, and there has been a subtle softening of its aggressively "macho" character – although it must be said that the women who have been able to make their mark are no less forceful than their male colleagues. Male chauvinism and sexual harassment are still widespread but tend to be covert rather than overt, and any foreign visitor who treats a US businesswoman patronizingly can expect not only her antagonism but the disapproval of many of her male colleagues. This is particularly true in industries such as publishing, where women are a major force.

There are now many women graduating from the business schools. In 1973 the number of women attending business school was only

9.2% of the total; today the figure is probably around 30%. At Harvard Business School, the proportion went to over a quarter in 1983 and has stayed around that level. More significantly, of 30 targets ranked high on headhunters' lists, two were women, according to a 1986 article in *Fortune*. But one worked in retailing and fashion, the other in newspapers; jobs in the top echelons of sectors such as manufacturing have been much harder to come by – although the need to conform with federal legislation has forced big US groups to be clearly seen not to operate discriminatory policies.

Companies can less and less afford the social costs of operating in a discriminatory way – not to mention the costs of lost talent, a loss clearly shown by women who, frustrated by big companies, are setting up on their own. The number of woman-owned businesses rose by 30% in a recent six-year span. Whether self-employed or company employee, the American businesswoman is as dedicated to her work as any man.

The business method

Visitors to the USA are often struck by the vigorous pace of American business. Briskness is not universal in US corporations; it goes against the leisurely grain of the Deep South. But as a rule the American businessman values dynamism and the "go-getter" is much admired. Yet ideas and fashions in American business are as mobile and changeable as the personalities – fixed ideas about US business are always being disproved by US business executives themselves.

Business thinking

Behind the briskness and dynamism of US business lies a surprisingly thoughtful attitude. American executives take their work far more seriously than their European counterparts. Typically, they are aware of current thinking on business methods and philosophy to a degree that is rare elsewhere.

Gurus and fashions The American manager is a great reader of business books and avidly follows the example of the latest management guru. Fashions such as the current emphasis on innovation and entrepreneurial ability – "intrapreneuring" in the mid 1980s jargon – spread rapidly and last a few years before giving way to the next wave. It pays visitors to the USA to be aware of the management ideas currently in vogue. The ideas sometimes seem bizarre and are often ephemeral, but they should not be taken lightly; American business people take them as seriously as every other aspect of business life.

Introspection Equally symptomatic of the thoughtful approach of the American executive is the almost obsessional concern with every issue that affects the corporation or the individual manager. Managers today are deeply worried about, for example, the excessive aggression of the new MBAs graduating from business school, smoking by managers (some companies pay for managers to go on anti-smoking courses), and the role of "whistle-blowers" in alerting boards to corporate wrongdoing.

Control and direction

Paradoxically, in a business world that worships pace and dynamism, US corporations tend to go about their business with extreme deliberation. The phrase "paralysis by analysis" was coined in the USA, and exhaustive analysis will normally feature in any transaction or plan. The approach is encouraged by business school training, in which "numerate" or finance-based,

disciplines predominate.
Significantly, management methods based on statistical techniques originated in the USA, and it is in American business that they are still used most intensively. Every project is subjected to rigorous financial scrutiny, and American managers are invariably well-versed in operating budgets and tend to be trained in the most up-to-date management accounting methods.

Heroes and "bean-counters" Ironically, despite the attention paid to financial detail, it is not the financial controllers who are most admired in US business; a corporation's accountants are dismissively known as "bean-counters." Now, as in the past, it is the risk-takers, the entrepreneurs, who provide the American business world with its inspiration. The heroes of the day are the young adventurers who have powered the rise of Silicon Valley in California and made many fortunes in the process. They provide the model for many large and apparently sober-minded companies today. Nevertheless, even the most visionary apostle of the high-tech heroes ties business practice firmly to financial realities.

The search for talent

US business has a great deal of faith in individual talent, and corporations go to enormous lengths to establish whether a future manager has the right qualities for the job – and are prepared to pay the right person handsomely once found. Tough "pressure" interviews are common, and psychological testing, too, has been vigorously developed. The background of every candidate is studied with almost excessive thoroughness.

"Headhunting" Corporations looking for someone to fill an important executive post not only closely scrutinize candidates who apply to them, but also closely observe their rivals or other industries in search of the right person. When they have found their "man," they are quite prepared to offer substantial financial inducements to tempt him/her away. The services of headhunting consultancy firms, who prefer to be known as "executive search firms," are widely used, and these firms have become very influential. Secrecy is of the essence when headhunting, and many Americans consider it highly unethical. But it has become a marked feature of US business life. Ambition is a much-admired and often ruthlessly exercised quality, and headhunters exploit the pursuit of ambition in a highly-organized manner. Although many managers deplore some of the results of headhunters' work, they use their services frequently – one of several examples from the business world of lip-service being paid on issues of principle. Criticism of headhunting centers on the way it encourages job-hopping, lessens corporate loyalty and pushes up salary levels. All three developments, though, are prominent features of US business life. Top salaries, in particular, have been rising very fast: CEOs received an average 22% more in 1985 than in the previous year; all top executives saw pay increase by an average of 12.7%; but middle managers won only a 6% rise. This is indicative of the present pressure on middle management and of the premium exacted by "high-fliers" for their frequent changes of job.

A fair fight?

On the face of it, competing businesses seem fairly friendly toward each other. But often the welcoming handshake conceals a deadly rivalry restrained only by the limits of what works. The past saw plenty of collusion in price-fixing, market-sharing and the like – and although these have long been highly illegal, it is clear that they have not vanished entirely. Far more common, however, is ruthless fighting for market share and other advantages.

The thin line between industrial espionage and true market research is often crossed – examples even include flying spy planes over the plants of a rival company, or hiring a key employee solely for the secrets that he or she may possess.

Most people in US business think of themselves as highly ethical, but their behavior tends to be ruled more by pragmatism than by any rigid moral code. It is hard to keep dishonesty and law-breaking altogether out of a system that makes the pursuit of wealth its central objective.

Managerial privilege Under the influence of the Japanese example, US managers have taken many initiatives designed to involve workers more in their work and to encourage a more open and democratic atmosphere on the shop floor. However, the enthusiasm of managers for this approach, in practice as opposed to theory, is less than wholehearted. Managers want to manage; and reluctance to share authority is most marked within company management itself. Power-sharing is rare, and insistence on the prerogatives and privileges of executive rank is conspicuous.

The meeting

The advent of advanced electronic means of communications has done nothing to lessen the American enthusiasm for face-to-face contact. Meetings of all shapes and sizes, from the business breakfast to the monster convention, take place in endless profusion.

Setting up a meeting First encounters with a potential client or customer may be set up by either side. Whoever proposes the meeting is likely to suggest the other side's office as a meeting place, but there is no firmly established protocol. Many kinds of location are acceptable, and convenience is usually the most important criterion.

"On-campus" meetings Most business meetings take place "on campus," in the company's own offices. Big corporations tend to have lavish rooms for any normal size of meeting, plus handsome and spacious offices for their senior executives. These often have a seating area designed for the informal conversations that are the basic form of business meeting. Executives may stay in shirtsleeves if they want to put the visitor at ease – but they usually come straight to the point, and expect visitors to do likewise.

Board presentations Because of the size and spread of US corporations, executives are accustomed to large-scale meetings – and also to inquisitorial, even brutal questioning in front of their peers. For presentations to the board or any other top executive meeting, technical standards are very high. It is therefore essential to prepare any presentation with great thoroughness, to try to anticipate awkward questions, to be fully armed with relevant facts and figures, and to spend whatever is necessary to obtain visual aids of "professional quality" – the two words that sum up the ideal, and often the reality, of US management.

"Off-campus" meetings With convenience and time at a premium, meetings often take place at airports, many of which often have very well-equipped business lounges. Similarly, US executives often arrange meetings in hotels or conference centers, either because their own office facilities are inadequate or occupied, or because secrecy is paramount. The "downtown" hotels, in the city centers, are kept in business by business – and are used by locals as much as by out-of-town visitors. "Convention" hotels can have 2,000 or more bedrooms, and their conference and allied facilities go far beyond the norm in Europe.

The large-scale meeting, of course, has to be off-campus. Conventions play an important part in American business life, whether they are in-house – typically, a sales convention for far-flung sales people, or the annual assembly of the company's managers in overseas subsidiaries – or huge rallies of executives from many firms in the same industry. These rallies commonly take place in resort hotels, in places like Florida, or even abroad, as well as in the huge convention hotels in New York, Chicago, and other major cities. Recreation and friendly camaraderie are usually to the fore at these gatherings; and social encounters play as important a part in the business relationship as more formal meetings. They used to be very "macho" affairs, and women found themselves isolated – but as more and more women join the executive ranks, the male club atmosphere is beginning to break down. Visitors should not be fooled by the emphasis on leisure; the purpose of these gatherings is as serious as anything else in US business.

Business meals

The social element in American business is strong, and dining or lunching together is often a vital part of the business relationship. In fact, more important deals are probably clinched over the dining table than over the desk.

The working breakfast, a symbol of the overriding dedication to business, is an American invention, popularized to overcome the problem of there being only one lunch in a day. Breakfast does not intrude into the working day, and being a simpler, less variable meal interferes with the conversation less than lunch does. The location is generally a hotel or club. The working breakfast has proved so valuable that some especially sought-after Wall Street tycoons schedule two "power" breakfasts, one after the other, with separate guests.

Business lunches can be as long and alcoholic and leisurely as in London and Paris, but this is by no means typical. The standard business lunch is often preceded – but not accompanied – by drinks, and even the preliminary cocktail is often waived nowadays in favor of mineral water. The menu is lighter (and the price often lower) than for dinner in the same restaurant, and executives rarely expect to be at table for more than an hour and a half; a little more than an hour is typical.

Dinner invitations are less common than those for lunch and are likely to be social rather than business occasions. Visitors from out of town are more often invited to dine than locals. American traditions of hospitality insure that foreign visitors especially are rarely left to their own devices in the evening. This applies particularly in the many American cities where restaurants of a high standard are hard to find.

Asking visitors home either for dinner or for lunch at the weekend is a common practice. These invitations are important and should not be refused, even though the main purpose is usually ostensibly social rather than business. Social relationships are an important part of US business life; the American executive is highly gregarious and likes nothing more than to introduce people to each other – and the friendliness is seldom artificial.

Company hospitality takes many forms. US corporations, for example, are much more heavily engaged in cultural or sports sponsorship than European firms and often use such events to entertain business guests. On the whole it is wisest to accept. The social mixing – whether at a museum private view, a football game or a charity gala – will help to cement the business connection.

Company dining rooms, while perhaps less widespread than in Europe, can be very luxurious.

In most firms – especially in manufacturing – executives do not have a separate dining room, so a private meal usually has to be held outside at a restaurant or hotel.

Making contact

American executives are usually very accessible compared to their counterparts elsewhere in the world, and it is usually clear from a person's title exactly what his/her role in the corporation is – with certain exceptions (see *Corporate hierarchies*). Finding the right contact is usually simple, and following up, if the meeting has any future, rarely presents problems.

Using the phone American business lives on the phone – often the public phone. Any public place, such as an airport, will have far more phone booths than can be found in other countries. The most ambitious travelling managers keep in touch not only by voice, but also by connecting up their portable computers. Credit cards can be used for phoning from many airports and hotels. However, most phones accept only US phone cards, and if you have a local subsidiary, it is worthwhile asking them in advance to arrange a phone card for you.

Letter writing As in all matters of business etiquette, the safest course is to veer toward the formal. First names are ubiquitous in America. But if that stage of familiarity has not been reached, "Dear Mr......:" is proper for men and, unless you know what title she prefers, "Dear Ms......:" for businesswomen. Note also that a *handwritten* "Dear Mr......:" is unusual in the US and may be regarded as an insult rather than a sign of respect. Always write to thank a contact for seeing you or for any entertainment; and keep business letters short and to the point – US business letters are, for foreigners, often startling in their brevity. The safe ending for letters is "Sincerely yours."

Returning hospitality

Hospitality should always be returned, if possible. The principle is to reciprocate in kind. If invited to lunch at a smart restaurant, you should offer a meal in a similar establishment. Asking your hosts to dinner – with spouses, if they came to the original date – is perhaps the best response.

Gifts and commissions In many firms, this issue is taken out of the outsider's hands by detailed corporate policies. Most companies forbid the acceptance of any gifts of substance. Cash payments are totally out of the question. Although bribery and corruption are unfortunately sometimes found in American business, these are exceptions, not to be either expected or encouraged by visitors. Small gifts, however, are acceptable. If invited home, always take flowers, or chocolates. Bottles of drink are safe gifts for all purposes.

Dressing for business

The variations in US business dress are as extreme as those in management style and follow much the same pattern. Thus, the West Coast company that favors a very loose, collegiate, trendy management style also has casual dress as its uniform – say, jeans, sneakers, and tieless colored shirts. At the other end of the spectrum, Wall Street bankers tend to dress extremely conservatively in dark pinstripe suits. The safest course is to dress in a somewhat formal manner: suits of conservative shades for men – and very possibly for women too. The tailored, mannish suit is popular female business wear, originally a weapon in the battle to establish women as equals of men, though women's dress is softening nowadays. Women high in the executive ranks tend to shun suits.

Exceptions to suits are found – for example, conservative sport jackets and slacks. But whatever the coat, a tie is nearly always worn with the shirt. Lower ranking executives in the West, at least, do favor more colors and patterns than, say, English executives and wear shoes that would not be found in some more old-fashioned business environments. But the overall effect should still be subdued.

The business media

The USA has the most vigorous and comprehensive business press in the world – an inevitable reflection of the dominant force of business in the national life.

Newspapers and journals

The two leading business publications in the USA are indisputably the daily newspaper the *Wall Street Journal* (which has a national circulation) and the weekly magazine *Business Week.* The *WSJ* is an institution central to US business life, and every American with more than a passing interest in the business world scans its pages each day for relevant news. Its daily "Heard on the Street" column inside the back pages is a must for investors. It looks oddly old-fashioned and lacks analytical depth in its ordinary financial and business news, but its features are outstanding, and its nationwide sale gives it great influence. *Business Week*, too, is highly respected – a light, digestible magazine that manages to be remarkably authoritative. It is concise, well-written and fast in spotting new trends.

Coverage in the heavyweight nationals – the *Washington Post*, the *New York Times* and the *Los Angeles Times* – varies but is generally sound and thorough. Weekly news magazines, such as *Time*, can be surprisingly informative and entertaining on business issues. *The Economist* is now also printed in the USA, to which it devotes much coverage.

Biweekly magazines The top biweeklies, *Forbes* and *Fortune*, are both large and rich. *Forbes* calls itself "the drama critic of American business." It has great stock market influence and reports more widely than the others, but its coverage is unsystematic, and it is of less use to business people in general than to investors. *Fortune* addresses itself to the top management audience and its in-depth analyses can be excellent.

Local magazines and closely targeted publications are a relatively recent phenomenon and are the best introduction to the business scene in any of the big metropolitan areas. Some of the business monthlies have reputations beyond their immediate circulation area. Would-be and actual entrepreneurs are served by *Inc* and *Venture*. New York has a very glossy monthly, *Manhattan Inc*, which runs articles on the city's business heroes.

Financial coverage in the USA is extensive. The two leading Wall Street magazines are *Barron's*, a weekly from the *WSJ* stable, which is full of statistics and authoritative but has a punchy style, and *Institutional Investor*, a monthly which gives a broad coverage of the financial scene. There are also countless investment newsletters. Influential letters range from the various *Kiplinger Letters* and *Boardroom Reports* to the myriad specialist publications such as the *Gallagher Reports*, which covers the Madison Avenue advertising community.

Trade publications for specific audiences are, by and large, the best in the world. Their coverage is the best way of finding out rapidly what is happening in any market.

Broadcast media

TV has an influence more pervasive than any other US medium, and many people in business make a point of watching the early evening TV news in particular. The early morning TV shows, such as NBC's *Today*, are also watched by many in the business community, while morning "drive-time" radio programs have large audiences, and standards of reporting (for example on stock market moves) can be high. Specialist business programs, such as the *Nightly Business Report* and Public Broadcasting's *Wall Street Week* are also well thought of.

Cultural Awareness

A historical perspective

From the moment the first European settlers stepped on to the shore of the wilderness continent, inhabitants of the New World have seen America as a land of opportunity – a land where those with the will and talent to succeed can carve out their own niche in the world no matter what their background. Such is the American dream and, from the hardy pioneers who trekked westwards into the unknown in the 19th century to the entrepreneurs who "make it good" in business today, Americans have maintained an unquenchable faith in the future and themselves that has given American society a unique dynamism and restlessness.

Early colonists

When Christopher Columbus first "discovered" the New World in 1492, there were already more than a million Indians living in North America. But the Indians' culture and their past were swamped by the European colonists who followed in Columbus' wake across the Altantic. Europeans called the newly discovered continent "America" after the Italian explorer Amerigo Vespucci, but it was the English, Dutch and French in the north and the Spanish in the South who made the first, pioneering settlements in the new land.

The first permanent English settlement, founded on Chesapeake Bay in 1607, was called Jamestown, after the British king. But Americans were rarely so deferential again. Among the earliest settlers were many Puritans braving the New World to practise their religion free from the opposition they faced at home, and for centuries America seemed the promised land for the poor and the persecuted of Europe.

Yet the relentless Anglo-Saxon expansion provoked conflict with the equally ambitious French and Spanish, resulting in New World squabbles echoing Old World animosities. Seventy years of intermittent wars ended by treaty in 1763, in England's favour. Canada and all the territory east of the Mississippi River became English. Twenty years later, they were lost.

Revolution and expansion

Until then, most colonists considered themselves loyal subjects of the Crown, serving in its armies against the Catholic kings. But in imposing what it regarded as postwar order, which involved taxation and enforcement of regulations designed to ensure the continued hegemony of English shipping and trade, Westminster hastened the inevitable revolution. The rebellious colonists voiced their defiance with a Declaration of Independence in 1776, and the British immediately went to war against their truculent offspring.

In the way of such uprisings, the colonists' fight was the rebellion of a minority, for a third of the population remained loyal to England and at least as many others held themselves aloof. But with the defeat of General Cornwallis in 1781 at Yorktown, Virginia, victory fell on their side. Independence achieved, the colonists set about welding the loose confederacy of 13 states into a united country and drew up the remarkable republican Constitution which still provides the country's basic laws and system of government.

The experiment in republican democracy began in 1787, and its territory almost immediately doubled when, in 1803, president Thomas Jefferson bought from Napoleon the French territory west of the Mississippi called Louisiana.

The adolescent nation prematurely flexed its muscles with Britain again in the War of 1812, a three-year effort that left its borders exactly the same. But the following years saw the United States almost bursting with national pride and "good feeling". Soon, pioneers and their families were loading covered wagons and heading west across the continent to seek a better life. Their struggles form the core of the mythology of American history and even today remain the inspiration for the pioneering spirit and restless mobility of the American people. In their eagerness, however, the American settlers swept aside Indians and Spaniards alike, convinced of their own "manifest destiny" to conquer the continent.

Civil war

As the immigration rolled on, festering internal conflicts began to erupt and the long and bitter feud between the North, with its mixed economy, and the South, dependent on slave-worked plantations, exploded into violent conflict. For the South, it was the election of an anti-slavery, northern president, Abraham Lincoln, that was the final straw; they withdrew from the Union in 1861. The terrible civil war lasted four years, leaving an indelible scar on the national memory and the defeated South in ruins.

The victorious Union embarked upon a remarkable era of invention and technological development. A transcontinental railroad was completed in 1869. The telegraph was introduced, and in rapid sequence, electrical generating and distribution systems, the telephone, the radio, motion pictures, the phonograph, the airplane.

Boom and bust

Industry boomed as a result of this fevered creativity and America finally caught up with the Industrial Revolution that had begun in England over a century before.

The country developed rapidly, and with a domestic vitality that now equalled or surpassed that of other industrialized nations, American ambition once again spilled over its borders. Hawaii, Cuba, Puerto Rico, the Philippines and the vital Panama canal zone were all gathered under the US umbrella, and America at last began to see itself as a world power. Although it remained aloof for three years from the great war that embroiled Europe between 1914 and 1918, its isolationism evaporated in a paroxysm of jingoism in 1917 when over 2m Americans went to war across the Atlantic.

Throughout the early 20th century, American troops were routinely landed in Panama, Nicaragua, Guatemala and Mexico to install governments or put down unrest. Such actions were the source of persistent anti-American sentiments. At home, amendments to the Constitution in 1920 granted the female vote and prohibited the manufacture and sale of alcoholic beverages – which succeeded only in promoting lawlessness and the rise of organized crime. In a lighter vein was the boom in consumer goods, and the rise of the "dream palaces," the cinemas that seduced Americans with the dream of a better world. But the dream and the economic boom of the "Roaring 20s" was shattered with the collapse of the Wall Street stock market in 1929 and, hard on its heels, the Depression.

The Depression, which threw 13m out of work – combined with the drought that turned the Great Plains into a Dust Bowl – tempered the buoyant optimism that had been so much a part of the US culture, and undermined faith in the capitalist system. Franklin D. Roosevelt, elected president in 1933, introduced his "New Deal" and began to install the components of a partial welfare state.

The war and after

The depression did not truly end until the US began to gear up for World War II. Emerging five years later as the only participant whose homeland was unscathed, America was unquestionably the single greatest world power. But fear of the communists and the Soviet Union grew, worsened by an anti-communist war in Korea. The "Cold War" abroad that followed was paralleled by a witchhunt for communist sympathizers at home. As the 1950s passed, and these tensions lessened, US trade and industry achieved new heights – building on a new technological base, and making the most of the gap left by the war-damaged economies of Europe and Japan – and Americans became prosperous as never before. As the USA became a richer place, it became one where the poor and the racially disadvantaged began to demand their share; in the 1960s civil rights marchers took to the streets, and the federal government launched a "War on Poverty."

The economic strains caused by the growth of the welfare state, and the political strains caused by a disastrous war in Vietnam, began to shake Americans' belief in themselves and their institutions. The exposure of abuse of government power in the Watergate scandal further deepened the malaise. It was not until the election of a robustly patriotic president, Ronald Reagan, in 1980, that the country began to "feel good about America" once more. Despite a federal deficit that is barely under control, a sustained trade imbalance and the political embarassments of the Iran arms scandal, the people are as optimistic and confident in the late 1980s as their Constitution-writing forbears in the 1780s.

Chronology

1607	First English settlement at Jamestown.
1636	Harvard College founded.
1770	Protests against English taxes and regulations culminate in the "Boston Massacre."
1776	Declaration of Independence.
1781	Lord Cornwallis surrenders to Franco-American forces at Yorktown, Virginia.
1787	US Constitution completed.
1789	George Washington inaugurated as first president.
1812	War with Britain over maritime trade.
1835	The Colt revolver is patented.
1836	Texas declares independence from Mexico. Fall of the Alamo
1861	Abraham Lincoln elected president. Civil War begins.
1865	The Southern Confederacy surrenders. Lincoln assassinated.
1870	John D. Rockefeller founds Standard Oil.
1896	Henry Ford makes his first car.
1903	First flight by Wright Brothers.
1913	Panama Canal opens.
1917	US enters war in Europe ensuring victory for the allies.
1929	Stock Market collapse triggers worldwide economic depression.
1932	Franklin D. Roosevelt president
1941	Japan attacks Hawaii. US enters World War II.
1945	World War II ends in Pacific.
1950	Joseph McCarthy embarks on campaign against communists in government. Korean War begins.
1953	Korean War ends in truce.
1958	USA launches its first space satellite.
1959	Alaska and Hawaii become the 49th and 50th states.
1962	USA confronts USSR over Cuban missile bases. USA sends military contingent to Vietnam.
1963	President John F. Kennedy assassinated.
1969	USA lands astronaut on moon.
1973	Watergate scandal exposed. President Nixon resigns.
1976	Bicentenary of independence.
1980	Ronald Reagan elected president

Beliefs, attitudes and lifestyles

Living in a country of very large distances and a wealth of personal options, Americans may well appear not only mobile, but restless: one out of five moves residence every year and a majority have called some fourteen different places "home" in the course of their lifetime. A readiness to change is manifest in personal relationships as well, with half the marriages ending in divorce. Everyone is from somewhere else: being a native New Yorker in New York is thought to be worth remarking on. And everyone seems to be going someplace as well. With all their material wealth, most Americans are committed to the pursuit of happiness with an energy which often leaves them, as they are the first to admit, little time to enjoy the fruits of their success.

Family, church and community

For all the stresses it has suffered in the current generation, family remains the focus for Americans. Multiple divorce and complex custody arrangements, however, can often give it new and unusual forms. Few American families escape completely from the uncertainties of their role in times of rapidly changing social and moral standards. Many Americans may turn to psychology for help, but most still will look for guidance from organized religion. Protestantism in a profusion of sects – Episcopalian (the American version of Anglicanism) – Methodist, Baptist, Dutch Reformed (Calvinist), Quaker and Unitarian – is the majority faith although Catholicism is the largest single religion. Fundamentalist churches, so called for their close and often literal reading of the Bible and accent on personal commitment, were once mostly in isolated rural communities, but now, thanks to the power of television and radio, command large followings over wide areas outside the major metropolitan centers. While religion forms an important strand of a shared cultural heritage in most countries and is part of social life even for nonbelievers, it is a very private matter for most Americans. The constitutional separation of church and state not only guarantees religious freedom to every persuasion; it scrupulously denies any of them a place in civic life. For many Americans today, religion still provides a link to earlier loyalties and the community they grew up in.

Class and race

Americans pride themselves on being free of class-consciousness. This does not mean, however, that distinctions are not routinely made between "them" and "us," or newcomers not scrutinized for clues and signals of their standing, rank or status. Yet there is much to be said for the Americans' claim, for there are almost as many criteria for judging one's neighbor as there are groups or communities in the culture, and no concensus among them across the country or even across town. Americans are quick to respect or praise achievement: but they react very negatively to those who claim deference as a matter of right. If Americans feel a quiet pride in the "classlessness," however, they are often sensitive to the tragedy which racism has brought into their history, and still grapple with its legacy.

The legacy of slavery Held as slaves in a country which declared that all men were created equal, American blacks (as they prefer to be called) were released from bondage into a twilight world of legal citizenship but social oppression. In the name of civil rights, and in alliance with many white sympathizers, they have struggled since the 1950s to emerge from the figurative as well as literal ghetto to which racial prejudice had condemned them. They have made surprising progress in such a short time and against such deeply-ingrained resistance: black mayors have been elected not only in Chicago and Washington, but in major cities of the deep South and black congressmen represent constituencies which have not changed much since Reconstruction. Great universities and major corporations actively recruit blacks and "positive action programs" discriminating in their favor are an accepted part of up-to-date personnel practice. Yet the legacy of generations of poverty and exclusion from mainstream society is not easy to overcome.

The plight of minorities Blacks are not America's only targets of racial feeling. Mexican-Americans in the Southwest, Hispanics in Florida and New York, and Native Americans (indigenous Indians) have all felt the chill of inhospitality or the violence of outright hostility. The open display of racial prejudice is generally unacceptable and racial epithets are strictly taboo. But grumbling is sometimes heard about the growing bilingualism in New York and other cities at the compulsory provisions which government and the business community have adopted.

The war of the sexes

The feminist revolution of the 1960s and 1970s, while not unique to the United States, was carried forward here with a characteristic readiness to follow the argument wherever it might lead. The feminist movement argued that the rights of women were not being served in a society where women earned 40% less, on average, than men and only 2% of management at or above the rank of vice-president are women. To the confusion of some men and the chagrin of others, they sought access to work – whether policeman or astronaut – to which their skills entitled them, and vigorous campaigns brought at least the legal right to equal pay, if not the fact. But there was much more at stake than simply equal pay or equality in the job market. Many women felt they also had a right to the dignity men seemed to reserve for themselves, and in a fashion typically American, proceeded to demand it. They asked to be spared the tiresome and degrading belittlement which passes for flirtation in many settings. They believed that decision about abortion belonged to them, and was not the province of society's moral guardians. The feminist movement reached a highpoint in the mid 1970s, and its achievements were significant. But the vilification of women involved in the movement, and the positive advances made, have softened the approach in the 1980s, an era known by many women as "post-feminist". Moreover, the price of the changes can be high for liberated American women; conflicts between family responsibilities and career are not always easily resolved.

Sexual liberation With the example of the black and feminist liberation movements before them, homosexuals in recent years have also asserted their right to the respect of the community and equal treatment by law. In some communities, notably San Francisco, they formed political pressure groups which had to be reckoned with by anyone seeking office. Liberation from the sexual mores of small-town America or from the taboos of religious upbringing also brought pornography into the open market, merchandized by the underworld, perhaps, but distributed under protection from the First Amendment (guaranteeing freedom of speech). More recently, dark clouds have gathered over this proliferating liberation. AIDS is now recognized to threaten tragedy to the population at large, and society waits nervously for medical technology once more to rescue it from one of the crueller caprices of nature.

Regionalism

Most generalizations about so large and varied a country are difficult to justify: this is only slightly less so when speaking about its individual regions. Thus the small-town, farm-based, conservative Midwest is also the home of historic American populism and suspicious of Eastern money and central government. The older states of the Northeast, home to the American establishment and its long established universities, also contains a major complex of cities which became the frontier for millions of immigrant pioneers from Europe. The South still savours its self image as a land of easy grace and elaborate courtesy, while others remember its history of racial and religious bigotry, its poverty and rural backwardness. Neither picture will make much sense to the visitor who sees the energy of cities like Atlanta, the cosmopolitanism of New Orleans, the Cuban and Caribbean influence in Miami, and a general political melée in which militant blacks, fundamentalist pastors and aggressive young entrepreneurs jostle each other for influence and power. The Southwest retains the scenery of the western films, but the cowboy ethos has been applied to herding oil wells and stock portfolios. Texas alone is larger than many countries in the world and richer than most, despite the recent difficulties caused by a weakening of world oil prices. The West Coast, oriented toward Asia as the East Coast is toward Europe, has been the center of radical politics and radical life-styles. Yet Orange County near Los Angeles is the heartland of American political conservatism, Silicon Valley the center of high-tech enterprise and the universities among the most respected in the world. All the images are true – but so are the contradictions: regionalism exists, but its character is a matter of interpretation.

Education

America was an early leader in the movement for universal free education. Today, while not a matter of constitutional guarantees, this benefit is viewed by most people as a kind of right and is required for all children by state law.

Schools

Education is entirely in the hands of the state and the local community and most of the bill is met at the community level. Education is free at public (tax supported) primary schools (the first eight or nine year-long grades) and secondary or high schools (four further years). Provision of schools for children younger than five years of age varies according to the finances and circumstances of the community. The overwhelming majority of American children attend such free schools but prestigious, fee-paying institutions are sprinkled about the country. In recent years, parents concerned about the quality of free schooling available in inner cities have turned to private schools as a solution. Private or public, American schools are conceived as an educational service to the children, their parents and the community: parent power is not only accepted but welcomed through the local Parent Teacher Association attached to every school. Since education is regarded as a universal benefit, conscientious schools attempt to serve the needs and talents of each individual child rather than some abstract standard of intellectual excellence. The result may seem to foreigners a puzzling mix of frivolity (baton-twirling and driver education) with more recognizable disciplines of traditional learning. Where schools are well-run and well-supported by the community, the quality of public education rivals any in the world and can offer opportunities seldom available elsewhere.

College

After high school, students can move on to college, and over half of them do. With more than 3,500 colleges and universities to choose from, Americans have come to look on a bachelor's degree rather than high school graduation as the natural termination of school life. There is an institution for every taste: alongside the old, prestigious and rich establishments, such as Harvard, Yale, Princeton, Columbia and Amherst, there is a profusion of privately funded and state-supported schools that range from vast educational plants offering the most advanced training available, to small, intimate academies which emphasize personal instruction and a taste for the humanities. Although university education has become commonplace, it is an expensive proposition and represents a continuing drain on the finances of families with college-bound children. State universities charge fees far below those of their private counterparts where the bill for one student can easily soar into five figures and is rising every year. Loans, grants and scholarships, and part-time work are frequently required to meet the cost, but most Americans believe it is an acceptable price to pay for the cash value a degree is thought to have in the job market. The link which Americans tend to make between education and earning power is also reflected in their preference for the oversubscribed prestige schools. As the bachelor's degree becomes a commonplace of middle-class citizenship, more and more graduates are pursuing an educational advantage in postgraduate study, particularly for professional degress in law (JD) and business (MBA), but also for the less exploitable dignity of the PhD.

Living standards

America is a very rich country indeed and evidence of its wealth is spread through all regions. Measured by the availability of decent to excellent housing, the wealth of appliances and the ubiquity of the automobile, the middle majority may well be accounted affluent by any of the world's standards. Yet expenses of medicine, care for the aged and higher education can seriously erode the security of many families, and most balance their checkbooks carefully in a continuing pursuit of higher expectations.

Rich and poor

The allegation of materialism often made against Americans probably arises from the profusion of consumer goods available to them. In fact, most Americans tend to be consumers, rather than collectors, and even the home with two (or more) cars and a well-kept swimming pool may well lack the artifacts of material value which serve as evidence of affluence in other societies. Although there are certainly exceptions, most Americans shy away from conspicuous display; the fun of wealth is in winning it in the first place. Despite its high proportion of millionaires, America's cities and rural areas often show the bitter aspect of poverty and squalor. Some urban ghettos are among the worst in the developed world, and jobless communities where the sun has set on once powerful industries are a depressing counterpoint to luxury skyscraper apartments and the vast stretches of comfortable, leafy suburbs. Neither its wealth nor its poverty provides a true yardstick for the measure of the "real" America: it is both.

Work and leisure

Americans not only believe in work, they give every evidence of enjoying it and have even invented the working breakfast in their impatience to get down to the day's business. While the clear desk, the three-hour lunch and the short day are perks of advancement in some countries, the higher an American executive advances up the ladder, the harder the expected slog.

Sport Golf offers probably the most popular release and can be played on innumerable and often excellent courses. Tennis has witnessed a boom in recent years while Americans of both sexes have become enthusiasts of fitness and exercise. Basketball may continue to be the most attended sport, thanks to its place in the high school sports program, but professional baseball, and more important, professional football command the most devoted following. Foreigners will need explanations of the fine points to appreciate either, but any one of 200 million Americans will be glad to oblige.

Leisure pursuits Americans enjoy dining out – and tend to make an occasion of it regardless of the quality of the food. They are proverbially hospitable and invite the most recent of acquaintances to their homes as a matter of course. Such entertainment is, as a rule, a relaxed affair, keeping with the unspoken American suspicion that formality is a brake on friendliness.

Vacations Getting away from it all is not difficult in a land of tens of thousands of lakes, vast expanses of excellent beach and areas of wilderness which would surprise those who are familiar only with the major cities. Many own a second home, or manage to rent one, where the wife and children can retreat during the long summer holidays. The Labor Day weekend, which ends the school vacation, probably witnesses more families on the move than at any time since the barbarian invasions. As the children grow up and arrange their own holidays, many Americans embark on world travel. Europe is the usual first port of call, but few destinations are exempt from their benign curiosity.

Meeting and getting on

Most Americans like to think of themselves as both friendly and forthright, and try to live up to the image as best they can. Greetings are always extended warmly, hands are shaken firmly, and they remember other people's names. They will normally signal the invitation to call them by their first names and are likely to lead the way by example. Titles are seldom used, except by way of establishing responsibility, and titles seldom used in direct address to members of one's own business family (but always to "Senator," and so forth). Policemen are always addressed as "officer" and "sir" is used only when a most respecful formality (or its opposite) is intended.

Shyness and diffidence in others makes most Americans slightly uncomfortable and somewhat guilty for having failed to put someone at his ease. They do not mind a moderate tardiness at social events (in fact they normally count on it), but they do not like to waste business time unnecessarily either. Both in homes and in offices, it is no longer possible to assume that smoking is acceptable. In recent years, too, the consumption of spirits seems to have declined and there is a heightened sensitivity to the needs of those with "a drinking problem." Outside the office, however, alcohol still provides much of the lubricant for conversation.

City by City

Introduction

The map below shows the cities featured in detail in the city by city guide and locates them in their time zones. There are four standard time zones in the continental United States. Reading from East to West they are Eastern, Central, Mountain and Pacific. Each zone is one hour earlier than its eastern neighbor, so that in California, for example, it is three hours earlier than in New York.

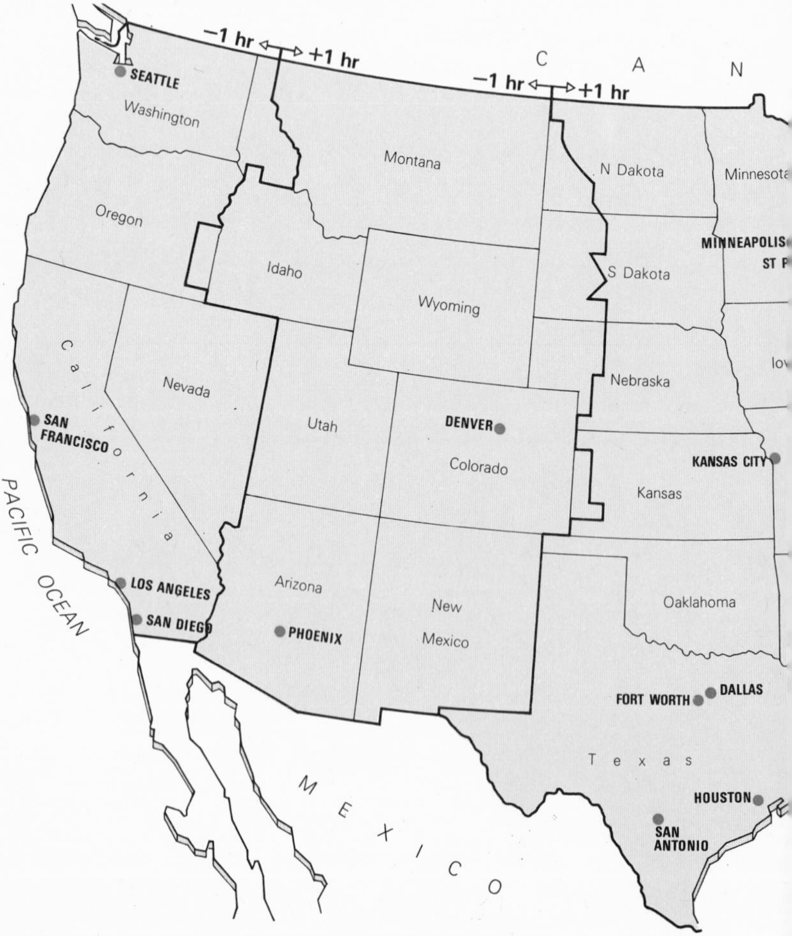

Each city guide follows a standard format: information and advice on arriving, getting around, city areas, hotels, clubs, restaurants, bars, entertainment, shopping, sightseeing, sport and fitness, and a directory of local business and other facilities such as secretarial and translation agencies, couriers, hospitals with 24-hour accident and emergency departments, and telephone-order florists. There is also a map of the city center locating recommended hotels, restaurants and other important addresses.

For easy reference, all main entries for hotels, restaurants and sights are listed alphabetically.

Atlanta	p102
Boston	p110
Chicago	p122
Cleveland	p141
Dallas	p149
Fort Worth	p158
Denver	p162
Detroit	p169
Houston	p177
Kansas City	p186
Los Angeles	p192
Memphis	p208
Miami	p214
Minneapolis/St Paul	p222
New Orleans	p230
New York	p238
Philadelphia	p278
Phoenix	p288
Pittsburgh	p294
St Louis	p300
San Antonio	p307
San Diego	p313
San Francisco	p319
Silicon Valley	p334
Seattle	p337
Washington	p343
Baltimore	p359

ATLANTA

Area code ☎ 404

Atlanta is the home of Coca-Cola and the economic center of Southeastern USA. Founded in 1837, the town was a main distribution point for troops, munitions and supplies during the Civil War – and later for building materials during Reconstruction – because three railroads converged here. Today, three interstate highways – 75, 85 and 20 – intersect at Atlanta, and Hartsfield Airport is a major domestic and international hub. Major companies such as Subaru, Yamaha, IBM, Panasonic and Canon have manufacturing, distribution or headquarters here, along with Cable News Network, SuperStation 17, Delta Air Lines, Georgia-Pacific and Lockheed-Georgia. The city's banks – Citizens and Southern Corporation and SunTrust – are among the region's most important.

Atlanta was the hometown of Dr Martin Luther King. Today the city's government is predominantly black, and the rights of minority groups are now accepted.

Arriving

Hartsfield Atlanta International Airport

Hartsfield has two huge terminals, North and South, each with four concourses, A, B, C and D, at which domestic flights arrive. In addition, North Terminal has an international concourse.

Signposting throughout the airport is good, but it is a long walk from the international gates to Customs and Immigration; baggage carts are available free. A transportation mall connects the domestic concourses; if you arrive or leave on a domestic flight, use the mall's computer-controlled train for easy, rapid, free transit to and from all the domestic gates and baggage claim. Customs and Immigration take about 20min normally – 30min when more than three flights arrive simultaneously. North Terminal services include currency exchange, 9–5; multilingual information center; duty-free shops and restaurants. Airport information ☎ 530 6600.

Air freight carriers include *Flying Tiger* ☎ 530-2400, *Airborne Express* ☎ 765-1420 and *Emery* ☎ 762-1673; they use the airport's separate air freight terminal.

Nearby hotels *Holiday Inn Crowne Plaza*, 1900 Sullivan Rd, College Park 30337 ☎ 997-2770 TX 3510603. *Marriott Airport*, 4711 Best Rd, College Park 30337 ☎ 766-7900. *Ramada Renaissance*, 4736 Best Rd, College Park 30337 ☎ 762-7676 TX 7581801.

City link Downtown Atlanta is 9miles/14km away, a 30min drive on I-85 North.

Car rental Driving is the best way to get around if your business takes you out of downtown. Eight agencies have desks in the airport: Hertz ☎ (800) 654-3131; Avis ☎ (800) 331-1212; Budget ☎ (800) 527-0700; Alamo ☎ (800) 327-9633; National (800) 227-7368; General ☎ (800) 327-7607; Dollar (800) 421-6868; and Thrifty ☎ (800) 367-2277.

Taxis Dependable companies include Yellow Cab ☎ 523-8746, Checker Cab 351-8255 and American Cab ☎ 688-5656. Be wary of using others; some drivers have a limited knowledge of the city, drive suspect vehicles and may overcharge.

Bus The Atlanta Airport Shuttle ☎ 524-3400 operates a good service to downtown and outlying hotels. Shuttles leave Ground Transportation Area in the North Terminal every 20min, 4.30am–12.30am for downtown hotels, 7am–9pm for Buckhead hotels.

Bus MARTA (Metropolitan Atlanta

Rapid Transit Authority) buses depart every 18min for Lakewood Rapid rail station, where you transfer to a train to downtown. It is the cheapest but slowest way to get to your hotel.

Getting around

If your business is downtown, walking is easy and enjoyable. But if you have to go to any outlying area, drive or take a cab. Public transportation is excellent downtown, but limited elsewhere.

Driving Rush-hour traffic (7.30–9 and 4.30–6) is congested, but the freeway system makes for easy movement at other times. Parking is limited around downtown office buildings.

Rail MARTA trains run every 9min and will take you anywhere in the business district quickly and safely.

Bus MARTA's buses run every 15min, and the drivers are courteous and knowledgeable.

Taxi see *City link.*

Limousine *Sun Belt Limousine* ☏ 524-3400 is considered the most professional; 24hrs. *Classic Coach* ☏ 455-3000 is also highly regarded.

Area by area

Most major corporations are downtown, but the Perimeter is gaining prominence and prestige as office towers are built along I-285, the multi-lane superhighway circling the city. The growth started at Perimeter Center, the intersection of I-285 and Ashford-Dunwoody. Cumberland, where I-285 meets Cobb Parkway (US 41), is a major office and retail center. Distribution

■ HOTELS		● RESTAURANTS		◆ BUILDINGS AND SIGHTS	
A	Hilton and Towers	A	Abbey	A	Chamber of Commerce
B	Hyatt Regency Atlanta	B	Aunt Fanny's Cabin	B	Main Post Office
C	Hyatt Regency Ravina	C	Bones	C	Southern Bell/Bell South
D	Mariott Marquis	D	Carsleys		Corporation Headquarters
E	Omni International	E	Coach and Six	D	CNN Center
F	Ritz Carlton Atlanta	F	La Grotta	E	Georgia – Pacific
G	Ritz Carlton Buckhead	G	Mary Mac's		Corporation Headquarters
H	Waverly	H	Morton's	F	Fox Theater
I	Westin Peachtree Plaza	I	Peasant Uptown		

G Federal Reserve Bank of Atlanta
H Georgia Institute of Technology
I State Capital
J Martin Luther King Historic District

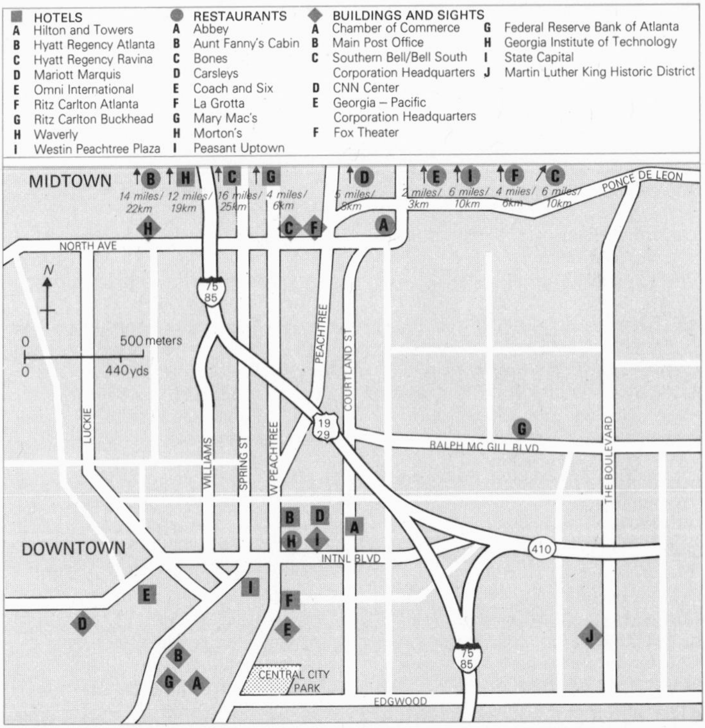

companies have taken over the I-85 corridor into Gwinnett County, where Norcross is the area's high-tech center.

Downtown This area is bounded by Baker Street to the N, Memorial Drive to the S, Courtland Street to the E and International Boulevard to the W. Five Points is the center of the city's Financial District. Peachtree Center, between Ellis and Baker streets, is a high-prestige area for law and accounting firms and banks.

Buckhead Once housing Atlanta's wealthy merchants only in summer, Buckhead is now both a business and residential area. Many of the executive homes remain; others have given way to high-rises. The center of Atlanta's advertising and public relations firms, it has fashionable restaurants and nightclubs.

Midtown AT&T, BellSouth, Coca-Cola and IBM all have offices in midtown, between 10th Street and Pershing Point.

Hotels

Atlanta's development as a major convention city has resulted in the building of several new hotels.

Hilton and Towers $$$
255 Courtland St NE 30043
☎ 659-2000 TX 804370 • 1,224 rooms, 60 suites, 4 restaurants, 4 bars, 1 coffee shop
The Hilton and Towers is one of Atlanta's longest established business hotels. Nikolai's Roof atop the Towers is popular with Atlanta's chief executives. A complete business center has been added, including computer services, word processing, copy machines and secretarial help. Pool, tennis, health club, jogging, whirlpool, sauna • 50 meeting rooms, fax, translation, teleconferencing, computer rental, recording facilities.

Hyatt Regency Atlanta $$$
265 Peachtree St, 30303 ☎ 577-1234 TX 542485 • 1,165 rooms, 53 suites, 4 restaurants, 1 bar, 1 coffee shop
An African trading dock, with cotton bales, drygoods and staff in khaki outfits and pith helmets, welcomes you to the Atlanta Hyatt. The lobby lounge has live entertainment. All rooms have jacuzzis and mini-bars. Hairdresser • health club, pool • 27 meeting rooms.

Hyatt Regency Ravinia $$$$
4335 Ashford Dunwoody Rd 30346
☎ 395-1234 TX 6827201 • 399 rooms, 41 suites, 1 restaurant, 2 bars, 1 coffee shop
This glass and granite de luxe hotel is used by top companies. The fully-glassed boardroom has a stunning panorama of the surrounding 10-acre forest. All rooms have desks and telephone-computer hookups. The Hyatt Regency Ravinia is ideal for business in DeKalb, Cobb and Gwinnett counties. Health club, tennis, jogging paths • 20 meeting rooms.

Marriott Marquis $$$$
265 Peachtree Center Ave 30303
☎ 521-0000 TX 6712053 • 1,471 rooms, 5 restaurants, 1 bar, 1 coffee shop
Part of architect John Portman's 12-block urban village, this Marriott is a city landmark. Its 48-floor indoor atrium is breathtaking. The city's major corporations, especially in the high-tech industries, use the Marquis for meetings and to house guests. Service and facilities are outstanding. Clerical and medical services • pool, hydrotherapy pool, sauna, health club • 45 meeting rooms.

Omni International $$$
1 Omni International, Marietta St 30335 ☎ 659-0000 TX 542380 • 430 rooms, 31 suites, 2 restaurants, 3 bars, 1 coffee shop
On the western fringe of the central business district, the Omni International has a strong following of business travellers. Its rich wood-

paneled lobby and comfortable rooms are welcoming. The building adjoins CNN Center, home of Cable News Network and the Chamber of Commerce. The Omni Sports Arena is nearby; the Georgia World Congress Center is next-door. The hotel's Italian restaurant, Bugatti, is suitable for business lunches. Gift shops • arrangements with nearby health club • 14 meeting rooms.

Ritz-Carlton Atlanta **$$$$**
181 Peachtree St NE 30303
☏ 659-0400 ⓉⓍ 543291 • 412 rooms, 22 suites, 2 restaurants, 2 bars, 1 coffee shop
Just a block from Peachtree Center, the distinctive Ritz-Carlton is the choice of many discriminating business travellers. It has a residential quality and excellent service. Suites have crystal chandeliers, pianos and jacuzzis. Club-level floors have private access and concierge. The restaurant and café are excellent for business and entertaining, and the piano bar is a hospitable sanctuary for unwinding after hours. Shops • arrangements with next-door health club, tennis, golf • 15 meeting rooms.

Ritz-Carlton Buckhead **$$$$**
3434 Peachtree Rd 30326 ☏ 237-2700 ⓉⓍ 549251 • 500 rooms, 28 suites, 3 restaurants, 2 bars, 1 coffee shop
In uptown Atlanta's most fashionable district, this Ritz-Carlton has a wide-ranging social and business clientele. The front entrance has crystal chandeliers and marble-faced pillars; fireplaces in the lobby lounge and main-level bar create a clubby ambiance. The café, very suitable for business luncheons, has a pianist and a jazz band, 5–7. Sauna, jacuzzi, pool, exercise room • 18 meeting rooms.

Waverly **$$$$$**
2450 Galleria Pkwy 30339
☏ 953-4500 ⓉⓍ 701565 • 489 rooms, 44 suites, 4 restaurants, 3 bars
With spectacular views of the lush rolling North Georgia hills and a 14-story atrium, this hotel has very large rooms with handsome mahogany furniture. The Waverly is especially convenient for aerospace industry business in Marietta. There are good shopping centers close by. Health club • 19 meeting rooms.

Westin Peachtree Plaza **$$$**
210 Peachtree St 30343 ☏ 659-1400 ⓉⓍ 804323 • 1,035 rooms, 43 suites, 3 restaurants, 5 bars, 1 coffee shop
The Westin dominates Atlanta's skyline with its sparkling glass exterior, matched internally by marble floors. The Peachtree Ballroom accommodates up to 2,000, and is frequently used for meetings and parties by the city's largest corporations. The Sun Dial Restaurant is a favorite for social and business entertaining. On the tri-level dining area, the Savannah Fish Company draws lunch crowds from nearby law and accounting firms and the merchandise marts next door. The Georgia World Congress Center is an easy four-block walk up International Boulevard. Health club, pool • 39 meeting rooms, fax.

Clubs

The *Capital City Club* is the center of Atlanta's business network. Numbered among the members of this men-only club are many chief executive officers and company presidents. The *Cherokee Club* attracts a range of professional people. The *Georgian Club* is mainly executives of corporations around the Northern Perimeter. The *Atlanta City Club* is middle management from banking, accounting, advertising and public relations. The *Commerce Club*'s varied membership uses it for business luncheons and meetings. *Horseshoe Bend Country Club*, *Piedmont Driving Club*, and *Dunwoody Country Club* are exclusive bastions of Atlanta society.

Restaurants

The city's business community is constantly on the lookout for new clients and contacts, and a new eating experience as well. In the main, when Atlantans leave work at the end of the day, they are out to make profitable contacts and so spread their culinary nets wide rather than patronizing two or three favorite restaurants.

Abbey $$$
163 Ponce de Leon Ave ☎ 876-8532 • D only • AE CB DC MC V *• reservations essential • jacket required*
A good choice for entertaining clients in an unusual setting. In this church-turned-restaurant, the excellent food is served by attentive waiters wearing monks' robes.

Aunt Fanny's Cabin $$
2155 Campbell Rd, Myrna ☎ 436-5218 • D only Mon–Sat, L and D Sun • AE CB DC MC V
International visitors enjoy the Cabin because it conjures up images of the *Gone with the Wind* era; waitresses and waiters dress in the garb worn by slaves and servants before the Civil War. It also provides authentic "down-home" Southern cooking and true Southern hospitality.

Bones $$$$
3130 Piedmont Rd ☎ 237-2663 • D only Sat and Sun • AE CB DC MC V
The autographed caricatures of local and international celebrities indicate that Bones has a following of business people and entertainers. The thick T-bones and spartan atmosphere of plain tables and chairs make it suitable for working lunches or easy-going evenings.

Carsleys $$$$
Courtyard of Tower Place, Piedmont Rd at Peachtree ☎ 261-6384 • closed Sun • AE CB DC MC V
Light and breezy in California style, Carsleys is quiet and good for business conversation over an excellent lunch. A jazz group makes evening business discussions more difficult, but keep this in mind for an off-duty outing. Located in Buckhead, it attracts the young television and advertising crowd.

Coach and Six $$$
1776 Peachtree St ☎ 872-6666 • L Mon–Fri, D Fri–Sun; AE CB DC MC V *• reservations essential • jackets required for dinner*
The Coach and Six is an Atlanta tradition, the restaurant you will be taken to when impressions count. Investment bankers, politicians, lawyers and professionals like the opulent surroundings for lunch as well as for evening entertaining.

La Grotta $$$$
2637 Peachtree Rd ☎ 231-1368 • closed Sun D • AE CB DC MC V *• reservations essential • jacket required*
La Grotta is unquestionably the city's best Italian restaurant. Its cramped, modest quarters, below an apartment building in Buckhead, belie the quality of the food. La Grotta is heavily used by business groups for evening entertainment (but not for talking business).

Mary Mac's $
224 Ponce de Leon Ave ☎ 874-4747 • closed Sat • no credit cards • no reservations
Lawyers, bankers, politicians, secretaries, construction workers and truck drivers all love Mary Mac's. Mary Margaret Lupo, a leader in the local community, can seat over 200 in her massive dining room. Fried chicken, creamed corn, collard greens, fried okra and cornbread all make this a must if you want true Southern cooking. Your suggestion to have lunch here will be appreciated by locals, but do not plan a lengthy business discussion; guests are

expected to enjoy a good meal and give others the same opportunity.

Morton's $$$$

245 Peachtree Center Ave ☎ 577-4366 • D only Sat; closed Sun • AE CB DC MC V • jacket required

Heavy wooden tables and chairs, wooden plank floors and photographs of Al Capone and his contemporaries recreate an atmosphere of America's Prohibition era. Your order is taken by a waiter who rolls a cart to your table so that you may select your cut of Midwest prime beef or Wisconsin milk-fed veal. The menu also features fresh whole Maine lobster.

Peasant Uptown $$$

3500 Peachtree Rd NE in Phipps Plaza ☎ 261-6341 • AE CB DC MC V

An excellent choice for a casual business lunch or an intimate off-duty evening, the Peasant Uptown has a friendly atmosphere. Attentive waiters serve innovative American dishes.

Bars

For quiet discussions, the best meeting places are those bars within the city's better hotels, such as the café/bar at the *Ritz-Carlton Buckhead*, which offers low-key jazz nightly.

Entertainment

Nothing much happens downtown after dark. Most business people – local and visiting – go to Buckhead or the Perimeter where locals gather in fashionable bars and discos.

Nightclubs *The Limelight Entertainment Complex*, 3330 Piedmont Rd NE ☎ 231-3520 has been the trendsetter for Atlanta's nightclubs. The sound system makes conversation impossible; this is a place for people who want to dance. *Club Rio*, 195 Luckie St NW ☎ 525-7467 is Latin-style, with dancing on three levels (one with live entertainment). It is the only nightspot in the downtown area that attracts local business men and women away from the Buckhead bars. *Studebakers*, Courtyard of Tower Place, Piedmont Rd at Peachtree ☎ 266-9856 attracts those who want to dance the night away. *Dante's Down the Hatch*, 3380 Peachtree Rd NE ☎ 266-1600 has a jazz trio; *Elan*, 4505 Ashford Dunwoody Rd NE ☎ 393-1333 is the favorite of middle and upper management. *The Punch Line*, 280 Hildebrand Dr NE ☎ 252-5233 features internationally famous comedians.

Theater and music The *Robert W Woodruff Arts Center* ☎ 892-2414 houses a variety of arts groups and the High Museum of Art; the *Alliance Theater* ☎ 892-2414, the *Atlanta Ballet* ☎ 873-5811, *Atlanta Symphony Orchestra* ☎ 892-2414 and *Atlanta Children's Theater* ☎ 892-2414 are based here. The *Fox Theater* ☎ 892-5685 hosts such performers as Bob Hope and Carol Channing.

Shopping

Lenox Square in Buckhead is *the* center for shopping. The sprawling complex features Neiman-Marcus, Macy's, Atlanta-based Rich's and a host of fine specialty shops. *Phipps Plaza*, across Peachtree from Lenox, is anchored by Lord & Taylor's, and also has smart boutiques. The suburbs are dotted with "regional" malls, such as *Gwinnett Place*, 30 miles N of downtown Atlanta on I-85 N; *Towne Center*, about the same distance up I-75 N in Cobb county; *Southlake* and *Shannon* malls in South Atlanta; and *Perimeter Center* (see *Area by area*). Rich's and Macy's also have downtown stores.

Sightseeing

Atlanta sightseeing includes pre-Civil War homes, battlegrounds, museums, mountain landscapes and theme parks.

Carter Presidential Center President Carter's library depicts his life and administration, as well as previous administrations, in film, exhibits and documents. *1 Copen Hill. Open 9–5, Sun 12–5.*

Cyclorama A 50ft-high, 400ft-circumference painting in the round, with three-dimensional figures, sound and light effects, and narration of the 1864 Battle of Atlanta. *In Grant Park. Open 9–4.30.*

Kennesaw Mountain National Battlefield Park Kennesaw is the site of a crucial engagement in the 1864 Civil War Battle of Atlanta. *Old Hwy 41, Marietta ☎ 427-4686. Open 8.30–5.*

Little Five Points/Inman Park About 3 miles/5km from downtown, this residential and commercial area is a showplace of Victorian architecture. Atlanta entrepreneur Joel Hurt laid out this "garden neighborhood" and built the nation's first trolley line to his building downtown.

Martin Luther King, Jr, Historic District A two-block area that includes the Nobel Peace Prize winner's birthplace and the Center for Non-Violent Social Change. *501 Auburn Ave ☎ 524-1956.*

Roswell Founded in 1830, this quaint little town has many pre-Civil War houses. Group tours can be arranged through the Roswell Historical Society ☎ 992-1665.

Wren's Nest The home of Joel Chandler Harris, creator of the Uncle Remus tales and characters – Br'er Rabbit, Br'er Fox, Tar Baby and others. *1050 Gordon St SW ☎ 753-8535. Mon–Sat, 9.30–5; Sun, 2–5.*

Guided tours

Atlanta Tours Inc, 157 International Blvd ☎ 522-4299 has guided tours of the city and Stone Mountain. Helicopter tours are available from *Dooley Helicopters Inc*, 2003 Flightway Dr, Chamblee ☎ 458-3431.

Out of town

Madison contains Civil War-period houses so beautiful that General Sherman refused to burn them; an hour E of Atlanta on I-20. *Stone Mountain Park*, on Highway 78, E of Atlanta, is the world's largest relief sculpture; the mounted figures of Confederacy President Jefferson Davis and Confederate generals Robert E Lee and Stonewall Jackson are carved into the face of the largest known granite mass. Attractions include a laser show.

Spectator sports

Basketball, baseball and football are the main sports preoccupations.

Baseball The *Atlanta Braves* play at the Atlanta-Fulton County Stadium ☎ 577-9100 Apr–Oct.

Basketball The *Hawks* play at Omni Coliseum ☎ 681-3605.

Football The *Falcons* appear at the Atlanta-Fulton County Stadium ☎ 588-1111.

Keeping fit

Health clubs *Downtown Athletic Club*, 1 CNN Center ☎ 577-2120; *Holiday Fitness Center* at Lenox ☎ 262-2120; *Australian Body Works*, 4385 Roswell Rd NE ☎ 255-2217 and 5486 Chamblee Dunwoody Rd ☎ 393-0828.

Golf Visitors can play at Georgia's *Stone Mountain Park* 498-5717; *Adams Park*, 2300 Wilson Dr SW ☎ 753-6518; *Bobby Jones* 384 Woodward Way NE ☎ 355-9049. Also, at *Candler Park* 585 Candler Park NE ☎ 373-9265; *Chastain Park* 216 W Wieuca Rd NE ☎ 255-0723; and Pine Isle *Lake Lanier Islands* ☎ 945-8921.

Tennis *Bitsy Grant*, 2125 Northside Dr NW ☎ 351-2774, *Chastain Park*, 140 W Wieuca Rd NE ☎ 255-1993, *Piedmont Park* ☎ 872-1507 and *Stone Mountain Park* ☎ 498-5600.

Local resources

Business services

LM Palm Associates, 2470 Windy Hill Rd, Marietta ☎ 952-5185 provides a complete range of business services.

Photocopying and printing *Franklin's Copying Service*, 135

International Blvd ☏ 522-7100; *Tucker Castleberry Printing*, 226 Luckie St ☏ 525-8654; *Alphagraphics*, 6 Decatur St ☏ 523-2679, offers self-service computer graphics and typesetting for reports and presentations; *Kwik-Kopy* gives quick turnaround and has several locations, including 120 Marietta St ☏ 525-9771.
Secretarial *Barbara H Taylor* ☏ 581-1949 and *Business World* ☏ 391-9460 offer equally efficient service.
Translation *Inlingua Translation* ☏ 266-2661, *Berlitz Translation* ☏ 261-5062.

Communications

Local delivery *Sonic Delivery* ☏ 633-8090, *Dependable Courier Service* ☏ 352-8160, and *Mid-Georgia Courier* ☏ 991-1084.
Long-distance delivery *Federal Express* ☏ 452-0314, *Airborne Express* ☏ 765-1400 and *Purolator Courier* ☏ (800) 645-3333.
Post office The downtown office is at 100 Marietta St ☏ 525-2178.
Telex *Omnicomp, Inc.* ☏ 393-2372.

Conference/exhibition centers

Facilities are provided at the *Georgia World Congress Center* ☏ 656-4150 and the *Southern Conference Center* ☏ 892-6000. Best and most convenient meeting arrangements are made through the hotels.

Emergencies

Hospitals *Georgia Baptist Medical Center* ☏ 653-4000, *Northside Hospital* ☏ 256-8000, *Grady Memorial Hospital* ☏ 589-4307.
Pharmacies *Reed Discount Drugs*, 14 Peachtree St NW ☏ 659-2046 and 55 Marietta St NW 688-0231.

Government offices

Atlanta City Government ☏ 658-6000; *City of Atlanta Economic Development* ☏ 659-4567; *US Dept of Commerce* ☏ 347-70000; *US Customs* ☏ 763-7125; *US Immigration and Naturalization Service* ☏ 331-5158.

Information sources

Business information The *Atlanta Chamber of Commerce* ☏ 521-0845 helps with economic and demographic data; The *Business Council of Georgia* ☏ 223-2264 and *Department of Industry and Trade* ☏ 656-3590 are sources for state-wide information.
Local media The *Atlanta Journal* (morning) and The *Constitution* (afternoon) give local, regional and state coverage. The *Gwinnett Daily News* and *Marietta Daily Journal* concentrate on Gwinnett and Cobb county news, respectively. The *Atlanta Business Chronicle* is a weekly tabloid of local business news. For magazine coverage, *Business Atlanta* ☏ 256-9800 is aimed at the region's business leaders; *Georgia Trend* ☏ 522-7200 covers the state and Southeast.
Tourist information The *Atlanta Convention and Visitors' Bureau* ☏ 521-6600 is the definitive source of tourist information. The *Georgia State Tourism Office* ☏ 656-3590 is also helpful.

Thank-yous

Florists *Blumenhaus Florist*, 1 Piedmont Center ☏ 237-6466; *Execuflower Service*, 5299 Roswell Rd ☏ 252-5151; *Peachtree Flowers*, 4280 Peachtree Rd ☏ 266-8800.
Gift baskets *Atlanta Wine Company*, 320 Pharr Rd NE ☏ 261-4422; *The Butler Did It*, 3820 N Druid Hills Rd ☏ 325-3296; *Baskets of Cheer*, 4470 Chamblee Dunwoody Rd ☏ 457-5001.

BOSTON

Area code ☎ 617

Boston – still often called the Hub, after Oliver Wendell Holmes's 1858 description of its State House as the "hub of the solar system" – is as jealous of its commercial, cultural and social diversity as of its place as a crucible of American history. From colonial, mercantile beginnings, it has developed via shipping and manufacturing into a world leader in education, banking, mutual funds and insurance, medicine, publishing and high-tech. Home of the Kennedys and Harvard, cradle of Democratic politics and the Red Sox, Boston was once described as a society where the Lowells spoke only to the Cabots and the Cabots spoke only to God. Even in today's property-based economy, that is still how native Bostonians regard themselves and their city. It is a city firmly rooted in its past, where the descendants of the founding families – the Brahmins, as they came to be called – are still among the most powerful and influential voices in America.

Arriving

Logan International Airport

All international flights arrive at Volpe International Terminal; domestic flights arrive at three others. It usually takes less than 30min to clear Customs and baggage inspection.

The airport has five restaurants; more interesting, however, are the live lobsters sold throughout the airport which can be shipped on dry ice to any destination within the USA. Many airlines provide executive lounges.

The international terminal has multilingual interpreters and currency exchange is available on ground level, Mon–Sat, noon–9.30; Sun, 1–9. A second currency exchange desk, in Terminal C, is open daily, 11.30–9.30. Air cargo ☎ 561-1610. General information ☎ 973 5500.

Nearby hotels *Hilton Inn*, Logan Airport 02128 ☎ 569-9300.
Ramada Inn–Airport, 225 McClellan Hwy 02128 ☎ 569-5250.

City link Logan is only 2 miles/3km from downtown and getting into the city is easy. Taxis are convenient, but for city center destinations the subway is quicker during peak hours, 7–9, 4–6, and much cheaper.

Subway Take the free Massport shuttle bus to the airport Blue Line subway station from which it is a 10–15min ride to Government Center/downtown Boston.

Taxi Cabs line up outside each terminal. At non-peak times the journey should take no more than 15min; fare about $10. During rush hours, traffic jams at the Callahan Tunnel can add at least 20min.

Car rental Boston is a city where you do not need a car, unless your business is with some of the many high-tech firms along Route 128 (see *Area by area*). Rentals can be arranged at the ground level of all terminals.

Limousine service is available from all terminals.

Bus A shuttle bus operator, *Airways Transportation Co* ☎ 267-2981 serves all major downtown hotels.

Getting around

Boston remains a city for walkers for two very good reasons – the street layout is complicated and parking is difficult. From anywhere in downtown Boston, a brisk 10–15min walk ought to take a visitor to most local destinations.

Taxi Boston cab drivers are notorious for asking passengers for directions to their requested destination, and one-way systems sometimes make circuitous routes necessary. Do not expect to flag a cab down in the street; it is best either to phone ahead or use a hotel taxi stand. Reliable companies are *Boston Cab* ☏ 536-5010; *Checker Cab* ☏ 536 7000; and *Red Cab* ☏ 734-5000.

Limousine *Fifth Avenue Limousine* ☏ 286-0555 caters to the city's corporate high rollers; *Commonwealth Limousine Service* ☏ 787-5575 also runs a sophisticated fleet.

Subway The MBTA, locally known as the T, has four lines: the Red Line runs N–S, from Cambridge to Mattapan or Quincy; the Blue Line runs from the NE into downtown; the Green Line has several branches operating from downtown to the W and SW; and the Orange Line is a N–S line. Park Street Station is the major downtown transfer point for Red and Green Line trains.

Area by area

Downtown and Back Bay Boston's business life is centered on downtown – home of most financial, legal and political offices – and adjacent Back Bay, where Boston's well-to-do live alongside the insurance companies, advertising and public relations agencies and retail stores in this traditional brownstone area.

The heart of Back Bay is bounded by Arlington Street, Massachusetts Avenue and Beacon and Boylston streets. The main thoroughfares are Commonwealth Avenue, for long one of the choicest and most expensive residential addresses, and Newbury Street, the city's most fashionable shopping district.

Fine houses in Marlborough and Beacon streets have now been transformed by Boston's young professionals, as rocketing costs forced most of the students who once lived there to move out beyond Kenmore Square to other more affordable areas in the W.

Despite development, downtown and Back Bay remain solid reminders of the city's past. The brick and granite buildings of Faneuil Hall and Quincy Market in downtown's Financial District date from the city's second mayor, Josiah Quincy, and one of the area's de luxe hotels is nothing less than the old Federal Reserve Bank.

The waterfront, once a bustling historic seaport, now has luxury condominiums and retail stores; while in Back Bay's South End – home of Boston's gay community, as well as numerous well-heeled residents – brick townhouses and wrought-iron streetlamps are overlooked by the modern marble and glass of Copley Place.

Beacon Hill With its gas-lit streets, mansions and townhouses, Beacon Hill preserves an atmosphere enjoyed by 18thC Brahmins, whose descendants still dominate city life.

North Slope Traditionally the "wrong" side of the hill, North Slope houses mainly writers, academics and intellectuals who choose to keep the Charles River between their homes and their Cambridge workbases of Harvard, MIT and Radcliffe.

Route 128 is so dense with shiny buildings and corporate headquarters that the road – which encircles the city – has become known as "America's Technology Highway." At a time when California's Silicon Valley has been hit by slump, the western stretch of Route 128, between the towns of Needham and Burlington, is lined with headquarters of such firms as Prime Computer, Wang, Raytheon, Digital and Honeywell.

Cambridge is a blend of academic, art-oriented and corporate life, the headquarters of such enterprises as Lotus, Polaroid, Arthur D Little and Draper Laboratories. Its twin focal points – bustling Harvard Square and the tranquil Harvard Yard nearby – have been supplemented recently by the slick retail complex of Charles Square.

Other areas W of Boston are the wealthy, gracious tree-studded residential towns of Brookline, Newton, and Chestnut Hill.

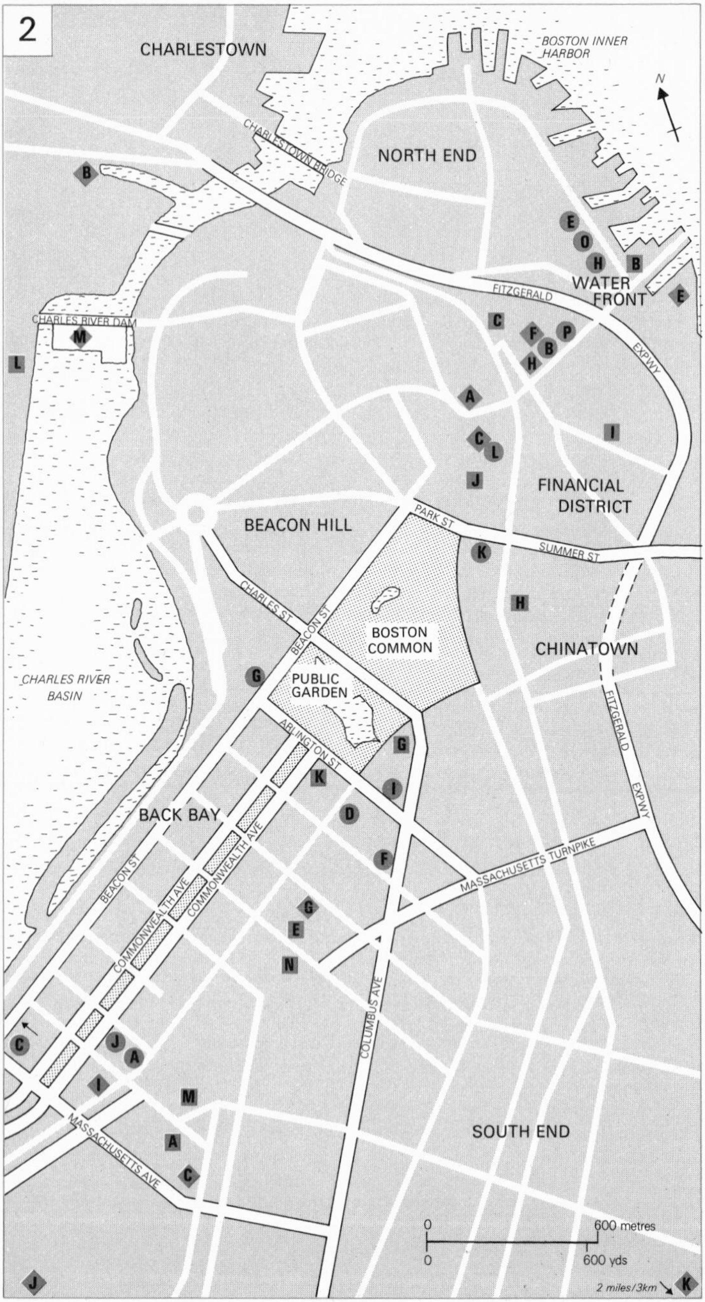
2
CHARLESTOWN
BOSTON INNER HARBOR
N
CHARLESTOWN BRIDGE
NORTH END
WATER FRONT
FITZGERALD
EXPWY
CHARLES RIVER DAM
FINANCIAL DISTRICT
BEACON HILL
PARK ST
SUMMER ST
CHARLES ST
BEACON ST
BOSTON COMMON
CHINATOWN
CHARLES RIVER BASIN
PUBLIC GARDEN
ARLINGTON ST
FITZGERALD
EXPWY
BACK BAY
MASSACHUSETTS TURNPIKE
BEACON ST
COMMONWEALTH AVE
COMMONWEALTH AVE
COLUMBUS AVE
MASSACHUSETTS AVE
SOUTH END
0
600 metres
0
600 yds
2 miles/3km

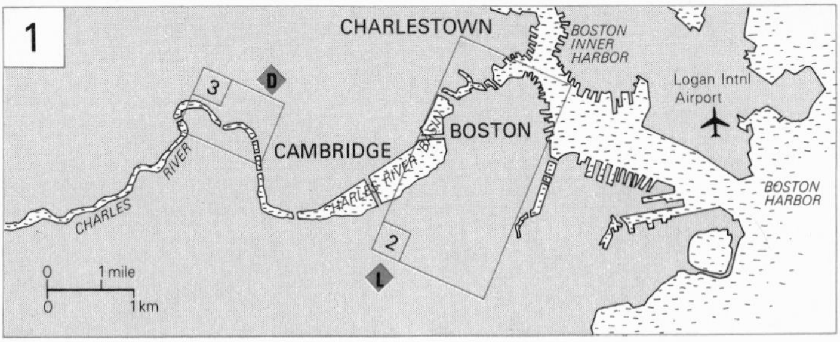

■ HOTELS
A Back Bay Hilton
B Boston Marriott Long Wharf
C Bostonian
D Charles
E Copley Plaza
F Embassy Suites
G Four Seasons
H Lafayette
I Meridien
J Omni Parker
K Ritz Carlton
L Royal Sonesta
M Sheraton Boston
N Westin

● RESTAURANTS
A Allegro on Boylston
B Bay Tower Room
C Bertucci's
D The Colony
E Davide
F Grill 23
G Hampshire House
H Jasper's
I Legal Sea Food
J L'Espalier
K Locke-Ober
L Maison Robert
M Michela's
N The Ocean Club
O Sally Ling's
P Tatsukichi

◆ BUILDINGS AND SIGHTS
A City Hall
B Northeast Trade Center
C Kerstein Business Library
D Harvard University
E Harvard Graduate School of Business Administration
F Faneuil Hall
G John Hancock Observatory Tower
H Where's Boston?
I Institute of Contemporary Art
J Isabella Steward Gardner Museum
K John F Kennedy Library
L Museum of Fine Arts
M Museum of Science

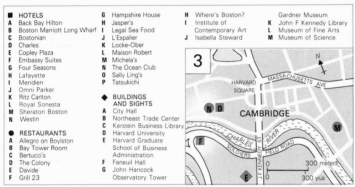

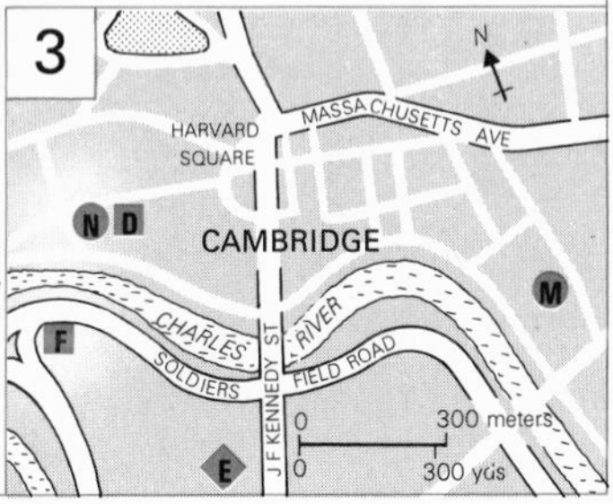

Hotels

Traditional premier hotels like the Ritz-Carlton and the Copley Plaza, and newer upscale competitors, such as the Four Seasons and the Westin provide amply for the needs of Boston's business visitors.

Back Bay Hilton $$$$
40 Dalton St 02115 ☎ 236-1100
[TX] 951858 • 338 rooms, 1 restaurant, 4 bars, 1 coffee shop
A modern high-rise, this typical Hilton caters and efficiently to the business community. Boodle's, a dining room specializing in mesquite-grilled steaks and seafood, is very popular among local executives. Pool, health club, arrangements with golf and tennis clubs • 14 meeting rooms.

Boston Marriott Long Wharf $$$$$
296 State St 02109 ☎ 227-0800
[TX] 928065 • 360 rooms, 2 restaurants, 2 bars
Though sporting what is arguably the city's ugliest façade, this brick hotel has an ultra-modern interior (featuring painted steel pipes in the open lobby), a prime waterfront location, and is convenient to the Financial District, Government Center and other downtown business addresses. Rooms on the seventh floor are equipped with large dining areas which can double as work spaces. Gift shops • pool, health club • 17 meeting rooms, recording facilities.

Bostonian $$$$$
Faneuil Hall Mktpl 02109
☎ 523-3600 [TX] 948159 • 153 rooms, 6 suites, 1 restaurant, 1 bar

Overlooking historic Faneuil Hall Marketplace, the Bostonian is the city's smallest luxury hotel and aims at meticulous but unobtrusive personal service. There are two wings, the contemporary Bostonian wing and the more rustic Harkness wing. Rooms are small but well-decorated, with oversized baths, jacuzzis, and TVs concealed in armoires. The rooftop restaurant, Seasons, is one of Boston's best for a quiet business meal. Lobby shops • use of nearby health club (pool and tennis) • 1 meeting room.

Charles $$$$$
1 Bennett St 02138 ☏ 864-1200
TX 857417 • 256 rooms, 44 suites, 2 restaurants, 2 bars
This personable new Georgian-style hotel in Cambridge has a quaint New England flavor. With its antiques and four-poster beds, it draws an urbane, sophisticated clientele, many of them academics visiting the nearby Kennedy School of Government. All suites have a small sitting room well-suited for business meetings, and those on the tenth floor have telephones equipped for computer modems. The hotel has a well-equipped third floor conference center, and some floors are reserved for non-smokers. Rarities, the hotel's sleek dining room, serves *nouvelle* dishes, and the live jazz at the Regattabar is the best in town. Smart shops • health spa and salon with indoor lap pool, exercise room, aerobics studio • 12 meeting rooms.

Copley Plaza $$$$
138 St James Ave 02116
☏ 267-5300 TX 951858 • 375 rooms, 26 suites, 2 restaurants, 3 bars, 1 coffee shop
The Plaza opened in 1912 and is Boston's *grande dame*, complete with French period furnishings, carved mantels and gilded ceilings. Sited on Copley Square, it attracts an especially well-heeled clientele from Back Bay and Beacon Hill, and is a nucleus of high level business and social activity in the city. The Plaza Bar, with its tropical plants and Oriental screens, is a Boston institution, quiet enough for serious business talks. Barber, beauty salon, jewelers, perfumery • 12 meeting rooms, Federal Express, translation, notary public.

Embassy Suites $$$$
400 Soldiers Field Rd 02134
☏ 783-0090 • 310 suites, 1 restaurant, 1 bar
A relative newcomer to the Boston scene, the city's only all-suites hotel is well located for visitors with business in Cambridge. The 15-story atrium lobby makes for an impressive entrance. Suites have refrigerators and living rooms that can be used for meetings or entertaining. The Ambassador Grille serves *nouvelle cuisine* in a subdued country club-like atmosphere and is a good choice for quiet conversation. Non-smoking suites • pool, sauna, jacuzzi, arrangements with nearby health club • 8 meeting rooms.

Four Seasons $$$$$
200 Boylston St 02116 ☏ 338-4400
TX 853349 • 288 rooms, 13 suites, 2 restaurants, 2 bars
Guest rooms in Boston's newest status hotel are graced with cherry furniture and formal English chintzes; many have separate work areas off the bedroom. The brown oak, candlelit Aujourd'hui specializes in classical French cuisine updated for the health-conscious 1980s. Pool, weights, whirlpool, sauna, massage • 9 meeting rooms, fax.

Lafayette $$$$
1 Ave de Lafayette 02111
☏ 451-2600 TX 853840 • 430 rooms, 41 suites, 2 restaurants, 1 bar
This 22-story Swissôtel has four atriums, a central location and a Continental flavor. Its Le Marquis restaurant is one of the best hotel dining rooms in the city. Non-smoking floor • pool • 12 meeting rooms.

Meridien $$$$$
250 Franklin St 02110 ☎ 451-1900
TX 940194 • 326 rooms, 22 suites, 2 restaurants, 2 bars
The Renaissance-style Meridien – located in the old Federal Reserve Bank – has 153 different room styles including loft bedrooms with downstairs living rooms. Julien serves creative cuisine in an Old-World setting and the Meridien's bar has been described by *Boston Magazine* as "the best place to have a drink and make a deal." Gift and flower shops • health club with pool, jacuzzi, aerobics, sauna • 8 meeting rooms, fax, recording facilities.

Omni Parker House $$$$$
60 School St 02108 ☎ 227-8600
TX 7103216707 • 541 rooms, 14 suites, 4 restaurants, 4 bars, 1 coffee shop
The home of Boston cream pie and Parker House rolls, this downtown hotel evokes a warmer atmosphere than most city hotels, from the mahogany walls and gilt ceilings down to the polished brass doors. Its Financial District location makes the Parker House central to all downtown offices as well as Government Center. Downstairs, the Last Hurrah is a turn-of-the-century saloon where local politicians meet for lunch and dinner; upstairs, the elegant Parker's serves Continental fare; and for after-dinner drinks, the quiet of Parker's Bar is ideal for talking business or relaxing. Non-smoking rooms, florist, gift shop • 14 meeting rooms.

Ritz-Carlton $$$$$
15 Arlington St 02116 ☎ 536-5700
TX 940591 • 202 rooms, 48 suites, 2 restaurants, 2 bars
Gentility and privacy reign supreme at the Ritz, where white-gloved elevator operators and call buttons for room service still matter. Guests are world travellers – Prince Charles stayed here during Harvard's 350th anniversary – and are treated accordingly. For years, professionals have flocked to the Ritz Bar, a local institution with an unobstructed view of the Public Garden and the best martini in town. The main dining room is the epitome of proper Bostonianism, and the downstairs café is *the* place for power breakfasts. Jewelers, gift shop, florist, dress shop • rooftop health club with sauna and massage • 10 meeting rooms.

Royal Sonesta $$$$
5 Cambridge Pkwy, Cambridge 02142
☎ 491-3600 • 400 rooms, 12 suites, 2 restaurants, 2 bars
Guest rooms are crisp and contemporary in this expensively renovated Art Deco-style building overlooking the Charles River. The location provides easy access to Harvard, MIT and Mass General Hospital. The Rib Room serves creative Continental dishes and has one of the best views in town. Barber, gift shop • pool, reduced rates at nearby health and racquetball club • 13 meeting rooms, computers, modems, software packages, copy center, library.

Sheraton Boston and Towers $$$$
39 Dalton St 02199 ☎ 236-2000
TX 940034 • 1,207 rooms, 75 suites, 4 restaurants, 4 bars
Although lacking the cachet of Boston's more established hotels, the Sheraton's central location and its dining room, Apley's, combine to attract many visiting executives. Pool, exercise equipment, jacuzzi • 41 meeting rooms, conference center, computer modems.

Westin $$$$
10 Huntington Ave 02116 ☎ 262-9600
TX 948286 • 800 rooms, 44 suites, 3 restaurants, 3 bars, 1 coffee shop
A far cry from the quaint or understated, the Westin has a convenient location, handsomely appointed pastel-colored rooms and a well-heeled professional clientele. Non-smoking floor, florist, gift shop, jeweler • pool, health club • 23 meeting rooms.

Clubs

Socially, the legacy of the Brahmins continues to thrive in the *Somerset Club* and its male-only members – who are said to be responsible for the founding of the equally august *Union Club*. The *Harvard Club* is also privileged, but women can join. Many bankers and lawyers are members. Its downtown location offers a breathtaking view of the city. Playing second string to the Harvard at double the price is the *University Club*, whose members are mostly Ivy Leaguers who didn't go to Harvard. The *Tavern Club* is where Boston's artists and writers converge these days.

Restaurants

A city once known for fresh fish, baked beans and other native New England staples, in recent years Boston has experienced something of a culinary boom with the focus on first-rate ethnic and *nouvelle* establishments. For important business entertaining the top hotel restaurants are the safest choice.

Allegro on Boylston $$$
939 Boylston St ☏ *236-0200 • closed Sun • AE MC V*
Its sleek, pastel interior, Italian *nuova* cuisine and sizzling social scene in the bar helped this Art Deco-style restaurant carve a niche among both the conservative three-piece-suit set and the arts and fashion crowd. Acoustics make conversation difficult.

Bay Tower Room $$$$
60 State St ☏ *723-1666 • closed Sun • AE CB DC MC V • jacket and tie required • reservations essential*
This dimly lit, 33rd-floor supper club provides an impressive setting for business deals either to be made or celebrated, though it is noted more for its sweeping views of the Boston Harbor than for its cuisine.

Bertucci's Pizza and Bocce $
799 Main St, Cambridge ☏ *661-8356 • MC V*
A Boston favorite, Bertucci's specializes in wood-fire-baked pizzas with toppings such as ricotta, roasted peppers and eggplant. Though family-oriented most evenings, this is a popular lunch spot for Cambridge business people and academics.

Colony $$$$
384 Boylston St ☏ *536-8500 • closed Sun, Mon • AE MC V • reservations essential*
Modern cuisine based on traditional New England foods is served amid the refined trappings of a wealthy turn-of-the-century Brahmin home. Service is black-tie without being stiff; strong selection of wines.

Davide $$$
326 Commercial St ☏ *227-5745 • closed 10 days late Aug • AE DC MC V • jacket recommended, no pipes or cigars • weekend reservations essential*
Davide's pretty setting and sophisticated northern Italian fare have won acclaim from local restaurant critics and the waterfront business crowd.

L'Espalier $$$$
30 Gloucester St ☏ *262-3023 • closed Sun; Mon in summer • AE CB DC MC V • jacket required*
You can expect the best in *nouvelle cuisine* and formal service at L'Espalier. Depending on mood and the type of deal being struck or celebrated, you can choose the ornate downstairs room or relax in the more club-like atmosphere above.

Grill 23 $$$$
161 Berkeley St ☏ *542-2255 • closed Sat and Sun L • AE CB DC MC V • jacket and tie required • weekend reservations essential*
The steaks and prime beef are the biggest draw, and the clubby

atmosphere makes the Grill a good choice for business lunches. The clientele includes executives from nearby insurance companies, publishing houses and advertising agencies, as well as Back Bay shoppers.

Hampshire House $$$
84 Beacon St ☏ 227-9600 • AE CB DC MC V • jacket required • reservations essential
Brahmin in tone, this Victorian-style dining room is particularly inviting in winter, with its hospitable fireplace, window seats overlooking the Public Garden, and a menu that's as hearty and conservative as the clientele. The Oak Room Bar and Café serves lighter fare.

Jasper's $$$$
240 Commercial St ☏ 523-1126 • closed Sun • AE CB DC MC V • jacket and tie required
Jasper White, one of the city's premier chefs, perfected his culinary skills at nearby Seasons (see *Hotel restaurants*). His menu is *nouvelle*, service is gracious and the atmosphere simple, contemporary and chic. Downtown professionals swear by the *prix fixe* lunch (Fridays only).

Legal Sea Foods $$
Park Plaza Hotel ☏ 426-4444 • AE • no reservations
Legal's downtown branch (there are two others) is the restaurant Bostonians love to hate. They hate the long lines, the erratic service and the pay-first-eat-later policy. But they love the fish enough to keep going back. The working crowd who cannot afford to wait for a table often heads to the bar for chowder, raw oysters and clams.

Locke-Ober $$$$
3-4 Winter Pl ☏ 542-1340 • closed Sun L • AE CB DC MC V • jacket and tie required • reservations essential
This is quintessential Boston, from the carved mahogany and floor-length white aprons of the waiters, to the crystal sconces, leather chairs and Continental menu. This is where the business elite meet to eat; private dining rooms on the 3rd floor are popular among local executives and politicians from State House.

Maison Robert $$$
45 School St ☏ 227-3370 • closed Sat L, Sun in summer • AE CB DC MC V • jacket and tie required • reservations essential
A good choice for business entertaining, this is the closest Boston gets to an authentic French tone. It is pretty and proper, without being stuffy. Downstairs, Ben's Café provides a bistro-like setting, and in summer a terrace café opens onto the old City Hall courtyard.

Michela's $$$
245 1st St, Cambridge ☏ 494-5419 • closed Sat L, Sun • AE CB DC MC V • reservations essential
Michela's Art Deco-style décor provides a cool meeting place for northern Italy and southern California. Its first-rate classics include goat cheese lasagna and ravioli with squid ink. The restaurant is a favorite with the architects, engineers and computer programmers of Kendall Square. Lunch prices are a fraction of those from the dinner menu.

Ocean Club $$
5 Bennett St, Charles Sq, Cambridge ☏ 576-0605 • AE CB DC MC V • weekend reservations essential
The décor is tropical, with polished wood floors, lots of plants and black-and-white photos of ocean scenes. Staff are young and stylish; the seafood is simple and well-prepared. Business interests dominate at lunch; dinner attracts the city's celebrity couples and young professionals.

Sally Ling's $$$$
256 Commercial St ☏ 227-4545 • closed Sat and Sun L • AE DC MC V • jacket required

With tuxedoed waiters and fresh-cut flowers, Sally Ling's has the grandeur of a Chinese palace, and cuisine to match. The Newton Center branch is similarly upscale, but less expensive.

Tatsukichi $$

189 State St ☎ 720-2468 • closed Sun • AE CB DC MC V

Sushi and *sashimi* are the main specialties here, but the menu includes other Japanese dishes such as *tempura* and *teriyaki*. The downstairs Foreign Affairs lounge is a popular downtown after-work spot with live music and cocktail food.

Hotel restaurants

Several of the area's best restaurants are in the city's de luxe hotels. Examples are *Seasons* on the rooftop of the Bostonian, *Boodles* in the Back Bay Hilton, *Rarities* at the Charles, and *Aujourd'hui* in the Four Seasons. In the same league are *Café Fleuri* at the Meridien, *Le Marquis* at the Lafayette, *Parker's* in the Parker House, the genteel main dining room of the Ritz-Carlton, and *Apley's* at the Sheraton.

Bars

The watering holes favored for business meetings are in the top hotels – *Parker's Bar* in the Parker House; the *Plaza Bar*, at the Copley Plaza; the old federal bank vault at the Meridien; and the *Ritz* in the Ritz-Carlton. For the social crowd, there is a very lively scene. Back Bay's most stylish bars include the *Commonwealth Grille*, where you can gaze on the latest models, fashionable photographers and rock musicians; *Joe's American Grill*, which is popular with ad agency boomers; and the *Allegro on Boylston* (see *Restaurants*). Cambridge's beautiful people use the *Ocean Club* (see *Restaurants*), the *Reggatabar* and *Harvest*.

Entertainment

Theater In recent years, Boston has evolved as a try-out town for Broadway shows. Major theaters include the *Shubert* ☎ 426-4520, the *Colonial* ☎ 426-9366 and the *Wang Center for Performing Arts* ☎ 482-9393. For local theater at its strongest, check out the *American Repertory Theater* ☎ 547-8300 and the *Huntington Theatre Company* ☎ 266-3913.

Music The *Boston Pops* start their season in May; and the world-class *Boston Symphony Orchestra*, conducted by Seiji Ozawa, performs at Symphony Hall Oct–Apr; in July it moves to Tanglewood ☎ 266-1494.

Nightclubs Most of Boston's nightclubs are frequented by a post-graduate clientele. The city's premier disco is *Metro*, 15 Lansdowne St ☎ 262-2425, which features state-of-the-art everything, from lasers to acoustics. *The Jukebox*, 275 Tremont St ☎ 542-1123, is the best of the local 1950s and '60s dance clubs; and the *Links Club*, 120 Tremont St ☎ 423-3832, caters to a very preppy crowd. For music, *Nightstage*, 823 Main St, Cambridge ☎ 497-8200, is the place for big names in blues and jazz.

Shopping

Back Bay is Boston's most stylish shopping district with elegant 19thC storefronts, art galleries, furriers and pricey boutiques along *Newbury Street*. The monolithic pink-marbled *Copley Place* is anchored by Neiman-Marcus and filled with such internationally known designer shops as Gucci, Tiffany's, Ralph Lauren and Yves St Laurent. Nearby *Downtown Crossing* is Boston's oldest shopping center, with department stores Filene's and Jordan Marsh. At *Filene's Basement* you can buy anything from furs to Brooks Brothers suits at greatly reduced prices. *Faneuil Hall Marketplace* is the city's top tourist destination, with scores of bars, shops and restaurants.

The food emporium is located inside the Quincy Market Building, where you can pick up everything from raw oysters to Chinese spare ribs. More of the same are in the adjacent *Marketplace Center*.

The Mall at Chestnut Hill, which includes Bloomingdale's, Filene's, Crate & Barrel and two high-class home furnishings stores (Adesso and Domain), is by far the best of the suburban malls.

In Cambridge, *Charles Square* has an interesting collection of small boutiques; and *Harvard Square* is packed with bookstores and gift and clothing boutiques. Also in the square are two small malls, The Garage and The Galleria, and the Harvard Coop, which sells all kinds of Harvard University paraphernalia and has one of the largest record selections in New England.

Sightseeing

Arnold Arboretum 265 acres of parkland with plants and trees (more than 7,000 varieties), and spectacular floral displays in the spring. *The Arborway ☎ 524-1718. Hours vary.*

Institute of Contemporary Art No permanent collection, but a changing range of imaginative temporary exhibits. The building – an old firehouse renovated by local architect Graham Gund – is worth seeing on its own merit. *955 Boylston St ☎ 266-5151. Open Tue–Sun, 11–7; closed Mon.*

Isabella Stewart Gardner Museum Rembrandts, Raphaels, Whistlers, Sargents and Matisses are displayed in the carefully preserved period rooms of a Venetian-style palazzo. *280 The Fenway ☎ 734-1359. Open 1–5.30, Tue to 9.30; closed Mon.*

John Fitzgerald Kennedy Library Films and exhibits depicting the life of the late president are featured in this contemporary waterfront museum. *Columbia Point on Dorchester Bay ☎ 929-4523. Open 9–5.*

John Hancock Observatory Tower In addition to the sweeping view of Boston, the 60th-floor observatory has a photo exhibit and a breathtaking film of the city taken from a helicopter. *Copley Sq ☎ 247-1976. Open 9–11; Sun from 10.*

Museum of Fine Arts The MFA's collections of European paintings – notably French Impressionists – and American art from the 18th and 19th centuries, are particularly strong. The museum has 43 Monets in addition to canvases by Manet, Renoir and Pissarro. American artists represented include Winslow Homer, John Singer Sargent, Fitz Hugh Lane, Edward Hopper and Mary Cassatt. There is also a vast collection of Asian art – T'ang Dynasty porcelain to Egyptian mummies. *465 Huntington Ave ☎ 267-9300. Open Tue–Sun, 10–5; Wed to 10; West Wing only Thu and Fri to 10.*

Museum of Science Astronomy, anthropology, medicine, music, electronics, computers and earth sciences are all represented. The Hayden Planetarium has a regularly changing program. *Science Park, on the Charles River Dam ☎ 723-2500. Open Tue–Thu, 9–4; Fri, 9–10; Sat, 9–5; Sun, 10–5.*

"***Where's Boston?***" This 50-minute multi-media show serves as a slick introduction to Boston. *60 State St ☎ 367-6090. Shown on the hour, daily 10–5; 10–8 in summer. Also shown at the Copley Place Cinema, 110 Huntington Ave ☎ 266-1300.*

Guided tours

Boat tours to Cape Cod and around the Harbor Islands are operated by *Bay State Cruises* ☎ 723-7800, the *Mass Bay Line* ☎ 542-8000 and *Boston Harbor Cruises* ☎ 227-4320. *AC Cruise Line* ☎ 426-8419 offers whale watches and daily sailings to Gloucester in the summer. Jazz, classical, and contemporary musicians are the specialty of *Water Music Inc* ☎ 876-8742. Cruises last about 3hrs.

Bus tours of Boston, Lexington and Concord are operated by *Brush Hill Tours* ☎ 287-1900 and *Gray Line Tours* ☎ 426-8805. Other tours include Cape Cod and Martha's Vineyard.
Helicopter tours *Boston Skyview* ☎ 770-4770.
Walking tours of Boston and the historic *Freedom Trail* are offered by various organizations; for information ☎ 536-1400.

Spectator sports

Baseball American League's *Red Sox* play at Fenway Park ☎ 267-8661.
Basketball The world champion *Celtics* play at the Boston Garden ☎ 227-3200 Oct–Jun.
Football The *New England Patriots*, the region's only professional team, play at the Sullivan Stadium in Foxboro ☎ 262-1776.
Horse racing Races every Mon, Wed, Fri and Sat year-round at *Suffolk Downs* ☎ 567-3900 in E Boston.
Ice hockey The *Bruins* face off at the Boston Garden ☎ 227-3200.
Running The Boston Marathon, a 26.2-mile/42km run is held on Patriots Day, in mid-Apr.

Keeping fit

In good weather, Bostonians head for the Esplanade, a grassy knoll with clearly marked paths for bikers and joggers on the banks of the Charles River. Bicycles can be rented from *Community Bike*. 490 Tremont St ☎ 542-8623.
Health clubs Many hotels have their own fitness centers or have arrangements with private clubs. Among the local clubs open to visitors are the *Boston Athletic Club*, 653 Summer St ☎ 269-4300; the *Boston Racquet Club*, 10 Post Office Sq ☎ 482-8811; the *Cambridge Racquet Club*, 215 1st St, Cambridge ☎ 491-8989; the *YMCA*, 316 Huntington Ave ☎ 536-7800; and the *YWCA*, 140 Clarendon St ☎ 536-7940.
Boating Instruction is provided at the *Boston Sailing Center* ☎ 227-4198; the *Charles River Canoe Service* ☎ 965-5110; *Community Boating* ☎ 523-1038; and *Europa Windsurfing* ☎ 497-0309. The *Boston Harbor Sailing Club* ☎ 523-2619 has power boats.
Golf The most prestigious private clubs are the *Country Club* in Brookline and *Pine Brook Country Club* in Weston. Public courses include the *Fresh Pond Golf Club*, 691 Huron Ave, Cambridge ☎ 354-9130; the *Ponkapoag Golf Course*, Rte 138, Canton ☎ 828-0645; and the *Martin Golf Course*, Concord Rd, Weston ☎ 894-4903.
Tennis There are public courts at *Lee Pool*, Charles St (across from Mass General Hospital) ☎ 523-9746, and *Foss Park*, McGrath Hwy ☎ 666-9236.

Local resources

Business services

Firms which offer complete services, convenient locations and prompt turnaround include *Boston Mimeo & Stenographic Service Inc*, 50 Broad St ☎ 482-4696; *Office Plus*, 6 Faneuil Hall Mktpl ☎ 367-8335; and *The Skill Bureau*, which has two locations – 129 Tremont St ☎ 423-2986 and 1384 Mass Ave, Cambridge ☎ 661 6699.
Photocopying and printing *Copy Copy* ☎ 267-9267 is at 815 Boylston St, across from the Prudential Center, and at several other locations; *Sir Speedy Instant Printing* ☎ 267-9711 is equally efficient with branches near Government Center, in the Financial District and in Brookline. Both companies offer pick up and delivery.
Secretarial Reliable agencies include *Accountemps* ☎ 423-1200 and *Kelly Services* ☎ 542-4040.
Translation *Berlitz Translation Services* ☎ 266-6858 and *Linguistic Systems, Inc* ☎ 864-3900

Communications

Local delivery *Choice Courier* ☎ 787-2020 and *Bay State Couriers*

☏ 625-5890. *Marathon Messenger Company* ☏ 266-8990 is Boston's most reliable bicycle courier system.
Long-distance delivery *Federal Express* ☏ 662-0200 or *Emery Worldwide* ☏ 569-6101.
Post Office General information ☏ 654-5083; the downtown office is at 647 Summer St ☏ 654-5489; the Back Bay office is at 390 Stuart St ☏ 654-5688.
Telex *Boston Telex* ☏ 576-5788.

Conference/exhibition centers

Facilities are provided at the *Bayside Exposition Center*, 200 Mt Vernon St ☏ 265-5800, which has meeting rooms for 4,000; *Boscom*, Commonwealth Pier ☏ 350-6600 has meeting rooms for 10–2,500 as well as complete food and beverage service, advanced audio-visual systems and teleconferencing capabilities; and the *Park Plaza Castle*, corner of Arlington and Stuart ☏ 426-2000, is a National Historic Landmark with towers, turrets, moats, and 20,000 square feet of exhibition space.

Emergencies

Hospitals *Mass General Hospital*, 55 Fruit St ☏ 726-2000; *Brigham and Women's Hospital*, 75 Francis St ☏ 732-5636; *Mt Auburn Hospital*, 330 Mt Auburn St, Cambridge ☏ 492-3500. Mass General does not accept credit cards. For dental emergencies, the *Mass Dental Society* ☏ 237-6511 makes referrals. For doctor referral, call the *Mass Medical Society* ☏ 893-4610.
Pharmacies *Phillips*, 155 Charles St ☏ 523-4372, is open 24hrs.

Government offices

US Dept of Commerce/International Trade Division ☏ 223-2314; *US Customs* ☏ 223-6519; *US Immigration and Naturalization Service* ☏ 723-3202.

Information sources

Business information *Greater Boston Convention and Visitors Bureau* ☏ 536-4100; the *Mass Dept of Commerce and Development* ☏ 727-3201.
Local media *Out of Town News*, Harvard Square ☏ 354-7777 carries the city's widest selection of international newspapers and magazines. The *Boston Globe* and the *Boston Herald* newspapers provide city and regional coverage. The *Globe* is Boston's white-collar daily with special business sections on Tue and Wed. *Boston Magazine* is an authoritative monthly on the political, cultural and social scene. *New England Business* is a slick monthly survey of area powerbrokers.

Thank-yous

Florists *Winston Flowers*, 131 Newbury St ☏ 536-6861; *The Greenhouse*, 569 Boylston St ☏ 437-1050; and *Victorian Bouquet Ltd*, 53 Charles St ☏ 367-6648. All accept credit card orders by telephone.
Gift baskets *The Cheers Group* ☏ 720-0102 specializes in personalized corporate gift baskets.

CHICAGO

Area code ☏ 312

Birthplace of the skyscraper and fertile breeding ground of a whole school of modern architecture, Chicago is a city of skypunching buildings; it is no accident that the world's tallest office building is Chicago's Sears Tower. The Windy City – so named as much for the hot-air rhetoric of its politicians as for the gusts blowing in from Lake Michigan – is America's Second City, after New York, but in temperament it is second to none. Still the nation's major railroad hub, it has seen economic decline on a massive scale, as the traditional steel industry died; it has experienced political upheaval and racial violence; crime is no stranger. But it is, as Carl Sandburg wrote, a big-shouldered city. Meatpacking has given way to hamburger merchandising; families like the Astors and the Pullmans have been replaced by the Crowns, Swifts and, wealthiest of all, the Pritzkers, of Hyatt Regency. Its docks handle some 82m tons of freight a year; its airport 50m passengers. It has a gross product of $88bn, from industries as diverse as conventioneering and furniture-making, mail order and tool and diemaking, transportation and fast food. But it is also the city of the Chicago Symphony Orchestra and the world-renowned Art Institute of Chicago; its university is an established intellectual, medical and scientific center, home of nuclear physics and the Manhattan A-bomb Project. It is, too, a city of well-defined ethnic communities – Irish Bridgeport, Polish Albany Park and Hispanic Pilsen, for example – as well as areas of great wealth like North Shore. If the business pace is less frantic than Manhattan's, it is no less intense and profitable.

Arriving

All international and most domestic airlines use Chicago's busy O'Hare International, 20 miles/32km NW of the Loop. An increasing number of domestic travellers, however, use the smaller Midway Airport, 8 miles/13km to the SW, and while corporate planes make use of the two major airports, more convenient is tiny Meigs Field, a mere 2 miles/3km from the downtown Loop.

O'Hare International Airport

O'Hare, genuinely one of the world's busiest airports, is currently going through a massive renovation, some of which is due to be completed in 1987, some of which has not yet started. It has three terminals – 2, 3 and 4. Terminal 1 has been demolished to make way for United's new domestic terminal; 2 and 3 are largely domestic, but they also handle Lufthansa, Swissair, Air France and British Airways. US airlines also use 2 and 3 for international departures. Terminal 4, a converted parking garage, is being used temporarily for all other international flights. A new international terminal is due to be completed by 1992.

O'Hare does not suffer from chronic weather delays, but traffic volume is a major problem. During the afternoon and evening peak periods, departing planes are frequently backed up for more than an hour, and arrivals have to stack to wait for a break in traffic.

On the ground, passengers are guided smoothly through Customs and Immigration, especially if you use the Green Channel, with nothing to declare; the airport's signposting is especially good. For international flights, baggage pick-up is close to passport control, but it is a long walk from most gates to the domestic baggage claim areas. American Airlines' N7 gate is the closest to the cab ranks. Luggage trolleys can be rented for $1, and there are speedwalkers to parking garages and car rental desks. You can estimate 45min from arrival hall to cab.

The airport is well-served for bars and restaurants, but most close at midnight. Repeat travellers patronize the restaurants in the O'Hare Hilton, which is part of the 2/3 terminal complex. If you come into Terminal 4, it is a short walk across the road to the Hilton.

The interim international Terminal 4 does have currency exchange facilities 8am–8pm, Mon–Fri. Mobile carts tour the domestic terminals 2 and 3 to meet incoming international flights.

Nearby hotels *O'Hare Hilton*, O'Hare International Airport ☏ 686-8000 TX 9177360. Only a 15min indoor walk from the farthest gate, with excellent business facilities and suprisingly quiet despite its location. *Hyatt Regency O'Hare*, 9300 W Bryn Mawr Ave ☏ 696-1234 TX 282503. A 5min bus trip from the airport, with an extensive business service center (teleconferencing, secretarial, fax and telex facilities) and 41 meeting rooms.

City link *Taxi* For someone with a lot of baggage, the best way downtown is without doubt by cab, but travelling by road is a nightmare for much of the day and especially during rush hours – 7–9.30, 3.30–7 – when the city's expressways are heavily congested. (Most European flights arrive just in time to meet that rush.) Driving then can take an hour or more; on Fridays two hours. Flights can be, and are, missed. Road repairs are scheduled throughout 1987–88, so expect the congestion to be made worse by lane closures.

Yellow, Checker and independent cabs line up at the lower level of each terminal. Trips downtown cost at least $25, and off-peak travel time should be no more than 40min.

Bus The real alternative to a cab is the Continental Air Transport ☏ 454-7800 which provides service to many of the downtown hotels and costs about $7. But you may have a several hundred yards' walk to its departure point from your baggage claim area.

Subway The quickest way downtown during rush hour for someone with little baggage and a good knowledge of the city is provided by the comfortable 24hr rapid transit rail link which takes about 35min and costs $1. Pedestrian tunnels on the lower level of each terminal lead to the station. State and Washington or State and Monroe stations are close to most downtown hotels, but occasionally you may find it difficult to find a cab when you come up onto the street. As a general rule, the service is used by locals, though it is not recommended, especially at night.

Car rental If you arrive during rush hour do not rent a car at the airport; there are plenty of rental car outlets downtown. Car agencies such as Hertz, Budget and National have booths at terminals 2 and 3.

Limousine Limousines are plentiful; see *Getting around*.

Midway Airport

This no-frills airport is significantly smaller, less crowded and easier to get through than O'Hare. With only one three-concourse terminal, it has no international carriers, but Midway, Northwest, America West, Southwest and Chicago Air all operate domestic flights. Midway is popular with corporate and private planes, cargo companies and express mail services.

City link A rapid transit link to Midway is still in the planning stages, but rush-hour traffic in this part of town is not quite so bad as that on the Kennedy Expressway; the trip downtown should take about 20min.

Car rental Major car rental firms like Budget, Hertz, Avis and National

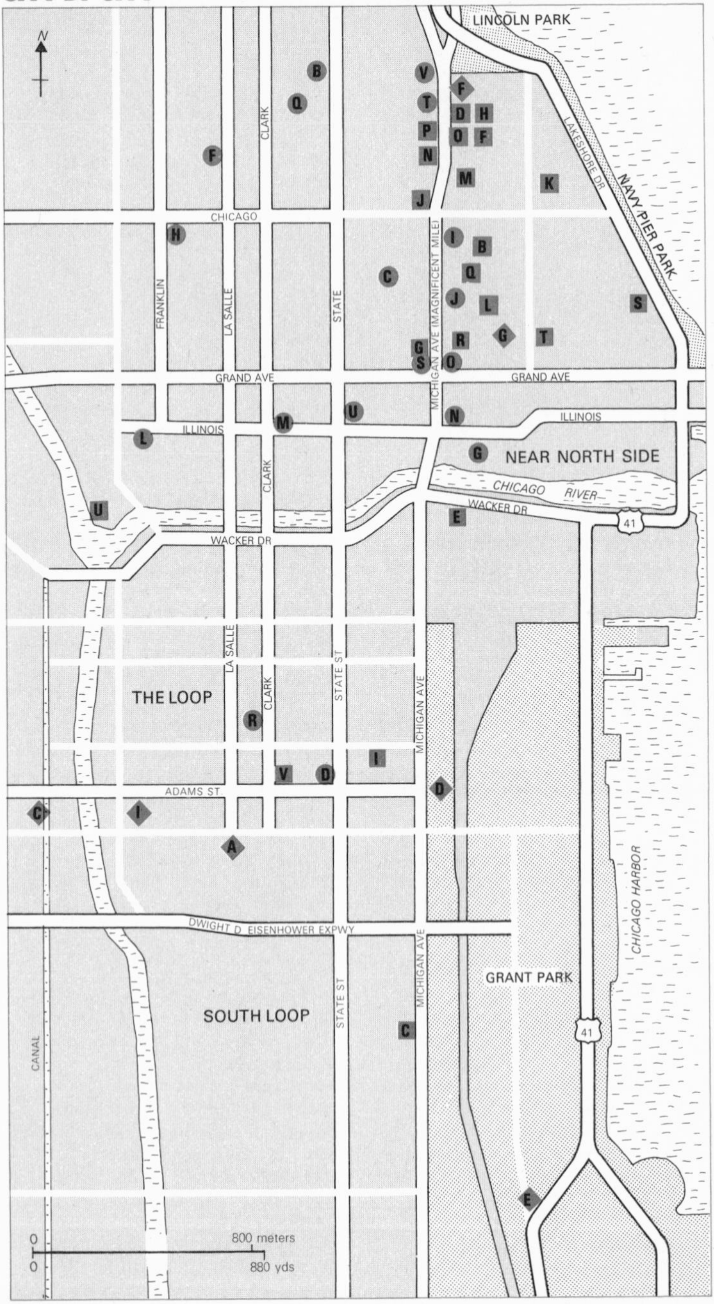
N
LINCOLN PARK
CLARK
LAKESHORE DR
NAVY PIER PARK
CHICAGO
MICHIGAN AVE (MAGNIFICENT MILE)
FRANKLIN
LA SALLE
STATE
GRAND AVE
GRAND AVE
ILLINOIS
ILLINOIS
NEAR NORTH SIDE
CLARK
CHICAGO RIVER
WACKER DR
41
WACKER DR
LA SALLE
STATE ST
CLARK
MICHIGAN AVE
THE LOOP
ADAMS ST
DWIGHT D EISENHOWER EXPWY
CHICAGO HARBOR
MICHIGAN AVE
STATE ST
GRANT PARK
SOUTH LOOP
41
CANAL
0
800 meters
0
880 yds

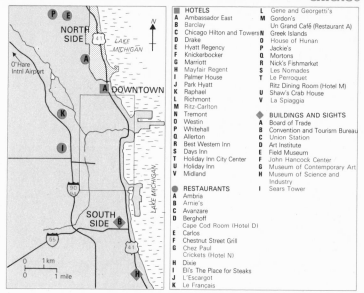

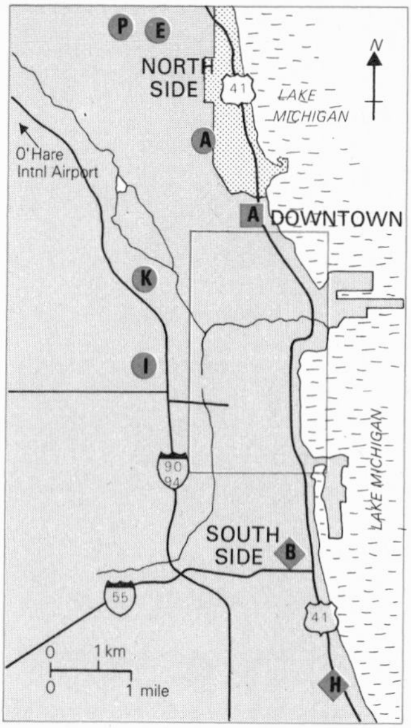

■ HOTELS
A Ambassador East
B Barclay
C Chicago Hilton and Towers
D Drake
E Hyatt Regency
F Knickerbocker
G Marriott
H Mayfair Regent
I Palmer House
J Park Hyatt
K Raphael
L Richmont
M Ritz-Carlton
N Tremont
O Westin
P Whitehall
Q Allerton
R Best Western Inn
S Days Inn
T Holiday Inn City Center
U Holiday Inn
V Midland

● RESTAURANTS
A Ambria
B Arnie's
C Avanzare
D Berghoff
Cape Cod Room (Hotel D)
E Carlos
F Chestnut Street Grill
G Chez Paul
Crickets (Hotel N)
H Dixie
I Eli's The Place for Steaks
J L'Escargot
K Le Français
L Gene and Georgetti's
M Gordon's
Un Grand Café (Restaurant A)
N Greek Islands
O House of Hunan
P Jackie's
Q Mortons
R Nick's Fishmarket
S Les Nomades
T Le Perroquet
Ritz Dining Room (Hotel M)
U Shaw's Crab House
V La Spiaggia

◆ BUILDINGS AND SIGHTS
A Board of Trade
B Convention and Tourism Bureau
C Union Station
D Art Institute
E Field Museum
F John Hancock Center
G Museum of Contemporary Art
H Museum of Science and Industry
I Sears Tower

have booths at the airport.
Bus Stopping at all major Loop hotels, Continental Air Transport ☏ 454-7800 is fast and convenient and costs about $6. They also provide a shuttle to O'Hare for around $10. CW Limousine Service ☏ 493-7800 has vans to Hyde Park (the South Side home to the University of Chicago) and O'Hare for under $10.
Taxi The trip to the Loop and Near North Side locations should cost no more than $15.
Limousine Stationed just outside the terminal entrance, United Limousine ☏ (800) 833-5555 will bring you to southerly destinations such as Indiana.
Helicopter Aviation Red Carpet Services Inc ☏ 284-2897.

Rail station

Union Station An imposing structure just W of the Loop and the Chicago River, between Jackson and Adams streets, Union Station is one of America's most famous old railroad terminals. It is a major Amtrak hub with trains leaving daily for all points E, S and W. Private sleepers and other first-class accommodations are available from Chicago. Amtrak information ☏ 558-1075. The Burlington Northern, Milwaukee Road, Norfolk and Western commuter lines also use Union Station. (For other commuter lines see *Getting around.*) Although the building's exterior recalls the grandeur of the railroad's heyday, its interior is an uncomfortable mix of old and modern, but is currently undergoing renovation. First-class Amtrak travellers have their own waiting room across from the ticket counter; eating spots are generally undistinguished. The station is within easy walking distance of the Loop and is a short cab ride away from many hotels.

Getting around

Most major hotels are an easy walk or short cab ride from the Loop, the city's corporate headquarters, so renting a car is unnecessary unless your business takes you out into the suburbs. Whatever your means of transport, navigating is easy since the city is built on a simple grid system. Madison Avenue cuts it N–S; State Street divides it E–W. Each mile has 800 house numbers, so an address which begins 3200 North is near Belmont Avenue, 4miles/6.4km N of Madison. Halsted Street is 800 West, a mile W of State. (The system breaks down in parts of the South Side.)

Public transportation All subway lines originate in the Loop and some travel in between the lanes of major expressways, speeding by rush-hour traffic jams. Bus and el (elevated train) fares run about $1, while transfers between lines are 25 cents; drivers accept bills.

Taxi Cabs are easy to find in major business districts, except when the weather is bad. There is also a convenient taxi stand at the S end of N Michigan, opposite the Wrigley Building – on the E side by the bridge. Most drivers are helpful and do not take advantage of visitors, though it is advisable to make sure they put the meter on at the start. If you are going to a suburb which is not contiguous with the city, ensure that the cab driver knows where you are going and check the price basis first; meter rates do not always apply. To order a cab by telephone, call *Yellow and Checker Cab* ☏ 829-4222 or *American United Cab* ☏ 248-7600.

Limousine Chauffeured limousines are readily available and are often cheaper than taxis for long distance trips. Two recommended limousine services are: *Carey Limousine Service* ☏ 663-1220 and *Chicago Limousine Service* ☏ 726-1035.

Car rental The major rental firms have offices both downtown and at the airport. If you decide to rent, the lowest downtown parking rates are at the municipal Monroe Street parking garage near Lake Shore Drive.

Area by area

Chicago's business center is confined to the Loop, the LaSalle Street financial district and the Near North Side. N along Lake Michigan lies the Gold Coast, a prestigious residential area for wealthy professionals. Lincoln Park, New Town and Old Town begin a few blocks farther NW. Overlapping ethnic neighborhoods, each with its own commercial life and industrial pockets, are on the outskirts. Farther out are the suburbs, in Cook, DuPage, Kane, McHenry and Will counties.

The Loop Technically, the Loop is the area within the imposing elevated track, but Chicagoans use the term loosely; often the Loop proper is seen as the area bounded by the river on the N and W, and stretching to 12th Street in the S, Michigan Avenue in the E.

There is also a newly-gentrified southern section known as South Loop, stretching from Van Buren to 12th. Newspapers and locals sometimes refer to the area N of Madison as North Loop. Most of the city's major office towers and complexes line Michigan Avenue, Dearborn Street and curving Wacker Drive. State Street – "that great street" – is now a major pedestrian shopping district. By night, however, the Loop is quieter, although an upper-class residential influx in the past decade has introduced new life. There are lakefront condominiums with dazzling views and new developments like the eye-catching River City, Dearborn Park and Presidential Towers in the S and W sectors. Several blocks away, LaSalle Street is a canyon lined with massive buildings that house the city's banks and financial institutions. It is bounded on the S by the Chicago Board of Trade, the city's prominent commodity market.

Near North Side Anything N of the Chicago River and S of North Avenue is considered Near North, although there is no agreed single definition. Streeterville, the Gold Coast with its renovated robber baron mansions, and N Michigan Avenue's

Magnificent Mile are home to many fashionable shops and restaurants. It is a bustling area, both day and night, especially around Rush and Division streets with their bars, restaurants and outdoor cafés. The ultra-rich live in beautiful old apartment buildings tucked away between the John Hancock Building and Water Tower Place, the fashionable inner-city atrium mall. IBM Plaza, the Chicago Tribune Tower, the Sun-Times Building and the huge wholesale Merchandise Mart are all on the N bank of the Chicago River. Northwestern University's law and medical schools are here, although the University's main campus is in Evanston, the first suburb N of the city.

South Side Amid miles of Polish, Irish, Lithuanian and black communities is Hyde Park, home of the University of Chicago and a middle and upper middle-class enclave. It is the city's most successfully integrated community. Farther S over the border in Indiana, steel mills spew smoke and yellow flames into the sky; but in SE Chicago, the old manufacturing smokestack is dying fast.

O'Hare Airport area Many corporations have re-located to parts of the city and suburbs around O'Hare, creating a self-contained thriving business district. Major concerns like National Can and Motorola line the Kennedy Expressway, and modern business complexes stretch along the Northwest and Tri-State tollways. The Zenith Corporation is located on the Tri-State.

Suburbs Tax concessions have persuaded some big firms to move their headquarters to the suburbs. The Oak Brook area, W of the city in wealthy DuPage County, has attracted a number of major corporations; McDonald's and Waste Management have their headquarters there. Their top executives tend to live along the affluent and exclusive 20-mile/32km North Shore. Mansions and palatial homes occupied by families of Crowns, Swifts and others dot the shoreline from Evanston N to Winnetka, Lake Forest all the way to Lake Bluff. In terms of increasing prestige and indicators of wealth and success, a ranking of suburbs would be Highland Park, Wilmette, Lake Forest, Kenilworth, Glencoe and, at the peak of the social scale, Winnetka. Barrington Hills, farther W, is also very exclusive.

Hotels

Many of Chicago's hotels are convention-oriented, but the city also has internationally acclaimed hotels, such as the Drake, Ritz-Carlton and the Mayfair Regent, as well as its share of smaller European-style hotels. All types offer a variety of convenience and comfort for the business traveller, and the best have comprehensive business facilities such as telex, fax, audio-visual equipment and in-house secretarial services. The opening of several new hotels is anticipated in 1987 and 1988: watch out for the Nikko, Swissôtel, Four Seasons and Fairmont.

Ambassador East **$$$$$**
1301 N State Pkwy 60610
☎ 787-7200 ⓉⓍ 2212120 • 238 rooms, 50 suites, 1 restaurant, 1 bar, 1 coffee shop

Located slightly out of mainstream Chicago hotel land, the Ambassador East compares with New York's Carlyle – super elegant, but uptown. It attracts a high society and show business clientele: expect jet setters, film stars and rock groups. Frank Sinatra is a frequent guest; Lauren Bacall and Humphrey Bogart honeymooned here. A considerable part of the building is comprised of residential suites. The hotel restaurant, the Pump Room, has been a Chicago institution for 60 years; booth number one is *the* place to be seen. Health club • 8 meeting rooms, fax.

Barclay **$$$$**
166E Superior St 60611
☎ 787-6000 TX 270527 • 12 suites, 1 restaurant/bar
A small modern European-style hotel just off Michigan Avenue catering to executives. Its suites are French Provincial in style; most have kitchens and many have conference areas, sunken living rooms and spectacular views. The hotel's suites make it particularly useful for in-room business meetings; it is used by visiting headhunters for the same reason. The hotel is named after the 40-year-old private dining club which it houses; guests automatically become members during their stay. Exercycles for use in suite • 5 meeting rooms.

Chicago Hilton and Towers **$$$$**
720 S Michigan Ave 60605
☎ 922-4400 TX 797297 • 1,613 rooms, 148 suites, 4 restaurants, 3 bars
The flagship of the Hilton empire, this gargantuan hotel recently underwent a $200m renovation which has given the interior a much-needed face lift. Situated S of Chicago's downtown area, and with many of the city's best known cultural attractions nearby, its regal Grand Ballroom hosts many a political get-together. The hotel's restaurant, Buckingham's, is a popular business rendezvous. Non-smoking rooms, shops • jogging track, pool, jacuzzis, weight training • 55 meeting rooms, word processors, fax, computer rental and modems, business reference library, transcription, answering machines.

Drake **$$$$**
140 E Walton Pl 60611 ☎ 787-2200
TX 270278 • 535 rooms, 65 suites, 4 restaurants, 2 bars
One of the great hotels of the 1920s, the Drake is the *grande dame* of Chicago's hostelries, catering equally to weary travellers and society and business guests. (Nancy Reagan stays here; the President prefers Palmer House Towers.) The Drake retains old-fashioned concepts of service and positively pampers guests staying on the exclusive 10th floor, refuge to numerous heads of state. Many of the rooms and suites have the best lake views in Chicago. The concierge has a reputation for being able and willing to do or arrange just about anything. The illustrious Cape Cod Room (see *Restaurants*) continues to get top marks as a fish restaurant; the Captain's Club and a glamorous bar area are also popular retreats. The Drake also has one of the city's best afternoon teas. Shopping arcade, barber, florist • arrangements with nearby health club • 18 meeting rooms.

Hyatt Regency **$$$$**
151 E Wacker Dr 60601
☎ 565-1234 TX 256237 • 2,019 rooms, 200 suites, 5 restaurants, 4 bars
The immensely popular Hyatt is a dependable favorite with executives both for its convenient downtown location and its extensive business services. The modern interior is done in true Hyatt style, with acres of glass, the sensation of sheer size, fountains and the trademark lobby waterfall. Jacuzzis are also offered in some of the suites, as are open fires. Gift shops • arrangements with 2 nearby health clubs • 38 meeting rooms, teleconferencing, fax.

Knickerbocker **$$$$**
163 E Walton St 60611 ☎ 751-8100
TX 206719 • 256 rooms, 27 suites, 1 restaurant, 1 bar, 1 coffee shop
Retaining the sumptuous and slightly flirty feel of the 1920s, the Knickerbocker's elegant lobby and guest rooms make a pleasant and much sought after retreat from the hectic bustle of the city outside. The clientele is decidedly well-heeled and

privacy is much valued. Its lobby houses the Limehouse Pub (see *Bars*), a delightful piano bar. Health club • 12 meeting rooms.

Marriott **$$$$$**
540 N Michigan Ave 60611
☎ 836-0100 [TX] 9102211360 •
1,100 rooms, 2 restaurants, 3 bars, 1 coffee shop
As its room numbers suggest, this Marriott is geared to conventions; but its address at the S end of N Michigan is convenient to the Loop and Gold Coast attractions alike. Thirty-four meeting rooms.

Mayfair Regent **$$$$$**
181 E Lake Shore Dr 60601
☎ 787-8500 [TX] 256266 • Regent International • 174 rooms, 30 suites, 2 restaurants, 1 bar
An elegant Old World-style hotel, more intimate and European than the Drake, the Mayfair Regent maintains a standard of comfort achieved only by a guest-to-staff ratio approaching one-to-one. Recently refurbished, the ambiance is more that of an elegant urban mansion than a hotel, with hand-painted Chinese murals and Louis XVI desks in the lobby, and flowers everywhere. Many rooms have lake views. Le Ciel Bleu is an undoubtedly elegant dining spot; the Palm, too, gets high marks as one of the city's traditional steak and seafood restaurants. Health club • 3 meeting rooms.

Palmer House **$$$**
17 E Monroe St 60690
☎ 726-7500 [TX] 382182 • Hilton • 750 rooms, 70 suites, 2 restaurants, 2 bars
The Palmer House ought to be the best business address in Chicago. This 1920s barn of a hotel, with its towering frescoed lobby, is host to Democratic Party functions and is magnificently situated in the heart of the Loop; it is but a step from the art museum. There are restaurants (nothing great, nothing awful) of every description and a good many shops. The staff at the serried ranks of check-in desks are efficient and courteous; the laundry works; the phones work; the rooms are comfortable and refurbished. But this is a Hilton convention hotel, and that sets the tone. It can take 30min to get on one of the dozen-odd elevators. So do not be fooled when you learn that statesmen stay here – they are in the very acceptable Towers complex, with its key-access elevators and special business facilities! Barber, jeweler • health club, pool, steam room, massage, arrangements with nearby tennis club • 68 meeting rooms, teleconferencing, notary, fax, translation, recording facilities.

Park Hyatt **$$$$$**
800 N Michigan Ave 60611
☎ 280-2222 [TX] 256216 • 255 rooms, 37 suites, 1 restaurant, 1 bar
Located just a few steps from Water Tower Place, the opulent Park Hyatt's lobby drips with Oriental rugs and objets d'art, a theme continued in the spacious guest rooms. Service is consistently good. The La Tour restaurant has a wine list with over 40 champagnes. A vintage Rolls-Royce is available for guest use, as is a $2,000-a-night penthouse complete with library and dining room. Non-smoking floor • access to 2 nearby health clubs • 6 meeting rooms.

Raphael **$$$**
201 Delaware Pl 60611 ☎ 943-5000 [TX] 206511 • 100 rooms, 78 suites, 1 restaurant, 1 bar
An elegant European-style small hotel at a good address off N Michigan Avenue, directly behind the John Hancock Building. Surprisingly, its comfortable suites cost less than rooms at other de luxe hotels. Its personalized service keeps guests coming back. A print of Raphael's Madonna of the Chair watches over the tiny chapel-like lobby; the lounge and restaurant are equally intimate. Three meeting rooms.

Richmont $$$
162 E Ontario St 60611 ☎ 787-3580 • 190 rooms, 13 suites, 1 restaurant, 1 bar
A useful alternative for someone on a tight expense account, the Richmont has a quaint charm missing at the huge, modern convention hotels. Conveniently just off N Michigan Avenue, this intimate spot has a staunchly loyal following who gladly do without frills such as room service, to enjoy the quiet and cozy feel reminiscent of a small European hotel. Two meeting rooms.

Ritz-Carlton $$$$$
160 E Pearson St 60611 ☎ 266-1000 TX 206014 • 411 rooms, 84 suites, 1 restaurant, 1 bar
The Ritz-Carlton is the favored Chicago hotel of many. The combination of location, the remarkable atrium, a fine dining room and excellent Four Seasons service, together with large and well-furnished rooms, put the Ritz-Carlton, with its unusual 12th-floor lobby in Water Tower Place, in the top rank of international hotels. Security is among the city's best. Gift shop, hairdresser, barber • health spa with pool • 6 meeting rooms, fax.

Tremont $$$$$
100 E Chestnut 60611 ☎ 751-1900 TX 255157 • 130 rooms, 9 suites, 1 restaurant, 1 bar
Yet another Chicago institution, the Tremont is a stone's throw from Michigan Avenue and has discreet European charm and old-fashioned elegance – as displayed by the collection of antique prints and Flemish vases. Guest rooms are unusually spacious, excellent for paperwork. Many have working fireplaces – a real status feature – and comfortable overstuffed chairs. The hotel restaurant, Crickets (see *Restaurants*) has several private rooms. The hotel prides itself on its special facilities for women executives. Arrangements with nearby health club • 4 meeting rooms.

Westin $$$$$
909 N Michigan Ave 60611 ☎ 943-7200 TX 206593 • 730 rooms, 2 restaurants, 2 bars
Due in part to its excellent site on N Michigan Avenue, right in the heart of the Magnificent Mile, the Westin is always busy with business people, conventioneers and professional sports players. Although it is not considered a top business address, its ultra-modern interior and up-to-the-minute facilities make this one of Chicago's most popular convention hotels. Oversize beds and wet bars available in most rooms. Rooftop pool, health club • 18 meeting rooms, fax.

Whitehall $$$$$
105 E Delaware Pl ☎ 944-6300 TX 255157 • 223 rooms, 13 suites, 1 restaurant, 1 bar
This renowned independently owned hotel has the feel of a private club. Owner John B Coleman also has the Tremont, the New York Ritz-Carlton and the Ritz in Washington DC. Rooms show great attention to detail; several have jacuzzis. The Whitehall Club restaurant is open only to members and guests. Health club • 6 meeting rooms, fax.

OTHER HOTELS
Allerton ($$$) *701 N Michigan Ave ☎ 440-1500.*
Best Western Inn of Chicago ($$$) *162 E Ohio St ☎ 787-3100.*
Days Inn ($$$) *644 N Lake Shore Dr ☎ 943-9200.*
Holiday Inn City Center ($$$) *300 E Ohio St ☎ 787-6100.*
Holiday Inn ($$$) *Merchandise Mart Plaza, 350 Orleans St ☎ 836-5000.*
Midland ($$$) 172 W Adams St *☎ 332-1200.*

Clubs

Most of Chicago's establishment lunching takes place within the city's private clubs, many of which are only just beginning to admit women, and even then only with restrictions. The clubs are central to business life in the city, and some of the rooms in the top clubs are stunning. The *Chicago Club* is arguably the best and most prestigious; women are now admitted as guests. The (mainly Jewish) *Standard Club* is in the same league and has similarly tight entry procedures. In either club, your host will be part of Chicago society and active in charity work or the arts. The *Tavern Club* is a favorite with corporate executives and many of the city's leading Democrats, media moguls and artists. The *Union League Club,* nicknamed the Republican Club, is an alternative for politicians. Its wood-paneled dining room is a favorite with judges and lawyers. The *University Club* and the *Chicago Athletic Association,* which attract a wide range of professionals, have less exclusive membership policies. Two private yacht clubs, the *Columbia* and the *Chicago,* also have dining facilities. The club with the best food is the *Mid-America,* which has a faithful following among those in the creative industries such as publishing and the media. Uptown clubs are the highly esteemed *Casino,* dominated by women, providing good food, and more socially than business oriented; the *Raquet Club* is favored by the city's top families, particularly for Sunday brunch, and is used for business and pleasure. In addition, there are various executive lunch clubs in large office buildings – such as the *M&M* in the Merchandise Mart and the *Metropolitan* in Sears Tower.

Restaurants

Chicagoans love to eat out. The business lunch is a much-valued tradition, and the best restaurants are jammed noon–1.30. Dinner is from 5.30 to 10, closing earlier in the winter. In the past few years a whole new crop of restaurants has sprung up, in addition to the city's classic eating institutions: outdoor cafés transform the city into a Midwestern Paris in summer, and the ethnic bistros reflect the city's immensely varied immigrant culture. Most of the restaurants listed here are on the Near North Side and on the North Side. North Loop and Loop restaurants are geographically the most practical for lunch.

Ambria $$$$
2300 N Lincoln Park West
☎ 472-5959 • D only; closed Sun • AE CB DC MC V • jacket required
Chicago's fashionable make reservations at least two weeks ahead to dine on excellent *nouvelle cuisine.* Set in the Belden Stratford Hotel just off Lincoln Park, Ambria has an intimate atmosphere perfect for negotiations or celebrations.

Arnie's $$$
1030 N State St ☎ 266-4800 • AE CB DC MC V • no reservations
The other half of Morton's, distinctive, plush and fashionable, is a Chicago institution. Steaks and fish are the main fare, although it also has a famous hamburger bar. A good place to unwind, but not recommended for a quiet business dinner. Arnie's brunch is famous citywide.

Avanzare $$$
161 E Huron St ☎ 337-8056 • D only Sat and Sun • AE DC MC V • jacket preferred
In a high-rise lobby just off Michigan Avenue, Avanzare couples serious northern Italian cuisine with a relaxed Continental atmosphere. This is a good spot for quiet business discussion, especially in the intimate, 10-table room upstairs.

Berghoff $$
17 W Adams St ☎ 427-3170 • closed Sun • no credit cards • no reservations
Even when the wind chill factor is well below zero, there are lines outside the Berghoff at lunch time. For 85 years, waiters in white aprons and black jackets have served reasonably-priced German and American dishes, sandwiches and beer, and businessmen and lawyers have hobnobbed in its well-appointed bar and two huge dining rooms. Not a first-time choice for visitors wishing to entertain.

Cape Cod Room $$$
140 E Walton Pl (in Drake Hotel) ☎ 787-2200 • AE CB DC MC V
Cozy, dark and comfortable, this New England-style seafood restaurant is on the lower level of the Drake hotel. It has red checkered tablecloths, wood floors, a chowder bar and a happy hubbub. The Cape Cod is always full and remains one of Chicago's most desirable dining spots. Only two seatings for dinner, 5 and 8.

Carlos $$$$
429 Temple, Highland Park ☎ 432-0770 • D only; closed Tue • AE CB DC MC V • jacket and tie required • reservations essential
A small, intimate restaurant, Carlos's subtle *nouvelle cuisine* offerings more than make up for the 45min drive from the Loop. Owner Carlos is especially proud of his private sitting room and 10-person dining room upstairs, which has the simple, comfortable feeling of a private house, and is a fine place to entertain North Shore business associates. The wine list is long and expensive, but good.

Chestnut Street Grill $$
845 N Michigan Ave ☎ 280-2720 • AE DC MC V
A first-class modern fish restaurant, in Water Tower Galleria, with a splendid list of California wines. Unusually, you can drink vintage wine by the glass.

Chez Paul $$$
660 Rush St ☎ 944-6680 • D only Sat and Sun • AE CB DC MC V
This dark, rather earnest French restaurant helped to pioneer the move in Chicago away from meat and potatoes – and deserves some respect simply for that. And there are hordes of businessmen here at lunchtime, negotiating away to their hearts' content, blissfully unaware that their favorite watering hole is not exactly a gastronome's paradise.

Crickets $$$
100 E Chestnut St (in Tremont Hotel) ☎ 280-2100 • AE CB DC MC V
Taking its cue from New York's 21 Club, on which its design and general ethos is loosely based, Crickets's *raison d'être* is not purely gastronomic. It has a fiercely loyal clientele of socialites (who may or may not also be business moguls) who love it because it's their place. Serious-minded gourmets find the food OK, but not exceptional; the wine list first class, but very expensive; the service reliable and gracious. So, Crickets is an institution; it's fun; it's good for the ego; but it's not Chicago's best restaurant by a long shot.

Dixie Bar & Grill $$$
225 W Chicago Ave ☎ 642-3336 • AE DC MC V • no dinner reservations
The Art Deco look, open-hall setting and crowded bar do not create a sense of intimacy, but nonetheless Dixie is a recent, popular entry on the Chicago restaurant scene, especially favored by the city's businessmen and aldermen. Good cajun food is the staple. At dinner, New Orleans and Chicago-style jazz is played.

Eli's the Place for Steak $$$
215 E Chicago Ave ☎ 642-1393 • AE DC
Another Chicago tradition. Eli's is recognized for its fine steaks, prime rib, a nationally known cheesecake and famed Liver Eli. Recommended for business dinners, but perhaps less enticing for social occasions, Eli is

nevertheless a favorite with visiting movie and sports stars.

L'Escargot **$$$**
701 N Michigan Ave ☎ 337-1717 • AE DC MC V • jacket required
With its brasserie-style tone and reasonable prices, this L'Escargot, in the Allerton Hotel, is a very acceptable and genuinely French alternative in the good provincial class. It offers a set lunch and decent wines. Also at 2925 N Halsted ☎ 525-5522 where it is a big local favorite with Near Northsiders.

Le Français **$$$$$**
269 S Milwaukee Ave, Wheeling ☎ 541-7470 • D only; closed Mon • AE CB DC MC V • jacket required • reservations essential
Top executives, lawyers and doctors dine at Jean Banchet's charming cottage in this NW suburb 35 miles/56km from downtown. It is not the sort of place a business visitor is likely to have time to visit alone, but if you are invited there, you will be eating in one of the finest restaurants in the country.

Gene & Georgetti's **$$$**
500 N Franklin ☎ 527-3718 • closed Sun • AE CB DC
Although many of Chicago's business*men* would claim G&G's provides the best and biggest steaks in town, its aggressively macho atmosphere rules it out for women dining together. Although not elegant, it has a loyal and extremely eclectic following. Actually getting your reserved table may be difficult if you are not known.

Gordon's **$$$**
512 N Clark ☎ 467-9780 • D only Sat • AE CB DC MC V
The warm atmosphere of this 1840s building is an unexpected bonus; the Continental menu is in itself sufficient reason for choosing it. Both fun and businessy, it is a good place to unwind, enjoy a meal and still talk terms.

Un Grand Café **$$$**
2300 N Lincoln Park West ☎ 348-8886 • D only; closed Sun • AE MC V • no reservations
Located next door to Ambria in the same hotel, and created by Mr Rich Melman (also responsible for Shaw's Crab House and PJ Clarke's – see *Bars*), Un Grand Café is a French bistro. The crowd tends to be urbane and sophisticated, and the restaurant is becoming increasingly popular as a chic place to dine. A 10min drive N of the Loop.

Greek Islands **$$**
200 S Halsted St ☎ 782-9855 • AE CB DC MC V • no reservations
At night, the Greek Islands has a jovial feel with casually dressed clientele interspersed with opera-lovers headed for the Lyric Opera just across the river. A popular lunch and after-work spot. Good traditional Greek food.

House of Hunan **$$**
535 N Michigan Ave ☎ 329-9494 • AE CB DC MC V • jacket preferred
In the heart of the busy Magnificent Mile, the House of Hunan is a convenient spot for a working lunch or dinner. The food is American Chinese; the atmosphere soft, cool and quiet.

Jackie's **$$$$**
2478 N Lincoln Ave ☎ 880-0003 • closed Sun and Mon • AE CB DC MC V • reservations essential
Intimate, with closely set tables, this is not the place for private talks, but the food makes up for that. Intricate and decidedly *haute cuisine* is the hallmark of Jackie Etcheber's (ex Le Français) smart uptown restaurant. Jackie's is the top choice for many of Chicago's committed foodies.

Morton's **$$$$**
1050 N State St, Newbury Plaza ☎ 266-4820 • D only; closed Sun • AE CB DC MC V
This other half of Arnie's is a rather more formal, but not altogether

quiet, restaurant. Its expensive steaks are said to be the best in the city, and the shellfish is also good.

Nick's Fishmarket $$$$
1 First National Plaza ☎ 621-0200 • L only Sat; closed Sun • AE CB DC MC V • jacket preferred
Fresh seafood specialties and a Caribbean islands atmosphere make this one of the top seafood restaurants in town. Fresh abalone and *mahi-mahi* top the list. Popular for business luncheons, but not in the same league as Shaw's.

Les Nomades $$$$
222E Ontario ☎ 649-9010 • D only; closed Sun and Mon • no credit cards • jacket and tie required • weekend reservations essential
An intimate bistro-like private club in a signless red-brick town house. You have to be a member to eat here, says idiosyncratic Jovan Trobyeevic; but he adds that most international visitors are welcome. If you are invited, you will not only enjoy your meal (with imaginative wines) but also know that your host thinks highly of you.

Le Perroquet $$$$$
70 E Walton St ☎ 944-7990 • D only Sat; closed Sun • AE CB DC • reservations essential
Generally rated the tops, Le Perroquet is certainly one of Chicago's finest and most elegant restaurants – and its grandest. The *nouvelle cuisine* is served in a third-floor dining room, accessible only by private elevator. An invitation here means that your host is pulling out all the stops.

Ritz Dining Room $$$$
160 E Pearson St, Water Tower Place ☎ 266-1000 • D only Sat • AE CB DC MC V • dinner reservations only
The Ritz-Carlton's dining room is certainly Ritzy and everything you might hope for from a grand hotel restaurant – even if it wouldn't be a committed gourmet's first choice.

Shaw's Crab House $$$
21 E Hubbard St ☎ 527-2722 • D only Sat and Sun • AE CB DC MC V • lunch reservations only
Tucked away in a dark street around the corner from the downtown IBM Plaza, Shaw's is a mélange of styles: formal 1930s décor and taped '40s and '50s jazz music. The seafood is strictly first-rate. Ensconced in Shaw's comfortable booths are top executives from Chicago's major television stations and partners of its most prestigious legal and financial firms. After work the young professional crowd frequents the place. Melman again.

La Spiaggia $$$$
980 N Michigan Ave ☎ 280-2750 • AE CB DC MC V • reservations essential
At one of the most fashionable addresses in the North Loop, the glass-dominated La Spiaggia is consciously glamorous. The northern Italian cuisine includes everything from *vitello tonnato* – and lots of fish – to a locally famous thin-crusted pizza. Service, on the other hand, can be slow.

Rib joints
Chicago is famous for tender barbequed pork and beef ribs. Two of the classier rib restaurants are *Carsons: The Place for Ribs*, 612 N Wells St ☎ 280-9200 and *Randall's*, 41 E Superior St 280-2790. *Larry's Prime Rib*, 100 E Ontario ☎ 787-5000 is considered among the best for rib roasts.

Deep-dish pizza
Chicago is the self-proclaimed birthplace of deep-dish pizza; stuffed with meats and vegetables of your choice, one or two slices are enough for most appetites. Try *Giordano's*, 747 N Rush St ☎ 951-0747; *Bacino's on Wacker*, 75 E Wacker Dr ☎ 263-0070; or *Pizzeria Due*, 619 N Wabash Ave ☎ 943-2400.

Bars

While most business is dealt with in the recesses of the city's private clubs, there are some local bars that attract a strong business clientele. Among the best is *The Berghoff Café*, 17 W Adams St, which is conveniently located in the Loop. It is packed nightly with the off-duty business crowd; a bit too noisy for any serious conversation, but nonetheless a real Chicago institution dating back to 1898. The black and white tiled floor is often thick with bulging briefcases, making it difficult to walk the length of the bar. Excellent bar food as well. *P J Clarke's*, 1204 N State Pkwy, sister to the club of the same name in New York, is popular with the business community and politicians as well as the occasional athlete and actor. Like its New York counterpart, it has a rustic, turn-of-the-century look and is a popular after-work spot. *Gold Star Sardine Bar*, 666 N Lakeshore Dr, has an elegant, dark 1940s décor; regulars include personalities from CBS studios across the street. The plush couches and armchairs of the *Limehouse Pub*, 163 E Walton St in the Knickerbocker lobby (see *Hotels*), are often used for talking shop. *Miller's Pub*, 23 E Adams St, is an unpretentious place with a late night license, food until 3am and a long bar. Its round tables are favorite haunts for Chicago football players and sports celebrities. *Benchers*, in the Sears Tower, is an often-used spot for the local business force, while both *The Sign of the Trader*, 141 W Jackson in the lobby of the Board of Trade, and the *Broker's Inn*, 323 S LaSalle, are hotbeds of financial talk. *Bynion's*, 327 S Plymouth Ct near the Federal Building, attracts a sedate lawyer crowd.

Entertainment

Chicago's entertainment offerings are many and varied, as befits the cultural capital of the Midwest. To find out what's on, pick up a free copy of the *Chicago Reader*, Friday entertainment supplements to the *Chicago Tribune* or the *Sun-Times*, a *Chicago Scene* and/or *Chicago Magazine* at any newsstand.

Ticket agencies To book a show or concert, call either the box office or *Theater Tix* ☏ 853-0505; major credit cards accepted. Half-price tickets are available for cash on the day of the performance at the *Hot Tix Booth*, 24 S State, Mon, 12–6; Tue–Fri, 10–6; Sat, 10–5.

Theater and ballet The Chicago theater scene enjoys a growing national reputation. The *Goodman Theater* in the Art Institute of Chicago complex, 200 E Colombus Dr ☏ 443-3800 is known for fine performances of classic and new productions. Pre- and post-Broadway productions can be seen at the *Shubert Theater*, 60 E Balbo and at the *Aria Crown*, McCormick Pl at 23rd and Lake Shore Dr ☏ 791-6000. For classics by such as Ibsen and Shaw, try the *Court Theater*, 5706 S University at the University of Chicago Hyde Park ☏ 753-44720.

The Maria Tallchief-directed *Chicago City Ballet* ☏ 943-1315 is highly regarded but has no permanent home of its own. A blend of jazz and ballet can be seen at the *Hubbard Street Dance Company*, 218 S Wabash ☏ 663-0850.

Cinema First-rate cinemas include those in *Water Tower Place* ☏ 649-5790 or the newly-renovated *Chicago Theater*, 175 N State St. For arty offbeat movies, there is the *Fine Arts Theater*, 410 Michigan ☏ 939-3700; *Facets Multimedia*, 1517 W Fullerton ☏ 281-9075; and the *Biograph Theater*, 2433 N Lincoln ☏ 348-4123 where bank robber John Dillinger was gunned down by the FBI in 1934.

Music The renowned *Chicago Symphony Orchestra*, under the direction of Sir Georg Solti, plays at Orchestra Hall, 220 S Michigan ☏ 435-8111. The *Lyric Opera Company* ☏ 346-0270 is at the grand Civic Opera House in the Loop. The CSO gives free outdoor concerts in

Grant Park at the Petrillo Bandshell in summer; for information ☎ 744-3315.
Blues Chicago is the world's blues capital. Two favorite North Side clubs are *Lilly's*, 2513 N Halsted ☎ 525-2422 and *Kingston Mines*, 2548 N Halsted ☎ 477 4646, both open until 4am. The *New Checkerboard Lounge*, 423 E 43 St ☎ 373-5948 is in a rougher neighborhood but is still a favorite haunt of the Rolling Stones and BB King when they are in town.
Jazz Top quality jazz can be heard at midday or between 5 and 8pm at *Andy's*, 11 E Hubbard St ☎ 642-6805. For late night jazz with a touch of elegance, Joe Segal's *Jazz Showcase* in the Blackstone Hotel, 636 S Michigan Ave ☎ 427-4300 is the place. For up-to-the-minute information ☎ 666-1881.
Nightclubs and comedy Chicago politicians and celebrities tend to be seen in *The Limelight*, a wildly decorated, renovated church at 632 N Dearborn ☎ 337-2958. The *Faces Club*, 940 N Rush ☎ 943-0940 is a more conventional disco; *Crosscurrents*, 3206 N Wilton ☎ 472-7884 has good cabaret. More risqué is the revue at the *Racoon Club*, 812 N Franklin ☎ 943-1928. The *Second City* comedy troupe has been host to many of the nation's finest comedians, who started out on its stage at 1616 N Wells ☎ 337-3992; make reservations well in advance.

Shopping

Though State Street has lost some of its former glory as the most famous shopping street in America's Midwest, it still is a thriving shopping center, lined with clothes and shoe shops and two of Chicago's prestigious department stores, *Carson, Pirie, Scott*, 1 S State St, and *Marshall Field's*, 111 N State St.
Clothing More exclusive shops have moved across the river to Michigan Avenue on the Near North Side. A walk down N Michigan Avenue's Magnificent Mile takes you past *I Magnin*, *Neiman-Marcus*, *Bonwit Teller*, *Saks Fifth Avenue*, *Burberry's*, *Gucci*, *Stanley Korshak* and many others.

In both areas, the traditional stores are looking to stiff competition when Bloomingdale's finally opens its doors for the first time in Chicago.
Shopping malls *Water Tower Place*, 845 N Michigan, is a popular inner city atrium mall, named after the ornate original Chicago water tower standing nearby, one of the few buildings to survive the disastrous 1871 fire. Its seven floors house over a hundred shops, including *Lord & Taylor's* and another branch of *Marshall Field's*, as well as various children's shops, of which the best are *FAO Schwarz*, *Beagle and Company* and *Beauty and the Beast*. You can find sporting goods of every imaginable type at *Morrie Magees*, an eight-floor sports emporium at 620 N LaSalle St.
Crafts *The Museum Shop* at the Art Institute of Chicago sells jewelry, posters and art books; the *Illinios Artisan's Shop* on the second level of the State of Illinois Center is a good place to find handmade Illinois craft articles.
Music *Jazz Mart*, 11 E Hubbard, has an extensive selection of tapes and records; *Rose Records*, 214 S State, covers the whole musical spectrum.
Books *Kroch and Brentano's*, 29 S Wabash, is the city's best bookstore and the country's second busiest after New York's 5th Avenue *Barnes & Noble*, with excellent, knowledgeable service and a regular stock of more than 125,000 titles.

Sightseeing

The places listed are all within easy reach of the business traveller and can be fitted into a busy daytime schedule.
Art Institute of Chicago Truly one of the world's finest art museums. With its notable collection of French Impressionists – including works by Monet, Pisarro and Renoir

– the Institute, right in the heart of downtown, is reason enough in itself to visit the city. Its new wing houses a fine collection of medieval and Renaissance art and its collection of prints is unique. You have to ask to see them, but where else would you be allowed to touch these magnificent works and wonder at the skill and craftsmanship from medieval times to the present day? Among its rarer exhibits is a collection of delicate and exotic paperweights, donated by a local real estate speculator, the late Arthur Rubloff. Other exhibits include the renovated old Stock Exchange Trading Room, now displaying Marc Chagall's stained glass; the Thorne Miniature Rooms; and a fine showing of Oriental and medieval art. Avoid weekends. *Michigan at Adams St ☎ 443-3600. Open Mon, Wed and Fri, 10.30–4.30; Tue, 10.30–8; Sat, 10–5; Sun, noon–5.*

Field Museum of Natural History Exhibits include everything from precious stones and the origins of man to a Pawnee lodge and dinosaur skeletons. Architecture buffs would find the Stanley Field Hall, with its soaring coffered ceiling and superb Ionic capitals, worth visiting even if it were empty. *Roosevelt Rd and S Lake Shore Dr ☎ 922-9410. Open 9–5.*

John Hancock Center This imposing 100-story office and residential building has an observation deck on the 95th floor, providing an unbeatable view of the North Loop. Have a drink at Images, on the 96th floor, or a memorable, if expensive, meal in the city's loftiest restaurant, The 95th. *875 N Michigan Ave. Open 9am–midnight.*

Museum of Contemporary Art Occupying an old bakery and housing seven galleries, this forum for untried and/or controversial exhibits of neon, video and *avant-garde* art includes works by Alexander Calder and Picasso. *237 Ontario ☎ 280-2660. Open 10–5; Sun, noon–5; closed Mon.*

Museum of Science and Industry Chicago's top tourist attraction is an echoing cavern filled with gadgets, levers, computers and other hands-on devices which visitors can use to find out about scientific principles and the latest technological advances. Major drawing cards are the full scale underground coal mine, a 16ft replica of a human heart, a half-acre model train set and the only German U-boat captured during World War II. *57th St and S Lake Shore Dr ☎ 684-1414. Open Mon–Fri, 9.30–4; Sat, Sun and holidays, 9.30–5.30.*

Sears Tower The 110-story Tower is the world's tallest building, and though the upper floors are often encased by clouds, on clear days the 103rd-floor skydeck offers magnificent panoramas of the downtown area 1,300ft below. In clear weather you can see as far as the neighboring states of Indiana, Wisconsin and Michigan. *Wacker and Adams St. Open 9am–midnight.*

Guided tours

The Chicago Architecture Foundation, 330 S Dearborn ☎ 782-1776 organizes walking, bike, bus and river tours taking in many of the most significant examples of Chicago architecture. *Crescent Helicopters* ☎ 944-2301 have flightseeing programs; and for an escorted tour of the city's cultural heritage, try *Culture Bus* ☎ 836-7000.

Out of town

Frank Lloyd Wright Home and Studio Foundation, 951 Chicago Ave, Oak Park ☎ 848-1978. One of America's leading and seminal architects, Wright designed 25 buildings in suburban Oak Park, just W of the city limits, 25min from downtown. Around the corner is the childhood home of Ernest Hemingway, at 600 N Kenilworth. *The Indiana Dunes National Lakeshore* starts 65 miles/90km S of the city along Lake Michigan. Magnificent sand dunes, some reaching up to 70ft high, stretch all the way along the coast for a distance of about 100 miles/60km.

During the warm months there is a lovely nature walk through a preserved prairie.

Spectator sports

Baseball, football and horse racing are the city's three prime spectator sports interests.

Baseball The *Chicago Cubs* play in ivy-covered Wrigley Field, 1060 W Addison St ☎ 281-5050; afternoon games are a popular diversion for well-heeled business types and city employees. Mayor Richard Daley was a keen fan of the *White Sox*, who play in Comiskey Park, 324 W 35th St ☎ 924-1000.

Basketball The *Bulls* play in an exciting, but often unsuccessful, style at Chicago Stadium, 1800 W Madison St ☎ 733-5300.

Football The *Bears*, the city's new major obsession and source of pride, are based at 250 N Washington St, Lake Forest ☎ 663-5100 though they play at Soldiers Field just S of downtown near the Field Museum.

Horse racing Horse racing remains a fervently attended sport in Chicago. The city has three tracks: *Hawthorne*, 3501 S Laramie, Cicero ☎ 652-9400; *Maywood Park*, North and 5th avenues, Maywood ☎ 343-4800; and *Sportsman's Park*, 3301 S Laramie, Cicero ☎ 242-1121.

Ice hockey The *Black Hawks* have a stoutly loyal following despite their losing ways; games are at Chicago Stadium, 1800 W Madison St ☎ 733-5300 Oct–Apr.

Polo Prince Charles is an occasional player at international games at the Oak Brook Polo Club, 1000 Oak Brook Rd, Oak Brook ☎ 654-3060.

Soccer The *Sting*, the city's contribution to soccer, play all their games indoors at the Chicago Stadium. Ticket information ☎ 245-5425.

Keeping fit

There are dozens of health clubs in Chicago. Many hotels either have their own facilities or provide arrangements with nearby clubs, but the city is also tailor-made for outdoor activities. Swimming at the 28miles/44km of beaches and jogging along the many lakeside paths are just a few possibilities.

Health clubs Most private clubs will let non-members use their facilities for a daily fee, ranging from $5–15. Facilities range from swimming and jogging tracks to weightlifting and aerobics. The *East Bank Club*, 500 N Kingbury St ☎ 527-5800 is the city's most prestigious health club, where Richard Daley Jr and well-known Chicagoans jog around the track. Guests must be accompanied by a member. Other places for the exercise conscious include *Charlie Club*, 112 S Michigan Ave ☎ 726-0510; *Chicago Health and Racquetball Club*, 111 E Wacker Dr ☎ 861-1220 and 300 N State St ☎ 321-9600; *Combined Fitness Center*, 1235 N LaSalle St ☎ 787-8400; *McClurg Court Sports Center*, 333 E Ontario ☎ 944-4546.

Beaches North Avenue Beach, Fullerton Avenue Beach and Oak Street Beach are particularly good for swimming and tanning, all within 10min of the Loop.

Bicycling and jogging There are good jogging paths along the shore from the Loop S to 57th Street (not recommended after dusk) and from the Loop N to Evanston (about 11 miles/19km – usually safe up to Wilson Avenue even at night). There are several concessions in Lincoln Park where bikes may be rented. Some hotels have rental bikes.

Golf It has been said that Chicago has more golf courses than any other major metropolitan center in the United States, but unfortunately the best are well out in the suburbs. Some hotels offer guest privileges at private clubs, and there are ten golf courses within the city, including nearby *Waveland* in Lincoln Park ☎ 294-2274.

Raquet sports There are over 600 outdoor tennis courts, the most convenient of which are in Lincoln Park and the lakeshore just N. Many

Loop-area health clubs also offer tennis and squash for a fee. For tennis ☎ 294-2314.
Sailing Fantastic sailing and outstanding views of the city are possible from the open water off Navy Pier, but nasty storms can kick up without much warning. Check weather ahead of time with US Coast Guard ☎ (219) 949-7440. Good rentals from *City Sailors* ☎ 935-6145.

Local resources

Business services

Most of the major hotels provide or can arrange basic business services for the visitor, and Chicago has no lack of firms offering extensive help for the travelling executive.
Audio-visual *Midwest Visual Equipment Co* ☎ 236-5076; *PC Rents* ☎ 951-1700; *Rent Com, Inc* ☎ 678-7000; *Audio Visual Services* ☎ 836-1000.
Photocopying and printing *Pandick Technologies*, 208 S LaSalle St ☎ 236-0200 provides 24hr service. *Instant Printing Corp*, 200 S Clark St ☎ 726-6275 is also in the Loop.
Secretarial Dependable temporary agencies include *Kelly Services* ☎ 853-3434 and *Insta-Temps* ☎ 664-0622.
Translation *Inter Lingua* ☎ 782-8123, *Berlitz* ☎ 782-7778.

Communications

Local delivery The best service is generally had from *Arrow Messenger Service* ☎ 782-6688. Also *Chicago Messenger Service* ☎ 666-6800 and *Cannonball Inc* ☎ 337-1234.
Long-distance delivery *Federal Express* ☎ 559-9000; *DHL Worldwide Express* ☎ 456-3200; *Emery Worldwide* ☎ 635-6111.
Post office The main post office is at 433 W Van Buren St ☎ 886-2420 or 886-2480; post offices close early on Saturday.
Telex *Western Union/Telex* ☎ (800) 325-6000.

Conference/exhibition centers

Extremely large and only 5min from the Loop is *McCormick Place on the Lake*, 2300 S Lake Shore Dr ☎ 791-7000. *O'Hare Exposition Center*, 9301 Bryn Mawr Rd, Rosemont ☎ 629-2220 is close to the airport.

Emergencies

Hospitals *Northwestern Memorial Hospital*, Superior and Fairbanks ☎ 649-2000; AE MC V. *Henrotin Hospital*, 111 W Oak St ☎ 440-7700; no credit cards. *Resurrection Hospital* (near O'Hare), 7435 W Talcott Ave ☎ 774-8000; V only. *Michael Reese Hospital and Medical Center*, 31st and Lake Shore Dr ☎ 791-2000; AE MC V. Doctor referral ☎ 670-2550; dental referral ☎ 726-4076.
Pharmacies *Walgreen Drug Store*, 757 N Michigan Ave ☎ 664-8686 has a 24hr prescription service.
Police The two main downtown stations are at 1121 S State St (police headquarters) ☎ 744-6230 and 113 W Chicago Ave ☎ 744-8230.

Government offices

US Dept of Commerce/International Trade Division ☎ 353-4450; *US Customs/Commercial Importations–Personal Importation*, 230 S Dearborn St ☎ 353-6150; *US Immigration and Naturalization Service* ☎ 353-7334.

Information sources

Business information The *Chicago Association of Commerce and Industry*, 200 N LaSalle St ☎ 580-6900 offers assistance in locating everything from audio-visual equipment to videotext directories. The *Chicago Convention and Tourism Bureau*, McCormick Pl on the lake ☎ 225-5000 is the best source of convention information.
Local media There are two major daily papers, The *Chicago Sun-Times* and the larger *Chicago Tribune*. Both lean towards a conservative editorial line, although the latter leans slightly more to the center. The *Tribune* is

known for its international coverage while the *Sun-Times's* forte is city politics.

Rizzoli's, a bookstore on the 3rd level of Water Tower Place, has daily papers from France, Italy, Germany and England, plus a good selection of foreign language books. Foreign papers are also available at the newsstand on the corner of Rush and Oak streets. Among magazines, *The Chicago Reader* and *Chicago Magazine* provide general information about the city, while Crain's *Chicago Business* is an invaluable source of local business news.

Tourist information *Chicago Tourism Council* ☎ 644-6610; *Visitors' Eventline* ☎ 225-2323; *Weather* ☎ 976-1755.

Thank-yous

Florists *Floral Fashions Inc* ☎ 829-0353; *A Lange Florist and Greenhouse* ☎ 236-3777.

Wine merchants *Sam's at the Barway* ☎ 664-4394; *Zimmerman Liquors* ☎ 322-0012.

Specialty shops *Marshall Field's*, 1 N State St ☎ 781-1000 has hand-dipped chocolate which they will send anywhere in the world; also their Frango mints make a good gift. *Let Them Eat Cake*, 948 N Rush St ☎ 951-7383 has *petits fours* and custom-made cakes.

CLEVELAND

Area code ☎ 216

Cleveland's traditional heavy industries – steel production, oil refining, shipping and railroads – were the foundations upon which men like John D Rockefeller, Samuel Mather and Marcus Hanna built their fortunes in the 18th and early 19th centuries, providing work for the thousands of immigrants whose children and grandchildren comprise much of the city's population today. The city still retains some elements of that smokestack economy, but it is also rapidly developing a service sector. The Cleveland Clinic – where the heart by-pass was developed – is now the area's largest private employer, treating patients from around the world; Jones Day Reavis & Pogue, one of the country's biggest law firms, is headquartered here; leading accountants Ernst & Whinney are in Cleveland; AmeriTrust NA is one of the Midwest's most important financial institutions; and Case Western Reserve University's polymer-chemistry departments work jointly with the region's burgeoning plastics industry to create and develop new technologies and applications for its products.

Arriving

Cleveland Hopkins International Airport

CHI, 10 miles/16km SW of downtown, has three concourses (A, B and C) with a total of 42 gates radiating out from the central terminal. Movement from plane to cab is usually quick and trouble-free, thanks to good signposting. All passengers from outside the USA arrive at concourse A, Gate 9, and there is an international travellers' lounge across from Gate 6. Clearing Immigration and Customs generally takes 15min – but may take 1hr if more than one flight arrives around the same time. General information ☎ 265-6000.

Dining facilities are sometimes quite cramped and offer only standard airport fare. Currency can be exchanged at the Society National Bank Mon–Fri, 10–2. Free emergency translation services and document translations are available at the airport office of the Nationality Services Center of Cleveland ☎ 781-4560. Taxi stands, limousine pick-up and shuttle buses to rental-car lots are just outside the baggage-claim area.

Nearby hotels *Marriott West Airport*, 4277 W 150 St 44135 ☎ 252-5333: very acceptable. *Sheraton Hopkins Airport*, 5300 Riverside Dr 44135 ☎ 267-1500: very close to the airport RTA station.

City link *Car rental* The normal 20min drive to downtown can be an hour-plus nightmare during the morning rush 7.30–9.30, and even worse from downtown to the airport in the evening rush 3.30–7, but car rental is a necessity if business will take you outside the downtown area. Eight national rental agencies have desks or courtesy phones in the central terminal, near the baggage claim area.

Taxi Cabs are available outside the baggage claim area. The fare to downtown is about $10.

Limousine Regular, scheduled service to downtown is provided by Airport Limousine Service ☎ 267-8282.

Rail There is a Regional Transit Authority (RTA) station at the airport: follow the signs from the baggage-claim area. Rapid transit trains take only 20min to Public Square; the exact fare ($1), preferably in coins, is required. This is the easiest, fastest and least expensive way to go if you have little baggage and are staying downtown.

Getting around

The city is bisected into E and W by Ontario Street, which runs through Public Square, but the West Side is usually considered to be the area W of the Cuyahoga River. Streets (generally numbered) run N–S, avenues (all named) run E–W. Lake Erie lies to the N.

Walking If your business and hotel are both downtown, you can usually walk to your destination just as easily as drive or take a cab.

Driving If you have a car, you can find street maps and get advice in the Visitors' Bureau Information Center, at the street-level main entrance to the Terminal Tower on Public Square. If possible, get a garage or parking lot space; police give tickets *and* tow away illegally parked cars downtown.

Try to avoid the busy Interstates 90, heading E or W, and 71 and 77, heading S, during the evening rush. You can turn right at a red light, unless it is signposted otherwise. All drivers and front-seat passengers must wear seat belts.

Taxi Cabs are available only in front of major hotels, at the corner of E 9th Street and Euclid Avenue, and by phone; they are not allowed to pick up in the streets. Companies include *Yellow/Zone Cab* ☎ 623-1500 and *Americab* ☎ 881-1111.

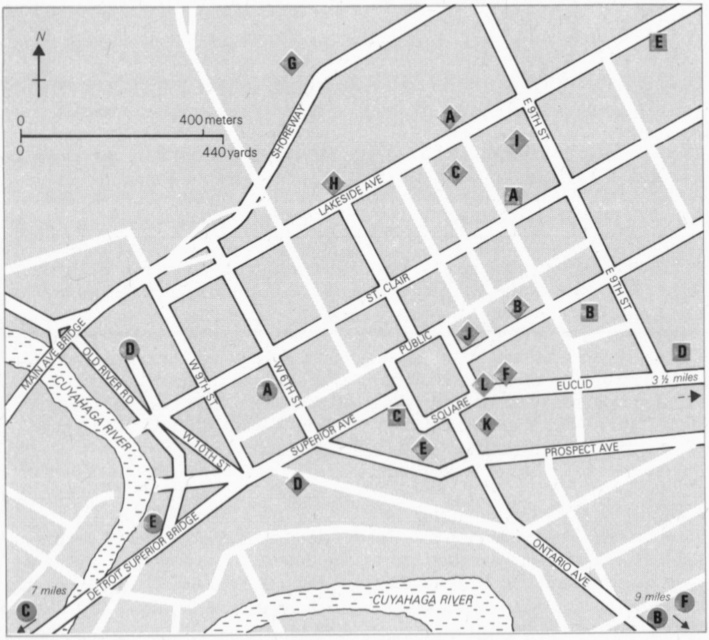

■ HOTELS
A Bond Court
B Hollenden House
C Stouffer
D Clinic Inn
E Holiday Inn Lakeside

● RESTAURANTS
A Burgess Grand Café
French Connection (Hotel C)
B Giovanni's
C Heck's Cafe
D Sammy's
E Watermark
F Z

◆ BUILDINGS AND SIGHTS
A Cleveland City Hall
B Cleveland Public Library
C Public Hall
D State Office Building
E Visitors' Bureau (Terminal Tower)
F The Arcade
G Cleveland Municipal Stadium
H County Courthouse
I Federal Building
J Federal Courthouse
K May Company
L Standard Oil Building

Limousine *National Limousine Service* ☏ 289-0800 has cars with cellular telephones; *Century Limousine* ☏ 234-4097 provides 24hr service.

Bus and train *RTA* ☏ 621-9500 runs "loop" buses (25 cents) on routes covering most of downtown; schedules and route maps are posted at many stops and are available at an information center at 2019 Ontario St, just S of Public Square. Fares throughout greater Cleveland are 85 cents on local buses; $1 on express buses and rapid transit trains.

Area by area

Downtown The skyline is dominated by the 52-story Terminal Tower and the new 45-story headquarters of Standard Oil, both on Public Square – elegant and bustling by day; nearly deserted and possibly dangerous for lone pedestrians by night. A short walk up Euclid Avenue brings you to the intersection with E 9th Street, where most of the city's major banks and national law firms have headquarters. Five blocks further E is Playhouse Square, with many restaurants and three restored vaudeville theaters that are Cleveland's ballet, opera and repertory-theater centers.

New office buildings and office/retail complexes have sprung up at the northern end of E 9th Street, near St Clair and Lakeside avenues. Along Lakeside Avenue, from Ontario to E 9th, are city, county and federal government buildings, and the Public Auditorium Convention Center.

Six blocks W and a block N of Public Square lies the warehouse district, where sturdy 19thC buildings are being furnished for housing, office and commercial use. The Flats, in the Cuyahoga River valley, is a burgeoning dining and entertainment area.

University Circle Farther E on Euclid, beginning at E 85th Street, are the Cleveland Play House Complex (designed by native Philip Johnson), the Cleveland Clinic and University Circle, an academic and cultural district.

West Side To the W of the Cuyahoga is Ohio City, an enclave of Victorian homes and distinctive restaurants. Running along the lakeshore through the West Side's suburbs are the yacht clubs and marinas of the boating set; to the SW rapidly growing office complexes and high-tech industrial parks are taking over. The new International Exposition Center (I-X), a huge convention and trade-show hall, is also to the SW, minutes from the airport.

Suburbs E of University Circle you will find Cleveland Heights, Shaker Heights, Hunting Valley and Gates Mills – undoubtedly Cleveland's classiest addresses.

Hotels

Because cabs are not available on the street, visitors – especially those with two or more appointments scheduled for the same day – would be wise to make proximity to destination their first criterion in choosing a hotel in downtown Cleveland. In general, hotel dining facilities are adequate, but sampling one or more of the area's growing number of good restaurants involves little extra effort or expense.

Bond Court **$$$**
777 St Clair Ave NE 44114
☏ 771-7600 • 480 rooms, 40 suites, 1 restaurant, 2 bars, 1 coffee shop
One of the top downtown hotels, along with Stouffer Tower City Plaza. The Bond Court is very central and is especially convenient to the Convention Center, city and federal offices and many of the newer office buildings on the N side of downtown. Luxury multi-level

suites have two work areas, multiple phone lines with computer modem facility and brass beds. Twenty meeting rooms.

Hollenden House $$$
610 Superior Ave NE 44114
☎ 621-0700 • 502 rooms, 27 suites, 1 restaurant, 2 bars, 1 coffee shop
Less obviously for senior managers, the Hollenden nonetheless provides excellent in-house athletic facilities, including pool, sauna and weight room, and is just a short walk from the city's financial and legal heart. Massage • 14 meeting rooms.

Stouffer Tower City Plaza $$$$
24 Public Sq 44113 ☎ 696-5600
TX 752889 • 496 suites, 1 restaurant, 1 bar, 2 coffee shops
Previously the undisputed leader, the Stouffer is being challenged by the Bond Court. But this is still Cleveland's most elegant hotel and in some ways it is still the better address: certainly it has the best restaurant, the French Connection (see *Restaurants*). The Stouffer is part of the Terminal Tower complex on Public Square, convenient to public transit, dining and the entertainment district. The large suites have ample space for in-room meetings and business entertaining. Twenty meeting rooms.

OTHER HOTELS
Clinic Inn ($$) *2065 E 96 St 44106 ☎ 791-1900.* Popular with medics and academics visiting Cleveland Clinic.
Holiday Inn Lakeside ($$) *1111 Lakeside Ave 44114 ☎ 241-5100.* Indoor pool, sauna, weight room.

Clubs

The *Union Club*, oldest and most exclusive of Cleveland's downtown clubs, is a bastion of the establishment. Sometimes maligned as stuffy and insular, it nonetheless remains popular for business breakfasts, important lunches and even business meetings downstairs in the barbershop. The *Cleveland Athletic Club* has good fitness facilities and two dining rooms. It has reciprocal agreements with more than 50 other American clubs and is the preferred venue for noontime business-cum-racquetball encounters. The *Mid-day Club* is mostly professional; the spacious dining room (for breakfast, lunch and private dinners) offers a bird's-eye view of the city.

Restaurants

From the Mexican, Greek and Italian offerings you would expect to find in any cosmopolitan city, to authentic Hungarian, Thai and South American food, Cleveland offers the business traveller a wide choice of cuisines. The establishments listed, which attract regular clientele, are recommended for business meetings or entertaining.

Burgess Grand Café $$$
1406 W 6th St ☎ 574-2232 • AE MC V
This Victorian-inspired restaurant is especially popular with downtown business people for breakfast meetings. It has an all-mahogany bar in a renovated building in Cleveland's burgeoning Warehouse District. The food is a mix of French and Italian.

French Connection $$$$
24 Public Sq ☎ 696-5600 • closed Sun • AE CB DC MC V • jacket required
The smartly chic dining room of the Stouffer Tower City Plaza (see *Hotels*) is one of Cleveland's best restaurants. Both the classic Continental cuisine – the menu changes seasonally – and formal service are good, and can be enjoyed from tables overlooking Public Square. Booths and discreet

partitions provide privacy for business discussions.

Giovanni's $$$$
25550 Chagrin Blvd, Beachwood ☎ 831-8625 • D only Sat; closed Sun • AE DC MC V • jacket required
This is Cleveland's best Italian restaurant – some say its best overall. Giovanni's has well prepared (sometimes tableside) northern Italian cuisine and an extensive wine list. An impressive choice for business entertaining. Plush and sympathetic, this is one of the city's restaurants where deals are often struck.

Heck's Café $$$
19300 Detroit Rd, Rocky River ☎ 356-2559 • AE DC MC V
Housed in a former Art Deco movie theater 7 miles/11km from downtown, Heck's offers a stylish location for entertaining convenient to the airport and the most interesting *nouvelle cuisine* on Cleveland's West Side.

Sammy's $$$$
1400 W 10th St ☎ 523-5560 • D only Sun • AE CB DC MC V • reservations essential
Known for its fish dishes and unusual sauces, its pastas, produce from its own 10th Street Market and its homemade sorbets, Sammy's is one of Cleveland's "in" places for business lunches and dinners. Located on the renovated waterfront, it is fashionable and crowded every day, especially in summer. The raw fish bar and the view of the Cuyahoga River are features.

Watermark $$$
1250 Old River Rd ☎ 241-1600 • AE DC MC V
An airy converted warehouse with an all-glass wall providing striking views of the Cuyahoga River. The menu features a number of mesquite-grilled dishes, seafood and some memorable desserts. Close by to Sammy's and with a similarly businessy clientele.

Z $$$
Tower East, 20600 Chagrin Blvd, Shaker Heights ☎ 991-1580 • D only Mon and Sat; closed Sun • AE MC V
A minimalist white décor in a building 20min from downtown, designed by the founder of the Bauhaus School, Walter Gropius. Only abstract art adds the odd splash of color to a restaurant that is as sophisticated as its food. Voted Cleveland's top restaurant, the cuisine is California *nouvelle* (all entrées – fish, beef, veal and chicken – are grilled). Zachary Bruell's wine list is both extensive and expensive.

Bars

Cleveland is not especially noted for its nightlife except for the hangouts of the young professional crowd in the Flats, on the banks of the Cuyahoga River. For somewhere pleasant to enjoy a drink and a quiet business conversation, the downtown hotel lounges are best. For something more lively, however, try the suburbs.

Recommended bistros on Cleveland's East Side include *Gamekeeper's Tavern*, 87 West St, Chagrin Falls ☎ 247-7744 where drinks (and dinner) are served on an outdoor patio in the summer, indoors before a fire in cooler weather; *Nighttown*, 12387 Cedar Rd, Cleveland Heights ☎ 795-0550 a landmark watering hole and restaurant; *Noggin's*, 20110 Van Aken Blvd, Shaker Heights ☎ 752-9280 a popular East Side eatery whose bar features fresh seafood and interesting wines by the glass; and *Club Isabella*, 2025 Abington Rd, University Circle ☎ 229-1177 offering light fare and live jazz nightly 9–1.

On the Near West Side, you could try the *Ohio City Tavern*, 2801 Bridge Ave ☎ 687-0505 a former stagecoach stop and inn.

Entertainment

Theater and music Clevelanders are proud of the attention and money they have given to support classical music, ballet and dance. The *Cleveland Orchestra* plays weekends Oct–May at Severance Hall ☎ 231-1111, Jun–Sep at Blossom Music Center ☎ 566-9330. *Blossom*, 45min out of town, where one can picnic casually on the lawn or sit in comfort in the pavilion, also hosts rock and pop acts during the summer. Big-name entertainment, ranging from comedy to jazz, can be seen in the round at the *Front Row Theater* ☎ 449-5000. The city's newest entertainment facility, *Play House Square Center* ☎ 241-6000 comprises three restored historic theaters: the Ohio, State and Palace. The Center is used by the *Cleveland Ballet*, *Cleveland Opera*, *Great Lakes Theater Festival*, a professional classical-repertory company with a summer-only season, and touring Broadway shows and modern dance troupes. With a Sep–Jun season, the country's oldest professional regional theater, the *Cleveland Play House* ☎ 795-7000 offers yet more high-quality dramatic fare.

Shopping

Whatever you want to buy, you do not have to go far to find it. Two established department stores – *May Co* and *Higbee's* – are on Public Square, and there is an array of specialty shops in two downtown historic landmarks: *The Arcade*, 401 Euclid Ave, and *Tower City Center* in Terminal Tower. The most notable mall is *Beachwood Place* (Saks and other high-quality men's and women's fashion shops) on the East Side at the intersection of Cedar and Richmond roads, where you will also find the newly renovated and very posh *La Place* mall; and, on the West Side, *Beachcliff Market Square*, an interesting mix of boutiques at 19300 Detroit Rd, Rocky River.

Sightseeing

Cleveland Metroparks Zoo Revitalized in the past ten years by such new exhibits as Birds of the World, African Plains and the Aquatic Center, this is something you can't do in 1hr, but it is worth visiting if you have time. *3900 Brookside Pk ☎ 661-6500. Open daily 9–5; summer to 7.*

Cleveland Museum of Art Highly regarded around the world for its general collections, this is an excellent museum with an admirable collection of Picassos. Also worth seeing are the Old Masters and Oriental galleries. *11150 East Blvd, University Circle ☎ 421-7340. Open daily exc Mon; hours vary.*

Cleveland Museum of Natural History Ohio's largest natural science museum features permanent exhibits on dinosaurs, prehistoric American Indians and gemstones. *Wade Oval, University Circle ☎ 231-4600. Open Mon–Sat, 10–5; Sun, 1–5.*

Crawford Auto-Aviation Museum Two hundred beautifully restored antique automobiles and a smaller number of historic planes. *10825 East Blvd, University Circle ☎ 721-5722. Open Tue–Sun; hours vary.*

Municipal stadium Home of the Cleveland Indians and Browns, the stadium is a monument to 1930s architecture. *585 W 3rd St.*

USS Cod This World War II submarine made seven patrols, sinking about 30,000 tons of Japan's fleet. *N Marginal Rd between E 9th St and Burke Lakefront Airport ☎ 566-8770. Open end May–early Sep, Mon–Fri, 11–4; Sat and Sun, 1–5.*

Western Reserve Historical Society Twenty period rooms recreate life in the Ohio region from 1770–1920. *10825 East Blvd, University Circle. Tue–Sat, 10–5; Sun, 12–5.*

West Side Market One of the largest Old World-style indoor/outdoor markets, which has more than 100 traders selling everything from vegetables to baked goods and smoked meats. *Lorain Ave at W 25th St ☎ 664-3386. Mon and Wed, 7–4; Fri and Sat, 7–6.*

Guided tours

Best Conventions ☎ 781-8819 organize group bus and walking tours; *Executive Arrangements* ☎ 991-8333 provide custom tours of Greater Cleveland by bus, van, limo or vintage car; *Holiday Boat Charters* ☎ 771-2628 take you on the water – Lake Erie or the Cuyahoga or Rocky rivers; *North Coast Tours* ☎ 579-6160 have both standard and custom bus or walking tours; and *Trolley Tours of Cleveland* (May–Oct) ☎ 771-4484.

Spectator sports

Cleveland is a busy sports city, with the emphasis on football. The offer of a seat in a corporate box at any of the sporting venues is a compliment.

Baseball The *Cleveland Indians* play at Municipal Stadium, 585 W 3rd St ☎ 861-1200.

Basketball The *Cavaliers* are at the Coliseum, 2923 Streetsboro Rd, Richfield ☎ 659-9100.

Football The *Browns* kick off at Municipal Stadium, 585 W 3rd St ☎ 696-5555.

Horse racing *Northfield Park Raceway* Rte 8, Northfield ☎ 467-4101 is open year-round for harness racing; *Thistledown*, Emery and Warrensville Center roads, North Randall ☎ 6621-8600 has thoroughbred racing Mar–Dec.

Soccer The *Force* play at the Coliseum, 2923 Streetsboro Rd, Richfield ☎ 247-4740.

Keeping fit

Greater Cleveland has an abundance of parks offering an array of recreational activities for free or for a modest fee. Health club facilities are offered at most hotels, or they will have arrangements with a nearby club.

Beaches Public beaches can be found at Edgewater Park on the W and Euclid Beach on the E – part of the system of *Cleveland Lakefront State Parks* ☎ 881-8141.

Cross-country skiing Although primarily a preserve for 6,000 varieties of trees, plants and flowers, *Holden Arboretum* ☎ 946-4400 is also laced with cross-country ski trails.

Golf Among the many public golf courses in the area are those operated by *Cleveland Metroparks* at its Rocky River, Brecksville, Bedford and North Chagrin reservations ☎ 351-6300.

Jogging The *Cleveland Metroparks* have all-purpose trails for jogging, hiking and biking. Rocky River, Big Creek, Brecksville, Bedford, South Chagrin, North Chagrin and Euclid Creek reservations are also popular. For information ☎ 351-6300.

Tennis *Racquet Club East* ☎ 464-7122 in Bedford Heights is one of the only clubs with indoor courts open to the public.

Local resources

Business services

Complete secretarial, word processing and answering services are available at *Executive Center*, 14650 Detroit Ave, Lakewood ☎ 221-2561; *Headquarters Companies* (pick-up and delivery), 23200 Chagrin Blvd, Beachwood ☎ 831-8220, and 25000 Great Northern Corporate Center, North Olmsted ☎ 777-0000; and *Statler Office Service*, 1127 Euclid Ave ☎ 566-8050.

Photocopying and printing *Original Copy Centers* ☎ 861-0620 (pick-up and delivery); *Kinko's*, 1832 Euclid Ave ☎ 589-5679 and 1990 Ford Dr, University Circle ☎ 229-5679; and *Kwik Print*, 1278 W 9th St ☎ 696-5000.

Secretarial Reliable temporary help can be obtained through *Kelly Services*, 7550 Lucerne Dr, Middleburgh Heights ☎ 243-8292 and *Olsten Services*, 2000 E 9th St ☎ 861-1900.

Translation *A Technical Translation Service*, 38355 Chimney Ridge Dr, Willoughby Hills ☎ 942-3130; *Berlitz Translation Services*, 815 Superior Ave NE ☎ 861-0950; and *International Business Translations*, 17149 Rabbit Run Dr, Strongsville ☎ 238-6140.

Communications

Local delivery *Bonnie Speed Delivery* ☏ 696-6033; *Executive Delivery Systems* ☏ 861-4560.
Long-distance delivery *Federal Express* ☏ 361-0872 and *Purolator* ☏ (800) 645-3333; for international deliveries, *DHL* ☏ 836-9130.
Post office The downtown (and main) office is open Mon–Fri, 8–6.30 at 2400 Orange Ave ☏ 443-4199.
Telex *Action Telex*, 20900 St Clair Ave ☏ 531-9111; and *A SOS Telex*, 1127 Euclid Ave ☏ 566-8050.

Conference/exhibition centers

Most of Cleveland's larger hotels offer conference and meeting facilities. *Center One*, 35000 Curtis Blvd, Eastlake ☏ 953-8000, *Quail Hollow Inn*, I-90 and Rte 44, Painesville ☏ 352-6201, and *Ramada Aqua Marine Resort*, 216 Miller Rd, Avon Lake ☏ 933-2000 all provide a country-club setting for business meetings. For more information, consult the *Convention and Visitors' Bureau of Greater Cleveland*, 1301 E 6th St ☏ 621-4110.

Emergencies

Hospitals The following hospitals operate 24hr emergency rooms: *Mt Sinai Medical Center*, 1 Mt Sinai Dr, University Circle ☏ 421-4000; *St Vincent Charity Hospital*, 2351 E 22nd St ☏ 861-6200; and *University Hospitals*, 2074 Abington Rd, University Circle ☏ 844-1000. For dental emergencies, call *National Dental Center*'s 24hr help-line ☏ 289-6900.
Pharmacies *Revco Discount Drug Center* is a major local chain with many locations open Mon–Sat till 10pm.
Police *Cleveland Police* ☏ 621-1212; *Cuyahoga County Sheriff* ☏ 443-6085.

Government offices

Cleveland City Hall ☏ 664-2000; *Cuyahoga County Administration* ☏ 443-7000; *Ohio Dept of Commerce/Real Estate Division* ☏ 622-3100; *US Dept of Commerce/International Trade Administration District Office* ☏ 522-4752; *US Customs* ☏ 522-4287; *US Immigration and Naturalization Service* ☏ 522-4770.

Information sources

Business information The *Greater Cleveland Growth Association*, 790 Huntington Building ☏ 621-3300 provides information about the local economy and business practices.
Local media The *Plain Dealer* is a daily morning newspaper with local, national and international coverage. The *Sun* newspapers are a chain of weeklies serving Cleveland suburbs. Crain's *Cleveland Business* is a bi-weekly business journal. *Cleveland Magazine* is a monthly general-interest publication. Another monthly magazine, *Northern Ohio LIVE* covers the arts, entertainment and dining-out. Cleveland's public radio station, *WCPN-FM* (90.3), features news and public affairs during the morning and evening rush hours.
Tourist information The *Convention and Visitors' Bureau of Greater Cleveland* operate a Visitors' Information Center in the Terminal Tower, near the main entrance. Or call the Bureau's Fun Phone ☏ 621-8860 for a listing of current entertainment and special events.

Thank-yous

Florists *Alexander's Flowers* ☏ 292-4500; *Jones-Russell Florist* ☏ 621-8545; and *Segeln's* ☏ 791-8900 accept credit card orders by telephone.
Gift baskets *Cheese World* (imported and domestic cheeses) ☏ 371-8841; *Completely Nuts* (assorted nuts) ☏ 589-0666; *Feren Fruit Basket Co* (gourmet fruit and meats) ☏ 431-8700; and *Shaker Square Beverages Inc* (fine wines) ☏ 561-5100.

DALLAS

Area code ☎ 214

Despite the TV series, Dallas has been involved more in trade than in oil since it was established in 1841. Biggest among the city's major sources of revenue is its wholesale merchandise trade, which attracts more than half a million buyers a year to markets selling home furnishings, clothing and information-processing, among other products and services. Dallas is also a major defense electronics and armaments center, earning over $10bn annually. The area now has more than 400 high-tech firms, including Electronic Data Systems, Texas Instruments and Tandy. Its concentration of insurance company headquarters is the second largest in the country, and it has become one of America's most significant financial centers. Established wealth outshines new money, and culture is important for the quality of life sought by its inhabitants. Conservative in politics, its city fathers owe their status more to family name than party allegiance. Sitting right on the edge of the prairie, Dallas has extreme weather – over 105°F (30°C) in summer and traffic-paralyzing ice storms in winter.

Arriving

Dallas/Fort Worth International Airport

Dallas/Fort Worth Airport is suitably gigantic for a Texan facility, with seven unconnected terminals arranged in a double row along International Parkway. The airport is midway between Dallas and Fort Worth – together known as the Metroplex – and is serviced by all major domestic and international airlines, as well as commuter and charter flights. International flights arrive at Terminal 2E or 2W; there are currency exchanges and Customs in both. For domestic travellers it should take about 30min from arrival to leaving the airport – an hour if Customs and Immigration have to be cleared.

An electric transport system, Airtrans, transfers passengers from one terminal to another, to remote parking lots, and to the on-site airport hotel, AMFAC.

Nearby hotels *AMFAC* ☎ 453-8400. *Hilton*, 1800 Hwy 26E ☎ 481-8444. *Marriott*, 8400 Freeport Pkwy ☎ 258-4800.

City link The trip into Dallas from the airport takes about 40min; 1hr in rush hours, 7–9 and 4–6. To Fort Worth, allow 30min, 50min in rush hours. Bus, limousine and taxi services are near baggage claim areas at terminals 2E, 3E, 4E and 2W.

Taxi The best way to get into town, taxis are available 24hr at all upper level curbside exits. Fares to downtown Dallas and Fort Worth are about $25.

Bus Shuttle services to Dallas include The Link ($8–10), Tours by Stan ($7), Trailways and VIP Transport ($10). Shuttles to Fort Worth include Bluebird Transportation ($6) and Citran's Airporter ($6). Bus services generally run 8am–10pm. Pick-up points are clearly marked, but service can be infrequent (every half hour) and slow.

Car rental Getting out of the airport can be confusing; take a taxi downtown and rent there. However, four national agencies are open 24hrs with offices at the airport's N and S entrances: Avis ☎ 574-4100; Budget ☎ 574-3300; Hertz ☎ 574-2000; and National ☎ 574-3400.

Limousine These should be reserved in advance: Carry/Regal Limousine ☎ 358-1388; Texas Taxi ☎ 827-7900; Limousines by Jan ☎ 279-4192; and Royal Limousine ☎ 522-3290.

Helicopter Contact Airport Assistance ☎ 574-4420.

Getting around

Unless your business will keep you in the walkable downtown area, where there are plenty of taxis, a rental car is the best and most convenient method of getting around. Dallas is spread out, and is criss-crossed by freeways and expressways.

Car rental See *City link* for rental companies and telephone numbers.

Taxi Taxis cannot be hailed on the street; telephone in advance and allow 15–25min for pick-up. Try *Surtran* ☎ 263-8528; *Terminal Cab* ☎ 350-4445; and *Yellow Cab* ☎ 426-6262.

Limousine See *City link*.

Bus The bus system is not recommended, except on *Hop-A-Bus* downtown routes.

Area by area

Downtown The heart of Dallas's central business district is its downtown concentration of major banks, law and brokerage firms, and corporate headquarters. It includes business offices, historic sites, commercial buildings and institutions such as City Hall, the Public Library, the Museum of Art, Farmers' Market, JFK Memorial (and the Book Depository, from which the shot that killed Kennedy is thought to have been fired) and the original Neiman-Marcus store.

East Dallas Old-established neighborhoods in East Dallas – Swiss Avenue, Munger Place and Lakewood – have a wealth of historic buildings and parks. Most East Dallas residents have lived there for generations, though younger professionals are increasingly buying and restoring the old property.

Highland Park and the Golden Corridor Ten minutes N of downtown, the exclusive township of Highland Park is the city's top residential district, with a concentration of the city's founding families and old wealth. It also has the Southern Methodist University and Exall Lake. Other esteemed neighborhoods – such as Oak Lawn, Bluff View and University Park – plus restaurants, shops and office buildings, are strung along the North Dallas Tollroad, known as the Golden Corridor.

Far North Dallas As the tollroad crosses I-635 into Far North Dallas,

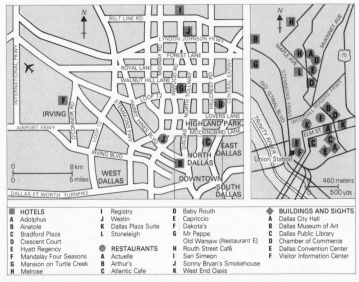

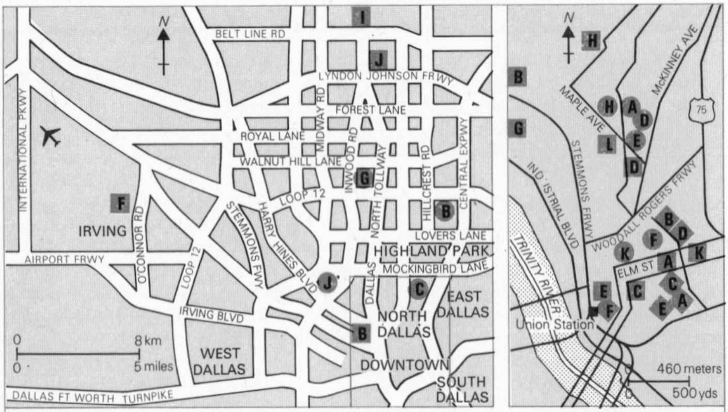

■ HOTELS	I	Registry	D	Baby Routh	◆	BUILDINGS AND SIGHTS
A Adolphus	J	Westin	E	Capriccio	A	Dallas City Hall
B Anatole	K	Dallas Plaza Suite	F	Dakota's	B	Dallas Museum of Art
C Bradford Plaza	L	Stoneleigh	G	Mr Peppe	C	Dallas Public Library
D Crescent Court				Old Warsaw (Restaurant E)	D	Chamber of Commerce
E Hyatt Regency	●	RESTAURANTS	H	Routh Street Café	E	Dallas Convention Center
F Mandalay Four Seasons	A	Actuelle	I	San Simeon	F	Visitor Information Center
G Mansion on Turtle Creek	B	Arthur's	J	Sonny Bryan's Smokehouse		
H Melrose	C	Atlantic Cafe	K	West End Oasis

chic new shopping centers and modern residential developments stretch northwards. Far North Dallas is the city's major area of new wealth, home of Dallas's population influx.

South and West Dallas South Dallas, largely a black community that includes Old City Park, and West Dallas, gateway to Texas Stadium in Irving, combines industrial development with mainly low-income residential neighborhoods. West Dallas also has two major business centers, the Infomart – a computer and high-tech facility – and Market Center – a large wholesale forum. Oak Cliff, just across the Trinity River, is being redeveloped; it is the home of the Dallas Zoo. On the city's western outskirts, midway between downtown and the airport, lies Las Colinas, an enclave of major business headquarters, luxury hotels, country clubs and affluent residential areas.

Hotels

Because Dallas's major business locations are not confined to downtown, the hotels listed serve diverse working communities: downtown, Cedar Springs, Market Center, North Dallas and Las Colinas.

Adolphus **$$$$$**
1321 Commerce St 75202 ☎ 742-8200 TX 84530 • 415 rooms, 20 suites, 3 restaurants, 2 bars, 1 coffee shop
In the heart of downtown on the crossroads of Commerce and Akard, the landmark Adolphus is one of Dallas's most convenient addresses. Prominent guests have included heads of state, international celebrities and VIP entrepreneurs. An extensive concierge staff will provide for practically any need. The French Room is an opulent dining room, an excellent choice for an important meal. The Clark Hatch Fitness Center offers a full range of fitness equipment and activities. Twenty meeting rooms.

Anatole **$$$$**
2201 Stemmons Frwy 75207 ☎ 748-1200 TX 730475 • Loews • 1,620 rooms, 145 suites, 11 restaurants, 8 bars
A magnet for much of the city's substantial convention trade, the Anatole dominates the skyline of Dallas's Market Center area and offers a good mix of business and sports facilities. The Verandah Club is an exceptionally elegant spa and health center. Fifty-eight meeting rooms.

Bradford Plaza **$$**
Jackson and Houston St 75202 ☎ 761-9090 • 116 rooms, 6 suites, 1 restaurant, 1 bar
An intimate European-style hotel offering privacy and quiet, the Bradford is conveniently sited in downtown's West End. Rooms are spacious; suites have desks and typewriters. Two meeting rooms.

Crescent Court **$$$$$**
400 Crescent Court 75201 ☎ 871-3200 TX 275555 • 190 rooms, 28 suites, 1 restaurant, 1 bar
The area's young business professionals have made Beau Nash one of the city's foremost business restaurants. The rest of this new hotel measures up equally well. All rooms have three telephones and large desks; message service is prompt. Special staff are assigned to the Crescent's six meeting rooms and 14-seat boardroom, equipped with the latest multi-media technology. European spa, pool.

Hyatt Regency Dallas **$$$**
300 Reunion Blvd 75207 ☎ 651-1234 TX 732748 • 947 rooms, 49 suites, 2 restaurants, 3 bars, 1 coffee shop
Conveniently near the West End, this ultra-modern architectural landmark with its light-studded revolving

tower is the choice of many visiting business travellers. Efficient, well-trained staff. Non-smoking floors • health club, pool, tennis, jogging track • 25 meeting rooms.

Mandalay Four Seasons $$$$$
221 S Las Colinas, Irving 75039 ☎ 556-0800 [TX] 794016 • 412 rooms, 12 suites, 2 restaurants, 3 bars, 1 coffee shop
This modern hotel is located in Las Colinas and is convenient for the airport, downtown businesses, and Texas Stadium. Enjolie, its first-rate dining room, is often used by senior executives for entertaining, and those that stay in the Mandalay are assured of high levels of service, as well as good business and sports facilities. Health club, golf, tennis, pool • 12 meeting rooms, fax, teleconferencing.

Mansion on Turtle Creek $$$$$
2821 Turtle Creek Blvd 75219 ☎ 559-2100 [TX] 794946 • 129 rooms, 14 suites, 2 restaurants, 1 bar
The restored Sheppard-King mansion – an Italianate villa – comprises the hotel's excellent bar and restaurant area; the rooms were built in 1981. Filled with *objets d'art* and handsome reproduction furniture, the Mansion caters to an older, wealthier clientele. The visitors' register often reads like a Who's Who in America. The Mansion restaurant, thought by some to be the city's best, features American *nouvelle* dishes and attentive service. Pool, arrangements with local country club • 8 meeting rooms.

Melrose $$$
3015 Oak Lawn Ave ☎ 521-5151 • 185 rooms, 1 restaurant, 1 bar
Though less sumptuous than the Mansion, the Melrose has spacious bathrooms, mahogany furniture, ceiling fans and separate sitting areas in each room. Just to the N of downtown and only a few minutes from Market Center, it offers personalized service and is popular with women executives. Arrangements with downtown health club • 5 meeting rooms.

Registry $$$
15201 Dallas Pkwy 75248 ☎ 386-6000 [TX] 795515 • 516 rooms, 37 suites, 4 restaurants, 3 bars
This comfortable hotel is a good choice if you have business in North Dallas, and it is surrounded by shops, boutiques, restaurants and nightclubs. In addition to the business concierge, a lobby concierge is on duty 24hrs. Health club, tennis • 24 meeting rooms.

Westin $$$$
13340 Dallas Pkwy 75240 ☎ 934-9494 [TX] 630182 • 430 rooms, 14 suites, 3 restaurants, 1 bar
Located in the Galleria Shopping Mall, the Westin is the most impressive place to stay in North Dallas. Blom's is a highly respected restaurant; the excellent Sunday brunch is much patronized by locals. Health club, pool, nearby tennis, squash • 13 meeting rooms, fax, express mail service.

OTHER HOTELS

Dallas Plaza Suite ($$$) *1933 Main St 75201 ☎ 741-7700.* An intimate, all-suite hotel in eastern downtown, near the San Jacinto Tower; a short walk to the arts district.

Stoneleigh Terrace ($$$) *2827 Maple Ave 75201 ☎ 871-7111.* This Cedar Springs hotel often has celebrity guests.

Clubs

The following are the most elite of Dallas's clubs: *Bent Tree Country Club, Brook Hollow Golf Club, Cipango Club, City Club, Dallas Club, Dallas Country Club, Dallas Petroleum Club, Dallas Women's Club, Northwood Club, Preston Trail Golf Club* and *Willow Bend Polo and Hunt Club.*

Restaurants

Some of Dallas's best restaurants are in the big hotels. In particular, the Adolphus Hotel's *French Room*, *Enjolie* at the Mandalay Four Seasons and the Mansion on Turtle Greek's excellent *Mansion* dining room are nearly always filled with expense-account diners. Many restaurants close by 10pm.

Actuelle $$$$
2800 Routh St, suite 125 ☎ 855-0440 • D only; closed Sun • AE CB DC MC V
The newest entry in the current explosion of New American Cuisine establishments, this sleek restaurant in a gazebo-like pavilion overlooks the courtyard of the Quadrangle. A nearly flawless regional menu with touches of international sophistication is masterfully prepared by one of the city's top chefs.

Arthur's $$$$
8350 N Central Expressway, Campbell Center ☎ 361-8833 • D only Sat; closed Sun • AE CB DC MC V • jacket required
Renowned for its steak and seafood selections, Arthur's provides a formal dining atmosphere that is very popular for business entertaining. The maitre d' is sensitive to requirements for privacy or prime seating.

Atlantic Café $$$
4566 McKinney Ave ☎ 559-4441 • AE CB DC MC V
Some locals swear the Atlantic Café serves the best seafood in this landlocked city. With an attractive setting of polished brass and dark wood trimmings, the restaurant's cozy booths are ideal for quiet conversation during lunch or dinner.

Baby Routh $$$
2708 Routh St ☎ 871-2345 • AE CB DC MC V
An offshoot of the highly touted Routh Street Café (see later), this casual restaurant attracts a fashionable crowd. Its *nouvelle* American dishes are best described as "country chic."

Capriccio $$
2616 Maple ☎ 871-2004 • AE DC MC V • jacket required
This beautiful old Texan house has been well restored and now offers stylish comfort and better-than-average northern Italian dishes. An informal restaurant, Capriccio nonetheless sees a lot of business deals transacted over the *linguini* and *zabaglione*.

Dakota's $$$
500 N Akard ☎ 740-4001 • D only Sat • AE DC MC V
Though a bit noisy for prolonged conversation, Dakota's is nevertheless a continuing success which draws Dallas's own VIPs as well as visiting celebrities. Serving a selection of grills – mainly steaks, chops and seafood – the below-ground restaurant is a good choice for entertaining clients.

Mr Peppe $$$
5617 Lovers Ln ☎ 352-5976 • D only; closed Sun • AE CB DC MC V • jacket required
In this long-established but unpretentious café, the Swiss owner provides good French food and personal service at relatively modest prices. The noise level is rarely above a whisper – though not oppressively silent.

Old Warsaw $$$$$
2610 Maple ☎ 528-0032 • D only • AE CB DC MC V
With its dark, plush décor, background classical music and a fine Continental cuisine, Old Warsaw was the city's ultimate dining experience in the not-so-distant past. Many of the old guard still consider it Dallas's

top spot, and will be favorably impressed by an invitation to dine here.

Routh Street Café **$$$$**
3005 Routh at Cedar Springs
☎ 871-7161 • D only; closed Sun • AE MC V • reservations essential
The best in Dallas according to many of the city's younger professionals, Routh Street Café offers a chic setting and Southwestern food with a *nouvelle* flair. The imaginative menu changes daily, and the all-American wine list has much to commend it.

San Simeon **$$$**
2515 McKinney Ave at Fairmount
☎ 871-7373 • AE CB DC MC V
Sought out for its well-balanced dishes adapted from regional and ethnic traditions, San Simeon also wins honors for its impeccable service and superior wine list.

Sonny Bryan's Smokehouse **$**
2202 Inwood Rd ☎ 357-7120 • B and L only • no credit cards or reservations
A lot of restaurant reviewers have proclaimed Sonny's the best barbeque joint – and one can see why. Ambiance is next to nil, and the seating is either at a secondhand schooldesk or out in the car, but the ribs are excellent. Definitely an off-duty place, but well worth visiting.

West End Oasis **$$$$**
302 N Market ☎ 698-9775 • D only Sat; closed Sun • AE CB DC MC V • jacket preferred
French/American food is suavèly served in this restored warehouse, *the* place for watching Dallas's "beautiful people." It is also one of the few top restaurants which will close its doors to host private parties, so check that it is open to the public on the night you plan to go.

Bars

The classier, more subdued bars are found mainly in the city's better hotels, restaurants and private clubs, such as the bar in the Beau Nash of the Crescent Court (see *Hotels*). Other good meeting places include North Dallas's *Gershwin's*, 8442 Walnut Hill Ln, featuring solo vocalists; and *Moctezuma's*, 3202 McKinney Ave, serving the best margaritas in town. *Andrews*, 7557 Greenville Ave, has exposed brick and Tex-Mex nibbles. Also worth visiting are the *Hard Rock Café*, 2601 McKinney Ave; *Plus Fours*, 2504 McKinney Ave; *Strictly Tabu*, 4111 Lomo Alto; and *SRO*, 2900 McKinney Ave. North Dallas's *La Cave*, 2926 N Henderson, and the *Grape*, 2808 Greenville Ave in East Dallas, are both quiet wine bars useful for after-hours discussions.

Entertainment

Except for the hotels' numerous lounges and cozy bars and the permanently charged West End historic district, streetlife in downtown Dallas fades with the setting sun. Greenville Avenue, Highland Park's Knox Street, Beltline Road in Far North Dallas and McKinney Avenue then come alive, offering dozens of bars, discos and nightclubs. In addition, Dallas has a varied selection of live theater, music and dance performances.

For information on what's on, call the *Cultural Arts Info Hot Line* ☎ 385-1155 or check the "Weekend" sections in Friday editions of *Dallas Morning News* or the *Times Herald. D* magazine also has entertainment information. For tickets contact *Ticketron* ☎ 265-0789.

Music, theater and dance The widely acclaimed *Dallas Symphony Orchestra* performs at the Music Hall, State Fair Grounds ☎ 565-9100, tickets ☎ 692-0203. For other musical events, the *Dallas Civic Music Association* performs in the McFarlin Auditorium at SMU ☎ 526-6870; *Dallas Grand Opera*, 13601 Preston Rd ☎ 661-9750, tickets ☎ 691-7200; the *Dallas Opera*, Majestic Theater, 1925 Elm St ☎ 979-0123, tickets ☎ 871-0090; and *Dallas Summer Musicals*, State Fair Box

Office, 6021 Berkshire Ln ☏ 691-7200. The Frank Lloyd Wright-designed *Dallas Theater Center*, 3636 Turtle Creek Blvd ☏ 526-8210 is headquarters for one of the city's oldest performing arts companies, while the *Arts District Theater* also stages DTC productions.

Live theater is also available at the *Dallas Repertory Theater*, NorthPark Center ☏ 369-8966; *Greenville Avenue Theater*, 2914 Greenville Ave ☏ 824-2552; *New Arts Theater*, 702 Ross Ave at Market St ☏ 761-9064; *Plaza Theater*, 6719 Snider Plaza ☏ 363-7000; and *Theater Three*, 2800 Routh St ☏ 871-3300.

Regular programs are presented by the *Dallas Ballet* at the Majestic Theater, 1925 Elm St ☏ 744-4430 and the *Southern Methodist University School of the Arts* ☏ 692-3146.

Nightclubs The best clubs include *Dick's Last Resort*, Ross and Record streets in the West End historic district ☏ 747-0001; it offers Dixieland jazz. *Emerald City*, 4908 Greenville ☏ 361-2489 is another jazz spot; a coat and tie are required. *The Longhorn Ballroom*, 216 Corinth ☏ 428-3128 is the most authentic country dance hall. *Poor David's Pub*, 1924 Greenville ☏ 821-9891, presents oldies-but-goodies, such as Mary Travers. The best show in town is usually at the *Venetian Room* at the Fairmont Hotel, Ross and Akard ☏ 720-2020.

Shopping

Miracle Mile in Lover's Lane (Inwood Road to Douglas Avenue) has some of the city's most exclusive designer boutiques and three top specialty stores for women: The Gazebo, Lou Lattimore and Marie Leavell. Another area for top designer wear is *Highland Park Village*. Along *Oak Lawn*, Turtletique and Loretta Blum are favorites of Dallas women; Alexander Julian and Harrison's have good menswear. Two other popular men's shops – Marvin Brown and Pockets – are on *Greenville Avenue*.

Dallas's biggest and best shopping malls are all N of Northwest Highway (Loop 12), with hundreds of retail shops plus branches of most major national department stores. *NorthPark Center* has the largest Neiman-Marcus suburban branch store, as well as Lord & Taylor, The Carriage Shop and Ann Taylor. *The Galleria* also has Ann Taylor, plus Macy's, Marshall Field's and Saks Fifth Avenue. Nearby Valley View Mall has Bloomingdale's.

The renowned Neiman-Marcus and Sangar-Harris are both headquartered *downtown*, as is Brooks Brothers.

The *Farmers' Market*, 1010 S Pearl Expressway, is one of the largest outdoor markets in the country, with an eclectic assortment of produce and other Texan goods. Grand Prairie's huge flea market, *Trader's Village*, 2602 May Field Rd, operates at weekends 8–sunset.

Dallas has a network of wholesale fashion outlets; a copy of *The Underground Shopper*, available at newsstands and bookshops, will guide the bargain hunter.

Sightseeing

Arboretum and Botanical Gardens Two former Dallas estates make up this 66-acre garden complex overlooking White Rock Lake. After touring the gardens, drive around the lake (9 mile/14.5km). *8525 Garland Rd at Whittier ☏ 327-8263.*

Dallas Museum of Art Highlights include pre-Columbian art, Old Masters, modern American works, Oriental and Oceanic collections and the Reves Decorative Arts Wing. *1717 N Harwood ☏ 922-0220. Open 10–5, Tue–Sat; 10–9, Thu; noon–5, Sun.*

Dallas Public Library Photograph and art collections, special exhibits, recordings, a cable television studio and an auditorium. *1515 Young St ☏ 749-4400. Guided tours (45min) at 11 and 1, Sat; at 3, Sun.*

DeGolyer Estate An historic mansion sits in the eastern part of the city. In nearly 43 acres bordering White Rock Lake it has a good art collection and beautiful grounds. *8525 Garland Rd ☏ 324-1401. Open daily exc Mon.*

Fair Park Home of the three-week long Texas State Fair each October, the fairgrounds are filled with Art Deco architecture, and provide a permanent home to many Dallas museums as well as the Dallas Music Hall and the Cotton Bowl. The museums, including the Aquarium and the Museum of Natural History, are open daily and most are free. *Grand Ave ☏ 565-9931.*

Meadows Museum of Art owns a fine collection of Spanish art: more than 100 paintings by such artists as Velazquez and Goya. *Southern Methodist University ☏ 692-2516. Open 10–5, Mon–Sat; 1–5, Sun.*

Old City Park Historic homes and replica buildings – such as a doctor's office, depot, pioneer cabins, hotel, general store and school – re-create a semblance of early northern Texas communities. The park is close to downtown and has an excellent restaurant, Brent Place, serving lunch daily. *Gano and St Paul ☏ 421-7800. Open Tue–Fri, 10–4; Sat and Sun, 1.30–4.30; closed Mon.*

Guided tours

Dallas Silver Cloud Tours, 4200 Herschel Ave ☏ 521-1664. *Execservice Unlimited*, 2701-A Fondren Dr, University Park ☏ 691-1166 specializes in custom group tours. *Gray Line of Dallas and Fort Worth*, 4110 S Lamar ☏ 824-2424 provides the most variety in daily, regularly scheduled city tours. *Kaleidoscope Tours*, 3131 Turtle Creek Blvd ☏ 522-5930 gives comprehensive and customized sightseeing area tours.

Spectator sports

Dallas is enthusiastically sports-minded, and local business deals are often settled at the Texas Stadium, where many companies hold corporate boxes.

Baseball The *Texas Rangers* ☏ 273-5100 play at Ranger Stadium, next door to Six Flags Over Texas, Apr–Sep.

Basketball The *Mavericks* appear at Reunion Arena, 777 Sports St ☏ 748-1808, Sep–Mar.

Football The Dallas *Cowboys* play at Texas Stadium ☏ 438-7676.

Rodeo The best venue is the *Mesquite Championship Rodeo*, I-635 at Military Pkwy, Mesquite ☏ 285-8777; Apr–Sep, Fri and Sat at 8.30pm.

Soccer *Sidekicks Soccer* take over Reunion Arena Nov–Apr ☏ 760-7330.

Keeping fit

Health clubs *President's Health & Racquet Clubs* have 15 locations in Greater Dallas providing gyms, swimming pools, indoor tracks and advanced training equipment. The *Turtle Creek President's Health Club*, 3301 McKinney ☏ 871-7700 is particularly prestigious.

Bicycling Locally popular bike trails skirt Bachman Lake on Northwest Highway and White Rock Lake on Garland Road; Turtle Creek Drive in Highland Park is also often used. Bicycle rentals are available from *Hundley Recreation Center*, 3240 W Lawther (at White Rock Lake) ☏ 823-6933, and *Inwood Cycle*, 3750 W Northwest Hwy ☏ 357-7625 (near Bachman Lake).

Golf Some of the best public courses are *Cedar Crest* ☏ 943-1004, *Grover Keaton* ☏ 388-4831, *Stevens* ☏ 946-5781 and *Tenison* ☏ 823-5350.

Horseback riding The following stables offer daily riding: *Benbrook Ranch & Stables*, W of Dallas off I-20 ☏ (817) 249-1176, and *Wagon Wheel Stables*, D/FW Airport ☏ 462-0894.

Tennis Tennis courts are scattered across the city in parks and near recreation centers. To find the public courts most convenient to your hotel and to make reservations ☏ 428-1501 Mon–Fri, 8.15–5.15.

Local resources

Business services

Photocopying and printing *Red-E-Print*, 8383 Stemmons Fwy ☎ 637-2532 (near Market Center); *Century Printing*, 701 N St Paul ☎ 741-3191; *Quik Print*, 1 Main Pl ☎ 741-1425, also 513 N Ervay (downtown). *Cliff's Printing & Instant Copy Shop*, 5307 E Mockingbird ☎ 826-8911; *Minute Man Press*, 11617 North Central at Forest ☎ 363-2876 (North Central area). *Cliff's Printing & Instant Copy Shop*, 12810 Hillcrest ☎ 980-4714 (Far North Dallas).
Secretarial *Executive Secretarial Services*, Walnut Hill at Greenville ☎ 750-1111; *AMS Secretarial Service*, 6200 N Central Expwy, suite 226 ☎ 363-7824; *Capital Secretarial Services*, 401 Capital Bank Bldg ☎ 823-7950.
Translation *Berlitz*, 15340 Dallas Pkwy ☎ 387-4487; *Language Bank*, Dallas Council on World Affairs, World Trade Center ☎ 744-3109.

Communications

Local delivery *The Secretary's Choice*, 3720 Walnut Hill Ln ☎ 352-1732; *Wingtip Couriers*, 910 N Central Expwy ☎ 826-8690.
Long-distance delivery *Emery Airfreight* ☎ 574-6300; *Federal Express* ☎ 358-5271; *Sky Courier* ☎ (800) 336-3344; *United Parcel Service*, 10155 Monroe ☎ 350-3342.
Post office *Main post office*, 400 N Ervay ☎ 767-5648; open Mon–Fri, 8–5. *D/FW office*, at SW-end of the airport ☎ 574-2685, offers 24hr service for express mail; for other services Mon–Fri, 8–5.
Telex *Action Telex*, 6350 LBJ Fwy, suite 165-E ☎ 661-2913; *Southwest Data Terminals*, 11052 Shady Trail, suite 207 ☎ 956-7744.

Conference/exhibition centers

The largest facility is the *Dallas Convention Center*, 650 S Griffin St ☎ 658-7000, with banquet and meeting rooms, plus large exhibition areas.

Emergencies

Hospitals *Baylor University Medical Center*, 3500 Gaston; emergency ☎ 820-2501, doctor referral ☎ 820-3312. *Medical City Dallas*, 7777 Forest Ln; emergency ☎ 661-720, doctor referral ☎ 661-7072. *Presbyterian Hospital*, 8200 Walnut Hill Ln; emergency ☎ 696-7863. *St Paul Medical Center*, 5909 Harry Hines Blvd, emergency ☎ 879-2790, doctor referral ☎ 879-3099.
Pharmacies *Sun Rexall Drugs*, 4101 Bryan at Haskell ☎ 824-4539; *Eckerd Drugs*, 2320 W Illinois Ave ☎ 331-5466; both are open 24hr.
Police (also fire and ambulance) ☎ 744-4444.

Information sources

Business information *Dallas Chamber of Commerce*, 1507 Pacific Ave ☎ 954-1111.
Local media The *Dallas Morning News* and the *Dallas Times Herald* are the two local dailies; a Southwest edition of the *Wall Street Journal* is also available. The monthly *D* magazine and the Chamber of Commerce's *Dallas Magazine* both contain helpful advice on sights, restaurants and entertainment.
Tourist information *Dallas Convention and Visitors' Bureau*, Dallas Chamber of Commerce, 1507 Pacific Ave ☎ 954-1111.

Thank-yous

The following companies accept telephone orders and major credit cards.
Florists *Biggerstaff Flowers*, 900 18th St ☎ 423-2501; *Bullard's Flowers*, 4529 McKinney Ave ☎ 528-0383; *North Haven Gardens* (FTD), 7700 Northhaven Rd ☎ 691-6751; *Petals & Stems*, (downtown) in the Fairmont Hotel ☎ 720-4009.
Gift baskets *Goodies From Goodman* (food), 12102 Inwood Rd ☎ 387-4804.

FORT WORTH

Area code ☎ 817

Only 30 miles/48km from Dallas, Forth Worth is moving from its traditional reliance on land, cattle and oil to high tech, and has attracted the headquarters of Tandy, and the Advanced Robotics Research Institute. It also houses the headquarters of American Airlines and divisions of Burlington Northern Railroad and General Motors.

Arriving

(See DALLAS)

Getting around

Taxi Don't expect to be able to hail a cab; telephone ahead. Try *American Cab Company* ☎ 332-1919.

Car rental Rental firms at the airport include: *Avis* ☎ 335-3211; *Budget* ☎ 336-6600; *Hertz* ☎ 335-7000; and *National* ☎ 335-1030.

Limousine The major firms are *CandleRidge Limousine* ☎ 294-8747; *Carey Limousine* ☎ 263-7298; and *Barron Limousines* ☎ 263-8611.

Bus *CITRAN*, the public transport service, has a free zone downtown and a 75 cent basic fare elsewhere.

Area by area

Downtown is the central business district and where the best hotels are found. Landmarks are the glass Texas American Bank Tower; the post office; Texas & Pacific Railway Passenger Station; and the twin towers of the Tandy Corporation.

Northside Just 3min N of downtown, this historic district once had the world's largest livestock market.

Eastside New middle-class, residential area on the I-30 artery to Arlington; headquarters of the Advanced Robotics Research Institute.

Southside Texas Christian University, the Colonial Country Club and pockets of elegant residential development – old and new. Berkeley and Ryan Place in particular are monied residential areas.

Westside The city's oldest and most affluent residential areas – Westover Hills and River Crest – are here.

Hotels

All the hotels listed are downtown, with the exception of the Stockyards Hotel in Northside.

Hilton $$$

1701 Commerce 76102 ☎ 335-7000 • 434 rooms, 4 suites, 3 restaurants, 2 bars

Over-shadowing the Water Gardens, the Hilton has recently been stylishly restored. Centerstage, serving mainly grills, has window booths well-suited for business conversation. Pool, jacuzzi • 19 meeting rooms.

Hyatt Regency $$$$

815 Main St 76102 ☎ 870-1234 TX 794826 • 482 rooms, 34 suites, 2 restaurants, 3 bars

Formerly the Hotel Texas, the Hyatt's historic exterior is complemented by a contemporary interior. Its restaurant, the Crystal Cactus, serves gourmet food. The Hyatt Business Center provides a full-time secretary and a range of other services. Health club • 18 meeting rooms.

Stockyards $$$

109 E Exchange Ave 76106 ☎ 625-6427 • 50 rooms, 2 suites

The renovated Stockyards is popular with business travellers. Built in 1907, it has a grand oak staircase and a comfortable lobby, with leather Chesterfield sofas and handwoven rugs. Three meeting rooms.

Worthington $$$$

200 Main St 76102 ☎ 870-1000 • 509 rooms, 64 suites, 2 restaurants, 1 bar

A most elegant hotel geared to business travellers, it provides full concierge service, in-house translation and currency exchange. Pool, sun-deck, health club, jacuzzi, sauna, roof-top tennis • 30 meeting rooms.

Clubs

Fort Worth's most exclusive country clubs are the *Colonial River Crest* and *Shady Oaks*. Downtown there is the *Petroleum Club*; *Fort Worth Club*; the high-powered *Century II Club* and the *City Club*.

Restaurants

Fort Worth is not a gourmet's paradise, but the following establishments supply good Tex-Mex, barbeque and Continental fare.

Angelo's $
2533 White Settlement Rd ☏ 332-0357 • closed Sun • no credit cards • no reservations
This Fort Worth institution, with its gruff service and sawdust-strewn floor, offers the best barbeque in town. Angelo's is a casual spot where you can be in, fed and out in 20min.

Balcony $$
6100 Camp Bowie Blvd ☏ 731-3719 • closed Sun • AE CB DC MC V
Natives recommend this restaurant for its good classic Continental cuisine; best dishes include tournedos and fresh fish. Good for business *têtes à têtes.*

Carriage House $$$
5136 Camp Bowie Blvd ☏ 732-2873 • closed Sun D • AE CB DC MC V
The highly-regarded Carriage House is one of Fort Worth's oldest restaurants, and one of the few open for Sunday brunch. Continental food.

Joe T Garcia's $$
2201 N Commerce ☏ 626-4356 • L only Sun • no credit cards • no reservations
Though the lines are always long at this casual Tex-Mex emporium, Joe T's is unbeatable for a relaxed evening. Fort Worth executives are as comfortable here as at the Carriage House, but because of the first-come-first-served policy, regard it as an off-duty spot or for a very relaxed business lunch or dinner.

Michel $$$
3851 Camp Bowie Blvd ☏ 732-1232 • D only Sat; closed Sun and Mon • AE CB DC MC V • reservations essential
The city's top restaurant, Michel offers attentive service and a superior menu of Continental and regional specialties.

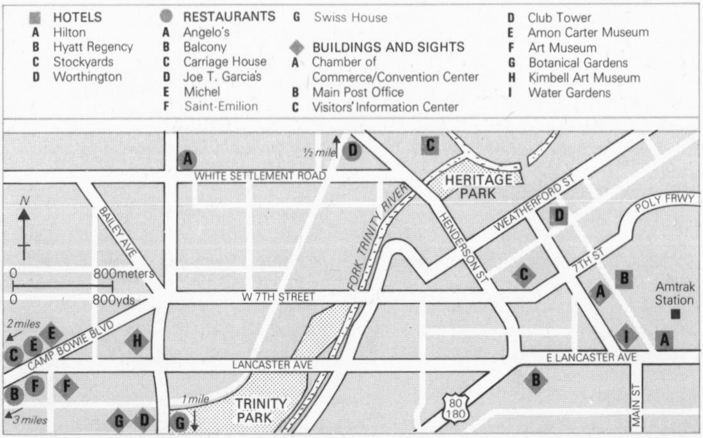

Saint-Emilion $$$
3617 W 7th St ☏ *737-2781* • *AE CB DC MC V*
A small restaurant with a good selection of grilled meats, including wild rabbit and lamb, plus an above-average choice of desserts. A quiet spot for business discussions.

Swiss House $$
1541 Merrimac Circle ☏ *877-1531* • *D only; closed Sun* • *AE CB DC MC V*
A bastion of Fort Worth's establishment because of the good Continental food and cozy piano bar atmosphere. Another good choice for business.

Bars

For quiet conversation, you have to use the lounges of Fort Worth's major hotels, but *Rangoon Racquet Club*, 4936 Camp Bowie Blvd, is an exception to the town's otherwise raucous bar scene, attracting the well-heeled. The intimate piano bar at the Swiss House (see *Restaurants*) is popular. *Billy Miners*, 150 W 3rd St, and *The Ice House*, 4600 Dexter, are two other popular spots, though more casual and lively.

Entertainment

Fort Worth has two major draws: the playhouse, *Casa Mañana*, and *Billy Bob's Texas*, described as the world's best – and largest – country rock club. For what is on locally check the entertainment section of the *Fort Worth Star Telegram* or *Fort Worth Magazine*.

Music At the Tarrant County Convention Center, abbreviated TCCC, 111 Houston: *Fort Worth Ballet* ☏ 921-6133; *Fort Worth Opera* ☏ 731-0833; *Fort Worth Symphony Orchestra, Fort Worth Symphony Pops* and *Fort Worth Chamber Orchestra* ☏ 921-2676. *Cliburn Concerts* are played at several different locations ☏ 738-6509 or 738-6536. *Johnnie High's Country Music Revue* plays at the Will Rogers Auditorium, 3401 W Lancaster Ave ☏ 481-4518, every Sat at 7pm.

Nightclubs *Billy Bob's Texas*, 2520 N Commerce ☏ 625-6491 is a colony of 46 bars, indoor rodeo, restaurants, dance floor and VIP club. *Caravan of Dreams*, 312 Houston St ☏ 877-3000 has a jazz and blues club, theater and cinema. *White Elephant Saloon*, 106 N Exchange ☏ 624-0357 blasts country music – sometimes live.

Shopping

Sundance Square on Main Street, downtown has book and video shops, boutiques and restaurants. *The Balcony of Ridglea*, 6333 Camp Bowie, has fashion boutiques. Major shopping malls are *Hulen Mall*, 4800 S Hulen St and *Ridgmar Mall*, 2060 Green Oaks at I-30; on the Southside, there is the *Seminary South*.

Sightseeing

Amon Carter Museum specializes in 19th and 20thC American art. There is also an extensive photograph collection. *3501 Camp Bowie Blvd* ☏ *738-1933. Tue–Sat, 10–5; Sun, 1–5.30; closed Mon.*

Art Museum A fine collection of modern 20thC art. *1309 Montgomery St* ☏ *738-9215. Tue, 10–9; Wed–Sat, 10–6.*

Botanical Gardens The gardens include 114 acres of rose gardens based on Versailles, and a Japanese garden. *3220 Botanic Garden Dr* ☏ *870-7686. Daily, 8–sunset.*

Kimbell Art Museum Collections of pre-Columbian sculpture, Oriental and African art, and European paintings. *3333 Camp Bowie Blvd* ☏ *332-8451. Tue–Sat, 10–5; Sun, 1–5; closed Mon.*

Spectator sports

Baseball The *Texas Rangers* play at Arlington Stadium, I-30 ☏ 273-5222 or 273-5100.

Rodeo For weekly, year-round rodeo, *Kow Bell Indoor Rodeo* ☏ 477-3092 in nearby Mansfield; Sat and Sun 8pm for rodeo; Mon and Fri, bull riding.

Keeping fit

Health clubs *Gym & Trim*, 6225 Sunset Dr in Ridglea. *President's Health & Racquet Clubs*, 6833-A Green Oaks Rd in West Fort Worth ☎ 738-8910.

Golf Visitors can play at *Meadow Brook*, 1815 Jensen Rd ☎ 457-4616; *Pecan Valley*, Ben Brook Lake ☎ 249-1845; *Rockwood*, 1851 Jacksboro Hwy ☎ 624-1771; and *Sycamore Creek*, 2423 E Vickery ☎ 535-7241.

Tennis *Mary Potishman Lard Tennis Center*, 3609 Bellaire Dr (on the TCU campus) ☎ 921-7808. The *McLeland Tennis Center*, 1600 W Seminary ☎ 921-5134.

Local resources

Business services

Photocopying and printing *The Printing Store*, 5821 Camp Bowie ☎ 731-1121; *Quik Print*, 600 Houston St Mall ☎ 336-2533; *Speedicopy*, 2913-A W Berry St at Cockrell ☎ 924-0176.

Secretarial *Fort Worth Executive Center*, 777 Taylor St, suite 8000 ☎ 336-0800; *Ridglea Telephone & Secretarial Service*, 5608 Malvey Ave ☎ 732-7151.

Translation *AAA Spanish Translation Service*, 4504 Wilson Ct ☎ 237-7588; *American Translations Co* ☎ 451-8899.

Communications

Local delivery *Mail Call* ☎ 737-7151; *Metrocall Messengers* ☎ 572-4303; *Security Couriers*, 325 N Riverside Dr ☎ 831-6381 or (800) 442-6398.

Long-distance delivery *Federal Express* ☎ 332-6293.

Post office *Main post office*, 251 W Lancaster ☎ 334-2920; open Mon–Fri, 8.30–5.

Telex *American Telephone and Satellite*, 1340 Main St ☎ 481-7322; *Western Union* ☎ 335-8251.

Conference/exhibition centers

Tarrant County Convention Center, 1111 Houston St; *Cowtown Coliseum*, 123 E Exchange Ave ☎ 624-1101; *Will Rogers Coliseum* ☎ 335-0734.

Emergencies

Hospitals *All Saints Episcopal Hospital*, 1400 8th Ave ☎ 926-2544; *John Peter Smith Hospital*, 1500 S Main ☎ 921-3431.

Pharmacies *Hall's Pharmacy*, 1008 Pennsylvania ☎ 336-7281 or 700 W Rosedale ☎ 877-3677; open 24hrs.

Police (and fire) ☎ 274-2511.

Government offices

Texas Consumer Credit Commission ☎ 263-2016; *Small Business Administration* ☎ 334-3777; *Better Business Bureau* ☎ 332-7585.

Information sources

Business information *Fort Worth Chamber of Commerce*, 700 Throckmorton St ☎ 336-2491.

Local media The *Fort Worth Star Telegram* and the *Fort Worth News Tribune* are daily newspapers. For a magazine format there is *Aura Magazine*, *Fort Worth Magazine* and *The Longhorn Scene.*

Tourist information *Fort Worth Convention and Visitors' Bureau* ☎ 336-2491; *Fort Worth Visitor Information Center*, 124 E Exchange Ave.

Thank-yous

Florists *Gordon Boswell Flowers*, 1220 Pennsylvania ☎ 332-1345; *Petals*, 4919-A Camp Bowie Blvd ☎ 738-0934.

Gift baskets *Fruit Basket Boutique* 5677-D Westcreek Dr ☎ 292-8295; *Coffee etc*, 6328 Camp Bowie Blvd ☎ 731-9069.

DENVER

Area code ☎ 303

A natural hub for business and government, Denver is the largest urban center in an eight-state area as well as Colorado's state capital. Although many of the city's petroleum-based businesses have suffered from the oil recession, there has been an influx of high-tech companies along Colorado's Front Range, which extends from Fort Collins in the N to Colorado Springs in the S. The biggest employers in the metropolitan area include AT&T, Martin Marietta/Denver Aerospace, Mountain Bell, Adolph Coors Companies, Public Service Company of Colorado and IBM, and the state is now home to about 1,100 manufacturing and R&D firms, including Rockwell International, Digital Equipment, Hewlett-Packard, Ampex and Cobe Labs.

Arriving

Stapleton International Airport

Stapleton has one main terminal with four unusually long adjoining concourses and congestion can be extreme in the early morning and evening, and on Friday and Sunday evenings especially. A major inconvenience is that trolleys are not available, except in the Customs area. Porters are stationed at baggage claim areas and at curbside check-ins. There are several restaurants and a 24hr cafeteria; currency exchange is in Concourse C, level 2 (6am–9pm). Couriers at the airport include *JCI* ☎ 363-6688, *Federal Express* ☎ 892-7981 and *Pony Express* ☎ 573-9202. Air cargo is handled by *Flying Tigers* ☎ 398-2330.

Nearby hotels *Airport Hilton*, 4411 Peoria ☎ 373-5730; *Clarion*, Quebec St 80207 ☎ 321-3333/3203.

City link *Taxi* The quickest way to get downtown, only 6 miles/9.5km away, is by cab – usually no more than a 15min drive, 30min in rush hour (7.15–8.15 and 4.30–5.30). Cabs are readily available from the lower level by the baggage claim area.

Car rental If your business will take you throughout the wide-ranging metropolitan area, it is best to rent a car. Major car rental companies have booths at the airport's lower level: *Hertz* ☎ 355-2244, *Avis* ☎ 398-3725, *Dollar* ☎ 398-2323 and *National* ☎ 321-7990.

Limousine Stretch limos to downtown and SE Denver locations are provided by Airport Limousine ☎ 398-2284 but you may have to wait more than 30min for pick-up.

Getting around

With the Rocky Mountains providing an unmistakable western orientation, Denver is quite easy to negotiate. If your business is mainly in the downtown area, walking and the free shuttle – which runs along the 16th Street Mall from Broadway Street to lower downtown – are by far the easiest ways of getting about. Traffic is not particularly heavy except during rush hours, and parking is readily available. E–W roads are generally avenues; N–S roads are streets. E–W numbering of addresses begins at Broadway, N–S at Ellsworth Avenue. The main N–S freeway is I-25, the E–W route is I-70.

Car rental If you don't rent at the airport, local firms include *Thrifty* ☎ 388-4634, *Mister Motors* ☎ 798-0861 and *Holiday Payless* ☎ 399-2886.

Taxi Taxis do not cruise the streets, but can be found outside major downtown hotels. For a reservation, call *Yellow Cab* ☎ 292-1212 or *Zone* ☎ 861-2323.

Limousine *Prince Limousine* ☎ 295-7411 offers a 24hr service.

Bus Not recommended; for information ☎ 778-6000.

Area by area

Downtown The downtown is slightly disorienting as it runs at a NE–SW diagonal while the rest of the city conforms to a N–S, E–W grid. As Denver's financial hub, 17th Street is thick with law firms, oil companies and major financial offices. The 16th Street Transitway Mall, a block S, has most of the city's department stores.

Lower downtown At the western end of the downtown area, lower downtown, once the city's sleaziest district, has been extensively renovated and gentrified; it is now a choice retail area and is home to interior designers, architects and other creative businesses. Larimer Square's prestigious Victorian renovations attract shoppers and sightseers; the updated Tivoli Brewery shopping complex just off Larimer Street, a block from Larimer Square, is another smart shopping district. Sakura Square, on 19th Street between Lawrence and Larimer, is the center of Denver's large Japanese community.

Capitol Hill E of downtown is Capitol Hill, once a most desirable residential site and today a mix of restored Victorian homes and small businesses, plus numerous government agencies and office buildings, and Restaurant Row, where you can find many of the city's newest and best restaurants. Though safe by day, the area has a high crime rate; take care after dark.

Cherry Creek North Cherry Creek North, near 1st Avenue and University Boulevard, has the city's highest concentration of art galleries, chic restaurants and high-fashion boutiques. Nearby Polo Club, Country Club and Hilltop are prime Denver residential enclaves.

Denver Tech Center To the S is an area now known as the Denver Tech Center (DTC) because of its many high-tech businesses.

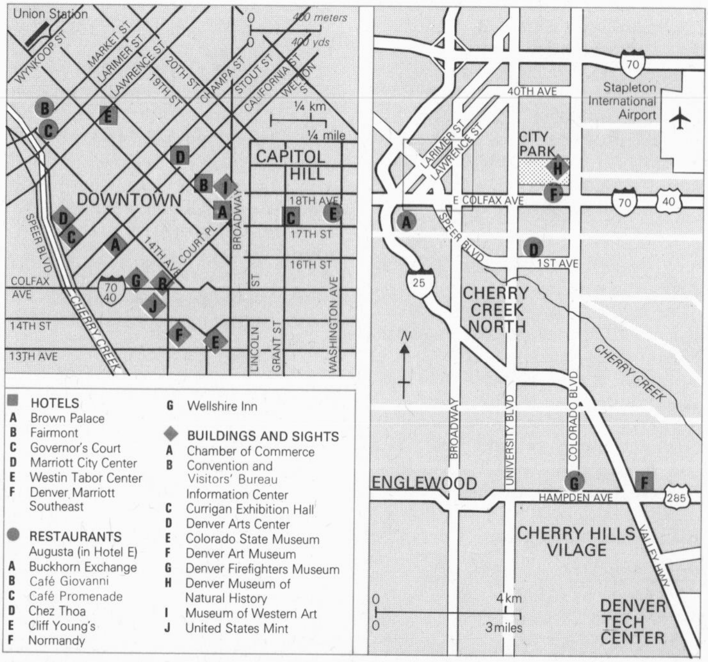

The suburbs

Cherry Hills Village, S of Denver, is the city's most affluent suburb, with expensive homes, open spaces and a criss-crossing of bridle trails. *Englewood* is a major commercial and activity center; *Lakewood*, to the W, is recreational and family-oriented. *Littleton*, 10 mile/16km S of downtown is the base for several national firms such as Martin Marietta and the Manville Corporation. *Aurora* is the major employment center in the eastern metropolitan area.

Evergreen, 30 miles/48km SW, is a retreat where high-income executives enjoy mountain living. *Boulder*, 40min NW on the edge of the Rocky Mountains, is a university town – cultured, pricey, youthful and educated, with several major high-tech businesses, including Hewlett-Packard, IBM and Kodak.

Hotels

Since 1892, the Brown Palace has hosted royalty, presidents and celebrities. Today it faces stiff competition from several luxury downtown hotels.

Brown Palace $$$$

321 17th St 80202 ☎ 297-3111 TX 454416 • 461 rooms, 20 suites, 4 restaurants, 2 bars

The Brown is Denver's grandest hostelry. Because it is built as a triangle, some rooms are spacious, others more cramped; ask not to be given a corner room. The Brown provides a high degree of personalized service, and its Victorian décor is both cozy and inviting. An excellent concierge takes care of most business travellers' needs. Gift shops, car rental • sauna, whirlpool, nearby health club • 11 meeting rooms.

Fairmont $$$$

1750 Welton St 80202 ☎ 295-1200 TX 9109312669 • 530 rooms, 27 suites, 3 restaurants, 4 bars

Close to the financial district, the Fairmont has great style. Rooms are exceptionally spacious and well-equipped, and have ample working space; suites are ideal for small meetings. The Marquis restaurant is quiet and highly valued by both local and visiting executives. Pool, tennis, jogging track, arrangement with nearby health club • 13 meeting rooms, teleconferencing.

Governor's Court $$$

1776 Grant St 80202 ☎ 861-2000 • 149 rooms, 43 suites, 1 restaurant, 1 bar

This hotel offers oversized guest rooms, all with a conference table, wet bar, private balcony and two phones. The refined Governor's Table is ideal for quiet dinners and business talk. Pool • 9 meeting rooms.

Marriott City Center $$$$

1701 California St 80202 ☎ 297-1300 TX 9109312284 • 612 rooms, 2 restaurants, 3 bars, 1 coffee shop

The centrally located Marriott occupies the lower 20 floors of the ARCO Building. All rooms have good views of either the city or the Rockies. The hotel's restaurant, Mattie Silks', is popular with the downtown business crowd. Pool, hydrotherapy pool, sauna, games room, indoor tennis • 25 meeting rooms.

Westin Tabor Center $$$$

1672 Lawrence St 80202 ☎ 572-9100 TX 4970844 • 420 rooms, 14 suites, 2 restaurants, 2 bars, 1 coffee shop

The Westin opened only in 1985, and is the focal point of the Tabor Center retail and office complex. Rooms are spacious and many are furnished with reproduction antiques; each room has a refrigerator. The formal

Augusta restaurant (see *Restaurants*) is a local favorite with corporate executives. Health club, pool, hot tub, sauna, racquetball courts, exercise room • 19 meeting rooms, fax.

OTHER HOTELS

Denver Marriott Southeast ($$$) *I-25 and Hampden Ave* ☎ *758-7000* TX *9109312595.* Near Denver Tech Center.

Clubs

The *University Club*, the city's most prestigious club, and the *Denver Athletic Club* are popular dining spots for downtown business people. The beautifully decorated *Petroleum Club* offers spectacular views, but it does not buzz with the same activity as in years past. The *Metropolitan Club* caters largely to business people with offices in SE Denver.

Restaurants

Although locally grown beef is still a favorite, it has been joined by more sophisticated Continental fare; California wines dominate most lists. All restaurants listed provide a no-smoking area, and almost none impose dress codes.

Augusta $$
1672 Lawrence St ☎ *572-7222 • AE CB DC MC V*
One of Denver's best, this restaurant is popular both for business lunches and evening entertaining. The emphasis is on American cuisine – steaks, chops, roast beef, big salads, shrimp cocktails – with a rôtisserie for duckling and rabbit. The décor is elegant Art Deco.

Buckhorn Exchange $$
1000 Osage St ☎ *534-9505 • closed major holidays • AE CB DC MC V*
Denver's oldest restaurant is an institution, its walls overflowing with Western memorabilia, including period figurines, costumes and vintage photos. Buffalo burgers, pot-roast sandwich, and elk steak are specialties. A good choice for working lunches, though slightly out of the downtown center.

Café Giovanni $$$
1515 Market St ☎ *825-6555 • AE CB DC MC V • reservations essential*
Occupying a Victorian warehouse in lower downtown, Giovanni's serves Continental cuisine to the cream of local society in opulent surroundings. Highly recommended for power lunches or dinners, or for first-class entertaining.

Café Promenade $$
1424 Larimer St, Larimer Sq ☎ *893-2692 • AE CB DC MC V • lunch reservations essential*
The Promenade has been a local legend from the moment it opened more than 20 years ago. It is a favorite for business lunches and pre- and post-theater meals; the cuisine is mainly Italian.

Chez Thoa $$$
158 Fillmore St ☎ *355-2323 • AE MC V*
Between downtown and the Denver Tech Center, Chez Thoa offers elegantly presented French Vietnamese cuisine. It is especially popular with the younger business professionals in the area's numerous computer-based firms and is intimate enough for private conversation.

Cliff Young's $$$
17th Ave at Washington ☎ *831-8900 • AE CB DC MC V • reservations essential*
On the fringes of the Capitol Hill area, in Restaurant Row, Cliff Young's has great cachet and is an impressive choice for either lunch or dinner entertaining. Its wine list is extensive; its menu varied; its presentation unsurpassed.

Normandy $$
1515 Madison at Colfax Ave
☎ 321-3311 • closed Mon and first week in Jul • AE CB DC MC V
Styled after a French country inn, the Normandy has several small rooms, subdued lighting, a provincial French menu and one of Denver's largest wine lists. A good choice for talking business or entertaining.

Wellshire Inn $$
3333 S Colorado Blvd ☎ 759-3333 • closed Memorial and Labor days • AE CB DC MC V
Between downtown and the Denver Tech Center in the luxurious setting of a former country club, the Tudor-style Wellshire overlooks an 18-hole golf course and is patronized by local executives who find its high-backed booths and private seating areas. This is a good dinner spot, and its clubby bar is an excellent ice-breaker.

Bars

For after-hours business talk, local executives prefer the *Brown Palace*'s lobby bar which serves champagne and caviar 5–8pm. More low key is the hotel's dark and intimate *Ship Tavern*, a Denver tradition since the turn of the century. The *American Grill*, 1670 Broadway at 17th St, draws downtowners on weekdays for after-hours drinks. *My Brother's Bar*, 2376 15th St, is popular with younger professionals; good hamburgers.

Entertainment

For news of what's on, look at the *Rocky Mountain News* and the *Denver Post* Friday editions.
Theater and music The *Denver Arts Center*, 14th and Curtis ☎ 893-3272 is the major cultural center for the Rocky Mountain region. The *Helen G Bonfils Theater Complex*, part of the Center ☎ 893-4200, has its own repertory company. Avant-garde theater can be seen at *Germinal Stage Denver* ☎ 296-1192. The *Denver Symphony Orchestra* ☎ 592-7777 performs at Boettcher Concert Hall. The *Corner Room* in the Oxford Hotel, 1600 17th St, features jazz.
Nightclubs The Fairmont's *Moulin Rouge* has top-name entertainment accompanied by dinner or drinks. The *Comedy Works*, 1226 15th St in Larimer Sq ☎ 595-3637, also serves dinner.

Shopping

Downtown shops are interspersed with office buildings along the 16th Street Mall, served by free, circulating shuttles. Along the route are major department stores such as *May D & E*, *Denver*, *Joslins* and *JC Penney*. *Homer Reed*, 1717 Tremont Pl ☎ 298-1301, is a traditional men's store. Generations of women have found designer labels and high fashion at *Montaldo's*, 1630 Stout ☎ 629-1111. Also downtown is *Kohlberg's* ☎ 292-4578 with an excellent selection of Indian jewelry and crafts, and a resident Indian silversmith. Seventy shops, including *Brooks Brothers*, and 16 restaurants are enclosed in *The Shops* at Tabor Center ☎ 534-2141 an indoor retail complex on the 16th Street Mall. Two blocks S is *Larimer Square*, a one-block collection of boutiques and restaurants, housed in restored Victorian buildings on Denver's oldest street. The *Cherry Creek North* area, on 2nd and 3rd avenues between Josephine and Steele streets, is full of boutiques featuring high fashion, home decorations, jewelry and crafts.

Denver has two main sports stores: *Dave Cook Sporting Goods* ☎ 892-1929 near Larimer Square, and *Gart Brothers*, 1000 Broadway ☎ 861-1122. For cowboy gear, try *Miller Stockman*, 1409 15th St or *Sheplers* at I-25 and Orchard Rd.

Sightseeing

The most important sights in the city are the Denver Art Museum, the Natural History Museum and the Larimer Square area. If you have time, visit the Rocky Mountain National Park.

Colorado State Museum This modern museum provides a panorama of Colorado's history. *1300 Broadway* ☎ *866-3682.* Open *Tue–Sat, 10–5.30; Sun, noon–4.30.*
Denver Art Museum This 28-sided, fortress-like structure has collections of Spanish-American and Southwestern art, as well as an outstanding collection of American Indian art. *100 W 14th St* ☎ *575-2793. Open Tue, Thu, Fri and Sat, 9–5; Wed, 9–8; Sun, noon–5.*
Denver Museum of Natural History Dinosaurs that span entire rooms and lifelike dioramas are the principal attractions. It also has a four-story-screen IMAX theater. *17th St and Colorado Blvd* ☎ *370-6363. Open 9–5.*
Museum of Western Art One block from the Brown Palace Hotel, this private collection of Western paintings and sculpture includes works by Frederic Remington and Georgia O'Keeffe. *1727 Tremont Pl* ☎ *296-1880. Open Tue–Fri, 10–6; Sat, 10–5.*
United States Mint Throughout the summer, lines form for free, 20min tours of this mint which produces 5bn coins a year. *W Colfax Ave at Cherokee St* ☎ *844-3582. Open Mon–Fri, 8–3.*

Guided tours

Bus tours *Gray Line* ☎ 289-2841 runs a 2½hr bus tour of Denver's highlights. *Historic Denver* ☎ 534-1858 offers driving and walking tours.

Out of town

W of Denver, off 6th Avenue, *Red Rocks Park and Amphitheater* offers a panoramic view of Denver and the plains. Farther W, off I-70, is the *Buffalo Bill Museum and Grave.* About an hour out of Denver on I-25 is Colorado Springs and the *US Air Force Academy*, one of Colorado's most-visited attractions. In the same area are the *Cheyenne Mt Zoo*, the *Will Rogers Shrine* and many special-interest museums.

Spectator sports

Baseball *Denver Zephyrs* appear at Mile High Stadium ☎ 433-8645.
Basketball NBA Denver *Nuggets* play at McNichols Sports Arena ☎ 893-3865.
Football The *Broncos* play at Mile High Stadium ☎ 433-7466.

Keeping fit

Denver's dry, sunny climate lends itself to a wide variety of outdoor sports. Most of the city's major hotels have in-house fitness facilities or arrangements with private clubs. Local clubs open to visitors include the *International Athletic Club*, 1630 Welton St ☎ 623-2100 and the *YMCA*, 25 E 16th Ave ☎ 861-8300.
Golf There are six municipal courses. Most scenic is *Wellshire* ☎ 756-6318 with 18 holes, rental equipment and a good restaurant and lounge.
Jogging paths border Cherry Creek and the Platte River; together they extend for some 20 miles/32km.
Skiing Skiing begins within an hour W of Denver. Some of the closest resorts are *Loveland* ☎ 571-5580, *Keystone* ☎ 534-7712 and *Winter Park* ☎ 447-0588. Cross-country skiing is popular in the mountains (inquire at *Keystone* ☎ 468-2316 or *Snowmass* ☎ 892-7100) and – for the short time that snow remains on the ground in Denver – in the *Cherry Creek Reservoir* area as well.
Tennis The city has more than 150 public courts, including the 20-plus courts at *Gates Tennis Center* ☎ 355-4461.

Local resources

Business services

Two conveniently located firms that offer comprehensive, prompt services are *The Typehouse* ☎ 572-3486 and *Downtown Business Service* ☎ 777-2447.
Photocopying and Printing *Dodge*, 1240 14th St ☎ 623-8193, *Hirschfeld Press*, 5200 Smith Rd ☎ 320-8500 and *Stop & Go Printing*, 1800 Glenarm Pl ☎ 296-7867; all will pick up and deliver.

Secretarial Reliable agencies include *Kelly Services* ☎ 623-6262 and *Accountemps* ☎ 629-1010.
Translation *Berlitz Translation Services* ☎ 399-8686.

Communications

Local delivery *Speedy* ☎ 292-6000.
Long-distance delivery *United Parcel Service*, 6355 E 50th Ave ☎ 289-5311; *Federal Express* ☎ 892-7981.
Post office General information ☎ 297-6000. The main downtown station at 1823 Stout St ☎ 297-6016 is open 7–5.30; the Terminal Annex ☎ 297-6455 6.30am–9pm, with 24hr express mail.
Telex and telegram *Comspec Corporation* ☎ 773-3553 provides telex, TWX, and E-Mail services; for telegrams contact *Western Union* ☎ 573-6606.
Fax *American Fax Mail* ☎ 893-5656 has same day pick-up and delivery; *Network Facsimile Service* ☎ 320-8444 is open 24hrs with pick-up and delivery.

Conference/exhibition centers

Denver's major conference facility is the downtown *Currigan Exhibition Hall*, 14th and Champa ☎ 892-1112. The *Denver Merchandise Mart*, 451 E 58th Ave ☎ 292-6278 also hosts exhibitions.

Emergencies

Hospitals *Merry Medical Center*, 1650 Fillmore St ☎ 393-3000; emergency ☎ 393-3600. *Rose Medical Center*, 4567 E 9th Ave ☎ 320-2121; 24hr emergency ☎ 3290-2455. Emergency dental treatment is available at *St Anthony Central Dental Office*, 4231 W 16th Ave ☎ 629-3648. For doctor referral call *Med Search*, a free service of St Joseph Hospital ☎ 866-8000.
Pharmacies *Medisave Pharmacy*, 2 S Broadway ☎ 744-2721 has a 24hr answering service and is open Mon–Sat, 9–6; Sun, 11–3.
Police ☎ 534-2424.

Government offices

US Dept of Commerce/International Trade ☎ 844-3246; *US Customs* ☎ 361-0712; US *Immigration and Naturalization Service* ☎ 844-3526.

Information sources

Business information The *Denver Chamber of Commerce*, 1301 Welton St ☎ 534-3211 is a comprehensive source of business information.
Local media The *Denver Post* (business pullout Mon) and *Rocky Mountain News* (business pullout Tue), are both morning dailies providing national, regional and local coverage. For magazines, *Denver Business* and the *Rocky Mountain Business Journal* cover business; the *Daily Journal* publishes legal and construction news editions; *Colorado Business Magazine* covers area business developments. *Denver Magazine* profiles the city and its people, while *Colorado Homes & Lifestyles* features the state's architecture, leisure, and life-style.

The News Gallery, 13th and Sherman ☎ 830-2229, sells papers from around the country as well as a large selection of magazines. The *Tattered Cover Book Store*, 2930 E 2nd Ave ☎ 322-7727, also has an extensive magazine rack. Denver's *Central Library* is only a few blocks from the heart of downtown at 1357 Broadway ☎ 571-2052.
Tourist information The *Convention and Visitors' Bureau Information Center*, 225 W Colfax Ave ☎ 892-1505, provides special-event planning information, and an exhaustive collection of brochures.

Thank-yous

Florists Credit card orders are welcome at the *Brown Palace*, 335 17th St ☎ 292-3893 and *DE Miller* ☎ 399-3403.
Gift baskets *A Tisket A Tasket* ☎ 985-5297 accepts orders for personalized gift baskets, as does *Basket-Grams* ☎ 777-6676 and the *Brown Palace* ☎ 292-3893.

DETROIT

Area code ☏ 313

Detroit is dominated by the auto industry and its related suppliers and distributors. American Motors, Chrysler, Ford, General Motors and Volkswagen of America have headquarters here, as do Allied Automotive and Fruehauf. Non-related companies include American Natural Resources, Unisys, the Budd Company, Federal Mogul, K-Mart and Stroh's Brewery. The city's 20th century history is largely the story of car-makers, from the first Henry Ford and his contemporaries – Dodge, Olds and Fisher – to Henry Ford II and Lee Iacocca, who saved Chrysler from extinction in the early 1980s. The city covers some 900 square miles/2,300 sq km. For the business visitor, it can be like having appointments in Cologne, Dusseldorf and Bonn during a single trip to the German Rhineland, such is the measure of distance between Dearborn, Southfield and Troy, three of the major corporate and manufacturing areas. Only the financial center remains downtown near the still-busy Detroit River.

Arriving

Detroit Metropolitan Airport

DTW has two connected domestic terminals, with a Marriott hotel between them and concourses radiating out from each. The usual food, bar, telephone, gift and other services are available in both terminals. Mutual of Omaha booths provide office and messenger services, desk space to rent, as well as insurance and currency exchange. American Airlines, Delta, Northwest and United have first-class lounges. The international terminal is small; most overseas visitors clear Customs and Immigration at other points of entry. Information ☏ 942-3550.

Nearby hotels *Detroit Marriott*, Detroit Metropolitan Airport 48150 ☏ 941-9400. *Airport Hilton*, 31500 Wick Rd, Romulus 48174 ☏ 292-3400. *Holiday Inn*, 31200 Industrial Expressway, Romulus 48174 ☏ 728-2800. *Ramada*, 8270 Wickham Rd, Romulus 48174 ☏ 729-6300. *Sheraton*, 8600 Merriman Rd, Romulus 48174 ☏ 728-7900. All have courtesy pick-up service.

City link A car is really needed by anyone whose business is not confined to downtown. It is a 30min drive to downtown, 20min to Dearborn, 40min to Southfield, 60min to Troy.

Car rental All major companies have booths at the airport: Hertz ☏ 729-5200; Avis ☏ 942-3450; National ☏ 941-5030; Dollar ☏ 942-1905; and Budget ☏ 258-5877.

Taxi To get a cab, call as soon as you can – even before you claim your baggage. Reliable firms include Somerset Cab ☏ 689-9090 and Radio Cab ☏ 491-2600. Fares are about $15 to Dearborn, $21 downtown, $35 Troy.

Getting around

The metropolitan area has an excellent highway system, with rush hours 7.30–8.30, 4–5.30.

Taxi For short trips, taxis can be a useful alternative to driving yourself, but do not expect to hail a cab in the street: call ahead. *Checker Cab Co* ☏ 963-7000 has the largest fleet; alternatively try *Pacific Cab* ☏ 541-6880.

Car rental If you do not rent at the airport, major firms can be contacted easily from most business hotels. Parking is difficult and expensive downtown, but readily available elsewhere.

Limousine *Limousine Service* ☏ 471-0980.

Bus Services are limited and generally unreliable.

Area by area

Metropolitan Detroit has several business centers: downtown for conventions and financial firms; New Center, 3 miles/5km N, home of General Motors; Highland Park, 3 miles/5km farther, Chrysler's base; and Dearborn, 12 miles/19km W, Ford's administrative and manufacturing headquarters. Troy and Southfield are developing rapidly.

Downtown The downtown business area stretches half a mile N of the Detroit River between John Lodge and Chrysler freeways, marked US-10 and I-75 respectively. In this compact district are the Renaissance Center, the older established corridors of the Penobscot Building and the headquarters of American Natural Resources. Major Detroit banks, utility companies and accounting, insurance, legal and brokerage firms have offices in downtown.

Other areas Ford World Headquarters is at Michigan Avenue and Southfield Road, *Dearborn*, with dozens of Ford offices nearby. *Southfield*, along Northwestern Highway, is home to American Motors, Federal Mogul and Allied. *Troy* has K-Mart's world headquarters on Big Beaver Road and elegant shops in Somerset Mall. *Birmingham*, due N of Detroit on Woodward Avenue, is the center of an affluent residential area. Many of the city's oldest families live in *Grosse Pointe*; chief executives tend to be in *Bloomfield Hills*; middle managers live in western and northwestern suburban cities like Birmingham, Troy, West Bloomfield and Rochester.

Windsor, Ontario

Business travellers sometimes stay in or visit the small Canadian city of Windsor, a 5min drive across the river from downtown. GM, Ford and Chrysler have plants there. Non-US visitors should check whether they need a visa to enter and that their US visa allows re-entry. (Most visas are multiple entry.)

Hotels

Detroit has three major riverfront hotels in downtown – the Westin, Pontchartrain and Omni – all on the same block. In Dearborn there is the high-rise glass of the Hyatt Regency or the genteel warmth of the Dearborn Inn. The other suburban areas are served mostly by the chains and suite hotels.

Dearborn Inn $$$

20301 Oakwood Blvd, Dearborn 48124
☏ 271-2700 • 171 rooms, 6 suites, 2 restaurants, 1 bar, 1 coffee shop

Ford executives who like old-fashioned comforts opt for this red-brick inn, built by Henry Ford in 1931. It is still a center of Dearborn social life and is popular with many local business people for lunch or after-work cocktails in the Early American Room. The Snug bar is also much favored. Bedrooms are small and filled with antiques and the hotel's Georgian-style elegance and ambiance are complemented by good leisure facilities. Gift shop • pool, tennis, arrangements with nearby health club and golf course • 7 meeting rooms.

Hyatt Regency Dearborn $$$

Fairlane Town Center, Dearborn 48125
☏ 593-1234 TX 235613 • 766 rooms, 42 suites, 3 restaurants, 3 bars, 1 coffee shop

Connected by monorail to the adjacent Fairlane shopping mall, this contemporary crescent-shaped hotel with a 16-story atrium lobby and bronze-mirrored walls is owned and frequented by Ford Motor Company. La Rôtisserie offers fine food and good service, and Guilio's restaurant

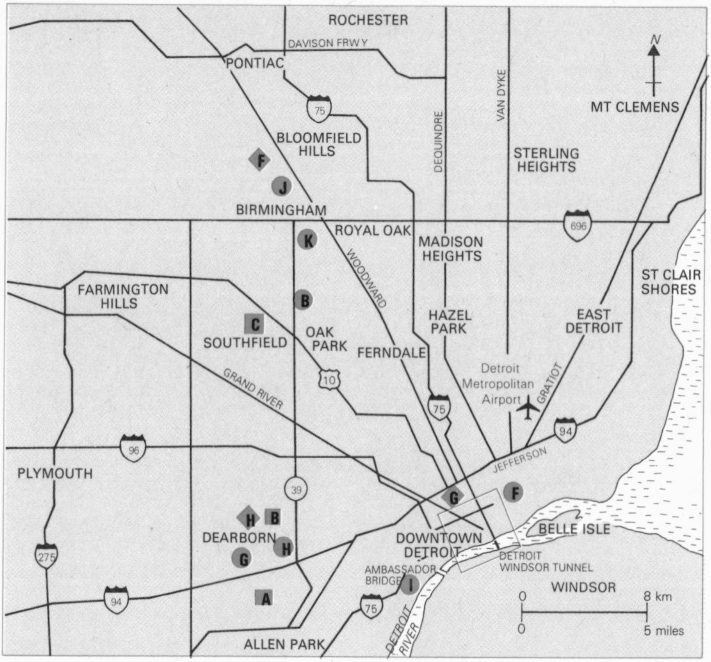

is much used by Ford and other office workers. There is dancing in the rooftop Rotunda at night. Gift shop, florist • pool, sauna, whirlpool, arrangements with nearby health club • 30 meeting rooms.

Michigan Inn $$$$
16400 JL Hudson Dr, Southfield 48075 ☎ 559-6500 • 412 rooms, 12 suites, 2 restaurants, 1 bar, 1 coffee shop
On the edge of a large and slightly seedy shopping area, but with good freeway access, this full-service low-rise hotel is well-appointed, and its Benchmark restaurant has a fine menu. Southfield alternatives are chain hotels like the high-rise Holiday Inn and Hilton or suite hotels. Beauty/barber salon, gift shop, florist • pool, tennis, putting green, sauna • 18 meeting rooms.

Omni International $$$$
333 East Jefferson Ave 48226 ☎ 222-7700 TX 5106002912 • 240 rooms, 18 suites, 1 restaurant, 1 bar
Smaller and more residential in feel than others in the city, this modern hotel is part of Detroit's attempt to revitalize downtown. It occupies 21 floors of the Millender Center and is connected to the Rennaissance Center by a skywalk. The restaurant, 333 East, is smart, with a menu featuring *nouvelle cuisine*. Pharmacy • tennis, jogging, racquetball, pool, sauna, massage, weight training equipment • 4 meeting rooms.

Pontchartrain $$$$
2 Washington Blvd 48226 ☎ 965-0200 TX 8102215227 • Crescent Hotels • 385 rooms, 36 suites, 2 restaurants, 2 bars
The glass-sided "Pontch," as locals call it, overlooks the river and is close to the convention center on Jefferson Avenue. It gives first-class personal service, and its bars, seafood restaurant and Friday night rooftop jazz concerts are popular with downtown business people. Gift shop, complimentary executive

HOTELS		RESTAURANTS	H	Fairlane Charley's	◆	BUILDINGS AND SIGHTS
A	Dearborn Inn	A	Caucus Club		Steak House	A	City-County Building
B	Hyatt Regency Dearborn	B	Golden Mushroom	I	Kyoto Japanese	B	Cobo Hall
C	Michigan Inn	C	Joe Muer Sea Food		Steak House	C	Visitors' Information Center
D	Omni International	D	London Chop House	J	Peabody's	D	Renaissance Center
E	Pontchartrain	E	Pontchartrain Wine Cellars	K	Restaurant	E	Tiger Stadium
F	St Regis	F	Van Dyke Place		Duglass	F	Cranbrook Educational Institute
G	Westin	G	Chambertin			G	Detroit Institute of Arts
H	Days Inn Detroit		Early American Room			H	Greenfield Village;
	Downtown		(Hotel A)				Henry Ford Museum

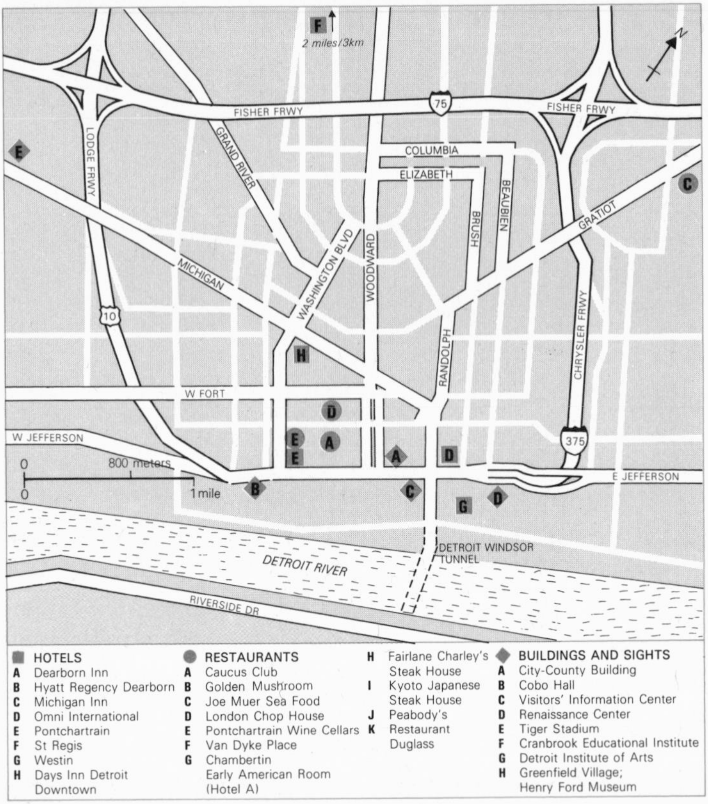

limousine in the downtown area and to GM and Ford offices • health club/spa, pool • 9 meeting rooms, teleconferencing.

St Regis $$$$
3071 W Grand Blvd 48202
☎ *873-3000* ℡ *235500 • Rank Hotels • 109 rooms, 8 suites, 1 restaurant, 1 bar*
After a period of decline, this once-excellent establishment has been restored and now caters primarily to General Motors executives, who can simply walk across the skyway bridge to GM World Headquarters. Its rooms have sleeping areas separate from the lounge/meeting space. The St Regis has an elegant dining room, and offers afternoon tea, Sunday brunch, a summer outdoor café

(noisy, but pleasant), and evening piano music in the lobby. Its discreet bar is a favorite for after-business drinks. Four meeting rooms.

Westin $$$$
Renaissance Center on Jefferson at St Antoine 48243 ☎ *568-8000* ℡ *755156 • 1,321 rooms, 69 suites, 2 restaurants, 4 bars, 1 coffee shop*
Detroit's biggest and best for big conventions, the Westin is a popular choice for senior executives with business in the Renaissance Center. Labyrinthine passages lead off the vast and confusing atrium lobby to adjacent RenCen office towers. The 73rd-floor Summit restaurant revolves, and the main dining room, La Fontaine, is very highly regarded.

The Westin has by far the best downtown business services, including word-processing and typewriter rental. Adjacent shopping mall (with post office) • health club, pool, sauna, jacuzzi, outdoor jogging track • 27 meeting rooms.

OTHER HOTELS

Days Inn Detroit Downtown ($$) *231 Michigan Ave 48226 ☎ 965-4646.* A 287-room high-rise on the trolley line five blocks N of the river and convention center.

Clubs

The finest Detroit clubs, catering to highly placed CEOs and executive VPs, are the *Detroit Athletic Club*, 241 Madison ☎ 963-9200 and the *Detroit Club*, 712 Caff ☎ 963-8600. Both offer dining, reading and meeting rooms; the former also has facilities for swimming and handball, and recently bowed to changing times and began admitting women members. Another old-line club, the *University Club*, 1411 E Jefferson ☎ 567-9280 is located in its own building and offers members a soothing, dark-paneled retreat where they can read by cozy fireplaces. A somewhat younger crowd can be found at the *Renaissance Club*, 2000 Renaissance Center ☎ 259-4700 and the *Fairlane Club*, 5000 Woodview ☎ 336-4400. The latter, located in Dearborn, caters to the Ford upper echelon, while GM people are more likely to frequent the *Recess Club* in the Fisher Building ☎ 875-3554 across from GM Headquarters in downtown Detroit. For reporters, television and public relations people, the *Detroit Press Club*, 516 Howard ☎ 962-3090 provides a more informal atmosphere, and is the site of many of the city's press conferences.

Restaurants

Metropolitan Detroit has two distinct dining styles: international cuisine in cosmopolitan, often hotel-based, settings; and tiny neighborhood restaurants that reflect the varied heritage of the city's auto workers. Many restaurants are of the steak and chop variety.

Caucus Club $$

150 W Congress, 17 Penobscot Bldg ☎ 965-4970 • D only Sat, L only Mon; closed Sun • AE CB DC MC V

Local executives meet here for chophouse-style food, a good wine list and prompt service in a warm, clubby setting. An old local favorite, on the ground floor of the Penobscot Building, the Caucus has always attracted a weighty business crowd.

Golden Mushroom $$$

18100 West Ten Mile Rd, Southfield ☎ 559-4230 • D only Sat; closed Sun • AE CB DC MC V

Chef Milos Cihelka was the first Master Chef in the USA, and many community names come here to enjoy the low-calorie, low-cholestoral cuisine and excellent wines. It is just as renowned for its superb, calorie-packed pâté. Especially popular for business lunches in the Southfield area. The atmosphere is informal, and its mahogany booths ensure privacy.

Joe Muer Sea Food $$

2000 Gratiot Ave ☎ 567-1088 • D only Sat; closed Sun • AE CB DC MC V • no reservations

The lines outside are testimony to the popularity of Detroit's oldest seafood restaurant. The atmosphere is informal and relaxing, the fish superb. They do not take reservations but will serve you a cocktail as you wait.

London Chop House $$$$

155 West Congress St ☎ 962-0278 • closed Sun • AE CB DC MC V

This atmospheric basement

restaurant is where you are most likely to see Detroit's high flyers and international celebrities. It is a good place to impress downtown clients, and the Continental cuisine is much acclaimed.

Pontchartrain Wine Cellars $$
234 Larned ☏ 963-1785 • D only Sat; closed Sun • AE CB DC MC V
This intimate downtown French-style bistro is usually packed with business people and leaders of Detroit society. The menu includes outstanding veal and seafood dishes, and the wines are excellent.

Van Dyke Place $$$$
649 Van Dyke ☏ 821-2620 • L only Mon; closed Sun • AE MC V • reservations essential
You have to make a reservation at least six weeks ahead for dinner, a week ahead for lunch at this highly esteemed and elegantly restored mansion on the city's East Side. One of the city's best restaurants, with an extensive and choice wine list, the Van Dyke is an ideal place to celebrate a successful deal.

Other restaurants
Around the Fairlane Center and Ford World Headquarters in Dearborn are the *Kyoto Japanese Steak House*, 18601 Hubbard Dr ☏ 593-3200 and *Fairlane Charley's*, 700 Town Center Dr ☏ 336-8550, both popular local choices for informal meals. Ford people with business to discuss head to the quiet tables of the *Early American Room* at the Dearborn Inn, 20301 Oakwood Blvd ☏ 271-2700 or to the *Chambertin* in the Holiday Inn, 22900 Michigan Ave ☏ 278-6900. Residents of the affluent northern suburbs favor *Restaurant Duglass*, 29269 Southfield Rd, Southfield ☏ 424-9244 and *Peabody's*, 154 S Hunter Blvd, Birmingham ☏ 644-5222.

Bars
Business people who want to meet just for a cocktail or beer and a quiet talk tend to choose the bars in the city's hotels – whether it is a small booth in the atrium lobby of the *Westin*, a wing chair in the Golden Eagle lounge of the *Dearborn Inn*, the lobby of the *Omni*, or a corner table at the *Kingsley Inn*, 1475 N Woodward, Bloomfield Hills. But apart from the hotels, there are *Galligan's*, 519 E Jefferson, across the street from Renaissance Center, especially the roof bar in summer; *River Rock Café*, 673 Franklin, in Rivertown E of Renaissance Center, with a main floor bar and balcony bar for rock music lovers; and there is video music in the bar at *Monroe's*, 508 Monroe atop Trappers Alley in Greektown.

Entertainment
The *Detroit Symphony Orchestra* plays at Ford Auditorium on the riverfront in winter ☏ 567-9000, outdoors at Meadow Brook Music Festival on the Oakland University campus in Rochester in summer ☏ 377-3316. Major rock music events are held at *Cobo Arena* or *Joe Louis Arena* on the riverfront or N at *Pine Knob*. Touring Broadway shows come to the *Fisher Theater* in the New Center ☏ 872-1000 or *Masonic Auditorium*, 500 Temple, downtown ☏ 832-2232.

Shopping
Three huge shopping centers dominate the suburban scene: *Fairlane Town Center*, Dearborn; *Twelve Oaks Mall*, Novi; and *Lakeside Center*, Sterling Heights. The *World of Shops* in the Renaissance Center has boutiques and shops selling everything from gourmet food to clothes; *Trappers Alley*, at Festival Marketplace in Greektown, has scores of specialty and novelty shops. *Maple Road*, in Birmingham, is one of the area's most pleasant shopping streets.

Sightseeing
For many business visitors based in outlying areas, sightseeing must include a trip downtown to see the

modern development of Detroit's inner city. Farther afield, some travellers take advantage of Canada's proximity and attend the Shakespeare theaters in Stratford, Ontario or go to Ann Arbor, beautiful home of the University of Michigan.
Cranbrook Educational Institute Includes a science museum, art gallery and gardens. *500 Lone Pine Rd, Bloomfield Hills ☎ 645-3210.*
Detroit Institute of Arts Impressionist, Dutch-Flemish and African art, plus personal effects of Louis XIV and Diego Rivera murals of the auto world. *5200 Woodward ☎ 833-7900.*
Greenfield Village This 260-acre village, together with the *Henry Ford Museum*, comprise the biggest single indoor-outdoor museum complex in North America; to see everything would take at least two days. The village has the house where Henry Ford was born, Thomas Edison's Menlo Park laboratory, the Wright brothers' bicycle shop and Harvey Firestone's farm. *23 Oakwood Blvd, Dearborn ☎ 271-1620.*

Spectator sports

Baseball The *Detroit Tigers* play at Tiger Stadium, Trumball at Michigan Ave ☎ 962-4000.
Basketball The *Pistons* appear at the Silverdome, 1200 Featherstone, Pontiac ☎ 338-4500.
Football The *Lions* kick off at the Silverdome, 1200 Featherstone, Pontiac ☎ 335-4151.
Horse racing The two most popular tracks are *Hazel Park Harness Raceway*, 1650 East Ten Mile Rd, Hazel Park ☎ 398-1000 and *Ladbrokes Detroit Race Course*, 28001 Schoolcraft Rd, Livonia ☎ 525-7300.
Ice Hockey Detroit's *Red Wings* play at Joe Louis Arena, 600 Civic Center Dr ☎ 567-6000.

Keeping fit

Most Detroit hotels have pools and either a fitness center or arrangements for guests with private health clubs. Some Dearborn hotels have guest privileges at the Fairlane Club ☎ 336-4400 which has indoor and outdoor tennis courts.
Jogging Downtown fitness fanatics congregate on Belle Isle, and there are frequent city marathons.
Sailing You can rent sailboats and motorboats at St Claire Shores.
Skiing When the snow is right, Mt Brighton ☎ 229-9581 is just a 1hr drive from downtown; an alternative is Alpine Valley, W of Pontiac ☎ 887-4183.
Golf *Oakland Hills Country Club* is considered by some the area's best private club. Public courses include the *University of Michigan* course in Ann Arbor ☎ 663-5005; the *Oakland University* course N in Rochester ☎ 370-4150; and the *Rackham* in Huntington Woods ☎ 398-8430.

Local resources

Business services

Photocopying and printing There are copy shops all over downtown Detroit, but for pick-up and delivery contact *National Reproductions Corp*, 443 E Larned ☎ 961-5252 which has 12 offices metro-wide, with at least one providing 24hr service. In downtown, *American Speedy Printing Center*, 525 E Jefferson ☎ 963-3600 is open 24hrs.
Secretarial *Employers Temporary Services Inc*, 11220 Whittier Ave ☎ 372-7700; *Kelly Services Inc*, 100 Renaissance Center, Suite 1650 ☎ 259-1400.
Translation *Berlitz Translation Service* ☎ 874-2777 downtown; ☎ 642-9335 northern suburbs.

Communications

Local delivery *Direct Delivery*, 34th floor, Book Bldg ☎ 962-0202 for same-day metro-wide deliveries. *United Parcel Service* ☎ 261-8500 is used by many firms for reliable next-day local service, but they need 24hrs notice for pick-up.
Long-distance delivery *Federal Express* ☎ 961-8771. *Purolator* ☎ (800) 645-3333 is popular for Canadian destinations.

Post office The main downtown office, 1401 W Fort ☎ 226-8675 has a 24hr stamp machine; Dearborn office, 3800 Greenfield Rd ☎ 337-4728. The Troy office, 2844 Livernois ☎ 689-6262 and the Southfield office, 22200 W 11 Mile Rd ☎ 357-3310 both have a 24hr self-service lobby.
Telex *Financial Exchange of Michigan*, 536 Shelby ☎ 962-7296.

Conference/exhibition centers
Cobo Hall, on the riverfront downtown, has 400,000 square feet of exhibition space and will almost double that by 1988. Contact *Detroit Civic Center*, 7 Washington Blvd ☎ 224-1010, or *Metropolitan Detroit Convention and Visitors' Bureau* ☎ 259-4333.

Emergencies
Hospitals *Henry Ford Hospital*, W Grand Blvd ☎ 876-2600 is in New Center area; for emergencies or doctor appointments ☎ 593-8100 in Dearborn, ☎ 254-1670 in Sterling Heights, ☎ 689-5200 in Troy and ☎ 661-4100 in West Bloomfield. AE MC V accepted. *Beaumont Hospitals* ☎ 288-8000 in Royal Oak and ☎ 828-5100 in Troy accept MC and V.
Pharmacies *Perry Drugs* has metro-wide locations open daily; some are open 24hr, including that at 5650 Schaefer, Dearborn ☎ 581-3280.
Police City of Detroit, 1300 Beaubien ☎ 224-4400; Dearborn ☎ 943-2240; Oakland County Sheriff ☎ 858-5000; Wayne County Sheriff ☎ 224-2222; state police ☎ 256-9636.

Government offices
US Federal Information Center ☎ 226-7016; *US Customs* ☎ 226-3158; *US Dept of Commerce/International Trade* ☎ 226-3650; *City of Detroit* ☎ 935-4700.

Information sources
Business information *Greater Detroit Chamber of Commerce*, 150 Michigan Ave ☎ 964-4000 offers information about local companies and development prospects.
Local media *Detroit Free Press* is the city's morning daily favored by liberal readers; *Detroit News*, a morning and afternoon daily, is larger and more conservative. Both have daily business pages and Sunday business sections. *Metropolitan Detroit* and *Detroit Monthly* are magazines with good coverage of the city's dining and entertainment scene.
Tourist information *Metropolitan Detroit Convention and Visitors' Bureau*, 100 Renaissance Center, Suite 1950 ☎ 259-4333. For a recorded list of current events ☎ 298-6262. For state information contact *Michigan Travel Bureau* ☎ (800) 292-2520.

Thank-yous
Florists Floraline International, *1 Parklane, Dearborn* ☎ *(800) 221-4417* provides a 24hr flower or gift basket service.
Gift baskets Detroit Sampler Co, *11849 E Seven Mile Rd* ☎ *527-0080* takes telephone credit card orders.

HOUSTON

Area code ☎ 713

Although Houston is the nation's third largest port, a center for international finance, home of Texas Medical Center, NASA, dozens of major corporations and a wide range of manufacturing enterprises, the city's economy is driven by oil and oil-related industries. The oil recession had a profound effect, changing Houstonian attitudes from permanent optimism to introspection. To counter its economic collapse, the city demands relatively low taxes and no corporate or personal income tax. Developers have cut rents to fill empty office space in exchange for long-term leases; housing is inexpensive and many developers from both inside and outside the city are investing in cheap real estate, waiting for oil and the city to make a comeback.

Since the oil business went into decline, diversification has become the trend. Scientific and biotechnological companies have started in far north Houston; the Texas Medical Center continues to expand; and Clear Lake in SE Houston is the home of the commercial space industry. Major firms include Texas Commerce and First City banks; law firms Vinson & Elkins and Baker & Botts; engineering and construction companies Brown & Root and Turner, Collie and Braden; and developers such as Walter Mischer, Gerald Hines, Kenneth Schnitzer and Friendswood Corporation. It is a city where even the most important chief executive is likely to take a business visitor (especially an international one) home to meet his family or to his club.

Arriving

Houston Intercontinental Airport

IAH has three terminals, A, B and C, and a hotel between B and C. Each terminal has a 24hr bar and coffee shop, and lounges for first-class passengers. Terminal A handles domestic, B and C international flights. The three terminals and the Marriott Hotel are linked by a free, 24hr "people mover." Clearing Customs takes 60–90min. Currency exchange is available in each terminal. The white paging telephones provide 24hr multilingual information. Airport information ☎ 230-3000.

Nearby hotels *Hilton Houston Airport*, 500 North Belt E 77060 ☎ 931-0101. *Hotel Sofitel*, 425 N Beltway 8 ☎ 445-9000. *Marriott Intercontinental Airport*, 18700 Kennedy Blvd 77032 ☎ 443-2310. *Sheraton Crown*, 15700 Drummet Blvd 77032 ☎ 442-5100.

City link Depending on the time of day, road construction and weather conditions, it can take 45min–2hrs to make the 22-mile/35km journey into downtown Houston. Cabs, buses and limousines are available at the S exit of each terminal near the baggage claim area; rental car and helicopter service are also available. Getting to the airport in the evening rush hour is such a nightmare that the helicopter journey is well worth the fare. Ask your airline or travel agent if a discount is available.

Taxi The fare to downtown Houston is about $25, though passengers may share a cab.

Bus An express bus service is run by Texas Bus Lines ☎ 523-8888 every 20min to four stops: the downtown Hyatt Park Regency, the Galleria–Post Oak area, the South Main terminal and (exc Sat and Sun) Greenway Plaza.

Rental car Rental cars are available at the W exit of the baggage claim area in each terminal. Companies include Avis ☎ 443-2130; Hertz ☎ 443-0800; National ☎ 443-8850; and Dollar Rent-A-Car ☎ 449-0161. *Helicopter* Air Link ☎ 975-8989 services depart every 30min, Mon–Fri, from Terminal C, gate 17. Helicopters land at the West Chase Hilton near the Galleria, and at the Park 10 complex on I-10 in Far West Houston. The fare is $45.

William P Hobby Airport

Accessible by either the 610 Loop or I-45, Hobby Airport is 9 miles/14km SE of downtown and is used by domestic and commuter services.
City link *Hobby Airport Limousine Service* ☎ 644-8359 is available to downtown for $4. For rental cars, *Avis* ☎ 641-0531; *Hertz* ☎ 941-6821; *Ashbaugh* ☎ 649-2751; and *National* ☎ 641-0533.
Nearby hotel *Hobby Airport Hilton*, 8181 Airport Blvd 77061 ☎ 645-3000.

Getting around

Three major arteries intersect Houston: highway 59 and Interstates 10 and 45. (Houstonians often refer to freeways by their names rather than their numbers.) Loop 610 circles the city, and is often the best choice for getting quickly to your destination. If possible avoid major streets, especially Westheimer, and all freeways during rush hours (7–9, 4–6; Fri 3–7).
Car rental A car is essential for travelling in Houston. See *City link* for the two airports.
Taxi Taxi fares in sprawling Houston can be very high. You cannot hail a cab on the street, but the following companies are reliable: *Liberty Cab* ☎ 695-6700, *Yellow Cab* ☎ 236-1111 and *Sky-Jacks* ☎ 523-6080.

Area by area

Houston is sharply divided, with the Hispanic and black working classes living on the E side of town, close to the Ship Channel and manufacturing and construction sites. SE suburban towns such as Pasadena, Deer Park and Galena Park are where blue-collar workers live. The middle class has moved to the SW, W and to the far northern suburbs. The major freeways are lined with office blocks.
The Loop The 610 Loop is a vital part of the freeway system, and serves as a geographical boundary, with homes, businesses and cultural activities designated as being inside

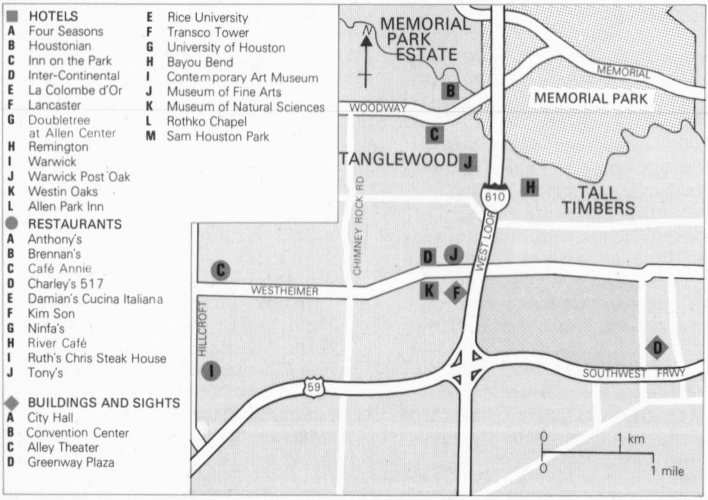

or outside the Loop. Although most of the biggest corporations, banks and law firms are situated downtown, the Galleria–Post Oak district, just outside the Loop on the W side, is a major office and shopping area. Greenway Plaza, inside the Loop on US highway 59, is another important business and entertainment center.

Montrose and the Heights Inside the Loop are Houston's older, more established neighborhoods. Few live downtown, which is mainly deserted after dark. The Montrose area just W of downtown has the museums, galleries, top-class nightclubs and restaurants, as well as some sleazier zones. To the N of the city center is the Heights, where many grand 19thC houses have been restored.

River Oaks River Oaks, inside the Loop to the W of downtown, is the homebase of Houston wealth. Established in the 1920s, the area displays both the good taste and the vulgarity of oil money.

Other areas Some small inner-city neighborhoods such as Courtlandt Place and the area around Rice University have been elegantly maintained, and are a little more subdued than River Oaks. Young professionals have gentrified the modest – though high-priced – homes in the neighborhood of West University Place. Many wealthy Houstonians prefer the Memorial area, with ranch-style houses on large, pine-filled lots to the W of River Oaks and outside the Loop. Other Houston professionals live to the SE in Clear Lake, near the NASA complex. The area has good boating and fishing, yet is only a 30–45min drive to downtown and even nearer the petrochemical plants that line the banks of the 50-mile/80km Ship Channel.

Hotels

Houston hotels have been hit hard by the oil recession. The once-grand Shamrock Hilton is to become a parking lot; the downtown Sheraton has closed. But the hotels that do remain are thoroughly geared to the needs of the business traveller.

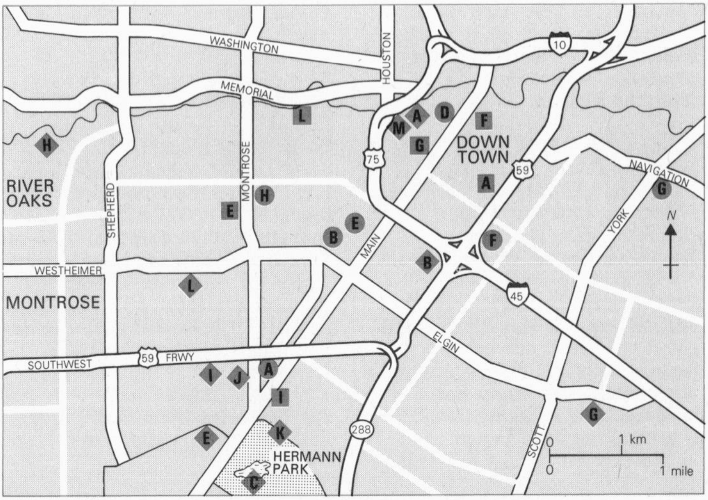

Doubletree at Allen Center $$$$
400 Dallas 77002 ☏ 759-0202
TX 762544 • 353 rooms, 32 suites, 2 restaurants
Formerly owned by the French Meridien chain, the Doubletree is downtown across the street from the Public Library and close to City Hall. With marble floors, tapestries and exotic flowers, it still retains its sophisticated French elegance. The dining room is a comfortable place for a working lunch. Good business center with copy machines and secretarial services. Access to nearby health club • 6 meeting rooms.

Four Seasons $$$$
1300 Lamar St 77010 ☏ 650-1300
TX 784653 • 377 rooms, 140 suites, 3 restaurants, 2 bars, 3 coffee shops
Convenient to the George R Brown Convention Center, the contemporary Four Seasons has become an important downtown meeting place. Visiting politicians drop in on the city council's weekly breakfast club, which often meets in the coffee shop. Business people use the quiet and comfortable first-floor bar and restaurant for lunch. Complimentary limousine service to downtown, antique store • pool, whirlpool, sauna, access to nearby health club • 12 meeting rooms, fax, translation, teleconferencing, recording facilities.

Houstonian $$$$
111 North Post Oak Ln 77024
☏ 686-2626 TX 791810 • 229 rooms, 17 suites, 2 restaurants, 2 bars
The Houstonian Hotel and Conference Center was built for the fitness-conscious business traveller. On a wooded, 22-acre lot near the Galleria area, the Houstonian offers guests access to fitness center facilities including two swimming pools, racquetball, tennis and basketball, and a jogging trail. The Houston Press Club gathers in the second-floor bar Thursday evenings. Thirty three meeting rooms, computer rentals.

Inn on the Park $$$$
4 Riverway 77056 ☏ 871-8181
TX 794510 • 344 rooms, 10 suites, 1 restaurant, 1 bar
One of the Four Seasons chain, this hotel is noted for its black swans and contemporary outdoor sculpture. It has a fine *nouvelle cuisine* restaurant, an English pub and a health club with swimming, cycling and jogging. Thirteen meeting rooms, fax, translation.

Inter-Continental $$$$
5150 Westheimer 77056 ☏ 961-1500
TX 755704 • 476 rooms, 42 suites, 2 restaurants, 4 bars
In the heart of the Galleria shopping district, the Inter-Continental is another favorite with fitness enthusiasts. The hotel is decorated in marble and hardwood with art by contemporary Houston artists. Rooms have three phones, including one in the bathroom (bathrooms also have color TV). The hotel aims to appeal particularly to the businesswoman; there are full-length mirrors, hairdriers and skirt hangers in each room. Drugstore, hair salon, gift shops • health club, pool, tennis, sauna, whirlpool, racquetball • 9 meeting rooms.

La Colombe d'Or $$$$$
3410 Montrose 77006 ☏ 524-7999
TX 272525 • 6 suites, 1 restaurant
In the Montrose center, La Colombe d'Or is a refurbished mansion, with just six suites. Each has a separate dining room and all except the spacious penthouse are furnished with French antiques and open fireplaces. There is a well-stocked library and excellent restaurant, with Continental cuisine and an extensive wine cellar. The clientele is thoroughly VIP.

Lancaster $$$$
701 Texas Ave 77002 ☏ 228-9500
TX 790506 • 85 rooms, 8 suites, 1 restaurant

When West Texas oilman T Boone Pickens comes to town to work on a takeover, he first takes over a suite at the tiny downtown Lancaster. The rooms are charmingly decorated, and each has three or four telephones and a sitting area adaptable for small meetings. The crowded grill is a popular lunch spot. Computers are available on request. Access to nearby health club • 3 meeting rooms.

Remington $$$$$
1919 Briar Oaks Ln 77027
☎ 840-7600 TX 765536 • 221 rooms, 27 suites, 3 restaurants
An intimate hotel decorated in marble, wood and French tapestries, the Remington offers excellent personalized service. Bankers from the nearby Galleria area often hold business breakfasts and lunches here; private dinners for up to eight can be arranged in the wine cellar. Adjacent to the heliport. Five meeting rooms, law library, teleconferencing.

Warwick $$$$
5701 Main 77251 ☎ 526-1991
TX 762590 • 250 rooms, 49 suites, 3 restaurants
Across from the Museum of Fine Arts on the edge of Hermann Park, and a short cab ride to the Texas Medical Center, the Warwick is elegantly furnished, with European wood paneling and Aubusson tapestries. It is the first choice for many visiting corporate VIPs, politicians and celebrities. Complimentary health-club facilities at the nearby Houston Club • 7 meeting rooms.

Warwick Post Oak $$$$
2001 Post Oak Blvd 77056
☎ 961-9300 TX 795315 • 455 rooms, 63 suites, 2 restaurants, 2 bars
In a parklike setting, the Post Oak has Oriental furnishings in the public areas; the rooms are country French in style, with telephones on the ample desks as well as by the bed. Seven meeting rooms.

Westin Oaks $$$$
5011 Westheimer 77056 ☎ 623-4300
TX 4990983 • 400 rooms, 20 suites, 2 restaurants
The Westin's large rooms are decorated in earth tones and pastels; some are furnished with antiques and all have well stocked refrigerators. Useful for those with business in the Galleria, the hotel is within the huge shopping mall. Non-smoking rooms • pool, health club • 11 meeting rooms, fax.

OTHER HOTELS

Allen Park Inn ($$$) *2121 Allen Pkwy 77019 ☎ 521-9321.* About a mile from the downtown area; 24hr restaurant.

Restaurants

Houston restaurants tend to specialize in regional and ethnic foods: Creole, barbeque, seafood, Chinese, Vietnamese and Mexican. The emphasis is not so much on elegant service and elaborate recipes, as on big servings, fresh ingredients, lots of liquor and wine, and a casual atmosphere.

Anthony's $$$$
4611 Montrose ☎ 524-1922 • closed Sun • AE MC V
This Montrose lunch spot is the favorite of Houston's smart social set. Excellent antipasti, pasta, crab and salmon.

Brennan's $$$$
3300 Smith ☎ 522-9711 • AE CB DC MC V • jacket required
The Brennan family became famous for Creole food in New Orleans, and maintains its tradition in Houston. In a beautifully renovated brick house just S of downtown, the restaurant

attracts many business diners. The seafood and the Sunday brunch are especially recommended.

Café Annie $$$
5860 Westheimer ☎ *780-1522 • L only Sat and Sun; closed Mon • AE CB DC MC*
Even his competitors call owner-chef Robert Del Grande the most innovative restaurateur in town: his regional experiments include redfish baked in a sesame crust with coriander and Texas venison with chestnut ravioli. There is a quiet bar at the front, and the dining room tables are well-spaced.

Charley's 517 $$$$
517 Lousiana ☎ *224-4438 • L only Sat; closed Sun • AE CB DC MC V • jacket and tie required*
A huge wine list, a gleaming, mirrored interior and the best lamb around attracts the business community at lunchtime and theater, symphony- and opera-goers in the evening. One of the few fine restaurants downtown.

Damian's Cucina Italiana $$$
3001 Smith ☎ *522-0439 • L only Sat; closed Sun • AE DB DC MC V*
This boisterous restaurant is not a fancy spot, but is still a favorite for casual business entertaining and top-class Italian food.

Kim Son $
1801 St Emmanuel ☎ *222-2461 • AE DC MC V*
Vietnamese immigrants have introduced their cuisine to Houston. Kim Son, one of several Vietnamese restaurants, is large, modestly priced and slightly noisy; it is used by many Houston businessmen as well as Vietnamese locals. Recommended are barbequed pork with vermicelli, spring rolls with shrimp and fresh mint, and fresh crabs with lemon and black pepper.

Ninfa's $
2704 Navigation Blvd ☎ *228-1175 • AE CB MC V*
In a poor Hispanic neighborhood, this was the first of Ninfa Laurenzo's chain of popular restaurants, and is still preferred by many business people. The specialties are *tacos al carbon* with flour tortillas, washed down with powerful margaritas or Mexican beer.

River Café $$
3615 Montrose ☎ *529-0088 • D only Sat • AE CB DC MC V*
The River Café is an established meeting place for artists and journalists, with a fine bar, plenty of elbow room and a mesquite grill that offers fish, steak and sausage with inventive sauces.

Ruth's Chris Steak House $$$
6213 Richmond ☎ *789-2333 • D only Sat • AE CB DC MC V*
With oil company logos plastered on the walls, this steak house was the independent oilmen's meeting place until the oil depression. It still offers massive pieces of well-marbled, aged beef and powerful martinis.

Tony's $$$$
1801 S Post Oak Blvd ☎ *622-6778 • D only Sat; closed Sun • AE CB DC MC V • jacket and tie required*
With its mixture of Continental and *nouvelle* dishes, its huge wine cellar (with over 100,000 bottles), and its resident gossip columnist (Maxine Messinger of the *Houston Chronicle*), Tony's is *the* place to be seen in Houston, and one that will impress any top-ranking client or contact.

Clubs

The *Coronado* is the meeting place of the city's biggest names. The *Petroleum Club* attracts corporate oil executives. One of the city's oldest clubs, the *Houston*, is often used for working breakfasts. Many lawyers belong to the *Ramada Club*, and up-and-coming business people lunch at the *Houston City Club*, a short drive from downtown at Greenway Plaza. The city's two most important country clubs are the *Houston Country Club* and *River Oaks*.

Bars

Hotel bars are the business favorites for a quiet drink. *Remington's*, in particular (in the hotel of the same name) is known for its wide selection of cognac and port. Of the independent bars, *La Carafe*, 813 Congress, in one of Houston's few 19thC buildings downtown on Market Square, features Piaf and Streisand on the jukebox, and a varied clientele. *Grif's Inn*, 3416 Roseland, is the Montrose sports bar. *Paradise Bar and Grill*, 401 McGowen, on the edge of downtown, is a meeting place for professionals and liberal politicians. *Marfreless*, 2006 Peden, offers classical music, sofas, dim lighting and elegant décor. *Cody's*, 3400 Montrose, has a 10th-floor view and is a popular after-work spot. Houston is also the home of the "ice house," a beer joint that grows up around a tiny grocery store. Most are working-class establishments, but *Timothy's Montrose Icehouse*, 2009 W Dallas, is much used by local actors and artists.

Entertainment

Houston has top-class companies in opera, ballet, symphony and theater, and the opening of the twin-theater Wortham Center in 1987 gives the opera and ballet a glamorous new base. Houston also has several comedy clubs, and a wide variety of touring performances. For information and tickets, contact *Showtix* ☎ 227-9292 or *Ticketron* ☎ 526-1709.

Nightclubs The most famous nightclub in the area – in Pasadena, to the SE – is *Gilley's*, 4500 Spencer Hwy ☎ 941-7990 which has top country performers. *Rockefeller's*, 3620 Washington ☎ 861-9365 attracts top rock 'n' roll and blues musicians; *Fitzgerald's*, 2706 White Oak ☎ 862-7580 is its rival, with everything from country to jazz. *Anderson Fair*, 2007 Grant ☎ 528-8576 is a folk coffeehouse from the 1960s. For a more relaxed, elegant evening *Cleo's Twenty-One*, 1947 Gray ☎ 521-9209 is a dinner club offering light jazz piano. More lively is the jazz upstairs at the *Blue Moon*, 1010 Banks ☎ 523-3773.

Theater and music The biggest and best theaters are the *Alley*, 615 Texas ☎ 228-8421, *Chocolate Bayou* ☎ 528-0119 and *Stages*, 3201 Allen Pkwy ☎ 527-8243. The *Houston Grand Opera*, the *Houston Symphony* and the *Houston Ballet* all have strong national reputations; contact *Showtix* ☎ 227-9792. The *Society for Performing Arts* ☎ 227-1111 showcases outstanding musical performers.

Sightseeing

Houston is not a city of great scenic beauty, although visitors may want to visit the island city of Galveston, an hour's drive away on I-45, for its Strand, the square-rigged ship *Elissa* and its wooden houses photographed by Cartier-Bresson.

Astrodome The world's first domed stadium is now the nation's smallest, but the guided tour is still popular; wear walking shoes. *8400 Kirby ☎ 799-9544. Tours at 11, 1 and 3.*

Bayou Bend The beautifully landscaped former home of philanthropist Ima Hogg is filled with American and Texan antiques. *1 Westcott Dr ☎ 529-8773. Tours (2hr) by reservation only.*

Contemporary Arts Museum The polished aluminum siding conceals exhibition space for contemporary artists of national and regional fame. *5216 Montrose ☎ 526-3129. Open Tue–Sat 10–5; Sun, noon–6.*

Museum of Fine Arts features Italian Renaissance painting and an outstanding collection of Frederic Remingtons. There is also a growing sculpture garden by Isamu Noguchi and a first-class photographic collection. *1001 Bissonnet ☎ 526-1361. Open Tue–Sat, 10–5; Thu, 10–9; Sun, noon–6.*

Museum of Natural Science Displays of oil technology and the gem and mineral collection are the museum's high spots. *1 Hermann Circle Dr in Hermann Park ☏ 526-4273. Open Mon–Wed, Fri, 9–5; Sat, 9–6; Sun, 12–6.*

NASA–Lyndon B Johnson Space Center It is a 45min drive on I-45 from downtown to rockets, spacecraft and moonrocks at the visitors' center; tours of Mission Control by reservation. *2102 NASA Rd 1 ☏ 483-4321. Open 9–4 daily exc Christmas • guided tours hourly beginning at 10.*

Rothko Chapel This ecumenical chapel houses 14 paintings by the modern master Mark Rothko. Barnett Newman's sculpture, the Broken Obelisk, is outside. *1401 Sul Ross ☏ 524-9839. Open 9–6.*

Sam Houston Park Run by the Harris County Historical Society, the downtown park has six restored 19thC buildings filled with antique furniture and decorative arts. *Bagby and Lamar ☏ 956-0480 or 759-1292. Open Tue–Fri, 10–4; Sat, 11-3; Sun, 2–5 • tours every 30min.*

Guided tours

The *Port of Houston* ☏ 225-4044 offers a free, 2hr boat tour of the Houston Ship Channel, artery of much of the city's wealth. Reservations are needed at least two weeks in advance.

Spectator sports

Baseball The *Houston Astros* play at the Astrodome ☏ 797-1000.

Basketball The *Rockets* are at the Summit ☏ 627-0600.

Football The *Oilers* play at the Astrodome ☏ 797-1000.

Keeping fit

Health clubs Most Houston hotels have either facilities or arrangements with a nearby club. The most prominent are the *Houstonian*, on the same grounds as the hotel ☏ 680-3330; the *Texas Club*, 601 Travis (downtown) ☏ 227-7000; and the *Downtown YMCA*, 1600 Louisiana ☏ 659-8501. *Hank's Gym*, 5320 Elm, Bellaire ☏ 668-6219 is for serious bodybuilders.

Basketball *Fonde Recreation Center*, Sabine at Memorial ☏ 222-5191 has the best pick-up basketball games in town, with college and professional athletes occasionally taking part.

Bicycling Bicycles can be rented from *Recycled Cycles* ☏ 977-1393. There is a good bike path from the Sabine Street Bridge downtown along Buffalo Bayou.

Golf The central public courses are at *Memorial Park* ☏ 862-4033 and *Hermann Park* ☏ 529-9788.

Jogging The most popular jogging track is a partially shaded 3-mile/5km loop in Memorial Park, 4 miles/6.5km from downtown; another lines Buffalo Bayou from downtown. The heat and humidity can be overwhelming, however.

Tennis The best public tennis facilities are the municipally-run *Memorial Park Tennis Center* ☏ 641-4111 with 18 courts, showers, lockers and a pro shop.

Local resources

Business services

Inside the Loop, *SRC Secretarial*, 5615 Kirby Dr ☏ 522-5926 offers 24hr service and a full range of typing and transcription. Also inside the Loop is *Legal Documents, Etc*, 4101 San Jacinto ☏ 524-9401. Hotels in the Galleria area frequently call *Nancy Sellers and Associates*, 770 S Post Oak Ln ☏ 961-3223. Full services plus conference rooms are available in the Galleria area at *One Riverway*, an executive suite service at 1 Riverway ☏ 840-8611.

Photocopying and printing *Kinko's* offers cheap photocopying services downtown at 1430 San Jacinto ☏ 654-8161 and two other locations. *Kwik-Kopy* has offices downtown ☏ 659-1054, Galleria ☏ 960-9392 and at many other locations.

Security Unarmed, plainclothes bodyguards (in Texas only

uniformed officers are allowed to carry firearms) are available through *Minuteman Security* ☎ 266-5400.
Translation *Berlitz Translation Services*, 3100 Richmond ☎ 529-8110; *ILS-International Language Service*, 5959 Westheimer ☎ 783-1035; and *Compu Tran Inc*, 4801 Woodway ☎ 552-0155.

Communications

Local delivery *Early Bird* ☎ 957-1119 offers low rates. *A & E* ☎ 225-0941 is one of the city's longest established services.
Long-distance delivery *Federal Express* ☎ 667-2500; *Emery* ☎ 820-0056; or *Purolator* ☎ 672-0941.
Post office The downtown office is at 401 Franklin ☎ 227-1474. For airport mail information ☎ 226-3408.
Telex/telegram *Via Telex Company*, 9525 Katy Frwy (I-10) ☎ 461-9849; *Western Union International*, 5444 Westheimer ☎ 626-0676.

Conference/exhibition centers

For information, contact the *Greater Houston Convention and Visitors' Council*, 3300 Main St ☎ 523-5050.

Emergencies

Hospitals *Hermann Hospital*, 1203 Ross Sterling Ave ☎ 797-4011; *Houston Northwest Medical Center*, 710 FM (Farm to Market Road) 1960 West ☎ 440-1000; *Methodist Hospital*, 6565 Fannin ☎ 790-3311; and *St Joseph Hospital*, 1919 LaBranch ☎ 757-1000. For dental emergencies the *Houston District Dental Society* ☎ 961-4337 makes referrals. For doctor referral, *Harris County Medical Society* ☎ 790-1885.
Pharmacies *Eckerd Drugs*, 2434 University ☎ 523-6611 is open 24hr. Another major chain is *Walgreen*, 822 Main (downtown) ☎ 223-1513.

Government offices

US Dept of Commerce/International Trade Administration ☎ 229-2578; *US Small Business Administration* ☎ 660-4401; *Passport Assistance* ☎ 229-3600; *US Customs Entry of Merchandise* ☎ 226-2308; *US Customs Tourist Information* ☎ 443-5910; *Immigration and Naturalization* ☎ 750-1637.

Information sources

Business information The *Houston Chamber of Commerce*, 1100 Milam ☎ 651-1313 and the *Houston Economic Development Council* ☎ 651-7200 provide city business and marketing data. To help businesses interested in relocating or expanding in Houston, the city has established the *One Stop Business Service* ☎ 663-7867.
Local media The *Houston Chronicle* and the *Houston Post* are the local daily newspapers. The *Chronicle* is larger and offers more complete coverage of business. The *Houston Business Journal* is a weekly all-business newspaper. *Guy's Newsstand*, 3700 Main ☎ 528-5731 and *Westheimer News*, 6437 Westheimer ☎ 781-7793 offer large selections of out-of-town publications. *Texas Monthly* magazine offers the most reliable and complete guide to what's on. *Ultra* covers the activities of the wealthy social set.

Thank-yous

Florists Houston's society florist is *Leonard Tharp*, 2705 Bammel Ln ☎ 527-9393. *The Empty Vase*, 2439 Westheimer ☎ 529-9969 does custom designs. *Arrangements*, in Chelsea Market ☎ 520-6679 features avant-garde floral designs and unusual gifts.
Gift Baskets *Basketful of Goodies* ☎ 688-9414 will deliver baskets filled with chocolates, caviar, paté, wine, fruit and nuts.

KANSAS CITY

Area codes: Missouri ☎ 816, Kansas ☎ 913

Once the major starting point for the wagon trains of settlers migrating West, Kansas City now ranks as the economic center of the American breadbasket. Agriculture, especially wheat, is big business yet the city ranks second only to Detroit in car and truck manufacture. Other major industries include farm equipment, frozen food storage and distribution and greeting card publishing. The largest single employer is the federal government, which has many regional offices in Kansas City; the leading corporations are General Motors, Hallmark Cards, TWA and Ford. The metropolitan area, with almost 1.4m residents, crosses the state line dividing Kansas and Missouri. Most of the financial corporations are in Kansas City, Missouri; the industries and factories are in Kansas City, Kansas. Johnson County, Kansas – about 20 miles/32km from downtown – has become an important corporate area. Unless otherwise stated, the area code for telephone numbers is 816.

Arriving

Kansas City International Airport

Each of KCI's three C-shaped terminals has its own restaurant, shop and information booth. Baggage retrieval is adjacent to each gate on the same level of the building and it is only a short walk from disembarking to the terminal exits. Airport information ☎ 243-5200; cargo ☎ 891-8434.

Nearby hotels *Kansas City Marriott Hotel*, 775 Brasilia St 64153 ☎ 464-2200. *Airport Hilton Plaza Inn*, 8801 NW 112th St 64153 ☎ 891-8900. *Holiday Inn KCI*, 11832 Plaza Circle 64153 ☎ 464-2345. *Sheraton Kansas City Airport Hotel and Conference Center*, 7301 NW Tiffany Springs Rd 64153 ☎ 741-9500.

City link The airport is about 30–40min by road NW of downtown.

Car rental Unless your business is confined to downtown, car rental is advisable; most major firms have desks at KCI.

Taxi Except for late at night, taxis are plentiful. Agree on a fare ($20–25) before setting off.

Bus KCI Express ☎ 243-5950 operates to Kansas City and Johnson County. If your hotel is at the end of the route, the journey can take over 2hrs.

Getting around

Greater Kansas City follows a grid pattern with numbered streets running E–W and named streets N–S. Parking is both cheap and plentiful.

Taxi Taxis can be difficult to find on the street. The biggest companies are *Airport Bus and Limousine Service* ☎ 921-6683; *Quicksilver Taxi and Airport Service* ☎ 262-0905; and *Metropolitan Transportation Services* ☎ 471-5000.

Bus *Kansas City Area Transportation Authority* ☎ 221-0660. For Johnson County ☎ (913) 469-8223.

Trolley *Kansas City Trolley* ☎ 221-3399 runs services between downtown, Crown Center, Country Club Plaza, Westport and Barney Allis Plaza.

Area by area

Downtown The main business area lies just S of the Missouri River and E of the Kansas River and the state line. Legal, financial and related businesses are located here, as well as the main convention facilities. Several blocks S of route 70 is Crown Center, a prestigious development financed by Hallmark Cards, which contains dozens of stores, restaurants, two luxury hotels, apartments and an office complex.

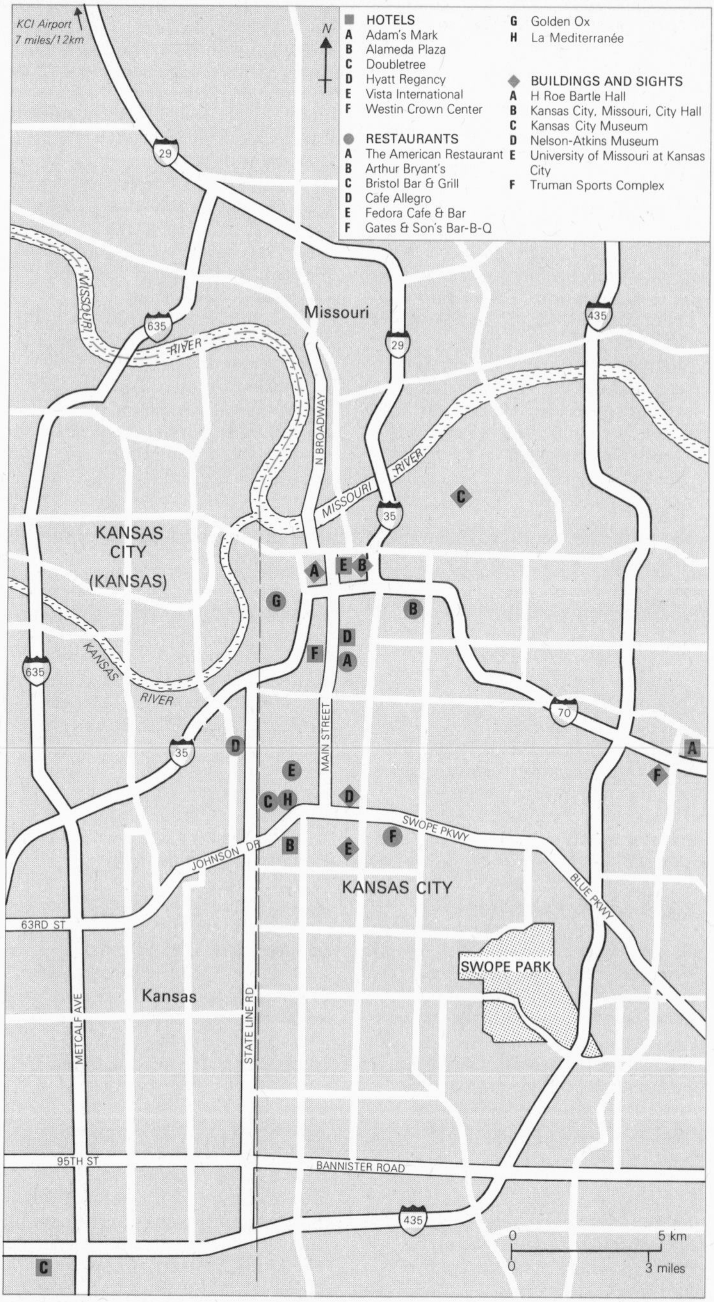

KCI Airport 7 miles/12km
N
HOTELS
A Adam's Mark
B Alameda Plaza
C Doubletree
D Hyatt Regancy
E Vista International
F Westin Crown Center
RESTAURANTS
A The American Restaurant
B Arthur Bryant's
C Bristol Bar & Grill
D Cafe Allegro
E Fedora Cafe & Bar
F Gates & Son's Bar-B-Q
G Golden Ox
H La Mediterranée
BUILDINGS AND SIGHTS
A H Roe Bartle Hall
B Kansas City, Missouri, City Hall
C Kansas City Museum
D Nelson-Atkins Museum
E University of Missouri at Kansas City
F Truman Sports Complex
29
635
435
Missouri
MISSOURI RIVER
N BROADWAY
35
KANSAS CITY (KANSAS)
KANSAS RIVER
70
MAIN STREET
SWOPE PKWY
JOHNSON DR
BLUE PKWY
KANSAS CITY
63RD ST
SWOPE PARK
Kansas
METCALF AVE
STATE LINE RD
95TH ST
BANNISTER ROAD
0 5 km
0 3 miles

Between route 35 and the Missouri River, City Market is where the region's farmers converge every Saturday.

Country Club Plaza About 3 miles/4.8km S of Crown Center, this 14-block district, with its tiled roofs, pastel-colored buildings, wrought ironwork and fountains, is full of shops and restaurants. It is also an important business center and is home to the Kansas City Board of Trade and the world's largest winter wheat market.

Westport Square The original starting point for wagons rolling westward, this area – a few blocks N of Country Club Plaza – has been extensively renovated and is now crammed with bars, restaurants and stores. It is very fashionable with the city's young professionals who have cultivated its casual atmosphere and established it as the center of Kansas City nightlife.

Mission Hills Close to Country Club Plaza, this is Kansas City's most exclusive, mansion-packed residential area. Close rivals are Country Club District, Roanoke and Rockhill.

Overland Park Many telecommunications, insurance and engineering firms have been wooed across the state line to Overland Park in Johnson County. Together with Leawood and Lenexa, it is also a residential area much favored by the young up-and-coming.

Hotels

Most of the de luxe, business-oriented hotels used by international visitors are downtown or in the Country Club Plaza area.

Adam's Mark **$$$**
9103 E 39th St, Missouri 64133
☎ 737-0200 • 370 rooms, 2 restaurants, 2 bars
Close to the Truman Sports Complex, this modern hotel is less formal and corporate-oriented than many, but it is nevertheless used for local meetings and conventions. Health club, pool, tennis • 17 meeting rooms.

Alameda Plaza **$$$**
401 Ward Pkwy, Missouri 64112
☎ 756-1500 • 400 rooms, 1 restaurant, 2 bars, 1 coffee shop
This very comfortable hotel was President Reagan's headquarters in 1976. The décor is Spanish and its elegant rooms overlook the fountains and statues of Country Club Plaza. It is extremely popular with local residents, especially for Sunday brunch. Health club, tennis • 18 meeting rooms.

Doubletree **$$$**
10100 College Blvd, Overland Park, Kansas 66210 ☎ (913) 451-6100 • 357 rooms, 4 restaurants
Nestled among the trees, this spacious modern hotel in Overland Park caters to many regional conventions as well as local business people. Gift shop • pool, racquetball, outdoor track • 11 meeting rooms, fax.

Hyatt Regency **$$$$**
2345 McGee, Missouri 64108
☎ 421-1234 [TX] 434022 • 727 rooms, 2 restaurants, 1 coffee shop
Rebuilt after the collapse of a skywalk in 1981, the Hyatt is now one of the city's most chic hotels. It has a popular lobby bar, J Patrick's Lounge, and the Peppercorn Duck Club serves some of the finest food in town. Non-smoking floor, gift shop • health club, pool, exercise equipment • 18 meeting rooms.

Vista International **$$$**
200 W 12th St, Missouri 64105
☎ 421-6800 [TX] 442354 • 572 rooms, 2 restaurants, 1 bar
One of Kansas City's premier hotels, the Vista is especially convenient for the main downtown convention sites. The lobby, with its nine-tier

waterfall, is a well-known local meeting place, as is the 12th Street Rag jazz club. The Harvest Restaurant attracts many corporate diners, and the Vista's executive lounges are well equipped for business visitors. Non-smoking rooms, florist, gift shops • health club, pool, tennis • 19 meeting rooms, fax.

Westin Crown Center $$$$
1 Pershing Rd, Missouri 64108 ☎ 474-4400 TX 426169 • 724 rooms, 50 suites, 5 restaurants, 3 bars
This de luxe hotel is part of the Crown Center Complex. Its lobby incorporates the limestone face of the hill upon which the hotel is built and features a winding stream, a five-story waterfall and tropical rain forest. It also has three lounges with live entertainment, and there is a panoramic view of downtown from the Top of the Crown restaurant. Non-smoking floors, gift shop • health club, tennis, pool, putting green, exercise equipment • 8 meeting rooms.

OTHER HOTELS
Quarterage ($) *560 Westport Rd, Missouri 64111 ☎ 931-0001.*

Clubs

The most prestigious downtown club is the men-only *River Club* at 611 W 8th St ☎ 221-5353. Others with business significance are the *Kansas City Club*, located in a stately 14-story building at 1228 Baltimore ☎ 421-6789, and the *University Club* at 918 Baltimore Ave ☎ 474-6000. Highly esteemed country clubs in the metropolitan area are the *Kansas City Country Club*, 62nd St and Indian Ln ☎ 362-8103; the *Carriage Club*, 5301 State Line ☎ 363-1124; the *Mission Hills Country Club*, 5400 Mission Dr ☎ (913) 722-5400; *Indian Hills Country Club*, Tomahawk Rd and Cherokee Ln ☎ (913) 362-6200; and *Blue Hills Country Club*, 777 W Burning Tree Dr ☎ 942-3292.

Restaurants

Many of the city's best restaurants are located in Country Club Plaza. The city is best known for its steaks.

American Restaurant $$
200 E 25th St ☎ 471-8050 • D only; closed Sun • AE CB DC MC V
Atop Crown Center, the American offers sweeping views of downtown and serves dishes such as Gulf shrimp creole, rock salt hobo steak and braised South Dakota pheasant in juniper sauce. The décor is modern, the atmosphere private and relaxed.

Arthur Bryant's Barbeque $
1727 Brooklyn Ave ☎ 231-1123 • no credit cards
This unsalubrious restaurant is a "must" for devotees of pork ribs and brisket beef sandwiches. The secret of its success lies in Mr Bryant's unique spicy, peppery sauce.

Bristol Bar & Grill $$
4740 Jefferson ☎ 756-0606 • D only Sun • AE CB DC MC V
A great place for oysters or broiled salmon, the Bristol, with its Victorian architecture and modern art, is a favorite of the city's young professionals for a brunch, snack or a business meal. The back room is particularly striking, with a huge Tiffany leaded-glass dome.

Café Allegro $$
1815 39th St ☎ 561-3663 • D only Sat; closed Sun • AE DC MC V
Much frequented by the city's upper crust, the Allegro has menus offering everything from Cajun to *nouvelle* American cuisine. It is a place for social rather than serious business entertaining.

Fedora Café & Bar $$
210 W 47th St ☎ 561-6565 • AE DC CB MC V
This Art Deco, European café-style

restaurant, serving Continental cuisine, attracts the trendy business set in Country Club Plaza. Although fairly formal, it can be too noisy for serious talk.

Gates & Son's Bar-B-Q $
1141 Swope Pkwy ☎ 921-0409 • no credit cards
This is one of several branches of Gates's which specialize in barbequed beef. Although in the fast-food category, they are popular with local business people addicted to sausage and sliced beef.

Golden Ox $$
1600 Genessee ☎ 842-2866 • AE DC MC V
Located in the center of the stockyards, near Kemper Arena, the Golden Ox is a good choice for informal meals. Its steaks are said by many to be the best in town.

La Mediterranée $$
4742 Pennsylavania ☎ 561-2916 • D only Sat; closed Sun • AE CB DC MC V
This restrained elegant restaurant in Country Club Plaza is one of the best for private business meals. The cuisine is Continental, the wine list extensive.

Bars

Kansas City has no shortage of bars, particularly in Country Club Plaza or Westport Square. The Plaza is a little more formal and attracts an older crowd than Westport, which is very lively at weekends.

Entertainment

Kansas City is renowned for jazz, and its theater, ballet and opera are all keenly supported.
Theater and music The *Midland Center for the Performing Arts*, 1228 Main St, presents touring Broadway hits; the *Missouri Repertory Theater*, 4949 Cherry, performs year-round on the University of Missouri at Kansas City campus; the *Starlight Theater* in Swope Park, an outdoor amphitheater, features musical comedy and concerts May–Sep. Drama and musical productions are staged at the *Music Hall in the Municipal Auditorium*, 1310 Wyandotte Street; the *Lyric Theater*, 11th and Central streets; and the *Folly Theater*, 300 W 12th St. *Tiffany's Attic*, 5028 Main St, and *Waldo Astoria*, 7428 Washington, are the city's two dinner playhouses.
Jazz Some of the most popular clubs are the *Bristol Bar & Grill* (see *Restaurants*) and those at the Westin, Vista and Hyatt hotels. *Jazz Hotline* ☎ 931-2888.

Shopping

Country Club Plaza, Crown Center and Westport are the leaders among the city's several shopping areas. *Westport* runs from Main St to Southwest Trafficway and from 39th to 43rd streets. The area has dozens of small boutiques, specialty stores and art galleries. *Country Club Plaza*, at 47th St and JC Nichols Pkwy, has more than 100 shops, top-name stores and boutiques. *Crown Center*, at Pershing Rd and Grand Ave, has three floors of boutiques, specialty shops and Halls, one of the city's finest department stores.

Sightseeing

Harry S Truman Library and Museum The museum houses many of Truman's personal and official papers. *Hwy 24 at Delaware St, Independence, Missouri ☎ 833-1225.*
Harry S Truman National Historic Site This is where President and Mrs Truman lived for most of their life together. *219 N Delaware St, Independence, Missouri ☎ 254-2720.*
Kansas City Museum The 72-room mansion formerly owned by the lumber giant RA Long, features regional history exhibits, a natural history hall and a planetarium. *3218 Gladstone Blvd ☎ 483-8300.*
Nelson-Atkins Museum of Art An outstanding Oriental collection and a fine restaurant. *4525 Oak ☎ 561-4000. Closed Mon.*

Guided tours
Kansas City Sightseeing ☏ 833-4083 offers individual and group tours. *Missouri River Queen Boat Excursions* ☏ 842-0027 operate May–Nov.

Spectator sports
Baseball The *Kansas City Royals* play at the Truman Sports Complex ☏ 921-2200.
Football The *Chiefs* are also based at the Sports Complex ☏ 924-2500.

Keeping fit
Bicycling Bikes can be rented in summer at Swope Park.
Golf *River Oaks*, 140th St and US-71, in Grandview, Missouri ☏ 966-8111.
Jogging Tracks include *Penn Valley Park*, near Crown Center, and the *Jacob L Loose Park*, near the Alameda Plaza.
Tennis The city has more than 200 public courts, including several near Country Club Plaza.

Local resources
Business services
Firms offering complete services include *Executive Center* ☏ (913) 341-2399; *Corporate Way* ☏ 345-8020; and *Corporate Office Concepts* ☏ (913) 362-8321 or 451-8338 or 362-0567.
Photocopy and printing *Buzz Print*, downtown office at 105 W 11th St ☏ 842-0889; *Sir Speedy*, 1101 Grand St ☏ 421-7137 offers pick-up and delivery service; and *Quik Print*, 910 Walnut ☏ 421-3780 and 2000 Main ☏ 421-2760.
Secretarial *Kelly Services* ☏ 561-3585; *AAA Secretarial Service* ☏ 531-4615; and *Jerry Schreiner Secretarial Service* ☏ 421-2550.
Translation *Berlitz Translation Services* ☏ 561-8303 and *Technical Translation Services* ☏ 648-3732.

Communications
Local delivery *Express Delivery Service* ☏ 471-2340.
Long-distance delivery *Federal Express* ☏ 421-4681.
Post office The main office is at 315 Pershing Rd ☏ 374-9270, after 5 ☏ 374-9135.
Telex *Western Union* ☏ 471-7440.

Convention/exhibition centers
Downtown convention facilities include the *Municipal Auditorium, H Roe Bartle Hall* and *Barney Allis Plaza* ☏ 421-8000; and just E of the state line is the *American Royal Center* ☏ 421-6460.

Emergencies
Hospitals *St Lukes Hospital*, 4400 Wornall Rd ☏ 932-2000; *Menorah Medical Center*, 4949 Rockhill Rd ☏ 276-8000; *Research Medical Center*, 2316 E Meyer Blvd ☏ 276-4000.
Pharmacies *Revco Discount Drug Centers* and *Osco Drug Stores* have many branches throughout the city.

Government offices
US Dept of Commerce/International Trade Administration ☏ 374-3141; *US Customs* ☏ 471-8530; *US Immigration and Naturalization Service* ☏ 891-0603.

Information sources
Business information *Kansas City Convention and Visitors' Bureau* ☏ 221-5242 or (800) 523-5953; *Chamber of Commerce* ☏ 221-2424.
Local media *Time For News* newsstand at 1310 Main St carries one of the city's widest selections of out-of-town newspapers and magazines. The *Kansas City Times* is the morning daily. Its afternoon sister is the *Star*.

Thank-yous
Florists *Fiddly Fig*, 6324 Brookside Plaza ☏ 363-4313 and *Jasmine The Florist*, 4771 Jefferson ☏ 756-2111.
Gift baskets *Crabtree and Evelyn of London*, 505 Nichols Rd ☏ 531-6468; *The Best of Kansas City*, 6233 Brookside Plaza ☏ 333-7900.

Los Angeles

Area code ☎ 213

Los Angeles is a sprawling giant of megapolitan proportions, with a bewildering array of individual communities crammed together in an area that covers nearly 400 square miles/640 sq km. Projected to be America's largest city by the year 2000, LA is a lotus land that began as a Spanish mission and became a last frontier, a mecca of opportunity. Americans and Europeans move to LA for the year-round sunshine, the variety of work and entertainment, and because they think it will be fun. Others come for work – mainly in retail and service industries – from Latin America, Southeast Asia, Mexico and Iran. The population comprises approximately 53% white, 26% Hispanic, 13% black and 8% Asian.

Aerospace, defense, real estate, finance and tourism are all major industries, but entertainment is dominant. Many of the big-name studios and networks are now part of megacorporations: Columbia Pictures is owned by Coca-Cola; ABC by Capital Cities; and NBC belongs to General Electric. Beyond the self-contained world that is Hollywood, oil, banking and real estate have played a large part in shaping Los Angeles. Atlantic Richfield (ARCO), the Getty Trust and Occidental Petroleum have their headquarters in the city, with landmark high-rises downtown, in Westwood and in the San Fernando Valley.

Banking has made downtown LA the second-largest financial community in the USA, and its skyline is dominated by Bank of America, First Interstate, Security Pacific and Wells Fargo; a new Pacific Stock Exchange opened in 1986. Big names in real estate include Fred Sands, Bruce George and John Douglas. Most recent money comes from Japanese developers eager to invest in land unavailable at home and Japanese bankers seeking US mergers. TRW, Hughes Aircraft, Northrup and Burroughs represent some of the area's contribution to the US defense program.

Arriving

In addition to its international airport, Los Angeles also has four suburban airports: Burbank Airport to the N in the San Fernando Valley; John Wayne Airport S in Orange County; Ontario Airport (60 miles/96km E); and the smaller Long Beach Airport to the S.

Los Angeles International Airport

Reconstructed for the 1984 Olympics, LAX has seven terminals clustered around a horseshoe layout; inter-terminal buses run every 15min. Along the right are West Coast airlines; the left side houses national airlines such as American and United; and at the top of the horseshoe is the impressive, glass-structured Tom Bradley International Terminal.

Some gates are a distance from the entrance/exit, and access from the street is complicated; it is better to have someone meet you outside the nearby baggage area on street level. Allow an hour to get through Customs and Immigration, double that during the peak travel season May–Sep. Business centers at

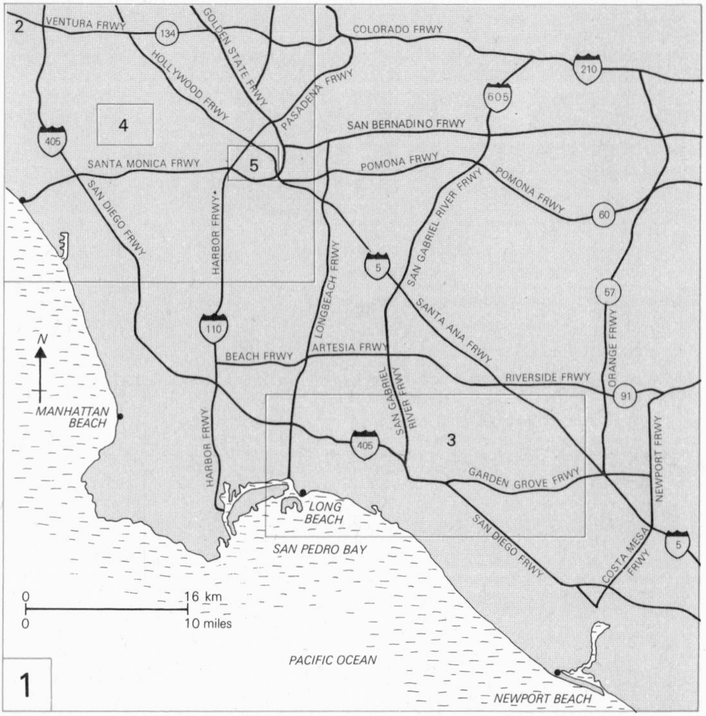

Terminals 1, 4 and 7 provide mailing, secretarial, telex and notary services, computer rental, baggage storage and conference rooms for up to eight people ☎ 646-5252.

Nearby hotels *Sheraton Plaza La Reina*, 6101 W Century Blvd 90045 ☎ 642-1111. *Marriott*, 5855 W Century Blvd 90045 ☎ 641-5700. *Hyatt*, 6225 W Century Blvd 90045 ☎ 670-9000. *AMFAC*, 8601 Lincoln Blvd 90045 ☎ 670-8111. At *Skytel*, a mini-hotel in the southmost part of the International Terminal, you can rent a tiny room by the hour to take a nap, shower, watch TV or make phone calls.

City link LAX is 25 miles/40km SW of downtown LA; the drive takes 60min, 45min off-peak.

Car rental A car is a necessity in LA. All major companies have desks at the airport, and prices are no higher than in town. Pre-arrival reservation is advisable. If you want something different, Budget ☎ 659-3473 rents Ferraris, Rolls-Royces and other exotic cars at prices to match. Rent-A-Wreck ☎ 478-0676 has a fleet of second-hand cars at only slightly lower rates; their shuttle service to and from the airport is available Mon–Fri, 9–4 only.

Taxi Cabs line up outside the baggage claim areas at all airport terminals.

Bus A Supershuttle fleet of vans patrols the airport regularly, providing an inexpensive door-to-door service to any LA destination. Use the Supershuttle phone in the baggage claim area or ☎ 777-8000 to make a reservation.

Limousine The Celebrity Airport Livery ☎ (800) 235-3248 has vans and limousines for airport pick-up.

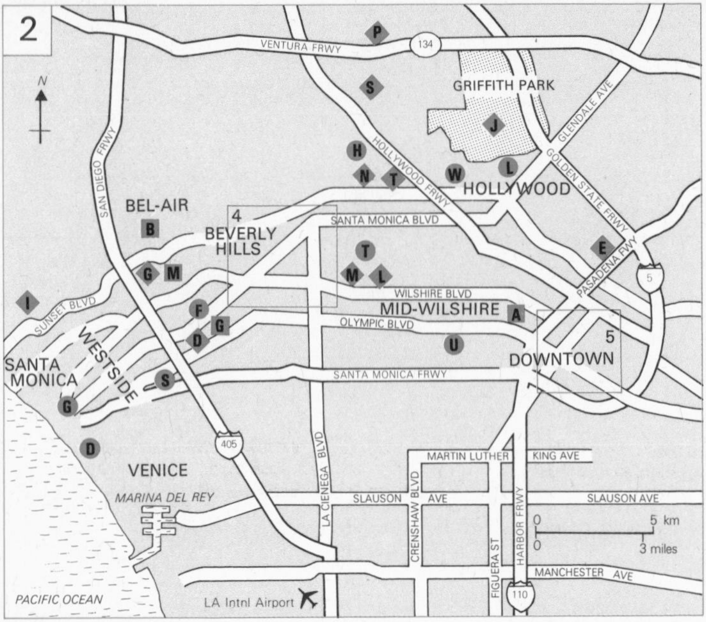

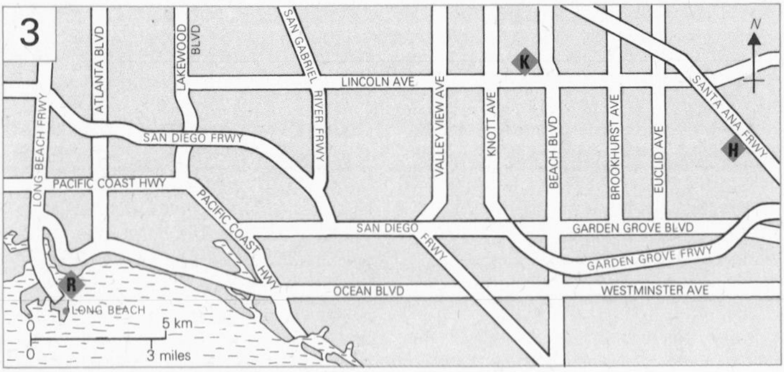

HOTELS
- **A** Ambassador
- **B** Bel-Air
- **G** Century Plaza
- **M** Westwood Marquis

RESTAURANTS
- **D** Chinois on Main
- **F** Harry's Bar
- **G** Michael's
- **H** Musso & Frank Grill
- **L** La Petite Chaya
- **S** Valentino
- **T** Canter's
- **U** El Cholo
- **W** La Villa Taxco

BUILDINGS AND SIGHTS
- **D** Century Plaza Towers
- **E** Dodger Stadium
- **G** UCLA
- **H** Disneyland
- **I** Getty Museum of Art
- **J** Griffith Park Observatory and Museum
- **K** Knotts Berry Farm
- **L** La Brea Tar Pits
- **M** LA County Museum of Arts
- **N** Mann's Chinese Theater
- **P** NBC Studios
- **R** Queen Mary, Spruce Goose
- **S** Universal Studios
- **T** Walk of Fame

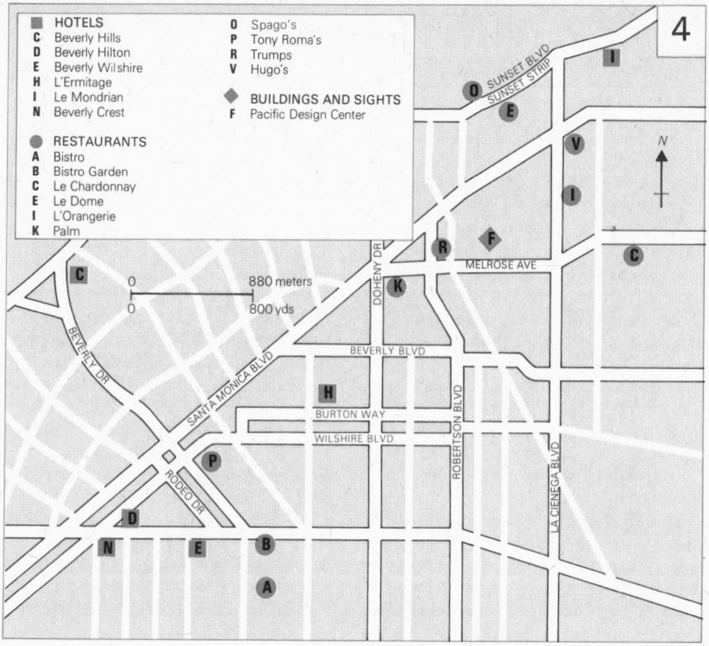
4
HOTELS
C Beverly Hills
D Beverly Hilton
E Beverly Wilshire
H L'Ermitage
I Le Mondrian
N Beverly Crest
RESTAURANTS
A Bistro
B Bistro Garden
C Le Chardonnay
E Le Dome
I L'Orangerie
K Palm
O Spago's
P Tony Roma's
R Trumps
V Hugo's
BUILDINGS AND SIGHTS
F Pacific Design Center
SUNSET BLVD
SUNSET STRIP
MELROSE AVE
DOHENY DR
BEVERLY BLVD
BURTON WAY
WILSHIRE BLVD
SANTA MONICA BLVD
BEVERLY DR
RODEO DR
ROBERTSON BLVD
LA CIENEGA BLVD
0 880 meters
0 800 yds
N

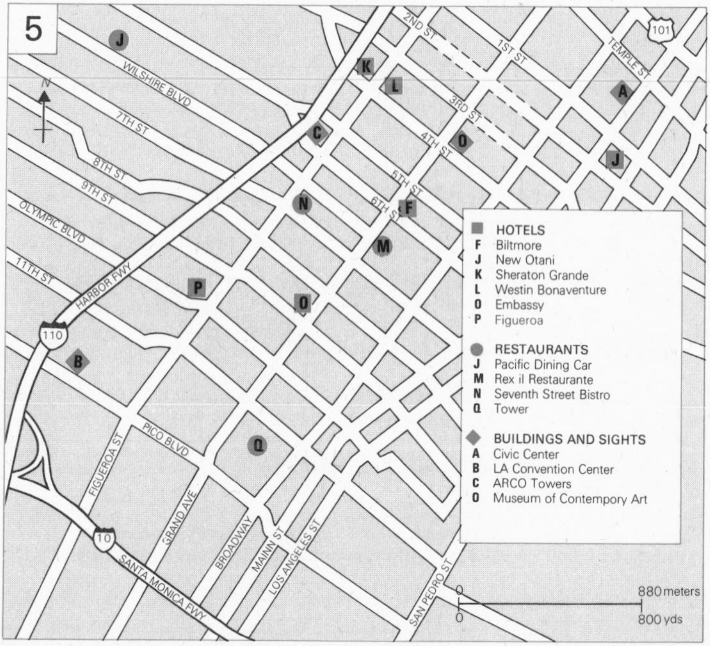
5
WILSHIRE BLVD
7TH ST
8TH ST
9TH ST
OLYMPIC BLVD
11TH ST
HARBOR FWY
110
2ND ST
1ST ST
TEMPLE ST
101
3RD ST
4TH ST
5TH ST
6TH ST
PICO BLVD
FIGUEROA ST
GRAND AVE
BROADWAY
MAINN ST
LOS ANGELES ST
SAN PEDRO ST
10
SANTA MONICA FWY
HOTELS
F Biltmore
J New Otani
K Sheraton Grande
L Westin Bonaventure
O Embassy
P Figueroa
RESTAURANTS
J Pacific Dining Car
M Rex il Restaurante
N Seventh Street Bistro
Q Tower
BUILDINGS AND SIGHTS
A Civic Center
B LA Convention Center
C ARCO Towers
O Museum of Contempory Art
0 880 meters
0 800 yds
N

Getting around

Everyone drives in LA and although the city's freeway system is fairly efficient, rush hour (7.30–10am, 3–7pm) extends a 15min drive into a 45min crawl. Thirty freeways and 13 highways criss-cross greater LA, and virtually every part of the city is within 10min of the freeway system. The freeways, especially routes 405 and 11, are often congested. If you get impatient on the 405, take Sepulveda Boulevard; Figueroa Street is a good alternative to Route 11.

Thomas' Road Guide, a spiral-bound book of detailed maps, is an indispensable aid for visiting drivers. Look out for pedestrians approaching crosswalks: you risk an instant penalty if you don't stop.

Taxi Drivers do not have a reputation for good service. Many are recent immigrants who speak little English, take circuitous routes and often charge whatever they think the market will bear. Finding a cab in the street is generally difficult, so call *Celebrity Cab* ☏ 934-6700, *LA Checker Cab* ☏ 481-1234 or *United Independent Taxi* ☏ 653-5050.

Limousine Undoubtedly the most comfortable and efficient, although expensive, way to get around. *Music Express* ☏ 849-2244 is the best of the larger firms; *White Tie* ☏ 553-6060 is the city's largest service; *Primetime* ☏ 208-0760 is smaller.

Bus Except for buses operating in the downtown area, public transportation is not useful for the business visitor.

Area by area

Dorothy Parker described Los Angeles as "63 suburbs in search of a city." These are the most important of its myriad communities.

Downtown Originally an immigrant gateway to California, the area bounded by the Harbor Freeway and Los Angeles Street and between Sunset and Venice boulevards now comprises the city's business (but not show business) heart. Landmarks include the moated Water and Power Building on 1st Street, residential Bunker Towers, the shiny Westin Bonaventure Hotel and the twin ARCO Towers. The SW corner houses the headquarters of IBM, American Express and the real estate developer Grubb and Ellis. Flower Street is the center of banking and finance and the home of several corporations with Oriental and Middle Eastern connections. Seven blocks E at 9th and Los Angeles is the garment district, and farther E still are the produce and flower markets. Los Angeles Civic Center, which includes City Hall and the Court and Records buildings, is in the NE corner of downtown. Bordering it on the N and E are the ethnic communities of Chinatown, Little Tokyo and the Mexican area.

Mid-Wilshire Lying between downtown and Beverly Hills, mid-Wilshire has been colonized by some businesses, mainly legal, clerical and employment firms. Landmark buildings include Texaco, Pacific Telephone and Cannon Films headquarters. N of Wilshire, from Wilton Street to La Brea Avenue, Hancock Park and Larchmont Village are elegant, monied residential districts for prosperous downtown executives, with wide, tree-lined streets.

Hollywood Today's Hollywood is a far cry from the romanticized, illusionary image generally fostered. Since the Hollywood Freeway sliced across the city, the area has become principally one of sleazy shops and runaway teenagers. But some remnants of former splendor remain. Paramount Studios still preside on Melrose Boulevard, and Warner Holly Studios now occupy the old Goldwyn studios on Santa Monica Boulevard.

West Hollywood A city incorporated in its own right, West Hollywood is a burgeoning, prosperous business and residential area. It has a strong gay population, a busy art and design trade and is the headquarters of talent agencies like ICM and APA.

Beverly Hills Money – both the acquisition and the spending of it – is the key to Beverly Hills. There is no limit to how much you can spend or what you can buy. The area has little industry, but there are many lawyers, doctors and plastic surgeons, besides entertainment industry agents and the corporate offices of film production companies.

Century City W of Beverly Hills, Century City has an opulence of its own. When 6th Street and Wilshire Boulevard began to lose their luster as fashionable business addresses, many of LA's advertising and design agencies – for example, J Walter Thompson – moved W. The area also has many entertainment-associated firms (lawyers, accountants and management specialists), along with Tri-Star Pictures, HBO cable channel, talent agency CAA and Blake Edwards. The twin Century Plaza Towers, the most eye-catching of the modern skyscrapers, house publishers (Larry Flynt, for example) and show business agents, as well as executive headhunters and banking and insurance conglomerates. ABC Entertainment Center is also there. Across the street are the Century Plaza Hotel and smart outdoor Century City Shopping Center.

Bel-Air Heavy with Hollywood money and prestige, Bel-Air is the fortress home of America's show business elite.

Westside Westside generally refers to anything W of the San Diego Freeway (405) and includes Westwood, West LA, Brentwood, Santa Monica and Venice. The area is heavily residential, peopled primarily by young professionals who seek the cleaner air and outdoor activities the beach brings. Most of the area's businesses are small and service-oriented, but there are pockets of corporate activity.

Next to 405 and adjacent to Beverly Hills and Century City, *Westwood* has a handful of residential high-rises and a large federal complex. At night the streets of Westwood Village, a 12-block shopping, eating and movie-going district, are packed with UCLA students, and others seeking entertainment.

West LA is primarily a middle-class renters' high-rise residential neighborhood. To the N is *Brentwood*, wealthy and "suburban" in feel, and home to the World Bank and many celebrities who shun Beverly Hills. Primarily a beach resort, *Santa Monica* has some corporate concerns, including Rand Corp, law firms and high-tech companies.

Malibu, Venice, Marina Del Rey To the N of Santa Monica, on the coast, is Malibu, where celebrities, entertainment executives and others who are simply wealthy live in beachfront homes. South of Santa Monica, Venice – the focal point for hippies in the 1960s and artists in the 1970s – is now a trendy-but-funky amalgam of characters. The boardwalk (on ocean's edge) is the weekend showplace for bikers, skaters and beachers. Farther S, Marina Del Rey, LA's main boating center, has many boating/nautical support-product companies as well as high-tech industries.

Other areas

N of LA, the *San Fernando Valley*, a massive residential overspill, has developed a personality of its own, although many residents still drive into the city daily to work. Route 101, which starts as the Hollywood Freeway and becomes the Ventura Freeway, has the Universal City complex, which includes Universal Studios, the Universal Amphitheater and MCA Records.

S of LA, orange groves have been transformed into the metropolis of *Orange County*, where high-tech and aerospace/defense-related industries have a significant presence.

Hotels

Most of the hotels listed are clustered in Beverly Hills or downtown. If your business takes you to the suburbs, downtown, with its access to freeways, is the best choice.

Ambassador $$$$
3400 Wilshire Blvd 90010 ☎ *387-7011* TX *9103212941 • 460 rooms, 40 suites, 3 restaurants, 3 bars, 1 coffee shop*
Discreet, with a faded, historical air, the Ambassador is a respectable alternative to the glass and chrome of downtown, only 2 miles/3km away. The hotel occupies a 23-acre site, with gardens and superior health club and Olympic-size pool. Ample business facilities make it a popular choice for conventions. Gift shops, post office, jewelers, barber, florist • jacuzzi, sauna, putting green • 17 meeting rooms, fax.

Bel-Air $$$$$
701 Stone Canyon Rd 90077 ☎ *472-1211* TX *674151 • 92 rooms, 33 suites, 1 restaurant*
This secluded hotel in LA's wealthiest area attracts the international patrician set who value understated luxury and personal service. Each room in the mission-style building has its own fireplace and exterior entrance, and most have walled patios useful for small meetings. The elegant dining room is especially popular for afternoon tea and Sunday brunch. Florist, complimentary limo • pool • 1 meeting room.

Beverly Hills $$$$$
9641 Sunset Blvd 90210 ☎ *276-2251* TX *691459 • 325 rooms, 2 restaurants, 1 coffee shop*
The pink stuccoed Beverly Hills offers a prestigious base for top-drawer executives and movie moguls. Many rooms have patios, and there are also small poolside cabanas ideal for business entertaining or meetings. The Polo Lounge is *the* place to spot celebrities and is a favorite for important business deals. Pharmacy, florist, jeweler, barber, car rental • tennis, pool • 7 meeting rooms, screening room, translation.

Beverly Hilton $$$$
9876 Wilshire Blvd 90210 ☎ *274-7777* TX *194638 • 626 rooms, 50 suites, 5 restaurants, 2 bars, 2 coffee shops*
Although it has less cachet than the Beverly Wilshire and is less convenient for central Beverly Hills, the Hilton is admirably efficient with an extensive range of services and facilities, including a good business center. Many entertainment and social functions are held here, and Trader Vic's is popular with the entertainment crowd; Mr H does a thriving Sunday brunch. Boutiques, barber, beauty salon, florist • pool, health club • 24 meeting rooms, notary public, fax, translation, teleconferencing, computers, computer modems, business reference library.

Beverly Wilshire $$$$
9500 Wilshire Blvd, Beverly Hills 90212 ☎ *275-5282* TX *698220 • Regent International Hotels • 453 rooms, 76 suites, 2 restaurants, 3 bars, 1 coffee shop*
Across Rodeo Drive, the Beverly Wilshire is favored by celebrities and high society, as well as senior executives. Rooms are well-appointed and dignified; those in the newer wing both vary in style and cost more. The Hideaway, serving traditional and Mexican cuisine, is a popular luncheon spot for the business community. Florist, barber, jeweler, bookstore • pool • 8 meeting rooms, fax.

Biltmore $$$$
515 S Olive St 90013 ☎ *624-1011* TX *677686 • 728 rooms, 28 suites, 4 restaurants, 2 bars*

LA's *grande dame* hotel is beautifully appointed, well-maintained and has an extensive art collection throughout the rooms and halls. Adjacent to the new 24-story Biltmore Tower office building and only a block's walk from the ARCO Towers, it is nearer California Plaza than other downtown hotels. Its wide range of services and facilities make it popular with those who want something more personal than the Bonaventure. Bernard's has long been one of LA's greatest hotel restaurants and it is much used by lunching bankers, lawyers and PacTel executives. Bank, gift shop, pastry shop • tennis at adjacent racquet club, pool, jacuzzi, massage • 18 meeting rooms.

Century Plaza $$$$
2025 Ave of the Stars, Century City 90067 ☏ 227-2000 ⊠ 698664 • 1,072 rooms, 75 suites, 4 restaurants, 3 bars, 1 coffee shop
Although principally a convention center, this is the LA hotel that has been used by politicians, diplomats and every US president since it opened in 1966. It is Century City's only hotel, and its new Tower complex houses one of LA's best hotel business centers, offering fax, telex, multilingual personnel, business library, computerized airline info system, secretarial, word-processing and transcription services, typewriter, dictaphone and personal computer rental, modems, VCRs, copy service, MCI Mail, Dow Jones reports and Federal Express. Shopping arcade, car rental counters • 2 pools, outdoor jacuzzi, guest privileges at adjacent health club, tennis and golf nearby • 30 meeting rooms.

L'Ermitage $$$$
9291 Burton Way, Beverly Hills 90210 278-3344 ⊠ 698441 • 114 suites, 1 restaurant, 1 bar
The emphasis here is on individualism, high-quality accommodation, service and luxury. The public rooms are graced with Chagalls, Renoirs, Van Goghs, and Miró sculptures. All the suites have separate sleeping areas, wet bar, private terraces, fully equipped kitchen and multi-line telephones and can accommodate small business meetings. Complimentary limo • rooftop pool, mineral water spa, solarium • 2 meeting rooms, teleconferencing.

Le Mondrian $$$$
8440 Sunset Blvd, West Hollywood 90069 ☏ 650-8999 ⊠ 182570 • 188 suites, 2 restaurants, 1 bar
Named after the Dutch artist Piet Mondrian, this 12-story suites-only hotel has little chance of ever blending into Hollywood's Sunset Strip backdrop. Its façade sports a huge surrealistic mural and the arty feel is continued into the lobby with a display of works by contemporary artists. Each suite has three telephones with up to five lines, and all are suitably adapted for business meetings or entertaining. Beauty salon (men and women), complimentary limo • pool, jacuzzi • 3 meeting rooms.

New Otani $$$$
1st and Los Angeles 90012 ☏ 629-1200 ⊠ 677022 • 448 rooms, 10 suites, 3 restaurants, 2 bars, 1 coffee shop
Appropriately located in the center of Little Tokyo, the luxurious New Otani caters especially to Japanese executives. It has traditional Japanese suites and a delightful half-acre garden. The Thousand Cranes serves *tempura* and *sushi*; Commodore Perry's specializes in steaks and seafood. The Music Center, City Hall and the courts are within walking distance. Sauna, jacuzzi, massage • 8 meeting rooms.

Sheraton Grande $$$$$
333 S Figueroa St 90071 ☏ 617-1133 ⊠ 677003 • 470 rooms, 60 suites, 4 restaurants, 2 bars
Popular with upper management, the Grande has unusually high standards

for a Sheraton. Rooms are spacious and well-equipped for working, and there is a butler on every floor. Like the Bonaventure, the Sheraton is connected to some of LA's high-rises by walkways. Errand service • pool, arrangements with nearby health club • 17 meeting rooms, fax, translation, teleconferencing, recording facilities.

Westin Bonaventure **$$$$**
404 S Figueroa St 90071
☏ 624-1000 TX 677628 • 1,474 rooms, 100 suites, 4 restaurants, 2 bars
Designed by John Portman, the Bonaventure is one of downtown LA's most distinctive landmarks. Its five futuristic glass cylinders are linked by skywalks to the twin ARCO Towers, the Wells Fargo Building and the World Trade Center. A convention hotel with extensive facilities, the Bonaventure has a five-level mall, a maze of freeway-like passages and more than 50 shops and boutiques. There are five executive floors and two for non-smokers. The views from the rotating Top of Five Restaurant on the 35th floor are exceptional, perhaps more memorable than the food. Tennis at adjacent racquet club, pool • 26 meeting rooms, exhibit hall, fax.

Westwood Marquis **$$$$$**
930 Hilgard Ave 90024 ☏ 208-8765 TX 181835 • 256 suites, 2 restaurants, 2 bars
Westwood's premier hotel is located in a residential neighborhood within walking distance of the Village. The ambiance is European and intimate, the service attentive and discreet. Guests tend to be in advertising or entertainment. Florist, hairdresser, complimentary limo • 2 pools, sundeck, hydrotherapy tubs, massage, sauna, jacuzzi • 6 meeting rooms.

OTHER HOTELS

Beverly Crest ($$$) *125 S Spaulding Dr ☏ 274-6801.* A comfortable low-profile hotel in Beverly Hills.
Embassy ($$) *851 S Grand Ave ☏ 622-3200.* Stay here when you can't get a room at the Figueroa.
Figueroa ($$) *939 S Figueroa St ☏ 627-8971.* Comfort, facilities and ambiance make this downtown hotel a contender in the luxury class.
Other There are a few motels and hotels in the beach cities just S of LAX and lots near the big theme parks in Anaheim.

Clubs

Established powerbrokers belong to the city's oldest gentlemen's club, the *California Club*, while the up-and-coming are members of the *Jonathan Club*, which has premises downtown and a beach house in Santa Monica. More reluctantly than other clubs in the city, both have opened their doors to minorities, but neither admits women.

The *LA Athletic Club* has extensive gym/workout facilities, fine bedrooms and a very good lunch room. Membership is non-exclusive, but most members are over 40 rather than young bloods. The *University Club*, open to anyone who has a college or university degree, does a brisk lunch and dinner business. So does the *Petroleum Club*, where the membership now extends beyond the petroleum, oil and gas industries. In mid-Wilshire, the *Los Angeles Club*, one of the city's biggest, is much used by the local Korean business set. The *Regency Club* in Westwood has some top names from politics and entertainment.

Of the many suburban country clubs, the oldest and most prestigious is the *LA Country Club.* It has many members in common with the California Club: the only women admitted are members' wives, and they have to use a separate entrance. S of Beverly Hills, the *Hillcrest Country Club* was established by Jews who could not join the LACC. The *Bel-Air Country Club* is the place that positively welcomes people from the entertainment industry.

Restaurants

LA's casual atmosphere and abundance of restaurants means that business can and does go on all day – at lunch, dinner and even breakfast. Lunch venues are generally determined by geography, so although most of the best restaurants are in West Hollywood, downtowners tend to eat at a few local restaurants and clubs. The entertainment industry goes to Sunset and Santa Monica boulevards, and suburban industries like aerospace and high-tech have their own neighborhood favorites.

Bistro $$$
246 N Canon Dr, Beverly Hills
☎ 273-5633 • closed Sun • AE CB DC MC V • jacket preferred
An old Beverly Hills standard, the Bistro caters to the political, business and Hollywood communities, and is the venue for many parties, charity functions and society affairs. The interior is attractive, the dining room open but discreet. Food is very good French/Continental.

Bistro Garden $$
176 N Canon Dr ☎ 550-3900 • AE CB DC MC V
Sister to the Bistro, but trendier, this eating house is priced lower and does a hefty business lunch trade.

Le Chardonnay $$$
8284 Melrose Ave, West Hollywood
☎ 655-8880 • closed Sun • AE CB DC MC V
A lovely turn-of-the-century bistro whose French/Californian cuisine is made distinctive by the wood rôtisserie and mesquite grill. Le Chardonnay's lunch is dominated by both the entertainment and advertising industries.

Chinois on Main $$$
2709 Main St, Santa Monica
☎ 392-9025 • AE DC MC V • reservations essential
Chinois, Wolfgang Puck's second restaurant, opened in 1982 to the same kind of outrageous success as his first, Spago's. This "experiment" combines French and Chinese cuisine, producing delightful results. The iridescent green and maroon interior, designed by his wife, is as beautifully exotic as the food. Tables are somewhat close together, and the place gets noisy at night. Weekends require a four-week reservation.

Le Dôme $$$
8720 Sunset Blvd, West Hollywood
☎ 659-6919 • AE CB DC MC V
A tasteful restaurant featuring good French food influenced by California cuisine. Le Dôme's Sunset Strip location makes the restaurant popular with agencies, production companies and celebrities. Tables offer enough privacy for quiet conversations. The lunch and after-hours drinks are workmanlike; things get more elegant after 8.

Harry's Bar $$$
2020 Ave of the Stars ☎ 277-2333 • D only Sun • AE MC V
Related to the Harry's in Venice, Florence and San Francisco, this is the premier restaurant in Century City. Fine northern Italian food is served in casual, elegant surroundings. The intimate and quietly chatty dining room is popular.

Michael's $$$$
1147 3rd St, Santa Monica
☎ 458-3800 • AE CB DC MC V
Everybody who's anybody has eaten at Michael's, still one of the most important dining rooms in Greater LA. White umbrellas in a garden setting are the backdrop to the Californian/French cuisine, which includes a variety of char-broiled meats, fish and fowl. The wine list has many classics. A good choice for business discussions.

Musso & Frank Grill **$$$**
6667 Hollywood Blvd, Hollywood
☎ 483-6000 • closed Sun • AE CB DC MC V
This, the oldest restaurant in Hollywood, caters mainly for the lower-profile, older showbiz crowd, as well as businessmen who value the restaurant's lack of trendiness. The specialty is American food served with a minimum of fuss. Spacious wooden enclosed booths afford privacy and discretion.

L'Orangerie **$$$$**
903 N La Cienega Blvd, West Hollywood ☎ 652-9770 • D only • AE CB DC MC V
An impressive restaurant, both in its traditional French food and the opulent surroundings. Seafood and delicacies are flown in from France. Formal ambiance is heightened by exotic plants and high ceilings. Open for dinner only, L'Orangerie is best for social or celebratory meals. The clientele includes wealthy people from all walks of life.

Pacific Dining Car **$$$**
1310 W 6th St ☎ 483-6000 • MC V
One of LA's few 24hr restaurants, the Dining Car attracts downtown regulars for early breakfast as well as dinner. Steak is its main feature. Large tables and booths and unfussy service make it a good place to spread papers and linger.

Palm **$$$$**
9001 Santa Monica Blvd, West Hollywood ☎ 550-8811 • AE CB DC MC V
Food and atmosphere are modeled on the New York original, with sawdust on the floor, a crowded dining room and slightly hyper service. Old Hollywood stalwarts and city powerbrokers eat here; excellent steaks and French fries are the pick of the menu.

La Petite Chaya **$$$$**
1930 Hillhurst Ave, Hollywood
☎ 665-5991 • AE CB MC V
French/Japanese cuisine is a hybrid that continues to grow in popularity in LA. La Petite Chaya's claim to fame, and one they are proud of, is that they are the original. Best are the *sashimi* creations prepared in the French manner. Décor is understated, the clientele discreet. Employees from the nearby ABC Studios use it for lunch.

Rex il Ristorante **$$$$**
617 S Olive St ☎ 627-2300 • closed Sun • AE CB DC MC V • jacket required • reservations essential
Located in the glamorous Oviatt Building, and reeking of old money from places like San Marino and Hancock Park, the Rex has a discreet atmosphere. The food is *nouvelle* Italian, delicate and attractively presented, complementing the smoked etched glass and shining black décor.

Seventh Street Bistro **$$$**
815 W 7th St ☎ 627-1242 • D only Sat and Sun • AE CB DC MC V
A hot downtown spot at both lunch and dinner, the Bistro is the new favorite of many top executives and show-business types. Its French-style food and its growing popularity have contributed to the growth of the downtown scene.

Spago's **$$$$**
1114 Horn Ave, West Hollywood
☎ 652-4025 • D only • AE DC MC V • reservations essential
Wolfgang Puck, who is both chef and owner, has greatly influenced Californian cooking with his creative combinations of fresh and unusual herbs and vegetables with grilled meat, fish and fowl. Located on the Sunset Strip, Spago's is one of LA's biggest celebrity hangouts. Big and noisy, it is a place to see and be seen. But even with a reservation you may have to wait.

Tony Roma's **$$**
9404 Brighton Way, Beverly Hills
☎ 278-1207 • AE CB DC MC V

Part of an international chain, Tony Roma's has reliably good ribs and delicious onion rings. The Beverly Hills location offsets the decidedly funky, proletarian feel, but you come here for the spicy sauce, not the snob appeal. Lunch is busy and Tony's is open until 1.30am.

Tower $$$
Transamerica Center, 1150 S Olive St ☏ 746-1554 • AE CB DC MC V • jacket required
The Tower is a well-respected French restaurant atop the 32-story Transamerica Center. Fish is the house specialty, and there is an ample wine cellar. A lunchtime favorite for downtown executives, where business can be discussed without being overheard.

Trumps $$$
8764 Melrose Ave ☏ 855-1480 • closed Sun except for afternoon tea • AE V
A chic art-gallery-land spot with a striking interior and appealing French/Californian cuisine, Trumps is impressively contemporary but too noisy for serious talk.

Valentino $$$$
4313 Pico Blvd, Santa Monica ☏ 829-4313 • closed Sun • AE CB DC MC V
Owner Piero Selvaggio's charm and enthusiasm have made this one of the best Italian restaurants in LA, with inventive food and a wine list of more than 1,100 varieties from France, Italy and California. Valentino is a popular choice for Fortune 500, IBM and McDonnell Douglas executives.

Working breakfasts
Breakfast is an important meal in LA. Most high-profile industry breakfasts take place in the city's top hotels; senior studio executives get together in the pink recesses of *Beverly Hills's Polo Lounge* or on the terraces of the Bel-Air. In the "others" category, *Hugo's*, 8401 Santa Monica Blvd ☏ 654-3993 is popular and *Canter's*, 419 N Fairfax Ave ☏ 651-2030, a 24hr deli in the heart of the traditional Jewish district, is an LA institution.

Mexican eating
California has many good, cheap Mexican restaurants. Two of LA's best are *El Cholo*, 1121 S Western Ave ☏ 734-2773 (there's always a wait of at least 20min, but the lounge is comfortable) and *La Villa Taxco*, 4444 Sunset Blvd ☏ 665-5751.

Bars
Los Angeles, by and large, is not a city renowned for bars. The *Cock 'n Bull*, 9170 Sunset Blvd ☏ 273-0081 is lively, traditional and has a loyal clientele. The *Polo Lounge* at the Beverly Hills Hotel, 9641 Sunset Blvd ☏ 276-2251 is the haunt of Hollywood moguls, and the *Grande Avenue Bar* ☏ 624-1011 at the Biltmore, is the smartest of the downtown hotel bars. A few restaurants have good or interesting bars – for example *The Ginger Man*, 369 N Bedford Dr, Beverly Hills ☏ 273-7585 owned by film duo Patrick O'Neal and Carroll O'Connor. Out in Santa Monica, *Merlin McFly's*, 2072 Main St ☏ 392-6468 is always busy on weeknights; at weekends its clientele is mainly singles and young professionals. Also in Santa Monica is the rowdy *Kings Head*, 116 Santa Monica Blvd ☏ 451-1402 an English-style pub frequented by the substantial local British émigré population.

Entertainment
The best source for news of what's on is either of two free weeklies, the *LA Weekly* and the *LA Reader*. *Ticketmaster* ☏ 480-3232 and *Ticketron* ☏ 216-6666 sell tickets to all concerts, shows and sporting events. *Equity Ticket Agency* ☏ 629-1241 and *Murray's* ☏ 234-0123 are ticket brokers who can arrange choice seats, at higher prices.
Cinemas Impressive theaters

include the *Mann Chinese* (see *Sightseeing*), the *Pacific Cineramadome*, 6360 Sunset Blvd ☏ 466-3401 and the *Plitt* in Century City ☏ 553-4291.

Nightclubs Many clubs – most notably, the *Comedy Store*, 8433 Sunset Blvd ☏ 656-6225 and the *Improvisation*, 8162 Melrose Ave ☏ 651-2583 – feature comedians every night. The Improv has dancing Sun and Mon. The *Vine St Bar & Grill*, 1610 Vine St ☏ 463-4375 is a supper club with top-class vocal and jazz acts. The *Variety Arts Center* downtown, 940 S Figueroa St ☏ 623-9100 has several simultaneous shows, including comedy and music.

Theater and music The biggest, most luxurious stage theater is the *Shubert* in Century City ☏ 553-9000 where major Broadway shows appear. Downtown, the *Music Center* ☏ 972-7211 has three venues, the largest of which – the Dorothy Chandler Pavilion – hosts the LA Philharmonic Orchestra. In Hollywood, the Art Deco *Pantages* puts on plays and musicals; *James Doolittle Theater* ☏ 410-1062 specializes in classic plays and one-man shows.

One unique feature of LA is the large number of equity waiver theaters, which because they seat 99 or less can ignore union rules and restrictions. For the city's hordes of struggling actors, writers and directors, they offer a chance to work in legitimate theater. The *Greek Theater* ☏ 216-6666 is an impressive outdoor bowl built into the side of a hill; it has top musicians Apr–Oct. For rock'n roll, there is the Art Deco *Palace* ☏ 462-3000.

Shopping

Rodeo Drive and *Wilshire Boulevard* in Beverly Hills are the most exclusive shopping districts, with some stores open only by appointment. *Melrose Avenue* is the city's liveliest, most contemporary shopping area. New-wave and second-hand clothing mix with smart shops such as Olivia Newton-John's Koala Blue, and there are others selling gifts, records and 1950s furniture. At night, their neon signs are pure art. The *Beverly Center* at La Cienega and Beverly boulevards ☏ 854-0074 is a major shopping mall, with department stores and boutiques, as well as 25 restaurants and a 16-movie theater complex. The *Westside Pavilion*, Pico Blvd and Overland St in West LA, is one of the city's newest malls. Some of the restaurants, like Crayons on the street level, have unique, wild décor, and the Samuel Goldwyn Theater has impressive neon.

Downtown The wholesale *jewelry district* is clustered around the International Jewelry Center on Hill St at 6th; the *garment district* is around the Cooper Building on Los Angeles and 9th St; and there are the *wholesale flower market* on San Pedro at 7th and the *product market* S on San Pedro. High-rise lobby malls include the *Bonaventure* at 404 S Figueroa, the *ARCO Plaza* at 505 S Flower, and the *Broadway Plaza* at 700 S Flower. In Little Tokyo, traditional vendors, at the *Japanese Village Plaza* on 2nd and Central, merge with luxurious high-tech toy and electronic stores (at Weller Court on 2nd and San Pedro).

Movie memorabilia *Larry Edmunds Book Shop*, 6658 Hollywood Blvd ☏ 463-3273 has one of the area's most extensive collections of film reference books and memorabilia.

Sightseeing

Hollywood landmarks Only the most avid movie buff will not be disappointed by the famous Hollywood landmarks. The only must is *Mann's Chinese Theater* (formerly Grauman's), 6926 Hollywood Blvd ☏ 464-8111 where Cary Grant, Jimmy Durante and Trigger have left their respective foot, nose and hoof prints in the cement pavement; there, too, is the *Walk of Fame*, where bronze stars are

inlaid in the pavement to commemorate Hollywood's greatest.
Studio tours N over the Hollywood Hills are two half-day studio tours: the *Universal Studios Tour*, 3900 Lankershim Blvd, Universal City ☏ (818) 777-5444 is more of an amusement park ride than "peek-behind-the scenes"; the *NBC TV Studio*, 300 W Almeda Ave, Burbank ☏ (818) 840-4444 is more technical and less anecdotal.
Griffith Park For a spectacular, panoramic view of LA, Griffith Park's Observatory can't be matched. The Observatory has a set of museum-like displays, while the Planetarium's telescope is open from sunset until late, with three shows a night at 6.30, 9.15 and 10.30. The park (Visitors' Center ☏ 665-5188) offers a wide selection of activities, from golf and tennis to sunbathing, hiking and the Zoo. *Observatory, Vermont Ave ☏ 664-1191. Opens 11.30am Mon–Fri; 12.30 Sat and Sun.*
Museums Below Hollywood in mid-Wilshire are the *La Brea Tar Pits*, 5801 Wilshire Blvd ☏ 936-2230 a wellspring of natural tar that seeps still onto surrounding roads; fossils found in the tar are on show. Next to the Tar Pits is the city's major museum, the *LA County Museum of Art*, 5905 Wilshire Blvd ☏ 937-2590. The *Getty Museum of Art*, 17985 Pacific Coast Hwy, Malibu ☏ 454-6541 is one of the richest in the USA; reservations required. The recently established *Museum of Contemporary Art*, 250 S Grand Ave ☏ 382-662, a striking adjunct to California Plaza, houses 20thC art. S of downtown are the *Museum of Science and Industry* ☏ 744-7400 with "touch" displays, NASA-loaned space and satellite equipment and IMAX (image maximation) films which project onto a five-story screen with a six-channel stereo system.
Theme parks Nothing is quite like *Disneyland*, 50 miles/80km S in Orange County. Allow a whole day; 1313 Harbor Blvd, Anaheim ☏ (741) 999-4565. *Knott's Berry Farm*, 8039 Beach Blvd, Anaheim ☏ (741) 220-5200 is a good second. In Long Beach, you can visit the *Queen Mary*, Pier J ☏ 435-3511, now permanently docked alongside *Spruce Goose*, the world's largest all-wood aircraft, built by Howard Hughes.

Guided tours

Starline Tours, 6845 Hollywood Blvd ☏ 463-3131 offer the best combination of tours and service. *Gray Line Tours Co*, 6333 W 3rd St ☏ 481-2121 are a national chain. Hollywood tours include *Fantasy Tours*, 1721 N Highland Ave ☏ 469-8184 whose open double-decker buses cruise the landmarks. *Hollywood on Location*, 8644 Wilshire Blvd ☏ 659-9165 publishes a daily listing of TV and film shoots with detailed maps. Walking tours through the lands of LA heritage are conducted by the *LA Conservancy*, 849 S Broadway ☏ 623-2489.

Spectator sports

Baseball Dodger Stadium, 1000 Elysian Park Ave ☏ 224-1500 is home to the LA *Dodgers*; the California *Angels* play at the Anaheim Stadium, 2000 State College Blvd, Anaheim ☏ (714) 937-6700.
Basketball The *Lakers* appear at the Forum ☏ 674-6000; the San Diego *Clippers* at the Sports Arena ☏ 748-6131.
Football The LA *Raiders* kick off at the Coliseum, 3911 S Figueroa St ☏ 747-7111; LA *Rams* play at Anaheim.
Soccer The LA *Lazers* can be seen at the Forum, Manchester Blvd, Inglewood ☏ 674-6000.
Horse racing *Santa Anita Park*, Huntington Dr and Baldwin Ave, Arcadia ☏ (818) 574-7223 has a heavy schedule of winter racing and is a social highspot. *Hollywood Park*, Century Blvd ☏ 677-7151 also has winter racing. Summer racing is at *Del Mar*, Jimmy Durante Drive off Hwy 5 ☏ (619) 755-1141 right on the beach.

Keeping fit

Most hotels have extensive private facilities and/or arrangements with specialized clubs. The *Wilshire YMCA*, 225 S Oxford Ave ☏ 386-8570 has limited facilities, but the new and very smart *Downtown YMCA*, 401 S Hope St ☏ 624-2348 provides a full service. Both sell daily passes. *Nautilus Plus*, 888 International Tower at Figueroa and 9th ☏ 488-0095 has an extensive range of facilities, including weight machines.

Beaches From Malibu to the highly populated South Bay and beyond, there is a string of large public beaches. *Will Rogers Beach*, N on the Pacific Coast Hwy at Topanga Canyon Blvd, has a large parking lot and a comfortable mixed crowd. Southward *Santa Monica Beach*, the easiest to get to at the end of Rte 10, usually sees a colorful ethnic group. *Venice Beach* has a discreet topless bathing area. *Manhattan Beach* and those to the S, like Huntington, are popular with surfers.

Cycling The bike path that runs down along the ocean's edge from Santa Monica to Palos Verdes is the area's favorite biking spot. Cyclists are also permitted in Griffith Park, though some of the hills are steep.

Jogging Alongside the oceanfront bike path is a pedestrian path popular with joggers. Other options are the clifftop *Pacific Palisades Park*, overlooking the ocean (Ocean Blvd in Santa Monica); *San Vicente Blvd* (extending from Ocean Blvd 4 mile/6.5km to Brentwood Center); and a 4-mile/6.5km hilly path at *UCLA*. In the city itself, both *Griffith Park* and *Echo Park Lake* are used by joggers.

Golf There are a dozen LA municipal courses. If you can't get in to *Rancho Park*, 10460 W Pico Blvd ☏ 838-7373 try *Wilson* or *Harding*, Griffith Park Dr ☏ 663-2555. The *Riviera Country Club*, 1250 Capri Dr, Pacific Palisades ☏ 454-6591, home of the PGA Championship Open, is one of the few private clubs that allow non-members ($100 a person).

Racquet sports The *Sports Connection* chain ☏ 652-7440 rents courts by the hour. Public tennis courts include *The Tennis Place*, 5880 W 3rd St ☏ 931-1715 and *Riverside Tennis* at Griffith Park ☏ 661-5318.

Local resources

Business services

Several LA-based firms offer a full range of business services. *Fingerprint*, 8467 Melrose Pl ☏ 653-2082 is an electronic page-processing center providing comprehensive desktop publishing facilities. *Modern Secretarial*, 2813 La Cienega Blvd ☏ 870-5882 offers a full range of services, while *California Transcribing*, 6010 Wilshire Blvd ☏ 857-5566 include in-house dictation machines, word-processing and optical scanning.

Photocopying and printing *Charlie Chan Printing* is a reliable chain with an office in the Union Bank Bldg, 445 S Figueroa ☏ 622-1231 that does pick-up and delivery; there are two more downtown sites on Wilshire Blvd ☏ 381-1301 and 380-6121; and dozens throughout the city.

Secretarial *Electronic Office Personnel* ☏ 934-8211, *Olsten Temporary Services* ☏ 385-8367 and *Stivers Temporary Personnel* ☏ 386-3440 are reliable firms.

Translation *Academie Language Center* ☏ 651-1670, *Inlingua Language & Translation* ☏ 386-9949 and *Berlitz Language Center* ☏ 380-1144.

Communications

Local delivery *Super Messenger Service* ☏ 469-2744 and *Rocket* ☏ 469-7155 are both reliable.

Long-distance delivery *Federal Express* ☏ 687-9767; *DHL* ☏ 973-7300.

Post office The *Worldway Postal Center* at LAX, 5800 W Century Blvd, is open 7am–8pm, but the Express Mail window is open 24hrs. The *Terminal Annex* downtown is at

900 N Alameda St ☎ 617-4641 open 7am–9pm.
Telex *ITT World Communications* ☎ 269-9191; *Nanosec* ☎ (800) 227-4247; *West Coast Telex & Secretarial* ☎ 463-0903.
Fax *Nanosec* ☎ (800) 227-4247; *Action Telex* ☎ 653-9361.

Conference/exhibition centers

Most hotels have meeting facilities, and several specialize in conventions. Downtown LA also has the *Convention Center*, 1202 S Figeuroa St ☎ 741-1151 a municipal facility with a main exhibition hall and several smaller rooms. The *California Conference Center*, 1329 S Hope St ☎ 746-7393 hosts smaller meetings.

Emergencies

Hospitals *Good Samaritan*, 616 S Witmer St ☎ 977-2121; *Cedars Sinai*, 8700 Beverly Blvd ☎ 855-5000; *UCLA Medical Center* ☎ 825-9111. For dental emergencies, the *LA Dental Society* ☎ 481-2133 makes referrals; the *USC Medical Center*, 12300 N State St ☎ 226-2622, offers short-term, 24hr assistance.
Pharmacies *Horton & Converse* has about a dozen stores; some stay open late, all deliver. The downtown store is at 201 S Alvarado St ☎ 413-2424 open 9–5; Beverly Hills, 9730 Wilshire Blvd ☎ 272-1034 open 8.30–5; and mid-Wilshire, 3875 Wilshire ☎ 382-2236 open until 2am.
Police *Downtown*, 251 E 6th St ☎ 485-3294; *Beverly Hills*, 450 N Crescent Dr ☎ 550-4951.

Government offices

City of LA information ☎ 485-3891; *California Dept of Commerce/Business Development* ☎ 735-3680; *US Dept of Commerce/International Trade Administration* ☎ 209-7612; *Immigration and Naturalization* ☎ 894-2119.

Information sources

Business information *LA Area Chamber of Commerce* ☎ 629-0711 covers downtown; *Wilshire Chamber of Commerce* ☎ 386-8224 includes Hollywood; *Los Angeles West Chamber of Commerce* ☎ 475-4574 has good information on Westside and Greater LA.
Local media LA's most comprehensive and international magazine and newspaper store is the *Universal News Agency*, 1655 N Las Palmas Ave ☎ 467-3850. The *Los Angeles Times* has a business section daily (including weekends) with complete stock listings. The *Los Angeles Herald Examiner* is smaller in size and circulation. *Los Angeles* is a glitzy regional magazine; *California* is a well-written monthly. *KNX* (1070 *AM*) and *KFWB* (98 *AM*) are all-news radio stations.
Tourist information *Greater Los Angeles Visitors' and Convention Bureau*, 515 S Figueroa St ☎ 624-7300; *Visitors' Information Center*, ARCO Plaza ☎ 689-8822.

Thank-yous

Florists *Pete's Flowers*, 6260 Sunset Blvd ☎ 466-4060 services entertainment corporations like MCA and Motown and supplies fruit packs and gourmet baskets, locally and abroad. *Downstairs Greenery & Florists* has three downtown locations: ARCO Plaza ☎ 485-1171, Bonaventure ☎ 620-0601 and California Mart ☎ 628-0107.
Gift baskets A corporate favorite is *San Antonio Winery*, 737 Lamar St ☎ 2123-1401, for wine, pâté and cheeses. *Ultimate Nut & Candy*, Farmer's Market, 3rd and Fairfax ☎ 938-1555 provides candies, chocolate-covered nuts and fruits and popcorn combinations. *Classic Gourmet Baskets* ☎ 262-1740 will send fruit and jam baskets.

MEMPHIS

Area code ☎ 901

Memphis, an old Southern city with an easy tempo, is an important distribution center, a launching pad for entrepreneurs and the crucible of rock 'n'roll. The city sits on a high bluff beside the Mississippi River in the extreme SW tip of Tennessee. It is the urban center of an agricultural region that includes parts of Mississippi, Arkansas, Missouri and Tennessee, and its economic base is closely tied to agriculture. It also houses the headquarters of such national corporations as Holiday Inns, Federal Express, Dunavant Enterprises and Schering-Plough. The population is about 1m.

Arriving

Memphis International Airport

MIA has few international flights, but busy domestic services operate daily 6.30am–11.30pm. The three-concourse terminal building has a business center (in the center concourse across from TWA), offering secretarial, computer, telex and telecopying services, 7–5 Mon–Fri. There is a full-service travel agency, 7–7 Mon–Fri, 8–5 Sat. Western Union, money order and travellers' check services are available.

Nearby hotels *Sheraton Skyport Inn*, on the mezzanine level of the airport's W and E concourses ☎ 345-3220. *Sheraton Airport Inn*, 2411 Winchester Rd (in airport grounds) ☎ 332-2370.

City link The airport is about 20min in rush hour by road from the city's major business centers. Most major hotels offer a courtesy car service, obtainable through direct telephones in the baggage claim areas.

Taxi Cabs stand outside the baggage claim areas. There is a $5 minimum charge for airport trips, and it's advisable to negotiate in advance.

Car rental All the major companies have booths near the baggage claim area in each concourse, but lower rental rates are available in the city.

Getting around

The best way to get around in Memphis is by car. The city is spread out, and taxis are relatively expensive. Buses are slow and rarely run late at night.

Driving Parking is not a major problem, but there are occasional rush-hour traffic jams in major business areas, 7.30–8.30 and 4–5.30. In most areas roads form a grid pattern, with streets running N–S and avenues E–W. For information on hazardous road conditions or for emergency help, contact the *Tennessee Highway Patrol* ☎ 386-3831.

Taxi You cannot hail a cab on the street. *Yellow Cab* ☎ 526-2121 is recommended.

Limousine Cadillac limousines may be hired from *Yellow Cab* ☎ 526-8358.

Bus The routes of the municipally owned bus system (MATA) are not useful for business travellers. For information ☎ 274-6282.

Area by area

Memphis began as two separate ports, Memphis and South Memphis, which were merged in 1840. The major business, government and financial center is in downtown along the Mississippi River. Development and restoration are underway, and a section within Parkways Boulevard in downtown has been developed as a medical and research zone. Farther E, a second major business center has grown up at the intersection of the interstate by-pass and Poplar Avenue. Residential areas spread throughout the city. Some of the most fashionable include Central Gardens, East Memphis, and new areas farther E, among them River Oaks.

Hotels

The city where Holiday Inns were born is still the headquarters of the international chain and has seven Holiday Inns, including the flagship Crowne Plaza. For traditional ambiance and prestige, however, the choice is the Peabody.

Crowne Plaza $$$
250 N Main St 38103 ☏ 527-7300 • Holiday Inn • 406 rooms, 14 suites, 2 restaurants, 2 bars
Designed primarily as a convention hotel, the 18-story Crowne Plaza overlooks the Mississippi River and is connected to the Memphis Convention Center. Car rental and airline desks • indoor pool, whirlpool, sauna, exercise room • 6 meeting rooms.

French Quarter Inn $$$
2144 Madison Ave 38104 ☏ 728-4000 • 69 suites, 1 restaurant, 1 bar
Modern, all-suite and luxurious, this hotel is adjacent to the restaurants, bars and shops of Overton Square in midtown. Within walking distance of Overton Park, it draws much of its clientele from the medical center. All suites have jacuzzis and their own bars. Weight room, good location for jogging • 2 meeting rooms.

Hyatt Regency $$$
939 Ridgelake Blvd 38119 ☏ 761-1234 ⓉⓍ 533299 • 380 rooms, 10 suites, 1 restaurant, 1 bar
This contemporary 27-story hotel is in a beautifully landscaped office development in the center of the city's eastern business section. Rooms have mini-bars and coffee-making equipment. Car rental desks • pool, complimentary admission to local health spa • 31 meeting rooms.

■ HOTELS
A Crowne Plaza
B French Quarter Inn
C Hyatt Regency
D Peabody
E Residence Inn

● RESTAURANTS
Dux (Hotel D)
A Folk's Folly
B Justine's
C Palm Court
D Rendezvous

◆ BUILDINGS AND SIGHTS
A City Hall
B Chamber of Commerce
C Memphis Convention Center
D Mid-South Coliseum and Liberty Bowl Stadium
E Information Center
F Beale Street Historic District
G Chucalissa Indian Village
H Court Square
I Dixon Gallery and Gardens
J Graceland
K Memphis Brooks Museum of Art
L Victorian Village

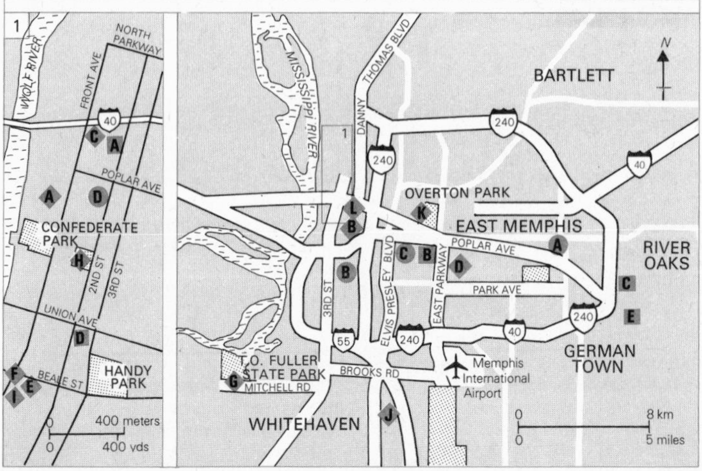

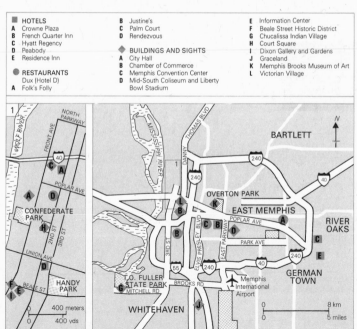

Peabody $$$$
149 Union Ave 38103 ☎ 529-4000
TX 558503 • 454 rooms, 24 suites, 4 restaurants, 3 bars
A few decades ago the Peabody was *the* hotel in the region. It then fell on leaner times, and was closed for renovation in the 1970s. Now listed in the National Register of Historic Places, it is again *the* place to stay. Its elegance, ambiance and service make it important in city social life. Chez Philippe, an expensive, prestigious, formal French restaurant with excellent food and a harpist, is open for dinner daily except Sunday. Dux is a highly recommended spot for regional dining (see *Restaurants*). The Lobby Bar is perfect for afternoon tea or after-work cocktails (see *Bars*). Mallards is popular with the downtown crowd for lunch and offers the best in evening entertainment (see *Entertainment*). Shopping arcade
• pool, whirlpool, sauna, health club
• 23 meeting rooms.

Residence Inn $$$
6141 Poplar Pike Rd 38119
☎ 685-9595 • 106 suites
The Residence's all-suite complex offers the long-term business visitor apartment-like living. The longer you stay, the cheaper the rate. On the edge of five residential areas in the city's eastern business sector, the suites are in modern four-story townhouses. All have a living room with fireplace, dining area, equipped kitchen, separate bedroom or bedrooms and bath with jacuzzi. Grocery service
• sports court • 2 meeting rooms, transport to and from seminars within 2 miles/3km.

OTHER HOTELS
Memphis has many moderately priced hotels and motels clustered in the downtown area, around the medical center, near the airport and in the city's eastern business area near I-240 and Poplar Avenue. They include four *Hampton Inns*, *Holiday Inn's* new no-frills city hotels ☎ (800) 426-7866, and three *La Quinta Inns* ☎ (800) 531-5900.

Clubs
Memphis restaurants and bars have been able to serve alcohol only since 1969. As a result, much entertaining was done at home or in private clubs, a pattern that still holds. The *Memphis Country Club* (old-line club with a few guest rooms), *Chickasaw Country Club*, *Colonial Country Club* and *Ridgeway Country Club* are exclusive and offer golf, tennis, swimming and dining. The *Memphis Hunt and Polo Club* and *University Club* are in the same category, but have no golf course. The *Racquet Club of Memphis*, an athletic club with a non-exclusive membership policy and outstanding facilities, hosts the US National Indoor Tennis Championships.

Restaurants
Although a lot of business entertaining takes place in clubs, the city does have a wide variety of restaurants, including traditional no-frills lunchtime cafés, serving "down home" Southern turnip greens, cornbread and meat and vegetable specials. Try one if you want something out of the ordinary: the *Cottage* (midtown), *Cupboard* (midtown), *Little Tea Shop* (downtown) or the *Fourway Grill* (South Memphis).

Dux $$$
149 Union Ave (in the Peabody Hotel)
☎ 529-4000 ext 199 • AE CB DC MC V
Dux has been named one of America's best new restaurants by *Esquire*, *Playboy* and *USA Today*. Its attractive contemporary décor, regional specialties and well-spaced tables make it a favorite with the business set from breakfast to dinner.

Folk's Folly $$$
51 S Mendenhall ☎ 767-2877 • D only • AE CB DC MC V • jacket recommended
The best steaks in town are reputed to be served in this small, unpretentious converted house. It is popular for after-work business discussions.

Justine's $$$
919 Coward Pl ☎ 527-3815 • D only; closed Sun • AE CB DC MC V • jacket required
If you are in town for only one night and looking for an elegant dinner, Justine's is the place. Its Continental cuisine is served in the elegant and formal atmosphere of the Old Coward Place, built in 1843 in French colonial style.

Palm Court $$
2101 Overton Sq Ln ☎ 725-6797 • D only; closed Mon • AE CB DC MC V
Located in the center of Overton Square, a midtown area noted for its restaurants, shops and nightlife, Palm Court serves northern Italian cuisine to local *cognoscenti.* The atmosphere is pleasant and lively.

Rendezvous $$
52 S 2nd St (enter through back off Gen Washburn Alley) ☎ 523-2746 • D only Tue, Wed, Thu; closed Sun, Mon, and last 2 weeks in Jul and Dec • AE CB DC MC V • beer only; take your own wine
Memphis claims to offer the world's best pork barbeque (and even has an annual international barbeque contest to prove it). The Rendezvous is one of the city's leading barbeque joints: it is underground, filled with memorabilia and has a festive atmosphere.

Bars
The city's bars have developed only since 1969. Overton Square, at the intersection of Madison and Cooper in midtown, has several types: *Paulette's* for a quiet drink, *La Chardonnay* for wine, *Bombay Bicycle Club* for the after-work crowd, and *Studebaker's* for the younger set who want to dance. The eastern business section along Poplar Avenue, E of Perkins, is dotted with bars for after-work drinking; and Beale Street, downtown, offers lively nightlife for the later hours. *Peabody Lobby Bar* is the best spot for conversation, quiet piano music, an after-work drink, weekday afternoon tea (3–4.30pm) or a nightcap in opulent surroundings; open 11am–1am daily (see *Hotels*).

Entertainment
Memphis and music are inseparable. This was where Black blues were first written down by W C Handy; it was also where blues and country & western melded to form 20thC rock 'n' roll. Elvis Presley lived here. Outdoor concerts are held throughout the year, and several bars are also good for live music. *Mallards*, Peabody Hotel, 149 Union Ave ☎ 529-4140 is a favorite with both locals and visitors; 9pm–1.30am Tue–Sat. *Rum Boogie Cafe*, 182 Beale St ☎ 528-0150 is just as loud and packed until 1am each night.

The city has several good regional theater companies and is a stopping point for touring productions. The Symphony and Opera are also big attractions. For listings, consult *Memphis Magazine* or Friday's *Commercial Appeal.*

Shopping
Malls Three top-quality small downtown malls and two big regional malls provide for most needs. The small malls are *Chickasaw Oaks Plaza*, between Poplar Ave and Walnut Grove, just E of Tillman; *Park Place Mall*, Park Ave and Ridgeway; and *Peabody Galleria*, inside the Peabody Hotel (see *Hotels*). The two large regional malls are *Hickory Ridge Mall*, on Winchester between Hickory Hill and Ridgeway, and *Mall of Memphis*, I-240, Perkins Rd and American Way.

Specialty shopping Good shops for special regional items are *Alice Bingham Gallery*, 24 S Cooper ☏ 722-8665, regional art; *Burke's Book Store*, 634 Poplar ☏ 527-7484, Southern history and rare books; *Patt Kerr Inc*, 200 Wagner Pl ☏ 525-5223, lace designer clothes, phone for appointment; *Strings and Things*, 1492 Union ☏ 278-0500, music store that does custom work for many stars; and *Woman's Exchange*, 88 Racine ☏ 327-5681, handmade children's clothing.

Sightseeing

Beale Street In the early 1800s it was the main street of South Memphis; at the turn of the century it was the birthplace of the blues and today it is an entertainment and shopping district.

Chucalissa Indian Village Choctaw Indians demonstrate crafts in this reconstructed Indian village and museum operated by Memphis State University. Several different settlements of the temple-mound culture lived on the site. *1987 Indian Village Dr ☏ 785-3160. Open 9–5, Tue–Sat; 1–5, Sun.*

Court Square This two-acre park has been the symbolic center of Memphis for generations. It is surrounded by landmark buildings, including the Porter Building, Lincoln American Tower and the Tennessee Club Building. *Between 2nd St and Mid-America Mall on Court.*

Dixon Gallery and Gardens Set in 17 acres of gardens, this 1940s house has antique furniture, silver, crystal, porcelain, carpets and a collection of French and Impressionist paintings. *4339 Park Ave ☏ 761-5250. Open 11–5, Mon–Sat; 1–5, Sun.*

Graceland Elvis Presley lived here from 1957 to 1977 and is buried with his parents in the gardens. Guided tours of the house, Elvis Museum and other memorabilia. *3717 Elvis Presley Blvd ☏ 332-3322. Open Jun–Aug, 8–6; Mar–May and Sep–Oct, 9–5; Nov–Feb, daily exc Tue, 9–5.*

Memphis Brooks Museum of Art The city's fine arts museum features the Kress Collection of Renaissance art and 16th–20thC paintings, prints and sculpture. *In Overton Park ☏ 722-3500. Open Tue–Sat, 10–5; Sun, 1–5.*

Victorian Village The impressive townhouses in the 600 block of Adams were built during the second half of the 19thC when cotton was king and Memphis was booming. Two are public museums. *Fontaine House*, a restored French Victorian mansion built about 1871, features period antiques and clothing; its renovated carriage house is now a Continental-style restaurant. *680 Adams ☏ 526-1469. Open Apr–Dec, 10–4, Mon–Sat; 1–4, Sun; Jan–Mar, 1–4 daily.* The other museum, the *Mallory-Neely House*, is an Italianate Victorian mansion built about 1852, modified 1883, which contains original family antiques and furnishings. *652 Adams ☏ 523-1484. Open 1–4.*

Guided tours

Boat Tours *Memphis Queen Excursion Boats* ☏ 527-5694; 90min scheduled cruises on a paddlewheeler.

Bus Tours *Gray Line Tours* ☏ 942-4662. Half- or full-day city, Elvis, riverboat and nightclub tours.

Spectator sports

Baseball The *Chicks*, a farm team of the Kansas City Royals, play in Chicks Stadium near the intersection of Central and E Parkway ☏ 272-1687.

Basketball The Memphis State University *Tigers* are at Mid-South Coliseum ☏ 454-2331.

Football This is the real craze in Memphis, and fans have been eagerly awaiting the reorganization of the USF league which foundered some years ago. Some time in 1987 the local professional team, the *Showboats*, will be back on their home ground at Liberty Bowl Stadium ☏ 272-1214.

Keeping fit

Most hotels have pools and exercise facilities. While private clubs are usually the setting for business across the net or on the green, public facilities are available. The *Memphis Park Commission*, 2599 Avery ☎ 454-5759 operates the city's 9 public golf courses, 17 swimming pools and 8 tennis centers. The most convenient public golf courses are *Audubon*, 4160 Park Ave ☎ 683-6941, *Overton Park*, 2080 Poplar Ave ☎ 725-9905 and *Galloway*, 3815 Walnut Grove Rd ☎ 685-7805. The most convenient public tennis courts are *Leftwich-Audubon*, 4145 Southern Ave ☎ 686-7907 and *Rodgers*, 1123 Jefferson Ave ☎ 523-0094. The *Memphis Area Chamber of Commerce* (see *Information sources*) produces a free fishing guide to the area.

Local resources

Business services

Photocopying and printing *Kinko's Copies* ☎ 327-2679 has the best prices and will pick up and deliver. *Clarke's Quick Print* has branches city-wide.
Translation *Memphis State University Foreign Languages Dept* ☎ 454-2506 or *Memphis Public Library Literature Dept* ☎ 725-8825.

Communications

Local delivery *Mad Annie's Package Express Inc* ☎ 725-0194.
Long-distance delivery *Federal Express* ☎ 345-5044.
Post office Main branch, 555 S 3rd St at Calhoun, lobby with stamp machines and pick-up open 24hr.
Telex and telegrams *Western Union* ☎ 526-0141.

Conference/exhibition centers

For information contact *Memphis Convention and Visitors' Bureau* ☎ 526-1919. The *Agricenter International* ☎ 756-7777 specializes in agribusiness conventions and trade shows. Also *Memphis Convention Center* ☎ 576-1200; *Mid-South Coliseum* ☎ 274-7400; and *Shelby Farms Showplace Arena* ☎ 756-7433.

Emergencies

Hospitals Most Memphis hospitals have several locations and each has 24hr emergency room service. The largest are *Baptist/Central*, 899 Madison ☎ 522-5511; *Methodist/Central*, 1265 Union ☎ 726-7600; *Regional Medical Center*, 877 Jefferson ☎ 528-7100, public. All major credit cards accepted. For ambulance ☎ 458-3311. Doctor or dentist referral ☎ 527-3311.
Pharmacies *Super D* and *Walgreen's* have locations city-wide. In-hospital pharmacies are open 24hr.
Police 201 Poplar ☎ 528-2222.

Government offices

Mayor's Action Center ☎ 576-6500 and *County Assistance Center* ☎ 576-4580 provide information for business visitors.

Information sources

Business information *Memphis Area Chamber of Commerce*, 555 Beale St ☎ 523-2322 supplies economic data on the community and works with businesses considering expanding or relocating in the area.
Local media The *Commercial Appeal* is the city's major daily; The *Daily News* is the daily business paper; *Memphis Business Journal* is the weekly business paper. The *Memphis Magazine*, is a monthly.
Tourist information *Visitors' Information Center*, 207 Beale St ☎ 526-4880 open Mon–Sat, 9–5. LINC ☎ 725-8895. A service run by the public library.

Thank-yous

Florist *John Hoover Flowers and Fine Gifts* ☎ 274-1851. Credit cards accepted; same-day delivery.
Gift baskets *John Simmon's* ☎ 682-5517. Credit cards accepted; delivery service.

MIAMI

Area code ☏ 305

Long famous for its resorts, Miami is now an international banking hub, a leading import-export center and a major cruise base. It is America's gateway to the Caribbean and to Central and South America; many corporations have their Latin American divisions in the city, or nearby. In the 1960s Miami began to develop a decidedly Latin flavor. (Of the 1.85m who now live in the city, 43% are of Latin origin and 17% are black.) South Florida is still a haven for retirees, but in Miami they are concentrated in the northern suburbs.

Arriving

Miami International Airport

MIA is almost constantly under construction. International passengers arrive at Concourse E, which houses Customs and Immigration. Passengers collect their baggage at street level, near car rental desks, taxi stands and stations. There is a 24hr multilingual information service (Concourse E ☏ 871-7000), currency exchange and snack bars.

Nearby hotels *Doral Hotel and Country Club*, 4400 NW 87th Ave 33178 ☏ 592-2000. *Marriott*, 1201 NW Le Jeune Rd 33126 ☏ 649-5000. *Miami Airport Hilton*, 5101 Blue Lagoon Dr 33126 ☏ 262-1000. *Radisson Mart Plaza*, 836 Expressway and Milam Dairy Rd ☏ 261-3800. *Sheraton River House*, 3900 NW 21st St 33142 ☏ 871-3800.

City link It is about a 15min drive to downtown, 30min to Miami Beach.

Taxi and limousine Cabs are plentiful; Redtop Limousine vans leave the airport for downtown and Miami Beach every 20–30min at less than half the price of cabs ☏ 526-5764.

Car rental Most major firms have offices at the airport, but cars may be in short supply during holiday periods. For collection on arrival, it is advisable to book in advance. Rental car costs in Florida are the lowest in the country.

Getting around

A rental car with air conditioning gives the most freedom and comfort. But the highway system is confusing and clogged, so use cabs until your business is done, then rent a car to go exploring. With the exception of Coral Gables and Coconut Grove, the city follows a grid pattern: avenues run N–S and streets run E–W. Miami Avenue divides E from W; Flagler Street N from S. Streets and avenues are numbered from the dividing lines, and street numbers are followed by NW, NE, SW or SE.

Taxi Cab drivers are strictly regulated. They must be able to speak English, load and unload baggage, turn on the air conditioning upon request, and know significant Miami destinations. They are not allowed to recommend specific businesses or to solicit tips. Major companies are *Central Cab* ☏ 532-5555; *Metro* ☏ 888-8888; *Super Yellow Cab* ☏ 855-5555; and *Yellow* ☏ 444-4444.

Limousine *Redtop* ☏ 526-5764; *Executive Limousine Service* ☏ 940-5252.

Rail The *MetroRail* ☏ 638-6700 elevated train links downtown Miami to Hialeah and Kendall/South Miami and connects with the elevated *MetroMover*, which circles the downtown area.

Bus *Metrobus* covers most of surrounding Dade County and links with MetroRail. It is not recommended for the business visitor.

Area by area

Downtown Philip Johnson's Mediterranean-style Cultural Arts Center and IM Pei's Centrust Tower are the most striking buildings; others are the Arquitectonic

Condominiums along Brickell Avenue, the Southeast Financial Center and its Chopin Plaza neighbors, the Bayside Specialty Center (a waterfront market place around the Miamarina) and Isamu Noguchi's computerized fountain on Biscayne Boulevard in the newly-redesigned Bayfront Park. The Dade County Courthouse, the City of Miami offices and the Federal Building are downtown. Major businesses are law, import-export, banking and jewelry.

Dodge Island Freight handling and the cruise business are centered on Dodge Island Port, just E of downtown. The Metro Dade Cultural Center (housing the impressive new Center for the Fine Arts, the South Florida Historical Museum and the public library), the James L Knight Conference Center and the Gusman Cultural Center are close by the port. International banks, lawyers, accountants, and luxury condominiums share the waterfront along Brickell Avenue. A few blocks to the N, the Omni Plaza Venetia Complex has a major shopping mall, top-class hotels, restaurants and bars, apartments and a yacht basin.

Calle Ocho Cuban culture has revitalized the once deteriorating area to the W of Miami along SW 8th Street, called "Little Havana."

Miami Beach Across Biscayne Bay by causeway is Miami Beach, a narrow, 8 mile/13km-long island. The beach is now being rebuilt, hotels are being refurbished and the Art Deco South Beach area is enjoying a renaissance. The main thoroughfare is Collins Avenue.

Bal Harbour At the top of Miami Beach, this upmarket area contains hotels, high-rise condominiums, a shopping complex and restaurants.

Other areas Light manufacturing, clothing and interior design firms are based in an area 15 blocks N of downtown. Two miles/3km to the S

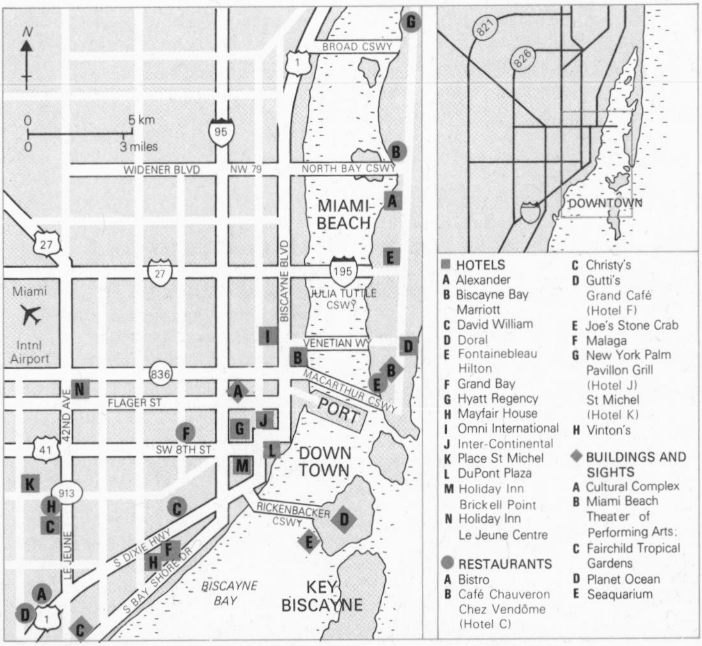

of downtown, along Biscayne Bay, is *Coconut Grove*, one of the oldest and most unusual of Miami communities. It is a gentle blend of black and white, gay and straight, business-minded and bohemian Miamians occupying rustic, shady neighborhoods around the bay. Wrapped around Coconut Grove to the W and S is the city of *Coral Gables*, home of more than 100 international businesses. *Key Biscayne*, across Biscayne Bay from Coconut Grove, is connected by a bridge to the mainland. It is divided equally among residences, top-class oceanfront hotels and public recreational facilities, including miles of tree-lined beach, a woody park, a golf course and a marina.

Hotels

Greater Miami is a tourist destination of such magnitude that you can expect to find a comfortable, reasonably priced, air-conditioned hotel room near your business destination.

Alexander $$$$$
5335 Collins Ave, Miami Beach 33140 ☎ 865-6500 [TX] 808172 • 211 suites, 2 restaurants, 3 bars, 1 coffee shop
This is the preferred business address in Miami Beach: a luxurious, low-key, oceanfront hotel with tropical gardens, and antique furniture in the lobby and suites. Dominique's is noted for its unusual appetizers, which include rattlesnake. Two pools, 4 jacuzzis, marina, jogging, watersports, golf and tennis nearby • 8 meeting rooms, teleconferencing.

Biscayne Bay Marriott $$$$
1633 N Bayshore Dr 33132 ☎ 374-3900 [TX] 525840 • 605 rooms, 2 restaurants, 2 bars
This Marriott overlooks the Intracoastal Waterway and Miami Beach. Veronique's, with inventive American dishes, is a decidedly genteel restaurant. The hotel's own marina has 220 boatslips. Pool, tennis, health club • 20 meeting rooms.

David William $$$
700 Biltmore Way, Coral Gables 33134 ☎ 445-7821 • 88 rooms, 2 restaurants
A European-style hostelry with a mostly Latin American clientele, the David William is noted for its restaurants. The 700 Club, quiet and conducive to conversation, has wood paneling and large bar; popular for business lunches. Chez Vendôme is elegantly French. One meeting room.

Doral $$$$$
4833 Collins Ave, Miami Beach 33140 ☎ 532-3600 [TX] 518928 • 334 rooms, 18 suites, 3 restaurants, 4 bars, 1 coffee shop
On the beach with views of the Atlantic Ocean and Biscayne Bay, the Doral is a luxurious hotel, catering to the convention and tourist trade. The 16th floor has 50 executive privilege rooms. Health club, jogging track, pool, aquasports club, access to Doral Country Club • 16 meeting rooms, courier service.

Fontainebleau Hilton $$$$$
441 Collins Ave, Miami Beach 33140 ☎ 538-2000 [TX] 519362 • 1,206 rooms, 63 suites, 7 restaurants, 4 bars, 1 coffee shop
The Fontainebleau is a convention hotel with a range of restaurants, from an Art Deco steakhouse to an outdoor café with a Calypso band. Rooms have a video network, mini bar and jacuzzi. Hairdresser, pharmacy, jeweler • health club, 2 pools, watersports, tennis • 21 meeting rooms, fax, translation.

Grand Bay $$$$$
2696 S Bayshore Dr, Coconut Grove 33133 ☎ 858-9600 [TX] 441370 • 200 rooms, 22 suites, 1 restaurant, 4 bars
The Italian-owned Grand Bay is just three blocks from the Mayfair Mall. The service is excellent and

unobtrusive. Regine's fashionable rooftop disco is open to members and hotel guests only. The Grand Café restaurant has a light and airy dining room and huge flower arrangements. Hairdresser • health club, pool, golf • 6 meeting rooms.

Hyatt Regency $$$
400 SE 2nd Ave 33131 ☎ 358-1234 ⊠ 514316 • 615 rooms, 36 suites, 2 restaurants, 3 bars
Situated downtown, with views of Biscayne Bay and the city skyline, this hotel is a favorite for conferences. Its Esplanade restaurant is a cosmopolitan spot serving fresh pompano and swordfish daily. Pool, arrangements with nearby health club • 30 meeting rooms.

Inter-Continental $$$$
100 Chopin Pl 33131 ☎ 577-1000 • 646 rooms, 34 suites, 5 restaurants, 1 bar, 1 coffee shop
This well-equipped, luxurious hotel is centrally located at Biscayne Bay. Its Pavillon Grill serves superb French food. Health club, pool, jogging trails, tennis • 13 meeting rooms, teleconferencing.

Mayfair House $$$$$
3000 Florida Ave, Coconut Grove 33133 ☎ 441-0000 ⊠ 153670 • 186 suites, 2 restaurants, 1 bar
The Mayfair House occupies the top two floors in a chic shopping arcade designed by artist/owner Ken Triester. The individually designed suites have dining areas and hot tubs. The Mayfair Grill has four dining rooms, each decorated with French and Oriental art. Rooftop pool • 3 meeting rooms.

Omni International $$$
1601 Biscayne Blvd 33132 ☎ 374-0000 ⊠ 515005 • 485 rooms, 50 suites, 2 restaurants, 2 bars, 1 coffee shop
Much favored by business travellers, especially from Latin America and the Caribbean, the Omni is part of the Omni Plaza/Venetia Complex. It overlooks Biscayne Bay and has 46 club level rooms. Dentist, hairdresser, optician • arrangements with nearby health club, rooftop pool, tennis • 21 meeting rooms.

Place St Michel $$$
162 Alcazar, Coral Gables 33134 ☎ 444-1666 • 25 rooms, 3 suites, 2 restaurants, 1 bar
This small hotel has a comfortable inn-like atmosphere. There are vaulted ceilings, tiled and parquet floors, a rooftop garden and individually decorated rooms. The Restaurant St Michel has a very Parisian tone. The hotel bar is popular with the after-work crowd. One meeting room.

OTHER HOTELS
DuPont Plaza ($$) *300 Biscayne Blvd Way ☎ 358-2541.*
Holiday Inn Brickell Point ($$$) *495 Brickell Ave ☎ 373-6000.*
Holiday Inn Le Jeune Centre ($$) *950 NW Le Jeune Rd ☎ 446-9000.*

Clubs

The *Miami Club*, the oldest of the downtown luncheon clubs, is also the most exclusive. The *City Club of Miami*, the newest of the business clubs, is conservative in membership selection; good for working lunches. The *Bankers Club*, with stunning views of the bay, has world-wide reciprocity with more than 150 clubs. Representing the growing Latin influence in the business community are the *American Club* and the *Big Five*, a consolidation of the five social clubs that dominated Havana society for 100 years. The *Standard Club* is one of the oldest and most enduring of the downtown clubs. The *University Club* is the stronghold of Miami's young male professionals; women are not admitted. The traditional establishment recreational clubs are the *Indian Creek Country Club* and Coconut Grove's *Biscayne Bay* and *Coral Reef* yacht clubs.

Restaurants

For business dining, look to Coral Gables, Coconut Grove, and Bal Harbour in the evenings; downtown becomes a desert after 5pm. At lunch, lawyers use *Sally Russell's*, the *VIP* or the *Standard* and *Bankers* clubs. Brickell Avenue executives walk to lunch at *Cye's Rivergate*, the *Brickell Villa Deli*, the *Brickell Emporium* or *Tobacco Road.*

Bistro **$$$**
2611 Ponce de Leon Blvd, Coral Gables
☎ 442-9671 • AE CB DC MC V
Small and friendly, the Bistro specializes in personalized service; it has many regular customers. Good, moderately-priced wine list.

Café Chauveron **$$$$$**
9561 E Bay Harbor Dr, Miami Beach
☎ 866-8779 • closed Jun–Oct • AE CB DC MC V • *jacket required*
Chauveron is one of southern Florida's very best restaurants, run by André, the son of Roger Chauveron (of New York's Chambord). Serving French cuisine in the grand manner, it is noted for soufflés; it also features duck and rack of lamb. There are dock slips for waterborne diners.

Chez Vendôme **$$$$**
700 Biltmore Way, Coral Gables
☎ 445-7821 • AE CB DC MC V
This classy French restaurant in the David William Hotel (see *Hotels*), popular with business and finance executives, has red velvet booths and elaborately framed paintings. Successful dishes include steak Diane, rack of lamb, duck with sherry and several good snapper recipes. The wine list is extensive.

Christy's **$$**
3101 Ponce de Leon Blvd, Coral Gables
☎ 446-1400 • AE CB DC MC V
Well-liked by local business people, Christy's has a quiet, masculine décor. The cooking is conservative: prime rib, fresh fish, and Caesar salad are specialties.

Gatti's **$$$**
1427 West Ave, Miami Beach
☎ 673-1717 • open daily exc Mon; closed May–Oct • AE CB DC MC V • *reservations essential*
Featuring northern Italian cuisine, Gatti's has been a family operation for 60 years. Housed in a stucco building, it is a haven for pasta fanatics. Canneloni, tortellini, fresh fish and scallops are specialties.

Grand Café **$$$$$**
2669 S Bayshore Dr, Coconut Grove
☎ 858-9600 • AE CB DC MC V
Grand Bay Hotel's Grand Café has a striking, open dining room and an attentive staff. Mediterranean dishes such as *cioppino* Grand Café (seafood in broth), grilled whole fish and an assortment of pastas highlight the menu. It also has splendid lamb chops and good crab soup.

Joe's Stone Crab **$$$**
227 Biscayne St, Miami Beach
☎ 673-0365 • open daily exc Mon; closed mid-May–mid-Oct • AE CB MC V • *no reservations*
Diners at this big, high-ceilinged South Beach restaurant run the risk of having to stand in line for an hour or two, particularly during the early crab season in the fall. Joe's is a Miami institution, noisy and ebullient, and famous for its stone crabs, which are brought in from the Florida Keys by Joe's fishing fleet.

Malaga **$$**
740 SW 8th St ☎ 854-9101 • AE CB DC MC V
Malaga captures the flavor of Hispanic Miami in a very traditional Spanish setting; there are two indoor dining rooms and a limited number of tables in a romantic outdoor courtyard area. Located in Little Havana, Malaga specializes in Cuban cuisine, including fish dishes, *paella* and squid casserole.

New York Palm $$$

9650 E Bay Harbor Dr, Bay Harbor ☎ 868-7256 • closed May–Sep • AE CB DC MC V • reservations essential

Ever since it opened in 1986, local business, political and showbusiness celebrities have used the Palm to entertain, discuss deals and impress. The menu is international, the décor elegant, the wine list almost as long as Miami Beach.

Pavillon Grill $$$$$

100 Chopin Plaza ☎ 372-4494 • AE CB DC MC V

The Pavillon Grill offers French cuisine, an extensive wine list and an elegant interior with green marble columns, leather chairs and mahogany paneled walls. Located in the Inter-Continental (see *Hotels*), its specialties include stuffed *escalope de veau* with wild mushrooms and shallots, and a ragoût of crustaceans with Pernod sauce.

St Michel $$$

2135 Ponce de Leon Blvd, Coral Gables ☎ 446-6572 • AE CB DC MC V

Located in the Place St Michel (see *Hotels*), this café restaurant is a lunch favorite of Coral Gables executives. Specialties include rack of lamb, duck with blackcurrants, veal scallopine Dijonaise and poached salmon with lobster.

Vinton's $$$$

116 Alhambra Circle, Coral Gables ☎ 445-2511 • closed Sun and holidays • AE CB DC MC V

Situated in the La Palma Hotel, the very romantic Vinton's – where each woman receives a long-stemmed flower and a foot pillow – serves Continental cuisine; on Monday there is a "gourmet night," with a multi-course *prix fixe* dinner. Bouillabaisse, salmon in sorrel sauce and duck with raspberry are the menu's highlights. No spirits, but a fine wine list.

Entertainment

Miami is noted for its extravagant floor shows, pari-mutuel betting (horses, dogs and jai alai) and, more recently, for sophisticated cultural attractions. In the winter season, the large beach hotels have headline acts and touring companies, from rock groups to symphony orchestras.

Nightclubs The top hotel clubs are the *Fontainebleau*, *Sheraton Bal Harbour*, *Eden Roc*, and *Diplomat*. Others include *Biscayne Baby*, 3336 Virginia St, Coconut Grove ☎ 445-3751, for rock 'n' roll; *Casanova's*, 740 E 9th St, Hialeah ☎ 883-8706, for Latin salsa/disco, with a mixed, dressy crowd; *Ciga Lounge*, on the mezzanine level of the Grand Bay Hotel, has an elegant jazz piano bar with ultra comfortable seating; *Les Violins*, 1751 Biscayne Blvd ☎ 371-8668, has extravagant Latin dance numbers and continuous entertainment; *Tobacco Road*, 626 S Miami Ave ☎ 374-1198, is the place for top-name blues bands.

Theater and music *Coconut Grove Playhouse* ☎ 442-2662 presents regional theater; *Miami Beach Theater for the Performing Arts* ☎ 673-5300 stages Broadway productions; and *Gusman Cultural Center* ☎ 372-0925 has a wide range of stage shows. In addition, the Gusman houses the *Greater Miami Symphony* ☎ 532-4421 and the *Greater Miami Opera Association* ☎ 854-1643.

Shopping

From Bloomingdale's at *The Falls* in S Miami to Macy's almost at the county line of Dade and Broward, Miami is one vast shopping center. The Falls is a delightful indoor/outdoor mall enclosing a series of ponds and waterfalls. Across from The Falls is a large warehouse area packed with discount shops. Off Kendall Drive, there is *Dadeland Shopping Center*; and *Coconut Grove* is good for stylish, offbeat or bohemian fashion and artifacts. *Bal Harbour Shops* is an elegant mall with branches of top US department chains. *Miracle Mile* in Coral Gables is lined with expensive designer shops and boutiques. *Downtown* Miami has a host of small discount shops; *Little Havana* is good for specialty foods and clothes. The *Omni Hotel and Mall* is favored by the fashionable, both for shopping and eating; *Mayfair Mall* is still developing.

Sightseeing

Fairchild Tropical Gardens America's largest botanical garden has more than 5,000 exotic plant varieties and a rain forest; take the guided tram ride. *10901 Old Cutler Rd, Coral Gables. Open daily exc Christmas, 9.30–4.30.*
Metrozoo An outstanding zoo with animals in natural habitats. Monorail and tram tours. *12400 SW 152nd St, Kendall. Open 10–4.*
Planet Ocean A multi-media science center devoted to the oceans of the world. *3979 Rickenbacker Causeway, Virginia Key. Open 10–4.*
Seaquarium Across the causeway from Planet Ocean, this 60-acre tropical marine aquarium has seals, manatees, whale and dolphin shows. *Rickenbacker Causeway, Virginia Key. Open 9–6.*

Guided tours

The coastal mansions and Biscayne Bay's islands can be seen on short cruises. The *Island Queen* leaves from Miamarina, 5th St and Biscayne Bay ☏ 379-5119; *Nikko's Gold Coast* cruises, 10800 Collins Ave ☏ 945-5461, also has frequent departures. For bus tours, contact *American Sightseeing Tours*, 4300 NW 14th St ☏ 871-4992.

Out of town

Disneyworld, in Orlando, is Florida's top tourist attraction. It is about a 4hr drive from Miami, but flights to Orlando take only ½hr. *Everglades National Park* is 40 miles/65km S of Miami on US-1; a world-famous tropical swamp and animal preserve. *Key West*, 180 miles/290km S of Miami on the Overseas Highway, is a colorful, somewhat bohemian town where Ernest Hemingway lived.

Spectator sports

Baseball The *Miami Marlins* play at the Miami stadium.
Football The *Dolphins* and the University of Miami *Hurricanes* are at the Orange Bowl, 1501 NW 3rd St ☏ 643-4700; a new stadium is to be completed in 1989.
Horse racing *Hialeah Park*, 4 E 25th St ☏ 885-8000 is almost as noted for its pink flamingos and beautiful setting as it is for its races. *Gulfstream Park*, US-1 at Hallandale ☏ 944-1242 and *Calder Race Course*, 21001 NW 27th Ave ☏ 625-1311 are not as scenic but have the horses.
Jai alai During the winter months, gamblers try their luck at jai alai, a fast-paced court game played at the *Miami Fronton*, 3500 NW 37th Ave ☏ 633-6400.

Keeping fit

Beaches *Hobie Beach*, *Crandon Park* (Rickenbacker Causeway) and *Bill Baggs Cape Florida State Park* are on Key Biscayne. *Venetian Pool* and *Matheson Hammock* (Old Cutler Rd) are in Coral Gables.
Bicycling For the cyclist there are more than 100 miles/160km of year-round paths. Rental shops include *Dade Cycle Shop*, 3043 Grand Ave, Coconut Grove ☏ 443-6075 and *Key Biscayne Bicycle Rentals*, 260 Crandon Park Blvd, Key Biscayne ☏ 361-5555.
Golf Many hotels offer guests golf privilege at private courses. Good local public golf courses include the *Biltmore*, 1210 Anastasia Ave ☏ 442-6485 in Coral Gables; the *Key Biscayne*, Crandon Blvd, Key Biscayne ☏ 351-9129; and *Palmetto*, 9300 Coral Reef Dr ☏ 238-2922.
Jogging Among the favorite jogging courses is *David T Kennedy Park* at 220 S Bayshore Dr.
Tennis Public tennis and raquetball courts are numerous at universities, schools and parks, and many major

hotels provide access to tennis either on their own courts or through arrangement with a private club.
Watersports and boating There are scores of marinas in Miami, and most have rental facilities for windsurfing, waterskiing, skin diving, sailing and deep-sea fishing.

Local resources

Business services

Firms that offer complete services include *Linguex*, suite 603, 95 Merrick Way ☎ 446-9289 and *Stephan Secretarial Service*, 2731 Ponce de Leon Blvd ☎ 444-8310 or 444-8311, both in Coral Gables.
Photocopying and printing *Kwik Copy* ☎ 358-1535 provide a convenient service for most areas of the city.
Secretarial *Adia Personnel Agency* ☎ 279-7111; *Advantage Personnel Agency* ☎ 264-7060.
Translation *Berlitz Translation Services* ☎ 371-3686 and *Interamerican Translating Services* ☎ 371-4283 are convenient for most parts of the city.

Communications

Local delivery *Choice Courier Systems* ☎ 949-0909; *Crown Courier Systems* ☎ 592-4000.
Long-distance delivery *Federal Express* ☎ 371-8500; *DHL* ☎ 592-8795.
Post office The post office at the Miami International Airport is open 24hrs. The downtown office is at 500 NW 2nd Ave ☎ 371-2911.
Telex *ITT Communications* ☎ 591-1065.

Conference/exhibition centers

Many of the larger hotels provide conference and meeting facilities. For other needs, consult the *Convention and Visitors' Bureau* ☎ 573-4300.

Emergencies

Hospital *Cedars Medical Center*, 1400 NW 12th Ave ☎ 325-5511; *Jackson Memorial Hospital*, 1611 NW 12th Ave ☎ 549-7137; *Mount Sinai Medical Center*, 4300 Alton Rd, Miami Beach ☎ 674-2222.
Pharmacies *Eckerd Drugs* has many stores, several open 24hrs.
Police *Metro-Dade Police*, 1390 NW 14th St ☎ 547-7472; *City of Miami Police*, 400 NW 2nd Ave ☎ 576-6111.

Government offices

Metro Government Directory ☎ 579-5900; *Florida Dept of Commerce/International Trade Division* ☎ 446-8106; *US Dept of Commerce* ☎ 536-5267; *US Customs* ☎ 536-5342; *Immigration and Naturalization Service* ☎ 536-5741.

Information sources

Business Information
The *Greater Miami Chamber of Commerce* ☎ 350-7700 is one of 28 chambers in the Miami area, and a good source for general local business information.
Local media The *Miami Herald* gives good local and regional coverage; the Spanish-language *Diario Las Americas* serves the Latin community; *Miami Review* provides an excellent business coverage, Mon–Fri. *Miami/South Florida* magazine highlights cultural, dining and entertainment life.
Tourist information The *Greater Miami Convention and Visitors' Bureau*, 4770 Biscayne Blvd 33137 ☎ 573-4300.

Thank-yous

Florists *Buning the Florist, Inc*, 2125 Biscayne Blvd ☎ 576-2800; *Exotic Gardens, Inc*, 4800 Biscayne Blvd ☎ 576-4500; *The Flower Tech*, 166 Alhambra Circle, Coral Gables ☎ 444-2192.
Gift baskets *How Sweet It Is*, 15425 SW 77th Ct ☎ 253-5810 and *The Sweet Treat Emporium*, 1565 Sunset Dr, Coral Gables ☎ 665-0233.

MINNEAPOLIS/ST PAUL

Area code ☎ 612

The twin cities of Minneapolis/St Paul are separated by the Mississippi River, the waterway that helped to build fortunes in lumber and flour milling. Today these interests are represented by General Mills, Pillsbury and International Multifoods, as well as by the technology titans Honeywell, Control Data and Minnesota Mining and Manufacturing (3M), which have headquarters here. Minneapolis is also the home of Northwest Airlines and the seat of the University of Minnesota, which has strong business, engineering and medical schools. It has close commercial and cultural ties with neighboring Canada.

The roots and lifestyles of the two cities are distinctly different. Minneapolis has a strong Scandinavian heritage, a dominant work ethic and a dislike of conspicuous alcohol consumption. St Paul, the smaller of the two, has the area's oldest names and oldest money, derived from railroad and lumber interests, plus a conservative Irish Catholic population. Its powerbrokers entertain in their homes and clubs rather than in restaurants and bars, as Minneapolitans do. St Paul is the seat of state government but it has traditionally relied on its twin for arts, dining, shopping and business, although new commercial complexes are bringing money and activity back to the once-stagnant city center.

Arriving

Minneapolis/St Paul International Airport

Most flights to and from MSP are domestic. Those that must clear Customs arrive at a secondary terminal, a quarter mile from the main building, making baggage claim a slow process. Facilities include currency exchange 6am–6pm, executive lounge, restaurants and car rental offices; all are in the main terminal. Inquiries ☎ 720-7171.

Nearby hotels *Granada Royal Hometel*, 2800 W 80 St ☎ 884-4811. *Registry*, 7901 24th Ave S ☎ 854-2244.

City link It is about 10 miles/16km to both downtown areas. Allow about 15min, 45min in the rush hour.

Taxi Cabs line up at the main terminal. The fare is about $18.

Limousine The Airport Limousine Service ☎ 726-6400 provides shared limos, leaving the airport every half hour; around $7.

Car rental Most agencies have airport offices but, unless you need to drive frequently between the two cities or to the suburbs, it is advisable to take a taxi or limousine.

Getting around

Minneapolis is laid out in a grid pattern with avenues – divided by Washington – running N–S and streets – divided by Nicollet – running E–W. Downtown St Paul is less orderly, but its avenues consistently run E–W and streets N–S.

Walking In Minneapolis, most downtown hotels, stores and office buildings are connected by a skyway system. Any area is safe during daylight, but downtown streets are deserted after office hours. After dark, avoid walking around Hennepin Avenue, the city's nightlife area, and Loring Park, and the Selby–Dale area of St Paul.

Taxi It is usually possible to hail a cab in either downtown, but they must be ordered by phone elsewhere; expect a wait in bad weather. *Airport Taxi* ☎ 721-6566, *Blue and White* ☎ 333-3331 and *Yellow* ☎ 379-7171.

Limousine *Airport Service* ☎ 726-6400, *Martin Services* ☎ 222-0555, *Executive Services* ☎ 378-3815.

Bus Minneapolis has no subway, and the *MTC* bus service ☏ 827-7733 is generally of little help to the business visitor, except for commuting to St Paul or the university.

Area by area

The *downtown Minneapolis* skyline is dominated by the 50-story Investors Diversified Services (IDS) in Nicollet Mall. Nearby are Cesar Pelli's Norwest Bank Tower, Saks Fifth Avenue and City Center, a 90-store shopping complex. The Mall stretches S past the Orchestra Hall and Convention Center, Loring Park and the Guthrie Theatre and Walker Art Center. Snaking N, Nicollet Avenue runs parallel with the city's financial institutions, government buildings and prestigious law offices to the E, and the recently gentrified arts-and-dining *Warehouse District* to the W, before reaching the broad Mississippi. Just across the bridge is *Riverplace*, a waterfront shopping and entertainment complex, and historic *St Anthony Main*, now a restored shopping–dining area.

International Market Square, a five-building showcase for interior design firms, lies just W of downtown. Sandwiched between the industrial and shipping compounds along the riverbank and the dual domes of the State Capitol and the cathedral, *downtown St Paul* is the home of prominent banks and insurance companies. The area includes Town Square, a shopping/dining/hotel complex, and Galtier Plaza, in the heart of the chic *Lowertown* arts-cum-warehouse district. Rice Park, just S, is a pretty square bordered by St Paul's showcase buildings: the Ordway Music Theater, St Paul Hotel, Landmark Center, the public library and civic center.

St Paul's upper crust occupy the imposing mansions on *Summit Avenue.* Young lawyers, foundation people and upper management types live in *Crocus Hill*'s Victoriana. *Highland Park*, a neighborhood to the SW, houses the more conservative, independent business executives. Big money, but not necessarily old, buys an estate in super-exclusive *North Oaks.*

Other areas

The university's East and West Bank campuses are bordered by *Prospect Park*, a coveted riverside neighborhood inhabited mainly by the university faculty. Doctors, lawyers and the town's intelligentsia are based in *Kenwood*, an enclave of smart homes surrounding several lakes 3 miles/5km S of downtown Minneapolis. At night its focal point, the S Hennepin and Lake Street intersection – known as Uptown – is alive with shopping and socializing young professionals.

An address in *Edina*, an inner-ring suburb 15min from downtown, denotes first-generation wealth. Farther out lie the wealthy *Wayzata* and *Orono* communities of chief executive officers.

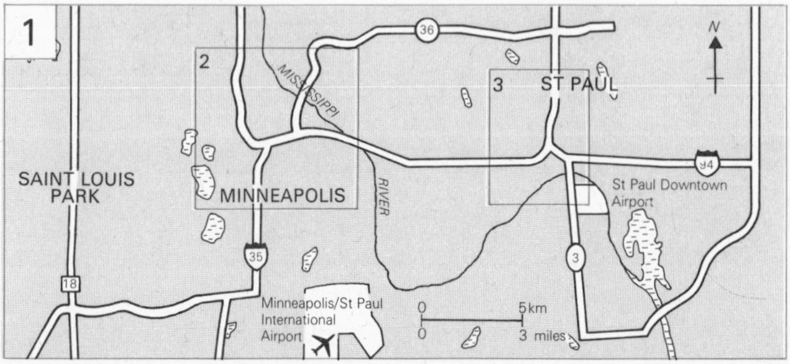

Hotels

In preparation for the completion in the early 1990s of the expanded Convention Center, Minneapolis hotels have been remodeled and refurbished. Except for a cluster on The Strip (Hwy 494, leading from the airport), they are mostly within a five-block downtown area.

Hyatt Regency **$$$$**
1300 Nicollet Mall, Minneapolis 55403
☎ 370-1234 TX 290413 • 479 rooms, 26 suites, 2 restaurants, 2 bars
Because of its size and location this is a popular choice for conferences and conventions. Behind the awesome fountain in the vast, atrium-like lobby is The Willows, a contemporary restaurant with the genteel atmosphere of a private club (see *Restaurants*). Drugstore, bank, travel agency, florist, non-smoking floor • pool, tennis • 21 meeting rooms, fax.

Marquette **$$$$**
710 Marquette Ave, Minneapolis 55402
☎ 332-2351 TX 9105761686 • 282 rooms, 16 suites, 3 restaurants, 2 bars
This modestly understated hotel, offering unusually spacious rooms, each with steam bath, is where VIPs receive Minneapolis's most deferential and accommodating service. Located on the 3rd–21st stories of the IDS pinnacle, it is connected by skyway to other business towers. Businessmen are attracted to the dark Marquis bar and the tiny, quiet Marquis restaurant,

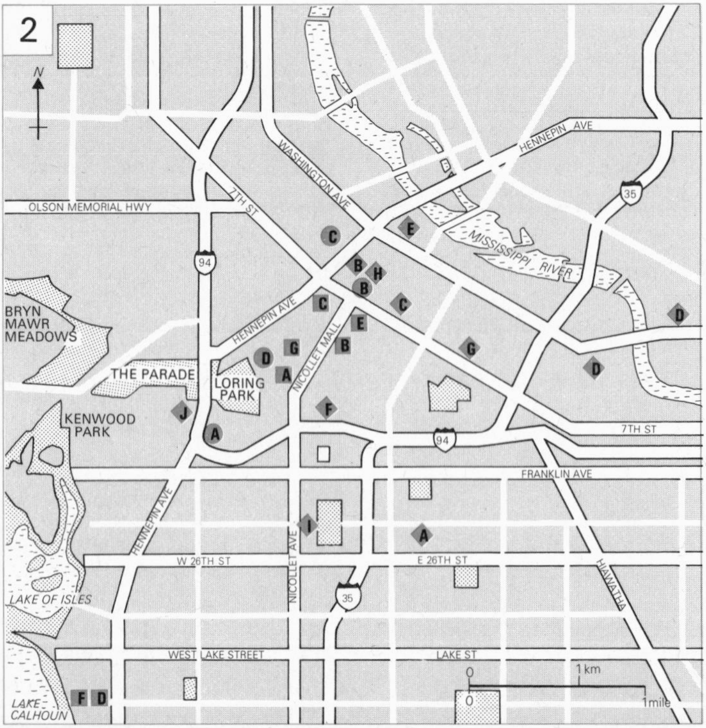

with its polished and tactful service. The Orion Room, on the 50th floor, offers the most spectacular view of the city. Discounted membership in nearby Greenway Athletic Club • 8 meeting rooms, teleconferencing, fax.

Marriott City Center **$$$$**
30 S 7th St, Minneapolis 55402
☎ 349-4000 • 602 rooms, 22 suites, 3 restaurants, 2 bars
A relative newcomer, the Marriott sits atop the shops of City Center and is connected to adjacent downtown buildings by skyway. Its atrium is a good spot for quiet discussion. The Fifth Season (see *Restaurants*), a greenhouse room serving what is arguably the city's finest cuisine at well-spaced tables, ensures uninterrupted business conversations. Rooms on the executive floor all have jacuzzis. Whirlpool, sauna, weightroom • 18 meeting rooms.

Northstar **$$$$**
618 2nd Ave S, Minneapolis 55402
☎ 338-2288 • Omni • 226 rooms, 2 suites, 2 restaurants, 1 bar
Located on the seventh story of the Northstar Building, this has a chinoiserie-laden lobby; a masculine, clubby restaurant, the Rosewood Room, much used by local bankers and attorneys. Excellent concierge • guest discounts at two athletic clubs • 6 meeting rooms, fax.

Radisson St Paul **$$$**
11 E Kellogg Blvd, St Paul 55101
☎ 292-1900 • 418 rooms, 22 suites, 3 restaurants, 3 bars
A popular choice in St Paul for conventions and conferences, despite its rather anonymous lobby and rooms. Le Carousel, a Continental dining room on the top floor, offers splendid views as well as music and dancing. Non-smoking floor, barber, gift shop • pool and guest pass to YMCA • 13 meeting rooms, fax.

Radisson South **$$$$**
7800 Normandale Blvd, Minneapolis 55435 ☎ 835-7800 • 578 rooms, 18 suites, 3 restaurants, 2 bars
Midway between the airport and downtown Minneapolis, the Radisson South caters to the convention trade as well as to the individual business traveller. Its remodeled marble lobby with scatter rugs and period furniture leads to the Spectator Lounge, a quiet discussion spot, and Aurora (see *Restaurants*). Travel agency, car rental, barber, gift shop, poolside cabana suites • whirlpool, sauna, pool, putting green, daily membership at Normandale Sports & Health Club • 17 meeting rooms.

Saint Paul **$$$**
350 Market St, St Paul 55102
☎ 292-9292 ⓧ 297008 • 253 rooms, 30 suites, 2 restaurants, 1 bar

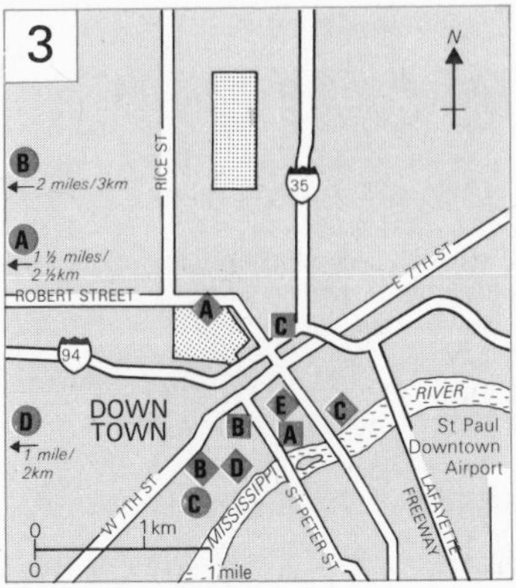

Key for Map 2

■ HOTELS
- **A** Hyatt Regency
- **B** Marquette
- **C** Marriott City Center
- **D** Hotel Sofitel
- **E** Northstar
- **F** Radisson South
- **G** Embassy Suites

● RESTAURANTS
- Aurora (Hotel F)
- Fifth Season (Hotel C)
- **A** 510 Restaurant
- **B** Murray's
- **C** New French Café
- **D** Nigel's
- Willow's (Hotel A)

◆ BUILDINGS AND SIGHTS
- **A** American Swedish Institute
- **B** Library
- **C** Courthouse
- **D** University
- **E** Main Post Office
- **F** Auditorium and Convention Center
- **G** Metrodome
- **H** Chamber of Commerce
- **I** Institute of Arts; Planetarium (Building B)
- **J** Walker Art Center

Key for Map 3

■ HOTELS
- **A** Radisson St Paul
- **B** Saint Paul
- **C** Embassy Suites

● RESTAURANTS
- **A** Blue Horse
- **B** Dakota Bar and Grill
- **C** Forepaugh's
- **D** Lexington

◆ BUILDINGS AND SIGHTS
- **A** State Capitol
- **B** Civic Center
- **C** Main Post Office
- **D** Library
- **E** Chamber of Commerce

This once-prestigious property had fallen on seedier times but is now splendidly renewed, with gilt, Persian carpets and marble in its intimate lobby. Its Rice Park location and link to the skyway system are major bonuses, as is the fine Franco-American restaurant, L'Etoile. Gift shop • nearby health club • 9 meeting rooms.

Sofitel **$$$$**
5601 W 78th St, Minneapolis 55435
☎ 835-1900 ⓉⓍ 290215 • 287 rooms, 11 suites, 3 restaurants, 1 bar
Only 10min from the airport, 15min from downtown Minneapolis, the Sofitel has a cosmopolitan air and a dedication to service that suggests its French parentage. It attracts more foreign business guests than most other area hotels. There is a six-story garden atrium, and its spacious rooms can be used for small meetings. La Terrasse, a chic, informal sidewalk café/bar, is famed locally for its onion soup. French deli/bakery, gift shop, barber • pool, sauna, whirlpool • 13 meeting rooms.

OTHER HOTELS
Hotel Luxeford ($$) *1101 La Salle Ave ☎ 332-6800* and **Embassy Suites ($$$)** *425 S 7th St ☎ 333-3111*: both centrally located in Minneapolis.
Embassy Suites ($$) *175 E 10th St ☎ 224-5400*: in St Paul, convenient to the State Capitol.

Clubs

Members of the *Minneapolis Club* are old names and old money, while the more egalitarian *Minneapolis Athletic Club* attracts aspiring young achievers. The *Tower Club*, atop the IDS, is favored by university alumni, and the *Greenway Athletic Club* is for young professionals of both sexes.

Across the river, an invitation to the prestigious *Minnesota Club* usually means lunch with St Paul's monied patricians and executive officers. The *St Paul Athletic Club* attracts the new entrepreneur as well as the sons of older business families; the *University Club*, more social than business-oriented, has the college-educated sons and daughters of old families as well as newer alumni.

Restaurants

Minneapolis financiers tend to lunch in the city's top-class hotel restaurants; in St Paul, business dining is generally conducted in private clubs. Socializing dominates the evening hours.

Aurora **$$$**
7800 Normandale Dr, Minneapolis
☎ 835-7800 • closed Sun • AE CB DC MC V
Set piece of the Radisson South hotel (see *Hotels*), the Aurora provides superb service and classy, creative food, often in California style.

Blue Horse **$$$**
1355 University Ave, St Paul
☎ 645-8101 • D only Sat; closed Sun • AE CB DC MC V
St Paul's finest restaurant has long been a favorite of powerbrokers and politicians. A savvy, professional staff understands the requirements of a private and perhaps protracted business meal. Seafood and California wines are specialties.

Dakota Bar and Grill **$$**
1021 Bandana Blvd E, Bandana Sq, St Paul ☎ 642-1442 • closed Sun D • AE CB DC MC V
In a renovated railroad roundhouse, the Dakota serves innovative California dishes. After 9, the room grows loud with live jazz.

Fifth Season **$$$**
30 S 7th St, Minneapolis ☎ 349-4000 • D only Sat; closed Sun • AE CB DC MC V • jacket required
Well-spaced tables in a choice garden atmosphere off the Marriott hotel's

atrium, combined with discreet, professional service and outstanding food, make this a highly desirable business eating place.

510 Restaurant $$
510 Groveland Ave, Minneapolis ☎ 874-6440 • D only Sat; closed Sun • AE CB DC MC V
The club preferred by the grand old Minneapolis names. An aura of quiet formality, underscored by pale gray walls and chandeliers, sets the tone for French-style dining. The wine list is excellent and staff helpful.

Forepaugh's $$
276 S Exchange, St Paul ☎ 224-5606 • AE CB DC MC V
Top executives from 3M often escort visiting associates to this quaintly restored Victorian mansion overlooking charming Irvine Park. The French-style food is served superbly.

Lexington $$
1096 Grand Ave, St Paul ☎ 222-5878 • closed Sun • no credit cards or checks
If St Paul's leaders are not at the Blue Horse, look for them at their other neighbourhood club, the Lex. Steaks and martinis are favored choices.

Murray's $$$
26 S 6th St, Minneapolis ☎ 339-0909 • AE CB DC MC V
Little has changed since this steakhouse opened in the 1940s, including its locally renowned silver butterknife steak and its career waitresses. The crush of patrons includes everyone from visiting celebrities to celebrating locals.

New French Café $$$
128 N 4th St, Minneapolis ☎ 338-3790 • AE CB DC MC V
The décor is aggressively stark in this warehouse hotspot, the service chatty, the food *nouvelle cuisine*, the clientele eager to see and be seen. The NFC is a food temple for the monied arts and foundation people.

Nigel's $$
15 S 12th St, Minneapolis ☎ 338-2235 • AE CB DC MC V
British and Canadian business travellers as well as the local upper crust favor this informal, garden-level café mainly because of its British-born owner, Nigel. Décor and menu are select American.

Willows $$$
1300 Nicollet Mall, Minneapolis ☎ 370-1234 • AE CB DC MC V
The Hyatt Regency hotel's de luxe restaurant is New York-style chic, and polished servers respect the requirements of a business meal. Ask for a banquette or wall table for extra privacy. Don't miss the duck or salad buffet.

Bars

Hotel bars are preferred for business meetings, but for socializing try *Figlio*, 3001 Hennepin Ave S ☎ 822-1688, much frequented by Uptown's young professionals; the *Monte Carlo*, 219 3rd Ave N ☎ 333-5900 (no credit cards), where wheeler-dealers mix with theatrical types; the *New French Bar*, around the corner from the café at 127 N 4th St ☎ 338-3790, very "in" with the city's bohemians; or *The Loon*, 500 1st Ave N ☎ 332-8342, packed with aspiring singles. In St Paul's, *Dixie*, 695 Grand Ave ☎ 222-7345 draws in mainly Crocus Hill WASPs; *Sweeney's* champagne bar at 96 N Dale ☎ 221-9157 attracts a young sophisticated crowd.

Entertainment

Minneapolis has always been the entertainment center for the area, but the building of the *Ordway Music Theater* has given St Paulites a top-class venue of their own. The weekly *Twin Cities Reader* covers what is on in both cities; *Arts Resource and Information Center* ☎ 870-3131.

Theater and music In Minneapolis, the *Guthrie* ☎ 377-6626 presents vivid stagings of classics and contemporary works.

Chanhassen Dinner Theater ☏ 934-1500 is noted for comedies and musicals. The *Carleton Celebrity Room* ☏ 854-9300 attracts top musical performers, and *Dudley Riggs' Theaters* ☏ 332-6620 offer fringe comedy. Musical director of the *Minnesota Orchestra* ☏ 371-5656 is Dutch-born Edo di Waart. The *St Paul Chamber Orchestra* ☏ 291-1144 is led by artistic director and violinist Pinchas Zukerman at the Ordway Theater, which is also the permanent home of the *Minnesota Opera.* The *Civic Center* stages rock and pop concerts.

Nightclubs *Rupert's,* 5410 Wayzata Blvd ☏ 544-5035, the area's classiest club, features jazz and big band music. *First Avenue,* 701 1st Ave N ☏ 332-1775, hosts funkier rock and jazz groups, and *Williams,* 2911, Hennepin Ave S ☏ 827-6271 attracts a younger Uptown crowd. All are in Minneapolis.

Shopping

Riverplace is the newest Minneapolis shopping complex; next to it, a brick factory building, *St Anthony Main,* has been converted into specialty shops. *Southdale,* a shopping mall S of downtown, is adjacent to the pricier and more exclusive offshoot, *The Galleria*; *Ridgedale,* its counterpart on the W of the city, has spawned the equally smart *Bonaventure.* The *Nicollet Mall* in downtown has scores of clothing and gift shops, all dominated by Dayton's department store. Across the street is *City Center,* a 90-shop complex ranging from exclusive models to mass-market wares. *Hello Minnesota,* 7 S 7th St, specializes in locally made gifts. *Byerly's Food Store* at St Louis Park, one of Minneapolis's major tourist attractions, has a cooking school, 24hr restaurant, ice cream, candy and bakery shops and a gift gallery stocked with Limoges and Lalique.

St Paul's downtown *Carriage Hill Plaza,* 14 W 5th St, is a good source of jewelry, fine chocolates and designer fashions. *Town Square,* in the city's center, has 70 mid-price shops and cafés as well as a branch of Dayton's. The *Victoria Crossing* complex at Grand and Victoria avenues is an intriguing warren of gift shops, bookstores and boutiques.

Sightseeing

Alexander Ramsey House Home of Minnesota's first territorial governor, affording a glimpse of cultivated Minnesota family life in the 1880s. *265 S Exchange St, St Paul ☏ 296-0100. Open Mon–Fri, 10–4; Sat and Sun, 1–4.30.*

American Swedish Institute Art and artifacts of Swedish heritage in Minnesota in an ornate 33-room mansion. *2600 Park Ave, Minneapolis ☏ 871-4907. Open Tue–Sun, noon–4.*

Minneapolis Institute of Arts An eclectic collection; strong points are the Rembrandts, Chinese jade collection and French Impressionists. *2400 3rd Ave S ☏ 876-3046. Open Tue–Sun, 10–5.*

Walker Art Center First-rate display of avant-garde art, plus superb giftshop and cafeteria with skyline vista. *Vineland Pl, Minneapolis ☏ 375-7600.*

Spectator sports

Baseball The *Twins* play at the Hubert H Humphrey Metrodome, 900 S 5th St ☏ 332-0386 and 375-7444.

Football The *Vikings* ☏ 333-8828 and University of Minnesota *Gophers* ☏ 373-3181 are based at the Hubert H Humphrey Metrodome.

Hockey The *Northstars* are at the Met Center, 8100 Cedar Ave S ☏ 853-9300.

Horse racing *Canterbury Downs* is the local racetrack, at Shakopee ☏ 445-7223.

Soccer The *Strikers* play at the Met Center ☏ 854-5450.

Keeping fit

Most hotels offer some form of fitness facilities. Among the public health clubs are those of the *Sports*

and Health Club chain at various locations in the area ☏ 927-5481. For aerobics, the status place is *The Sweat Shop*, 1620 Harmon Pl ☏ 375-9510.
Golf Public courses are found at the larger parks, such as *Highland Park* at Snelling and Montreal Ave, St Paul ☏ 699-3650. Minneapolis courses include *Hiawatha*, 4553 Longfellow Ave S ☏ 724-7715; *Meadowbrook*, 201 Meadowbrook Rd ☏ 929-2077; and *Theodore Wirth*, Plymouth Ave N and Wirth Pkwy ☏ 522-2817.
Racquet sports There are more than 200 public tennis courts. Indoor courts are available at *Normandale*, 6701 W 78th St ☏ 944-2434 and *Northwest*, 5525 Cedar Lake Rd ☏ 546-5474, both in Minneapolis.

Local resources

Business services

Your hotel is likely to be your best resource. For additional help call *AIE Support System*, 430 Oak Grove St ☏ 871-2914 and *Business Support Secretarial Services*, 9921 Lyndale Ave S ☏ 888-5979.
Photocopying and printing *Insty-Print* ☏ 379-0039.
Translation *Berlitz* ☏ 920-4100 and *Krollkraft* ☏ 934-1300.

Communications

Local delivery *Quicksilver Express Courier* ☏ 454-0360; *Road Runners* ☏ 644-8444.
Long-distance delivery *Federal Express* ☏ 340-0887; *PHC* ☏ 944-9780; *DHL* ☏ 944-9780.
Post office The main Minneapolis post office is at 100 S 1st Ave ☏ 349-4970. St Paul's main office is at 180 E Kellogg Blvd ☏ 725-7212. The airport office ☏ 293-3138 is open 24hrs.
Telex *ITT Communications* ☏ (800) 932-2200.

Conference/exhibition centers

The *Minneapolis Auditorium and Convention Hall*, 1403 Stevens Ave S ☏ 870-4436; *St Paul Civic Center*, 143 W 4th St ☏ 224-7361.

Emergencies

The *Minnesota Medical Assn* ☏ 378-1875 supplies lists of physicians, as does the *Minnesota Dental Assn* ☏ 646-7454.
Hospitals In Minneapolis: *Hennepin County Medical Center*, 701 Park Ave ☏ 347-3131; *Abbott Northwestern Hospital*, 800 E 28th St ☏ 874-4234; *Mount Sinai Hospital*, 2215 Park Ave ☏ 871-3700. In St Paul: *St Paul-Ramsey Medical Center*, 640 Jackson St ☏ 221-2121 and *United Hospitals*, 333 N Smith Ave ☏ 298-8755.
Pharmacies *Walgreen's*, 533 Hennepin Ave ☏ 333-8898 has a convenient downtown location; the branch at 12 W 66th St ☏ 861-7276 is open 24hrs.

Government offices

Minnesota Dept of Commerce ☏ 296-4026; *Minneapolis District, US Dept of Commerce* ☏ 349-3338; *US Customs* ☏ 349-3970; *Immigration and Naturalization* ☏ 725-7107 (evenings and weekends ☏ 222-8824).

Information sources

Business information The best sources are *Minneapolis Convention and Visitors' Commission*, 15 S 5th St ☏ 348-4313; *St Paul Convention Bureau* ☏ 292-4360.
Local media Minneapolis's daily newspaper is the *Star & Tribune*; St Paul's has the *Dispatch-Pioneer Press*. The *Twin Cities Reader* carries entertainment and dining guides.

Thank-yous

All of the following outlets accept credit card orders by telephone.
Florists *Bachmans* ☏ 861-7311; *Minneapolis Floral* ☏ 377-8080; *Holm & Olson* ☏ 222-7335.
Gift baskets *Bob's Produce Ranch* ☏ 571-6620; *Minnesota's Best in a Basket* (orders over $50) ☏ 920-8537; *Hello Minnesota* ☏ 332-1751; *Maud Borup Candies* ☏ 332-0008.

NEW ORLEANS

Area code ☎ 504

Located 90 miles/144km from the Mississippi River's delta into the Gulf of Mexico, New Orleans has long been a busy port, as well as a cultural mix of European, Central and South American, Caribbean and, more recently, Southeast Asian traditions. Spearheaded by offshore oil drilling in the Gulf, petrochemical companies dominate New Orleans's economy despite the recent fall in oil prices. Numerous oil companies have offices in the city and three Fortune 500 companies – McDermott, Freeport-McMoran, and Louisiana Land and Exploration – have headquarters here. Tourism generates some $2bn annually, 20% of which is attributed to the city's growing convention trade.

Arriving

New Orleans International Airport

Moisant (MSY) lies 15 miles/25km W of the downtown Central Business District (CBD). No gate is more than a 5min walk from the baggage claim area. Useful information booth near the Customs area exit. For information ☎ 464-0831.

Nearby hotels *Hilton New Orleans Airport*, 901 Airline Hwy ☎ 469-5000. *Holiday Inn Holidome*, 2929 Williams Blvd ☎ 467-5611. *Ramada Inn-Airport*, 1021 Airline Hwy ☎ 467-1381.

City link A cab is best, and sharing is an accepted practice.

Taxi A taxi can drop you off at your French Quarter or CBD hotel within 25min, 35min during the 4–6 peak and 50min in the morning rush hour 7–8.30. Cabs line up on the ground level to the right of the terminal exit. The fare is $18 for 1–3 people, $6 per person over that.

Bus Orleans Transportation Service "limousine" usually takes 45–60min; the fare is about $8. The much cheaper airport shuttle does not stop at major hotels and is not recommended at night.

Limousine London Livery ☎ 944-1984.

Getting around

New Orleanians do not talk in terms of N, S, E or W: directions are generally given as uptown, downtown, lakeside or riverside, relating to the Mississippi River and Lake Pontchartrain. If your business is restricted to downtown you can easily get around on foot.

Taxi Most hotels have taxi stands. Only in the French Quarter and business district do you have a good chance of hailing a cab on the street. Companies that have air-conditioned cabs include *Yellow Checker* ☎ 525-3311 or 943-2411 and *United* ☎ 522-9771 or 524-9606.

Bus *CBD Shuttles* No. 1 and No. 2 (Mon–Fri, 6.30–6) travel in opposite directions along a triangular path, including most important business addresses in Canal and Poydras streets. The *Vieux Carré Shuttle* (Mon–Fri, 5–7) is convenient for French Quarter locations on or near Chartres Street (pronounced "*Char*-ters"). The *St Charles Avenue Streetcar* cuts through the central district on its way uptown 24hrs a day; avoid using it at night.

Limousine *London Livery* ☎ 944-1934 and *Uptown Limousine* ☎ 861-7693 are among the city's best private limousine services.

Car rental is not recommended except for out-of-town journeys; New Orleans's multi-angle street grid and one-way system can be very confusing. However, the local offices of *Avis* are ☎ 523-4317; *Budget* ☎ 525-9417; *Hertz* ☎ 568-1645; and *National* ☎ 525-0416.

Walking For safety, avoid dark streets at night. The Bionville housing project near the French Quarter is notorious for muggings and murders; avoid at all times.

Area by area

Downtown comprises the French Quarter and Central Business District, where most major hotels, banks, law firms and government and corporate offices are concentrated. Among its landmarks are the venerable Cotton Exchange and Whitney Bank Building and the skyscraper offices of Amoco, Chevron, Exxon and Texaco. The prestigious, 53-story Place St Charles is the headquarters of Louisiana's biggest law firm, Jones-Walker.

The district's warehouse area has been revitalized recently by a spate of office and residential renovation. Between the warehouse district and the Mississippi River is the New Orleans Convention Center; and stretching for half a mile back to Canal Street is the new Riverwalk shopping center.

French Quarter Located on the site

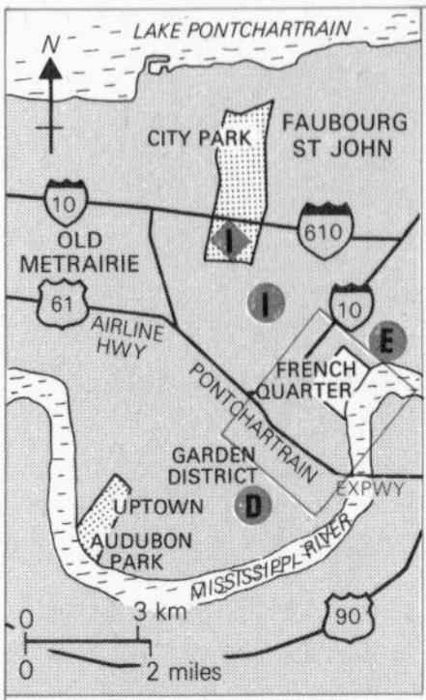

■ HOTELS
- **A** Fairmont
- **B** Intercontinental
- **C** Maison de Ville
- **D** Meridien
- **E** New Orleans Hilton
- **F** Pontchartrain
- **G** Royal Orleans
- **H** Royal Sonesta
- **I** St Louis
- **J** Westin Canal Place
- **K** Windsor Court
- **L** Holiday Inn Crowne Plaza
- **M** Holiday Inn French Quarter

● RESTAURANTS
- **A** Antoine's
- **B** Arnaud's
- **C** Bon Ton Café
- **D** Commander's Palace
- **E** Feelings Café D'Aunoy
- **F** Galatorie's
- **G** K-Paul's Louisiana Kitchen
- **H** Mr B's
- **I** Ruth's Chris Steak House

◆ BUILDINGS AND SIGHTS
- **A** City Hall
- **B** Municipal Auditorium
- **C** New Orleans Convention Center
- **D** Louisiana Superdome
- **E** Preservation Hall
- **F** Gallier House
- **G** Historic New Orleans Collection
- **H** Louisiana State Museum Complex: Jackson Square
- **I** New Orleans Museum of Art

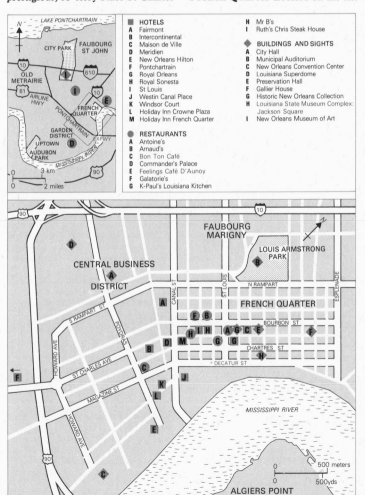

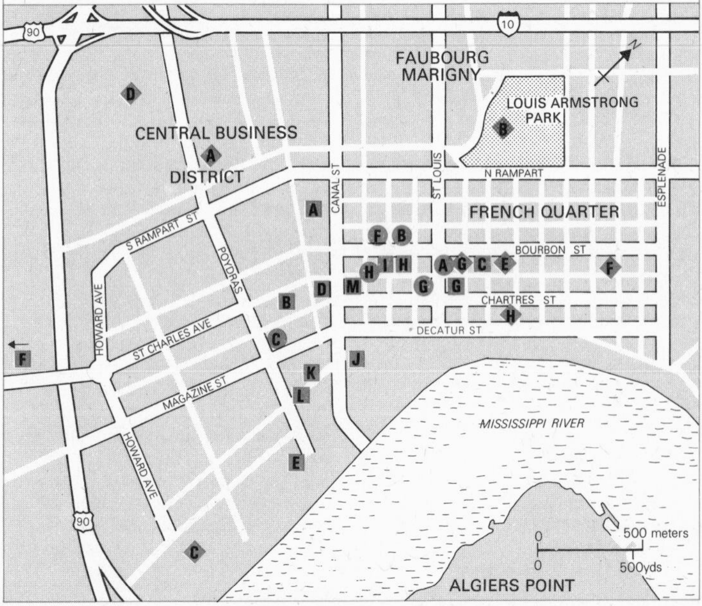

of the original city, the *French Quarter*, or *Vieux Carré*, still has a European look. Little remains from before the 19thC, but Creole cottages, built flush with the sidewalk around private courtyards – some of them visible from the street – give the area an unmistakable Old World flavor. The daytime hub of the Quarter is Jackson Square, with its permanent population of sidewalk artists; the pedestrian area in front of St Louis Cathedral is the stage for street performers. At night, the action moves to brash and bawdy Bourbon Street. Beyond Jackson Square the Quarter is mainly residential, with a large gay population and a number of gay bars.
Garden District About 2 miles/3km up St Charles Avenue from Canal Street, the Garden District is the most historic of New Orleans's wealthy areas. Many of its mansions date back a hundred years and are raised above ground to protect against flooding.
Uptown A mile or two farther up St Charles Avenue is a district combining the houses of the rich and many modest and even ramshackle dwellings – a legacy of the days when slaves lived on their owners' land.

Other areas

Adjacent to the French Quarter is *Faubourg Marigny*, a small neighborhood that houses many middle-income, old-time New Orleans families and a growing number of young professionals. *Algiers-Point*, on a spit of land across the Mississippi River, is also being gentrified. The *Lakefront* area on Lake Pontchartrain is typical modern suburbia, with sprawling condominiums and neatly manicured lawns. *Old Metairie* is New Orleans's oldest and most chic suburb.

Hotels

Almost all important hotels are in the downtown area, especially near the foot of Canal Street. Many of the best are ultra-modern, but some retain the city's distinctive European character.

Fairmont $$$$

University Pl 70140 ☎ 529-7111 TX 8109516015 • 730 rooms, 50 suites, 4 restaurants, 3 bars
The hotel's block-long lobby, with its gilded Greek Revival columns, opens onto the bustling Central Business District at each end. Rooms vary dramatically in size. The Sazerac is a popular business bar, and at night the Blue Room supper club offers high-quality entertainment. Barber and beauty shops • rooftop tennis • 22 meeting rooms.

Inter-Continental $$$$

444 St Charles Ave 70130 ☎ 525-5566 TX 58202 • 460 rooms, 44 suites, 2 restaurants, 2 bars
This imposing St Charles Avenue hotel is a harmonious blend of contemporary and old-time splendor. The hotel has an extensive collection of modern art displayed in its public rooms; a sculpture garden is set into the fifth-floor courtyard. Rooms are modern, spacious and well suited for working. Each has a minibar, and bathrooms have telephone, hairdrier and mini-TV. Barber and beauty shops • 7 meeting rooms, teleconferencing.

Maison de Ville $$$$

727 Toulouse St ☎ 561-5858 • 12 rooms, 2 suites, 7 cottages, 1 restaurant
The Maison de Ville caters mainly for clients who value their privacy and who appreciate intimate, Old World surroundings. The main house dates from the mid-19thC; the adjacent cottages (former slave quarters) are a century older. All rooms are furnished with antiques. Though the hotel has few in-house business services, its excellent

concierge can conjure up almost anything. Pool.

Meridien $$$$
614 Canal St ☏ 525-6500 TX 784465 • 505 rooms, 13 suites, 2 restaurants, 2 bars
Marble floors, shiny brass railings and a three-story atrium with a water cascade make this Air France-owned hotel one of New Orleans's most luxurious. The well-equipped business center offers complimentary secretarial services as well as the use of a photocopier, telex, fax, dictating equipment and a personal computer. Health club • 13 meeting rooms.

New Orleans Hilton $$$$
2 Poydras St 70130 ☏ 561-0500 TX 6821214 • 1,602 rooms, 86 suites, 3 restaurants, 4 bars, 2 coffee shops
With its river view and convenient location for the Convention Center, the Hilton is popular with conventioneers. Its Rivercenter Racquet and Health Club has a rooftop jogging track, 11 tennis courts, 7 racquetball courts and a squash court. There is direct covered access to the Riverwalk shopping area. Thirty-nine meeting rooms.

Pontchartrain $$$$
2031 St Charles Ave 70140 ☏ 524-0581 TX 266068 • 55 rooms, 20 suites, 1 restaurant, 1 bar, 1 coffee shop
Discreetly refined, the Pontchartrain is family-owned and operated, and has an international reputation for service. Café Pontchartrain is the number one breakfasting place for many of the city's business leaders. Arrangements with nearby health club • 1 meeting room.

Royal Orleans $$$$
621 St Louis St 70140 ☏ 529-5333 TX 58350 • Omni • 356 rooms, 24 suites, 2 restaurants, 4 bars
The huge lobby resplendent with mirrors, marble floors and beautiful floral arrangements, proclaims the luxurious standard of this French Quarter hotel, which is reflected in the consistently good service. Rooms are on the small side, but are charmingly furnished. The Rib Room is a well-established business lunching place. Beauty and barber salons, jeweler • 13 meeting rooms.

Royal Sonesta $$$$
300 Bourbon St ☏ 586-0300 TX 22361 • 380 rooms, 40 suites, 2 restaurants, 5 bars
Located in the heart of the French Quarter, the Royal Sonesta caters to the serious business traveller; its 35-room Tower, with concierge and reservation desk, is accessible only by private key. Despite its business orientation, however, the Royal Sonesta appeals also to the tourist, and it has something of a carnival atmosphere all year round. Pool, nearby health club, tennis, golf • 19 meeting rooms.

St Louis $$$$
730 Bienville St 70130 ☏ 581-7300 • 48 rooms, 4 suites, 2 restaurants, 1 bar
Small and charming, the St Louis is typically French Quarter in style. All rooms overlook a courtyard with fountain and have antique or reproduction French furnishings. One meeting room.

Westin Canal Place $$$$
365 Canal St 70130 ☏ 566-7006 TX 6711201 • 398 rooms, 41 suites, 3 restaurants, 2 bars
Among the Westin's attractions are its location, in the smart Canal Place shopping complex, and the magnificent river view from its 11th-floor lobby. Afternoon tea is accompanied by piano music. Pool, access to health club at the Meridien • 8 meeting rooms, fax.

Windsor Court $$$$
300 Gravier St ☏ 523-6000 TX 784060 • 58 rooms, 266 suites, 2 restaurants, 1 bar
Although it is one of the city's newest hotels, the Windsor Court has already acquired a loyal clientele,

including many senior executives. In the English manor-style lobby afternoon tea is accompanied by classical music. Many rooms have private balconies and most have refrigerators. Service is excellent. The swimming pool features an underwater music system. Seven meeting rooms.

OTHER HOTELS

Holiday Inn Crowne Plaza ($$$) *333 Poydras St* ☏ *525-9444.* Near CBD and Convention Center.
Holiday Inn French Quarter ($$$) *124 Royal St* ☏ *529-7211.* Just across Canal Street from CBD.

Clubs

New Orleans society revolves around the annual Mardi Gras celebrations and the 60-plus private clubs or "krewes," each of which sponsors its own parade every year. The most prestigious is *Rex*, whose leader is automatically recognized as the "King of Carnival." In business terms, the city has three important clubs: the Petroleum, the City and the Plimsoll. The *Petroleum Club* counts among its members top New Orleans's executives from virtually every major American oil company. Across from the Superdome, the *City Club* appeals more to political types, whereas the *Plimsoll Club*, in the World Trade Center, attracts the heavyweights in import-export. More socially-oriented is the *Boston Club*, 824 Canal St ☏ 523-2241.

Restaurants

Often loosely termed "Creole" or "Cajun," New Orleans's cuisine is a complex mélange of French, Spanish, Caribbean and African influences. The inhabitants consider eating one of life's more important activities and like to take their time over it, although the quick business lunch is growing in popularity, and some hotels provide inexpensive buffets.

Antoine's $$$$

713 St Louis St ☏ *581-4422 • closed Sun • AE CB DC MC V • jacket and tie required*
Antoine's has been serving Creole dishes to the monied classes since 1840. Huge, with dark wood walls, it is very suitable for quiet conversation. A table in one of the four private dining rooms is a local status symbol. With 35,000 bottles, Antoine's has New Orleans's largest wine cellar.

Arnaud's $$$

813 Bienville St ☏ *523-5433 • AE CB DC MC V • jacket and tie for dinner*
With its tiled floors, beveled glass and ceiling fans, Arnaud's has a turn-of-the-century ambiance. Fish is the specialty. The *prix fixe* luncheon is an excellent bargain. For a business meal, reserve one of the private dining rooms.

Bon Ton Café $$

401 Magazine St ☏ *524-3386 • closed Sat and Sun • AE MC V*
Although primarily a neighborhood restaurant, the Bon Ton is famed throughout town for its Creole food. Its festive atmosphere is better suited to off-duty than business entertaining. Specialties are the shrimp and crayfish dishes, turtle soup, and bread pudding – a New Orleans favorite.

Commander's Palace $$$

1403 Washington Ave ☏ *899-8221 • AE CB DC MC V • jacket and tie required • reservations essential*
Housed in a gracious ante-bellum mansion, this restaurant is popular with the city's upper crust. Dinnertime is always crowded, so reserve in advance. The cuisine is Creole and American – rated by some as the best in town. A good

choice for entertaining important clients.

Feelings Café D'Aunoy $$$
2600 Chartres St ☎ 945-2222 • closed Sun • MC V
The atmosphere is old New Orleans; the service brisk; the food consistently very good. The brick-walled courtyard provides ample privacy for quiet discussion.

Galatoire's $$$
209 Bourbon St ☎ 525-2021 • closed Mon • no reservations or credit cards • jacket and tie required after 5pm
Founded in 1905, Galatoire's is a favorite among old-line New Orleanians. With only a single, tile-floored dining room, the restaurant is charming but noisy and usually crowded, so consider it only for non-business dining.

K-Paul's Louisiana Kitchen $$$
416 Chartres St ☎ 942-7500 • D only; closed Sat and Sun • AE
The line outside the front door of this restaurant proclaims it as one of New Orleans's most popular – considered well worth the wait and the necessity (often) of sharing your table with strangers. Chef Paul Prudhomme's mastery of Creole-Cajun cooking is beyond dispute; but K-Paul's is more suitable for an off-hours meal than for business entertaining.

Mr B's $$$
201 Royal St ☎ 523-2078 • AE CB DC MC V
Just two blocks from Canal Street, in the French Quarter, Mr B's is *the* luncheon choice for many CBD professionals. Dark and masculine, with excellent Creole-American food.

Ruth's Chris Steak House $$
711 N Broad St ☎ 486-0810 • AE CB DC MC V
Ruth's is one of the city's busiest business lunch spots, crammed daily with many leading local business people and representatives of the judicial and political fields. The surrounding neighborhood is not the best; take a taxi.

Bars

Quite a lot of business is transacted in the city's better hotel bars, especially the *Sazerac* at the Fairmont, the *Rain Forest* atop the Hilton and the Royal Orleans's *Esplanade Lounge.* If you want to combine your business talk with a bit of New Orleans jazz, try the *Bayou Bar* in the Hotel Pontchartrain, a small piano bar much appreciated by locals. The wine bar uptown at *Flagon's*, 3222 Magazine St, is popular with young professionals. Tops among French Quarter bars is the *Napoleon House* at 500 Chartres St. *Pat O'Brien's*, 718 St Peter St, is probably New Orleans's most famous bar, worth exploring when you have some free time.

Entertainment

For weekly listings look at the "Lagniappe" (pronounced "lan-*yap*") section in Friday's *Times-Picayune*, or *Gambit*, a weekly free magazine available at newsstands and restaurants. Tickets can generally be obtained through *Ticketmaster* ☎ 888-4700.

Jazz and nightclubs The city's two top contemporary jazz clubs are *Snug Harbor*, 626 Frenchman St ☎ 949-0696, and *Tyler's Beer Garden*, 5234 Magazine St ☎ 891-4989. *Preservation Hall*, 726 St Peter St ☎ 522-2238, is famed for its traditional jazz and ancient musicians who play in a hot, musty, crowded room. Clarinetist Pete Fountain performs with his band in the *New Orleans Hilton* four days a week ☎ 561-0500.

Theater, music, ballet *The Saenger Performing Arts Center*, 143 N Rampart St ☎ 524-2490, a renovated movie palace, stages concerts and touring Broadway plays. The *Orpheum*, 129 University Pl ☎ 525-0500 is the home of the New Orleans Symphony. Local theater productions are performed at the *Contemporary Arts Center*, 900 Camp St ☏ 523-1216 and *Le Petit Théâtre du Vieux Carré*, 616 St Peter St ☏ 522-2081. Opera and ballet are staged in the *New Orleans Theater of the Performing Arts* in Louis Armstrong Park near the French Quarter ☏ 525-7615. The general warning about safety after dark applies to visiting any of these venues at night.

Shopping

Canal Place, near the foot of Canal Street, is New Orleans's most upmarket shopping center, with Gucci and Saks Fifth Avenue among the noteworthy stores. The popular Riverwalk development (see *Area by area*) is newer and larger. For food and amusing presents, go to *Jackson Brewery*, Decatur and St Peter streets, which has been transformed into a smart urban mall. Royal Street in the French Quarter is the place for antiques.

Sightseeing

The St Charles Avenue streetcar is the best way to explore the Garden District and uptown; its relaxing 7 mile/11km run takes you past some of New Orleans's most interesting sights.

Gallier House in the French Quarter offers a view of New Orleans upper class life in the mid-19thC, with original art and furnishings. *1118-32 Royal St. Open 10–4.30; closed Sun.*

Historic New Orleans Collection Ten galleries trace the city's history through documents, antiques, paintings, maps and memorabilia. The collection is housed in a maze of inter-connecting late-18thC houses. *Main gallery at 533 Royal St. Open 10–5, Tue–Sat.*

Louisiana State Museum Complex is on Jackson Square in the French Quarter – an historic group of buildings including the old Mint and Arsenal. *Open 9–5; closed Mon.*

New Orleans Museum of Art Located in City Park, NOMA has a world-class collection from Asia, Africa, Europe and America. The Fabergé egg collection is on display in the City Wing. *Open 10–5, Tue, Wed, Fri, Sat and Sun; 10–9, Thu; closed Mon.*

Guided tours

Boat tours *Cajun Bayou Cruise* The *New Orleans Steamboat Company* ☏ 586-8777 has 2hr and half-day cruises. The *Creole Queen*'s 3hr cruise ☏ 524-0814 includes a visit to the Beauregard Plantation House and the site of the War of 1812's Battle of New Orleans; *Honey Island Swamp Tours* ☏ 242-5877 visits one of the country's best-preserved water wilderness areas, 1hr out of town.

Bus tours *Gray Line Tours of New Orleans* ☏ 581-7222 operates a variety of tours.

Limousine tours *Allan's Limousine Service* ☏ 733-5466.

Walking tours *Friends of the Cabildo* ☏ 523-3939 conduct daily tours of the French Quarter.

Spectator sports

Football New Orleans is deluged each year with fans who come for the Sugar Bowl Classic, held in the Superdome ☏ 587-3663 on New Year's Day. The city's professional football team, the *Saints*, also play here.

Horse racing The *Fairgrounds*, 1751 Gentilly Blvd ☏ 944-5515 from Nov to Apr; *Jefferson Downs* at 1300 Sunset Blvd ☏ 466-8521.

Keeping fit

Most hotels have pools; some have fitness centers. The 18-station outdoor exercise circuit at Audubon Park is a local favorite but is not recommended after dark.

Health clubs The *YMCA* ☏ 568-9622 has weight rooms and exercise classes for men and women at its Lee Circle and Superdome branches. The Lee Circle Y also has

racquetball courts and a gym.
Bicycling Audubon Park has cycle paths and bikes to rent ☎ 861-2537.
Golf Public courses are at City Park ☎ 483-9397 and Audubon Park ☎ 861-9511.
Tennis Courts are widely available, again at City Park ☎ 482-2230 and Audubon Park ☎ 865-8638. The Hilton's tennis courts (see *Hotels*) are open to guests of any city hotel.

Local resources

Business services

For a comprehensive range of most business services try *Office Masters* ☎ 568-0871; for 24hr dictation ☎ 568-0874.
Audio-visual *AVW Audio Visual* ☎ 522-7937, *Jasper Ewing & Son* ☎ 525-5257.
Printing and photocopying *Accurate Letter Co* ☎ 522-9092; *Kinko's Copies* ☎ 581-2541 is open 24hrs.
Secretarial *Your Girl Friday* ☎ 822-8973.
Translation *Excel Services* ☎ 581-1123; *Professional Translators and Interpreters* ☎ 581-3122 provides US Court certified translators.

Communications

Local delivery *Choice Courier* ☎ 522-2678; *Constant Business Couriers* ☎ 523-4497.
Long-distance delivery *Federal Express* ☎ 523-6001.
Post office *Main post office*, 701 Loyola Ave ☎ 589-1111.
Telex and telegram *RCA Global Communications Service*, 2 Canal St ☎ 586-0485; *Western Union*, 334 Carondelet St ☎ 523-5453.

Conference/exhibition centers

New Orleans Convention Center, 900 Convention Center Blvd ☎ 582-3000 and *The Rivergate*, 4 Canal St ☎ 529-2861 both have meeting rooms and big exhibition spaces. New Orleans is a popular convention city, so plan several years in advance.

Emergencies

Hospitals *Charity Hospital*, 1532 Tulane Ave ☎ 568-2311; *Tulane Medical Center*, 1415 Tulane Ave ☎ 588-5263. For physician referral call *Touro-MD* ☎ 897-7777. 24hr emergency dental service is provided by the *Touro Infirmary*, 1401 Foucher St ☎ 897-8250.
Pharmacies *Walgreen Drug Store*, 900 Canal St ☎ 523-7201; the nearest 24hr drugstore is *Eckerd's*, 3400 Canal St ☎ 488-6661.
Police *New Orleans Police Department*, 715 S Broad St ☎ 821-2222.

Government offices

City Hall, 1300 Perdido St ☎ 586-4311; *US Customs*, 423 Canal St ☎ 589-6494; *US Dept of Commerce's Office of International Trade*, 2 Canal St ☎ 589-6546; *US Immigration and Naturalization Service*, 701 Loyola Ave ☎ 589-6533.

Information sources

Business information *The Chamber/New Orleans and the River Region*, 301 Camp St ☎ 527-6900, tells visitors what services are available and provides information about potential markets. The Chamber's Economic Development Council ☎ 527-6946 specializes in economic research.
Local media *The Times-Picayune/The States-Item* is New Orleans's only daily newspaper. *Where* and *Go* are useful magazines for visitors; *New Orleans Magazine* is feature-oriented.
Tourist information *The Greater New Orleans Tourist and Convention Commission*, 1520 Sugar Bowl Dr ☎ 566-5011 provides general information about the city.

Thank-yous

Florists *Carrollton Flower Market*, 838 Dublin St ☎ 866-9614; *Harkins the Florist*, 1601 Magazine St ☎ 529-1638.
Wine *Martin Wine Celler*, 3827 Baronne St ☎ 899-7411.

NEW YORK

Area codes: Manhattan and Bronx ☎ 212; Brooklyn, Queens and Staten Island ☎ 718; New Jersey ☎ 201 (north) ☎ 609 (south); Connecticut ☎ 203; Long Island ☎ 516. Telephone numbers in this city guide are 212 unless otherwise indicated.

Though New York is not America's capital city, it is without doubt its city of capital. Money – especially the relatively new foreign investment flowing in through the city's exchanges – is the power that has revitalized the city, restructured much of the nation's business through complex financial transactions, and created the 24-hour business day. If anything characterizes New York, it is not muggings, subway crime or Central Park after dark; it is the pace that obliges even the most temporary business visitor to seek to shave a minute or so off the walk to the next meeting. New York is the city that invented the power breakfast, an occasion that has little to do with eating, but a great deal to do with winning – contracts, companies, kudos and power.

New York was always a busy place, a bustling seaport; it still is one of the world's busiest ports. But it has lost its manufacturing edge, and many of the best-known corporations have moved their headquarters to the suburbs or to cheaper cities elsewhere. Now New York belongs to the money-movers, the real-estate developers, and the supporting cast in communications, image-making and advertising.

Away from the wharves, Manhattan thoroughfares have given their names to entire industries. Seventh Avenue – Fashion Avenue – is the center of American fashion, and Madison Avenue means advertising and promotion. Wall Street, of course, has been the seat of the nation's financial activity since the forerunner of the New York Stock Exchange was founded under a buttonwood tree on that street in 1792.

The pursuit of success and self-advancement has produced a business culture renowned for its extreme pressures, tough standards and high compensation. New MBAs or young lawyers at the foot of a long corporate ladder routinely work 80-hour weeks with starting salaries of more than $50,000. But life in New York is more expensive than anywhere else in the USA. City taxes are high, and rents easily top $2,000 a month for a one-bedroom apartment in a doorman-protected building on a good Manhattan block. And both dining out and maintaining the corporate wardrobe are expensive. Even play is intense in the Big Apple. City health clubs are full of weight-lifting bankers; Central Park full of jogging media planners. Many top executives leave Manhattan early on Friday afternoons in summer; they are headed for weekend homes out of town. Younger strivers, when they can escape their offices early enough, make for whatever is the latest fashionable nightspot to socialize, dance, drink and impair their efficiency for the next morning.

New York is a city of startling contrasts, where extreme wealth flourishes alongside poverty more typical of Third World countries.

Imported nannies wheel imported baby carriages in elegant little parks just a stone's throw from cacophonous avenues; subway travellers read both the brash *New York Post* and the restrained *New Yorker*. Outside a multi-milllon dollar Broadway musical or the glittering headquarters of a multinational corporation you will find an altogether different kind of financial dealer – the hustler.

Though the old Park Avenue WASP elite has not really ruled New York for a considerable time, one legacy at least of the city's history remains: the enormous bureaucracy which attempts to govern it, accused often of corruption, seldom of efficiency. But after its brush with fiscal disaster and near-bankruptcy in the 1970s, the city has only struggled back to solvency and improved many of its municipal services.

New York City is made up of five boroughs: Manhattan, which has 20% of the city's 7m population, the Bronx, Brooklyn, Queens and Staten Island. The metropolitan area also includes counties in New Jersey, immediately across the Hudson River; Westchester County, N of the Bronx; Fairfield County in Connecticut; and Nassau County on Long Island.

Arriving

Three airports serve the metropolitan area: J F Kennedy International (JFK) and LaGuardia (LGA) in Queens, and Newark International (EWR) in New Jersey.

Domestic travellers will find it quicker to get into Manhattan from LaGuardia. International travellers are likely to find that airline schedules dictate their arrival at JFK, even though Immigration and Customs formalities may take less time at Newark. Journey times into town from Newark and JFK are similar.

If you have an urgent connection to make, half-hourly helicopter flights taking 10–20min connect JFK and LaGuardia, and JFK and Newark; you cannot fly direct between LaGuardia and Newark. You can still save time by flying into midtown and catching a flight out to the other airport. For inquiries contact *New York Helicopter* ☏ 972-5680 or (800) 645-3494.

By road allow at least 90min to get between Newark and both the other airports (you have to cross Manhattan). Even the 3-mile/5km journey from LGA to JFK may take an hour at peak times. *Carey Transportation* ☏ (718) 632-0500 or 286 9766 operate a half-hourly LGA–JFK bus service. *Salem Limousines* ☏ (718) 656-4511 serve all three airports.

J F Kennedy International Airport

JFK handles international and medium- and long-haul domestic services. International flights arrive at either the International Arrivals Building or the Pan American, American, British Airways or TWA terminals.

International passengers first go through US Public Health, Immigration and Naturalization formalities, then baggage claim and finally Customs. If you are one of the first off the plane and have only hand baggage, you can be out of the airport in less than 30min; otherwise, allow an hour. Clearance is usually slowest at the International Arrivals Building; allow up to 2hrs; in summer, it can take longer.

All terminals have places to eat, drink and buy gifts or duty-free goods. If you expect to have a long wait, the airline executive or VIP

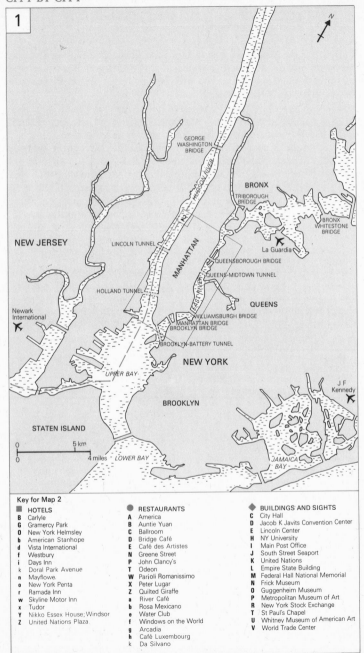

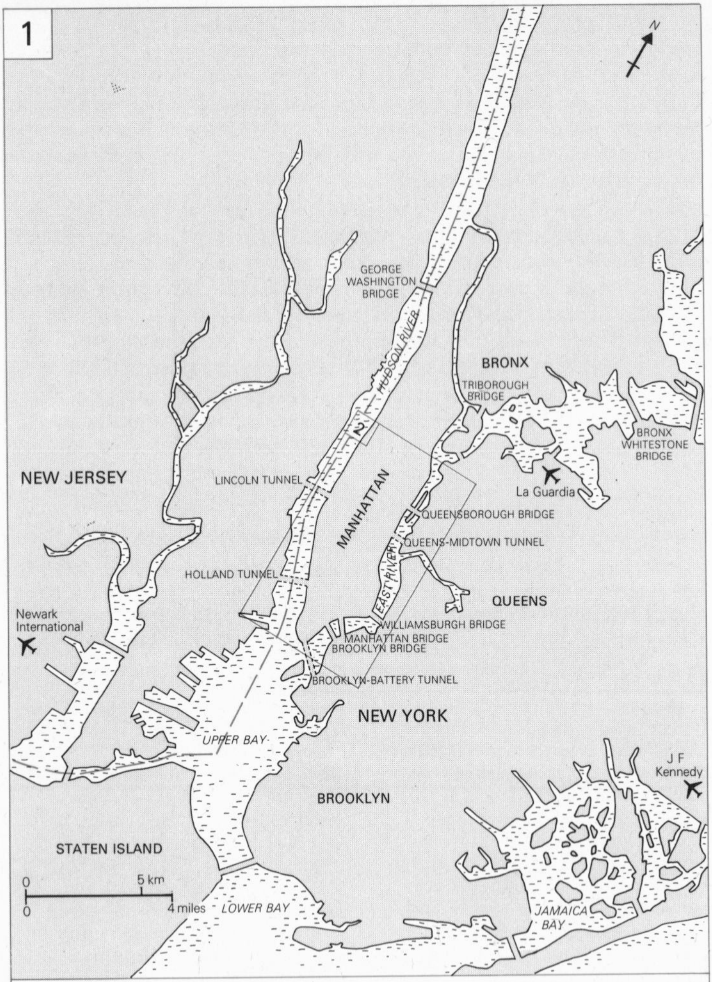

Key for Map 2

HOTELS
- **B** Carlyle
- **G** Gramercy Park
- **O** New York Helmsley
- **b** American Stanhope
- **d** Vista International
- **f** Westbury
- **i** Days Inn
- **k** Doral Park Avenue
- **n** Mayflowe.
- **o** New York Penta
- **r** Ramada Inn
- **w** Skyline Motor Inn
- **x** Tudor
- **Y** Nikko Essex House; Windsor
- **Z** United Nations Plaza

RESTAURANTS
- **A** America
- **B** Auntie Yuan
- **C** Ballroom
- **D** Bridge Café
- **E** Café des Artistes
- **N** Greene Street
- **P** John Clancy's
- **T** Odeon
- **W** Parioli Romanissimo
- **X** Peter Lugar
- **Z** Quilted Giraffe
- **a** River Café
- **b** Rosa Mexicano
- **e** Water Club
- **f** Windows on the World
- **g** Arcadia
- **h** Café Luxembourg
- **k** Da Silvano

BUILDINGS AND SIGHTS
- **C** City Hall
- **D** Jacob K Javits Convention Center
- **E** Lincoln Center
- **H** NY University
- **I** Main Post Office
- **J** South Street Seaport
- **K** United Nations
- **L** Empire State Building
- **M** Federal Hall National Memorial
- **N** Frick Museum
- **O** Guggenheim Museum
- **P** Metropolitan Museum of Art
- **R** New York Stock Exchange
- **T** St Paul's Chapel
- **U** Whitney Museum of American Art
- **V** World Trade Center

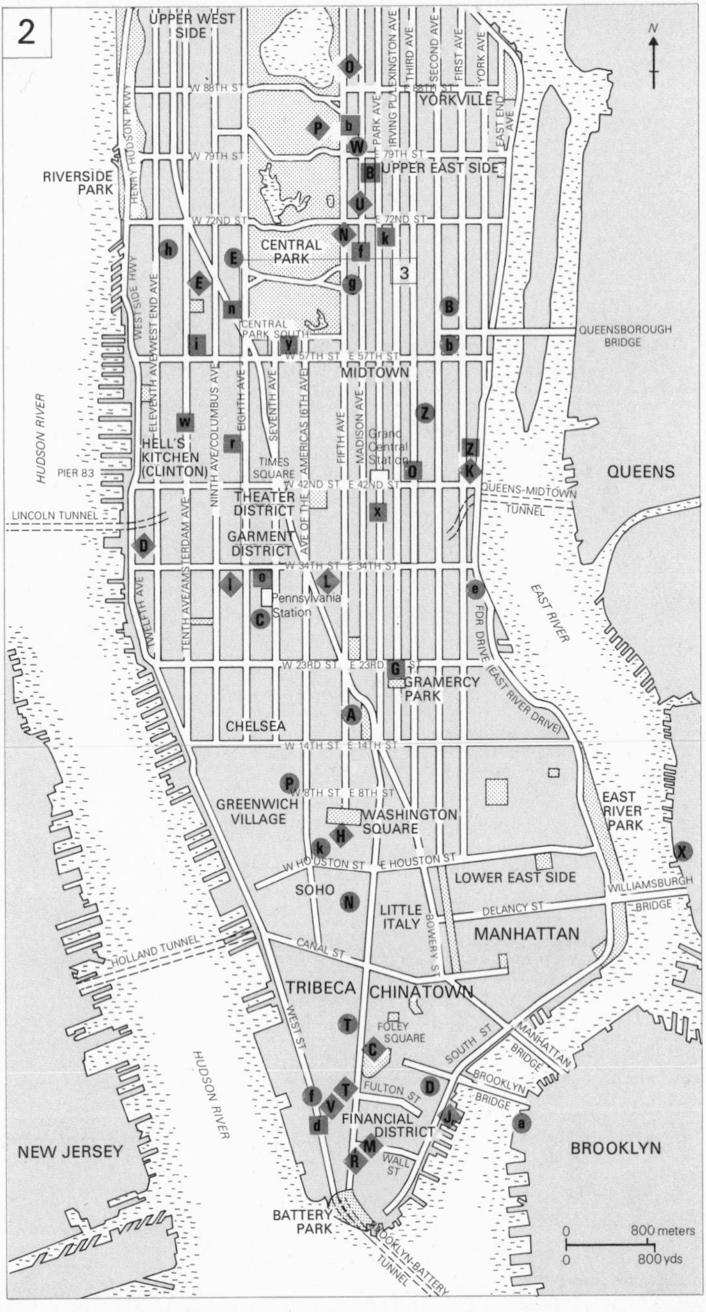
2
UPPER WEST SIDE
W 88TH ST
W 79TH ST
W 72ND ST
RIVERSIDE PARK
HENRY HUDSON PKWY
PARK AVE
LEXINGTON AVE
IRVING PL
THIRD AVE
SECOND AVE
FIRST AVE
YORK AVE
EAST END AVE
YORKVILLE
E 79TH ST
UPPER EAST SIDE
E 72ND ST
CENTRAL PARK
3
WEST SIDE HWY
WEST END AVE
CENTRAL PARK SOUTH
QUEENSBOROUGH BRIDGE
W 57TH ST
E 57TH ST
MIDTOWN
HUDSON RIVER
ELEVENTH AVE
NINTH AVE/COLUMBUS AVE
EIGHTH AVE
SEVENTH AVE
AVE OF THE AMERICAS (6TH AVE)
FIFTH AVE
MADISON AVE
Grand Central Station
HELL'S KITCHEN (CLINTON)
TIMES SQUARE
PIER 83
W 42ND ST
E 42ND ST
QUEENS
QUEENS-MIDTOWN TUNNEL
THEATER DISTRICT
LINCOLN TUNNEL
GARMENT DISTRICT
TENTH AVE/AMSTERDAM AVE
W 34TH ST
E 34TH ST
Pennsylvania Station
TWELFTH AVE
FDR DRIVE (EAST RIVER DRIVE)
EAST RIVER
W 23RD ST
E 23RD ST
GRAMERCY PARK
CHELSEA
W 14TH ST
E 14TH ST
W 8TH ST
E 8TH ST
GREENWICH VILLAGE
WASHINGTON SQUARE
EAST RIVER PARK
W HOUSTON ST
E HOUSTON ST
LOWER EAST SIDE
SOHO
LITTLE ITALY
WILLIAMSBURGH BRIDGE
DELANCY ST
BOWERY ST
MANHATTAN
HOLLAND TUNNEL
CANAL ST
TRIBECA
CHINATOWN
WEST ST
HUDSON RIVER
FOLEY SQUARE
SOUTH ST
MANHATTAN BRIDGE
BROOKLYN BRIDGE
FULTON ST
FINANCIAL DISTRICT
NEW JERSEY
WALL ST
BROOKLYN
BATTERY PARK
BROOKLYN-BATTERY TUNNEL
0
800 meters
0
800 yds
N

3
CENTRAL PARK
CENTRAL PARK SOUTH
FIFTH AVE
MADISON AVE
PARK AVE
LEXINGTON AVE
65TH ST
63RD ST
61ST ST
N
W 57TH ST
E 57TH ST
EIGHTH AVE
BROADWAY
SEVENTH AVE
AVE OF THE AMERICAS (SIXTH AVE)
W 55TH ST
E 55TH ST
MIDTOWN
W 53RD ST
E 53RD ST
W 51ST ST
E 51ST ST
W 48TH ST
E 48TH ST
THEATER DISTRICT
W 44TH ST
E 44TH ST
Grand Central Station
TIMES SQUARE
W 42ND ST
E 42ND ST
W 37TH ST
E 37TH ST
GARMENT DISTRICT
0
400 meters
0
400yds

Key for Map 3

HOTELS					
A	Algonquin	**a**	Sherry-Netherland	**R**	Lutèce
C	Doral Tuscany	**e**	Waldorf-Astoria	**S**	Il Nido
D	Dorset	**g**	Westin Plaza	**U**	Oyster Bar and Restaurant
E	Drake Swissôtel	**h**	Best Western Milford Plaza	**V**	Palio
F	Essex House	**j**	Doral Inn	**Y**	Petrossian
H	Grand Hyatt New York	**l**	Edison	**c**	Russian Tea Room
I	Helmsley Palace	**m**	Halloran House		Sea Grill (Building S)
J	Inter-Continental	**p**	Omni Park Central	**I**	Christ Cella
K	Lowell	**q**	Quality Inn Lexington	**J**	Jean Lafitte
L	Marriott Marquis	**s**	Roosevelt		
M	Mayfair Regent	**t**	Salisbury		BUILDINGS AND SIGHTS
N	Morgan's	**u**	Shelburne Murray Hill	**A**	Carnegie Hall
P	New York Hilton and Towers	**v**	Sheraton City Squire	**B**	Chrysler Building
Q	Omni Berkshire Palace			**F**	NY Convention Center and Visitors' Bureau
R	Park Lane		RESTAURANTS		
S	Parker Meridien	**G**	Le Cirque	**G**	NY Public Library
T	Pierre	**H**	La Cote Basque	**Q**	Museum of Modern Art
U	Plaza Athenée	**I**	Le Cygne	**S**	Rockefeller Center
V	Regency	**J**	Darbár		
W	Ritz-Carlton	**K**	Felidia		
X	St Moritz-on-the-Park	**L**	Four Seasons		
Y	St Regis Sheraton	**M**	Gloucester House		
Z	Sheraton Centre and Towers	**O**	Hatsuhana		
		Q	Kitcho		

lounges are the best places to be. In the International Arrivals Building there is a shared executive lounge and a wide range of services, including a general information counter in the main lobby ☎ (718) 656-7990 and two baggage storage areas ☎ (718) 995-2228. A 24hr currency exchange is on the second floor (other terminals close at 8.30); there is a dental suite in the east wing ☎ (718) 656-4747.

Nearby hotels *International Hotel* at JFK 11436 (Trusthouse Forte) ☎ (718) 995-9000 TX 4972701. *Airport Hilton*, 138-10 135 Avenue, Jamaica, Queens 11436 ☎ (718) 322-8700 TX 971962. *Marriott*, 135-30 140 St, Jamaica, Queens 11437 ☎ (718) 659-6000 or (800) 228-9290 TX 980879.

City link JFK is in the borough of Queens, 15 miles/24km E of Manhattan. During peak hours (7–10, 3–7) the only quick transportation is a helicopter.

Helicopter Most major airlines have arrangements with New York Helicopter Corp ☎ 972-5680 or (800) 645-3494 which provides for a free flight to the heliport at E 34th St in midtown Manhattan. The free service (which operates also to Newark International Airport in some cases) is available only to certain categories of passenger – for example, British Airways Concorde, 1st Class and Super Club. Other categories pay a $10 surcharge. TWA offers a similar service; but Pan Am has its own flights to the Metroport (60th Street and York Avenue) or to Newark. Pan Am 1st Class and Clipper passengers travel free; others have to pay $10. Pan Am passengers who prefer to fly by New York Helicopter to E 34th Street are charged $10. The standard local New York Helicopter fare for airline passengers who do not qualify for a discount is $58. Check that you are covered by the free service when making reservations.

Taxi Cabs provide the most convenient way to get into the city and cost only about $25. Taxis wait outside all terminals; there can be shortages during peak arrival periods (late morning and late afternoon). The ride to midtown takes about 30min with no traffic delays, but can take 90min during rush hours. After 3pm, the usual route through the Queens-Midtown Tunnel has only one in-bound lane, and many drivers prefer to cross the Triboro Bridge to minimize hold-ups. Because the meter fare is a combination of time and distance, if Triboro is the quicker route, it may not add much to the fare.

Limousine Limousines (especially Fugazy) are often available outside terminals and, shared, should cost

less than a cab. Otherwise you can call ahead for a limo to meet you (see *Getting around* for reliable firms).
Bus Services operated by Carey Transportation ☏ (718) 632-0500 leave every 15–30min, 6.30am–12.30am, fare $8. You can get off at various midtown locations including Grand Central Terminal.

Bus services advertised in hotels often make many stops, and whether your stop is first or last can make a difference of 30min travel time.
Subway The JFK Express ☏ (718) 858-7272 leaves every 20min, 5.30am–12.30am, and takes 45min–1hr; fare $6.50. It involves both an airport bus ride (stopping at every terminal) and a long subway trip with frequent stops on the West Side of Manhattan along the IND subway system routes. It can be delayed and is useful only in rush hour.
Car rental A car is almost always an encumbrance in Manhattan, but all the major firms have desks at JFK.

LaGuardia Airport

LGA, named after the former mayor, Fiorello H LaGuardia, is on the East River in Queens, 8 miles/13km from midtown. The airport is busiest in the early morning, late afternoon and evening, when cabs into town can be scarce and traffic problems are most likely. Long walks to baggage claim are common. Only limited foreign currency exchange is available. The large gift shops offer a wide selection, but do not expect a bargain, or anything unusual.
Nearby hotels *Holiday Inn*, 100-15 Ditmars Blvd, E Elmhurst, Queens 11369 ☏ (718) 898-1225. *Sheraton Inn at LGA*, 90-10 Grand Central Parkway, E Elmhurst, Queens 11369 ☏ (718) 446-4800.
City link The fastest way into midtown Manhattan is by helicopter; otherwise use a cab or bus.
Helicopter The standard fare for services operated by New York Helicopter Corp ☏ 972-5680 or (800) 645-3495 is $58 (plus tax), but many major airlines have special arrangements for certain categories of passenger, whereby the helicopter fare is waived altogether, or only a $10 surcharge need be paid. Check the circumstances when your reservations are made. Flights leave from American Airlines baggage claim on the lower level (7.13am–9.43pm) and land at the midtown heliport, E 34th St.
Taxi It takes 20–45min by cab into midtown and costs about $20 including tolls. The Queens-Midtown Tunnel is the most direct route, but is often snarled with traffic; because the meter fare is a combination of time and distance, the longer Triboro Bridge route may be faster and may not add much to the fare.
Bus Carey Transportation ☏ (718) 632-0500 runs buses to Grand Central Terminal every 15min, 6.45am–12.30am; fare $6. Many hotels have a shared van service; if your hotel is the last stop, it can add 30min to the trip.
Subway The subway is not a recommended way into town; it is the cheapest ($2) but slowest (at least 2hrs). The Q33 bus connects LaGuardia and the Queens–74th Street subway station, which is on the Flushing line to Grand Central Terminal and 5th Avenue.
Car rental Having a car in Manhattan is rarely an advantage, but all the major firms have desks at the airport.
Limousine See *Getting around.*

Newark International Airport

Newark, about 16 miles/25km from midtown, is comparatively uncrowded and problem-free. Terminals A and B and the North Terminal handle domestic flights; international and long-haul domestic flights go through Terminal C. Customs and Immigration seldom take more than 1hr, but long walks to baggage claim are common.

Modern, comfortable facilities are available in Terminals A, B and C. Coffee shops and newsstands are

located both landside and airside. Currency exchange is available, but rates are generally poor, especially in Terminal C. Transit buses run between the two. North Terminal has a book shop, coffee and bar facilities and currency exchange.
Nearby hotel *Howard Johnson*, S Haynes Avenue, Newark, NJ 07114 ☎ (201) 824-4000 or (800) 654-2000.
City link Helicopter is the fastest way into Manhattan; taxi or bus are the only other ways, unless you rent a car.
Taxi Flat rates apply from Newark into the city (but not if you are going from New York to the airport). To midtown Manhattan, the fare is about $25–30. There is an additional charge for East Side destinations above 14th Street. The cab ride takes about 30min (at least 1hr at peak times).
Limousine See *Getting around* for reliable firms.
Bus Olympia Trails ☎ 964-6233 runs buses to World Trade Center or Grand Central, every 20min, 5am–1am. NJ Transit ☎ (201) 762-5100 or (800) 722-2222 operates to Port Authority Bus Terminal every 15–30min, 24hrs.
Helicopter The standard fare for services operated by New York Helicopter Corp ☎ 972-5680 or (800) 645-3495 is $58, but you may have to pay only a $10 fee if your airline has arrangements with NYHC. Some air fares include free helicopter shuttle. Check when making your reservations. Flights leave from Terminal A Gate 21 (Piedmont counter) and land midtown at the E 34th Street heliport.

Rail stations

The city's two railroad stations – Grand Central and Pennsylvania – are used more by daily commuters from the suburbs than by long-distance travellers. At both, beware of hustlers who will take your bags, offer to get you a cab and then demand several dollars: they are illegal and can be dangerous.
Grand Central, on 42nd St at Park Avenue, serves upper New York State and Connecticut. The huge c.1903 Beaux Arts terminal has many shops and concessions, and it connects with both the Grand Hyatt (see *Hotels*) and the Pan Am Building. The terminal, though generally well organized, is dirty and many homeless people live there. IRT subway trains 4, 5 and 6 stop there, and you can connect with a shuttle train to Times Square. The Oyster Bar (see *Restaurants*) is useful for business lunches. Information ☎ 523-4900 and 532-1358.
Pennsylvania The modern, underground Penn Station serves Long Island and New Jersey, as well as more distant points on the Amtrak lines. The 7th Avenue, Broadway and 8th Avenue subway lines all stop there. Information: *Amtrak* ☎ 736-4545, *Long Island Railroad* ☎ (718) 454-5477.

Getting around

Manhattan's predominantly grid-like layout is simple to understand outside Greenwich Village and the area below Canal Street. Numbered streets run E–W and numbered avenues run N–S. The E–W street designations are centered on 5th Avenue. Broadway, following an old Indian trail, cuts a long diagonal across the grid. North is referred to as uptown, south is downtown – crucial when asking directions.

Walking is often the quickest and most pleasant way to get around. For longer journeys the subway is quicker during peak hours (7–10, 4–6). At other times, use taxis.
Walking In general, a fit New Yorker with little or no baggage would walk any distance up to 15 blocks – except in bad weather. Calculate walking time at about 1min per N–S block, 2min per E–W block. Heavy traffic means that you should cross roads as and when the green light shows, rather than sticking to what seems to be the most direct route. Avoid areas with few

pedestrians, especially Central Park, after dark. Ask for directions: most New Yorkers are glad to help.

Taxi Going crosstown averages 15min without traffic problems, but there are ridiculous delays at lunchtime and in the rush hours. From midtown to the Financial District takes about 20min, but at peak times very much longer.

Many drivers are recent immigrants. They are required to pass language and city knowledge tests, but they may speak English poorly and sometimes do not know their way around. Yellow medallion cabs are subject to city-controlled testing and fare regulations. Nevertheless, many cabs are scruffy, and few are air-conditioned. A cab is available when the center of its roof sign is lit, and medallion drivers must by law take you to any of the city's five boroughs, or to Westchester County, Nassau County or Newark International Airport. Special rates apply on such trips and are posted in each cab. Make a point of being inside the cab before giving your destination, especially if it is outside Manhattan. If a "gypsy" cab (an unregulated ordinary car of any color with a "Livery" or "Car Service" sign on the dashboard) is all you can get, at least make sure to agree the fare in advance.

In the early evening (5–7), cabs are very difficult to find in the street; on Friday evenings, it is almost impossible even to get one by phone. In wet weather, cabs may be found at main hotels, but be prepared for brusque treatment if the driver was hoping for a lucrative airport trip. Cabbies expect a tip of 15–20% of the metered fare.

Radio cabs There are two main types of radio-despatched unregulated cars available, the better of the two being almost limousine standard, although without the stretched body. Although their fares are usually higher than regulated cabs, they are clean, comfortable and air-conditioned: they may be worth the extra cost (except for long trips out to the suburbs).

Reliable, straightforward radio cab services include *Citywide Taxi* ☎ 295-1122; *Utog* ☎ 741-2122 and *XYZ Two-Way Radio* ☎ (718) 768-7333. The lesser-limousine services include *Fugazy Express* ☎ 762-9100; *Salem Limousines* ☎ (718) 656-4511; and *Scully's Angels* ☎ (718) 651-9400.

Limousine Full-scale limo service is available from *Cooper Rolls-Royce* ☎ 929-0094; *Fugazy Express* ☎ 762-9100; *London Towncars* ☎ 988-9700; and *Salem Limousines* ☎ (718) 656-4511.

Driving All major car rental companies have facilities at or near the three airports and in midtown, but it is not advisable to drive. Traffic is absurdly bad, and parking expensive.

Subway The subway operates 24hrs, but not all stations are served at all times. Its network covers Manhattan well, particularly in midtown; most of the lines run predominantly N–S.

The IND (Independent) lines (A, C, E, B, D and F trains) seem to have more delays and run less frequently than the IRT (Interborough Rapid Transit) lines (1, 2, 3, 4, 5 and 6 trains). However, IND trains are newer and safer.

The BMT line (Brooklyn–Manhattan) runs from lower Manhattan to Brooklyn and Queens, and so is less useful to the business visitor than the other two lines.

Distinguishing between local trains, which stop at all stations, and express trains, which do not, is important; generally, express trains run on the tracks in the center of a station, local trains against the walls. Local trains are more often air-conditioned and usually less crowded than express trains, and at rush hour they can also be faster.

The subway is often quickest in rush hours. In the evening, if you are heading for Brooklyn, you can avoid the appalling rush-hour crawl across the bridge by using the E-bound Nassau Street line.

Contrary to the subway system's reputation, its users do not regularly risk loss of life, limb or belongings. However, after 10pm empty trains do offer opportunities to criminals; in rush hours, watch out for pickpockets. If the car you are travelling in begins to empty, move to a fuller one. Always, even in rush hours, avoid deserted or infrequently used exits or entrances, even if they seem more convenient; stick with the crowds. On stations, outside rush hours, you can often wait in designated safe areas.

Free maps of the subway system are available at token booths.

Buses are the only form of public transportation going crosstown (E–W) in Manhattan; they generally operate on major cross streets (such as 14th, 23rd and 34th) as well as N and S, up and down most major avenues. Stops are frequent (every two blocks on N–S routes; every block crosstown). The exact fare ($1) in coins is required, but subway tokens are acceptable. Passengers may transfer to a connecting line without extra charge, provided they ask the driver of the first bus for a "transfer" when they get on.

City buses tend to be slow-moving, but in the summer most buses are air-conditioned.

Finding your way around

Use the following information to pinpoint the whereabouts of your next appointment. For N–S avenues the rule is to take the address number, drop the last digit (472 becomes 47), divide by 2 and add or subtract the number shown on the table below. For E–W street addresses see the diagram to find which block a particular address is on.

Central Park occupies the blocks between 5th Avenue and Central Park West and stretches from 59th Street to 110th Street. N of 59th Street, 8th Avenue becomes Central Park West; 9th Avenue becomes Columbus Avenue; 10th Avenue becomes Amsterdam Avenue; 11th Avenue becomes West End Avenue; and 12th Avenue becomes Riverside Drive.

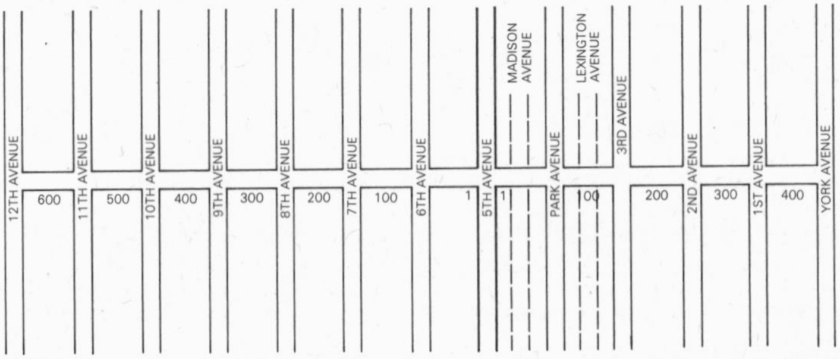

Avenues A, B, C and D	+3	Avenue of the Americas	+24	Edgecombe Avenue	+134
1st Avenue	+3	7th Avenue	+12	Ft Washington Avenue	+158
2nd Avenue	+3	above 110th St	+20	Lenox Avenue	+110
3rd Avenue	+10	8th Avenue	+10	Lexington Avenue	+22
4th Avenue	+8	9th Avenue	+13	Madison Avenue	+26
5th Avenue		10th Avenue	+14	Manhattan Avenue	+100
up to 200	+13	Amsterdam Avenue	+60	Park Avenue	+35
201-400	+16	Audubon Avenue	+165	Pleasant Avenue	+101
401-601	+18	Broadway (23rd to 192nd St)	−30	Riverside Drive – divide bldg	
601-775	+20	Central Park West – divide		no. by 10, then up to 165th St	+72
776-1286 – cancel last figure, then	−18	bldg no. by 10, then	+60	St Nicholas Avenue	+110
1287-1500	+45	Columbus Avenue	+60	Wadsworth Avenue	+173
		Convent Avenue	+127	West End Avenue	+60

Area by area

New York's most important and most prestigious business areas are from 42nd Street to 57th Street and 3rd Avenue to 6th Avenue in midtown, and in the Wall Street area downtown. Certain industries have distinct territories: for example, garment-making is in the W 30s, music in the W 60s, jewelry in the W 40s. Although many city professionals commute from the suburbs, luxurious residential areas still remain on the Upper East Side (on Park and 5th Avenue) and West Side (along Central Park West).

New York developed historically by growing northward along Manhattan Island from the Battery. In the older areas, the grid street plan does not exist, and visitors without a good map may get lost.

Influxes of immigrants in the early part of this century created many ethnic enclaves: Little Italy and Chinatown in lower Manhattan; the German community in Yorkville on the Upper East Side; a Ukrainian outpost in the East Village; black Harlem and Spanish Harlem uptown. With a housing shortage and spiralling rentals, however, today's arrivals tend to settle in the outer boroughs: Greeks and Koreans in Queens; Russians, Jamaicans and Haitians in Brooklyn, for example. Meanwhile, young professionals have gentrified some Manhattan neighborhoods and penetrated Brooklyn areas such as Park Slope, replacing bodegas and numbers shops with gourmet delis and singles bars. In the UN area, Beekman Place and Sutton Place, N of 48th Street, are among the city's most prestigious, most expensive residential neighborhoods, home to some of New York society's oldest families.

Financial District The Financial District, from the Battery N to City Hall, was once home to virtually all the city's banks and brokerage houses. Now, because of the difficulties of expanding in a cramped area and commuting to it, many banks and brokers have moved to midtown. Some firms have moved to the new World Financial Center, near the World Trade Center; but many, especially legal firms and those whose business is tied closely to the New York and American Stock Exchanges, securities and commodities, remain downtown. The population has tripled to 15,000 since 1975, but the area remains one of the city's most sparsely populated neighborhoods and is deserted after dark and at weekends.

Foley Square and Chinatown E from City Hall, N to Canal Street, is a warren of government buildings around Foley Square, and, E and N of that, Chinatown – a maze of busy streets, with Oriental restaurants and shops.

TriBeCa and SoHo To the W below Canal Street is the area known as TriBeCa (the TRIangle BElow CAnal), where artists and wealthier trend-followers have converted old factories and warehouses to living and working loft apartments. To the N is SoHo (SOuth of HOuston), similarly transformed into a neighborhood of lofts, wine bars, galleries and expensive shops.

Greenwich Village Between Houston (pronounced House-ton) and 14th Street, from the Hudson to beyond 4th Avenue, is one of the city's most attractive and interesting areas. The low brownstone buildings house upper middle class families, artists and writers, young professionals and older immigrants.

High rents mean that the Village is less bohemian than it was, but its numerous cafés and restaurants still give it an unmatched street life. New York University occupies many buildings in the central part of the Village around Washington Square. The West Village is the center of the city's gay life; the East Village, which lies E of Broadway towards Alphabet City (Avenues A, B, C and D), has pink-haired punks alongside old Ukrainians, Indian and macrobiotic eating houses next to old Russian borscht restaurants. The streets of Alphabet City with their after-hours clubs and illicit drug dealing can be dangerous, especially E of Avenue A.

Lower East Side and Little Italy S and E of Houston Street and S of Alphabet City is the Lower East Side, home to millions of mid-19th century European immigrants. Italians settled around Mulberry Street, creating Little Italy (still full of restaurants, *pasticcerie* and *caffè*). Farther E, European Jews came to crowded tenements and sweatshops; although many moved away when they prospered, the area is still predominantly Jewish, and Orchard Street still the best place in the city to find clothing bargains.

Gramercy Park The area between 14th and 23rd streets has engaging 19th- and early 20th-century architecture and two of the city's loveliest small parks, Stuyvesant Square (2nd Avenue at 16th Street) and Gramercy Park (Lexington Avenue at 20th Street). Gramercy Park is open only to residents of its quiet, expensive enclave.

Chelsea To the W lies Chelsea, a mixed neighborhood of young professionals and lower-income families that is rapidly developing.

Garment District Above 23rd Street and Chelsea, above the plant district (6th Avenue in the 20s) and W of the toy district (5th Avenue above 23rd Street) the jumble of decaying buildings, shabby offices and cheap diners meld almost imperceptibly into the Garment District, centered on 7th Avenue, above 34th Street. On weekdays, runners rush racks of garments through the streets, groups of people talk and argue at every door, limousines glide to the curbs and disgorge designer passengers. A fifth of the clothing made in the USA comes from this area.

Hell's Kitchen Above the Garment District in the W 40s and 50s is what was formerly known as Hell's Kitchen, now officially called Clinton. Its lurid reputation dates from shortly after the Civil War, when the Hell's Kitchen Gang ruled its streets. Although prostitution still thrives, today's residents are mainly Hispanic families, artists and writers. Manhattan Plaza, an apartment tower for musicians, actors and artists at 42nd Street and 10th Avenue, has helped to change the tone of the area.

Theater District Times Square and Broadway, center of New York's legitimate theater, are dazzling by night and sleazy by day. Pornography and its acolytes are rife along 42nd Street and 8th Avenue. In the side streets, bars and restaurants cater to Broadway crowds.

Midtown The heart of the midtown business district extends from 42nd to 57th streets, 6th Avenue (Avenue of the Americas) to 3rd Avenue. Glass-sheathed towers along the avenues, virtually all prestige addresses, house top firms in law, advertising, publishing and finance. Addresses E of 3rd Avenue, W of 6th Avenue, and on the side streets generally lack the clout of a tower-top suite or Rockefeller Center. But there are exceptions, such as the Gulf + Western Building at 59th Street and Central Park West, one of the few top business addresses outside the midtown area. And Park Avenue from 23rd to 42nd streets (called Park Avenue South below 34th) has experienced a bit of a renaissance, with advertising, publishing and other service firms discovering the charms of the area's quiet streets, good restaurants and office rents.

United Nations area Along the East River from 23rd to 57th streets, residential neighborhoods succeed one another up to and past the UN. These are generally older, quieter, more established neighborhoods: rentals rise the farther N you go.
Upper East Side The Upper East Side is primarily a residential area; as a rule of thumb, the farther S, the more prestigious. Top executives who choose to live in Manhattan tend to have addresses on 5th or Park avenues, or in a brownstone or townhouse on one of the side streets.
Yorkville The area above 79th Street and E of Lexington was originally settled by mid-European immigrants. However, in the past 20 years an influx of young, mainly unmarried professionals has changed the area, taking over blocks of nearly featureless high-rises interspersed with blocks of brownstone apartments in the E 70s, 80s and 90s.
Upper West Side Fifteen years ago, only Central Park West was thought respectable. Today, gentrification has transformed the other once-seedy avenues; owner-occupied and restored brownstones line the cross streets; Lincoln Center supports a host of auxiliary industries in the W 60s; and the poor who previously occupied the area have been pushed N towards Harlem. The area's best address is still Central Park West, where top-floor apartments can be as costly as those on the more staid east side of the park. Away from the park, the population is younger and more mixed.
Central Park Laid out in 1857, the 870-acre park is an oasis of greenery heavily used by joggers, picnickers, sports enthusiasts of all sorts, and families on weekends. It can be dangerous after dark and during less busy weekdays; above 86th Street, be particularly cautious at all times.
Brooklyn The city's largest borough, across the East River, has many lovely neighborhoods restored to residential splendor by young professionals and their families. Brooklyn Heights is now as expensive as Manhattan; Park Slope, farther E near Prospect Park, is evolving in the same way. Williamsburg, at the foot of the Manhattan Bridge, is home to many of the Hasidic Jews who work in the diamond district on W 47th Street.
Queens Most of Queens is traditionally lower middle class or light industrial. But Astoria has been "discovered," and its older ethnic character is changing. Forest Hills, former home of the US Open, is a delightful (and not inexpensive) residential neighborhood; Whitestone seems almost suburban in its greenery.

The suburbs

Many communities in Westchester County N of the city are almost empty of adults on weekdays. Scarsdale, Rye, Katonah and Mount Kisco are all commuter towns. Generally, towns farther from the city are more desirable, but beyond a certain distance their appeal drops sharply. Towns too close, such as Yonkers, are not favored.

Greenwich and Darien, in Fairfield County, Connecticut, are the archetypal residences of top corporate executives. Norwalk and Stanford are more middle-class and industrial.

Short Hills and Saddle River, New Jersey, have many middle- and upper-level executives who are driven to the city each day in private cars; others, like gentrifying Hoboken and Jersey City, are industrial lower middle class. Generally, the communities farther N and W, away from the Hudson River and the New Jersey Turnpike, are more expensive.

Long Island, like New Jersey, is more diverse than either Fairfield or Westchester. Older areas closer to the city, such as Manhasset and Roslyn, tend to be more expensive. Sands Point and Kings Point are predominantly Jewish; Locust Valley and Oyster Bay are mainly WASP. Huntington and Oyster Bay are home to many professionals.

Hotels

Nearly all New York hotels are geared to business clients, and the best ones are in midtown and the Upper East Side; in the Wall Street area, the only business-class hotel is the Vista at the World Trade Center. Expect to pay a minimum of $100 a night, and usually much more. Also, in addition to the usual $8\frac{1}{4}$% sales tax levied on your hotel bill, in New York you must also pay the additional taxes: a $2-per-room occupancy charge plus a 5% occupancy tax. Bear in mind that rooms on low floors are generally noisier; those without windows looking onto streets are generally quieter. Few city center hotels have in-house health club facilities or swimming pools: those that do have been noted.

Algonquin $$$
59 W 44th St (5th Ave) 10036
☎ 840-6800 TX 66532 • 160 rooms, 25 suites, 3 restaurants, 1 bar
The great attractions of this turn-of-the-century hostelry are its location (near Grand Central), lobby lounge (a venerable meeting place crowded with sofas and wing chairs) and amiable Blue Bar (see *Bars*). Its debits are the food (bland or worse), service (sullen or distracted), bedrooms (small, poorly equipped and with erratic plumbing) and elevators (slow). If you can, take a suite, which may be charmingly furnished. Still, there is that lobby, thick with literary and theatrical associations; Sir John Gielgud and Lord Olivier are among the hotel's regulars. It is ideal for afternoon tea or cocktails, especially with people from publishing or the theater. There is a 3pm check-out. Drugstore • 1 meeting room.

American Stanhope $$$$$
995 5th Ave (81st St) 10028
☎ 288-5800 TX 6720662 • 117 rooms, 94 suites, 3 restaurants, 1 bar
It's amazing what $26m can do to a pleasant but formerly unremarkable hotel. In 1986, the new owner cut the number of rooms by nearly half to create suites, and then filled them with buttery leather, silks, marble, Baccarat crystal and bath amenities by Chanel. All the suites have kitchenettes, two-line phones with hold buttons, and audio cassette players. Staff outnumbers clients by two-to-one, as well they should since this is the city's most expensive hotel. Six meeting rooms.

Carlyle $$$$$
35 E 76th St (Madison Ave) 10021
☎ 744-1600 TX 630692 • 114 rooms, 70 suites, 2 restaurants, 2 bars
This is the nearest Manhattan gets to having a European or Far Eastern grand hotel. Testimony to its desirability lies in the large number of permanently leased rooms, leaving barely 20% available to transients. Furnishings and accessories are harmonious blends of 16th–19thC regal conceits, but there are also discreetly concealed minibars, stereos, televisions and VCRs in every room. The staff is alert, attentive and available. The restaurant is an excellent choice for a business breakfast or lunch, but is probably not gastronomically distinguished enough to entice you for dinner. Bobby Short, singer and focal point of local society, holds court much of the year in the Café Carlyle (see *Entertainment*). Hairdresser • health club by arrangement • 2 meeting rooms.

Doral Tuscany $$$$$
120 E 39th St (Park Ave) 10016
☎ 686-1600 TX 640243 • 135 rooms, 16 suites, 1 restaurant, 1 bar
The relatively peaceful Murray Hill district S of Grand Central and E of 5th Avenue is home to several small, low-pressure hotels that do not treat guests as mobile cash-flow units. The

trade-off is slightly greater distance from the fevered midtown core, but this translates into only a few extra minutes' travel time. The Tuscany is exemplary of the breed, with extras including a variety of gadgets: in the lobby, a stock ticker; in the bedrooms, dressing alcoves with sinks and refrigerators, VCRs, three telephones, electric shoe-polishers and reclining lounge chairs. Rooms are spacious, with large desks, and most have exercycles. Arrangement with health club • 2 meeting rooms.

Dorset **$$$$**
30 E 54th St (6th Ave) 10019
☎ 247-7300 • 200 rooms, 1 restaurant, 1 bar
The discreet and stylish Dorset is an ideal choice for the business traveller who wants to visit the nearby Museum of Modern Art or the boutiques on 5th Avenue. The rooms (ask for one on the courtyard side) are pleasantly furnished and of a good size. The bar-café is a favorite with stars from nearby ABC at lunchtime.

Drake Swissôtel **$$$$$**
440 Park Ave (E 56th St) 10022
☎ 421-0900 TX 147178 • 583 rooms, 51 suites, 2 restaurants, 1 bar
The once-drooping reputation of this older hotel sparkles again under its new Swiss owners. The Park Avenue address was desirable, and the private rooms of the former apartment building always spacious. But the Swiss have opened up the cramped lobby, brightened the décor and improved the dining rooms. While the result isn't flashy, neither is it sedate. The Restaurant Lafayette is notable. Complimentary limo to Wall Street, clothing shop • health club by arrangement • 7 meeting rooms, fax.

Gramercy Park **$$$**
2 Lexington Ave (E 21st St) 10010
☎ 475-4320 TX 668755 • 350 rooms, 157 suites, 1 restaurant, 1 bar
Europeans have a particular fondness for this downtown hotel in a genteel neighborhood where Theodore Roosevelt lived as a child, though New Yorkers think it out-of-the-way and a little worn at the edges. But when image is unimportant or expense account tight, it is an amiable stopover with adequate rooms and a warm atmosphere. Ask for a room with a view of the park. Arrangements with nearby health club • 5 meeting rooms.

Grand Hyatt New York **$$$$$**
42nd St and Park Ave 10017
☎ 883-1234 TX 645616 • 1,197 rooms, 87 suites, 3 restaurants, 4 bars, 1 coffee shop
The Grand Hyatt's spectacular four-story atrium is as wide and long as a football field. It encloses a stepped waterfall, groves of potted trees and a huge hanging wire sculpture, all overwhelming the reception area, lobby and glassed-in bar cantilevered over the street. For the business traveller two floors are given to the Regency Club, with its private lounge, elevator and concierge. On another floor, 14 rooms provide combined conference and sleeping spaces. There is also a huge selection of high-class clothing, gift and jewelry shops. Bookstore, Federal Express • tennis courts in Grand Central • 8 meeting rooms, fax, translation.

Helmsley Palace **$$$$$**
455 Madison Ave (between 50th and 51st Sts) 10022 ☎ 888-7000 TX 640543 • 859 rooms, 105 suites, 3 restaurants, 2 bars
Harry Helmsley was prevailed upon to preserve and restore the Palace's existing late-19thC Italianate terraces, and his craftsmen did a superb job. Even if you are staying elsewhere, try the Gold Room for tea and Le Trianon for dinner; a pianist plays nightly in Harry's Bar. Bedrooms are comfortable, and all have remote-control TVs, electric shoe-polishers, minibars and clock radios. Guests in the special Tower

suites have full kitchens, special elevators, their own check-in area and other privileges. Hair salon, jeweler, boutique, antique shop • health club by arrangement • 7 meeting rooms.

Inter-Continental **$$$$$**
111 E 48th St (Lexington Ave) 10017 ☏ *755-5900* Ⓣ *968677 • 598 rooms, 88 suites, 2 restaurants, 2 bars*
Superbly situated for easy access to the UN and E midtown offices and restaurants, the former Barclay was erected in 1926 at the behest of the Vanderbilt family and was much favored by Gloria Swanson, Henry Cabot Lodge and Papa Hemingway. It has a measured European character, including the distinctive lobby birdcage and the high ceilings and generous proportions. Discriminating business people and notables from the creative and performing arts appreciate its serenity and privacy. Florist, pharmacy, men's shop, hair salon • arrangements at nearby health clubs • 16 meeting rooms, cable facilities, translation and interpreters.

Lowell **$$$$$**
228 E 63rd St (Madison Ave) 10021 ☏ *838-1400* Ⓣ *275750 • 8 rooms, 52 suites, 2 restaurants, 1 bar*
The Lowell is a leader in the Manhattan trend toward small, elegant inn-like hotels. An Art Deco façade on a tree-lined Upper East Side street insulates a clientele that includes corporate satraps, upper-level government officials and the occasional film and rock star. All rooms have kitchenettes (when making reservations, tell them what you'd like in the refrigerator). Suites are perfect for small meetings followed by a meal laid out on the marble table. Many of the rooms have working fireplaces, a rare status symbol. Service is highly personalized and includes a knowledgeable, multilingual concierge. One meeting room.

Marriott Marquis **$$$$$**
1535 Broadway (45–46th Sts) 10036 ☏ *398-1900* Ⓣ *6712057 • 1,876 rooms, 3 restaurants, 4 bars, 1 coffee shop*
This ungainly, futuristic fortress looming over Times Square does have a certain giddy bravado and no lack of amenities. The lobby is on the 8th floor! Hydrotherapy, health club, games room • 23 meeting rooms.

Mayfair Regent **$$$$$**
610 Park Ave (65th St) 10021 ☏ *288-0800* Ⓣ *236257 • 59 rooms, 142 suites*
The predominance of suites, many of them permanently leased, suggests the select clientele of this gracious building. The deliberate association with the patrician townhouses of London's Mayfair is entirely fitting. Instead of conventional bars and dining rooms, it offers cocktail service and afternoon tea in the lobby lounge, complete with fireplace. Adjacent to the entrance is the very fashionable Le Cirque (see *Restaurants*), which, although independently operated, functions as *de facto* dining room to the hotel's residents as well as to such regulars as Sylvester Stallone. The suites can accommodate small meetings.

Morgan's **$$$$**
237 Madison Ave (37th St) 10016 ☏ *686-0300* Ⓣ *288908 • 84 rooms, 30 suites, 2 restaurants, 1 bar*
Workers in the vineyards of investment banking and trust management are uneasy in the glossy, faintly slapdash surroundings of this flashy infant inn. Its appeal is to those who specialize in new-wave fashion and throw-away culture. Where calculated impermanence reigns, style is very much of the moment, and Morgan's delights in gadgets and worldly notions of fun décor: witness the VCRs in the bedrooms, the studied restraint of Franco-Italian settings of gray pinstriping and high-tech steel baths, the staff uniforms by Calvin Klein and Giorgio Armani. The cellar

restaurant is a California grill, offering meals until the small hours. One meeting room.

New York Helmsley $$$$$
212 E 42nd St (between 2nd and 3rd aves) 10017 ☎ 490-8900 TX 127724 • 781 rooms, 9 suites, 1 restaurant, 1 bar
Although far less grand than her Palace, this seems to be a particular pet of Leona Helmsley, who renamed it after her spouse and partner, as she did the off-lobby Harry's Bar. In truth, it is a rather conventional operation, enlivened by such trademark touches as the harpist in the "gourmet" restaurant and the big color TVs with remote control in the bedrooms. The UN is three blocks E; Grand Central one block W. Health club by arrangement • 5 meeting rooms.

New York Hilton and Towers $$$$$
1335 6th Ave (53rd St) 10019 ☎ 586-7000 TX 238492 • 1,802 bedrooms, 150 suites, 1 restaurant, 3 bars, 1 coffee shop
In the middle of a prairie, this colossus would constitute a good-sized town by itself. When all the rooms are occupied, the combined total of staff, guests and conventioneers can exceed 7,000. The six-story Executive Tower has its own express elevator, 24hr check-in and check-out, concierge, fully equipped boardroom, and private lounge. Tower bedrooms have three telephones – one on the bedside table, another in the bathroom, a third on the working-size desk. Beauty salon, barber, gourmet shop, drugstore, florist, jeweler • 49 meeting rooms, video teleconferencing, translation, computer modems, business library, fax, delivery service.

Nikko Essex House $$$$$
160 Central Park S (6th Ave) 10019 ☎ 247-0300 TX 7105815730 • 651 rooms, 64 suites, 1 restaurant, 1 bar
First-class, if not de luxe, the Essex House is now owned by Japan Airlines. With its prime location, a staff said to speak 18 languages, good housekeeping and the usual in-room gadgets, it is a notch above many chain hotels. Hairdresser, barber • complimentary passes to nearby racquet club • 14 meeting rooms, fax.

Omni Berkshire Palace $$$$$
21E 52nd St (5th Ave) 10022 ☎ 753-5800 TX 7105815256 • 415 rooms, 23 suites, 21 restaurants, 1 bar
The entrance opens onto a handsome lobby of tinkly mirrors, faceted glass and an emerald-green backdrop. To one side are the popular Rendez-vous bistro, the Atrium bar and a quiet formal restaurant, La Galerie. The pleasantly furnished bedrooms have large desks and telephones. Bathrobes, cable TV, morning coffee and newspaper and complimentary shoeshine are extra touches. One meeting room, computer rental, fax.

Park Lane $$$$$
36 Central Park S (5th Ave) 10019 ☎ 371-400 TX 668613 • Helmsley • 640 rooms, 22 suites, 1 restaurant, 1 bar
This is the Helmsley hotel where Harry and Leona actually live. Despite that, it is unexceptional, but worth considering for its views of Central Park from good-sized rooms. Expect first-class, though not grande luxe, comforts and appointments. The staff can be distant, but are usually helpful and efficient. Do not use the restaurant or room service. Four meeting rooms, computer rental, fax.

Parker Meridien $$$$$
118 57th St (6th Ave) 10019 ☎ 245-5000 TX 6801134 • 600 rooms, 100 suites, 2 restaurants, 1 bar
The opening of this Air France hotel was greeted with exultation by local Francophiles. The ambitious Chez Maurice restaurant and informal Le Patio were immediate successes, not

least as new power-breakfast venues. Rooms, although often small, are carefully conceived, including spa baths and minibars. The public rooms have a cool, Grecian look, warmed by flowers and feathery plants, and the in-house health facilities are exceptional, with pool, jogging track and racquet ball courts in addition to the usual features of sauna and weight equipment. Eight meeting rooms, fax, translation.

Pierre **$$$$$**
2 61st St (5th Ave) 10021
☎ 838-8000 TX 127426 • Four Seasons • 141 rooms, 56 suites, 1 restaurant, 1 bar
In character and clientele, the Pierre is akin to the Carlyle. Both count aristocrats and plutocrats among their enthusiasts; both aspire to the best of what is considered European standards of service; both go to considerable lengths to protect the privacy and security of their guests. The Pierre falls shorter of the mark, however, with a costly renovation that is more 5th Avenue than French. Reception varies from cheerful to occasionally aloof. Still, it is 15 blocks closer to midtown than the Carlyle and manages to project a convincing facsimile of the gracious era between the world wars. Florist, jeweler, barber, beauty salon • 7 meeting rooms, notary public, fax.

Plaza Athénée **$$$$$**
37 E 64th St (Madison Ave) 10021
☎ 734-9100 TX 6972900 • Trusthouse Forte • 124 rooms, 36 suites, 1 restaurant, 1 bar
One of New York's best new hotels. Rooms and suites are uncommonly comfortable, with reproductions of French period styles. TVs are hidden behind armoire doors, and among the conveniences are room safes, shoe trees, tie racks and individual temperature controls. Suites have kitchenettes, and some have terraces or solariums and extra bathrooms. Extraordinarily swift and comprehensive room service is aided by the placement of pantries on every floor. The ground-floor Le Régence restaurant is a sumptuous rendition of *belle époque* Paris. Fax.

Regency **$$$$$**
540 Park Ave (61st St) 10021
☎ 759-4100 TX 147180 • Loews Hotels • 252 rooms, 140 suites, 1 restaurant, 1 bar
The city's powerbrokers have made the Regency's 540 Park restaurant their number one breakfast venue. Otherwise, the hotel maintains the low profile preferred by people who do not require, or who abhor, visibility. Yet it is sheathed in marble, hung with rich tapestries, ablaze with huge vases of flowers, furnished with antiques and replicas of the fancies of Louis XV and lavished with gilded neo-baroque flourishes. All rooms have minibars, work desks and safes; many have kitchenettes, some have terraces. Meeting and banquet facilities are among Manhattan's most elegant. Excellent health facilities • 3 meeting rooms.

Ritz-Carlton **$$$$$**
112 Central Park S (6th Ave) 10019
☎ 757-1900 TX 971534 • 237 rooms, 30 suites, 1 restaurant, 1 bar
One of the growing number of small luxury hotels, the Ritz-Carlton has the air of an old-line East Coast club, with bleached pine, chintz, leather and mahogany as material for wing chairs and four-poster beds. In the Jockey Club restaurant, wood fires are accompanied by genre paintings of horses and overindulgent squires. The artful mock-rusticity attracts mainly a privileged but hard-working international set who are joined in conference by their New York peers in the restaurant and in the meeting rooms overlooking Central Park. Every bedroom has three telephones, with two lines. Drawbacks are the small lobby, limited public rooms and congested elevators. Four meeting rooms, fax.

St Moritz-on-the-Park $$$$
50 Central Park S (6th Ave) 10019 ☎ 755-5800 TX 66884 • 682 rooms, 90 suites, 1 coffee shop, 2 restaurants, 1 bar
Apart from its very central location, the best things about this old-timer are its street-level enterprises. Rumplemayer's is essentially an ice cream emporium, banked with stuffed animals. The sidewalk café looking down 6th Avenue and across to Central Park is one of the city's oldest. Upstairs, however, expect often cramped rooms, indifferently decorated. Choose it for tariffs lower than the name hotels in the immediate vicinity, especially when little time is to be spent in the room. Ask for a room on a higher floor with a park view. Five meeting rooms, fax.

St Regis Sheraton $$$$$
2 E 55th St (5th Ave) 10022 ☎ 753-4500 TX 148368 • 467 rooms, 84 suites, 2 restaurants, 1 bar
The builder of this genteel turn-of-the-century hotel was John Jacob Astor, the fourth-generation multimillionaire who went down with the *Titanic*. It was intended as a direct challenge to the original Waldorf-Astoria, and its regal Edwardian tone has been retained through many renovations. The King Cole Bar, with its famed Maxfield Parrish mural, is an enormously popular rendezvous for natives as well as tourists. No Manhattan hotel has a more exclusive roster of on-premises shops, including Bijan, Fred jewelry and Godiva. Conference and banquet rooms observe established standards of opulence. Its 5th Avenue location couldn't be better. Health club by arrangement • 9 meeting rooms, fax.

Sheraton Centre and Towers $$$$
811 7th Ave (52nd St) 10019 ☎ 581-1000 TX 421130 • 1,816 rooms, 67 suites, 2 restaurants, 2 bars, 1 coffee shop
Only the Hilton in New York is significantly larger than this vast, bustling, efficient and impersonal hotel, and the two have much in common – in this case The Towers (express elevators, a private lounge for breakfast and cocktails, and refrigerators and terrycloth robes in the bedrooms are the extras). The in-house bars and restaurants are filled with tourists and conventioneers; meet clients elsewhere. Pharmacy, gift and clothing shops, hair salon • health facilities at nearby Sheraton City Square • 36 meeting rooms, translation, recording facilities.

Sherry-Netherland $$$$$
781 5th Ave (59th St) 10022 ☎ 355-2800 • 54 suites, 46 rooms, 1 restaurant, 1 bar
Given its splendid site at the SE corner of Central Park, its majority of privately owned apartments and its reputation for civility and discretion, this is one hotel that feels no compulsion to keep up with the Carlyles and Pierres. It is also the city's only remaining major hotel not to accept credit cards. Captains of industry and notables of the silver screen find it the perfect bastion, as they hide in vast suites with working fireplaces and vistas of grass and skyscrapers glinting in the sun.

United Nations Plaza $$$$$
1 United Nations Plaza (44th St) 10017 ☎ 355-3400 TX 126803 • 444 rooms, 35 suites, 1 restaurant, 1 bar, 1 coffee shop
The striking angular blue-green towers that house this hotel have won architectural awards. They also contain offices and apartments, which is why rooms begin on the 28th floor and all have panoramic views. Given its association with and proximity to the UN, it is to be expected that the clientele and staff reflect that diversity. Many languages and dialects are spoken at the front desk, and that may account for the occasionally confused registration and check-out processes. Rooms are

sleekly comfortable, with few surprises beyond what is expected of a first-class establishment. Complimentary limo service to Wall Street, Garment District and theater engagements • pool, tennis, health club • 6 meeting rooms, notary public.

Vista International $$$$
3 World Trade Center 10048
☏ 938-9100 TX 661130 • Hilton • 727 rooms, 24 suites, 2 restaurants, 2 bars
This 1980s development is the only major local hotel conveniently placed for Wall Street visitors and is every bit equal to its contemporary uptown cousins. The smallest structure in the World Trade Center complex, it is only a few blocks from the two major stock exchanges and contains two of Wall Street's best restaurants – the American Harvest and The Greenhouse. On the 22nd floor, its health club has the best views to be obtained from the seat of an exercycle. Two executive floors provide a private lounge for breakfast and cocktails and an attendant to arrange airline, restaurant and hotel reservations. Since at least 85% of its customers are business people, every appropriate service is available including extensive conference facilities. Pool, jogging track • 16 meeting rooms.

Waldorf-Astoria $$$$$
301 Park Ave (49th St) 10022
☏ 355-3000 TX 666747 • Hilton • 1,850 rooms, 94 suites, 4 restaurants, 1 bar, 1 coffee shop
Long a synonym for New York glamor and sophistication, the Waldorf in recent years had slipped perceptibly, but the decline has been arrested by a multi-million-dollar reclamation. Art Deco details have been buffed and restored to former glory, the generally spacious rooms primped and brought to standard. Choose one of the 50 rooms in The Towers, a separate luxury section similar to those in the Hilton and Sheraton Centre, though with greater cachet. The lower floors are crowded with enough cafés and shops to fill a large village. The E midtown location is very desirable. Twenty-five meeting rooms, fax, translation, teleconferencing, computer rental, computer modems, recording facilities.

Westbury $$$$$
15 E 69th St (Madison Ave) 10021
☏ 535-6566 TX 125388 • Trusthouse Forte • 250 rooms, 50 suites, 1 restaurant
Erected as a post-Great War apartment house, the Westbury's conversion to hotel means spacious bedrooms with sometimes cramped baths. Public rooms are understated plush, glinting with cut-glass chandeliers and antique tapestries. It has the look, but not the attitude, of a London gentlemen's club that has reluctantly admitted women. There are few more distinguished addresses, and the Polo Lounge is one of the most accomplished of the city's hotel dining rooms, an especially good choice for brunch on Sunday. Five meeting rooms, fax.

Westin Plaza $$$$$
5th Ave (59th St) 10019
☏ 759-3000 TX 236938 or 620179 • 747 rooms, 88 suites, 6 restaurants, 3 bars
New Yorkers regard the Plaza with a sentimental affection that ignores the reality that it is no longer the epitome of gracious living. But the times, not the Plaza, have changed. Tea in the Palm Court is accompanied, as ever, by violins; the Oak Room continues to fill each evening with managers, entrepreneurs and "executive groupies." The restaurants are dated, still to undergo the trendy transformation of other hotel dining rooms. The location is still the best in New York. Florist, hair salon, barber, clothing and jewelry shops, cinema, art gallery • reduced rates at nearby health club • 11 meeting rooms, fax.

Windsor $$$$
100 W 58th St (6th Ave) ☎ *265-2100*
• *Helmsley* • *300 rooms*
This is one of Helmsley's less expensive hotels, but it is thoroughly acceptable for the business traveller who wants a good-sized, comfortable room without the full services of a grander establishment. No room service.

OTHER HOTELS

Regular visitors who are not worried about being flashy sometimes find that clubs like the Harvard Club (you need to be the guest of a member) provide everything you can get at, say the Algonquin, and are cheaper. The following hotels provide acceptable accommodation; usually at lower prices than most of the hotels given full entries.

Best Western Milford Plaza ($$$) *270 W 45th St (8th Ave) 10036* ☎ *869-3600* TX *177610.* In the Theater District, not far from the Garment District.
Days Inn ($$$) *440 W 57th St (10th Ave) 10019* ☎ *581-8100* TX *960473.* Near West Side television studios.
Doral Inn ($$$) *541 Lexington Ave (49th St) 10022* ☎ *755-1200* TX *236641.* Ask for a room on an upper floor as its 49th Street location can be noisy.
Doral Park Avenue ($$$$) *70 Park Ave (38th St) 10016* ☎ *687-7050* TX *968872.* Simple, modern and efficient, this hotel is convenient to midtown and lower midtown areas.
Edison ($$) *228 W 47th St (between 7th and 8th aves) 10019* ☎ *840-5000* TX *238887.* Close to Rockefeller Center and Theater District.
Halloran House ($$$$) *525 Lexington Ave (48th St) 10017* ☎ *755-4000* TX *668844.* Convenient to midtown banks and Park Avenue; near United Nations.
Mayflower ($$$$) *15 Central Park W (61st St) 10023* ☎ *265-0060* TX *968872.* Close to Lincoln Center, Carnegie Hall and West Side businesses, it offers large, comfortable and quiet rooms.
New York Penta ($$$) *401 7th Ave (33rd St) 10001* ☎ *736-5000* TX *9672643.* Near Madison Square Garden and Jacob Javits Convention Center.
Omni Park Central ($$$$$) *870 7th Ave (55th St) 10019* ☎ *247-8000* TX *42434.* Charmless but efficient and with easy access to West Side and Theater District business locations.
Quality Inn Lexington ($$$$) *511 Lexington Ave (48th St) 10017* ☎ *755-4400* TX *426257.* Convenient to midtown and the United Nations.
Ramada Inn ($$$) *790 8th Ave (48th St) 10019* ☎ *581-7000* TX *147182.* On sleazy 8th Ave, close to Broadway theaters and midtown, near Rockefeller Center. Rooftop swimming pool.
Roosevelt ($$$) *45 E 45th St 10017* ☎ *661-9600* TX *646229.* Near Grand Central, with extensive conference facilities and the popular Crawdaddy's restaurant, which the business community seeks out for its New Orleans-style seafood and gumbo.
Salisbury ($$$) *123 W 57th St 10019* ☎ *246-1300* TX *668366.* Across from Carnegie Hall, convenient to Lincoln Center. Good, spacious rooms but not smart.
Shelburne Murray Hill ($$$$) *303 Lexington Ave (37th St) 10016* ☎ *689-5200* TX *225666.* The all-suite arrangement is suitable for longer stays and provides workspace as well. Situated in a quiet neighborhood S of midtown.
Sheraton City Squire ($$$) *790 7th Ave (51st St) 10019* ☎ *581-3300* TX *640458.* Close to Broadway theaters and midtown.
Skyline Motor Inn ($$$) *725 10th Ave (50th St) 10019* ☎ *586-3400* TX *262559.* This Best Western is close to the Theater District, with easy access to the upper West Side.
Tudor ($$$) *304 E 42nd St 10017* ☎ *986-8800.* Close to United Nations and Grand Central.

Clubs

Clubs play a very important part in New York's business life. Members use them for lunchtime or after-hours discussions with colleagues and business visitors, and they are popular, especially with the financial community, for group meetings. Most of the principal clubs are in midtown. Some have been established especially for business users; others are for the alumni of the Ivy League colleges with rooms that members and their guests can stay in at much lower rates than those charged by midtown hotels; and there are the old-line social clubs, many of which still exclude women and minorities.

All except the business clubs have strict rules about conduct: guests are not allowed to pay for anything; tipping is forbidden; business papers are not to be displayed in public areas. Among those catering specifically to the business community are the *Boardroom*, 280 Park Ave ☏ 687-5858; the *Atrium*, 11 E 57th St ☏ 826-9460; and *Sky*, 200 Park Ave ☏ 867-9550.

Alumni of all ages use the Ivy League clubs: *Yale*, 50 Vanderbilt Ave ☏ 661-2070; *Harvard*, 27 W 44th St ☏ 840-6600; *Princeton*, 15 W 43rd St ☏ 840-6400; and the *University*, 5th Ave ☏ 247-2100. The old-line clubs, the *Union League*, 38 E 37th St ☏ 685-3800, *Knickerbocker*, 805 5th Ave ☏ 838-6700, and *Century*, 7 W 43rd St ☏ 944-0090 have prestige, but so, too, do the *New York Yacht Club*, 37 W 44th St ☏ 382-1000, *New York Athletic Club*, 180 Central Park South ☏ 247-5100, and the *Brook Club*, 111 E 54th St ☏ 753-7020. The Upper East Side's, *Links Club*, 36 E 62nd St ☏ 838-8181 is highly rated. Downtown clubs include the *Downtown Association*, 60 Pine St ☏ 422-1982 and *India House*, 1 Hanover Sq ☏ 269-2323.

Restaurants

For New Yorkers, business meals are primarily lunches, few with anything stronger than a glass of wine, and breakfasts, often starting as early as 7.30. Dinners – generally more lavish – are mainly for out-of-town clients or those who live in Manhattan. Lunch starts generally at 12.30, and dinners often end early (9–9.15) to allow commuters to get home. The city has an estimated 15,000 eating places, offering all types of cuisine, service, atmosphere and price. Most checks do not include a service charge; consider 17% a minimum, 20% standard. New Yorkers simply double the sales tax for a quick guide to what should be the minimum tip. If a captain has done more than simply take a meal order, he should be tipped separately – say, 25% of the basic tip. Many restaurants do not allow cigar and pipe smoking, though few offer no-smoking areas.

The city's ceaseless quest for novelty can be bewildering to the first-timer. Unconventional menus, custom or décor can cause some people to bristle, others to become expansive. There are still restaurants where a woman executive could be made uncomfortable by relentlessly masculine traditions. Beware, also, of unwittingly inviting a New Yorker to dine at a place where he or she has a regular table.

The listings here are dominated by established restaurants of sturdy reputation. They are primarily French, Italian or, the catchall hybrid, Continental.

America $$$
9-13 E 18th St ☏ *505-2110* • AE MC V
This feverishly popular new eating stable takes its name seriously: it is huge, flashy, exuberant and overwhelming. Most customers are young professionals in advertising and PR, and the 200-plus items on its menu include every real or contrived regional and ethnic cuisine from the Atlantic to the Pacific. Think of it as a visit to a natural phenomenon like Niagara Falls, and to hear yourself think, go at lunch.

Arcadia $$$$$
21 E 62nd St ☏ *223-2900 • closed Sun* • AE MC V
Featuring an idyllic Paul David mural of the seasons on three walls of the 50-cover dining room, Anne Rosenzweig's Arcadia has quickly become one of New York's hottest restaurants. The diminutive anthropologist is always in the kitchen, which produces thoughtful dishes of deceptive simplicity. Getting a table is a serious problem, although you may be luckier at lunch. The lobster sandwich snack is already legendary.

Auntie Yuan $$$$$
1191 1st Ave ☏ *744-4040* • AE
Essentially a Chinese restaurant, although it doesn't look or taste like one, this is one of midtown's most popular and stylish spots. The snappy décor is largely the color of anthracite, the better to highlight bud vases, napery, handsome table settings, attractively presented *nouvelle* Chinese cuisine and the equally handsome faces that hover above them. The management's cosmopolitan approach is underscored by the presence of a *cruvinet*, the device that allows the sale of wine by the glass from pricey bottles.

Ballroom $$$$$
253 W 28th St ☏ *244-3005 • closed Mon* • AE CB DC MC V
Superior Spanish tavern snacks called *tapas* are featured at the magnificent bar out front, where whole hams hang overhead: an excellent choice for pre-dinner drinks. The restaurant's slightly inconvenient location, not far from the Garment District, often mandates dinner, as well; besides *tapas*, there are conventional entrées. The separate nightclub at the back features offbeat jazz and cabaret.

Bridge Café $$$
279 Water St ☏ *227-3344* AE DC • *no reservations*
Ed Koch, noted trencherman and mayor of New York, is a regular patron of this winningly ramshackle tavern near the South Street Seaport. Once a disreputable sailors' bar, the 1801 woodframe building predates City Hall, a short walk away. Politicians, bureaucrats and Wall Streeters predominate at lunch. The informal bistro menu is supplemented by daily specials, brought to table by sometimes amateurish young people. Arrive early or late or expect a wait.

Café des Artistes $$$$$
1 W 67th St ☏ *877-3500 • D only Sat* • AE CB DC MC V • *jackets required*
There are few dining spots in Manhattan that can claim the graciousness of this café-restaurant. Leaded windows behind banks of greenery look out upon a tree-lined West Side street, while buffed wood paneling sets off large mirrors and Howard Chandler Christy's famed murals of voluptuous female nudes. There is a masculine tenor to the surroundings, though not aggressively so. The food is agreeable rather than *haute*, and tables are close, but the noise level is usually no more than a contented buzz. The middle-level executives (day) and neighborhood couples and concert-goers (evening) are sprinkled with stars and technicians from the nearby ABC studios. For greater privacy, choose the back room.

Café Luxembourg $$$$$
200 W 70th St ☎ 873-7411 • D only Mon–Fri • AE MC V
This zippy bistro near the Lincoln Center fills the locals' need for imaginative victuals in informal but striking settings. Full of mirrors, tiles, and late-1930s cafeteria-style trimmings, it burbles happily far into the night, the perfect destination before or after opera or ballet. The pre-dinner *prix fixe* menu is a bargain, the late supper an amusing parade of punkish peacocks and spangly creatures of the night.

Christ Cella $$$$$
160 E 46th St ☎ 697-2479 • closed Sun • AE CB DC MC V
This is a plain, aggressively masculine restaurant, serving extraordinary steaks, chops and onion rings to those with no expense account problems. Unfortunately the wine list is no match for the food.

Le Cirque $$$$$
58 E 65th St ☎ 794-9292 • closed Sun, Jul • AE CB DC *• jacket and tie required*
Powerhouse business people, politicians and scions of multi-generational fortunes mingle here with butterflies whose principal occupations are charity balls and shopping. Its closely set tables allow snatches of gossip about the mighty as well as the possibility of dipping an elbow into a neighbor's *pasta primavera*. The Franco-Italian-Continental cuisine is entirely secondary to the patrons, who are concerned more with forming proposals and skewering rivals. A place for top executives to entertain their counterparts.

La Côte Basque $$$$$
5 E 55th St ☎ 688-6525 • closed Sun, Jul • AE CB DC MC V *• jacket and tie required • reservations essential*
Owner-chef Jean-Jacques Rachou, who made his mark in Manhattan with the stylish, now-closed Café Lavandou, has returned La Côte Basque to the pinnacle of the city's French restaurants. His clientele are the same prosperous folk who lunch at Lutèce, Le Cirque and Le Cygne. Bernard Lamotte's naturalistic murals of the Basque coast are delightful, and there is even breathing space between tables. You should make reservations at least three days in advance for weekday meals and at least two weeks for Saturday dinner, which draws celebrants from a wider and somewhat less monied circle. The *prix fixe* luncheon menu costs barely half that of dinner.

Le Cygne $$$$$
55 E 54th St ☎ 759-5941 • D only Sat; closed Sun, Aug • AE CB DC MC V *• jacket and tie required*
It may have a smidgen less cachet than its peers – Le Cirque, La Côte Basque and their ilk – but that merely enhances the serenity of dining in this highly acclaimed spot, where you can make points and consider ripostes without raising your voice. Tables are well-spaced in a post-modernist setting of pearly grays and blues; service is attentive yet unobtrusive. The second floor is even more tranquil; one flight down from the main floor, the private room, with its racks of rare vintages, is perfect for highest-level dinner meetings requiring confidentiality.

Darbár $$$
44 W 56th St ☎ 432-7227 • AE DC MC V
The Darbár's Indian heritage is clear from its woven silk hangings and decorative objects of beaten metal, but they are used with a rare discretion far removed from the garish décor of many such restaurants. Beyond the friendly bar, the tables are comfortably proportioned and well apart, some of them separated by carved screens, which provide privacy.

Felidia **$$$$$**
243 E 58th St ☏ 758-1479 • D only Sat; closed Sun • AE CB DC MC V • jacket required
Menus without English translation require patrons to listen very closely to the waiters' explanations, but as the northern Italian specialties trundled from the kitchen normally range from excellent to exquisite, they are worth the effort. If you prefer, make friends with the paternal captain and leave decisions to him. The game and *porcini* are notable, and the wine list is good. A convivial place to meet clients or prospects.

Four Seasons **$$$$$**
99 E 52nd St ☏ 754-9494 • closed Sun, major hols • AE CB DC MC V • jacket required, no denims • reservations essential for Fri and Sat D
The venerable Four Seasons has skilfully adapted to stay in the main current of the volatile New York dining scene. Ensconced in a towering space in the landmark Seagram Building, it is now in its fourth decade. Menus have been adjusted to cater to the calorie- and health-conscious executive; the famed Grill Room is where powers in the "communications game" court each other at lunch, around the massive four-sided bar. Don't invite someone likely to have a regular lunch table, and don't go for dinner, when tourists and out-of-towners take over. In general, go only if invited.

Gloucester House **$$$$$**
37 E 50th St ☏ 755-7349 • AE CB DC MC V • jacket and tie required
The conventions of the traditional steakhouse are observed at this venerable fish house, through whose doors pass executives and millionnaires of a decidedly Establishment stripe. An unshowy lot, they betray no dismay with either the quasi-nautical décor or the breathtaking tariffs for seafood no better than that offered at Grand Central's Oyster Bar. What they want and get is the assurance of tranquility. Middle-aged and older businessmen dominate what amounts to a gentlemen's club; women are accorded courtesy, if not exactly welcomed.

Greene Street **$$$$**
101 Greene St ☏ 925-2415 • AE CB DC MC V
Situated in artsy, gentrified SoHo, Green Street has a large bar featuring wine by the glass, and a great brick-walled main room serving meals that deviate from the *nouvelle* canon primarily in the size of the portions. Nightly jazz, pop and cabaret performances follow at a loud amplification. Waiters and waitresses are generally well-trained and attentive, although most look ready to bolt at the first audition call. Best suited to off-duty drinks or dinner, or to celebrate wrapping up a deal.

Hatsuhana **$$$**
17 E 48th St ☏ 335-3345 • D only Sat; closed Sun • AE CB DC MC V
Consensus and its handy midtown location elevate this spot to most-favored *sushi–sashimi* status. Waiting for a table or a seat at one of the *sushi* bars is inevitable, especially at lunch, when no reservations are accepted. The presence of many Japanese nationals among the customers is reassuring, and patrons can see for themselves the supreme freshness of the ingredients as these are adroitly sliced, scooped and packaged by the solemn young chefs. Cooked entrées are also available.

Jean Lafitte **$$$**
68 W 58th St ☏ 751-2323 • D only Sun • AE CB DC MC V
The modern French bistro feel and acceptable provincial fare make this a good alternative midtown newcomer.

John Clancy's **$$$$**
181 W 10th St ☏ 242-7350 • D only • AE CB DC MC V

Clancy's open grills, fueled by mesquite or hickory coals, allow customers to witness the chefs at work, skewering or grilling whole shrimp, scallops, tuna, and, it seems, just about any other aquatic creature that takes the chef's fancy. Desserts are legendary. The only flaw in this attractive and popular Greenwich Village spot is the service, which can veer from exasperated to overly chummy. The upstairs room is quieter.

Kitcho $$$$
22 W 46th St ☎ 575-8880 • D only Sun; closed Sat • AE DC
Well before Americans were persuaded that raw fish was good to eat, Kitcho was garnering praise for the delicacy and authenticity of its Japanese cooking. While the *sashimi* and *sushi* are admirable appetizers here, there is more on offer, and mysterious combinations are prepared and served with understated artistry in a tranquil environment that abhors flash. Novices are guided gracefully through the unfamiliar enticements of the menu, and you can confidently leave decisions to the waitress. For extra privacy, book one of the *tatami* rooms.

Lutèce $$$$$
249 E 50th St ☎ 752-2225 • closed Sun, major holidays, Aug • AE CB DC • jacket and tie required • reservations essential
The stage for André Soltner's virtuoso *haute cuisine* performances (for which reservations must be made two or more weeks in advance) is a converted terrace house in midtown. Downstairs, the fabled Garden Room is the place to be seen; upstairs is good for relative privacy. The maestro moves easily among his patrons, with a word of welcome here, an off-menu suggestion there. His staff serves with neither *hauteur* nor unctuousness. The fixed-price lunch is the time to establish the parameters of a deal, the more ambitious and thrice-as-costly dinner to celebrate its closing.

Il Nido $$$$$
251 E 53rd St ☎ 753-8450 • closed Sun • AE CB DC MC V • jacket and tie required • reservations essential
Jockeying for position among the most honored Italian eateries in town, Il Nido is perceived to be slipping from the pack, but is still a place of contentment, judging by the hum of satisfied conversation and the relaxed attitudes of the conservatively dressed patrons that fill its rooms day and night. If they notice that they are swirling their pasta in surroundings that hint more of a Brittany farmhouse than Bolognese trattoria, it doesn't seem to matter. Seats are rare at lunch *or* dinner, even past closing hours. Book at least a day or two ahead.

Odeon $$$$
145 W Broadway ☎ 233-0507 • D only Sat; closed Christmas Day • AE V
With many of the area's best chefs engaged exclusively in corporate dining rooms, the downtown financial district is notoriously short of public restaurants of much verve or style. One solution lies in a brisk stroll N, to gentrified TriBeCa. This chrome-and-marble relic of the Depression–World War II era was swept out and polished up but otherwise left alone, and now offers lighthearted *nouvelle* dishes. The crowd is a giddy mix of stockbrokers and lawyers in three-piece suits, bearded and tweedy middle-aged artists, avant-gardists in fashion and the performing arts, and, late in the evening, androgynous beings who diligently outdo each other in outrageous apparel. Consider it for both low-pressure business lunches and off-hours diversion.

Oyster Bar & Restaurant $$$$
Lower Level, Grand Central Terminal ☎ 490-6650 • closed Sat, Sun • AE CB DC MC V
The now-fading European tradition of superior railway hotel restaurants was rarely copied in the USA, but the remarkably expensive Oyster Bar

is the exception. The specialty seafood, served in cavernous, vaulted rooms, is whatever was available from the wholesalers that morning. The buyer's reach is wide, including fresh turbot flown in from the North Sea and salmon from the Pacific Northwest. The kitchen starts running out of ingredients by mid-afternoon, so go after 1.30pm to avoid peak eating time, but before 2.30 to avoid shortages. The far Saloon room is smaller and marginally quieter.

Palio **$$$$$**
151 W 51st St ☎ 245-4850 • D only Sun; closed Sat • AE CB DC MC V
Entrance to this sparkling Italian restaurant is off the covered arcade of the new Equitable Center. Inside the doors is a stunning horseshoe-shaped marble bar, flanked by the vivid murals of Sandro Chia which are worth a visit for themselves. The kitchen has a light *nuova cucina* touch. A good choice for business lunches, with a heavy representation from the financial crowd. Dinners are social.

Parioli Romanissimo **$$$$$**
24 E 81st ☎ 288-2391 • D only; closed Sun, Mon • AE CB DC MC V • jacket and tie required • reservations essential
The quintessential Upper East Side Italian restaurant has several distinguishing marks – including an avoidance of Sicilian tomato sauces, a recognizable face or two every night, several limos in waiting, a large number of gentlemen in black silk suits with silver in their hair and gold in their shirt cuffs, an interesting décor that goes no farther than manly comfort, and daily specials unmentioned in the menu and revealed by the captain only after prodding. The switch from the old 1st Avenue address to these quarters altered the formula not a bit. Treatment of strangers is as evenhanded as is possible in a place with so many regulars.

Peter Lugar **$$$$$**
178 Broadway, Brooklyn ☎ (718) 387-7400 • no credit cards
Many steakhouse aficionados insist this is best-of-breed. It boasts a masculine, woody, *brauhaus* atmosphere and prime beef and chops seared precisely to order, with the option of lobsters of Godzilla proportions. Very popular with Wall Street denizens, it requires a taxi ride across the Williamsburg Bridge into a shabby Brooklyn neighborhood. Go only for lunch unless in the company of a local.

Petrossian **$$$$$**
182 W 58th ☎ 245-2214 • closed Sun • AE DC MC V • reservations essential
This sumptuous *fin de siècle* café offers an ideal light lunch or after-dinner snack comprising a few ounces of pearly Beluga caviar accompanied by papery-thin leaves of smoked salmon or perhaps a thick circle of *foie gras* embedded with truffles. The whole is best washed down with premium champagne or icy tumblers of Russian vodka. Convenient in central midtown, it attracts a meticulously tonsured and attired custom of international travellers and high-level corporate executives.

Quilted Giraffe **$$$$$**
955 2nd Ave ☎ 753-5355 • closed Sat, Sun, Jul • AE • jacket and tie required • reservations essential
If Lutèce has any peer, this is it. The original misguided décor of ceramic and stuffed giraffes has been stripped away, and steady hands at the skillets produce *nouvelle* dishes that have glorious flourishes refined by maturity and experiment. Its success and acclaim ensure some of the highest prices in town – a service charge is included in the bill so tips are optional – and the need to book two to three weeks in advance. As Chef Barry Wine proclaims, this is an "elegant, luxurious businessman's restaurant to celebrate the closing of a multi-million-dollar transaction."

River Café **$$$$**
1 Water St, Brooklyn ☎ (718) 532-5200 • AE CB DC MC V • jacket and tie required • reservations essential
Built on a barge moored in the East River beneath Brooklyn Bridge, the River Café provides an unobstructed vista of its magnificent span and of the lower Manhattan skyline. During lunch hours a launch shuttles customers from Wall Street, and open-air dining is available in good weather; ask about both when making your reservation. Its cuisine is a mildly inventive New American which comes a definite second to the view. Very popular with Wall Street financiers.

Rosa Mexicana **$$$$**
1063 1st Ave ☎ 753-7403 • AE CB DC MC V
Mexican cookery once had scant representation in New York, where aficionados were obliged to settle for watery guacamole and flaccid tortillas with fillings of uncertain origin. This sprightly *fonda*, much loved by the younger professional league, offers south-of-the-border dishes that do not involve blistering seasonings. Accept a table in the back room, to which no stigma is attached. Reservations are advisable but a wait in the ever-jolly bar is softened considerably by ingratiating house margaritas.

Russian Tea Room **$$$$$**
150 W 57th St ☎ 265-0947 • AE CB DC MC V • jacket required
A nightly rendezvous for the rich and famous, the Tea Room's clients include renowned concert artists and ballet masters, agents and movie stars, international bluebloods and royal pretenders. The less rich and not so famous are nevertheless treated well, provided they do not attempt to approach their more celebrated neighbors, which is why the likes of Woody Allen and Isaac Stern keep returning. The emerald jewel box of a room glints with the polished brass of dozens of clocks and samovars, and crimson banquettes do visual battle with rosy-pink napery. The emphasis is on blinis, caviar, herring, *shashlik* and borscht. Make every effort to get a booth in the main arena downstairs.

Sea Grill **$$$$**
Rockefeller Center, 19 W 49th St ☎ 246-9201 • AE CB DC MC V • jacket required • reservations essential
When the sunken iceskating rink that is centerpiece of the Rockefeller Center complex was rejuvenated, room was made for restaurants of greater ambition and pizzaz. This strikingly appointed room accommodates both business people and well-heeled tourists. Tables are well-spaced and the leather chairs uncommonly comfortable. The glassed-in kitchen with open grill produces chowders and seafood salads as well as charcoal-striped tuna steaks, sea bass and chicken. In warm months, there is outdoor dining on the drained rink. An excellent midtown choice for a business lunch; reserve ahead, especially for lunch.

Da Silvano **$$$$**
260 6th Ave (near Bleeker St) ☎ 982-2343 • D only Sat and Sun • no credit cards
Packed with tables that spill on to the sidewalk in summer, Da Silvano is, according to regulars, nothing less than the best Italian restaurant in Greenwich Village. Don't bother studying the printed menu; listen intently instead to the seemingly endless list of daily specials. Silvano's sauces are what make his place what it is – original, subtle, superb – and his venison and veal are also cooked to perfection. The Italian cheeses alone are worth a visit.

Water Club **$$$$$**
30th St (on the East River) ☎ 683-3333 • AE CB DC MC V • reservations essential
This two-decked, permanently moored barge has a working fireplace and outside dining deck, and a large

boat for dining and sightseeing is tied alongside in summer. The French chef skillfully fabricates regional American cooking styles, including New England clam chowder and Connecticut rabbit stew. During the week, the regular crowd comprises business people and senior medics from the nearby hospitals, especially at lunch. Weekends are social, particularly Sunday brunch. Men will feel more comfortable in a jacket, although it is not required.

Windows on the World $$$$$
1 World Trade Center (107th floor) ☏ *938-1100 • D only Mon–Fri • AE CB DC MC V • jacket and tie required*
The Center has three distinct dining areas. *The Restaurant* has a tiered, starship character with superb views of the city and competent Continental cuisine. At midday, it is a membership club, although outsiders can sometimes get in by paying a surcharge. At dinner and weekends, crowds are inevitable and so are waits, even with reservations. The adjacent *Hors d'Oeuverie* specializes in international appetizers, alternately highlighting Spanish *tapas*, Chinese *dim sum*, Indonesian *satay* and similar snacks. There are no views from the *Cellar in the Sky*, the showcase for Kevin Zraly's wine selections, but it serves the best food of the three Windows on the World restaurants, including a memorable seven-course *prix fixe* banquet accompanied by five different wines.

Power breakfasts
Growing numbers of top executives choose to hit the floor running every morning, and the business day grows even longer as a result, with power breakfasts playing a key role in New York business life. Since coffee shops are too noisily plebeian and conventional formal restaurants rarely open before noon, spacious hotel dining rooms profit from the phenomenon. The *Regency*, where the waiters will also make photocopies, and the *Carlyle*, used by investment bankers, are still the tops. A good breakfast can be had at the *Algonquin*. Other possibilities are joining the broadcast network biggies at the *Dorset*, or the tycoons and cosmopolites at Le Patio or Chez Maurice in the *Parker Meridien*. These power breakfasts have become so popular that reservations are generally essential. For addresses and phone numbers, see *Hotels*.

Afternoon tea
Now that many hotels serve afternoon tea – usually from 3 to 6 – executives are discovering its virtues as an alternative to working breakfasts, and as a way to escape office distractions. In the Gold Room of the *Helmsley Palace*, where a harpist performs from the balcony, Devonshire cream and scones lend an authentic touch. In the Palm Court of the *Plaza*, violinists are the musical backdrop. The splendid lobby of the *Mayfair Regent* offers "teas" that can include cappucino and excellent pastries. Other possibilities are the lounges of the *American Stanhope*, *Berkshire Place*, *Carlyle*, *Pierre*, *Algonquin*, *Inter-Continental* and *Plaza Athénée*. For addresses and phone numbers, see *Hotels*.

Wall Street dining
Good business-populated eateries scattered across lower Manhattan include *Tenbrooks*, 62 Reade St ☏ 349-5900; the 100-year-old *brauhaus*, *Suerken's*, 27 Park Pl ☏ 267-7389; *Ye Old Chop House*, 111 Broadway ☏ 732-6119; *Morgan Williams*, 1 Exchange Plaza ☏ 809-3150; *Harry's at Hanover Square*, 1 Hanover Sq ☏ 425-3412; and *Delmonico's*, 56 Beaver St ☏ 422-4747. On the eastern edge of the island is the South Street Seaport, riddled with dozens of bars, cafés and bistros. Some with loyal clientele are *Sloppy Louie's*, 92 South St ☏ 952-9657; *Sweet's*, 2 Fulton St ☏ 825-9786; and *Coho*, 11 Fulton St ☏ 608-0507.

Yet more French

Despite Manhattan's gastronomic diversity, the list of restaurants preferred by business people is overwhelmingly French. Useful alternatives to the ones given full entries are: *La Reserve*, 4 W 49th St ☏ 247-2993; *Chez Pascal*, 151 E 82nd St ☏ 249-1334; Provençal *Le Cherche-Midi*, 936 1st Ave ☏ 355-4499; and *Le Périgord Park*, 575 Park Ave ☏ 752-0050.

Steakhouses

When you can't get to or into *Peter Lugar*, choices include *The Palm*, 837 2nd Ave ☏ 687-2953, which is expensive and noisy and does not take reservations; it is as classy as its annex *Palm Too* (which does accept reservations) across the street; *Pietro's*, 232 E 43rd St ☏ 599-9090, which is Italianate; *Spark's*, 210 46th St ☏ 687-4855, known *inter alia* for its excellent wine list; *Assembly*, 16 W 51st ☏ 581-3580; *Smith & Wollensky*, 201 E 49th St ☏ 753-1530; and *Pen & Pencil*, 205 W 45th St ☏ 682-8660, thought by many to be the best.

Grills

Besides *John Clancy's* and the *Sea Grill*, you should try the designer burgers at *Hamburger Harry's* in TriBeCa, 157 Chambers St ☏ 267-4446 and 145 W 45th St ☏ 840 0566; the dashing *Gotham Bar & Grill*, 12 E 12th St ☏ 620-4020; the California-influenced *Batons*, 62 W 11th St ☏ 473-9510; *Ritz Café*, 2 Park Ave ☏ 684-2122; Tex-Mex *El Rio Grande*, 160 E 38th St ☏ 867-0922; the relentlessly trendy *Safari Grill*, 1115 3rd Ave ☏ 371-9090; pricey *Jams*, 154 E 79th St ☏ 772-6800; or the smoke-barbequed ribs at *Carolina*, 355 W 46th St ☏ 245-0058.

Chinatown

Chinatown's 200-plus eateries tend to be gaudy and cramped or gloomy and cramped, but their cooks are often as skilled as those in the fancier uptown establishments. Prices are much lower, however, and Chinatown is handy for the Financial District and the municipal and federal governmental offices of lower Manhattan. These restaurants are definitely not places to bring associates you wish to impress, but are admirable for working lunches or after-hours meals. Among the best are *Canton*, 45 Division St ☏ 226-9173; *dim sum* specialist *Hee Seung Fong* a.k.a. HSF, 46 Bowery ☏ 374-1319; *Hwa Yuan Szechuan*, 40 E Broadway ☏ 966-5534; and the Shanghai-style *Say Eng Look*, 5 E Broadway ☏ 723-0796. All these restaurants are near Chatham Square.

Other ethnic restaurants

Among the city's thousands of ethnic eating places the most agreeable for casual business or off-hours meals are the Cuban *Sabor*, 20 Cornelia St in Greenwich Village ☏ 243-9579; Brazilian *Cabana Carioca II*, 133 W 45th St ☏ 730-8375; Afghan *Pamir*, 1423 2nd Ave near 74th St ☏ 734-3791; Indonesian *Tamu*, 340 W Broadway in SoHo ☏ 925-2751; *Tibetan Kitchen*, 444 3rd Ave near 30th St ☏ 679-6286; Korean *Arirang House*, 28 W 56th St ☏ 581-9698; and Indian *Raga*, 57 W 48th St ☏ 757-3450.

Delicatessens

For fast food with an unmistakable New York flavor, try the overstuffed *pastrami* and corned beef sandwiches of its delis. Some are devoutly kosher, others not; but they all share a Jewish heritage. Convenient in midtown are the celebrity-studded *Stage*, 834 7th Ave; the nearby *Carnegie*, 854 7th Ave; *Kaplan's*, 59 E 59th St; and *Fine & Shapiro*, 138 W 72nd St. Most are open seven days and do not accept credit cards.

Bars

Manhattan's thousands of watering holes are packed from late afternoon to early morning. (They can legally remain open until 4am.) Most have clear identities and specific attractions. Few cater exclusively to business people, though many are used by executives unwinding after a long day, or meeting a contact before or instead of dinner. Unaccompanied men or women should feel comfortable in any of the following.

Originally a Prohibition speakeasy, the *21 Club*, 21 W 52nd St, has evolved into the lair of politicians, entrepreneurs and chief executive officers and their imitators. Although not a great restaurant, 21 is in its true glory as a bar. Its three parts are numbered 17, 19 and 21 from the joined terrace houses that comprise the establishment. If you are ushered into 17, you are clearly unknown to the management and appear unlikely to bridge the gap. In 21, your reputation precedes you or you look as if it should. If you are assigned to 19, the jury is still out.

Although better known as a restaurant, *Elaine's*, 1703 2nd Ave, is undoubtedly a bar in which to see some of America's big names. Its eponymous doyenne has always been fiercely protective of her pet clients – writers. Long before most of them became literary household names, she coddled and teased such lions as William Styron, Joseph Heller and George Plimpton. They have been augmented, over the years, by such diverse personalities as country singer Willie Nelson, Luciano Pavarotti, Albert Finney and Andy Warhol. To bask in such starlight – but not to stare or approach – arrive after 10 and snuggle up to the long bar right inside the door. If you are denied entrance, many of the same luminaries pass the fancier front-room bar of the *Russian Tea Room* (see *Restaurants*).

Celebrity-watching is also a preoccupation of the drinkers at the long mahogany bar of *Mortimer's*, 1057 Lexington Ave. The objects of their attentions tend to be high-profile fashion designers, musicians and Hollywood superagents. The other, yet-to-be-famous patrons are an attractive bunch, graduates of very select universities and amenable to conversation.

Hotel bars are often refuges for those out-of-towners too timid or listless to venture far from their rooms, and therefore are scorned by natives. Among the exceptions is the *Blue Bar* of the Algonquin, a haven for the theatrical and literary set; the *Oak Room* at the Westin Plaza, home to regulars talking in terms as sleekly groomed and wrinkle-free as their clothes. *Bemelman's* reflects the clientele of the adjacent *Café Carlyle*, 35 E 76th St ☎ 744-1600.

In lower Manhattan, no better view can be had than from *City Lights* ☎ 938-1100 on the 107th floor of the World Trade Center. About a quarter mile below is the *Market Bar* ☎ 938-1100, another magnet for Wall Streeters. And on the East River, the *South Street Seaport* complex has bars and cafés crammed with up-and-coming lawyers and brokers.

Beer aficionados should know about the *Peculier Pub*, 182 W 4th St ☎ 691-8667, which has more than 250 brews from across the USA and around the world.

Entertainment

New York offers every variety of entertainment imaginable, from the sublime, at Lincoln Center and Carnegie Hall, to Times Square and 42nd Street sleaze. A key rule is to call ahead, even if you think the event or spot will be uncrowded: unexpected publicity could draw throngs, stars change their plans, and ticket prices change at a moment's notice. Most hotels' concierge staff will arrange reservations.

For listings of events, plays, concerts, films and other performances, check *The New Yorker* and *New York* magazines, The *New*

York Times Friday "Weekend" section and the *Village Voice*.

Theater ticket agencies The Shubert organization, which owns most Broadway theaters, operates the *Telecharge* agency ☎ 239-6200 which handles tickets for shows in any Shubert-owned venue (with a small service charge per ticket). Telecharge accepts major credit cards, and will send tickets or have them held at the box office. Half-price tickets for Broadway and Off-Broadway shows are available on the day at *TKTS*, Broadway at 47th St or 2 World Trade Center ☎ 354-5800 (small service charge and long lines). *Ticketron* has outlets throughout the city ☎ 399-4444, cash only.

Broadway Broadway shows continue to attract the crowds despite rising prices. Tickets to the long-running musicals most popular with visitors are usually the most difficult to get, and discounted seats are seldom available.

Ballet, opera and classical music The main centers are *Carnegie Hall*, 57th St at 7th Ave ☎ 247-7800; *Metropolitan Opera*, Lincoln Center, Broadway at 64th St ☎ 362-6000; *New York State Theater*, *New York City Ballet* and *New York City Opera*, Lincoln Center ☎ 870-5570; and *Avery Fisher Hall*, Lincoln Center ☎ 874-2424.

Cinema New York has hundreds of cinemas, both first-run and art houses. Check the publications cited above for listings.

Piano bars and clubs For a less structured evening, many midtown hotels have piano bars with sophisticated musical entertainment, including Bobby Short's long-running Cole Porter-era act at the *Carlyle*, 35 E 76th St ☎ 744-1600. Jazz clubs such as the *Village Vanguard*, 178 7th Ave S ☎ 255-4037 and the *Blue Note*, 131 W 3rd St ☎ 475-8592 feature well-known artists and rising stars.

Nightclubs Hot discos in New York generally come and go in less than a year. Longer-lived exceptions include *Limelight*, 47 W 20th St ☎ 807-7850, in what used to be an Episcopal church, and *Palladium*, 126 E 14th St ☎ 473-7171. Expect cover charges of at least $15 and high drink prices. For comedy, try the *Improv*, 358 W 44th St ☎ 765-8268.

Shopping

You can buy literally anything you might ever want at almost any time of the day or night in New York, and you can buy it at almost any price. It is a city where someone always knows someone who "has it wholesale": discount stores abound, so much so that it is virtually unknown to pay the list price for, say, a camera or some electronic goods. It pays to ask your native contacts. In general, however, it is best not to be overwhelmed by the variety of the options, and either shop by neighborhood – going to a district, such as 7th Avenue or the Lower East Side for designer clothing bargains, for example – or simply go to one of the major department stores, such as Macy's or Bloomingdale's. But if you are really in a rush, stick to 5th Avenue where you can buy everything from exotic chocolates to books, furs to cigarettes and rare tobaccos, high fashion to extravagant jewelry, luggage to household goods, watches to wigwams. On the other hand, be aware that some 5th Avenue shops prey on tourists and unsuspecting visitors. In general, the stores and boutiques get more exclusive the farther N you walk from 34th Street.

Most shops open 10–6, with some of the large department stores staying open until 9 at least two nights a week. Most of the department stores are open Sundays, 12–5. Weekday mornings are the best times to shop; lunchtimes and Saturdays are extremely crowded. Most shops, even the smallest, are prepared to accept at least some credit cards, although a minimum purchase may be stipulated.

Shopping by area

Clothes 5th and Madison avenues for high fashion, 7th Avenue for bargains, SoHo and Greenwich Village for the more unusual.
Cameras and electronics 32nd Street near 6th Avenue (Camera World) and 32nd near 7th Avenue (Willoughby's – New York's largest camera store); 34th Street near Herald Square.
Diamonds and jewelry 47th Street between 5th and 6th.
Books 5th and Madison avenues, Broadway and Greenwich Village.
Antiques and art Madison Avenue between 57th and 80th. SoHo is good for avant garde galleries. Columbus Avenue on the Upper West Side is where you will find trendy shops selling bizarre items.

Shopping by name

Most of the ultra-fashionable shops are located on Madison and 5th avenues or on 57th Street. Among them are Tiffany's, Cartier, Bijan, Saks (5th Avenue); Henri Bendel and Courrèges (57th Street); and Yves St Laurent, Sonia Rykiel and Brooks Brothers (Madison).

Department stores and malls

Macy's, the world's biggest single store, is at W 34th St and Broadway. Also on 34th Street at 6th Ave is the city's largest shopping mall, a multi-level high-rise with each separate level bearing the name of traditional New York shopping meccas, Herald Square, 5th Avenue, Madison and Broadway among them. *B Altman*, 34th St between Madison and 5th Ave, *Lord & Taylor*, 5th Ave between 38th and 39th streets, and *Bergdorf Goodman*, 5th Ave at 58th St, are three other old established department stores with a decidedly upmarket stock. *Bloomingdale's* occupies the square block bounded by 59th and 60th streets and 3rd and Lexington avenues. *Trump Tower*, on 5th Avenue, has a selection of exclusive shops including Bonwit Teller.

Sightseeing

New York's main "sight" is, of course, Manhattan itself. Many American cities have impressive skylines, but none has the stunning impact of Manhattan's prodigious forest of towers. Spectacular views of the island can be enjoyed from the tops of the buildings themselves, from the water – on one of the ferries or tour boats – or from the opposite shores of the Hudson and East rivers; the view of the Financial District from Brooklyn Heights or the Brooklyn Bridge, an attraction in its own right, is especially recommended.

Many of the more familiar sights, such as the Statue of Liberty, cannot be visited quickly, but museums and the Wall Street area's historic sites are easily sampled by the traveller on a tight schedule.

American Museum of Natural History Four floors of exhibits illustrate the diversity of animal and human life – from a simple mollusk to the elaborate customs and sophisticated craftsmanship of the world's peoples. Realistic life-size dioramas show animals in their natural habitats, including a herd of African elephants and some formidable reptiles. The museum also has an outstanding collection of gems and minerals.

The adjacent *Hayden Planetarium* is the museum's department of astronomy. Its Theater of the Stars presents an hour-long show of celestial phenomena on a huge hemispheric screen; also "cosmic laser concerts." *Central Park West at 79th St ☏ 873-4225; Planetarium ☏ 873-8828. Open Mon, Tue, Thu, Sun 10–5.45; Wed, Fri, Sat, 10–9.*

Cloisters The building skillfully incorporates parts of several cloisters from southern French medieval monasteries – of which the most famous is St Michel-de-Cuxa – as well as fountains, doorways and the apse of a ruined Spanish chapel. The collection (part of the Metropolitan Museum of Art) includes reliquaries

Bird's eye views

World Trade Center The twin towers of the Center, each with 110 stories, are the second tallest buildings in the world (after the Sears Building, Chicago). From the enclosed observation deck of the World Trade Center on the 107th floor or (weather permitting) the open rooftop promenade, you can see 75 miles/120km or more on a clear day. *Tel 466-7377. Open 9.30–9.30.*

RCA Building In Rockefeller Center, the heart of midtown, the RCA building has a mere 70 stories, but its views of Manhattan are superb. *30 Rockefeller Plaza, between 49th and 50th St ☏ 489-2947. Open Apr–Sep, 10–9; Oct–Mar, 10.30–7.*

Empire State Building Once the world's tallest building, this graceful skyscraper still provides spectacular views from the 87th-floor observatory (open) or the 102nd floor (glassed-in). *350 5th Ave between 33rd and 34th St ☏ 736-3100. Open 9.30–midnight.*

and other liturgical objects. Among its chief treasures are the 15thC Unicorn Tapestries. It is located a long way uptown in Fort Tryon Park, 62 acres of greenery, which starts at W 192 Street and overlooks the Hudson. *Open Tue–Sat ☏ 923-3700.*

Federal Hall National Memorial This Greek Revival building, dating from 1842, occupies a site with many historical associations. The Colonial City Hall was founded here in 1699; and it's where the Stamp Act Congress later met to plan a response to British tax policies. Reconstructed after the Revolution, it became Federal Hall, the nation's first capitol, and George Washington was sworn in there as the first president. His statue overlooks Wall Street from the steps of the present building, which was built as a Custom House, later used as a Subtreasury of the Federal Reserve Bank, and is now a museum of New York history. *26 Wall St ☏ 264-8711. Open Mon–Fri, 9–5.*

Frick Collection Perhaps New York's most beautiful and visitable museum, the Frick has the advantage – if you are pressed for time – of being quite small; it is possible to view the collection in about an hour. It is also a good place to sit and think or plan your schedule in safety. Built in 1913 as the home of industrialist Henry Clay Frick, the mansion affords a glimpse of the life enjoyed by New York's millionaires in the early 20thC. Frick's outstanding collection of Old Masters – including masterpieces by Bellini, Titian, Holbein, Rembrandt, Vermeer, El Greco and Turner – are superbly displayed. There are delightful Boucher and Fragonard rooms and a collection of 16th–17thC Limoges enamel. *1 E 70th St ☏ 288-0700. Closed Mon; open Tue–Sat, 10–6; Sun, 1–6.*

Guggenheim Museum Of interest for its architecture as much as for the art it contains, the building – completed in 1959 – was designed by Frank Lloyd Wright and commissioned by Solomon R Guggenheim, who used the fortune he made in copper to support non-representational art. The building's design is a continuous oval spiral ramp which becomes smaller in diameter as it moves down; take the elevator to the top and move downwards along the ramp. The Guggenheim features the world's largest Kandinski collection. *5th Ave between 88th and 89th streets ☏ 360-3500. Closed Mon; open Tue–Sun, 11–5.*

Lincoln Center This impressive, classically-inspired complex houses the Metropolitan Opera, the New York City Opera, the New York City Ballet, the Lincoln Center Theater Company and the Juilliard School (music, dance and drama). Backstage tours of the Met are bookable in advance ☏ 582-3512. The Library and Museum of the Performing Arts is open free to the public and offers a variety of films, concerts and exhibitions. *65th St and Broadway ☏ 877-1800.*

Metropolitan Museum of Art The 236 galleries include collections of Greek, Roman and Egyptian antiquities, Islamic art, medieval European art, costume, arms and armor, prints and drawings, musical instruments, European painting and sculpture and decorative arts – including several furnished rooms. A new three-story wing is devoted to American art. It is impossible to get a comprehensive view on a single visit. Instead, choose two or three areas of special interest.

The medieval section on the first floor is particularly fine and includes a magnificent Spanish Baroque wrought-iron choir screen and Romanesque chapel.

An outstanding attraction of the Egyptian collection is the largely intact Temple of Dendur. In the Greek and Roman section, the Euphronios Krater, bought for $1m, is a superb example of red-figured pottery.

The Met's collection of European painting and sculpture includes masterpieces from all periods and schools. Among them are a *Madonna and Child* by Bellini, *Venus and the Lute Player* by Titian, El Greco's *View of Toledo*, and 33 works by Rembrandt, including *Aristotle with a Bust of Homer*. The 19thC collection in the André Meyer Galleries contains works by David, Delacroix, Turner and Rodin and many Impressionist and Post-Impressionist paintings.

The Michael C Rockefeller Wing of Primitive Art has 3,500 pieces donated by Nelson Rockefeller when his son died on an expedition to New Guinea in 1961. The exhibits cover Africa, the Pacific and the Americas.

The Lehman Pavilion contains a fine collection of Italian Renaissance and 19th and 20thC French art.

The American Wing houses the museum's extensive collection of American art, from colonial times to the present. Among the painters represented are Winslow Homer, Frederic Remington, Mary Cassatt, James Whistler, Georgia O'Keeffe and John Singer Sargent. American decorative arts are displayed in a series of period rooms, including a Duncan Phyfe Greek Revival parlor, a room furnished in the austere Shaker style and an earth-toned Frank Lloyd Wright living room overlooking Central Park. The spacious garden court that forms the entrance to the wing is embellished with Tiffany stained-glass windows. *5th Ave at 82nd St ☏ 535-7710 for recorded information, ☏ 870-5500 for other information. Open 9.30–5.15, to 8.45 Tue; closed Mon.*

Museum of Modern Art This extensive collection of modern art runs from Impressionism to Pop Art and includes paintings, sculptures, prints and drawings, architectural models, graphic design and films.

Among the museum's most important acquisitions are Van Gogh's *Starry Night*; Toulouse-Lautrec's *La Goulue at the Moulin Rouge*; several fine Cézannes; Picasso's *Les Demoiselles d'Avignon*; Chagall's poetic *I and the Village*; Piet Mondrian's abstract geometric compositions; and masterpieces by Matisse. There are also works by the Russian Constructivists and by Latin American painters, as well as by the more familiar School of Paris artists such as Modigliani and Braque and the Americans Edward Hopper and Andrew Wyeth (*Christina's World*). The exhibition of Braque and Picasso cubist pieces side by side is particularly impressive. Dado and surrealism are well represented by such artists as Arp, Magritte and Dali; abstract expressionism by Pollack, Kline and De Kooning. The museum's sculpture garden includes works by Rodin, Giacometti and Louise Nevelson. A self-service restaurant overlooks the garden; in warm weather you can eat outside. The museum shop is particularly good for books and gifts. *11 W 53rd St ☏ 708-9400. Open 11–6, to 9 on Thu; closed Wed.*

New York Stock Exchange Descended from an organization founded in 1792 under a buttonwood tree at Wall and William streets, the New York Stock Exchange now deals in the shares of nearly 1,600 companies. From the Visitors' Gallery one can watch the chaotic activity on the Trading Floor. Exhibits, recordings and guides explain the Exchange's history and workings. *20 Broad Street ☏ 656-3000. Open Mon–Fri, 9.30–4.*

Pierpont Morgan Library Originally the home of millionaire JP Morgan, this elegant building is now a museum housing his collection of rare books (including a Gutenberg Bible), illuminated manuscripts and medieval and Renaissance works of art. Like the Frick, its tranquil but imposing atmosphere makes it perfect for a breather. *29 E 36th St at Madison Ave ☏ 685-0008.*

Rockefeller Center This city-within-a-city includes 18 buildings, with a working population of 65,000. Still controlled by the Rockefeller family, the Center is the world's largest privately owned business and entertainment complex.

For visitors, the main attractions of the Center are the RCA Building, the Lower Plaza, which serves as an outdoor café in summer and an iceskating rink in winter, and Radio City Music Hall, an Art Deco palace famed for its elaborate stage shows. Tours of the Center, and of the radio and television studios of NBC (a subsidiary of General Electric), leave from the Guided Tour office on the main floor of the RCA Building, every day except Sun, 9.30–4.45 and 10–4 respectively ☏ 489-2947. Few television programs originate in New York; however, it is possible to attend some of those that do; forinformation ☏ 664-3055. Tours of Radio City Music Hall only, including backstage areas, start from the lobby; information ☏ 541-9436. The public areas of the Music Hall are included in the general tour of the Center. *RCA Building: 30 Rockefeller Plaza, between 49th and 50th St; Radio City Music Hall: 50th St at 6th Ave.*

St Patrick's Cathedral This graceful Neo-Gothic church presents a striking contrast to the massive modern towers that surround it. The bronze doors have bas reliefs depicting notable American Catholics; the stained-glass windows, some made in France, are especially noteworthy. *5th Ave between 50th and 51st St ☏ 753-2261.*

St Paul's Chapel The oldest church in Manhattan, St Paul's Chapel was completed in 1766. George Washington worshipped here while president; his pew is in the N aisle. It is now part of the parish of *Trinity Church*, which, when it was designed by the English-born architect Richard Upjohn in 1846, established Gothic as the fashionable American church style. *Broadway at Vesey St ☏ 602-0800.*

South Street Seaport This complex of piers, museums, galleries, shops, markets and restaurants on the East River is a redevelopment of the area that was the heart of New York's 19thC shipping industry. Carefully restored waterfront warehouses face a small fleet of sailing ships, some of which can be boarded, and there is an exhibition gallery. The schooner *Pioneer* offers 2 and 3hr cruises of the harbor, mid-May–mid-Oct. *South Street Venture Visitors' Center, 207 Water St. Ships and gallery open Mon–Sat, 10–6; Sun, noon–6.*

Statue of Liberty This 225-ton, 151ft statue, depicting Liberty holding the light of Freedom and the book of Justice, trampling the chains of Tyranny, was dedicated in October 1886. A gift from the French nation, it symbolized the promise of America to the newly arrived during the nation's greatest wave of

European immigration. Tourists crowd the statue, which was completely refurbished for the 1986 centenial celebrations. If you have two hours, it is worth visiting, especially for the view from the crown. *Circle Line Ferries ☏ 269-5755.*

United Nations Headquarters One of New York's major landmarks, the UN comprises five buildings, of which the most familiar are the slab-like Secretariat and the General Assembly Building with its gracefully sloping roof. Guided tours of the UN start from the Main Lobby of the General Asssembly Building and are conducted in many languages. At the Information Desk one can obtain tickets (free) to some UN meetings. *United Nations Plaza between 42nd St and 48th St ☏ 754-1234.*

Whitney Museum of American Art Marcel Breuer's cantilevered, granite-faced fortress contains an important collection of 20thC American painting and sculpture, including works by Hopper, Nevelson, Warhol and Calder. The museum's acquisitions policy is adventurous and its exhibitions controversial. The Whitney's program includes film showings and avant-garde dance. The museum now has branches in the Equitable Building on 7th Ave, where the murals of Thomas Hart Benton are featured; in the Philip Morris Building at 120 Park Ave; and downtown, 384 Broadway. The main building is on *Madison Ave at 75th St ☏ 570-3676. Open Tue, 11.30–8; Wed–Sat, 11–6; Sun, 12–6; closed Mon.*

Guided tours

Boat trips *Circle Line* ☏ 563-3200. Boats make a circuit of Manhattan Island, departing from and returning to Pier 83 at W 42nd St. The cruise, which operates Apr–Nov, takes about 3hrs and includes running commentary. In summer, twilight cocktail cruises can be spectacular on clear nights. A time-saving alternative is the *Staten Island Ferry*, which leaves from the Whitehall St pier, Battery Park ☏ 806-6940 every 20–30min, night and day, all year round. There's no commentary, but at 25 cents for a round-trip it offers good views of the Statue of Liberty, the Verrazano-Narrows Bridge and Lower Manhattan.

Bus tours *Gray Line* ☏ 397-2600. Bus tours, taking 2–8hrs, cost $12–26. Most leave from the terminal at 900 8th Ave (53rd St). Gray Line also organizes yacht cruises and helicopter tours.

Individual tours *Accent on Language*, 16 E 52nd St ☏ 355-5170. Provides tours in all major languages; all guides are licensed and experienced, and tours can be tailored to particular interests.

Spectator sports

Tickets for all metropolitan area professional sporting events can be bought in person at the *Ticketron* outlets around the city ☏ 399-4444; cash only. Midtown in Grand Central Terminal by Track 37, Mon–Fri, 9–5; downtown at J&R Music world, 23 Park Row, Mon–Fri, 9.30–5.30. *Teletron* ☏ 947-5850 handles credit card orders.

Baseball The city has two baseball teams and loyalties are sharply divided. The New York *Mets* (National League) play at Shea Stadium, Flushing Meadow, Flushing, Queens ☏ (718) 507-8499; the New York *Yankees* (American League) at Yankee Stadium, River Ave at E 161st St, Bronx ☏ 293-6000.

Basketball New York *Knicks* play at Madison Square Garden, 7th Ave at 32nd St ☏ 564-4400. The *New Jersey Nets* are at Byrne Meadowlands Arena, East Rutherford, NJ ☏ (201) 935-3900.

Football New York *Giants* and *Jets* play at Giants Stadium, Meadowlands ☏ (201) 935-8222.

Horse racing There is thoroughbred racing at *Aqueduct Race Track*, Rockaway Blvd, Ozone Park, Queens ☏ (718) 641-4700 and

Belmont Park Race Track, Hempstead Turnpike at Plainfield Ave, Elmont, Long Island ☏ (718) 641-4700. Harness races are held at *Roosevelt Raceway*, Old Country Rd, Westbury, Long Island ☏ (516) 222-2000 and *Yonkers Raceway*, Central and Yonkers avenues, Yonkers ☏ (914) 968-4200. *Meadowlands Racetrack*, Meadowlands, East Rutherford, NJ ☏ (201) 935-8500 features both types.
Ice hockey New York *Rangers* play at Madison Square Garden, 7th Ave at 32nd St ☏ 564-4400; New Jersey *Devils* at Byrne Meadowlands Arena, East Rutherford, NJ ☏ (201) 935-3900.

Keeping fit

Few reasonably priced sports facilities exist for visitors. Hourly court rates for racquet sports can be high and private reservations are difficult, but many hotel concierges can make arrangements with either nearby health clubs or outlying golf clubs. Some hotels have indoor sports facilities and health clubs.
Bicycling Central Park is the best area. Consider bicycling around the city only on weekends. Many large bicycle stores have bikes to rent: *Midtown Bicycle*, 360 W 47th St at 9th Ave ☏ 581-4500; *A&B Bicycle World*, 663 Amsterdam Ave at 92nd St ☏ 866-7600; or *Metro Bicycles*, 1311 Lexington Ave at 88th St ☏ 427-4450.
Golf Manhattan has no golf courses, but there are NYC-owned clubs in some of the outlying boroughs including Brooklyn ☏ (718) 965-6511 and Queens ☏ (718) 520-5311.
Racquet sports Many of the city's public tennis clubs also have racquetball courts and offer instruction in both; most of the city's squash clubs, however, are private. For tennis courts, expect to pay $22–46 an hour. *Wall Street Raquet Club*, Wall St at the East River ☏ 952-0760; *Village Courts*, 110 University Pl ☏ 989-2300; *Crosstown Tennis*, 14 W 31st St ☏ 947-5780; *Tennis Club at Grand Central Terminal*, 15 Vanderbilt Ave ☏ 687-3841; *Columbus Racquet Club*, 795 Columbus Ave ☏ 663-6900.
Riding *Claremont Riding Academy*, 175 W 89th St ☏ 724-5100. Horses, saddles and bridles provided, but riders must have boots and helmets. No beginners.
Running Runners flock to Central Park in good weather and bad; a favorite route of many circles the reservoir, just above 86th Street. Traffic in the streets and on the sidewalks can make running outside a park difficult or dangerous in many areas; consult a concierge for routes or call the *New York Road Runners Club* ☏ 860-4455.
Soccer and softball At weekends, many pick-up softball and soccer games happen spontaneously in Central Park; most welcome visitors. For *soccer*, walk towards the center of the park at 100th Street and look for the North Meadow soccer fields. For *softball*, try the area near the Sheep Meadow, below 72nd Street.

Local resources

Business services

The concierge at most business-class hotels can either supply or arrange services such as photocopying, printing, fax and secretarial and translation services. But there are many firms specializing in some or all of these services. For example, *Adia Personnel Services*, 41 E 42nd St ☏ 682-3438 and *IFD Secretarial and Printing Services*, 14 E 60th St ☏ 308-0049, both offer an extensive range.
Photocopying and printing *Mid-City Duplicating* specializes in legal work and has binding, offset printing and blueprint facilities. Free pick-up and delivery. Main office at 222 E 45th St ☏ 687-6699 open 24hrs. Also at 519 Madison Ave (51st St) ☏ 980-8585 and 136 William St ☏ 349-0880, both open 9am–midnight. *Pandick Technologies*, 85 5th Ave (16th St) and 150 Broadway ☏ 929-1600 is open 7 days, 24hrs,

and offers pick-up and delivery. *Xerox Reproduction Center*, 200 Madison Ave (36th St) ☎ 561-6700 offers complete copying, offset duplicating, color prints, transparencies, microfilm and fax.
Secretarial and translation *Accent on Language*, 16 E 52nd St ☎ 355-5170 offers foreign language typing and interpreting and translation services in all major European, Asian and Middle-Eastern languages. *Berlitz*, 866 3rd Ave (53rd St) ☎ 486-1212 or 61 Broadway ☎ 425-3866 offers multilingual word-processing and translation services.
Security *Burns International Security Services*, 10 Columbus Circle ☎ 397-6600 provides bodyguards and personal protection.

Communications

Local delivery Major banks and law firms use *Archer Services*, 855 6th Ave ☎ 563-8800 and *Bullit Courier*, 42 Broadway ☎ 952-4343 and 233 W 42nd St ☎ 221-3615; both offer 24hr service.
Long-distance delivery Major firms such as *Federal Express* ☎ 777-6500 and *DHL*, 1 World Trade Center ☎ (718) 917-8000 offer next-day delivery for most locations. *Associated Coast to Coast Couriers*, 233 W 54th St ☎ 489-0214 has 24hr domestic and international service, door to door. *Air Couriers International*, 251 5th Ave ☎ (800) 528-6070 has 24hr door-to-door service.
Post office The *General Post Office* at 421 8th Ave (33rd St) ☎ 967-8585 is open 24hrs. The 90 Church St post office ☎ 330-5297 is open for Express Mail until midnight.
Telex and fax *Telex Express International*, 29 John St ☎ (516) 348-5200, 24hrs, and *ITT Communications Services*, 67 Broad St ☎ 797-3000.

Conference/exhibition centers

Most of the city's business-class hotels offer conference facilities and can provide extensive assistance. The *New York Convention and Visitors' Bureau*, 2 Columbus Circle ☎ 397-8200 offers help and advice on convention facilities. The *Jacob K Javits Convention Center*, 11th Ave from 34th St to 39th St ☎ 216-2000 is the city's newest and largest exhibition center.

Emergencies

Currency exchange Practically all New York business-class hotels can provide 24hr currency exchange for their guests, though their rates are not usually the best available. Traditionally, many US banks have not offered currency exchange, but that situation is changing in many big cities. In New York, most of the banks at Rockefeller Center offer limited exchange facilities; others include *Bank Leumi*, 120 Broadway ☎ 602-9320, 579 5th Ave at 47th St ☎ 382-4407, and other locations; and the *Chemical Bank* branch at 5th Ave and 51st St. *American Express* travel service offices are open during normal business hours: 65 Broadway ☎ 493-6500; 150 E 42nd St ☎ 687-3700; 374 Park Ave ☎ 421-8240; and 822 Lexington Ave ☎ 758-6510.
Hospitals Virtually all New York hospitals have 24hr emergency rooms. The main ones include *New York Hospital*, 525 E 68th ☎ 472-5454 AE V; *Beth Israel Medical Center*, 10 Nathan D Perlman Pl (Stuyvesant Sq) ☎ 420-2840; *Lenox Hill Hospital*, 77th St and Park Ave ☎ 439-2345 AE CB MC V; *St Luke's Hospital*, 114th Amsterdam ☎ 870 6000 AE MC ; *Roosevelt Center*, 428 W 59th St ☎ 544-7000 AE MC. For dental emergencies call the *Dentist Emergency Service*, 172 E 4th St ☎ 677-2510 or 679-3966.
Pharmacies *Kaufman Pharmacy*, Lexington Ave at 50th St ☎ 755-2266, open 24hrs, accepts credit cards (AE MC) and will deliver.
Police For all emergencies (ambulance, fire or police) call 911; an operator will direct the call to the nearest station.

Government offices

New York City ☎ 566-4446; *US Immigration and Naturalization Service* ☎ 206-6500; *US Dept of Commerce*, 26 Federal Plaza ☎ 264-0634.

Information sources

Business information *The Chamber of Commerce for Trade and Industry*, 1 World Trade Center ☎ 432-1221 promotes international trade and offers some information to non-members. Nearly every country in the world maintains a chamber of commerce in New York. Most provide reference books, statistics and directories to non-members, sometimes at a charge. *British-American Chamber of Commerce*, 275 Madison Ave (39th St) ☎ 889-0680; *French-American Chamber of Commerce*, 509 Madison Ave, Suite 1900 ☎ 371-4466; *Italy–America Chamber of Commerce*, 350 5th Ave (33rd St) ☎ 279-5520; *Japanese Chamber of Commerce*, 145 W 57th St ☎ 246-9774; *Spain–US Chamber of Commerce*, 350 5th Ave (33rd St) ☎ 967-2170.

Local media The *New York Times* gives national, international and local coverage, with good features and a business section every day. The *Wall Street Journal* specializes in business and financial reporting, Mon–Fri. The *New York Post* is a tabloid afternoon daily, but it also carries the late stock market prices. The *New York Daily News*, also tabloid, is less lurid than the *Post*. The *Village Voice*, available weekly on Wed, gives left-of-center political and social coverage, and excellent entertainment listings. *Manhattan, Inc* aimed at the young, ladder-climbing business community. *The New Yorker* gives literary reviews, general commentary, cartoons and entertainment listings. *New York*, aimed at young professionals, has good entertainment listings and London's *Sunday Times*' crossword. *Crain's New York Business*, a weekly, covers local medium-sized firms.

AM radio stations WABC 770 news/talk; WCBS 880 all-news; WINS 1010 all-news; WMCA 570 phone-ins/talk/news; WNYC 830 information/talk; WOR 710 talk. WQXR 1560 *New York Times* station, classical/news

FM radio stations WBAI 99.5 listener-sponsored, no commercials; WNYC 93.9 public radio; WNYE 91.5 educational/talk. WNCN 103.4 classical; WQXR 96.3 *New York Times* station, classical/news

Television stations WCBS ch 2, WNBC ch 4, WNYW ch 5, WABC ch 7, WOR ch 9, WPIX ch 11, WNET ch 13.

Tourist information *New York Convention and Visitors' Bureau*, 2 Columbus Circle ☎ 397-8222 has many helpful brochures, but the staff are often quite busy. *New York State Dept of Commerce*, 230 Park Ave (46th St), Room 866 ☎ 309-0560 has information on tour packages and recreation. *Times Square Information Center*, 42nd St and Broadway or 2 Columbus Circle ☎ 397-8222 gives information on theater district events and shows.

Thank-yous

Florists *Flora Plenty*, 1135 1st Ave (62nd St) ☎ 254-7777 or 371-9099: charge by phone daily till 11pm. *Tiffany Florist* 162 E 23rd St ☎ 254-2758: charge by phone.

Wine merchants *Gourmet Liquor Shop*, 1118 Madison Ave (83rd St) ☎ 734-1400. *Park Lane Liquor Store*, 16 E 58th St ☎ 753-5160.

Special gifts Most department stores have personal shopping services which will put together a special gift package and arrange to have it delivered; *Bergdorf Goodman* is one of the best (see *Shopping*).

PHILADELPHIA

Area code ☎ 215

As the birthplace of the Declaration of Independence and the US Constitution, Philadelphia is the country's most historically important city. Yet though it once vied with London and other world centers of influence, much of the city's status and sense of urgency faded as the seat of government moved away, leaving it with little more than WC Fields's epitaph – "All in all, I'd rather be in Philadelphia".

Recent commercial real estate construction and retail development have done much to transform what had become a quaint Quaker haven into a forward-looking, economically vital city. Today it is an expanding metropolitan area of universities, colleges and medical schools and a major center for international enterprises, particularly those involved in health care, energy, pharmaceuticals, high tech, publishing, accounting and even, still, some "smokestack" industries. The area's big companies include Sun Oil, CIGNA, Bell Atlantic, DuPont, Campbell Soups, Alco Standard, Unisys, SmithKline Beckman, Scott Paper, Rohm & Haas, Commodore International, CertainTeed, Lea and Febiger, WB Sounders and Subaru of America.

Though nearly 90 miles/144km from the Atlantic, Philadelphia's seaport has a busy oil and cargo trade, and the local Navy repair yard is a major employer.

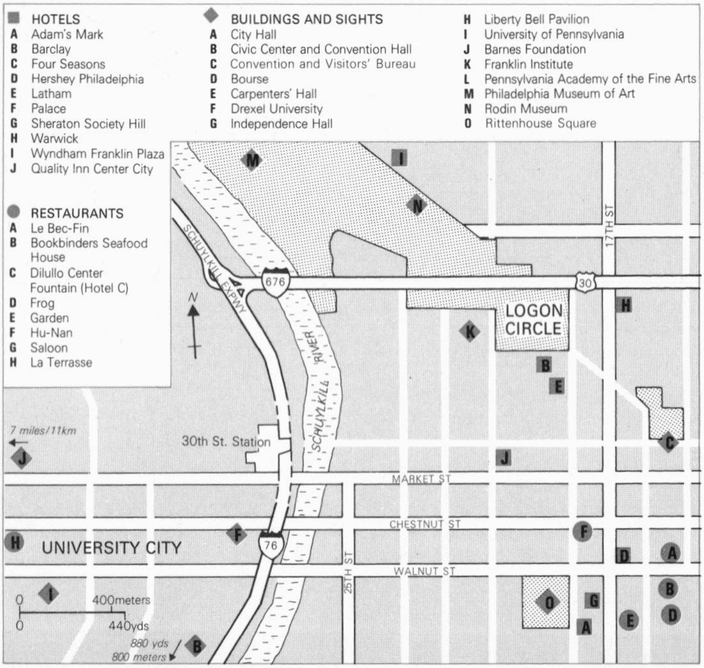

Arriving

Philadelphia International Airport

PHL is served by all major domestic carriers and a few international airlines. Passengers on other international carriers make domestic connections to Philadelphia after first clearing Customs at a major gateway airport such as New York.

PHL has two sections, a modern domestic facility and a single-story international terminal half a mile/1km away, linked by a free 24hr shuttle bus running every 5min. There are four domestic terminals (B, C, D and E). A new $75m combined domestic/international terminal (A) is expected to open in 1989.

The international terminal has multilingual staff; general (as well as airport) information is available daily 6am–midnight; and you can arrange car rental, obtain snacks and flight insurance, get currency changed and buy gifts.

The four domestic terminals, connected by a main corridor, offer flight insurance, currency exchange (6.30am–9.30pm) and multilingual information facilities (6am–midnight), mailing, American Express banking machines and a full-service dining room with cocktail lounge open 11.30–8. All terminals have bars, snack stands and gift shops. General airport information ☎ 492-3333.

Nearby hotels *Airport Hilton Inn*, 10th St and Packer Ave 19148 ☎ 755-9500. *Airport Ramada Inn*, 76 Industrial Hwy, Essington 19029 ☎ 521-9600. *Best Western Philadelphia Airport Inn*, International Airport 19153 ☎ 365-0700. *Embassy Suites Hotel*, 1 Gateway Center, 4101 Island Ave 19153 ☎ 365-5500.

City link Center City is approximately 8 miles/13km N of the airport, 15min by road in non-rush-hour traffic, 45min in morning and evening rush hours (7–8.30, 4.30–6). Best options are to take a taxi or, if you have only a small amount of luggage, the SEPTA Hi-Speed Rail line.

Taxi A taxi ride into Center City will cost about $15. Taxis are readily available at all terminals.

Limousine Van limos can be shared for about $12 per person. For

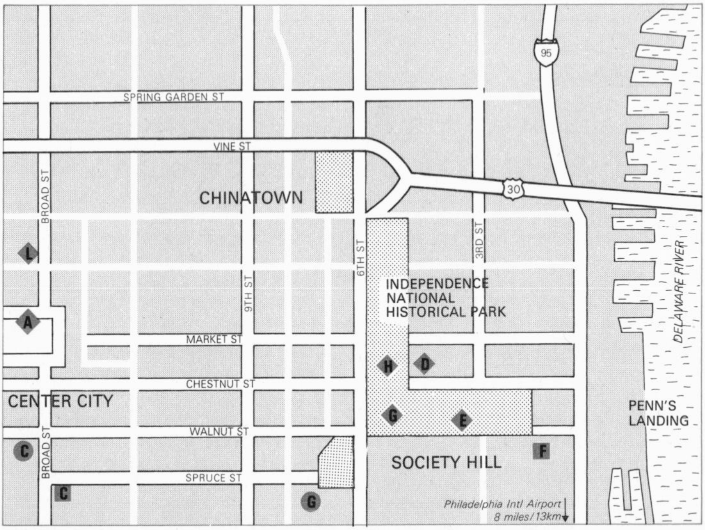

limousine service call Knights's Limousine ☎ 492-8402 or Casino Limousine ☎ (800) 452-1110.
Rail SEPTA's high-speed rail line to Center City takes about 20–25min and runs daily from the domestic terminal via 30th Street Station (30th and Market streets), Suburban Station (16th St and John F Kennedy Blvd) and Market Street East Station (10th and Market streets) from 6.10am to 12.10am for about $4. For information ☎ 574-7800.
Car rental Courtesy phones at street level in the baggage claim area of the domestic terminal connect directly to nearby offices of Hertz ☎ 492-7200, Avis ☎ 492-0900, National ☎ 492-2750, Budget ☎ 492-3915 and Dollar ☎ 365-1605.

Rail station

30th Street Station Though most business travellers arrive by air, 30th Street Station ☎ 824-1600 handles a good deal of business traffic, with its excellent Amtrak links to New York, Washington, Boston and other major East Coast cities. Located right in Center City, the station is a cavernous Art Deco building. Cabs are readily available outside; most downtown destinations are within 5–15min.

Getting around

The city's streets are laid out on a grid pattern, developed by William Penn more than 300 years ago. Numbered streets run N–S, named streets E–W.
Walking Philadelphia is a very walkable city, and most of the major business, entertainment, historical and cultural areas are within easy reach of each other. To go from City Hall, at Broad and Market, to Independence Hall, at 6th and Chestnut, is a brisk 20min walk. Many of the major office buildings are located between Broad and 20th, an area just six blocks wide.
Taxi It is safer to negotiate some parts of downtown – for example, Market Street just E of City Hall and the area just E of Broad Street – by taxi, daylight or dark. Cabs are plentiful on the streets before 5pm, but later it is advisable to call for one about 30min in advance: *Yellow Cab* ☎ 922-8400, *Quaker City Cab* ☎ 728-8000 and *United Cab Assoc* ☎ 625-2881.
Public transportation *SEPTA* operates commuter rail lines, buses, trolleys and subways to all parts of the city and suburbs. Base fare is about $1.25, although travelling to outlying suburbs costs more. Avoid all forms of public transportation at night in favor of taxis. Avoid the subway at all times.
Car rental Drivers unfamiliar with the city may have problems, for signposting is confusing and sparse; but if your business takes you to the outlying regions, car rental is advisable.

Area by area

In the city center, the main areas divide along financial, historical or sociological lines. Elsewhere there are distinct ethnic neighborhoods – for example, South Philly (Italian), Roxborough and Kensington (Polish and Irish), North Philadelphia (black) and Chinatown.
Center City Downtown has both commercial and residential interests. It houses most of the city's major corporations, banks, publishing houses, law and accounting firms, advertising agencies and government institutions. But in addition to high-rise office buildings, hotels and shopping areas, Center City's tree-bordered streets and grand avenues have historic sites, smart restaurants, apartment complexes, condominiums and townhouses. City Hall stands at the very core, at the intersection of Broad and Market streets, topped by a statue of the city's founder, William Penn. Prestigious Center City areas are the Rittenhouse Square area and Society Hill.
Chestnut Hill A suburb NW of Center City and bordering

Germantown, Chestnut Hill is a residential bastion of money and class, with big, graceful mansions, good restaurants and elegant shops overlooking the elite Chestnut Hill College.

Chinatown A huge and ornately oriental gateway marks the entrance to this neighborhood, NE of City Hall and bordering the site of the planned $450m Convention Center. The area offers a crowded array of colorful shops and restaurants.

Fairmount An established working-class area, Fairmount is now much sought after by young professionals for its Victorian mansions, townhouses and gracious, tree-shaded streets. It is also a fast-developing commercial area.

Germantown/Mount Airy The site of the colonial army's last battle with the British in 1777 is today an area of stately old mansions and churches, favored by the city's successful entrepreneurs.

Main Line Named after the railroad link to Center City, this affluent and highly regarded area of the W suburbs is the traditional home of Philadelphia's established society families. Main Line residents have a huge influence on the business and political dealings of the city.

Society Hill Years of restoration have made this area a living example of how Philadelphia looked in its colonial days. Elegant Georgian and Federal townhouses line the narrow, cobbled streets lit by old-fashioned Franklin streetlamps. Though largely residential, inhabited by some of the city's wealthiest and most powerful politicians, lawyers and corporate executives, Society Hill also has Philadelphia's major historic attractions, including Independence National Historic Park (see *Sightseeing*). Penn's Landing – where William Penn first set foot in the New World – is now a burgeoning tourist area with residential and commercial development.

University City Student and community life meet on the W bank of the Schuylkill River (pronounced Skoo-kull). The area includes 30th Street Station, the Ivy League University of Pennsylvania, the Wharton School of Business, the Civic Center, Drexel University and the city's major urban high-tech research and development center, the University City Science Center.

Hotels

Philadelphia's old mainstays such as the Bellevue Stratford and the Ben Franklin have gone, replaced by modern hotels, many of them along the Ben Franklin Parkway, W of Broad Street, convenient for the major Center City offices.

Adam's Mark $$$

City Ave and Monument Rd 19131 ☏ 581-5000 TX 7106701953 • 515 rooms, 67 suites, 2 restaurants, 3 bars

Philadelphia's second largest convention hotel (after the Wyndham), Adam's Mark is just outside Center City on City Line Avenue. Nonetheless, its attention to individual guests' needs makes it a firm favorite with business visitors. The décor is modern, and health facilities are extensive, with jacuzzi, saunas, health club, racquetball courts and two pools. Nine meeting rooms.

Barclay $$$$

18th and Locust 19103 ☏ 545-0300 TX 7106701009 • 240 rooms, 30 suites, 1 restaurant, 1 bar

Luciano Pavarotti, Bob Hope and Zubin Mehta are among those who enjoy the Barclay's prestigious location in Rittenhouse Square, convenient to Center City and the theater district. Its Old World charm, elegant lobby and well-proportioned rooms are among its other attractions. Nearby health club • 12 meeting rooms.

Four Seasons $$$$$
Logan Sq 19103 ☏ 963-1500
TX 00831805 • 370 rooms, 7 suites, 2 restaurants, 2 bars
The Four Seasons is Philadelphia's best and most prestigious hotel. With its beautifully landscaped garden and courtyard, numerous fountains and spacious, richly appointed lobbies, it is the place to stay if you want to make an impression. The good-sized rooms, furnished in Federal-period style, are easy to work in; the Fountain Room restaurant is often crowded with the city's corporate elite. Pool, whirlpool, sauna, massage, health club • 13 meeting rooms.

Hershey Philadelphia $$$$
215 South Broad St 19107
☏ 893-1600 TX 834374 • 450 rooms, 8 suites, 2 restaurants, 2 bars
In the heart of the theater and business district, the Hershey is immediately recognizable by its four-story, black-enameled, steel and glass atrium. The hotel has a private executive floor with its own lounge, concierge and sitting area. Pool, health club • 11 meeting rooms.

Latham $$$$
135 South 17th St 19103 ☏ 563-7474
TX 831438 • 141 rooms, 3 suites, 1 restaurant, 1 bar
The Latham offers a quieter and more intimate atmosphere than any other city hotel, though it doesn't stint on luxury. The tiny lobby is extremely ornate, and the very comfortable rooms have Louis XIV writing tables and sybaritic bathrooms. Nearby health club • 4 meeting rooms.

Palace $$$$
18th St and Benjamin Franklin Pkwy 19103 ☏ 963-2222 TX 902585 • Trusthouse Forte • 285 suites, 1 restaurant, 1 bar
An impressive guest register bears such names as President Gerald Ford, James Stewart and the late Princess Grace of Monaco. The all-suites complex is well equipped for business visitors. Each suite has a foyer, separate meeting/dining area, a bar, a sitting area with balcony and a bedroom with balcony. Outdoor pool, arrangement with nearby health club • 7 meeting rooms, fax, business reference library, translation, teleconferencing.

Sheraton Society Hill $$$$
1 Dock St 19106 ☏ 238-6000
TX 5106018655 • 365 rooms, 7 suites, 1 restaurant, 2 bars
The red brick façade of this new Sheraton complements the colonial architecture of surrounding historic Society Hill. The lobby, which includes a cocktail bar, is used for informal business get-togethers. Pool, tennis nearby, health club • 11 meeting rooms.

Warwick $$$$
17th and Locust 19103 ☏ 735-6000
TX 5106005742 • 180 rooms, 15 suites, 2 restaurants, 1 bar
The Warwick's 1920s lobby, with ornate Persian carpets and well-upholstered sofas, is an elegant place for informal business chat. Just a block from Rittenhouse Square, the Warwick is well placed for the city's main offices, shops and theaters. The hotel's Caribbean-style Polo Club is popular with younger professionals. Six meeting rooms.

Wyndham Franklin Plaza $$$
2 Franklin Plaza, 17th and Race 19103 ☏ 448-2000 TX 00834572 • 800 rooms, 53 suites, 4 restaurants, 3 bars, 1 coffee shop
Philadelphia's largest convention hotel, the Wyndham, is just by City Hall in the heart of Center City. The size and price of single rooms can vary dramatically, so check thoroughly before making a reservation. First-rate health club. Barber, hair salon, gift shops • 22 meeting rooms.

OTHER HOTELS

Quality Inn Center City ($$) *501 22nd St* ☏ *568-8300.*

Penn Center Inn ($$) *20th and Market* ☏ *523-0909.*

Clubs

Until recently, most of Philadelphia's noteworthy clubs were open to men only, but now even the ultra-conservative Union League accepts women members. Philadelphia is staunchly clubby, and many locals prefer to conduct business and entertain clients "at the club." Founded in 1834, the *Philadelphia Club*, 13th and Walnut, is the oldest gentlemen's club in the country and unswervingly maintains its Main Line high society ambiance. The distinguished *Union League*, Broad and Sansom, was founded in 1862 to support the Union cause and has evolved into a civic and business-oriented society. Dedicated to the preservation of American art, the *Peale Club*, 1819 Chestnut St, is part of the Pennsylvania Academy of the Fine Arts, and its members include some of the most highly esteemed names in Philadelphia. Younger professionals are in the majority at the *Racquet Club*, 215 South 16th St, which traditionally aims to "combine the gentility of the manor house with the heroics and sweat of a college gym."

Restaurants

Philadelphia's restaurants are much patronized by the business community and are extensively used for doing business. For an off-duty treat, try one of the locally-famous cheese steaks (thinly-sliced beef served on a roll with melted cheese and fried onions) at *Pat's Steaks*, 9th and Passyunk Avenue.

Le Bec-Fin $$$$$

1523 Walnut St ☏ *567-1000 • closed Sun; D only Fri and Sat • AE DC • jacket required • reservations essential*

Le Bec-Fin is unbeatable for business dining, especially if an impressive setting and top-class French food are needed. Its opulent surroundings and good service draw a well-groomed crowd of Main Line corporate executives and politicians. The lunch menu is considerably less expensive than the dinner *prix fixe*. Reserve weeks in advance, especially for Saturday dinner.

Bookbinders Seafood House $$$

215 15th St ☏ *545-1137 • closed Sat L • AE CB DC MC V*

A traditional seafood house crammed with captain's chairs, oak paneling and nautical paraphernalia, Bookbinders is a Philadelphia landmark and an established spot for business lunches. Do not confuse it with the old Original Bookbinders in Society Hill.

DiLullo Centro $$

1407 Locust St ☏ *546-2000 • AE CB DC MC V*

With an elegantly comfortable atmosphere in a renovated theater, DiLullo's has excellent northern Italian dishes. Its interior white wood half-walls allow privacy for business discussions without being claustrophobic. There is an imaginative wine list. With its convenient Center City location, this is a popular lunch spot for the local business community.

Fountain $$$

1 Logan Square ☏ *963-1500 • AE CB DC MC V • reservations essential*

Undisputedly the cream of Philadelphia's grand hotel restaurants, the Fountain in the Four Seasons is an excellent choice for entertaining. The tables allow quiet conversation; the French/American cuisine is top-notch. Reserve at least a week in advance for dinner.

Frog $$$
1524 Locust St ☏ 735-8882 • D only Sat • AE CB DC MC V
Another well-established Center City favorite for business lunches and dinners, Frog offers a well-prepared Continental menu. The converted townhouse is smartly low-key.

Garden $$$
1617 Spruce St ☏ 546-4455 • D only Sat; closed Sun • AE CB DC MC V
The stylish Garden – another converted Center City townhouse with antique tables and bar – is a traditional meeting place for business lunches; its many small rooms ensure privacy. The menu features aged prime grilled beef, seafood and homemade desserts.

Hu-Nan $$
1721 Chestnut St ☏ 567-5757 • D only Sun; closed Sat • AE CB DC MC V
The Hu-Nan's elegant blue-and-gold décor is a far cry from paper tablecloths and plastic chopsticks. Its Center City location makes it useful for working lunches.

Saloon $$
750 South St ☏ 627-1811 • D only Sat; closed Sun • no credit cards
This quaint Italian restaurant off the beaten track in the heart of South Philly is a cozy haven of rich wood paneling, Victorian antiques and brass. It is ideal for private conversation and has first-rate steak as well as Italian dishes.

La Terrasse $$
3432 Sansom St ☏ 387-3778 • AE CB DC MC V
The best restaurant in the University City area, La Terrasse offers fine French food in a casual setting and is likely to impress a business client or colleague.

Bars

The after-hours bar scene picks up considerably on Wednesdays and Fridays and plays an important role in Philadelphia's business activity. *Downey's*, Front and South streets, is an Irish pub popular with business executives after working hours. *Crickett*, in the Latham Hotel, 17th and Walnut, offers soft piano music and jazz and a more subdued setting for informal business chatter. *Carolina's*, 261 South 20th St, is a neighborhood bar-cum-restaurant in the affluent Rittenhouse Square area. It is very popular with younger professionals, as is *Houlihan's*, 18th St and Rittenhouse Sq. *The Fish Market*, 18th and Sansom, caters to the smart set, especially on Fridays before they head to the Polo Club at the Warwick. *Harry's Bar & Grill*, 22 South 18th St, is another pleasant, attractive after-work spot; jackets are required. The *Irish Pub*, 2007 Walnut St, is very informal and often noisy and packed; it is best used as an off-duty watering hole. *Dickens Inn*, 2nd and Pine at New Market, is a cheery English-style pub adorned with sketches, prints and other Dickensiana, which serves imported stout and ales.

Entertainment

Ballet, jazz and classical music dominate Philadelphia's entertainment attractions. For floor shows or headline acts, Philadelphians go to Atlantic City, 45min away. Major concerts and other entertainments are staged at *The Spectrum*, Broad St and Pattison Ave ☏ 336-3600. Check the monthly *Philadelphia* magazine, or the "Weekend" sections in the *Inquirer* or the *Daily News* for what's on. For tickets contact *Ticketron* ☏ 885-2515 or *Chargit* ☏ (800) 223-0120.

Theater and music The *Academy of Music*, Broad and Locust ☏ 893-1930, is home to the Philadelphia Orchestra, the Opera Company of Philadelphia, and the Pennsylvania Ballet, and also has top guest entertainers. The *Annenberg Center*, 3680 Walnut St ☏ 898-6791 is a performing arts center with three theaters for children's and professional theater, film, music and other presentations. The *Forrest Theater*, 11th and Walnut ☏ 923-1515 features touring Broadway musicals, as well as other short-running plays and concerts. The *Schubert Theater*, Broad and Locust ☏ 735-4768 also hosts performances of the Pennsylvania Ballet and other companies. The *Walnut Street Theater*, 9th and Walnut ☏ 574-3550 stages dramatic presentations, concerts, lectures, films, dance and experimental theater.

Cinema The city has some fine art cinemas, including the *Roxy Screening Rooms*, 2021-23 Sansom St ☏ 561-0114; the *Art Museum*, 26th St and Ben Franklin Pkway ☏ 763-8100 and the *Ritz Five*, 214 Walnut St ☏ 925-7900.

Nightclubs The *Bourse*, at 5th and Ranstead, is the renovated old Stock Exchange, now housing lots of trendy boutiques and chic restaurants, as well as the *Heartthrob Café* and *Philadelphia Bandstand*, providing dancing amid high-tech 1950s and 1960s décor. The *Polo Club*, at the Warwick Hotel on 17th and Locust, is Philadelphia's most favored nightclub among young professionals. *Flanigan's*, 2nd and South, is a nightclub/disco which is also popular with younger professionals. *PT's*, 6 S Front St, is much used by the local business community, and offers dancing, backgammon, wine bars and live entertainment. *Spectacles*, in the Sheraton Society Hill, 1 Dock St, has a clever, lighthearted décor which lends energy to one of the city's trendiest nightspots.

Shopping

In the Center City area, the *Gallery at Market East* spans Market Street from 8th to 11th streets, with major stores linked by hundreds of smaller shops and restaurants. The *Bourse*, 21 South 5th St, once the city's Stock Exchange, now has three floors of boutiques, gift shops and restaurants. *South Street*, a sort of Philadelphian Greenwich Village, has a wide variety of restaurants and shops selling everything from antiques to organic foods. *John Wanamaker's*, 13th St between Market and Chestnut, is Center City's most renowned department store. Other fashionable stores include *Brooks Brothers* at 15th and Chestnut, *Bonwit Teller* at 17th and Chestnut, *Nan Duskin* at 18th and Walnut, *Bailey, Banks, and Biddle* at 16th at Chestnut, *Saks Fifth Avenue* on Cityline Avenue and *Bloomingdale's* in the suburban malls at King of Prussia and Willow Grove.

Jewelers' Row is on Sansom St between 7th and 9th, and *Antique Row* is on Pine St between 8th and 13th streets.

Sightseeing

If time is limited, the "musts" among the city's many historic sites are Independence Hall, the Pennsylvania Academy of the Fine Arts, the Museum of Art and the Barnes Foundation.

The Barnes Foundation, in Merion, about 7 miles/11km W of Center City, has a world-class private collection of post-Impressionist art, including works by Matisse, Dégas and Van Gogh. Visit by reservation. *300 N Latches Lane, Merion ☏ 667-0290. Open Fri and Sat, 9.30–4.30; Sun 1–4.30; closed Jul and Aug.*

Franklin Institute features four floors of science and technology exhibits, America's largest public observatory, Fels Planetarium and a giant walk-through replica human heart. *20th St and Ben Franklin Pkwy ☏ 448-1200. Open Mon–Sat, 10–5; Sun, noon–5.*

Independence National Historic Park The area has more than 50 historically interesting attractions, including the *Betsy Ross House*, 239 Arch St; *Carpenters' Hall*, 320 Chestnut St; *Christ Church*, 2nd St above Market St; *Congress Hall*, 6th and Chestnut streets; *Independence Hall*, 5th and Chestnut; and the *Liberty Bell*, Market St between 5th and 6th. Most sites are open daily, 9–5; all are free. For additional information contact the Visitors' Center, 3rd and Chestnut ☏ 597-8974.

Pennsylvania Academy of the Fine Arts is the oldest museum and art school in the USA, exhibiting three centuries of American art. *Broad and Cherry ☏ 972-7600. Open Tue–Sat, 10–5; Sun, 11–5.*

Philadelphia Museum of Art More than 500,000 paintings, sculptures, drawings, prints and other examples of the decorative arts. *26th St and Ben Franklin Pkwy. Open Tue–Sun, 10–5.*

Rodin Museum has the largest collection of Rodin sculptures and drawings outside France. *22nd St and Ben Franklin Pkwy ☏ 787-5476. Open Tue–Sun, 10–5.*

Guided tours

Centipede Tours ☏ 735-3123 provides candlelight tours through Old Philadelphia and Society Hill beginning at historic City Tavern, 2nd and Walnut at 6.30pm. *76 Carriage Company* ☏ 923-8516 give horse-drawn carriage tours of Philadelphia's historic areas starting from Independence National Historical Park, 5th and Chestnut St, daily from 10 to 5; tours of Society Hill and Head House Square are from 7pm to midnight. *Fairmount Park Trolley Bus* ☏ 879-4044 offers guided tours of Fairmount Park, Society Hill and Independence National Historical Park in motorized re-creations of Victorian trolleys; times, routes and prices vary.

Out of town

Valley Forge National Park is about 25 miles/40km W of the downtown area in King of Prussia, where General Washington and his army spent the grueling winter of 1777-78.

Spectator sports

Philadelphians are sports-happy, and the Phillies (baseball) and the Eagles (football) are especially popular teams; games are usually sellouts.

Baseball The *Philadelphia Phillies* play at Veterans' Stadium (The Vet), Broad St and Pattison Ave, Apr–Oct ☏ 463-1000.

Basketball The *76ers* play at the Spectrum, across from The Vet, Oct–Apr ☏ 339-7676.

Football The *Eagles* play at The Vet, Aug–Dec ☏ 463-5500.

Horse racing *Garden State Park*, off Rte 70, Cherry Hill, NJ ☏ (609) 488-8400; thoroughbred season mid-Feb–mid-Jun, Mon–Sat; harness season Aug–Dec, Tue–Sat.

Ice hockey The *Flyers* play at the Spectrum from Oct–Apr ☏ 465-5000.

Keeping fit

Health clubs In addition to hotel clubs there are *Clark's Uptown Racquet Swim & Health Club* ☏ 864-0616; *Philadelphia Athletic Club*, 314 North Broad St ☏ 564-2002; and *Queen Village Racquetball & Fitness Club*, 325 Bainbridge St ☏ 922-7900.

Bicycling *Fairmount Park Bike Rental*, 1 Boat House Row ☏ 236-4359, daily Mar–Nov, weekends Dec–Feb.

Golf Municipal courses are open year-round, weather permitting: *JF Byrne*, 9500 Leon St ☏ 632-8666; *Juniata*, M and Cayuga Sts ☏ 743-4060; *Karakung*, 72nd and Lansdowne Ave ☏ 877-8707; *Franklin D Roosevelt*, 20th St and Pattison Ave ☏ 467-2418.

Jogging Most popular routes are along Kelly Drive and West River Drive in Fairmount Park.

Tennis There are over 100 free public tennis courts throughout Fairmount Park ☏ 686-2176. Also *Pier 30*, Delaware Ave and Bainbridge St ☏ 985-1234 (indoor courts).

Local resources

Business services

For comprehensive business services, convenient locations and prompt turnaround, try *Little Blue Computer Services*, 1518 Walnut St ☎ 545-3730 and *Control Data Business and Technology Center*, 5070 Parkside Ave ☎ 879-8500.

Photocopying and printing *The Printer's Places* ☎ 546-6562 and *Minuteman Press* ☎ 629-8505 are located throughout the city. Most will pick up and deliver.

Secretarial services *Kelly Services* ☎ 564-3110 and *Olsten Services* ☎ 568-7795 are both reliable temporary service agencies.

Translation *Language Bank* ☎ 879-5248; *Berlitz Translation Services* ☎ 735-8500; and *International Visitors' Center* ☎ 823-7261 or 879-5248.

Communications

Local delivery *Heaven Sent* ☎ 923-0929 and *Kangaroo Couriers* ☎ 561-5132 offer efficient service.

Long-distance delivery *Federal Express* ☎ 923-3085 and *Quick Courier Service* ☎ 592-9933 are dependable.

Post office The post office at 30th and Market ☎ 596-5577 is open 7–7 daily; the 9th and Market location ☎ 592-9610 is open 7–5, Mon–Sat.

Telex *World-Wide Business Centers*, 714 Market St ☎ 238-7000; *Western Union* ☎ (800) 527-5184.

Conference/exhibition centers

Many of the larger hotels provide conference facilities with audio-visual services and trained staff. For other needs, call the *Convention and Visitors' Bureau* ☎ 636-3300.

Emergencies

Hospitals *Hahnemann University*, Broad and Vine ☎ 448-7000; *Thomas Jefferson University*, 11th and Walnut ☎ 928-6000; *University of Pennsylvania*, 34th and Walnut ☎ 898-5000.

For specific health referrals, call the *Philadelphia Medical Society* ☎ 563-5343; *Philadelphia County Dental Society* ☎ 925-6050.

Pharmacies *CVS Pharmacies*, *Thrift Drug* and *Rite Aid Discount Pharmacies* are well-known chains with many locations.

Government offices

City Commerce Dept ☎ 686-3646; *Mayor's Office Information* ☎ 686-2250; *Pennsylvania Dept of Commerce* ☎ (717) 787-3003; *US Dept of Commerce* ☎ 597-3311; *US Customs Service* ☎ 597-4605; *US Immigration and Naturalization Service* ☎ 629-1637.

Information sources

Business information *Chamber of Commerce of Greater Philadelphia* ☎ 545-1234 is a good source of general local business information.

Local media Of Philadelphia's two daily newspapers, The *Philadelphia Inquirer* provides the best local and regional coverage. The *Daily News* is the other daily paper. *Focus* and the *Philadelphia Business Journal* are the major business-oriented magazines. *Philadelphia* magazine is the best source of the area's dining and cultural attractions.

Tourist information The *Philadelphia Visitors' Center*, 1525 John F Kennedy Blvd ☎ 568-6599 is the main information source for individual travellers and sightseers. The *Philadelphia Convention and Visitors' Bureau*, 1515 Market St ☎ 636-3300 is especially useful for groups planning conventions, trade shows or exhibitions.

Thank-yous

The following companies all offer regional deliveries and accept phone orders with major credit cards.

Florists *Flower World*, 30th Street Station ☎ 567-7100; *Society Hill Florist*, 713 Walnut St ☎ 925-5715.

Gift baskets *Stein*, 7059 Frankford Ave ☎ 338-7100; *The William Penn Shop* ☎ 561-5400 or 663-1012.

PHOENIX

Area code ☎ 602

Set in Arizona's Valley of the Sun, Phoenix is a city of tourism and high-tech. The sprawling network of individual communities remains a favored retirement zone and a fruit growing center, but its erstwhile kingpins, agriculture and copper, are on the decline, and electronics and publishing have moved in. The city has attracted many Midwest and East Coast corporations to its affordable land, magnificent climate and very healthy economy, among them McDonnell-Douglas (20min SE in Mesa); Greyhound; U-Haul International; Chandler's Inter-Tel; American Continental; and the Best Western International and Ramada Inns hotel chains. It is also an important military center, with Litchfield Park's Luke Air Force Base, Williams Air Force Base in Chandler and the Army and Air National Guard State Headquarters nearby.

Arriving

Sky Harbor International Airport

Sky Harbor has three terminals, and a $100m fourth terminal is planned for 1990. Traffic is mainly domestic, and the airport is easy to negotiate.
Nearby hotels *Sheraton Airport Inn*, 2901 Sky Harbor Blvd 85034 ☎ 275-3634. *Gateway Park*, 320 N 44th St 85008 ☎ 225-0500. *Quality Inn Airport*, 1820 S 7th St 85034 ☎ 254-9787.
City link It is a 10min drive to the heart of downtown, 15min during the 8–9 and 5–6 rush hours. Since Phoenix is very spread out, most travellers rent a car at the airport.
Car rental is available from all three terminals: Avis ☎ 273-3222, Hertz ☎ 267-8822, Dollar ☎ 275-7588 and American International ☎ 273-6181.
Taxi Taxis are available at all three terminals; agree a fare in advance.
Bus The 24hr Super Shuttle ☎ 244-9000 operates a door-to-door service throughout the Valley.
Limousine Sky Harbor Limousine ☎ 275-8501.

Getting around

Phoenix is an easy city to find your way around; except for Grand Avenue, the streets follow a grid system. Central Avenue is the dividing line, with avenues to the W and streets to the E.
Car rental If your business takes you to nearby communities like Scottsdale, Tempe and Mesa, you should rent a car (see *Arriving: City link*).
Taxi Taxis do not cruise the city's streets, so reserve ahead. Be sure to negotiate the fare in advance. Reliable firms are *Courier Cab* ☎ 244-1818; *Yellow Cab* ☎ 252-5252; *Checker Cab* ☎ 257-1818; *Arizona Taxi* ☎ 253-8294; *Village Cab* ☎ 994-1616.
Limousine *La Limousine Service* ☎ 242-3094; *Arizona Rolls-Royce Limousines* ☎ 267-7097; *Wild Bill's Limousine Service* ☎ 998-7711.

Area by area

Phoenix's financial district is on Central Avenue, between McDowell and Camelback streets, just minutes from downtown. The residential area closest to downtown is Encanto Park, which has the city's oldest houses, built 30–50 years ago. They have been gentrified and are now owned by lawyers and business leaders. The big-money homes are in Biltmore (to the N) and Paradise Valley. As a rule of thumb, N and E are home to affluent professionals; S and W are areas of blue-collar workers and minorities. In the NE lies Scottsdale, with numerous shops, restaurants, resorts and cultural centers. Academics live in Tempe, close to the university campus. Mesa is a strongly Mormon area.

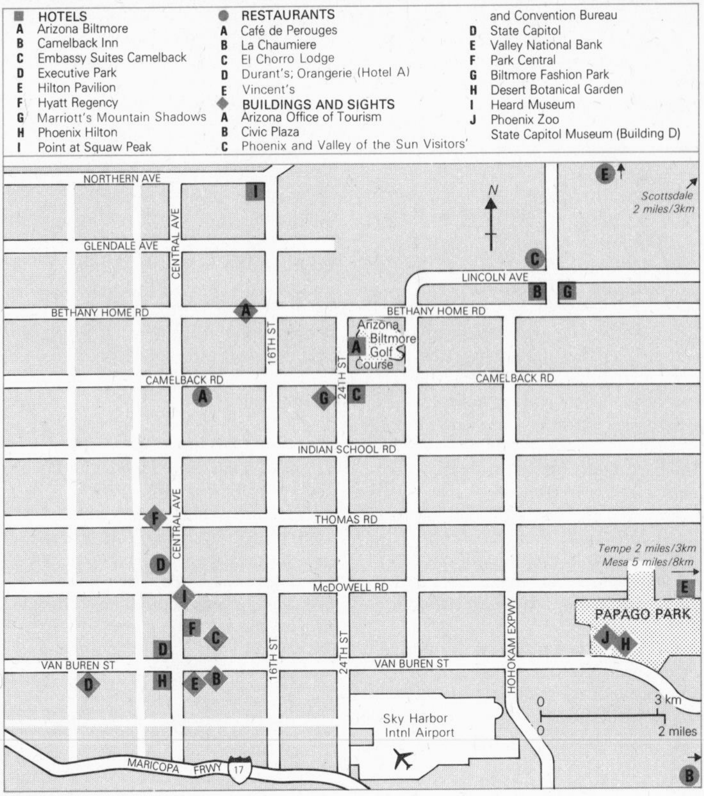

Hotels

The best hotels are in N Phoenix or Scottsdale, with golf courses, tennis courts, Olympic-size swimming pools and extensive meeting space. Between late May and mid-September hotel prices are cut by as much as 70%.

Arizona Biltmore $$$$$

24th St and Missouri Ave ☏ 955-6600 TX 165709 • 500 rooms, 78 suites, 4 restaurants

With a design inspired by Frank Lloyd Wright, this is the best of the Valley's top resort hotels. Occupying 39 acres of immaculate landscaped grounds, the Biltmore attracts celebrities, while its substantial business clientele appreciates the central location between downtown and Scottsdale. The Orangerie (see *Restaurants*) is highly recommended. Three pools, health club, golf, tennis • 15 meeting rooms, fax.

Camelback Inn $$$$

5402 E Lincoln Dr, Scottsdale 85253 ☏ 948-1700 TX 9109501198 • 401 rooms, 22 suites, 2 restaurants, 1 bar

A pretty resort hotel, the pueblo-inspired Camelback provides dramatic views of the nearby mountains. Guest rooms are not particularly lavish, but the public rooms are agreeably rustic.

Camelback has held the Mobil Travel Guide's five-star award for nearly two decades. Pool, golf • 20 meeting rooms, teleconferencing, recording facilities.

Embassy Suites Camelback $$$$
2630 E Camelback 85016 ☏ 955-3992 • 232 suites, 1 restaurant, 1 bar, 1 coffee shop
Located next to Biltmore Fashion Park, this hotel has a distinctive Art Deco look and a greenhouse-style lobby. The all-suite arrangement is particularly good for work or small meetings. There is easy access to downtown Phoenix and Scottsdale, and the airport is just 15min away. Golf arrangements with nearby club, pool • 8 meeting rooms.

Executive Park $$$
1100 N Central Ave ☏ 252-2100 • 106 rooms, 1 restaurant, 1 bar
This quiet hotel has a relaxed and homey atmosphere. Rooms are equipped with spacious desks and access for computer hook-up. Complimentary transportation to local office buildings • pool, jacuzzi • 11 meeting rooms.

Hilton Pavilion $$$
1011 W Holmes Ave, Mesa ☏ 833-5555 • 272 rooms, 122 suites, 2 restaurants, 3 bars
Decked out in white Italian marble flooring, tile fountains and Hawaiian koa wood, with an eight-story atrium lobby sprouting 50ft palm trees, the Hilton is well placed for appointments in the outlying SE suburbs. Health club, golf • 13 meeting rooms, teleconferencing.

Hyatt Regency $$$
122 N 2nd St 85004 ☏ 252-1234 TX 668347 • 727 rooms, 44 suites, 3 restaurants, 3 bars, 1 coffee shop
The Hyatt is frequently used by local corporations to house important visitors. Its revolving rooftop restaurant, Compass, affords a magnificent view of both desert and mountains, and Catina's bar is popular for business meetings. Health club, pool • 14 meeting rooms.

Marriott's Mountain Shadows $$$$
5641 E Lincoln Dr, Scottsdale ☏ 948-7111 • 339 rooms, 3 restaurants
At the base of Camelback Mountain and occupying 70 acres of desert gardens, the Marriott blends contemporary with Spanish and Indian design. Often used for conventions, it is an excellent place to relax as well as to work. Jacuzzis, pools, tennis, golf • 11 meeting rooms.

Phoenix Hilton $$$
111 N Central Ave 85004 ☏ 257-1525 • 450 rooms, 84 suites, 1 restaurant, 1 bar, 1 coffee shop
Convention-oriented, this Hilton provides a high standard of prompt, professional service. Happy hour at Clementine's is popular with the downtown business crowd. Health club, pool • 19 meeting rooms, computer modems.

Pointe at Squaw Peak $$$$
7677 N 16th St ☏ 997-2626 TX 4953529 • 600 suites, 4 restaurants
A modern luxury resort hotel given entirely over to suites and villas. Suites have spacious living areas, and the large dining tables in the de luxe villas are useful for small meetings. Six pools, golf, horseback riding, racquet sports, exercise room • 14 meeting rooms, teleconferencing.

OTHER HOTELS

Ramada Inn-Metrocenter ($$) *12027 N 28th Dr 85029 ☏ 866-7000.*
Westcourt ($$$) *10220 N Metro Pkwy E 85051 ☏ 997-5900 TX 706629.*

Clubs

Top people from all walks of life can be found at the *University Club*, 39 E Monte Carlo ☏ 254-5408, a sedate institution set on a residential, palm-lined street.

Restaurants

Downtown executives usually head uptown or over to neighboring Scottsdale for business meals, though they may use the *Golden Eagle* on the 37th floor of the Valley Bank Center, and the Phoenix Hilton's *Sand Painter*. Attorneys and judges from the nearby courthouse prefer the more casual *Greenhouse* or *Plaza Café*. Another good choice is the historic *1895 House*, with innovative dishes and an intimate atmosphere.

Café de Perouges $$$
4747 N 7th St ☏ 263-8000 • AE DC MC V
This charming restaurant is reminiscent of a French country inn. Service is unhurried, with classical music as a background. Younger business people often crowd the restaurant's glass-enclosed gazebo, on an "island" surrounded by water gardens.

La Chaumière $$$
6910 E Main St, Scottsdale ☏946-5115 • closed Sun May–Dec • AE CB DC MC V
A Scottsdale institution, serving top-class French creations. Service is impeccable and the numerous small dining rooms afford privacy for quiet conversation. Good wine list.

El Chorro Lodge $$
5550 E Lincoln, Scottsdale ☏ 948-5170 • closed mid-Jan–mid-Sep • AE CB DC MC V
In a scenic desert oasis with dramatic views of Camelback and Mummy mountains, the Lodge offers 1930s décor with fireplaces and wood beams, and casual dining on the outside patio. Much favored for weekday working lunches and Sunday brunch.

Durant's $$$
2611 N Central Ave ☏ 264-5967 • AE CB DC MC V
Durant's has been in business for business entertaining for more than 30 years. It offers generous portions of American food, with steak and prime ribs a specialty.

Orangerie $$$$$
24th St and Missouri ☏ 955-6600 • AE CB DC MC V
The Orangerie, in the Arizona Biltmore, has a reputation for excellence. The Continental menu is both varied and imaginatively prepared; game is a specialty. Good wine list.

Vincent's $$$$$
8711E Pinnacle Peak Rd, Scottsdale ☏ 998-0921 • D only; closed Sun and Mon in summer • AE DC MC V • reservations essential
Vincent's is *the* place to take a client you want to impress. The atmosphere is elegantly European; food is Franco-American *nouvelle.* Dress is more formal than in most Valley restaurants.

Bars

Phoenix bars are lively, but they tend to be frequented mainly by students, off-duty young professionals and tourists. Local executives use the bars of the main hotels, particularly the *Oasis Lounge* at the Camelback, *Catina's* in the Hyatt Regency and *Clementine's* in the Hilton. *Oscar Taylor's*, 2420 E Camelback Rd, is a restaurant bar also much used for talking over a drink.

Entertainment

To find out what's on and where, call the *Jazz Hotline* ☏ 254-4545, *Diamond's Select-A-Seat* ☏ 267-1246 or the *Scottsdale Center for the Arts* ☏ 994-2787.

Nightclubs Local and nationally known jazz musicians play at *Chuy's*, Mill Ave, Tempe ☏ 968-5568, while Top-40s and country & western tunes alternate at *Graham Central Station*, 4029 N 33rd Ave ☎ 279-3800. The cabaret show at *Yesterday's*, 9035 N 8th St ☎ 861-9080 features waiters, waitresses and audience participation; a commendable menu, too. *Mr Lucky's*, 3660 Grand Ave ☎ 246-0686 has crack country bands upstairs, rock 'n' roll downstairs. *Seekers Comedy Nite Club*, 4519 N Scottsdale Rd, Scottsdale ☎ 949-1100 features comics.

Theater, dance, opera The *Celebrity Theater* ☎ 267-1600, *Phoenix Symphony Hall* ☎ 264-4754, *Gammage Center at Arizona State University* ☎ 965-3434, *Scottsdale Center for the Arts* ☎ 994-2787 and the *Sundome* ☎ 975-1900 all attract big-name entertainers. *Phoenix Little Theater* ☎ 254-2151 has an ongoing series of hit plays, while dinner theater is available at *Max's* ☎ 937-1671. *Ballet West Arizona* ☎ 230-1140 hosts classical and modern dance performances. *Arizona Opera Company* ☎ 840-0841 and the *Arizona State University Lyric Opera Theater* ☎ 965-3398 both present commendable operatic performances.

Shopping

The *Borgata* in Scottsdale is styled after a medieval Italian village, with some 50 luxury boutiques and gourmet restaurants. One of the best shopping locations is the *Biltmore Fashion Park* with exclusive stores including I Magnin and Saks Fifth Avenue. Scottsdale's *Fifth Avenue Shops* include rows of art galleries, restaurants and specialty stores. A major renovation has breathed life back into midtown's open-air *Park Central Mall*. North Phoenix's *Metrocenter* has close to 400 stores and eateries. Mesa's *Fiesta Mall* is one of the area's most popular, featuring top chain stores, specialty shops, restaurants and bars.

Sightseeing

Desert Botanical Garden More than 10,000 plants; continuous guided tours. *1201 N Gavin Pkwy. Open 9–sunset.*

Heard Museum A collection of anthropology and primitive arts. *22 E Monte Vista Rd. Open 10–4.45; Sun, 1–4.45.*

Phoenix Zoo 1,000 or so animals, most in carefully reconstructed environments, located in the scenic Papago Park, a desert mountain preserve. *5810 E Van Buren. Open 9–5.*

Guided tours

Jeep tours The spectacular Arizona desert is well worth exploring by jeep safari. Recommendations include *Arizona Desert Jeep Adventures* ☎ 948-9192, *Arizona Awareness* ☎ 947-7852 and *Arizona Bound Jeep Tours* ☎ 994-0580.

Bus and van tours *All Round Valley Tours* ☎ 951-2110; *Champagne Cowboy Tours* ☎ 992-7791; *Windows on the West Tours* ☎ 840-8245. *Gray Line/Sun Valley Bus Lines* ☎ 254-4550 can accommodate large groups.

Aerial tours Take a leisurely view of the Valley with the *Unicorn Balloon Company of Arizona* ☎ 991-3666 or, for a swifter ride, *Paradise Valley Aviation* ☎ 998-7205.

Out of town

Grand Canyon is a 5–6hr drive from Phoenix, and its spectacular rock formations are the area's major tourist attraction. Reservations are a must if you plan to stay overnight; call Grand Canyon National Park Lodges ☎ 638-2631.

Spectator sports

Baseball The *Phoenix Giants* play minor league ball at Phoenix Municipal Stadium, 5999 E Van Buren ☎ 275-4488. In spring several major league teams train in Phoenix.

Basketball The *Suns* play Oct–May at Veterans Memorial Coliseum, 1826 W McDowell ☎ 263-7867.

Horse racing *Turf Paradise*, 1501 W Bell Rd ☎ 942-1101 has thoroughbred racing Oct–mid-May.

Keeping fit

Many hotels have extensive recreational facilities.
Golf Popular courses include *The Phoenician Golf and Tennis Resort*, 6255 E Phoenician ☎ 990-0029; *Arizona Biltmore*, 24th St and Missouri Ave ☎ 955-6600; *Orange Tree Golf Club*, 10601 N 56th St ☎ 948-3730; and *Papago Golf Course*, Papago Park ☎ 275-8428.
Tennis Public courts that are locally popular include *Encanto Park*, 15th Ave and Encanto Dr ☎ 253-3963; *Hohokam Tennis Center*, 1235 N Center St, Mesa ☎ 834-2149; and *Indian School Park*, 4289 N Hayden Rd, Scottsdale ☎ 994-2740.

Local resources

Business services

Photocopying and printing *Alphagraphics* ☎ 252-7002 is a nationwide chain known for dependable while-you-wait or same-day service. Many branches will pick up and deliver.
Secretarial *Manpower Temporary Services* ☎ 264-0237; *Temporaries Inc* ☎ 253-0880; *Employers Overload* ☎ 264-4080.
Translation *Berlitz Translation Services* ☎ 265-7333; *Professional Interpreters Corp* ☎ 998-8915.

Communications

Local delivery *Moody's Quick Courier Service* ☎ 861-2121; *Dial-a-Messenger* ☎ 274-6060.
Long-distance delivery *Federal Express* ☎ 254-4662; *Express Emery Worldwide* ☎ 273-7567; *DHL Worldwide Express* ☎ 244-9922.
Post office 4949 E Van Buren ☎ 225-3434 and downtown at 522 N Central Ave ☎ 261-4071.
Telex *Western Union* ☎ 258-0044.

Conference/exhibition centers

For large-scale conventions contact *Phoenix Civic Plaza* ☎ 262-6225.

Emergencies

Hospitals *Phoenix General Hospital*, 1950 W Indian School Rd ☎ 279-4411; *St Joseph's Hospital and Medical Center*, 350 W Thomas Rd ☎ 285-3000; *St Luke's Medical Center*, 180 E Van Buren ☎ 251-8100; *Good Samaritan Medical Center*, 1111 E McDowell Rd ☎ 239-2000; *Scottsdale Memorial Hospital*, 7400 E Osborn Rd ☎ 994-9616.
Pharmacies *Walgreen's*, *Long's* and *Drug Emporium* all have several locations in the area. Also *24 Hour Drugs*, 1023 E Indian School Rd ☎ 274-5981.
Police The main office is 620 W Washington ☎ 262-6151.

Information sources

Business information The *Phoenix Chamber of Commerce* ☎ 254-5521 is just one of 18 throughout the Valley. For information about a specific area, contact the *Arizona Chamber of Commerce* ☎ 248-9172. One of the most helpful sources of information is the *Phoenix and Valley of the Sun Visitors and Convention Bureau* ☎ 254-6500.
Local media The *Arizona Republic* and the *Phoenix Gazette* are the largest morning and afternoon daily papers serving the Valley. The monthly *Metro Phoenix Magazine* is an excellent local entertainment and events guide.
Tourist information *Arizona Office of Tourism*, 1480 E Bethany Home ☎ 255-3618; *Phoenix and Valley of the Sun Visitors' and Convention Bureau*, 505 N 2nd St, Suite 300 ☎ 254-6500.

Thank-yous

Florists *Phoenix Flower Shops*, 5012 E Thomas ☎ 840-1200; *My Florists, Inc*, 534 W McDowell ☎ 258-7401; *Cactus Flower* 10822 N Scottsdale Rd ☎ 948-1130.
Gift baskets For gift baskets filled with native products try the *Sphinx Date Ranch*, 6802 E McDowell Rd, Scottsdale ☎ 941-3468, or *Arizona Sun Products*, 7014 E 5th Ave, Scottsdale ☎ 941-9088.

PITTSBURGH

Area code ☏ 412

Once a gritty steel town, Pittsburgh is now a center of business, finance and education and home to such corporations as Westinghouse Electric, USX, Rockwell International and National Intergroup. As the steel industry declines, a service-oriented economy is taking over. Carnegie-Mellon University spearheads Pittsburgh's advances in computer software. But the city is still blue-collar in attitude despite the increase in white-collar workers and young professionals.

Arriving

Greater Pittsburgh International Airport

All international travellers arrive at Gate 45; baggage collection and Customs are just steps away. You can expect to be on your way in 30–45min. For those arriving on domestic flights, baggage collection can be as far as 10min from the arrival gate. Currency can be changed at *Tele-Trip* ☏ 264-4580, open daily 6am–10pm in the main concourse, and at the *Mutual of Omaha Service Center* in the main lobby. *Pittsburgh National Bank* has a branch in the main terminal, open 9.30–4. There is a full range of airport services; most close by 9pm but a restaurant is open 24hrs. For airport information ☏ 778-2525.

Nearby hotels *Airport Hotel*, GPIA Mezzanine Level 15231 ☏ 264-8000. *Hilton Airport Inn*, 1 Hilton Dr 15231 ☏ 262-3800. *Holiday Inn–Pittsburgh International Airport*, 1406 Beers School Rd 15108 ☏ 262-3600. *Sheraton Airport Hotel*, 1160 Thorn Run Rd, Coraopolis 15108.

City link It is a 30min drive to Pittsburgh's downtown Golden Triangle, though the morning and evening rush hours (7–9, 4–6) can add 30min.

Taxi Taxi stands are just outside both airport terminals; fare to downtown Pittsburgh averages around $20–25.

Car rental Avis ☏ 262-5160, Hertz ☏ 262-1705, Dollar ☏ 262-1300, Budget ☏ 262-1500 and National ☏ 262-2312 operate desks on the lower level of the main terminal.

Limousine Limo Center ☏ 923-165.

Bus Airport Limousine Service ☏ 471-8900 operates half-hourly in the morning and evening and every 20min in the afternoons, from 7am to 1am. Buses leave from the lower level of the main terminal and stop at most of the major downtown hotels; cost is around $6.

Getting around

Because Pittsburgh streets tend to follow topography, finding your way around the hills and rivers can be confusing. The downtown section is not large, however, and a visitor can easily cover most of it on foot.

Taxi There are not many cabs available on the street, so plan on phoning, with a 15–30min wait. Recommended firms include *Yellow Cab* ☏ 665-8100 and *Colonial Taxi* ☏ 833-3300.

Car rental See *City link.*

Subway The *Light Rail Transit System* operates only for three downtown stops, but is quick, reliable and free (before 7pm).

Bus The bus network mainly links the suburbs with downtown; it is not useful for the city center.

Area by area

Downtown The downtown business area is known as the Golden Triangle and is bordered by the Allegheny and Monongahela rivers. Its skyline is dominated by Philip Johnson's neo-Gothic glass tower for PPG Place, which holds numerous smart boutiques. Other older and no less extravagant architectural confections are scattered about, legacies from industrialists such as Frick, Carnegie and Mellon. The city's financial activity is centered on Grant Street.

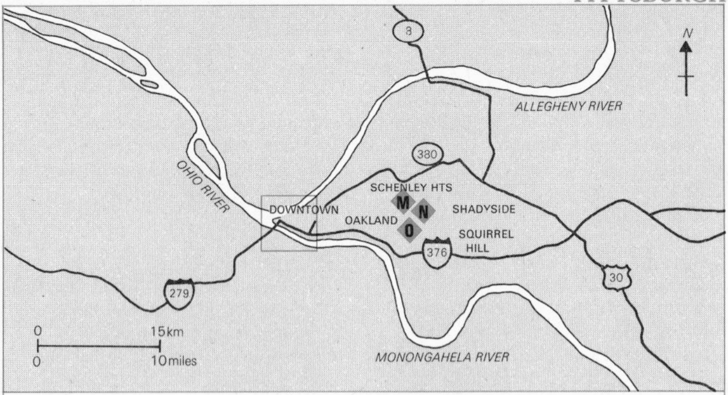

HOTELS

- **A** Hilton and Towers
- **B** Hyatt at Chatham Center
- **C** Sheraton at Station Square
- **D** Westin William Penn
- **E** La Vista
- **F** Bigelow
- **G** Marriott Inn

RESTAURANTS

- **A** Carlton
- **B** Common Plea
- **C** Grand Concourse
- **D** Hyeholde
- **E** La Normande
- **F** Top of the Triangle

BUILDINGS AND SIGHTS

- **A** Civic Center
- **B** Convention Center
- **C** Allegheny County Courthouse
- **D** City County Building
- **E** Gateway Towers
- **F** Heinz Hall
- **G** One Mellon Bank Center
- **H** Station Square
- **I** Three Rivers Stadium
- **J** US Steel Building
- **K** Aviary
- **L** Buhl Science Center
- **M** Carnegie Institute Museum of Art
- **N** Frick Art Museum
- **O** Phipps Conservatory

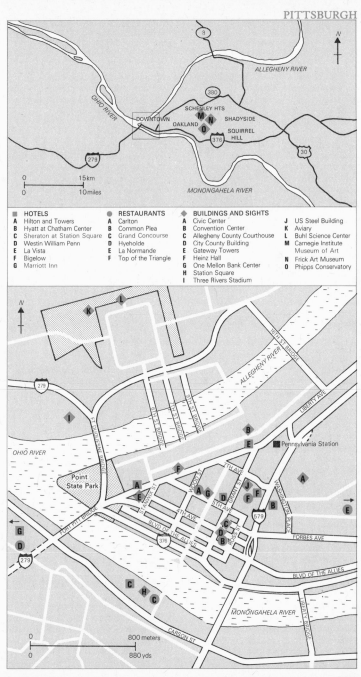

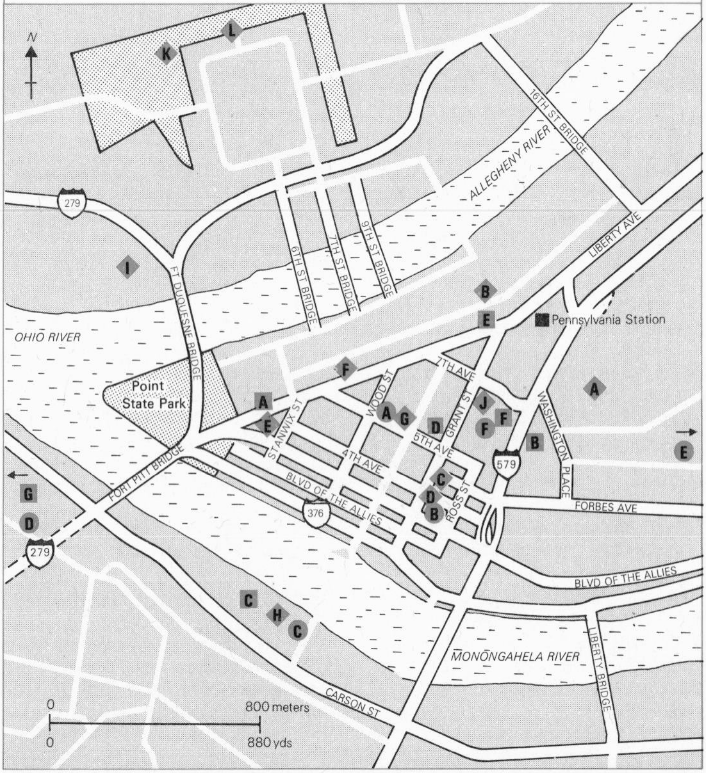

Just across the Monongahela River is Station Square, a converted railroad terminal with shops, restaurants and bars. This area also has a number of computer software firms. Also in the downtown area is Point State Park, 36 acres of gardens near where the Monongahela and Allegheny rivers converge to form the Ohio.

Oakland Just E of downtown is Oakland, site of the University of Pittsburgh and Carnegie-Mellon University, two of the city's seven major educational institutions. Most of Pittsburgh's high-tech industry is clustered around the university area. Just across Forbes Avenue from the Pitt campus's Cathedral of Learning is the Carnegie Institute (see *Sightseeing*).

Shadyside and Squirrel Hill Continuing E on Forbes Avenue will take you to Shadyside and Squirrel Hill, both fashionable neighborhoods which have recently seen a huge influx of young professionals. The area has many smart shops and restaurants, along with some of the city's most popular nightspots.

The suburbs

Old money and established families can be found in *Sewickley* and *Sewickley Heights*, two of the most affluent neighborhoods in eastern United States. Both are to the N of Pittsburgh on the Ohio River. Also in the N is *Fox Chapel*, another desirable residential area, with woodland and quiet country roads. Fashionable addresses S of Pittsburgh include *Mount Lebanon* and *Upper St Clair*.

Hotels

Pittsburgh has only a limited selection of hotels, most of which cater mainly to business travellers. All of the hotels listed below are within easy walking distance of most major corporation offices.

Hilton and Towers $$$$
Gateway Center 15222 ☎ 391-4600 • 800 rooms, 45 suites, 2 restaurants, 2 bars
On a downtown site overlooking the "big three" rivers, the Hilton is especially convenient for those with business in the towering Gateway Center. Sterling's restaurant, in the main lobby, is often filled with business diners. Barber, drugstore • health club • 21 meeting rooms, teleconferencing, translation.

Hyatt at Chatham Center $$$
112 Washington Pl 15219 ☎ 471-1234 TX 812364 • 404 rooms, 20 suites, 2 restaurants, 2 bars
Commanding a fine view of downtown Pittsburgh, the Hyatt is convenient to corporate headquarters and to the nearby Civic Arena. The Regency Club's two executive floors provide some of the city's choicest business-oriented accommodation; make sure you are given a room with adequate work space. Health club, pool, sauna, whirlpool • 7 meeting rooms.

Sheraton at Station Square $$$
7 Station Square Dr 15219 ☎ 261-2000 • 293 rooms, 53 suites, 2 restaurants, 2 bars
Just across the river from downtown, the Sheraton, with its futuristic lobby, is a favorite with business travellers dealing with the Station Square area's high-tech companies. Hairdresser, florist • sauna, jacuzzi, exercise equipment • 14 meeting rooms.

Westin William Penn $$$$
530 William Penn Way, Mellon Sq 15230 ☎ 281-7100 TX 866380 • 548 rooms, 47 suites, 1 restaurant, 1 bar
Wide corridors, wood paneling and lovely old furniture make the Westin the choice of visiting dignitaries and high-level executives. Its location is unbeatable, virtually across the street

from 18 major corporate headquarters. The Terrace Room, the city's number one spot for business breakfasts, is well suited for business lunches and dinners as well. Access to nearby health club, jacuzzi • 35 meeting rooms, fax.

La Vista $$$$
Liberty Ave at 10th St ☎ 281-3700 • Vista International • 615 rooms, 1 restaurant, 1 bar
This brand-new luxury hotel was scheduled to open in 1987. Across the street from the Convention Center, La Vista promises to offer first-class business facilities, including three executive floors.

OTHER HOTELS

Bigelow ($$) *Bigelow Sq 15219 ☎ 281-5800.* All-suite hotel in downtown.

Marriott Inn ($$$) *101 Marriott Dr, Crafton 15205 ☎ 922-8400 TX 7106442016.* Convenient for business in the SE suburbs.

Clubs

Old money and local powerbrokers can be found at the *Duquesne Club* downtown or the *Pittsburgh Athletic Association* in Oakland. Less exclusive is the *Rivers Club*, which has reciprocal membership with other health clubs.

Restaurants

Eating out in the city is mainly a lunchtime activity, since Pittsburgh's nightlife centers in the outskirts and suburbs. On pleasant days, many business lunchers walk to the numerous restaurants at Station Square.

Carlton $$$
Mellon Bank Center, Grant St ☎ 391-4099 • closed Sun • AE CB DC MC V
The Carlton specializes in prime meat, charcoal-broiled seafood and Cajun dishes. Tables are close together, but the restaurant remains a favorite with business people.

Common Plea $$$
308 Ross St ☎ 281-5140 • closed Sun • AE MC V • no dinner reservations
Near the courthouse, the Common Plea is another established luncheon spot. Seafood and veal are specialties. Seating on the ground floor is cramped; tables upstairs offer more privacy.

Grand Concourse $$$
1 Station Sq ☎ 261-1717 • D only Sat • AE CB DC MC V
One of the city's most attractive restaurants, the Grand Concourse is a renovated railroad station, with soaring ceilings and stained-glass skylights. Its booths are ideal for private business lunches or dinners. Seafood is the specialty.

Hyeholde $$$$
190 Hyeholde Dr, Coraopolis ☎ 264-3116 • D only Sat; closed Sun • AE DC MC V
Occupying an old country mansion, the classy Hyeholde offers expert cooking and excellent wines.

La Normande $$$$
5030 Centre Ave ☎ 621-0744 • D only; closed Sun • AE CB DC MC V • reservations essential
This fine French restaurant in Shadyside is always filled with local and visiting VIPs, and is an excellent choice for entertaining important clients. The weekday *prix fixe* is recommended. Le Bistro, next door and under the same management, offers similar fare less formally.

Top of the Triangle $$$
600 Grant St ☎ 471-4100 • AE CB DC MC V • reservations essential
The view – from the top floor of the US Steel Building – is superb; but the restaurant's main advantage for business people is its spaciousness, with large tables and booths designed for privacy. Cuisine is Continental.

Bars

Many say that the best drinks in town are found at *Froggy's*, 100 Market St, a favorite of young professionals. Local executives tend to head across the Monongahela River to *Chauncy's* at Station Square, South Side. Another popular after-hours spot is *Tramp's*, 212 Blvd of the Allies ☏ 261-1990, a former bordello; the *Top of the Triangle* bar (see *Restaurants*) is a good choice for working discussions. In the Southside, the Marriott's *Cahoots* bar has a loyal clientele.

Entertainment

Information about events can be found in the daily newspapers or in the weekly *In Pittsburgh*. Tickets can be bought at box offices or at the *Tix Booth*, Wood St between 5th and Liberty avenues ☏ 391-8368.

Jazz/nightclubs Most of the best jazz spots are bars and restaurants. The best-known is *Harper's* ☏ 391-1494; others include *Balcony* ☏ 687-0110 and *Brendan's Upstairs* ☏ 683-5656, both in Shadyside; *Hemingway's* ☏ 621-4100 in Oakland; and *Pyramid* ☏ 362-3022 in East Liberty. *Graffiti* ☏ 682-4210, in Oakland, offers a variety of jazz, classical, folk, rock and comedy. For straight rock 'n' roll try the *Decade* ☏ 687-7655 in Oakland.

Theater and music The *Pittsburgh Symphony*, *Opera* and *Ballet* all make their home at *Heinz Hall* ☏ 281-5000 or 392-4800. The *Pittsburgh Public Theater* ☏ 321-9800 and the *Playhouse Theater Center* ☏ 621-4445 offer entertainment ranging from classics to children's shows.

Shopping

The two established downtown department stores are *Kaufmann's* and *Horne's*. The smart shops at *Oxford Center* and *PPG Place* sell a wide and original variety of clothing, gifts and gadgets. Other stylish boutiques can be found at *Station Square* and along *Walnut Street* in Shadyside.

Sightseeing

Aviary A fine collection of tropical and domestic birds in natural settings. *W Ohio and Arch St ☏ 323-7234. Open 9–4.30.*

Buhl Science Center Includes science exhibits, a planetarium, a laser show and (during the winter) a huge model train exhibit. *Allegheny Sq ☏ 321-4302.*

Carnegie Institute Museum of Art A main Pittsburgh attraction, with a collection of paintings, sculpture, furnishings and other works of art. *4400 Forbes Ave, Oakland ☏ 622-3270. Open till 5; closed Mon.*

Frick Art Museum Good collection including Old Masters in an Oakland mansion. *7227 Reynolds St and S Homewood Ave ☏ 371-7766. Closed Mon and Tue.*

Phipps Conservatory Exhibits of orchids, cacti and tropical plants; also seasonal shows. *Schenley Park ☏ 622-6914.*

Guided tours

Boat tours The *Gateway Clipper Fleet* ☏ 355-7980 offers sightseeing and dinner-dance cruises. Boats leave from Monongahela Wharf at Station Square.

Bus tours *Lenzner Coach Lines*, Mt Nebo Rd, Sewickley ☏ 761-7000.

Spectator sports

Baseball The *Pittsburgh Pirates* play at Three Rivers Stadium on the North Side ☏ 323-1150.

Football Three Rivers Stadium is also the home of the *Steelers*. Many businesses have box seats here.

Hockey The *Penguins* play their games downtown at the Civic Arena, Washington Pl, Center and Bedford avenues ☏ 642-1800.

Soccer The Pittsburgh *Spirit* also play at the Civic Arena ☏ 642-1800.

Keeping fit

Most major hotels have facilities of their own or arrangements with local health clubs. The many parks are well used for jogging, walking and

impromptu softball or soccer games.
Health clubs *The Rivers Club*, 1 Oxford Center, Grant St ☏ 391-5227 and *The City Club*, 119 6th St ☏ 391-3300; both offer a full range of facilities, including racquet sports.
Bicycling Rental from *North Park* ☏ 935-1971 and *South Park* ☏ 835-5710.
Golf Some hotels have arrangements with local country clubs. *Schenley Park* in Oakland ☏ 622-6959 is one of the best public courses.
Jogging Two of the largest city parks, *Schenley Park* in Oakland and *Frick Park* in Squirrel Hill, have extensive jogging paths and are reasonably safe during daylight hours.
Tennis There are many public tennis and racquetball courts at local parks throughout the city.

Local Resources

Business services

Photocopying and printing *Quik Print Copy Shop* has several locations downtown, including 545 Liberty Ave ☏ 456-1060 and 207 Smithfield St ☏ 456-1067.
Secretarial *Add Staff Business Centers* ☏ 566-2020 and *Executive Office Services* ☏ 261-0900.
Translation *Berlitz* ☏ 471-0900 and *Inlingua* ☏ 391-3181.

Communications

Local delivery *Fleet Feet Messenger Service* ☏ 261-2675 and *Mercury Messenger Service* ☏ 391-2096.
Long-distance delivery Both national and international destinations are serviced by *Federal Express* ☏ 765-8900 and *DHL Worldwide Courier Express* ☏ 262-2764.
Post office The *Central Post Office*, at Grant and 7th ☏ 644-4500; open 24hrs.
Telex *Western Union* ☏ 288-0415.

Conference/exhibition centers

The city's major convention venue is the *David Lawrence Convention Center* ☏ 282-7711 run by the Pittsburgh Convention and Tourist Bureau.

Emergencies

Hospitals *Allegheny General Hospital*, 320 E North Ave ☏ 359-3252 is the closest hospital to downtown Pittsburgh. Also *Mercy Hospital*, 1400 Locust St ☏ 232-7555. Dental treatment is available at *Kaufmann's* dapartment store, 5th and Smithfield ☏ 232-2365.
Pharmacies *Thrift Drug*, Penn and 6th avenues.

Government offices

Pittsburgh Government Directory ☏ 255-2100; *US Dept of Commerce*, International Trade Administration, Federal Building ☏ 644-2850; *US Immigration and Naturalization Service* ☏ 644-3356.

Information sources

Business information The *Greater Pittsburgh Chamber of Commerce* ☏ 392-4500 will provide information on local businesses.
Local media The two local dailies are the morning *Pittsburgh Post-Gazette* and the evening *Pittsburgh Press*. The weekly *In Pittsburgh* is available free in many restaurants and shops. The monthly *Pittsburgh Magazine* is another source of information on local entertainment and dining.
Tourist information The *Pittsburgh Convention Bureau*, 4 Gateway Center ☏ 281-7711 is useful for up-to-the-minute information on Pittsburgh events. Open Mon–Fri, 9.30–5; Sat and Sun, 9.30–3; closed holidays. For a recorded message of current city activities ☏ 391-6840.

Thank-yous

Florists Florists who accept credit card orders include *Flowers by Salvy and Tom*, 813 Liberty Ave ☏ 281-1300; *Lubin and Smalley*, 126 5th Ave ☏ 471-2200; and *John McClements*, 925 Penn Ave ☏ 261-1041.

ST LOUIS

Area code ☎ 314

St Louis sits at the heart of the Midwest, at the confluence of the Missouri and Illinois rivers with the Mississippi; the city is in Missouri, but parts of the metropolitan area are in Illinois. Despite the song and the city's French fur-trading settler origins, you don't meet people in "St Louie" – you pronounce the "s"! St Louis has always been an important transportation hub – as an inland port, as a railroad center, and more recently as the intersection of four cross-country interstate highways and the site of a busy airport. Today its principal industries are aerospace and medicine. Major companies that have their world and corporate headquarters here include Monsanto, Ralston Purina, Emerson Electric, General Dynamics, Seven-Up, McDonnell-Douglas, Chromalloy American, Kellwood and Interco.

Arriving

Lambert-St Louis International Airport

STL is located 15 miles/24km from downtown St Louis. Its four passenger concourses lead to the main terminal's baggage claim area, adjacent to parking and public transportation: allow 30–60min for the whole operation. Hotel information can be obtained and reservations placed by using free phones in the baggage area. Other services include a bank (7.30–5; Canadian, British, French and German currencies) and various shops, restaurants and bars. For general and freight information ☎ 426-8000.

Nearby hotels *Henry VIII*, 4690 N Lindbergh 63044 ☎ 731-3040. *Park Terrace Airport Hilton*, 10330 Natural Bridge Rd 63134 ☎ 426-5500. *St Louis Airport Marriott*, I-70 at Lambert Airport 63134 ☎ 423-9700.

City link St Louis is a city in which a car is no handicap. All the major car rental firms have desks at STL.

Driving Expect about a 20min drive to downtown, 15min to the Clayton business district.

Taxi Laclede Cab is the largest and most frequently available taxi service ☎ 625-3456; Airport Cab ☎ 427-9348; Yellow Cab ☎ 361-2345. Fares average $12–18.

Limousine Airport limousine vans operate a 15min schedule to downtown and Clayton hotels, for about $6 per passenger.

Bus The Bi-State Bus Co has an express service that leaves every 45min.

Getting around

St Louis has excellent freeways and secondary highways, and most districts can be reached easily and quickly by car or cab. The city bus service is adequate, but slow. Roads lead into downtown like spokes on a wheel. Downtown's N–S streets are numbered; E–W streets have names.

Taxi *Yellow* cabs are available by phone ☎ 361-2345.

Walking The downtown business area is easily walkable; however, it is not advisable to go anywhere on foot after dark.

Area by area

Downtown is the city's hub and business headquarters. In addition it has St Louis's major hotels and best restaurants. Bounded by Market Street on the W, Convention Plaza Drive on the N, the Mississippi River to the E and US Highway 40 to the S, the downtown area is the location for major companies such as Ralston Purina, near Busch Stadium, and Southwestern Bell Corporation, in the heart of the rental business district.

Clayton Just 10min from downtown and 15min from the airport, Clayton

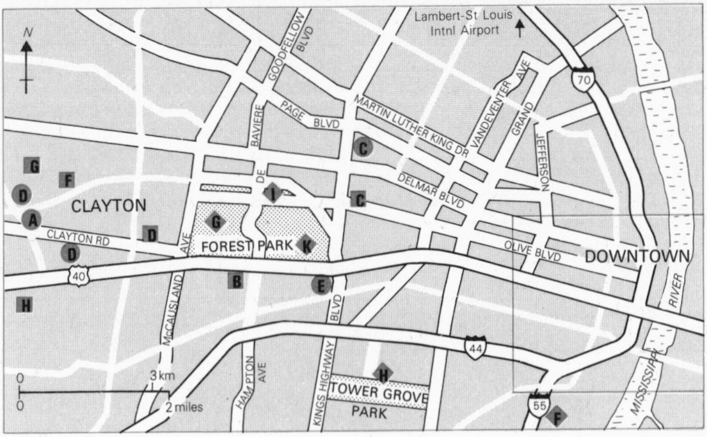

■ **HOTELS**
- **A** Adam's Mark
- **B** Breckenridge Inn
- **C** Chase Park Plaza
- **D** Cheshire Inn and Lodge
- **E** Clarion
- **F** Clayton Inn
- **G** Daniele
- **H** Doubletree
- **I** Embassy Suites
- **J** Marriott Pavilion
- **K** Omni International
- **L** Stouffer Concourse
- **M** Day's Inn at the Arch
- **N** Holiday Inn Riverfront
- **O** Radisson

● **RESTAURANTS**
- **A** Al Baker's
- **B** Anthony's
- **C** Balaban's
- **D** Busch's Grove
- **E** Dominic's Tenderloin Room (Hotel C)
- **F** Tony's

◆ **BUILDINGS AND SIGHTS**
- **A** City Hall
- **B** Convention and Exhibition Center
- **C** Visitors' Center
- **D** Busch Memorial Stadium
- **E** Gateway Arch
- **F** Anheuser-Busch Brewery
- **G** Art Museum
- **H** Missouri Botanical Garden
- **I** Missouri Historical Society
- **J** Old Courthouse
- **K** Science Center

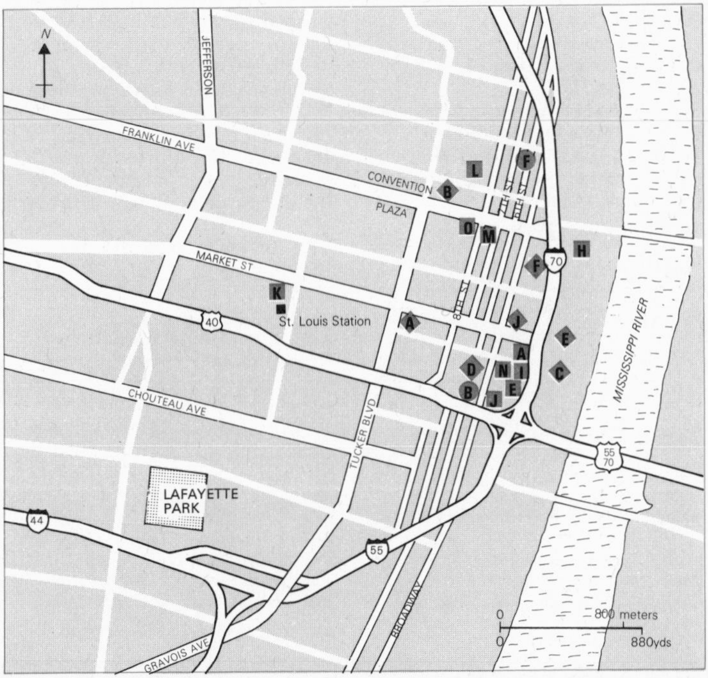

is both a business and wealthy residential area. Graybar Electric, Seven-Up and General Dynamics are among the top-ranking corporations based here. It has many good hotels and fine eating places.

West Port The West Port area, about 20 miles/32km from downtown, has retail stores, restaurants, hotels, office/warehouse buildings and light-industrial plants. The new West Port Plaza has European-style boutiques and a range of restaurants and entertainment.

Highway 40 Another business district is the corridor along Highway 40, W of West Port.

Hotels

St Louis is fast developing as a convention center, and as a result there has been a considerable growth in the number of hotels offering special services for the business visitor.

Adam's Mark $$$
314 N 4th St 63102 ☎ 241-7400 TX 9107640890 • 900 rooms, 89 suites, 6 restaurants, 2 bars
St Louis's newest luxury hotel, the Adam's Mark has indoor health facilities and a special level for VIPs, including private lounge and dining room. Pool, exercise equipment • 30 meeting rooms.

Breckenridge Inn $$$
1335 S Lindbergh 63131 ☎ 993-1100 TX 434383 • 257 rooms, 13 suites, 2 restaurants, 1 bar
This elegant French-style hotel is adjacent to the distinctive Plaza Frontenac shopping center and is convenient for visitors to IBM, Citicorp and Monsanto. Health club • 24 meeting rooms.

Chase Park Plaza $$
212 N Kingshighway (at Lindell) 63108 ☎ 361-2500 • 385 rooms, 31 suites, 3 restaurants, 3 bars
The *grande dame* hotel of St Louis, the Chase has all the amenities one would expect of a luxury hotel. It is conveniently located across from Forest Park. The Tenderloin Room is popular with locals for business entertaining. Barber, shops, pharmacy • 25 meeting rooms.

Cheshire Inn and Lodge $$
6306 Clayton Rd 63117 ☎ 647-7300 • 108 rooms, 10 suites, 2 restaurants, 2 bars
A splendid re-creation of an old English country inn, the midtown Cheshire is beautifully furnished with antiques in every room. Guests are shuttled to and from the airport in an English double-decker bus. Pool, health club • 6 meeting rooms.

Clarion $$$
200 S 4th St 63102 ☎ 241-9500 TX 2911010 • 825 rooms, 50 suites, 1 restaurant, 2 bars, 1 coffee shop
Recently expanded and redecorated, the Clarion is between Busch Stadium and the Arch downtown. Top of the Riverfront, the hotel's 28th-floor revolving restaurant, offers a spectacular view of the Mississippi. Pools, health club/spa and games room • 20 meeting rooms.

Clayton Inn $$
7750 Carondelet, Clayton 63105 ☎ 726-5400 • 220 rooms, 12 suites, 1 restaurant, 2 bars
This modern hotel provides good service, spacious rooms (all with work space) and fine facilities, and is a popular place to stay for those doing business in the Clayton area. Health club • 12 meeting rooms.

Daniele $$$$
216 N Meramec, Clayton 63105 ☎ 721-0101 • 90 rooms, 6 suites, 1 restaurant, 1 bar
Elegant, yet cozy, the Daniele has stylish European décor, a good

restaurant and a piano lounge. Pool, health club access • 2 meeting rooms.

Doubletree $$$
16625 Swingley Ridge Rd, Chesterfield 63107 ☏ 532-5000 • 224 rooms, 12 suites, 2 restaurants, 3 bars
A modern sprawling complex designed for business meetings, the Doubletree is set in a secluded spot, ideal for concentration and relaxation. Sports include racquetball, tennis, handball, fitness center, swimming and nearby golf. Twenty-five meeting rooms, lecture theater.

Embassy Suites $$$
901 N 1st St, Laclede's Landing 63102 ☏ 241-4200 • 300 suites, 1 restaurant
This all-suite hotel is on Laclede's Landing, a good place for dining and nightlife and easily accessible to downtown. Each suite has a refrigerator and bar. Pool, health club • 6 meeting rooms.

Marriott Pavilion $$$
1 Broadway ☏ 421-1776 TX 9107611029 • 671 rooms, 62 suites, 2 restaurants, 1 bar
The Marriott is as popular with the sports crowd as with corporate executives. Health club, pool • 23 meeting rooms, teleconferencing, business reference library.

Omni International $$$$
St Louis Union Station, 1820 Market 63103 ☏ 241-6664 TX 5006103807 • 550 rooms, 30 suites, 3 restaurants, 1 bar
The crown jewel of the refurbished Union Station, the Omni International is one of the best equipped downtown hotels for business travellers. Gift shop • pool, health club • 22 meeting rooms

Stouffer Concourse $$$
9801 Natural Bridge Rd 63134 ☏ 429-1100 TX 709107 • 400 rooms, 18 suites, 2 restaurants, 2 bars
This ultra-modern luxury hotel, just S of the airport, is popular with many of the city's business visitors. Health club, pool, tennis courts • 30 meeting rooms.

OTHER HOTELS
Day's Inn at the Arch ($) *4th and Washington 63102 ☏ 621-7900.* Comfortable and convenient.
Holiday Inn Riverfront ($) *200 N 4th St 63102 ☏ 621-8200.* Close to many downtown businesses.
Radisson ($$) *9th at Convention Plaza 63101 ☏ 421-4000.* Just across from the Cervantes Convention Center.

Clubs

St Louis's business network flourishes through the area's many country clubs. Most are in St Louis County, but the *Missouri Athletic Club* is a private men's club downtown, with elegant dining, meeting and health facilities. The most prestigious and exclusive "old money" clubs are *St Louis Country Club, Bogey Golf Club, Old Warson Country Club* and *Westwood Country Club.* Members of these include the city's businessmen and politicians. An invitation to lunch, dinner or a round of golf can be considered a mark of honor.

Restaurants

St Louis is well supplied with good restaurants, especially Italian ones; and a great deal of business is done in them – not only at lunchtime and in the evening, but also in the morning for breakfast.

Al Baker's $$$
Clayton and Brentwood, Clayton ☏ 863-8878 • D only; closed Sun • AE CB DC MC V
Well thought of for its Continental cuisine, fresh seafood and extensive wine list, Al Baker's is a good place for an important business dinner.

Anthony's $$$$
10 S Broadway ☎ 231-2434 • D only; closed Sun • AE MC V
A favorite with locals and visitors alike, Anthony's is a four-star restaurant specializing in light French cuisine, fresh seafood and excellent wine. The outstanding service and elegant, ultra-modern atmosphere make it equally suitable for a private business discussion or a romantic dinner.

Balaban's $$$
405 N Euclid ☎ 361-8085 • AE MC V
Considered *the* place to be seen in the Central West End, Balaban's features French dishes, Continental cuisine and fresh seafood in the dining room. The downstairs level gives added privacy. The glass-enclosed Parisian-style café provides an à la carte menu.

Busch's Grove $$
9160 Clayton Rd ☎ 993-0011 • closed Sun and Mon • MC V
A St Louis County favorite since the 1890s, Busch's specializes in prime ribs and offers a sound Continental menu. Besides the main restaurant there are individual screened cabins for outdoor dining.

Dominic's $$$
5101 Wilson on the Hill ☎ 771-1632 • D only; closed Sun and Mon • AE CB DC MC V
Dominic's serves Italian *haute cuisine* in opulent surroundings featuring marble statues and oil paintings. Tables are widely spaced. One of the best restaurants in St Louis.

Tenderloin Room $$$
Kingshighway and Lindell ☎ 361-2500 • D only Sat and Sun • AE CB DC MC V
Known for its prime steaks, the Victorian-style Tenderloin Room in the Chase Park Plaza hotel is a St Louis tradition. Chops, seafood and a fine dessert tray are all specialties of the house.

Tony's $$$$
826 N Broadway ☎ 231-7007 • D only; closed Sun and Mon • AE CB DC MC V • no reservations
Tony's is generally acknowledged to be the number one Italian restaurant in St Louis. Tony's takes no reservations, but locals feel a table here is well worth the wait.

Bars

There is no shortage of lounges and bars in the St Louis area. Besides those in the major hotels, some popular bars for talking business include *Laclede's Landing, Central West End, West Port Plaza* and *Union Station.* The "hot spots" include *Brio's*, a crowded disco in West County, and two *Houlihan's*, one in Union Station and one in the Galleria in Clayton.

Entertainment

Classical music, open-air theater, Broadway shows and, of course, Dixieland jazz are all important features of St Louis nighttime entertainment.

Theater The 1,800-seat *American Theater* ☎ 231-7000 brings the best of Broadway to St Louis. On the riverfront, *Goldenrod Showboat* ☎ 621-3311 is a floating dinner theater, staging vaudeville, melodrama and musical revues; often amusingly rowdy. The *Muny* ☎ 361-1900, a 12,000-capacity amphitheater, is the venue for music and plays, with appearances by entertainment's biggest names. The refurbished *Fabulous Fox Theater* ☎ 534-1111 is as much of an attraction as the shows it stages; it consistently hosts top-name stars and shows. *Westport Playhouse* ☎ 878-2424 is a theater in the round, where no seat is more than 30ft from the revolving stage. It offers mainly comedy and musicals.

Music The *St Louis Symphony Orchestra* ☎ 534-1700 is America's second oldest. Its season runs from fall to spring.

Shopping

St Louis is well-served with shopping malls. Two popular suburban centers are *Northwest Plaza* at St Charles Rock Rd at Lindbergh and the *Plaza Frontenac*, Clayton Rd at Lindbergh, which includes high-fashion stores such as Saks Fifth Avenue and Neiman-Marcus. *St Louis Center* is a huge mall in the central business district. But the "must-see" for any visitor is *St Louis Union Station*, a $140m renovation that is now a shopping and entertainment center.

Sightseeing

Anheuser-Busch Brewery Tours A 1hr tour of the world's largest brewery includes the famous team of Clydesdales, a look at the old brewhouse and a sampling of the products. *Broadway and Pestalozzi ☏ 577-2626. Open daily exc Sun and holidays.*

Art Museum A fine building in its own right, the St Louis Art Museum has more than 70 galleries of art treasures. *Forest Park ☏ 721-0067. Open daily exc Mon.*

Gateway Arch, the symbol of St Louis, is America's tallest memorial. Visitors are transported to an observation room, 630ft up. *11 N 4th St ☏ 425-4465.*

Missouri Botanical Garden, which has North America's largest Japanese Garden, also houses the Climatron, a domed greenhouse, and Mediterranean and desert houses. *4344 Shaw Blvd ☏ 577-5100.*

Missouri Historical Society Renowned, colorful exhibits focus on the history of St Louis, Missouri and the American West. Housed in the Jefferson Memorial Building, displays include advertising, firearms, the 1904 World's Fair and Charles Lindbergh memorabilia. *Forest Park ☏ 361-1424. Open Tue–Sun.*

Old Courthouse, dating back to the 1820s, was both the site of slave auctions and the location of the 1847 Dred Scott trial which further inflamed the controversy between North and South concerning slavery. It also houses the Museum of Westward Expansion. *At Gateway Arch ☏ 425-4465.*

Science Center comprises the McDonnell Planetarium, Museum of Science and Natural History and Medical Museum. *Forest Park ☏ 289-4400.*

Spectator sports

Baseball The *St Louis Cardinals*, play at Busch Stadium ☏ 421-3060.

Football The *Cardinals*, known as the Big Red, are also based at Busch Stadium ☏ 421-1600.

Ice hockey The *Blues* play their home games at the Arena Midtown ☏ 781-5300.

Soccer St Louis's *Steamers* are also at the Arena ☏ 821-1111.

Keeping Fit

Health clubs The YMCA downtown, 1528 Locust ☏ 436-4100 has an indoor pool, track, racquetball, and exercise equipment. *Vic Tanny International* ☏ 576-5355 has eight health clubs throughout the area.

Bicycling Forest Park in the city and Queeny Park in the country have bicycle paths. *Freewheelin'*, 6388 Delmar ☏ 721-5905 has bikes to rent.

Golf Two good public courses are in *Forest Park*, 9 and 18 holes ☏ 367-1337; and *Ruth Park*, 9 holes ☏ 727-4800.

Jogging *Forest Park* has numerous paths. Starting on *Wharf Street* below Gateway Arch, you can run 2 miles/3km along the river.

Tennis The *Dwight F Davis Tennis Center* ☏ 367-0220 in Forest Park is open during daylight hours.

Local resources

Business services

Firms that offer complete business support services include *Professional Business Centers*, 906 Olive, downtown ☏ 436-7335 and *Bradlie Business Service*, 222 S Bemiston, Clayton ☏ 726-2496.

Photocopying and printing *Quick*

Print, in Clayton ☏ 726-1110 and West Port ☏ 569-0994 offer free pick-up and delivery. Another choice is *PIP*, whose downtown location is at 620 Olive St ☏ 621-0991.
Photographers For commercial photography, call *Arteaga Photos Ltd*, 5212 Delor, S city ☏ 352-8345; for publicity shots, *Edwyn Studios* 38 N Euclid ☏ 361-4575.
Secretarial *Kelly Services* has eight offices ☏ 576-7787.
Translation *Berlitz Translation Services*, 200 Hanley ☏ 721-1070 and the *World Affairs Council of St Louis*, 212 N Kingshighway ☏ 361-7333.

Communications

Local delivery *Jiffy Express Package Delivery* ☏ 725-5600 has 24hr service in a 200-mile radius; *500 Courier System* ☏ 664-0643 provides a 1hr special service rush.
Long-distance delivery *Federal Express* ☏ 367-8278 or *Emery Worldwide* ☏ 423-4444.
Post office The main post office is downtown at 1720 Market ☏ 436-5255.
Telex *Western Union* ☏ 421-3967 or *Postal Center Telex International* ☏ 725-8300.

Conference/exhibition centers

For large groups or exhibits, contact the *St Louis Convention and Visitors' Bureau*, 10 Broadway ☏ 421-1023. The downtown *Cervantes Convention Center*'s L-shaped exhibit area contains 240,000 sq ft ☏ 342-5000. *Kiel Auditorium* has five assembly halls, 1400 Market ☏ 241-1010. Midtown's *Arena*, 5700 Oakland ☏ 644-0900 seats almost 20,000.

Emergencies

Hospitals *Washington University Medical Center* ☏ 362-5000 includes the Jewish Hospital of St Louis, the Children's Hospital and Barnes Hospital.
Pharmacies *Walgreen's* and *Medicare Glaser* have several locations, some open 24hrs.
Police *Police Dept–St Louis*, Clark and Tucker, downtown ☏ 231-1212.

Government offices

US Dept of Commerce District Office/International Trade Administration, 120 S Central Clayton ☏ 425-3302; *US Customs*, 120 S Central ☏ 425-3136; *US Immigration and Naturalization Service*, 210 N Tucker ☏ 425-4532.

Information sources

Business information The *St Louis Regional Commerce and Growth Association* (RCGA) is a major source of information and is downtown at 10 Broadway ☏ 231-5555.
Local media *St Louis Post-Dispatch* is the daily newspaper, with global and local coverage. The *St Louis Business Journal* reports area business and financial news. *St Louis Magazine* is a monthly featuring entertainment and cultural events.
Tourist information *St Louis Convention and Visitors' Bureau*, 10 Broadway, Suite 300 63102 ☏ 421-1023.

Thank-yous

Florists Credit card telephone orders are taken by *Tom Carr Florist*, 442 Mansion House Center, downtown ☏ 421-3769; *Town & Country Flowers*, 8127 Maryland, Clayton ☏ 862-2800; *Walter Knoll Florist*, 5501 Chippewa ☏ 352-7575.
Gift Baskets *Pfeifer's Party Pastries and Fine Wines*, 8021 Clayton Rd ☏ 725-2572; and *Professional Presents*, 14792 Timber Bluff Dr ☏ 532-0362.

SAN ANTONIO

Area code ☎ 512

Once little more than a historic tourist resort, the old Spanish city of San Antonio – site of the battle of the Alamo – is rapidly becoming a major industrial and business center. The city was out-distanced in the 1920s by oil-booming Dallas and Houston. But its diversified economy (government, tourism and services industries) spared it the worst of the Texas downturn of the mid-1980s, and new businesses are moving here. Five military bases, including Lackland, the US Air Force's only basic training facility, are important to the local economy, and corporate America is represented by Datapoint, Valero Energy and Fox-Photo. The population of just over 1m is young – average age about 28 – and 53% are Hispanic.

Arriving

San Antonio International Airport

SAIA is served by 15 major and numerous commuter airlines. Terminal 1, where most domestic flights arrive, is relatively new and efficient, and baggage can usually be claimed in less than 15min. International flights arrive at Terminal 2, where it may take travellers up to an hour to retrieve baggage and clear Customs. Information ☎ 821-3411.

Nearby hotels *San Antonio Marriott North*, NW Loop 410 at San Pedro ☎ 340-6060. *Embassy Suites Airport*, 10110 Hwy 281 ☎ 525-9999. *Amerisuites North*, 10950 Laureate Dr ☎ 691-1103. *La Quinta Airport East*, 333 NE Loop 410 ☎ 828-0781 or (800) 531-5900.

City link In normal traffic it takes about 15min to drive downtown. All the hotels listed provide a courtesy car. Otherwise take a taxi (about $11–13) or a VIA limo, which runs to the major hotels every 20–30min, 6am–midnight (about $5). All major car rental firms have counters in both terminals.

Getting around

Downtown San Antonio is compact, and it is possible to walk to almost any destination. However, for business beyond the city center, a taxi, limo or car is essential.

Taxi Cabs can rarely be hailed in the street, but there are usually lines at all major hotels and at taxi stands on the Paseo del Rio (Riverwalk) between E Commerce and Buena Vista. Taxi companies include *Yellow Cab* ☎ 226-4242, *United Taxi* ☎ 733-0852 and *Checker Cab* ☎ 222-2151.

Limousine *Fiesta Limousine* ☎ 431-5466; *Vintage Limousines* ☎ 680-1215.

Bus *VIA Metropolitan Transit* runs many routes out into the suburbs, but they can be time-consuming. Downtown, the VIA San Antonio streetcars run an efficient service on five routes. For further bus information ☎ 227-2020.

Walking The downtown area is easy and safe for walking, and it takes only 15–20min on foot from, for example, the Main Plaza E to Hemisfair. For other downtown locations follow the Paseo del Rio.

Area by area

The city is clustered around a horseshoe bend of the San Antonio River. From the center, the main streets fan out, following the meanderings of old Spanish roads. Superimposed on these is a system of interstate expressways.

Downtown San Antonio is marked by district boundaries – Market Square on the W and Hemisfair Plaza on the E. The city center, at the Alamo and Paseo del Rio, is a mix of business and tourist attractions. Its

1920s and 1930s skyscrapers, such as the copper-roofed Tower Life and ornate brass-decorated Nix Professional Building, are still the city's prestigious office addresses – although the newer glass-curtain wall buildings, Interfirst, One Riverwalk and Republicbank Plaza, have become fashionable. Paseo del Rio has been revitalized, and a pedestrian mall is being built.

North Star Mall and Loop 410 The mile-long enclosed North Star Mall is the focus of expansion to the N of the city. New business development is also spreading rapidly N along the interstate highway to San Pedro and out W along Loop 410.

Northwest suburbs The NW is in a growth stage, with new housing areas and several high-tech businesses, such as Sea World and Texas Research Park. The siting of the South Texas Medical Center, near Loop 410 to the NW, and the establishment of the university nearby have been the catalysts for expansion in this area.

Residential areas There are three prime residential areas in San Antonio. King William, just three blocks to the S of the city center, is a neighborhood of splendid 19thC mansions, each tastefully restored. Monte Vista, N of downtown, is distinguished and equally affluent. Alamo Heights, Terrell Hills and Olmos Park, just 10min to the NW of Monte Vista, are the prestige suburbs, collectively known by the "09" at the end of their zip code.

Other areas The W and S sides of the city are predominantly working class and Hispanic, with a few professional families. Eastside is mainly working class.

■ HOTELS
A Fairmont
B Four Seasons
C Hyatt Regency
D La Mansion del Norte
E La Mansion del Rio
F St Anthony Inter-Continental
G Wyndham
H Emily Morgan
I Hilton Palacio del Rio
J Marriott Riverwalk

● RESTAURANTS
Anaqua Room (Hotel B)
A Arthur's
B Chez Ardid
C L'Etoile
D La Provence
E PJ's Restaurant and Bar

◆ BUILDINGS AND SIGHTS
A City Hall
B Convention Center
C Visitor Information Center
D Alamo
E El Mercado
F La Villita

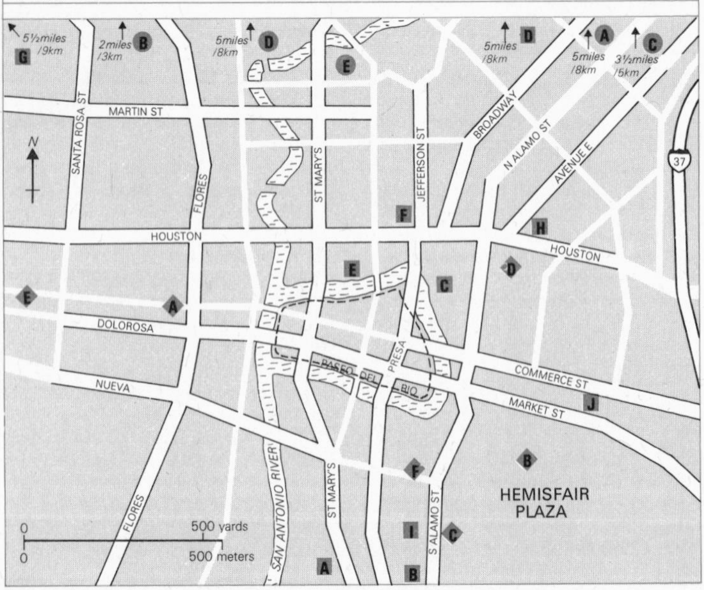

Hotels

Business hotels are becoming extremely competitive, and even the luxury establishments often have promotional packages.

Fairmont **$$$$**
401 S Alamo ☏ 224-8800
TX 5106018532 • 20 rooms, 17 suites, 1 restaurant, 1 bar
This meticulously restored three-story Italianate Victorian building garnered international attention as the heaviest building ever moved. The lobby is intimate yet splendid, with lots of Italian marble; the rooms are the best-appointed in San Antonio and have four-poster beds. Three meeting rooms.

Four Seasons **$$$$**
555 S Alamo 78205 ☏ 229-1000
TX 767381 • 242 rooms, 10 suites, 1 restaurant, 1 bar, 1 coffee shop
Although not so well endowed with business facilities as the Hyatt, the Four Seasons has an aura of serene elegance. Rooms have balconies overlooking tiled courtyards and lush grounds. Sauna, tennis courts, pool, croquet green • 14 meeting rooms, recording facilities.

Hyatt Regency **$$$$**
123 Losoya 78205 ☏ 222-1234
TX 767249 • 632 rooms, 30 suites, 3 restaurants
Modern and luxurious, the Hyatt is admirably located for downtown business and has a wide range of business facilities. Rooftop pool, reduced rates at downtown YMCA corporate health club • 17 meeting rooms.

La Mansión del Norte **$$$**
37 NE Loop 410 78216 ☏ 341-3535
TX 767478 • 292 rooms, 2 restaurants
For visitors doing business around the airport and the South Texas Medical Center, this is a convenient and comfortable option. The hotel has a fountain courtyard, complete with palms and banana plants. Pool • 8 meeting rooms, secretarial service.

La Mansión del Rio **$$$$**
112 College St 78205 ☏ 225-2581
TX 767478 • 24 rooms, 11 suites, 2 restaurants, 2 bars, 1 coffee shop
A hacienda-style hotel, La Mansión has excellent rooms overlooking the river. The inner courtyard, with its pool and scarlet bougainvillea, is a pleasant retreat. The hotel is always fully reserved a year in advance of the April Fiesta. Pool • 11 meeting rooms.

St Anthony Inter-Continental **$$$$**
300 E Travis 78298 ☏ 227-4392
TX 203481 • 227 rooms, 83 suites, 2 restaurants
Old-fashioned and distinguished, this lovingly restored turn-of-the-century hotel specializes in traditional, personal service. Roof garden • pool, weight room • 19 meeting rooms, fax, translation.

Wyndham **$$$**
9821 Colonnade 78238 ☏ 691-8888 • 328 rooms, 3 suites, 2 restaurants
Its polished granite façade and marble interior, furnished with chandeliers, Oriental rugs and masses of fresh flowers, give the Wyndham an air of *grande luxe*. It is conveniently located, just 10min from the airport and the medical center. Pools and jacuzzi, sauna, nearby racquetball club • 16 meeting rooms.

OTHER HOTELS

Emily Morgan ($$$) *705 E Houston ☏ 225-8486.* An elegant hotel near the Alamo.

Hilton Palacio del Rio ($$$) *200 S Alamo ☏ 222-1400.*
Just across from the Convention Center.

Marriott Riverwalk ($$$) *711 E Riverwalk ☏ 224-4555.* Conveniently located for downtown business.

Clubs

If you are doing business in San Antonio, there is a good chance that the deal may be clinched in one of the city's private clubs. Top of the list for those in business are the *City Club* and the *Plaza Club* – conveniently opposite City Hall and the resort of many top government officials. Both have reciprocal membership privileges within the Club Corporation of America. The atmospheric *Club Gireau*, in a restored limestone house, is up-and-coming; the *Argyle* is in the smart "09" district. The *San Antonio Country Club* is the oldest and most exclusive in town, but it plays only a peripheral role in the city's business life.

Restaurants

San Antonio has many informal Mexican eating places, but for important business meals, top executives choose one of the city's French restaurants.

Anaqua Room **$$**

555 S Alamo (in the Four Seasons Hotel) ☏ *229-1000* • *AE CB DC MC V*
The setting and food – Continental/French – are superlative. Ring-neck pheasants stride through the beautiful grounds and tiled courtyards.

Arthur's **$$**

4001 Broadway ☏ *826-3200* • *D only* • *AE MC V*
An elegant glass box overlooking the 300-acre Brackenridge Park, Arthur's has Oriental décor and Continental French cuisine. Specialties include New Orleans carpetbag steak (stuffed with fried oysters and served with béarnaise sauce).

Chez Ardid **$$**

1919 San Pedro ☏ *732-3203* • *AE MC V* • *jacket required at dinner*
This classic Italianate house has a skylit atrium and intimate, elegant side rooms. Its cool, restrained elegance and mainly French cuisine are popular with a young business clientele.

L'Etoile **$$**

6016 Broadway ☏ *826-4551* • *AE MC V*
Owned by the partnership that ran Place Vendôme in Washington DC, L'Etoile has a Parisian brasserie atmosphere, with brass ceiling fans and wooden balconies. The French menu is innovative, and the service is excellent.

La Provence **$$**

206 E Locust ☏ *225-0722* • *D only* • *AE DC MC V*
Expect conservative, classic French cuisine and excellent service in this converted 1920s mansion. The lamb is particularly good.

PJ's Restaurant and Bar **$$**

700 N St Mary's ☏ *225-8400* • *AE CB DC MC V*
A favorite business lunch and dinner place overlooking Riverwalk, PJ's specializes in Continental French cuisine. Its wine list is impressive, the menu inventive.

Tex-Mex

No visitor to San Antonio should leave without sampling the local Texan brand of Mexican food, "Tex-Mex," which features gooey, chili-smothered enchiladas.

Downtown, the best places to try Tex-Mex cooking are *Mi Tierra* ☏ 225-1262, 24hr, or *La Margarita* ☏ 227-7140 in El Mercado. Also downtown are the *Cadillac Bar* ☏ 223-5533, fashioned after its famous counterpart in Nuevo Laredo, Mexico, and *Mario's* ☏ 223-9602, the late-night spot for politicians.

Bars

San Antonio's bar life is concentrated in hotels and restaurants. Downtown there are numerous spots on the Paseo del Rio where you can sip a margarita. The city's young professionals flock to a revived area in the 3000 block of N St Mary's Street, where there is a row of trendy restaurants and bars ranging from the sedate to the funky.

Entertainment

Nightclubs offer dancing and live music, from country & western to jazz. *Jim Cullum's Jazz Band* is a permanent feature of the Hyatt Regency (see *Hotels*) from Fri to Sun. There is also jazz at *Arthur's* (see *Restaurants*). For soft rock, it's *PJ's Band* at One Riverwalk Place (see *Restaurants*).

Theater and music The *San Antonio Performing Arts Association* ☏ 224-8187 has a good record for attracting a variety of internationally known performers. The *San Antonio Symphony* ☏ 223-5591 also imports major stars and visiting conductors.

Shopping

In San Antonio the obvious shopping attractions are Mexican and Central American items. *Market Square, El Mercado*, W of downtown, is good for piñatas, curios and ceramics. Also downtown are two major stores – *Joske's* and *Frost's*. Out of town, *North Star Mall* on Loop 410 has major stores, including Saks Fifth Avenue and Marshall Field's.

Sightseeing

The Alamo, an early 18thC mission where Davy Crockett, Col James Bowie and 184 Texans fought off 5,000 Mexicans in the 1836 struggle for Texan independence, is on Alamo Plaza between Commerce and Houston streets. *La Villita* ("the little town") ☏ 299-8610 is a restored village reflecting San Antonio's Spanish origins. *King William* district is an area of exquisitely restored Victorian mansions along the river, just S of the city center. If you have time, you can follow the *Mission Trail*, which takes in San Antonio's 18thC missions including *Mission Concepción*, the oldest, and *Mission San José*, the best preserved. Missions open daily 9–6 ☏ 229-5701.

Guided tours

Bus tours *Alamo Tours* ☏ 735-5019, *Going Our Way Tours* ☏ 737-0318 and *Gray Line Sightseeing Tours* ☏ 227-5371.

Boat tours The *Paseo del Rio River Boats* ☏ 222-1701 provide daily, leisurely 30min trips along the downtown San Antonio River.

Horse-drawn carriages line up in front of the Alamo daily.

Out of town

The *LBJ Ranch* on US-290, 75 miles/120km from San Antonio, is a 200-acre ranch donated by President and Mrs Johnson and run by the National Park Service. Bus tours that include Johnson City and the working ranch start and end at the Visitors' Information Center, 317 Alamo Plaza ☏ 644-2241. About a 30min drive from San Antonio is the *Guadalupe River*, a cypress-lined waterway in the still unspoiled heartland of Texas.

Spectator sports

Baseball The *Dodgers*, a Class AA farm team for the Los Angeles Dodgers, play at VJ Keefe Field ☏ 434-9311 Apr–Aug.

Basketball The city's only major league club, the *Spurs*, play home games at the Convention Center Arena, Hemisfair Plaza ☏ 224-9578.

Keeping fit

The downtown YMCA, 903 N St Mary's ☏ 227-5221 has facilities to rival private health clubs, including swimming, aerobics, weight room and sauna.

Bicycling Bikes can be rented from the *Four Seasons* (see *Hotels*) and at *Brackenridge Park*. The 10-mile/25km San Antonio Missions Hike and Bike

Trail passes three of the four missions. Parts of the trail are isolated, so you will want company.
Golf Municipal golf courses include one at *Brackenridge Park* ☏ 821-3000 and *Oak Hills Country Club* ☏ 341-0823.
Jogging *Friedrich Park*, 21480 Milsa Rd, has splendid wilderness trails. Do not jog alone.
Racquet sports *McFarlin Tennis Center*, 1503 San Pedro ☏ 732-1223 is city-sponsored and has a nominal fee.

Local resources

Business services

For comprehensive services, the downtown best is *Headquarters Co* ☏ 226-7666. They will pick up and deliver. For a northside location, call *Susan Money Temporaries*, 8023 Vantage ☏ 525-8900.
Photocopying and printing *Kwik-Kopy Printing* has shops all over town – downtown ☏ 224-5589, northside ☏ 340-3488. They will pick up and deliver.
Translation *Berlitz Translation Services* ☏ 681-7050 and *East West Center* ☏ 344-2082.

Communications

Local delivery *Alamo Courier Service* ☏ 433-9133 or *SOS Express* ☏ 654-3111.
Long-distance delivery *Federal Express* ☏ 271-0561.
Post office The downtown post office is at 615 E Houston ☏ 227-3399. Special delivery ☏ 657-8524. All post offices open 8.30–5.
Telex *Telex Communiqué* ☏ 341-5248.

Conference/exhibition centers

The *San Antonio Convention Center*, a legacy of the 1968 San Antonio World's Fair, has two exhibition halls and 46 meeting rooms. The nearby *Arena* seats 15,389, and the *Theater of Performing Arts* 2,731.

Emergencies

Hospitals Downtown area, *Santa Rosa Hospital*, 519 W Houston St ☏ 228-2011; Northside area, *Methodist Hospital*, 7700 Floyd Curl ☏ 692-4000. All major credit cards are accepted.
Pharmacies *Eckerd Drugs* has branches in all areas. For 24hr service, *Revco* ☏ 690 1616.
Police *San Antonio Police Dept*, 214 W Nueva ☏ 299 7484.

Government offices

San Antonio City Hall, Military Plaza ☏ 299-7011; *US Customs*, International Airport ☏ 822-0471; *US Immigration and Naturalization Service*, 727 E Durango ☏ 229-6350.

Information sources

Business Information San Antonio has six chambers, the largest being the *Greater San Antonio Chamber of Commerce* ☏ 229-2100, which publishes a yearly guide to San Antonio.
Local media San Antonio has two major daily newspapers: *San Antonio Light* is serious and business-oriented; *Express-News* is more sensational but also has good business coverage. The best business magazine is the *San Antonio Magazine*; investigative articles are in the *San Antonio Monthly*.
Tourist information *Visitors' Information Center*, 317 Alamo Plaza ☏ 299-8155; open 9–5.30 daily.

Thank-yous

Florists *The Rose Shop*, 1903 San Pedro ☏ 732-1161, and *Kelly-Scherrer*, 326 W Josephine ☏ 735-6184; both are near downtown.
Gift Baskets *Creative Alternatives*, 2520 N Main Avenue ☏ 733-8551 and *Woven Hearts*, 1904 San Pedro ☏ 732-6088; both deliver. *Allen's Flowers and Gifts*, 2101 McCullough ☏ 734-6441 does food and wine baskets.

San Diego

Area code ☎ 619

Just a 30min drive from the Mexican border, San Diego is California's oldest city, its second largest and one of its fastest growing. Discovered by the Portuguese explorer Juan Cabrillo in 1542, it continues to attract new residents. Today's city is predominantly one of young people, mostly under 30, who enjoy a near-perfect climate and an easy southern Californian way of life. Aerospace giants Rohr Industries and General Dynamics have their headquarters here. Tourism contributes more than $2bn a year to the area's economy, and the Pacific Fleet injects $4.6bn more. Other important business sectors are electronics, agriculture and research institutes like the Salk Institute of Biological Studies and the Scripps Institution of Oceanography.

Arriving

San Diego Airport

SAN, known locally as Lindbergh Field, has two adjacent terminals, and the farthest gate in either is a 5min walk from the baggage claim. Baggage cart rentals (four quarters) are available. *Tele-Trip Insurance* ☎ 295-1501 operates a currency exchange and Western Union service daily 6.30–5. *California First Bank* (East Terminal ☎ 230-4340) is open Mon–Thu 8.30–4.30, Fri until 6, and there is a 24hr American Express cash dispenser outside the W end of East Terminal. Air freight services are listed in *Flighttimes*, a free brochure available throughout the airport.

Nearby hotels *Sheraton Harbor Island*, 1590 Harbor Island Dr 92101 ☎ 692-2265 (see *Hotels*).

City link *Car rental* It is a 5–10min drive to downtown. All major rental firms have desks in both terminals.

Taxi Taxis are available 24hrs at both terminals. The fare to downtown is about $4.

Bus The Airporter Express ☎ 231-1123 provides 24hr transportation to all major hotels.

Getting around

Car rental A car is by far the best method to get around. If you don't rent at the airport, the major firms also have offices downtown. Parking in downtown is easy, more difficult along the coast in summer.

Taxi Taxis have to be ordered by telephone. *Checker Cab* ☎ 234-4477, *Yellow Cab* ☎ 234-6161 and *Coast Taxi* ☎ 226-8294 are major companies.

Limousine *VIP Limousine* ☎ 299-7000 and *Capitol Limousine* ☎ 296-8373.

Area by area

Downtown In the legal, financial and governmental heart of the city, old buildings are being replaced by attractive hotels, office blocks, condominiums and boutiques. Many Victorian buildings are being restored, especially in the Gaslamp Quarter, the hub of all downtown activity. The $125m bayfront San Diego Convention Center is to be completed by mid-1989.

Balboa Park Bordering downtown to the NE, this site of two world fairs in 1915 and 1935 is where many of San Diego's museums, galleries, theaters and its Zoo are now located.

La Jolla San Diego's leading research institutes, high-tech research and development firms are located in this residential and business area just 10 miles/16km N of Balboa Park.

Point Loma, one of the more desirable neighborhoods, spreads over the hills of almost the entire peninsula between the ocean and San Diego Bay.

Coronado A 2-mile/3km bridge connects this island to the mainland.

North Island Naval Air Station occupies nearly half the area.
Mission Valley is the major shopping center. It stretches NE of Old Town and Mission Hills.
Mission Bay, 10min N of downtown, includes Mission Beach, a wealthy residential area, Pacific Beach and Mission Bay Park, a 4,600-acre aquatic park. In summer, the whole area is very crowded.
Other areas Many computer companies are located in Sorrento Valley, E of La Jolla. General Dynamics is at Kearny Mesa; and Chula Vista, to the S, is home to Rohr Industries.

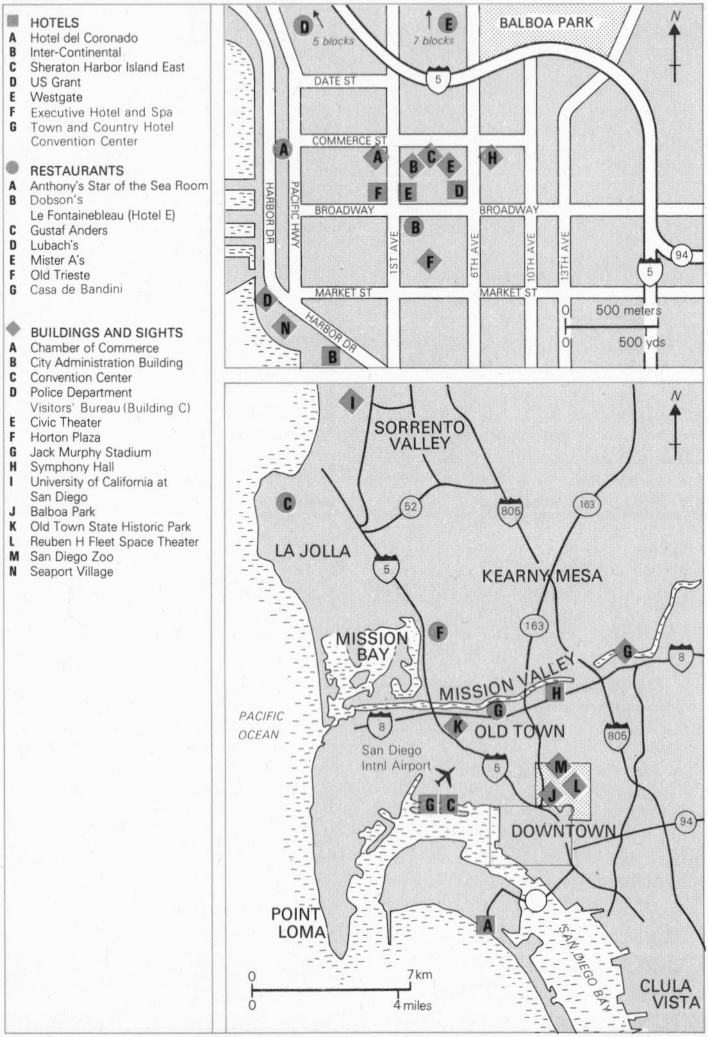

Hotels

Most of San Diego's top hotels are concentrated downtown and in Mission Valley. Several of them have a very extensive range of sports facilities.

Hotel del Coronado $$$$

1500 Orange Ave 92118
☏ 435-6611 • 643 rooms, 37 suites, 3 restaurants, 2 bars, 2 coffee shops

Long popular with US presidents, visiting celebrities and business travellers, this 19thC hotel is also where Marilyn Monroe made the movie *Some Like It Hot*. It is a graceful, turreted building with a perpetually busy lobby, paneled floor to ceiling in dark wood. Suites in the newer beachfront towers are particularly suited to business visitors who want room to work. Health clubs, 2 pools, tennis, power and sailboat rentals at adjacent Glorietta Bay Marina • 30 meeting rooms.

Inter-Continental $$$$

333 W Harbor Dr 92101 ☏ 234-1500 TX 695425 • 681 rooms, 40 suites, 2 restaurants, 1 bar

The striking Inter-Continental, with its mirrored façade, stands at the edge of San Diego Bay and has its own 19-acre marina. Oriental ceramics and other artworks decorate the marbled lobby and lounges; in the inner courtyard pathways meander beside trickling waterfalls. The rooms, which overlook the bay, are modern and comfortable. Hairdresser, gift shops • power boat rentals, 2 pools, 3-mile/5km jogging track, tennis, jacuzzi, sauna • 23 meeting rooms, fax.

Sheraton Harbor Island East $$$$

1380 Harbor Island Dr 92101
☏ 692-2265 TX 697120 • 669 rooms, 40 suites, 2 restaurants, 2 bars

The contemporary Sheraton East overlooks the multimillion dollar Harbor Island marina, and its Tower Club business center has the widest range of facilities of any hotel in the city. Rooms are furnished to a very high standard, and its Nautilus club complex has lighted tennis courts, health club, sauna, pool and a 5-mile/8km jogging track. The excellent Sheppards Restaurant serves French dishes. Forty meeting rooms, recording facilities.

US Grant $$$$

326 Broadway 92101 ☏ 232-3121 TX 183881 • 211 rooms, 62 suites, 2 restaurants, 1 bar

Built in 1910, the US Grant has a distinctly monied atmosphere. Its marble floors, handsome furnishings and the high standards of individual rooms are a strong magnet for its mainly business clientele. The formal Grant Grill and casual Grant Grill Lounge are both quiet and intimate. Complimentary limo to nearby health club • 15 meeting rooms.

Westgate $$$$

1055 2nd Ave 92101 ☏ 238-1818 TX 695046 • 212 rooms, 11 suites, 2 restaurants, 2 bars

Opulently elegant, this is the hotel with cachet in San Diego. Rooms have Louis XV and Louis XVI style furnishings and the bathrooms are in Italian marble. The lobby has Baccarat crystal chandeliers and a Steinway grand piano. White-gloved waiters serve the mainly business and international clientele in Le Fontainebleau (see *Restaurants*). Complimentary limo to nearby health club • 14 meeting rooms.

OTHER HOTELS

Executive Hotel and Spa ($$$) *1055 1st Ave 92101 ☏ 232-6141.*
Sheraton Grand ($$$$) *1590 Harbor Island Dr 92101 ☏ 291-6400.*
Town and Country Hotel-Convention Center ($$$) *500 Hotel Circle N ☏ 291-7131.*

Clubs

Downtown, the exclusive *Cuyamaca Club* and less smart *University Club* are both much used by judges, lawyers and finance executives. The prestigious old-money *San Diego Yacht Club* is in Point Loma. The *La Jolla Beach and Tennis Club* has a celebrity membership.

Restaurants

Many of San Diego's excellent seafood restaurants are on the waterfront downtown. The Old Town is best for Mexican food.

Anthony's Star of the Sea Room $$$$

1360 N Harbor Dr ☎ 232-7408 • D only • AE MC V • jacket and tie • reservations essential

Much used for business entertaining, Anthony's caters to an older, affluent clientele. Floor-to-ceiling windows look out on San Diego Bay. The menu is seafood-only; abalone is a specialty.

Dobson's $$$

956 Broadway Circle ☎ 231 6771 • D only Sat; closed Sun • AE MC V • reservations essential

A restored turn-of-the-century pub, this busy restaurant is much used by business people, politicians and leading lights of the local arts scene. Ask for a table upstairs to overlook the crowded bar.

Le Fontainebleau $$$

1055 2nd Ave ☎ 238-1818 • D only Sat • AE CB DC MC V • reservations 1 week in advance for Sat and Sun • jacket required

Antique French décor and excellent service make this San Diego's most elegant and formal restaurant. Located in the Westgate Hotel, it is popular for business lunches, entertaining and Sunday brunch. The classic French menu, with the emphasis on seafood, includes an excellently priced *prix fixe* meal.

Gustaf Anders $$$$

2182 Avenida de la Playa, La Jolla ☎ 459-4499 • MC V

Considered to be the most sophisticated and relaxed of the area's restaurants, Gustaf Anders serves Scandinavian and Californian cuisine. Sunday brunch here is highly recommended.

Lubach's $$$

2101 N Harbor Dr ☎ 232-5129 • AE MC V • jacket required • reservations essential

Popular for business lunches, Lubach's has been a top San Diego restaurant for more than 30 years. It has a heavily male atmosphere and a menu ranging from lobster thermidor to hamburgers.

Mister A's $$

2550 5th Ave ☎ 239-1377 • D only Sat and Sun • AE CB DC MC V • jacket required

Atop the 5th Avenue Financial Center, Mister A's commands a magnificent view of Balboa Park, downtown and San Diego Bay. Its exclusive air, leather upholstery and wood paneling make it a popular choice for business entertaining. It has an extensive and good wine list.

Old Trieste $$$

2335 Morena Blvd ☎ 276-1841 • D only Sat; closed Sun, Mon • AE CB DC MC V • jacket required • reservations essential

Much favored by San Diego's upper crust, this intimate restaurant serves excellent northern Italian cuisine with an emphasis on fish and veal. The service is also first-class.

Mexican food

Casa de Bandini ☎ 297-8211, which specializes in Mexican seafood, is the best outdoor Mexican restaurant in Old Town.

Bars

Popular with top executives are the *Grant Grill Lounge* (see *Hotels*), *Dobson's* (see *Restaurants*) and *Frenchy Marseilles*, 801 C St ☎ 233-3413. *The Butcher Shop*, 5255 Kearny Villa Rd, Kearny Mesa ☎ 565-2272, is a favorite with the aerospace and high-tech industry.

Entertainment

Good sources of information about current entertainment are *San Diego* magazine and the Sunday arts and the Friday weekend sections of the *San Diego Union*. The *Arts/Entertainment Hotline* ☎ 234-2787 provides recorded information. For tickets, contact *Teletron* ☎ 268-9686.

Music and theater The *San Diego Opera* ☎ 232-7636 attracts top international artists. Performances are at the Civic Theater in the *Convention and Performing Arts Center* ☎ 236-6510, which also hosts trade shows, exhibits, ballets, plays, musicals and rock concerts. The *Old Globe Theater* (a replica of Shakespeare's Globe Playhouse), *Cassius Carter Center Stage* and the outdoor *Festival Stage* comprise the *Simon Edison Center for the Performing Arts* in Balboa Park ☎ 239-2255.

Nightclubs *Pal Joey's*, 5147 Waring Rd ☎ 286-7873 has Dixieland jazz.

Shopping

Downtown's open-air *Horton Plaza* has movie theaters, art galleries, restaurants, four major department stores and more than 150 shops. Designer boutiques, trendy eateries and art galleries line the streets of La Jolla near Girard Avenue and Prospect Street. *Bazaar del Mundo* and the *Galleria* in Old Town have shops selling everything from South American textiles to gaily painted Mexican pottery.

Sightseeing

Balboa Park, covering more than 1,000 acres at the edge of downtown, contains the San Diego Zoo and most of the city's museums, including the Museum of Art, Natural History Museum, and the Reuben H Fleet Space Theater and Science Center. ☎ *239-0512 for opening times.*

Old Town Part of San Diego's original settlement can be visited in the Old Town State Historic Park. Guided 1hr tours ☎ 237 6770 leave daily at 2pm.

Reuben H Fleet Space Theater and Science Center features astronomy displays, simulated space flight, a giant screen IMAX theater. *1875 El Prado* ☎ *238-1168.*

San Diego Zoo 40min tram tours cover ground that would otherwise take a day to see. *Zoo Dr* ☎ *234-3153.*

Guided tours

Boat tours *Harbor Extension*, 1050 N Harbor Dr ☎ 234-4111 and *Invader Cruises*, 1066 N Harbor Dr ☎ 298-8066 operate daily cruises and winter whale-watching trips.

Out of town

Tijuana, an unattractive town, is just over the Mexican border in Baja California. In addition to its shopping market, the bullfights are a big attraction.

Spectator Sports

Baseball The *San Diego Padres* ☎ 283-4494 play in San Diego Jack Murphy Stadium.

Football The *Chargers* ☎ 280-2111 are at the Jack Murphy Stadium.

Horse Racing *Del Mar Racetrack* ☎ 755-1141 has thoroughbred racing late Jul–mid-Sep; closed Tue.

Keeping fit

Beaches *La Jolla Cove* has the most beautiful beach. *Coronado Beach*, has excellent swimming.

Bicycling There are many marked bike trails, including some in Balboa Park and around Mission Bay. You can rent from *Bicycleville*, 740 10th St, Imperial Beach ☎ 424-5565 and *Breez'n Bicycle*, 3969 Arista (near

Old Town) ☏ 296-3112.
Fishing Beach, pier and deep-sea fishing are available year-round.
Golf San Diego County has over 60 golf courses, of which *Torrey Pines Municipal*, 11480 N Torrey Pines Rd, La Jolla ☏ 453-0380 is the best of those open to the public.
Jogging Balboa Park has a marked course, and there is a popular run at E Mission Bay and Clairemont Dr.
Tennis The *Balboa Tennis Club* ☏ 295-9278 at the end of Texas St in Balboa Park has public tennis courts. *North Park Recreation Center*, 4044 Idaho St ☏ 296-4747 has outdoor courts.

Local resources

Business services

Headquarters Co, 701 B St (Imperial Bank Tower) ☏ 231-0206 and *The Total Office*, 964 5th Ave ☏ 544-1433; both provide comprehensive facilities.
Photocopying and printing *Sir Speedy*, 444 West C St ☏ 231-2799 and *PIP Printing*, 923 6th Ave ☏ 239-2079.
Secretarial *Victor Temporary Services* ☏ 279-7310 and *A Personal Touch* ☏ 238-1623.
Translation *Berlitz Translation Services* ☏ 297-8392.

Communications

Local delivery *Ambassador* ☏ 296-8501 and *Courier Express* ☏ 292-4668.
Long-distance delivery *Federal Express* ☏ 295-5545 and *DHL* ☏ 275-3890.
Post office Downtown office at 815 E St ☏ 232-5096; main office is at 2535 Midway Dr ☏ 221-3310.
Telex and telegram *ITT Communications* ☏ (800) 922-0184 and *Western Union*, 941 Broadway ☏ 236-0777.

Convention/exhibition centers

Convention and Performing Arts Center, 202 C St 92101 ☏ 236-6500. Open Mon–Fri, 8–5. *San Diego Convention and Visitors' Bureau*, 1200 3rd Ave, Suite 824 ☏ 232-3101.

Emergencies

Hospitals *Hillside Hospital*, 1940 El Cajon Blvd ☏ 297-2251 provides emergency dental treatment; cash payment required. During business hours, the *Dental Society Referral Service* ☏ 223-5391 helps locate dentists. *Mercy Hospital*, 4077 5th Ave ☏ 294-8111 and *UCSD Medical Center*, 225 Dickinson St ☏ 294-6222, have emergency rooms.
Pharmacies *Kaiser Hospital*, 4647 Zion Ave ☏ 584-5555 has a 24hr pharmacy. *Hillcrest Pharmacy*, 520 Washington ☏ 297-3993 and *Medicine Chest Pharmacy*, 2602 1st Ave ☏ 232-3161.
Police 801 W Market St ☏ 236-6566.

Government offices

City of San Diego information ☏ 236-5555; *US Dept of Commerce/International Trade Administration* ☏ 293-5395; *US Customs* ☏ 293-5360; *US Immigration and Naturalization Service* ☏ 233-7036.

Information sources

Business information The *Greater San Diego Chamber of Commerce*, 110 West C St, suite 1600 ☏ 232-0124.
Local Media The *San Diego Union* and *Evening Tribune* are the best dailies for local news; the *Los Angeles Times* prints a local edition with excellent national and international news coverage. *San Diego* magazine profiles people, culture and entertainment.
Tourist information The *International Visitor Information Center*, 11 Horton Plaza ☏ 236-1212 has multilingual staff. The *Visitors' Information Center*, Clairemont Dr and E Mission Bay Dr ☏ 276-8200.

Thank-yous

Florists *Snyder's*, 825 4th Ave ☏ 233-0779 and *Broadway Florists*, 800 Broadway ☏ 239-1228.
Gift baskets *Westgate Gourmet Shop* at the Westgate Hotel ☏ 233-4475.

SAN FRANCISCO

Area Code ☏ 415

First settled by the Spanish in the 18th century, San Francisco was acquired by the United States in 1847. It was a major Pacific Coast port from the 1849 Gold Rush until the 1960s, when Oakland made a successful bid for the containerized shipping business. Today, San Francisco's economy is dependent largely on the $1bn brought to the area by tourists and business travellers; government and service industries are the largest employers. Several of the nation's biggest corporations have major offices or headquarters in the city; among these are Chevron, Bank of America, Bechtel, McKesson, Wells Fargo, Levi Strauss, Castle and Cooke, and First Nationwide Financial. The wider Bay Area, which includes the cities of Oakland, Berkeley and Richmond, is dotted with big corporations, such as Safeway Stores, Intel, Apple Computer, Clorox, Advanced Micro Devices and World Airways. Stanford University and the University of California at Berkeley are the region's major institutions of higher learning.

San Francisco – never called "Frisco" – is one of the most distinctive and appealing American cities, despite the destruction wrought by the Fire of 1906. The natural beauty of its setting, overlooking San Francisco Bay and the Pacific; its temperate climate; and its relaxed, yet sophisticated, lifestyle attract millions of visitors annually, as well as many permanent settlers. Always a cosmopolitan city, it has the largest Chinese community outside Asia; in recent years many Hispanics, Filipinos and blacks have settled here. The city's large homosexual population is significant, both politically and economically.

Arriving

The Bay Area has three international airports – San Francisco, Oakland and San Jose – all within 1hr's driving time of San Francisco. There is a helicopter connection between San Francisco and Oakland airports; services operate Mon–Fri every 30–45min, 6am–10pm; Sat and Sun, 9.20–7.30.

San Francisco International

SFO's three terminals are connected by covered walkways, and it takes no more than 15–20min to walk from one end to the other. A free inter-terminal shuttle service circles the upper level (6am–midnight every 5min).

Domestic flights come into either the recently modernized North Terminal – which has the airport's only restaurant, a video games room, a Christian Science reading room, and a Bank of America cash machine – or the South Terminal, which is currently being renovated. Clearing Customs and Immigration at the International Terminal takes 30–60min, sometimes longer. Citibank and Bank of America branches are open for foreign currency exchange 7am–11pm, and there is a 24hr Citibank cash machine on the lower level. An AT&T Communications Center includes a conference room with teleconferencing capability and a fax machine; you can make long-distance calls 8am–10pm. The staff is multilingual.

The airport has many bars and coffee shops; barber and shower facilities are available during regular business hours. Hotel information, bus schedules, limousine and car rental services are opposite baggage claim areas. Airport information ☏ 761-0800.

Nearby hotels *Clarion*, 401 E Millbrae Ave, Millbrae ☎ 692-6363. *Hilton Inn*, San Francisco Airport ☎ 589-0770 ⊠ 172239. *Marriott*, 1800 Bayshore ☎ 692-9100. *Sheraton Inn*, 1177 Airport Blvd, Burlingame ☎ 342-9200.

City link There is no direct rail or subway connection to San Francisco, but the 16 miles/26km can be driven in under 20min – 40min in the 6–9 morning peak period. All bus, van and taxi stands are on the lower level near baggage claim. Car rental parking lot and inter-terminal shuttles are on the upper, departure level.

Taxi The fare from SFO to downtown is about $25.

Limousine Try Executive Limousine Service ☎ 593-0775 or Armadillo Limousine ☎ 665-1234.

Car rental Parking in San Francisco is either difficult or expensive, and a car is unnecessary for appointments in the downtown or financial districts. If you must rent, try Alamo ☎ 348-8666, which usually has the best rates.

Bus Airporter buses leave every 15min for the terminus at Ellis/Taylor (near the Hilton and Clift hotels) and every 30min for the Fisherman's Wharf and financial district hotels; fare about $6. SuperShuttle vans (maximum 7 passengers) deliver to any area in the city for $7; many hotels operate courtesy shuttle services. The Bay Area Rapid Transit (BART) subway system is also viable for East Bay destinations – look for a SamTrans bus No. 3B to get to the Daly City station.

Oakland International Airport

Oakland handles mainly local and domestic flights. Both terminal buildings have a bar and coffee shop; Terminal 1 has a cocktail lounge. Information ☎ 577-4015.

Nearby hotels *Hilton Inn*, 1 Hegenberger Rd, Oakland ☎ 635-5000. *Hyatt*, 455 Hegenberger Rd, Oakland ☎ 562-6100 ⊠ 335374.

City link The airport is 18 miles/29km from downtown via the Nimitz Freeway and the Bay Bridge. The drive should take no more than 25min, 10am–3pm and after 9pm; add 30min for the morning peak, 6–9am.

Subway During the day, the BART subway train is a quick alternative to driving – there is an AirBART shuttle connection to the Coliseum BART subway station (every 10min, 6am–midnight, Mon–Sat; 9am–midnight, Sun).

Taxi Bay Area Cab ☎ 563-3000; Yellow Cab ☎ 444-1234; Metro Yellow Taxi ☎ 444-4499. The fare to downtown is about $30.

Limousine Ambassador Limousine Service ☎ 881-0800.

Car rental See *San Francisco International Airport*.

Bus Oakland's limited bus service is not a serious option.

Getting around

The best strategy is to rent a car for out-of-town trips, but walk or use taxis and public transportation in town.

Walking The city center is compact, and walking is the best and most enjoyable way to get around, though it is often worthwhile to take a bus or cable car for a few blocks to avoid tramping up one of San Francisco's many hills. For longer distances, or in wet weather, take a taxi, bus or cable car.

Taxi You may not always be able to hail a taxi in the street; call ahead. Fares are about $2.50 for the first mile, $1.20 thereafter. *Yellow Cab* ☎ 626-2345, *Veteran's* ☎ 552-1300, *De Soto* ☎ 673-1414, *Checker* ☎ 885-5822.

Bus and cable car Cable cars operate between the financial district and the hotel area of Nob Hill. For advice on routes ☎ 673-6864. Bus services to Marin, Alameda and San Mateo counties are operated by *Golden Gate Transit* ☎ 332-6600, *AC Transit* ☎ 839 2882 and *SamTrans* ☎ 761-7000 respectively. Each

■ HOTELS
A Hyatt Regency

● RESTAURANTS
A Cadillac Bar
E Ferry Plaza Restaurant on the Bay
F Greens
G Harris' Restaurant
H Hayes Street Grill
K MacArthur Park
L The Mandarin
N Max's Diner
Q Tadich Grill
R Washington Square Bar and Grill

◆ BUILDINGS AND SIGHTS
C City Hall
D Embarcadero Center
E Federal Reserve Bank
F Ferry Building
G Ghirardelli Square
H Moscone Convention Center
I Pier 39
M Coit Tower
N Maritime Museum
O Museum of Modern Art
P Alcatraz Island
Q Yong Memorial Museum
R Asian Art Museum

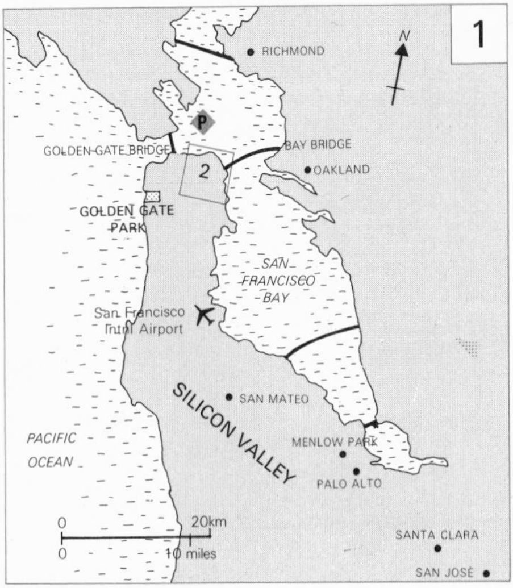

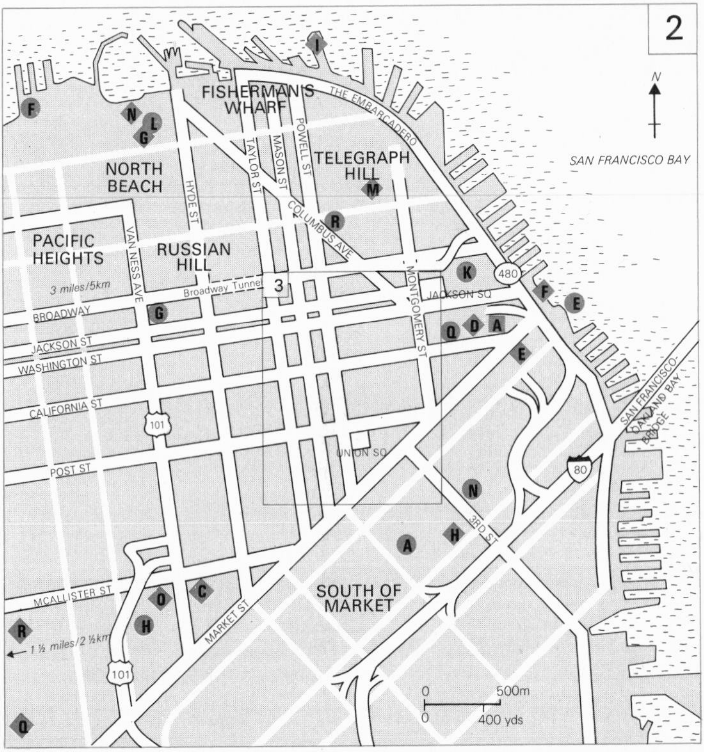

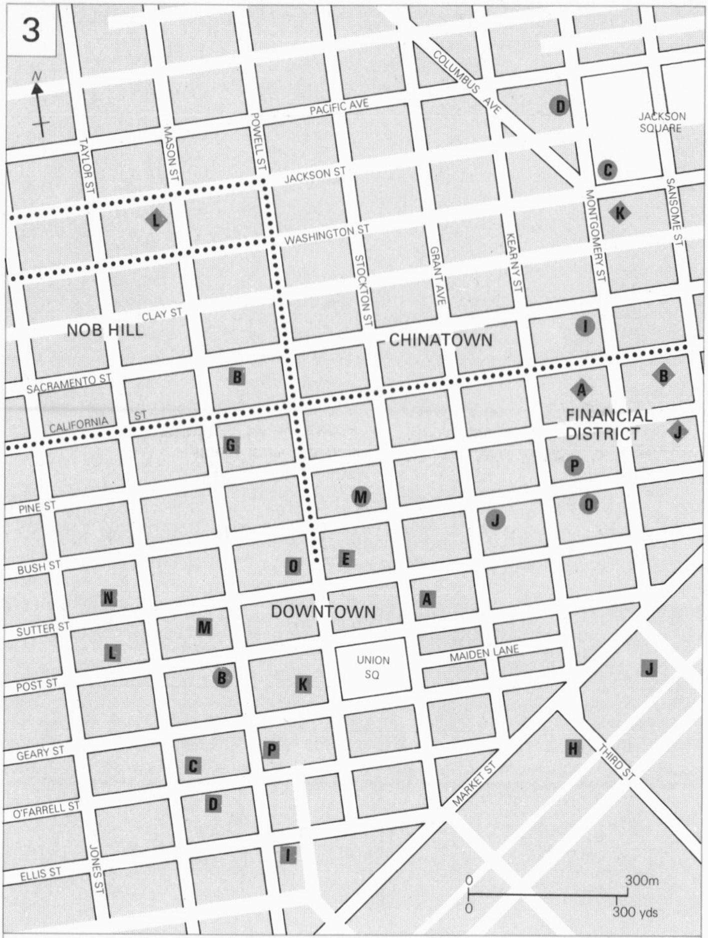

■ HOTELS
- A Campton Place
- B Four Seasons Clift
- C Fairmont
- D Hilton
- E Holiday Inn at Union Square
- G Mark Hopkins Inter Continental
- H Meriden San Francisco
- I Ramada Renaissance
- J Sheraton Palace
- K Westin St Francis
- L Andrews
- M Beresford
- N Canterbury/Whitehall Inn
- O Cartwright
- P King George

● RESTAURANTS
- Campton Place (Hotel A)
- B Donatello
- C Doros
- D Ernie's
- I Jack's
- J Le Central
- M Masa's
- O Orsi Restaurant
- P Sam's Grill and Seafood Restaurant

◆ BUILDINGS AND SIGHTS
- A Bank of America
- B Chamber of Commerce
- J Stock Exchange
- K Trans America Building
- L Cable Car Museum

●●●●● Cable car route

service has its own bus stops, or you can board at the Transbay Terminal on Mission at 1st Street.

Subway The *Bay Area Rapid Transit* (BART) ☎ 839-2220 connects San Francisco to East Bay communities. It is practical, fast and uncrowded outside peak hours, but it suffers from frequent breakdowns. Avoid empty cars and exits at night.

Rail A passenger train service connecting the peninsula cities between San Francisco and San Jose is run by *Caltrain* ☎ 557-8661. The

San Francisco terminus is at 4th and Townsend. It is advisable to call ahead to have a taxi meet your train.
Driving San Francisco has a serious shortage of on-street parking spaces, especially in the downtown and financial districts by day and North Beach at night. However, its simple grid pattern is easy to follow, and despite the hills, the direct route is often the quickest. Elevated freeways connect North Beach and the financial district to the Bay Bridge and both peninsular freeways (Hwy 101, I-280), but peak-hour traffic is heavy, and there are jams every day at the approaches to the Bay Bridge. Delays are frequently caused by accidents or, in winter, by heavy rainfall. Parking is expensive, but the following municipal garages are relatively cheap: *Civic Center Plaza* (enter on McAllister), 5th and Mission (enter on 4th), *Portsmouth Square* (enter on Kearny, between Clay and Washington), *Sutter/Stockton* (enter on Bush), *Union Square* (enter on Post), and *Vallejo Street* (between Powell and Stockton).
Limousine *San Francisco Limousine* ☏ 929-0759 or *Armadillo Limousine* ☏ 665-1234.

Area by area

San Francisco's neighborhoods are neatly delineated and easily identified. Business and commerce are concentrated in the NE corner, residential neighborhoods and suburbs to the W and S.
Financial district This area, a compact wedge between downtown and the Bay, extends from the Transamerica "pyramid," the tallest building in the city, to Market Street, with its easily identifiable high-rises. Montgomery Street is the district's historical center, and the 52-story Bank of America Building sits squarely at the intersection with California Street. The Embarcadero Center is at the bottom of California; the Stock Exchange is on Pine Street at Sansome; and the Federal Reserve Bank is on Market at Drumm.
Downtown San Francisco's main shops, hotels and theaters are downtown. Macy's, Neiman-Marcus, Saks and I Magnin's department stores surround Union Square; nearby Sutter Street and Maiden Lane have scores of galleries and boutiques.
"***Jackson Square***" There *is* no Jackson Square; the area is in fact a few city blocks of Gold Rush-era buildings preserved around Jackson at Sansome. The handsome brick warehouses, built before the 1906 fire, are now occupied by lawyers, advertising agencies, decorators and art dealers. A few blocks N, TV stations, advertising agencies and health clubs surround the all-brick offices of Levi Strauss at the foot of Telegraph Hill.
Chinatown Confined between the high-rises of the financial district and the slopes of Nob Hill, the densely populated residential and business area of Chinatown is a pedestrian corridor between downtown and North Beach and Fisherman's Wharf. It is customarily defined as lying within the eight blocks between Bush and Broadway, bounded by Kearny to the E and Powell to the W. Its Grant Avenue stores cater mainly to the tourist, but on Stockton Street the language, food and customs are authentically Chinese.
North Beach Most of the city's nightlife happens in North Beach's clubs, restaurants and *caffès* – many of them owned by descendants of the Italian immigrants who once dominated the area. Many architects and graphic designers have their offices here, and the area has a European atmosphere air by day. At night Broadway is a glittering array of contrasting neon signs advertising the entertainment and sex industry wares; but the street scene is good-natured and inoffensive.
South of Market Business concerns have begun to move in and upgrade this once low-rent district. It is the

center for the city's photographic, printing and audio-visual businesses. Interior design, furnishing and gift trade showrooms occupy the renovated warehouses of Showplace Square; marine repair and shipping businesses operate from the piers and dry docks S of the Bay Bridge.

Other areas

The expensive houses and apartments on the N slopes of *Telegraph Hill*, *Nob Hill* and *Russian Hill* have superb views of the Bay. *Pacific Heights* and *Presidio Heights* are considered the city's best addresses, despite the foggy summer weather. N of Lombard Street – "the crookedest street in the world" – the Mediterranean-style houses of the *Marina* face the Golden Gate Bridge, Alcatraz and the expensive yachts moored in St Francis Yacht Club. Across the Bay are the wooded hills of affluent *Marin County*, famous for its sybaritic, fashion-conscious lifestyle. The surroundings are bucolic, and the view of the city as one approaches the Golden Gate Bridge is striking: *Larkspur*, *Tiburon* and the charming former fishing village of *Sausalito* are convenient commuter areas. *East Bay* commuters have fine views of the city and the Golden Gate Bridge but the drawback of a long, slow journey into town. To the S of San Francisco, the pensinsula cities line El Camino Real, the original Spanish road which linked the 18th century missions. Some commuters make the trip each working day from as far away (1hr drive) as *Atherton* and *Menlo Park*, on the northern edge of Silicon Valley.

Hotels

Most of the city's major business hotels are conveniently within a 10min walk of Union Square – but walking in the area near the Hilton, for example, is not recommended at night. Because of San Francisco's popularity as a tourist and convention center, its room rates are generally comparable to those of New York and Los Angeles, and hotels are often booked up a month or more in advance.

Campton Place $$$$$

340 Stockton St 94108 ☎ 781-5555
TX 6771185 • 113 rooms, 10 suites, 1 restaurant, 1 bar

A block from Union Square and two blocks from the financial district, this small, well-appointed hotel woos the discriminating traveller with tasteful furnishings, fine art, personalized "anything-is-possible-at-any-time" service and an award-winning restaurant of the same name (see *Restaurants*). Membership at SF Tennis Club and Nob Hill Club • 2 meeting rooms.

Fairmont $$$$$

950 Mason St 94108 ☎ 772-5000
TX 9103726002 • 540 rooms, 60 suites, 6 restaurants, 6 bars, 1 coffee shop

This *grande dame* of San Francisco is familiar to TV viewers as the St Gregory of the *Hotel* series. A popular convention hotel, it is also a suitable choice for the individual business traveller. Barber and beauty salons, shops, travel agency, bank • spa and fitness center • 19 meeting rooms, teleconferencing via the hotel's own satellite dish.

Four Seasons Clift $$$$$

495 Geary St 94102 ☎ 775-4700
TX 340647 • 304 rooms, 25 suites, 1 restaurant, 1 bar

After a $5.5m refurbishment the classically stylish, 15-story Clift is fast becoming the most fashionable place to stay in San Francisco. Spacious rooms, excellent service, a fine French restaurant (with an alternative low-calorie, low-cholesterol menu) and the civilized Redwood Room bar are among its attractions. Two non-smoking floors • arrangement with nearby health club • 8 meeting rooms, computer modems, translation, teleconferencing.

Hilton $$$$
333 O'Farrell St 94102 ☏ 771-1400 ⓉⓍ 176180 • 1,544 rooms, 156 suites, 4 restaurants, 2 bars, 2 coffee shops
Close to the financial, theater and shopping districts, this is a major convention hotel. New rooms and meeting facilities are due to be completed by 1989. You can drive up and park close to your room if it is on one of the lower five floors, but a higher room in the remodelled 46-story tower may be more appealing. Heated outdoor pool • 25 meeting rooms, fax, teleconferencing.

Holiday Inn at Union Square $$$$
480 Sutter 94108 ☏ 398-8900 ⓉⓍ 9103722009 • 394 rooms, 6 suites, 1 restaurant, 1 bar
One of the more luxurious Holiday Inns, this is only one block from Union Square and three blocks from the financial district. The bells of passing cable cars make the lower rooms on Powell Street noisy. Non-smoking rooms • 9 meeting rooms.

Hyatt Regency $$$$$
5 Embarcadero Center 94111 ☏ 788-1234 ⓉⓍ 9103721018 • 711 rooms, 44 suites, 2 restaurants, 3 bars, 1 coffee shop
This modern hotel is the focal point of the Embarcadero Center business and shopping complex, at the edge of the financial district. The 20-story atrium lobby, filled with plants, trees, cafés and shops, has tea dances on Friday afternoons; the revolving rooftop bar and restaurant are good for conversation over a drink or meal. The two Regency Club floors, each with its own concierge, provide the business traveller with office facilities and luxury accommodation. Hairdresser, florist, shops • jogging and exercise courses, membership at SF Tennis Club • 5 meeting rooms.

Mark Hopkins Inter-Continental $$$$$
1 Nob Hill 94108 ☏ 392-3434 ⓉⓍ 340809 • 355 rooms, 42 suites, 2 restaurants, 2 bars, 1 coffee shop.
The Mark has long been one of San Francisco's most renowned hotels, and its top floor bar is particularly popular with business people and well-heeled tourists. Less extravagant than its Nob Hill neighbor, the Fairmont, the Mark has an air of quiet refinement. The cable car to the financial district stops outside the front door. Barber and beauty salon, gift shops, drugstore • membership at Nob Hill Club • 9 meeting rooms, fax.

Meridien $$$$
50 3rd St 94103 ☏ 974-6400 ⓉⓍ 176910 • 585 rooms, 26 suites, 2 restaurants, 2 bars
Two blocks from Union Square and one from the Moscone Center, the Meridien caters mainly for business visitors. The restaurant menu is excellent. Membership at SF Tennis Club • 8 meeting rooms.

Ramada Renaissance $$$$
55 Cyril Magnin St 94102 ☏ 392-8000 ⓉⓍ 755982 • 886 rooms, 90 club rooms, 39 suites, 2 restaurants, 2 bars
Opened in 1984, the 32-story Ramada has more than $1m worth of art throughout its public areas and is classier than most of its sister hotels. Unfortunately it is on the edge of the sleazy Tenderloin district, where walking during the day is not enjoyable, and at night quite unnerving. However, the Airport Bus Terminal is only one block away. Gift shops • health club, membership at SF Tennis Club • 20 meeting rooms.

Sheraton Palace $$$
2 New Montgomery St 94105 ☏ 392-8600 ⓉⓍ 340947 • 526 rooms, 60 suites, 1 restaurant, 3 bars, 1 coffee shop
The 100-year-old Victorian-style Sheraton, at the bottom of

Montgomery Street at Market, caters mainly to business travellers, who appreciate the larger-than-average rooms, the high ceilings and the proximity to the financial district and Moscone Center. The Palace was once the favorite of presidents and leading stars, such as Sarah Bernhardt. A business center is due for completion in 1988. Two travel agencies, shops, barber and beauty salons • arrangement with nearby health and tennis clubs • 23 meeting rooms.

Westin St Francis $$$$
335 Powell St 94102 ☎ 397-7000 ⊠ 278584 • 1,125 rooms, 75 suites, 3 restaurants, 4 bars, 1 coffee shop
Statesmen, politicians, literary lions and other celebrities stay at the St Francis, a quick three-block walk from the financial district and across the street from Union Square. Gift shops, barber and beauty salons, ticket agency • pool, gymnasium • 24 meeting rooms.

OTHER HOTELS

Andrews ($$) *624 Post St 94109 ☎ 563-6877.* Small, modern hotel two blocks from Union Square. Award-winning restaurant features American cuisine.
Beresford ($$) *635 Sutter St 94102 ☎ 673-9900 ⊠ 176088.* European-style hotel with small but comfortable rooms.
Canterbury/Whitehall Inn ($$) *750 Sutter St 94109 ☎ 474-6464, 227-4788.* Lots of antiques and an English décor, including a pub-style lounge.
Cartwright ($$) *524 Sutter St 94102 ☎ 421-2865 ⊠ 176579.* The rooms are small, but attractive, and the hotel has a loyal business clientele.
King George ($$) *334 Mason St 94102 ☎ 781-5050.* European atmosphere attracts many overseas visitors to this hotel.

Clubs

The *Bohemian Club* is one of San Francisco's most exclusive establishments, oriented to the conservative senior businessman and politician. The *Commonwealth Club* has more than 15,000 members, most of them lawyers, accountants and business people interested in current affairs. The club holds informative luncheon meetings every Friday to which visitors are welcomed; for information ☎ 362 4903. The *Press Club*, which now admits women, takes its members mainly from public relations and the press. *St Francis Yacht Club* ☎ 563-6363 is San Francisco's quintessential business and social club.

Restaurants

San Franciscans eat out a lot, and restaurants come and go almost as quickly as the fog. But in this food- and fashion-conscious city there are restaurants that have survived the test of time. Many are relaxed, in West Coast style; some are indisputably establishment, but all meet the sophisticated standards of cuisine that locals consider a hallmark of the city. Note that most stop seating patrons by 10–10.30.

Cadillac Bar $$
1 Holland Court ☎ 543-8226 • D only Sat; closed Sun • AE CB DC MC V
A short walk from downtown and a block from Moscone Center, this popular luncheon spot is also open for dinner and features mesquite-grilled seafood, Mexican specialties and loud music. A very noisy, but entertaining experience. Long, well-stocked stand-up bar, and a large after-work business crowd.

Campton Place Restaurant $$$$$
340 Stockton St (in Campton Place Hotel) ☎ 781-5155 • AE CB DC MC V • jacket and tie preferred for dinner

A comfortable, sophisticated restaurant offering imaginative, American food, served with considerable style. Breakfast daily.

Le Central $$
453 Bush St ☎ 391-2233 • closed Sun • AE MC V
This Parisian-style bistro/brasserie is still a favorite of local politicians, corporate executives and media personalities, though it has lost some of its ultra-fashionable status. Closely spaced tables discourage confidential business discussions.

Donatello $$$$
501 Post St (in Pacific Plaza Hotel) ☎ 441-7182 • closed L • AE CB DC MC V
A favorite with senior business people. The classic Italianate surroundings may be too imposing for a casual business meal but just right if a high-stakes business transaction is pending. Excellent northern Italian cuisine expertly prepared and served.

Doros $$$
714 Montgomery St ☎ 397-6822 • D only Sat; closed Sun • AE CB DC MC V
This award-winning restaurant serves excellent Continental cuisine. It is a popular haunt of advertising and media types, and its quiet atmosphere is very suitable for business conversations.

Ernie's $$$$
847 Montgomery St ☎ 397-5969 • D only • AE CB DC MC V • jacket and tie required
This plush, early Victorian restaurant specializes in *nouvelle cuisine* and has one of the best wine lists in the city. Formal yet pleasant service and exceptionally good food attract a loyal clientele, many of them from the financial district.

Ferry Plaza Restaurant on the Bay $$
1 Ferry Plaza, behind S end of Ferry Building ☎ 391-8403 • L only Sun–Wed; L and D Thu and Fri; D only Sat • AE CB DC MC V
A superb view of San Francisco Bay is a feature of this relatively new and spacious restaurant, which attracts a large business clientele.

Greens $$$
Building A of Fort Mason Center ☎ 771-6222 • D only Sun; closed Mon • no credit cards
With a good view of the Golden Gate Bridge, Greens sits on a pier in the Bay and serves fresh and imaginative vegetarian meals to a mix of residents and visitors, including many non-vegetarians. Popular with businesswomen for lunch, it is a 10min drive from downtown, but has abundant free parking.

Harris' Restaurant $$$
2100 Van Ness Ave ☎ 673-1888 • D only Sat and Sun • AE MC V • jacket required
This is San Francisco's best place for a steak dinner with all the trimmings. Aged beef from Harris's own ranch is perfectly cooked and expertly served in a comfortable Old West-style dining hall. Private dining rooms are available for small groups.

Hayes Street Grill $$$
320 Hayes ☎ 863-5545 • D only Sat; closed Sun • MC V
Located in the Civic Center area, this consistently fine seafood restaurant attracts a loyal crowd of city and government employees and politicians during the day; symphony- and ballet-goers at night. However, the tables are too close for private conversation.

Jack's $$$
615 Sacramento St ☎ 421-7355 • D only Sat and Sun • no credit cards • jacket and tie required
Established in 1864, this financial district institution specializes in French/Continental cuisine and caters largely to a business luncheon clientele. A place that is "famous because it is famous," it tends to

offer better service to steady customers than to newcomers, so accept an invitation from a regular, but look elsewhere if you are the host. Close seating makes conversation difficult, but private rooms are available.

MacArthur Park $$
607 Front St ☎ 398-5700 • D only Sat • AE MC V
California game and tasty barbequed ribs are the house specialties. Good local wines, an oakwood smoker and mesquite grill add up to a better-than-average California-style meal at a reasonable price. The bar is popular with the financial district crowd, especially right after work.

Mandarin $$$
900 North Point in Ghirardelli Sq ☎ 673-8812 • AE CB DC MC V
With an extensive variety of northern Chinese specialties, beautifully prepared and served amid Oriental antiques and museum-quality art, this is an impressive place to entertain a client. It has great views of the Bay, and its outstanding service has earned it a reputation as one of the best Chinese restaurants in a town noted for them.

Masa's $$$$$
648 Bush ☎ 989-7154 • D only; closed Sun and Mon • MC V • jacket required • reservations essential
The fine French *haute cuisine*, beautifully presented and served, is a San Francisco delight, but you must reserve early: three weeks ahead for a weekend, 1–3 days during the week. It is one of the few restaurants offering a traditional French cheese course. To enjoy it at room temperature, ask to have it set out when you order your entrée, since local health laws dictate that all dairy products be kept refrigerated.

Max's Diner $$
311 3rd St ☎ 546-6297 • AE MC V • no reservations
Huge quantities of the type of home-cooked food that much of America grew up on – meatloaf, mashed potatoes, roast turkey with stuffing and gravy – are served here very efficiently at reasonable prices. Its 1950s décor is complemented by jukebox "golden oldies." Breakfast is served from 7.30 during the week.

Orsi Restaurant $$$
375 Bush St ☎ 981-6535 • D only Sat; closed Sun • AE CB DC MC V
Although not as opulent as Donatello, Orsi's rarely disappoints with its northern Italian specialties and attentive service. Comfortable booth seating and widely spaced tables allow quiet conversation. A private cellar room is available for small groups.

Sam's Grill and Seafood Restaurant $$$
374 Bush St ☎ 421-0594 • closed Sat, Sun, holidays • MC V
Financial district workers appreciate the ample portions, reasonable prices and good, no-nonsense service here. It has been a favorite luncheon spot since 1867. Similar to the Tadich Grill in style and appeal – with polished wood and private rooms. It closes at 8.30.

Tadich Grill $$
240 California ☎ 391-2373 • closed Sat, Sun • no credit cards • no reservations
The granddaddy of business lunch restaurants, Tadich Grill is the oldest restaurant in California – established in 1849, the year of the Gold Rush. Its varied menu features charcoal-broiled fresh seafood, steaks and chicken. The huge counter bar – where you can also eat if you are in a hurry – makes the long wait bearable. It closes at 9.

Washington Square Bar and Grill $$
1707 Powell ☎ 982-8123 • AE MC V
A popular spot in North Beach for media personalities and politicians,

who enjoy its excellent food and convivial atmosphere. The fine Italian food, with constantly changing and imaginative daily specials, is served by tuxedo-clad waiters.

Bars

Bars play an important role in San Francisco's business life, and there is a wide variety of establishments from which to choose. For example, there are the young professionals' bars near Union Street, such as *Perry's* and *Balboa Café*; the conservative hotel bars downtown, such as *One Up Lounge* at the Hyatt and *S Holmes Esq Public House* at the Holiday Inn; and the gay-oriented bars and dance clubs S of Market around Folsom Street, such as *The Stud Bar* and *Febe's*. Popular after-work meeting places in the financial district and the Embarcadero Center include *The Royal Exchange* and *Harrington's*. The *Savoy Tivoli* is one of several noisy and colorful neighborhood bars in North Beach; and *The Condor* is one of the racier establishments on Broadway.

The *Carnelian Room*, 345 Montgomery, is perched on top of the Bank of America Building, 52 stories above the financial district; its recessed bay-window table seating provides a spectacular view and a measure of privacy. Expensive, but impressive. The *Cirque Room* at the Fairmont, 950 Mason St, serves cocktails, California wines and specialty coffee drinks in a splendid Art Deco lobby-level lounge. Perfect for afternoon tea or a quiet, early evening drink away from the crowds; the piano player's arrival at 9.30pm makes conversation difficult. The *Compass Rose*, in the Westin St Francis, is an attractive, fairly large bar which also serves a light lunch until 2.30, Mon–Sat. *Equinox*, in the Hyatt Regency, 5 Embarcadero Center, is San Francisco's only revolving rooftop lounge and provides a 360-degree view of the city. The seating is designed for one-to-one conversations.

Businesswomen from the financial district frequent the civilized *London Wine Bar*, 415 Sansome, which serves excellent local wines by the glass and fine light lunches. A good place to relax and enjoy great Dixieland jazz on the waterfront is the *Pier 23 Café*, Pier 23 at the Embarcadero. The *Buena Vista*, 2765 Hyde St at Fisherman's Wharf, claims to have invented Irish coffee.

One of the most relaxing and elegant bars in the city, the *Redwood Room* in the Four Seasons Clift, 495 Geary St, is a classic Art Deco cocktail lounge with original carved redwood panels and stylish light fixtures. At the top of Nob Hill, the *Top of the Mark*, in the Mark Hopkins, was the world's first "skyroom," offering a panoramic view of San Francisco and the Bay Area.

Entertainment

The "anything goes" spirit of the Barbary Coast which attracted Gold Rush miners, sailors and settlers more than a century ago still pervades today's "Baghdad-by-the-Bay." The greatest concentration of nightlife is in the North Beach/Broadway district, but nightclubs, discos and live music/dance clubs can be found in almost every section of the city. Yet San Francisco is not an all-night, non-stop town. Most restaurants stop seating guests at 10–10.30 and close by midnight. Last call in bars is 1.30, and there are few after-hours clubs; those that do stay open stop serving alcohol at 2. A recording of entertainment highlights is available 24hrs from the Convention and Visitors' Bureau – English ☎ 391-2001, French ☎ 391-2003, German ☎ 391-2004, Japanese ☎ 391-2101 and Spanish ☎ 391-2122.

Ticket agencies Both BASS ☎ 752-2277 (tickets) or 835-3849 (recorded information) and *Ticketron* ☎ 392-7469 (tickets) or 393-6419 (information) handle tickets for all kinds of sport, theater and concert events. *STBS*, on Stockton St downtown ☎ 433-7827, provides half-price, cash-only, in-person sales of unsold tickets for day-of-performance events.

Theater and ballet San Francisco has a rich theatrical tradition which is supported today by highly regarded repertory companies such as the *American Conservatory Theater* (ACT) company at the *Geary Theater*, 450 Geary St ☎ 673-6440, the *Curran Theater*, 445 Geary St ☎ 673-4400, the *Golden Gate Theater*, 25 Taylor St ☎ 775-8800, and the *Orpheum*, 1192 Market St ☎ 474-3800. "*Beach Blanket Babylon*" at *Club Fugazi*, 678 Green St ☎ 421-4222, is a cabaret-style production – no minors except on Sunday afternoon. The *San Francisco Ballet* is at the Opera House, Van Ness Ave and Grove St ☎ 621-3838.

Music Tickets for the *San Francisco Symphony*, Davies Hall, Van Ness Ave at Grove St ☎ 431-5400, are often available for subscription series performances on the day – in front of Davies Hall. The opera season extends from Sep to Dec and features one of the world's finest companies; performances are at the Opera House, Van Ness Ave and Grove St ☎ 564-3330.

Nightclubs The *Venetian Room* at the Fairmont ☎ 772-5163 and the *Plush Room* at the Hotel York ☎ 885-6800 are two good places to hear top-name entertainers perform in an intimate, supper club/cabaret atmosphere. *Alexis* ☎ 885-6400, atop Nob Hill near the Fairmont and Mark Hopkins, is an expensive bar-restaurant which features live gypsy music in the lounge. Comedy clubs are a San Francisco specialty, and one of the best is the *Punch Line*, 445 Battery St ☎ 397-7573, which features top local and national talent. *Finocchio's*, 506 Broadway ☎ 982-9388, is world famous for its 14 female impersonators. Top local and international jazz musicians perform at *Kimball's* Restaurant, 300 Grove St ☎ 861-5555.

Shopping

San Francisco's main shopping district, *Union Square*, has major department stores such as *Macy's*, Stockton at O'Farrell, and *Saks Fifth Avenue*, 384 Post St. Art galleries line both sides of Sutter Street; *Gumps*, 250 Post St ☎ 982-1616, is world famous for its jade and high-quality contemporary wares; *Shreve & Co*, Post St at Grant ☎ 421-2600, has fine jewelry and a courteous, knowledgeable staff; *Brooks Brothers*, 210 Post St ☎ 397-4500, is a must for high-quality, classic men's clothing; stylish, beautifully tailored and expensive designer clothes can be found at *Wilkes Bashford*, 336 Sutter St ☎ 986-4380. On the other side of the financial district, the four-building office/shopping complex *Embarcadero Center* has more than 175 retail shops, restaurants and art galleries. Farther down the Embarcadero is *Pier 39*, a collection of more than 130 specialty shops and restaurants only two blocks E of Fisherman's Wharf. Just W of the Wharf are three more large and lively shopping complexes: *The Cannery*, *The Anchorage* and *Ghirardelli Square*.

Sightseeing

No sightseeing tour of San Francisco is complete without experiencing the city's historic cable cars, renovated in 1982. Cars operate 6am–1pm, daily; fare $1.50.

Alcatraz Island A mile and a half/2.4km from Fisherman's Wharf, Alcatraz sits in the middle of San Francisco Bay and was once a federal prison. Excellent tours of the island, conducted by National Park Service rangers, afford views of the city and Golden Gate Bridge. Make sure to wear a warm coat, since it is always cold on the Bay.

Asian Art Museum The exhibits here include the priceless Avery Brundage collection of Oriental antiquities. *Golden Gate Park ☎ 668-8921. Closed Tue.*

California Palace of the Legion of Honor This art museum has

16th–20thC paintings, prints and sculpture, with special emphasis on 18th and 19thC France. Rodin's "The Thinker" collection is at the entrance. *Lincoln Park,* ☏ *221 4811. Closed Mon and Tue.*

Chinatown A walk along Grant Avenue between Bush Street and Columbus Avenue introduces the visitor to the most famous and colorful of San Francisco's ethnic neighborhoods. Separating the financial district from North Beach, Chinatown offers a fascinating mix of exotic shops, restaurants, food markets, temples, museums and businesses. The steadily growing community is spreading N into North Beach, buying up old established buildings and businesses and extending the Chinese culture into a predominately Italian neighborhood.

Coit Tower Shaped like a fire hose nozzle, this cylindrical tower stands atop Telegraph Hill and was built in 1933 as a monument to San Francisco's volunteer firemen. An observation platform at the top provides an excellent view of the city and the North Bay. *North Beach. Open 10–4.30.*

Fisherman's Wharf Although it ranks as San Francisco's most popular attraction, the Wharf is a mere shadow of its former self and is more a tourist trap than a working fishing community. Excellent year-round 75min sightseeing boat tours leave from Pier 39 (*Blue and Gold Fleet* ☏ 781-7877) and Pier 41 (*Red and White Fleet* ☏ 546-2800).

Golden Gate Bridge San Francisco's most famous Art Deco landmark is not golden in color but reddish-orange. It was completed in 1937 and measures 6,450ft across – the world's second largest suspended structure. Pedestrians and cyclists can cross free and enjoy an inspiring, if somewhat chilly, view of the Pacific Ocean on one side and San Francisco Bay on the other.

Golden Gate Park Once a wasteland of sand dunes, these 1,017 acres/4.1sq km are now the world's largest man-made park. Within its boundaries are the Steinhart Aquarium, Morrison Planetarium, California Academy of Sciences, MH de Young Memorial Museum, Asian Art Museum, Japanese Tea Garden, Conservatory of Flowers, Strybing Arboretum and Botanical Gardens, and the Chinese Pavilion. *Between Fulton St and Lincoln Way.*

MH de Young Memorial Museum contains collections of European and American art. *Golden Gate Park* ☏ *221-4811. Closed Mon and Tue.*

Museum of Modern Art This collection includes works by many major artists, such as Klee, Calder and Matisse, as well as a fine collection of photographs. *War Memorial Bldg, Civic Center* ☏ *863-8800. Closed Mon.*

Guided tours

Boat tours *Hornblower Yachts* ☏ 434-0300 offer regular dinner, lunch and brunch cruises in San Francisco Bay, from Pier 33 on the Embarcadero.

Bus tours *Agentours* ☏ 661-5200 has daily 4hr narrated tours in several languages. *American Express* ☏ 981-6293 has daily narrated tours including an 8hr tour of the wine country. Twelve tour plans are available from *Gray Line* ☏ 896-1515.

Limousine tours *Armadillo Limousine* ☏ 665-1234 offers personal – and expensive – tours of San Francisco and the wine country. Limos are equipped with telephones for travellers who need to combine business with pleasure.

Out of town

The Wine Country Located 44 miles/71km N of San Francisco, the vineyards of Napa and Sonoma counties comprise one of the best wine-growing regions of the world. Most wineries are geared to visitors, and many include restaurants and even accommodation.

Spectator sports

Baseball The *San Francisco Giants* play at Candlestick Park, 8 miles/13km S of the city off the Bayshore Freeway (Hwy 101) ☎ 467-8000. Downtown box office: 170 Grant Ave ☎ 982-9400. The *Oakland Athletics* are at Oakland Coliseum, across the Bay – a subway ride from the financial district – ☎ 638-0500. Tickets also available through BASS ticket agency at Embarcadero Records in Embarcadero Center ☎ 956-2204.
Football The *49ers* are two-time champions in recent years and are *the* hottest sports ticket in town. They kick off at Candlestick Park; box office ☎ 468-2249.
Horse racing *Bay Meadows Racecourse*, off Hwy 101, 20 miles/32km S of San Francisco ☎ 574-7223; *Golden Gate Fields*, PO Box 6027, Albany ☎ 526-3020, across the San Francisco-Oakland Bay Bridge.

Keeping fit

Many hotels provide free temporary membership at various health and tennis clubs with reasonable day rates. Among these clubs are *Physis*, 1 Post St ☎ 989-7310, the *San Francisco Tennis Club*, 5th and Brannan St ☎ 777-9000, the *Nob Hill Club*, at 950 California ☎ 397-2770, and *Symmetry*, 1 Market Plaza ☎ 495-3434.
Bicycling Most of the city's bike rental shops are located on Stanyan St at the E end of Golden Gate Park. The Pacific Coast Bicentennial Bike Map, available from *Caltrans*, 150 Oak St ☎ 557-1840, guides the cyclist along two scenic bike routes through San Francisco.
Golf The city has four public golf courses: the 9-hole, par 27 "pitch and putt" course in *Golden Gate Park* ☎ 751-8987; the 9-hole, par 32 *Fleming Course* ☎ 664-4690 in Harding Park; an 18-hole, par 72 course, also in *Harding Park* ☎ 661-1865; and *Lincoln Park Course* ☎ 221-9911, which offers 18 holes, a par 68, some fairly rough greens and magnificent views of the Pacific Ocean and the Golden Gate Bridge.
Tennis *The SF Parks Dept* ☎ 566-4800 maintains more than 100 free tennis courts.

Local resources

Business services

Complete business services can be provided on short notice by *Adia Personnel Services*, 44 Montgomery St, Suite 1250 ☎ 434-3810, which has 16 offices in the Bay Area; *Kelly Services*, 1 Post St, Suite 2150 ☎ 982-2200; and *Office Overload*, 44 Montgomery St, Suite 860 ☎ 434-3770.
Photocopying and printing The *Copy Factory*, 1 California St ☎ 781-2990, caters to convention and business persons' needs and is open 24hrs Mon–Fri and 9–5.30 on weekends. *Postal Instant Press* (PIP) has several locations downtown, including 44 Montgomery ☎ 421-7703 and 35 Taylor ☎ 441-1844.
Translation *Berlitz Translation Services*, 660 Market St, 4th floor ☎ 986-6474; the *International Translation Center*, 1550 California St, Suite 1 ☎ 885-1233, can translate from and into 55 languages.

Communications

Local delivery *Quicksilver Messenger Service*, 550 Beale ☎ 495-4360, guarantees a 1hr downtown delivery. Also offering 24hr, 7-day service via bicycle and van is *Special "T" Messsenger/ Delivery Service*, 322 6th St ☎ 861-0126. Also *Aero Special Delivery Service*, 242 Steuart ☎ 982-1303.
Long-distance delivery For overnight delivery of documents and packages under 150lbs to all 50 states, *Federal Express* ☎ 877-9000. For international delivery, *Emery Worldwide* ☎ 877-1822 or *DHL Worldwide Express* ☎ 697-9025. The *US Postal Service* ☎ 550-5240 offers Express Mail of up to 70lbs overnight, to major US cities. Open 8–5.

Post office The main post office is at 7th and Mission ☎ 556-2381.
Telex and fax The *HQ-Headquarters Companies* ☎ 781-5000 provides domestic and international telex and fax facilities in the financial district.

Conference/exhibition centers

San Francisco has three major convention facilities. The city's premier meeting place, *Moscone Center*, 747 Howard St ☎ 947-4000, is within walking distance of more than a third of the city's top hotels. The *Brooks Hall/Civic Auditorium* complex, 99 Grove St, Civic Center ☎ 974-4000, is the second largest facility downtown. The *Cow Palace*, Geneva Ave and Santos ☎ 469-6000, is a huge clear-span structure with a 100ft ceiling and 14,500 permanent seats. Another choice nearer downtown is the *San Francisco Concourse*, 635 8th St ☎ 864-1500.

Emergencies

Currency exchange The *Bank of America Foreign Exchange Office* at the airport keeps the longest office hours: 7am–11pm daily. Downtown, *Deak-Perera* is at 100 Grant Ave ☎ 362-3452, Mon–Fri, 9–5.
Hospitals *Pacific Presbyterian Medical Center*, Clay and Buchanan ☎ 923-3333, is close to downtown. *San Francisco Dental Office*, 132 Embarcadero ☎ 777-5115, offers immediate treatment of emergencies and is open 6 days a week, early mornings and evenings.
Pharmacies *Walgreens* has 21 stores in the city, including one open 24hrs at 3201 Divisadero ☎ 931-6417, and two locations downtown at 500 Geary Blvd ☎ 673-8413 and 135 Powell ☎ 391-7222, open Mon–Fri, 8–9; Sat, 9–5; Sun, 10–6.

Government offices

For *City and County of San Francisco* information ☎ 558-6161; *California State Governor's Office* ☎ 557-3326; *US Government* general information ☎ 556-6600; *US Customs* ☎ 556-4340.

Information sources

Business information *San Francisco Chamber of Commerce*, 465 California ☎ 392-4511, provides valuable information and assistance to non-residents interested in doing business in the city. The *San Francisco Convention and Visitors' Bureau*, at Hallidie Plaza, Powell and Market ☎ 391-2000, maintains a multilingual staff to aid the business traveller with literature and information.
Local media *Eastern Newsstand* carries a wide selection of newspapers and magazines and has five locations in the greater downtown area. One is at 3 Embarcadero Center ☎ 982-4425; another is in the Galleria Shopping Center at 50 Post St ☎ 434-0531. The *San Francisco Chronicle* is the morning paper (Herb Caen's column is a must read); the *San Francisco Examiner* comes out in the afternoon. The *San Francisco Business Journal*, published every Monday, covers industry, business trends, events and people in the Bay Area. *San Francisco Business* is a monthly magazine published by the San Francisco Chamber of Commerce ☎ 392-4511. *Key Magazine*, available free in many hotels, describes the weekly events in the city. *Teleguide* terminals throughout the city offer free electronic information on where to go, what to eat, where to shop, how to get there, and so on ☎ 957-2999.

Thank-yous

Florists/gift baskets *Podesta Baldocchi*, 1 Embarcadero Center ☎ 346-1300. There are many street-corner flower carts downtown.
Wine merchants Knowledgeable downtown merchants include *John Walker and Co*, 175 Sutter ☎ 986-2707; *London Wine Bar*, 415 Sansome ☎ 788-4811; and the *Wine and Cheese Center*, 205 Jackson ☎ 956-2518.

SILICON VALLEY

Area codes ☎ 408 and 415

You will not find Silicon Valley in many atlases; they have not kept pace with the developments that transformed this quiet agricultural area – real name, Santa Clara Valley – which stretches about 50 miles/80km from the quiet, serene and intellectual community of Palo Alto, home of Stanford University, 25 miles/40km S of San Francisco, to the still-sleeping San Jose, 30 miles/48 km farther. It was here that the silicon chip was developed – and multiplied. Today, what was once a quiet farming community of almond and orange groves is now the home of more than 3,000 electronics companies – from giants like National Semiconductor and Intel to small entrepreneurial set-ups. It is a saturated low-rise, high-tech area; the only way to get about is by car, despite the bumper-to-bumper jams. Leave plenty of time between appointments even if you seem to be going just down the block!

Arriving

From San Francisco International Airport it is 30min by car to Palo Alto and 1hr–90min to San Jose. Follow the signposts S on Highway 101 in the direction of San Jose; or use the longer, but often faster Interstate 280. Helicopters can be chartered in the Bay Area from *Helicopters Unlimited* ☎ (415) 632-9422. Or you can fly to San Jose International Airport (though its facilities are limited and baggage retrieval is slow). Car rental is a must: companies include *Hertz* ☎ (408) 297-9495, *Avis* ☎ (408) 297-8539, *Budget* ☎ (408) 288-8800 and *National* ☎ (408) 295-1344.

Nearby hotels *Holiday Inn Airport*, 1355 N 4th St ☎ (800) 465-4329. *Hyatt San Jose*, 1740 N 1st St ☎ (800) 228-9000 TX 357408. Le Baron, 1350 N 1st St ☎ (408) 288-9200. All are in San Jose.

Hotels

Most of the Valley's hotels are in San Jose or Palo Alto, both convenient for the towns of Sunnyvale, Cupertino, Santa Clara and Mountain View. All are geared to business needs; Silicon Valley is not a tourist region. Most have meeting rooms, personal computer rentals and Federal Express drop-offs.

Stanford Park Hotel $$$$

100 El Camino Real, Menlo Park ☎ (415) 322-1234 • 164 rooms, 12 suites, 1 restaurant, 1 bar

This smart new hotel near Stanford University has become popular with local companies for business presentations. Service is quiet and efficient. Each room is decorated in quasi-New England style with exposed wood. The lobby bar is a comfortable meeting area with unobtrusive piano entertainment. Pool, health club, sauna and jacuzzi • 3 meeting rooms.

Hyatt Palo Alto $$$$

4290 El Camino Real, Palo Alto ☎ (415) 493-0800 • 200 rooms, 1 restaurant, 1 bar

Located across the street from the Hyatt Rickey's, this offers slightly less expensive and less luxurious accommodation. The Echo restaurant is informal Italian, and Tempo's bar is popular for after-work drinks. Exercise room, pool, tennis.

Hyatt Rickey's $$$$

4219 El Camino Real, Palo Alto ☎ (415) 493 8000 • 350 rooms,

1 restaurant, 1 bar
The better of the two Hyatts, Rickey's has for some time been *the* choice of regular Valley visitors. Sprawling across 22 acres of ponds, pools, a croquet lawn, putting green and cabanas, it has a California-style charm, luxurious rooms and comprehensive conference facilities. Both J Patrick's bar and Hugo's restaurant are popular meeting places. Exercise room, pool, tennis.

Red Lion Inn **$$$$**
2050 Gateway Plaza, San Jose ☏ *(408) 279-0600 • 515 rooms, 10 suites, 1 restaurant, 1 coffee shop, 1 bar, 1 disco*
Next to San Jose Airport, well-appointed and a good business address, the Red Lion offers the visitor standard rooms and adequate restaurants. Hairdresser • pool, jacuzzi • 15 meeting rooms.

Restaurants

Good eating places tend to be very crowded, reservations are a must and often the food does not live up to the long wait. For good food, you have to drive 45min to San Francisco or try to get into the Mouton Noir or the Plumed Horse. MacArthur Park and the Lion and Compass are well-known (but noisy) Valley business meeting places.

Lion and Compass **$$$**
1023 N Fair Oaks Ave, off Hwy 101, Sunnyvale ☏ *(408) 745-1260 • D only Sat; closed Sun • AE CB DC MC V*
This is the pride of Silicon Valley, heavily patronized by senior executives from its high-tech neighbors. A tickertape service keeps the busy entrepreneur in touch with his investment portfolio over a glass of good California wine.

MacArthur Park **$$**
27 University Ave, Palo Alto ☏ *(415) 321-9990 • D only Sat • AE MC V*
A favorite of the local business community for lunch, drinks and dinner, this noisy restaurant is always buzzing. The large vaulted room used to be a part of the Palo Alto railroad station, but its high-tech computerized order-entry system puts it clearly in the heart of today's Silicon Valley. Waiters and waitresses carry handheld computers instead of paper. The atmosphere is jovial and relaxed; private rooms are available.

Le Mouton Noir **$$$**
Rte 9, Saratoga ☏ *(408) 867-7017 • D only; closed Sun • AE MC V*
Easily accessible from all Silicon Valley addresses, this French country-style restaurant has an unassuming but charming atmosphere. The menu changes frequently, and the wine list is comprehensive. Reservations required a week in advance for weekends.

Plumed Horse **$$$$**
Rte 9, Saratoga ☏ *(408) 867-4711 • D only; closed Sun • AE MC V • no jeans*
The Plumed Horse is often crowded, so reservations are advisable at least a day in advance. The cuisine is Continental, and the wine list includes some good California labels. Private rooms are available.

Bars and entertainment

The main bars for business purposes are Rickey's *J Patricks*, the bar at MacArthur Park, and *McFly's* in Cupertino, a favorite with Apple Computer people.

The Valley does have cinemas, but most business visitors prefer to spend their leisure time in San Francisco.

Shopping and sightseeing

The Valley has two major shopping malls; otherwise the choice is San

Francisco. *Vallco Fashion Park*, Stevens Creek and Wolfe Road, Cupertino, is a modern complex with major department stores, including I Magnin, and lots of specialty boutiques. *Stanford Shopping Center*, El Camino Real and Stanford University in Palo Alto, numbers Macy's, Saks Fifth Avenue, Neiman-Marcus and Nordstroms among its more than 200 stores.

If you have time for sightseeing, *Stanford University* campus grounds are beautiful, with large palm trees and an impressive quad. The Rodin sculpture garden is particularly pleasing.

Keeping fit

The principal private health club in the area is the *Decathlon Club*, 3250 Central Expressway, Santa Clara ☎ (408) 738-8743. Most companies have a membership policy.

Local resources

Business services

Complete business services are available from *Adams Joyce Secretarial Service* ☎ (415) 854-6800, in Menlo Park, and *Letter Shop*, 1573 Samedra, Sunnyvale ☎ (408) 245-0602.

Photocopying and printing *Copy Shop*, 581 University Ave, Palo Alto ☎ (415) 328-1272; *Kinko's*, 299 California, Palo Alto ☎ (415) 328-3381 and 1285 El Camino Real, Menlo Park ☎ (415) 321-4202. Kinko's also rents computers for desk-top publishing.

Secretarial *Adia Personnel Services* has offices throughout Silicon Valley: Palo Alto ☎ (415) 324-2771, Sunnyvale ☎ (408) 733-2882. Adia also offers technical and accounting temps. Also *Kelly Services* in Palo Alto ☎ (415) 326-0290.

Translation *Berlitz Translation*, Palo Alto ☎ (415) 323 0076; *Japanese Linguistic Service*, Redwood City ☎ (415) 321-9832.

Communications

Local delivery *Ultra Express* ☎ (800) 858-7299; *US Courier* ☎ (415) 495-0200.

Long-distance delivery *Federal Express* ☎ (415) 877-9000 or *Purolator Courier* ☎ (800) 645-3333.

Information sources

Business information The *San Jose Convention and Visitors' Bureau* ☎ (408) 295-9600 provides information about hotels, restaurants and local conference centres.

Local media The *San Jose Mercury News*, the Valley's daily newspaper, has detailed business coverage. The *San Francisco Chronicle*, the *San Francisco Examiner*, *USA Today* and the *Los Angeles Times* are also all available.

Thank-yous

Florist *Ah Sam*, 2645 S El Camino Real, San Mateo ☎ (415) 341-5611; *Stapleton Florist*, 452 Waverly, Palo Alto (415) 321-5390.

SEATTLE

Area code ☎ 206

Standing on Puget Sound in the extreme NW of the USA, Seattle – which began as a logging camp 150 years ago – is today a major import/export shipping terminal to the Far East. American President and Hanjin Container Lines are its largest port customers, and shipbuilding and repair are important to the region. Lockheed and Todd Shipyards are the field leaders. Other dominant corporations include the spacecraft giant, Boeing Aerospace; Boeing Commercial Airline; the heavy equipment manufacturer PACCAR; and lumber corporations Weyerhaeuser and Boise Cascade. Traditional industries like fishing and coal-mining have recently been joined by computer design specialists such as Microsoft, ensuring the area's continued economic growth. As the economic hub of the Pacific Northwest and Alaska, Seattle presently heads the national job-creation table.

Arriving

Seattle-Tacoma International Airport

Sea-Tac, 13 miles/21km S of downtown Seattle, has five arrival concourses surrounding the main terminal, and two satellite concourses connected to it by regular subway service; cars run every 2min. International flights arrive at South Satellite, which has Customs and Immigration services, interpreters in 21 languages, and currency exchange. Even at non-peak periods, it can take an hour to clear Customs. Moving sidewalks and escalators make it easy to get to the baggage claim area, which also has major car rental counters, telephone booths and Western Union. Desks, telephones and copy and telecopier machines are available in the business communications center in North Satellite. Bars close at 2am, but a cafeteria-style restaurant is open 24hrs.

Nearby hotels *Sea-Tac Red Lion Inn*, 18740 Pacific Hwy S ☎ 246-8600. *Hyatt Seattle* 17001 Pacific Hwy S ☎ 244-6000.

City link *Taxi* The most convenient way to get into downtown Seattle is by cab, which generally takes only 20–30min in morning and evening rush hour. The fare is about $20.

Bus The Airport Express Charter Bus, which leaves every 20min, costs approximately $5. There are also frequent Metro bus services.

Car rental The major car rental agencies have desks in the main terminal, but a car is useful only if you have business in outlying areas.

Getting around

The city's main business community, hotels, restaurants, shopping and entertainment are all conveniently located within the compact downtown area, though the city is quite hilly. Carry a map if you plan to walk any distance.

Taxi The most reliable firms are *Farwest* ☎ 622-1717, *Hanson* ☎ 323-0365 and *Yellow Cabs* ☎ 622-6500; all accept major credit cards.

Bus *Metro Transit* ☎ 447-4800 operates frequent services, and has an 18-block free zone downtown, from the waterfront to 6th Street, and from Jackson to Blanchard streets.

Monorail A monorail runs between the downtown shopping area at 4th Street and Pine and the Seattle Center.

Limousine *Elite Limousine Service* ☎ 575-2332 operates 24hrs.

Area by area

Downtown Most of the city's business headquarters are in the lively downtown area, with its plazas

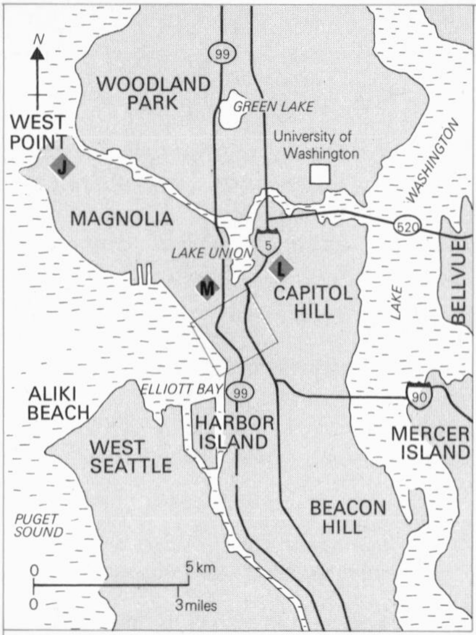

■ **HOTELS**

A Alexis
B Four Seasons Olympic
C Seattle Sheraton and Towers
D Sorrento
E Westin
F Edgewater Inn
G Holiday Inn Crowne Plaza
H Mayflower Park

● **RESTAURANTS**

A Cutters Bay House
B Ivar's Indian Salmon House
C Metropolitan Bar and Grill
D Ray's Downtown
E The Other Place

◆ **SIGHTS AND BUILDINGS**

A Chamber of Commerce
B Convention Centre and Visitors' Bureau
C Columbia Center
D Federal Building
E First Interstate Building
F IBM Building
G Kingdom
H Rainier Square/Rainier Tower
I Smith Tower
J Discovery Park
K Seattle Aquarium
L Seattle Art Museum
M Seattle Center

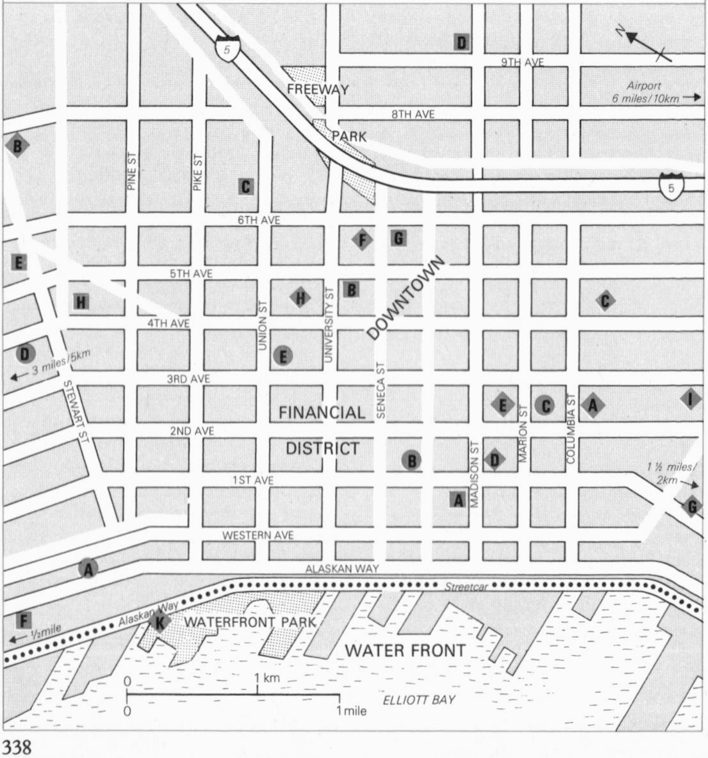

and parks. The 76-floor Columbia Center, Rainier Square/Rainier Bank Tower, the First Interstate Building at 1111 3rd Avenue and the IBM Building are among the most prestigious business addresses.

Other areas Old-money residential estates are the Highlands, N of downtown, and Broadmoor, E on Lake Washington. Windermere, Innis Arden and Laurelhurst are other areas with cachet. Young professionals have settled by Lake Washington.

Suburbs Immediately N of Seattle, Ballard was founded by Scandinavians and still retains its ethnic heritage. To the E across Lake Washington, and linked by bridge, is Bellevue, a high-tech area known as "Silicon Valley North."

Hotels

Most of the better hotels are downtown within easy reach of the business headquarters, restaurants and entertainment. Many have in-house business facilities. The hotels listed have meeting rooms for large groups, plus trained staff to make arrangements for conferences.

Alexis $$$
1st and Madison 98104 ☎ 624-4844 • 27 rooms, 27 suites, 2 restaurants, 1 bar
An attractive, turn-of-the-century building decorated with discreet good taste, the Alexis puts great emphasis on personal service. Rooms, furnished with antiques, are large enough to work in, and many have stoves or fireplaces. The Alexis Room is one of Seattle's top restaurants and a favorite meeting ground for big-league executives. Guest membership to Seattle Athletic Club and Rooftop Tennis • 2 meeting rooms, fax, translation.

Four Seasons Olympic $$$$$
411 University 98101 ☎ 621-1700 TX 152477 • 450 rooms, 48 suites, 2 restaurants, 1 bar
Opened in the mid-1920s, the Olympic was considered one of the best hotels in western America; now absorbed into the Four Seasons empire it is grander than ever. Just five blocks from the waterfront, it caters mainly for leaders of Seattle society, top executives and their visiting counterparts. Its luxurious, elegantly furnished rooms are highly suitable for working in or for small meetings. The health club is one of the city's best, and the Georgian Room is a much-favored and impressive corporate meeting place. Solarium, health club, sauna, massage • 13 meeting rooms, fax, translation.

Seattle Sheraton and Towers $$$$
6th and Pike 98101 ☎ 621-9000 TX 152981 • 888 rooms, 46 suites, 3 restaurants, 1 bar
A fine collection of works by Northwest artists is this Sheraton's *pièce de resistance.* As important for the business visitor is the Tower's well-equipped third-floor executive floor. Pool, health club, weight room, aerobics • 26 meeting rooms.

Sorrento $$$$
900 Madison 98104 ☎ 622-6400 TX 244206 • 76 rooms, 40 suites, 1 restaurant, 1 bar
Overlooking downtown and Puget Sound, this small hotel will appeal to guests who prefer personal service and ambiance to high-tech hustle. The comfort of its rooms, which are furnished with antiques, is complemented by the readiness of the concierge to arrange business services. The Hunt Club is a good choice for business dining, with a wide range of seafood. Guest membership to Seattle Athletic Club • 2 meeting rooms.

Westin $$$$

1900 5th Ave 98101 ☏ 728-1000 ⓉⓍ 152900 • 875 rooms, 47 suites, 3 restaurants, 1 bar

The twin 47-story towers of this downtown giant give panoramic views of the locale, and its sleekly renovated interior attracts much convention trade. The Palm Court is commendably opulent, and Trader Vic's is popular with local corporate leaders. Pool, sauna • 27 meeting rooms, fax.

OTHER HOTELS

Edgewater Inn ($$) *2411 Alaskan Way 98101 ☏ 728-7000. No AE.*
Holiday Inn Crowne Plaza ($$$$) *6th and Seneca 98101 ☏ 464-1980 ⓉⓍ 152032.*
Mayflower Park ($$) *405 Olive 98101 ☏ 623-8700.*

Clubs

The *Rainier Club* is Seattle's oldest and most prestigious club. The *Washington Athletic Club* offers accommodation, athletic facilities and excellent dining. The exclusive men-only *101 Club*, on the top floor of the 22-story WAC building, has the best view in town. The *College Club* has a mixed membership and *Women's University Club*, women only. The *Seattle Yacht Club* is the city's finest boating club.

Restaurants

Much of Seattle's business entertaining takes place in the better hotel restaurants such as the Alexis Room, the Sorrento's Hunt Club and the Georgian Room in the Olympic.

Cutters Bay House $$

2001 Western ☏ 622-7711 • D only Sun–Thu • AE MC V

Looking out over Elliot Bay, Cutters has become so popular for business get-togethers that reservations are advised. The fantastic view of Puget Sound and the Olympic Mountains, the casual ambiance and light pasta specialties make this an enjoyable spot for a working lunch or dinner.

Ivar's Indian Salmon House $$

401 NE Northlake Way ☏ 632-0767 • no credit cards

A visitor to the Northwest will enjoy this new experience: eating alder-smoked salmon, Indian-style, in an authentic tribal longhouse on the shore of Lake Union. Best used for informal, get-to-know-you dinners.

McCormick and Schmick's $$

1103 1st Ave ☏ 623-5500 • AE CB DC MC V

A comparatively new restaurant, though with the look and feel of a long-established one, McCormick and Schmick's specializes in seafood and grilled meats. Look especially for the oysters and Manila clams in season.

Metropolitan Bar and Grill $$

818 2nd St ☏ 624-3287 • D only Sat and Sun • AE MC V

In midtown, the Metropolitan is always crowded with the elite of the Seattle business community; and reservations are advisable. Steak is a specialty, but the menu changes daily.

Ray's Downtown $$

99 3rd ☏ 623-7999 • AE DC MC V

Ray has two excellent restaurants, but this is the one most used by local executives. His Boathouse is a 20min drive away in Ballard, but its stunning location on the Sound makes it well worth the effort, as does the first-rate seafood and prime rib.

Rosellini's 410 $$

4th Ave and Wall St ☏ 728-0410 • closed Sun • AE CB DC MC V

This Old World-style fish and

poultry eating house attracts locals as well as visitors. Service is always good; the French and northern Italian cuisine even more so. Its location right on the downtown edge makes it more suitable for dinner than lunch.

The Other Place $$$
96 Union ☎ 623-7340 • closed Sat L, Sun • AE MC V
Recently moved from farther along Union, this favorite spot has taken over an older building near Pike's Market, but retains its old elegance and quality of service. Even so, the style is sufficiently casual to appeal also to the younger professional. Now with water view, its emphasis has moved from game to seafood, though game is still featured. A separate lounge provides a good private spot for pre-dinner discussion.

Bars

Hiram's at-the-Locks, 5300 34th NW, overlooks the ship canal, a scenic place to watch the boats and meet the younger professional crowd. *J&M Café*, in the Pioneer Square area, is a rustic, turn-of-the-century saloon. The half-block-long bar of the *Metropolitan Bar and Grill*, 818 2nd St, downtown, is popular for after-work drinks. *Ray's Boathouse at Shilshole*, 6049 Seaview NW, offers a splendid view, wines and seafood.

Entertainment

The best sources of entertainment information are the Friday feature "What's Happening" in the morning *Seattle Post-Intelligencer* and the "Tempo" column of the evening *Seattle Times*. *Ticketmaster Northwest* ☎ 628-0888 and *Fidelity Lane* ☎ 624-4970 take MC and V telephone orders.

Theater and music Broadway shows and stars come to the *5th Avenue Theater*, 1308 5th ☎ 625-1900. *Pioneer Square Theater*, 512 2nd ☎ 622-2016, and the *Empty Space Theater*, 95 Jackson ☎ 467-6000, are more experimental. The *Gilbert and Sullivan Society* and *Seattle Repertory Theater* both perform at the Seattle Center's *Bagley Wright Theater* ☎ 443-2222. Also at the Center is the *Seattle Opera House* ☎ 443-4711, home to the Seattle Symphony and the Pacific Northwest Ballet.

Nightclubs *Backstage*, 2208 NW Market, presents both local and nationally known groups, ranging from rock to folk music. *Celebrity Bar & Grill* is a heavy favorite with the younger professional crowd. Located in Pioneer Square under Swannie's Bar & Restaurant, *Comedy Underground*, 222 S Main, has stand-up comedy acts. *Windjammers*, 7001 Seaview NW, has live bands.

Shopping

I Magnin, *Nordstrom* and *Frederick & Nelson* are on Pine Street at 5th and 6th. Expensive specialty shops, such as *Littler's* and *Talbot's*, are in Rainier Square, 4th and Union. The Waterfront has a long string of tourist shops. *Pioneer Square*, around 1st and Yester, is yet another specialty shop haven, for fruit, vegetables, seafood, handmade craft items and antiques.

Sightseeing

Discovery Park, site of the *Indian Cultural Center*, has a 2 mile/3km saltwater beach with hiking trails. *3801 W Government Way.*

Seattle Aquarium, one of the city's major attractions, has a variety of historical nautical exhibits as well as marine life. You can also walk through a dome surrounded by water and fish. *Pier 59, Waterfront Park ☎ 625-4358.*

Seattle Art Museum, specializing in African and Asian art, is at Volunteer Park. *1400 E Caler, adjacent to the city's Conservatory.*

Seattle Center, covering more than 70 acres, was built for the 1962 World's Fair, and now houses the towering 605ft Space Needle and the Pacific Science Center.

Guided tours
The *Goodtimes Harbor Tours*, Pier 56 ☎ 623-1445 make daily trips May–Oct. *Tillicum Tour*, Pier 56 ☎ 329-5700 travels twice daily May–Sep to Blake Island, a state park. *Underground Tour* ☎ 683-1511 offers guided walks along the original – now-subterranean – Seattle streets of 1899 in the Pioneer Square area.

Spectator sports
Baseball The *Seattle Mariners* ☎ 628-0888 play in the Kingdome.
Basketball The *Supersonics* ☎ 281-5850 are at the Seattle Center.
Football The *Seahawks* ☎ 827-9766 play at the Kingdome. The University of Washington team, the *Huskies* ☎ 543-2230, is also strongly supported.

Keeping fit
Health clubs *Metropolitan Health Club*, 1519 3rd Ave ☎ 682-3966 and *Nautilus Northwest Athletic Club*, 2306 6th ☎ 443-9944.
Bicycling Rentals from the *Bicycle Center* ☎ 525-8300.
Golf *Bellevue Municipal Golf Course*, 5500 140th St NE, Bellevue ☎ 885-6009; *West Seattle Golf Course*, 4470 35th St SW ☎ 932-9792.

Local resources
Business services
Photocopying and printing *Copy Mart Copy Centers*, 216 Stewart ☎ 728-7100.
Secretarial *Globe Secretarial*, 310 1st ☎ 624-3822.
Translation *Red Cross Language Bank* ☎ 323-2345 offers 24hr interpreting. *Berlitz Translation Services* ☎ 682-0312.

Communications
Local delivery *Farwest Taxi* ☎ 622-1717 or *Overland Transportation Service* ☎ 441-4555.
Long-distance delivery *Federal Express* ☎ 282-9766 and *National Courier System* ☎ 682-9315.
Post offices Downtown at 3rd and Union ☎ 442-6150; or at the airport ☎ 246-6788 open 24hrs.
Telex *Telex B&A Service* ☎ 633-3522.

Conference/exhibition centers
The *Seattle Center* has two auditoriums; *Kingdome*, the sports arena, is also available for large gatherings. A new *Convention Center* is to open in 1988.

Emergencies
Hospitals *Swedish Hospital Medical Center*, 747 Summit ☎ 386-6000; *Virginia Mason*, 925 Seneca ☎ 624-1141; and *Saint Cabrini*, Terry and Madison ☎ 682-0500. *Seattle-King County Dental Society* ☎ 624-4912 takes emergency calls 24hrs.
Pharmacies *Kelley-Rose* ☎ 622-3565 will deliver; *Fred Meyer*, 425 Broadway E ☎ 323-5256.

Government offices
Federal Information Center ☎ 442-0570; *US Customs* ☎ 442-4676.

Information sources
Business information *Chamber of Commerce* ☎ 447-7200 provides a wide range of business information. Potential investors can get help from the *Economic Development Council*.
Local media City news is supplied by the morning and evening *Seattle Times*. The *Seattle Daily Journal of Commerce* and the weekly *Seattle Business Journal* specialize in local business coverage.
Tourist information *Seattle-King County Convention and Visitors' Bureau* ☎ 447-4235.

Thank-yous
Florists *Crissey*, 416 University at 5th ☎ 728-6661; *Chas E Sullivan* ☎ 624-1300 open seven days.
Gift baskets *Au Delice that Gift of Class* ☎ 747-7541; *Totem Smokehouse Gourmet Seafood* ☎ 443-1710; *Cheers & Chocolates* ☎ 246-0253.

WASHINGTON DC

Area code ☏ 202; codes for nearby Virginia and Maryland are 703 and 301 respectively. Telephone numbers in this city guide are in Washington DC (District of Columbia) unless otherwise indicated.

As the nation's capital, Washington is, in many ways, the USA's most important city for business, given the role of government as a regulator of all commerce and industry, national and international. Virtually every major US corporation has an office of some sort in the Washington area, and nearly all US trade associations are headquartered here. In the past, Washington was dominated by government; Capitol Hill and Embassy Row were the city's major centers. Today, however, the private sector – corporations, lobbying groups and the like – predominates. Washington is a city obsessed by power, where lobbyists and politicians vie for influence, yet it is also a city relatively open in terms of access, especially by European standards. It is, above all, a town of bureaucrats and lawyers. Major employers are government, national trade associations, government contractors and law. It is head office of big defense contractors such as Martin Marietta, Atlantic Research Corporation and Fairchild Industries. Increasingly, it is also the headquarters of communications giants – like COMSAT, INTELSAT, Gannett and MCI. Washington is also an important center of learning, with several major universities, including George Washington, Catholic and Georgetown. Among the city's numerous tourist attractions are the White House, the Capitol, the Washington Monument, the Lincoln Memorial and some of the best museums in the world.

Arriving

Washington is served by Washington National Airport, Dulles International and Baltimore-Washington International. Because National is nearer downtown, it is the preferred airport for domestic flights. International travellers have the choice of Dulles or BWI, both about a 45min drive from the city.

Washington National Airport

National is situated just over 4 miles/6.5km from downtown Washington, across the Potomac River in northern Virginia. Handling about 40,000 passengers a day in cramped conditions, it is usually congested in the late afternoon and on Sunday night, but is nevertheless an easy airport to find your way around. Major renovation is scheduled for mid-1988 (to last 4–5 years), so there may be some inconvenience during this time. Passengers collect their baggage at street level; car rental desks, taxis and shuttle buses to car rental lots, long-term parking, and the Metrorail are all nearby. From plane to car can take only 15min, but baggage delays can double that during heavy traffic in late afternoon. A full banking service is available, Mon–Sat, 9–7; currency exchange, secretarial services, photocopying, telex/telegram and conference rooms are provided in a business services center, 7am–11pm daily. Information ☏ (703) 557-2045.

Nearby hotels *Crystal City Marriott*, 1999 Jefferson Davis Hwy, Arlington, VA ☏ (703) 521-5500. *Holiday Inn, National Airport*, 2799

Jefferson Davis Hwy, Arlington, VA ☎ (703) 486-1234. *Marriott Crystal Gateway*, 1700 Jefferson Davis Hwy, Arlington, VA ☎ (703) 920-3230.
City link *Taxi* The best way downtown is by taxi. It takes 15–20min, 35min in the rush hour 3.30–6. The fare is about $10. A cab ride to Dulles International costs about $30; to Baltimore-Washington Airport, closer to $40. It is advisable to agree the fare with the driver beforehand.
Subway The Metrorail station is only a short ride away on a free shuttle bus which runs from outside the baggage area.
Bus The Washington Flyer ☎ 685-1400 provides services to downtown Washington, Dulles International Airport, suburban Maryland and northern Virginia. A one-way ticket to downtown hotels is $5; round-trip $8. For Dulles International, the fares are $10 and $18.
Car rental Since cabs are readily available and relatively cheap to downtown (while parking lots are expensive), a cab is the better choice, but rental companies have desks at the airport: Avis ☎ (800) 331-1212; Hertz ☎ (800) 654-3131; National ☎ (800) 328-4567; Budget ☎ (800) 527-0700; and Dollar ☎ (800) 421-6868.

Dulles International Airport

Dulles is in northern Virginia, a 40–50min ride via the Dulles Access Road to downtown; in rush hour, it can take 15min more. The strikingly beautiful terminal, designed by Eero Saarinen, is easy to negotiate, and exiting usually takes about 15min (45min if you have to go through Customs and Immigration), though the new terminal scheduled for construction starting in 1988 could cause Customs delays.

For international travellers, Dulles has a business center on the ground floor; domestic travellers are catered to on the main floor at the E and W ends, 7am–11pm daily. Services include currency exchange, secretarial, photocopying, telex/telegram and conference rooms. There is a bank on the ground floor ☎ (703) 661-8861 and (703) 471-7498, open Mon–Fri, 9–1, 3–5. Concorde passengers to and from London can use British Airways' First Class lounge. Airport information ☎ (703) 471-4242.
Nearby hotels *Marriott-Dulles*, Dulles International Airport ☎ (703) 471-9500 or (703) 661-8411. *Ramada Renaissance Dulles*, 13869 Park Center Rd, Herndon, VA ☎ (703) 478-2900; 15min from airport. *Holiday Inn*, 1000 Sully Rd, Sterling, VA ☎ (703) 471-7411; limousine provided for the 10min ride. *Holiday Inn*, Fair Oaks Mall, 11787 Lee-Jackson Hwy, Fairfax County VA ☎ (703) 352-2525; limousine provided for the 25min ride.
City link If you are staying in downtown Washington, take either a cab or the Washington Flyer. Driving can be frustrating, and parking is expensive. There is no Metrorail from Dulles.
Bus The Washington Flyer ☎ (703) 685-1400 provides a fast bus service to downtown every 30min, fare $10 one way, $17 round trip. To National Airport, the fares are $10 and $18 respectively. The Flyer also serves northern Virginia and suburban Maryland.
Taxi Cabs to downtown Washington are available 24hrs ☎ (703) 471-5555. The fare is about $30.
Car rental Four major companies are represented: Avis ☎ (800) 331-1212; Hertz ☎ (800) 654-3131; National ☎ (800) 328-4567; and Dollar ☎ (800) 421-6868.

Baltimore-Washington International Airport

BWI lies about 10 miles/16km S of Baltimore and 30 miles/48km N of Washington on the Washington-Baltimore Parkway (I-95). It handles domestic and international traffic. Currency exchange, notary services, photocopying, secretarial services, communication services and

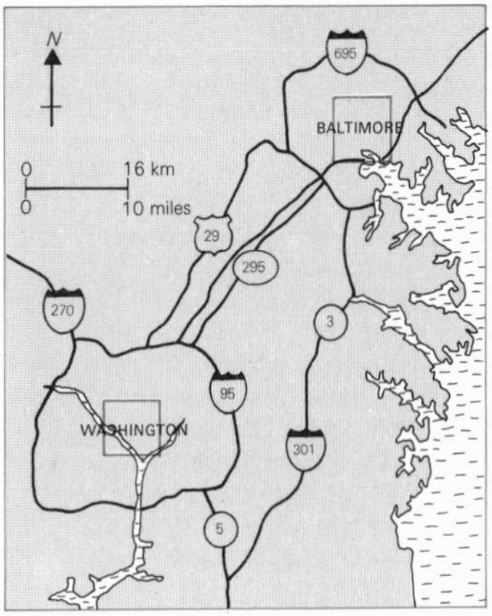

HOTELS

- **A** Embassy Row
- **B** Four Seasons
- **C** Grand
- **D** Hay-Adams
- **E** Jefferson
- **F** Madison
- **G** Mayflower
- **H** Park Hyatt
- **I** Ritz-Carlton
- **J** Sheraton Carlton
- **K** Sheraton Grand
- **L** Vista International
- **M** Watergate
- **N** Westin
- **O** Willard Inter-Continental
- **P** Georgetown Dutch Inn
- **Q** Quality Inn Downtown
- **R** Ramada Inn Central
- **S** Washington
- **T** JW Marriott
- **U** Omni Shoreham
- **V** Sheraton Washington
- **W** Tabard Inn
- **X** Washington Hilton and Towers

RESTAURANTS

- **A** Cantina d'Italia
- **B** Dominique's
- **C** Duke Zeibert's
- **D** Four Ways
  Jean Louis (Hotel M)
  Jockey Club (Hotel L)
- **E** Mr K's
- **F** Le Lion d'Or
- **G** Maison Blanche
- **H** Germaine's
- **I** Mel Krupin's
- **J** Morton's of Chicago
- **K** Le Pavilion
- **L** Potomac
- **M** 209 1/2
- **N** Vincenzo's
- **O** Joe and Mo's
- **P** Nora
- **Q** Old Ebbitt Grill
- **R** Sichuan Pavilion
- **S** Washington Palm

BUILDINGS AND SIGHTS

- **A** Convention Center
- **B** Tourist Information
- **C** Georgetown University
- **D** Lincoln Memorial
- **E** White House
- **F** Capitol
- **G** Corcoran Gallery of Art
- **H** Dunbarton Oaks
- **I** Hillwood Estate
- **J** Jefferson Memorial
- **K** Library of Congress
- **L** National Gallery of Art
- **M** Phillips Collection
- **N** State Department
  Diplomatic Reception Rooms
- **O** Smithsonian Institution
- **P** US Supreme Court Building
- **Q** Arlington National Cemetery
- **R** National Zoological Park
- **S** Pentagon
- **T** Washington Cathedral
- **U** Washington Monument

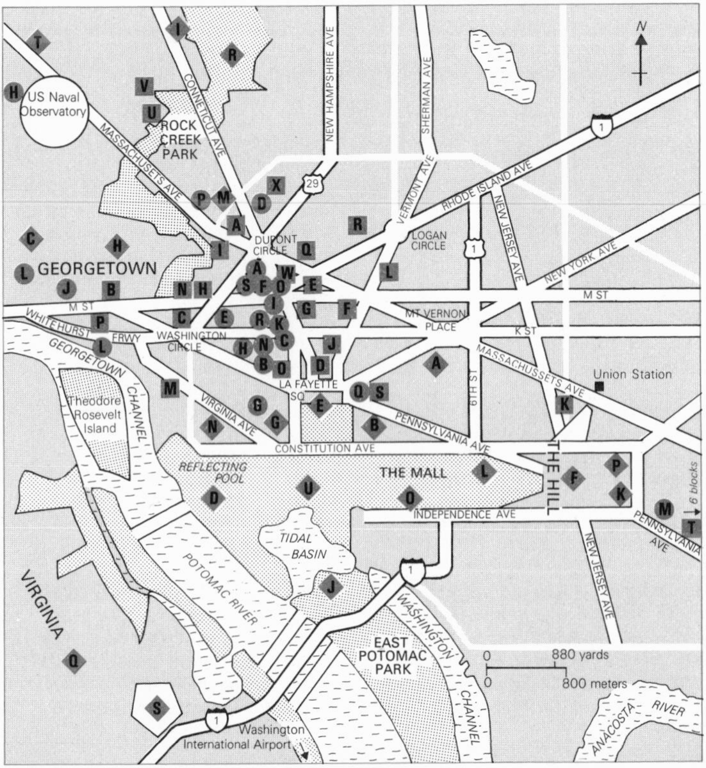

emergency cash are available at the Mutual of Omaha Service Center, Pier C ☏ (301)859-5997. Information (301) 859-7100.

Nearby hotel *International BWI* ☏ (301) 859-3300. Free shuttle bus from terminal to hotel.

City link *Taxi* Downtown Washington is a 45min drive from BWI; the center of Baltimore is just 15min by taxi. The fare to Washington is about $30, to Baltimore $12.

Rail Amtrak ☏ (800) 872-7242 provides services to Washington and Baltimore and other East Coast connections. Commuter rail service is provided by MARC ☏ (800) 325-7245. Free shuttle bus service is provided between the terminal and rail station.

Limousine BWI LIM Service ☏ 441-2345 provides a limo/bus service to the Washington Hilton, Capital Hilton and Greenbelt Terminal every 60min, 4.30am–midnight. The fare is $10 one way, $18 round trip.

Car rental Five car rental firms are represented at BWI: Avis ☏ (301) 859-1680; Budget ☏ (301) 859-0850; Dollar ☏ (301) 859-8950; Hertz ☏ (301) 859-3600; and National ☏ (301) 859-8860.

Union Station

Amtrak trains from points N, S and W, including an almost-hourly service from New York, Boston and other Eastern Seaboard cities, arrive at this imposing station near the Capitol, on Massachusetts Ave ☏ 484-7540. In recent years the station has been in what can charitably be called a state of flux, with the platforms reached via awkward stairways tucked behind a cavernous and unsuccessful "National Visitor Center." Currently the station is being completely renovated and will eventually contain restaurants and shops. In the meantime, arriving passengers will wish to go straight to the taxi rank or to the adjacent Metro station.

Getting around

Washington is designed in the shape of a wheel, with the Capitol building in the center and the streets radiating out like spokes. For the newcomer, driving can be a nerve-racking experience; and illegal parking is heavily penalized. The city is divided into quadrants, and streets are numbered and lettered consecutively; the diagonal streets are named after US states. Note that addresses repeat in all four quadrants; if travelling by taxi, you must specify which quadrant you require. The NW contains most of the city's important buildings, though the Capitol falls in the SE. If the numerous circles and squares cause driving difficulties, they also make walking a pleasure; it is practically impossible to get lost once you know the system. The best way to get around is on foot or by taxi, especially on Capitol Hill, where parking is almost exclusively by permit.

Taxi Cabs are readily available in downtown. Many drivers do not understand much English, though they do generally know their way around. Fares are reasonable and are calculated on a zone basis. (Virginia and Maryland taxis, however, are metered.) Do not be surprised if your driver stops to pick up another fare going in the same direction; likewise, do not hesitate to hail an occupied cab. New passengers have to pay the full zone fare, but additional members of the original party pay only a small premium. If you cannot hail a cab, you can call *Capitol Cab* ☏ 546-2450; *Diamond Cab* ☏ 387-6200; *Eastern Cab* ☏ 829-4222; or *Yellow Cab* ☏ 544-1212.

Subway The Metrorail's stations and trains are clean, quiet and comfortable; lines run throughout Washington and into northern Virginia and suburban Maryland. Fares range from 80 cents to $2.40. Ticket-selling is fully automated, occasionally making for annoying difficulties. You can buy a fare card

for various amounts, but the minimum is $1. Crisp dollar bills are needed for the ticket machines. The system operates 6am–midnight, Mon–Fri; 8am–midnight, Sat; 10–6, Sun. Information ☎ 637-7000.
Bus Metrobus ☎ 637-7000 operates in DC and in the Virginia and Maryland suburbs. It has 1,600 routes, and fares range from 75 cents to $1. Exact change or tokens are needed.
Car rental Major car rental companies have downtown offices: *Avis* ☎ 467-6588; *Budget* ☎ 628-2750; *Dollar* ☎ 296-3095; *Hertz* ☎ (800) 654-3131; and *National* ☎ 347-4772.
Limousine *Carey Limousine* ☎ 892-2000; *Orr's Limousine* ☎ 554-7997; *Admiral Limousine* ☎ 554-1000; and *International Limousine* ☎ 388-6800.

Area by area

When Major Pierre Charles L'Enfant was asked by President Washington to design the city in 1791, he placed the US Capitol building on the Hill to be the focal point of the city. It remains one of Washington's most visible and evocative landmarks.
Downtown Capitol Hill and Pennsylvania Avenue, which leads W to the White House, are dominated by huge Neo-classical government buildings. On the Hill, young Congressional staffers rub shoulders with countless tourists. Farther down Pennsylvania Avenue are the soberly dressed bureaucrats from the Department of Justice, Treasury, FBI and Federal Trade Commission buildings. Non-government businesses are concentrated around K Street and Connecticut Avenue, where lawyers, lobbyists and national trade associations throng the area – and its many business hotels and restaurants. The new Washington Convention Center occupies an entire block bounded by 9th, 11th and H streets and New York Avenue. ***Old Downtown*** is the city's fastest growing commercial sector, extending from just E of the White House almost to Union Station. In recent years it had become somewhat run-down, but its several department stores and new businesses, including luxury hotels, are thriving.
Georgetown Once a busy seaport with a thriving tobacco trade, Georgetown has many fine old Georgian and Federal-period townhouses where the city's social and political elite live and entertain. The area also has an array of ethnic restaurants strung along M Street and Wisconsin Avenue, plus a fine selection of fashion shops. To the E of Georgetown, Massachusetts Avenue runs into Dupont Circle, which has many lively shops and restaurants. The Washington Harbour development includes condominiums and offices, and is a good spot for strolling, with lovely views of the Kennedy Center and an excellent restaurant complex, the Potomac (see *Restaurants*).
Massachusetts Avenue The majestic stretch of this avenue running from Dupont Circle out past Rock Creek Park is known as Embassy Row. Here, and in the surrounding neighborhood, you will find most of Washington's embassies, many surrounded by spacious gardens. The area is also home to many senior executives and politicians.
Other areas Foxhall Road, in the Wesley Heights and Spring Valley area, is another prestigious address. Other expensive neighborhoods are scattered throughout Chevy Chase, Potomac and Bethesda in Maryland, and across the river in McLean, Virginia. Alexandria is another gentrified Virginia enclave, home to many Washington professionals. Its tone is similar to that of Georgetown, with gracious 18th and early-19thC houses and tree-shaded streets. King Street, in particular, contains numerous chic restaurants and trendy shops.

Hotels

Washington's top hotels cater well to the business traveller, with support services such as secretarial help and meeting and conference rooms readily available. All the hotels listed are in NW, not far from the Convention Center at 9th and H streets. Many have useful restaurants. Most have good security systems (the city's crime rate is high).

Capital Hilton $$$$$
1001 16th St NW ☏ 393-1000 Ⓣ 7108229068 • 549 rooms, 25 suites, 2 restaurants, 1 bar, 1 coffee shop
The fine location, just three blocks N of the White House, makes this hotel convenient for business. Rooms are unusually spacious. Two health clubs • 16 meeting rooms.

Embassy Row $$$$
2015 Massachusetts Ave NW 20036 ☏ 265-1600 Ⓣ 892650 • 168 rooms, 28 suites, 1 restaurant, 1 bar
Just off Dupont Circle, the Embassy Row is used by diplomats and CEOs seeking security and personable, attentive service. Its subdued Ambassador Grill serves *nouvelle cuisine*. Pool, nearby health club • 5 meeting rooms.

Four Seasons $$$$$
2800 Pennsylvania Ave NW 20007 ☏ 342-0444 Ⓣ 904008 • 167 rooms, 30 suites, 1 restaurant, 2 bars
Hard by Georgetown and just 12 blocks from the White House, on the edge of Rock Creek Park, this luxurious hotel is held to be one of the world's finest; be sure to get a room overlooking either the Chesapeake and Ohio Canal or the park. The handsome Aux Beaux Champs restaurant offers alternative calorie-, sodium- and cholesterol-reduced menus, as well as first-class Continental fare. Afternoon tea in the lobby (3–4.30) is a local favorite. Complimentary weekday limousine transportation • personalized exercise program, jogging path, arrangements with nearby health club • 5 meeting rooms, fax, teleconferencing, business reference library.

Grand $$$$$
2350 M St NW 20037 ☏ 429-0100 Ⓣ 904282 • 231 rooms, 31 suites, 3 restaurants, 1 bar
A European-style hotel, formerly the Regent, the Grand has a fine reputation, although service is thought to have slipped somewhat lately. Each bathroom has floor-to-ceiling marble panels, a large sunken tub, a separate shower and TV. All rooms have three telephones. Some of the suites have fine paintings, a jacuzzi and fireplace. The Promenade overlooking the courtyard is pleasant for tea or cocktails, and the Mayfair restaurant is smart and expensive. Health club, pool • 8 meeting rooms.

Hampshire Hotel $$$$
1310 New Hampshire Ave at N St 20036 ☏ 296-7600 Ⓣ 7108229343 • 54 suites, 36 rooms, 2 restaurants
This elegant small hotel prides itself on personal service. The 36 front-facing rooms all have balconies, and the décor is Oriental. The Hampshire has a good Creole restaurant, Lafitte. Breakfast is original, with spicy Creole omelets and *pain perdu.* Arrangements with nearby health club • 3 meeting rooms.

Hay-Adams $$$$$
1 Lafayette Sq NW 20006 ☏ 638-6600 Ⓣ 8229543 • 140 rooms, 18 suites, 3 restaurants, 2 bars
The Hay-Adams boasts that it is "an island of civility in a sea of power"; and the fashion publication *W* has said it is "as close as one can get to staying at the White House, short of being invited by the President." The rooms, some with fireplace, are tastefully furnished, and the view from the windows and balconies is of

Lafayette Square and the White House or the Washington Monument. The gentlemen's club-style English Grill and the John Hay Room offer Continental food (the former is a preferred eating place of Washington's financial community), but for breakfast try the Adams Room. Health club, jogging track • 3 meeting rooms.

Jefferson $$$$$
1200 16th St NW 20036 ☏ 347-2200 TX 248879 • 69 rooms, 39 suites, 3 restaurants
Small but distinguished, and just four blocks from the White House, the Jefferson was an apartment building until 1941. Its spacious rooms are attractively decorated; some have antique furnishings, including canopied beds. The Walter Annenbergs, Helen Hayes and Leonard Bernstein are among the hotel's discriminating guests. The staff are personable and attentive. The Hunt Club restaurant provides American cuisine in a warm, clubby atmosphere. Two meeting rooms.

Madison $$$$$
15th and M St NW 20005 ☏ 862-1600 TX 64245 • 330 rooms, 35 suites, 2 restaurants, 2 bars, 1 coffee shop
Not far from Dupont Circle and directly across the street from the *Washington Post* headquarters, the Madison has a 23-year record of good service and accommodation. All suites are furnished with antiques. The Montpelier Room serves traditional Continental dishes at rather elevated prices. Health club nearby • 9 meeting rooms.

JW Marriott $$$$$
1331 Pennsylvania Ave NW ☏ 393-2000 TX 7108229638 • 774 rooms, 51 suites, 3 restaurants, 1 bar
Recently refurbished as the flagship of the Marriott chain, the JW is big – and because of that, slightly impersonal; nevertheless, it is luxurious and conveniently located. The imposing lobby features expanses of marble flooring and gigantic crystal chandeliers. Plants and fresh flowers abound. The hotel connects with National Place, a popular shopping mall. Its smartest restaurant, the Celadon, features French/Chinese dishes. The National Café ranges from light snacks to full entrées, while the Garden Terrace has a jazz band. Barber, hair salon • health club • 22 meeting rooms.

Mayflower $$$$
1127 Connecticut Ave NW 20036 ☏ 347-3000 TX 892324 • 641 rooms, 83 suites, 2 restaurants, 1 bar
A $65m renovation has restored to this Washington landmark the Old World charm and status it had upon first opening in 1925. A Stouffer hotel, the Mayflower is ideal for engagements in the city's business district. Its airy Café Promenade does daily lunchtime buffets, but Nicolas is more intimate and stylish. Non-smoking rooms, gift shop, jeweler, barber, beauty shop • 19 meeting rooms.

Omni Shoreham $$$$
1500 Calvert St NW ☏ 234-0700 TX 7108220142 • 723 rooms, 47 suites, 1 restaurant, 1 bar, 1 coffee shop
The Art Deco Shoreham lies in Washington's NW district, just a short distance from the tranquil Rock Creek Park. It has recently undergone extensive redecoration. Service is both courteous and efficient. Pool, tennis, basketball • 22 meeting rooms.

Park Hyatt $$$$$
24th and M St NW 20037 ☏ 789-1234 TX 897105 • 100 rooms, 132 suites, 2 restaurants, 2 bars
This relatively new hotel has a full health club and 16,000 sq ft of conference and banquet space. The handsome suites and rooms have king-size beds, TV in the bathroom and multi-line telephones. Afternoon tea is served in the Tea Lounge 3–5; champagne and caviar are offered later. Non-smoking floor, hair salon

• pool, jacuzzi, sauna, exercise room
• 15 meeting rooms.

Ritz-Carlton $$$$$
2100 Massachusetts Ave NW 20008
☎ 293-2100 TX 263758 • 240 rooms, 30 suites, 1 restaurant, 1 bar
Formerly the Fairfax, the Ritz-Carlton has warmth and charm. Its Jockey Club (see *Restaurants*) and Ritz bar are as popular now as they were in the Kennedy era. Regulars include distinguished Europeans, corporate chiefs and media personalities. Nearby health facilities • 9 meeting rooms.

Sheraton Carlton $$$$$
923 16th St NW 20006 ☎ 638-2626 TX 440650 • 212 rooms, 38 suites, 1 restaurant, 1 bar
The Carlton is a throwback to a more gracious era, with a palm court lobby for afternoon tea and a wood-paneled wine bar frequented by K Street executives for after-work drinks. The dining room has an excellent reputation. Hair salon • arrangements with nearby health club • 7 meeting rooms, fax, translation.

Sheraton Grand $$$$
525 New Jersey Ave NW 20001
☎ 628-2100 TX 4970525 • 265 rooms, 32 suites, 2 restaurants, 1 bar, 1 coffee shop
As the only new luxury hotel on Capitol Hill, the Grand is ideal if your business is with Congress or one of the many associations, unions and government agencies nearby. The salmon-colored marble lobby has a glass atrium with a three-story garden trellis and waterfall. The rooms, including two floors for non-smokers, all have exercise equipment, personal computers, and telephones in bedroom and bathroom. Seven meeting rooms.

Sheraton Washington $$$$
2660 Woodley Rd NW ☎ 328-2000 TX 892630 • 1,505 rooms, 125 suites, 3 restaurants, 2 bars, 1 coffee shop
A giant of a hotel, the Sheraton Washington contains a mini-village of shops, while the Sunday brunch buffet is a veritable *grande bouffe*, with nearly 200 different items. Hair salon, post office • health club, pool • 38 meeting rooms.

Vista International $$$$
1400 M St NW 20005 ☎ 429-1700 TX 440237 • 300 rooms, 30 suites, 2 restaurants, 3 bars, 1 coffee shop
Soft background music – string quartet, piano or harpist – in the greenery-filled lobby sets the tone here, though the Vista's location is less than ideal; be wary of walking to the N or E after sunset. The American Harvest restaurant is Continental; the more casual Verandah does a good Sunday brunch. Health club • 11 meeting rooms.

Washington Hilton and Towers $$$$
1919 Connecticut Ave NW
☎ 483-3000 TX 248761 • 1,050 rooms, 80 suites, 2 restaurants, 2 bars, 1 coffee shop
About seven blocks N of Dupont Circle, the convention-oriented Washington Hilton is both modern and efficient. The health-conscious traveller is well catered to here, for the hotel offers an outdoor pool, jogging track, tennis courts and bike rental, plus a health club and game room. Thirty-one meeting rooms.

Watergate $$$$$
2650 Virginia Ave NW 20037
☎ 965-2300 TX 8220199 • 238 rooms, 3 restaurants, 2 bars
Part of the notorious Watergate complex, this Cunard hotel is just across the street from the Kennedy Center. The award-winning Jean Louis (see *Restaurants*) is generally considered the city's finest hotel restaurant. The Watergate Terrace, downstairs from the lobby, is popular with the Kennedy Center crowds in the evening, and Les Champs is good for a quick light meal.

Complimentary limousine to downtown 7–10am, hair salon, boutique shops • health club, pool • 7 meeting rooms.

Westin $$$$$
2401 M St NW 20037 ☎ *429-2400* TX *4979801 • 378 rooms, 38 suites, 2 restaurants, 1 bar*
Perhaps the Westin's strongest point is its fitness center, with exercise equipment, squash courts, lap pool, saunas, steamroom, whirlpool, massage and aerobic classes. The hotel also has conference facilities, including a soundproof theater equipped for worldwide video-conferencing. Non-smoking rooms • 15 meeting rooms, fax.

Willard Inter-Continental $$$$$
1401 Pennsylvania Ave NW 20004 ☎ *628-9100* TX *897099 • 395 rooms, 62 suites, 1 restaurant, 2 bars, 1 coffee shop*
Oliver Carr, a prominent Washington developer, has restored the Willard to its 1901 splendor, besides adding offices and boutiques. Two blocks from the White House, this was once the gathering place for politicians and literary figures, including Mark Twain. Its block-long lobby, Peacock Alley, where special-interest groups would gather in hopes of cornering politicians, is where the term "lobbyist" was coined. The turn-of-the-century wood-paneled Willard Room serves American food. The Round Robin Bar is a replica of the c.1850 black marble original. Fifteen meeting rooms, fax, translation, recording facilities.

OTHER HOTELS
Georgetown Dutch Inn ($$$) *1075 Thomas Jefferson St NW 20007* ☎ *337-0900.* Off M Street, near C & O Canal.
Quality Inn Downtown ($$) *1315 16th St at Massachusetts Ave NW* ☎ *232-8000.*
Ramada Inn Central ($$$) *1430 Rhode Island Ave NW 20005* ☎ *462-7777.*
Tabard Inn ($$$) *1739 N St NW* ☎ *785-1277.*
Washington ($$$$) *15th St and Pennsylvania Ave NW 20004* ☎ *638-5900* TX *7108220105.* Famous for its rooftop terrace, where from May to October you can admire the finest views in Washington.

Clubs

Washington clubs provide hidden, but powerful, opportunities to forge important business relationships – but mainly for men. The *F Street Club* is an exclusive dining club in the downtown area with about 400 members. For prominent scientists and literary figures, there is the all-male *Cosmos Club.* The traditional business, legal and banking community belong to the all-male *Metropolitan Club.* The prominent *University Club* recently opened its membership to women, and has meeting rooms as well as dining and athletic facilities. For women only, there is the *Sulgrave Club* on Massachusetts Avenue near Dupont Circle. Georgetown's *City Tavern Club* provides its members with an intimate townhouse atmosphere. Situated downtown on I Street is the discreet men-only *Alibi Club.*

Restaurants

Dining in Washington has moved away from steak and potatoes to more sophisticated fare, although quality does not always match prices. Many restaurants around K Street and Connecticut Avenue specialize in the business lunch, with prices equivalent to those in New York City. There is an ever-expanding range of ethnic restaurants. Georgetown's numerous exotic offerings lean towards the mass market, but those in Adams Morgan, just NW of Dupont Circle, are good value.

Cantina d'Italia $$$$$
1214-A 18th St NW ☏ *659-1830* • *closed Sat and Sun* • AE CB DC MC V • *reservations essential*
A northern Italian restaurant, popular for nearly 20 years with business people, the media and the diplomatic corps. The intimate atmosphere is maintained in a series of dimly-lit small dining rooms, and the changing menu offers good fish, veal and pasta. Extensive wine list.

Dominique's $$$
1900 Pennsylvania Ave NW ☏ *452-1126* • *closed Sun* • AE CB DC MC V
Just two blocks from the White House, this unusual restaurant – created by Dominique d'Erno – features a rather gaudy mélange of paintings and Washington memorabilia. In times past, this was a real showplace, though in recent years it has been surpassed by other, newer restaurants. It is still a favorite with Kennedy Center performers, however. The menu ranges from the traditional to the bizarre – including ostrich and rattlesnake.

Duke Zeibert's $$$
Washington Square Bldg, 1050 Connecticut Ave NW ☏ *466-3730* • *D only Sun* • AE DC MC V • *jacket required*
The owner came out of retirement recently to move his well-established restaurant into a new building with a view of Connecticut Avenue – though, that said, if you get the view, you are not in the preferred room. For 30 years this reliable steak and seafood house has been a second home for politicians, business leaders, athletes and media personalities, though the food is easily bettered in other nearby restaurants.

Four Ways $$$$
1701 20th St NW ☏ *483-3200* • AE CB DC MC V • *jacket and tie required*
The French food at Four Ways is attractive, as is the building itself – a grand oak-paneled mansion that is a historic landmark.

Germaine's $$$
2400 Wisconsin Ave NW ☏ *965-1185* • *D only Sat and Sun* • AE CB DC MC V • *reservations essential*
Serving well-prepared Asian dishes – incorporating Vietnamese, Korean, Chinese, Thai, Indian and Japanese influences, among others – Germaine Swanson's spectacularly successful restaurant is one of the best in Washington. The daily specials are the thing to watch for, as is the house specialty, pine cone fish. Good wine list.

Jean Louis $$$$$
Watergate Hotel, 2650 Virginia Ave NW ☏ *298-4488* • *closed Aug* • AE CB DC MC V • *reservations essential*
Regulars feel that you cannot beat the *nouvelle* creations prepared here by Jean Louis Palladin, one of America's most inventive and talented chefs. Go here for a special evening; expect to be pampered, and to pay plenty for it. Pastel peach walls and mirrors make the small room seem spacious. There is one seating per night with three-, four- and five-course meals available, and you can choose wines by the glass to accompany each course.

Jockey Club $$$$
Ritz-Carlton Hotel, 2100 Massachusetts Ave NW ☏ *293-2100* • AE CB DC MC V • *jacket and tie required*
This old Kennedy favorite has a warm, intimate atmosphere, with red leather banquettes and English hunting prints on the walls; and it remains well patronized by politicians and media types. Its crabmeat is renowned, its service laudable.

Joe and Mo's $$$
1211 Connecticut Ave NW ☏ *659-1211* • *closed Sun* • AE CB DC MC V • *lunch reservations essential*
An Old Downtown institution, this steakhouse has a loyal following among the city's leaders, although

one goes here to be noticed, not for the food, which is occasionally disappointing. On the other hand, the staff are courteous and efficient. Ideal for breakfast – imaginative and well-prepared – as well as for lunch.

Le Lion d'Or **$$$$**
1150 Connecticut Ave NW
☎ 296-7972 • D only Sat; closed Sun • AE CB DC MC V
Chef-owner Jean Pièrre Goyenvalle has maintained consistently high standards. Duck, quail and pigeon are specialties of his kitchen; the seafood and soufflés are also noteworthy. Dishes are classic French rather than *nouvelle*. The wine list is fairly priced.

Maison Blanche **$$$$$**
1725 F St NW ☎ 842-0070 • D only Sat; closed Sun • AE CB DC MC V • jacket and tie required
A favorite of the Reagan administration, the Maison Blanche is consistently rated as one of the city's better restaurants; a good table here undoubtedly lends status. The setting is plush. The waiters are helpful in guiding you to the excellent daily specials, and the long wine list offers some good things.

Mel Krupin's **$$$**
1120 Connecticut Ave NW
☎ 331-7000 • closed Sun • AE CB DC MC V • jacket and tie required
This comfortable downstairs restaurant – an archetypal steak and potatoes establishment with a loyal following – is a great place for catching up on gossip while enjoying the hearty food; the specials are the same each week. Recently, however, the restaurant's standards have slipped slightly.

Mr K's **$$$$**
2121 K St NW ☎ 331-8868 • AE CB DC MC V • jacket and tie required
Two white marble lions guard the entrance to this elegant restaurant in the city's business district. The food is Chinese, while the plush dining room (which includes a non-smoking area) has a pleasant European feel. The giant shrimp, quail and frogs' legs are splendid. Prices are steep, but the service is gracious.

Morton's of Chicago **$$$$**
3251 Prospect St NW ☎ 342-6258 • D only • AE DC MC V
Morton's is undoubtedly Washington's best steakhouse, and its white-walled dining room is always crowded with politicians, lobbyists and business people. It takes no reservations after 7pm. Huge portions.

Nora **$$$$**
2132 Florida Ave NW at R St
☎ 462-5143 • D only Sat; closed Sun • no credit cards
Fine American *nouvelle cuisine* is served here in a cozy setting with lace curtains and turn-of-the-century furniture. Typical dishes include smoked trout with horseradish sauce and roast chicken with mustard cream sauce.

Old Ebbitt Grill **$$**
675 15th St NW ☎ 347-4801 • AE CB DC MC V
Founded in 1856, Ebbitt's is the city's oldest saloon, although the present building is a recent reconstruction. It has Persian rugs, oak beams, marble floors and gas lamps. There is an oyster bar, the Old Bar and Grant's Bar, as well as two dining areas. There is a varied menu – everything from hamburgers to pasta, good fish, excellent desserts. It is also popular for breakfast.

Le Pavillon **$$$$$**
Washington Sq, 1050 Connecticut Ave NW ☎ 833-3846 • D only Sat; closed Sun • AE CB DC V • jacket required • reservations essential
A Lalique table stands in the foyer of this favorite of Washington society. Exquisite *nouvelle cuisine* is served here, and Chef Yannich Cam checks every dish as it leaves the kitchen. The service is attentive and discreet, and tables are suitably spaced for

privacy. However, some people feel the prices are rather high and the portions on the small side.

Potomac $$$
30th and K St NW ☎ 944-4200
• AE CB DC MC V
A new restaurant (or rather series of restaurants) built on the banks of the Potomac and with superb views of the river. The décor is flamboyant – fountains and chandeliers. The food is acceptable.

Sichuan Pavilion $$$
1820 K St NW ☎ 466-7790
• AE CB DC MC V
Although the restaurant is US-owned, the Sichuan's chefs are recruited from the People's Republic of China Chungking Service Bureau, which operates hotels and restaurants for visiting dignitaries and prepares state banquets. This is the best Chinese restaurant in Washington – elegant yet unpretentious. The food is always beautifully presented.

209½ $$$
209½ Pennsylvania Ave SE
☎ 544-6352 • D only Sat; closed Sun
• AE CB DC MC V
Perhaps the best restaurant on the Hill, this subdued dining room was the first to introduce Washington to American *nouvelle cuisine*. The prices are fairly modest, and the menu changes monthly – which keeps senators, congressmen and their aides coming back.

Vincenzo's $$$
1606 20th St NW ☎ 667-0047
• *closed Sun* • AE MC V
This pleasant Italian seafood restaurant serves excellent fresh fish, grilled or fried, and pasta – but no meat or cream sauces. The simple Adriatic décor features tiled floors and whitewashed walls.

Washington Palm $$$$$
1225 19th St NW ☎ 293-9091
• *D only Sat; closed Sun* • AE CB DC MC V • *reservations essential*
A southern cousin of New York's Palm restaurant, this is yet another stronghold of the city's business and political communities. The steaks are good, the lobsters succulent and truly jumbo-sized, the service friendly and reasonably efficient. Well recommended for working lunches.

Out of town
If time permits and you want a special treat, head for *Windows*, across Key Bridge in Rosslyn, Virginia, which offers a panoramic view of DC. The menu is also excellent. *L'Auberge Chez François* is a pleasant 45min drive through Virginia hunt country to Great Falls. Note, however, that you have to make your reservation two weeks ahead. The food is Alsatian, the atmosphere that of a French country inn.

Bars

Washington's hotel bars and lounges are much in use as work spills over from offices. The business elite favor the *Fairfax Bar* at the Ritz-Carlton, the classiest bar in town, with 18thC English paintings on the walls. Other favorite bars include *Bullfeathers*, 401 1st St SE, *the* gathering place for Hill staffers; the *Hawk & Dove*, 329 Pennsylvania Ave SE, close to the Capitol, with an old Irish tavern atmosphere; and *Jenkins Hill*, 223 Pennsylvania Ave SE, one of the longest bars in DC.

In the business district, the *Sign of the Whale*, 1825 M St NW, is an attractive English-style pub, popular with young professionals. *Rumors*, 1900 M St NW, is always crowded. Besides its two bars, it has an enclosed sidewalk café overlooking busy 19th Street.

In Georgetown, *Clyde's*, 3236 M St NW, is frequented by Washington politicos and their staff. Art Deco design and lively 1960s music make *F Scott's*, 1232 36th St NW, a local favorite. *Mr Smith's*, 3104 M St NW, is a Georgetown landmark, with an old tavern atmosphere.

Entertainment

The best sources of information are the "Weekend" section of Friday's *Washington Post* and the monthly *Washingtonian* magazine. For tickets contact *Ticketplace*, 12th and F St NW ☏ 842-5387. Cut-rate tickets are often available on the day of an event.

Music The *John F Kennedy Center for the Performing Arts* ☏ 254-3600 is a stunning building overlooking the Potomac River. With five halls, including the Opera House and the Concert Hall, it is the cultural hub of Washington. *Blues Alley* in Georgetown attracts student and diplomat jazz fans. During summer months there is a fine arts and music festival, featuring well-known performers, at *Wolf Trap Park*, about 45min out of town in the direction of Dulles Airport; for information ☏ (703) 255-1800. Summertime entertainment is also provided at the *Carter Barron Amphitheatre* in Rock Creek Park ☏ 426-6700.

Theater Washington's principal theaters are the *Warner* and the *National*; both stage Broadway productions. The *Folger Theater* is generally considered America's top Shakespearean playhouse. *Ford's Theater* has been restored to the way it was the night President Lincoln was shot. Comedy and drama are presented at the *Eisenhower* in the Kennedy Center.

Nightclubs The *Marquee Lounge* in the Shoreham Hotel has 1930s and '40s music; for '50s, '60s and '70s sounds, try *Déja Vu* on M Street.

Shopping

Formerly something of a fashion backwater, Washington has a growing number of smart shops. In the heart of the business district along Connecticut Avenue, you will find *Elizabeth Arden*, the *Tiny Jewel Box*, *Burberry's* and *Ralph Lauren Polo Shop. Kramer Books and Afterwards* is both bookstore and café. At 1840 L St NW there is *Brooks Brothers* men's shop. Department stores such as *Woodward & Lothrop*, known as "Woodies," *The Hecht Co* and fashionable *Garfinckel's* are in Old Downtown. Shopping malls include *The Shops* at National Place, 1331 Pennsylvania Ave, and *The Old Post Office*, just opposite.

If you have time, Georgetown has something for everyone – especially along Wisconsin Avenue and M Street. *Georgetown Park* has almost 120 shops and restaurants in an attractive converted warehouse. *Mazza Gallery*, on the border of DC and Chevy Chase, Maryland, on Wisconsin Avenue NW, is popular and has a Metrorail stop. In the same area are *Lord & Taylor*, *Saks Fifth Avenue*, *Saks-Jandel* and *Gucci*.

Sightseeing

Arlington National Cemetery Includes the Tomb of the Unknown Soldier, the Kennedy graves and Arlington House, home of General Robert E Lee until the Civil War. *Across the Memorial Bridge, in Arlington ☏ 629-0931. Open Apr–Sep, 8–7; Oct–Mar, 8–5.*

Capitol Half-hour tours of the Capitol set off every 15min, 9–3.45. US visitors can arrange with their congressman to get a pass to enter the chambers of the House or Senate to see Congress in action; non-US visitors will need some form of identification, such as a passport. *E end of the Mall ☏ 224-3121 or 225-6827. Open 9–4.30.*

Corcoran Gallery of Art Founded in 1859, this museum has a fine collection of American art, as well as works by European masters. *New York Ave and 17th St NW ☏ 638-3211. Tours from 10–4.30, Tue–Sun; 10–9, Thu.*

Diplomatic Reception Room, Department of State Exquisitely decorated room, with fine 18thC antiques; it is here that the secretary of state entertains foreign dignitaries. *2201 C St NW ☏ 632-3241. Tours at various times; reservations needed.*

Dumbarton Oaks This splendid Georgetown mansion houses Byzantine and pre-Columbian art.

1703 32nd St NW; gardens at 31st and R St. Open Tue–Sun, 2–5.

Executive Office Building This vast gray pile in Second Empire style, just W of the White House, houses various governmental offices. Not open to the public, but the exterior is worth a small detour for its architectural interest. *17th St and Pennsylvania Ave NW.*

Hillwood Estate The former estate of Marjorie Merriweather Post, located in the upper reaches of NW Washington. You can tour her home and see her large collection of Russian decorative arts, including Fabergé. *4155 Linnean Ave ☎ 686-5807. Tours $7; reservations required • closed Tue and Sun.*

Jefferson Memorial The graceful, domed monument is especially striking at night. Engraved on its walls are excerpts from Jefferson's writings, including the Declaration of Independence. *Tidal Basin end of 15th St SW.*

Library of Congress Built in 1897, the copper-domed Library contains more than 80m books and is one of the most spectacular buildings in Washington, an ornate Italian Renaissance/Beaux Arts design modeled after the Paris Opera House. *1st and E Capitol St SE ☎ 287-6700. Open Mon–Fri, 9–4; Sat, 8.30–5; Sun, 1–5.*

Lincoln Memorial Inspired by classical Greek architecture with columns representing the 36 states in the Union when Lincoln died. At the W end of the Mall. *23rd St NW between Constitution and Independence Ave. Open 24hrs daily.*

National Gallery of Art Situated on the Mall, this is one of the world's great art museums. The graceful West Building is a harmonious setting for an outstanding collection of Old Masters, particularly strong in the Italian, Dutch and Impressionist schools. The acclaimed new East Building contains modern art, includng works by Alexander Calder and Henry Moore. The Museum has a good cafeteria restaurant and presents free concerts on Sunday evenings. *4th–6th sts on Constitution Ave ☎ 737-4215. Open 10–5, Mon–Sat; 12–9, Sun.*

National Zoological Park Held to be one of the world's finest zoos, this forms part of the Smithsonian Institution (see below), though it is located in an extension of NW Washington's Rock Creek Park. The giant pandas Hsing-Hsing and Ling-Ling – a gift from China – are major attractions. A pleasant spot to spend a sunny afternoon. *3001 Connecticut Ave NW ☎ 673-4717. Open May–mid-Sep, 8–8 (grounds), 9–6 (buildings); mid-Sep–Apr, 8–6 (grounds), 10–4.30 (buildings).*

Phillips Collection Two blocks NW of Dupont Circle, this is a fine collection of art, featuring Impressionist and Post-Impressionist painting, in a lovely old red-brick house. *1600 21st St NW ☎ 387-2151. Open 10–5, Tue–Sat; 2–7, Sun.*

Smithsonian Institution The Smithsonian is a federally chartered, non-profit corporation comprising scientific, educational and cultural interests based mostly in Washington. Most of the buildings are along the Mall. The building known as the Castle is the headquarters and has a visitors' center ☎ 357-1300. The *Air and Space Museum*, held to be the world's most popular museum, has some fascinating films, as well as the Wright brothers' first airplane, Lindbergh's *Spirit of St Louis*, various space vehicles, and even the *USS Enterprise*, well known to all *Star Trek* fans. The *National Museum of American Art*, the *National Museum of American History* and the *National Museum of Natural History* all have excellent displays and exhibits. The *Freer Gallery* has the finest Far and Near Eastern art collection outside the Orient; and the *Hirshhorn Museum*, which displays modern art, has an outstanding sculpture garden. *1000 Jefferson Dr SW ☎ 357-2700. Most museums are open daily, 10–5.*

US Supreme Court This Neo-classical marble structure is one of the Capital's most impressive. The Court's sessions are open to the public. *1st and E Capitol St SE ☏ 252-3000. Open Mon–Fri, 9–4.30.*

Washington Cathedral A huge Gothic-style church (Episcopal), also known as the National Cathedral and, more accurately, the Cathedral Church of St Peter and St Paul. Still unfinished, it is a successful blend of French and English Gothic styles. The splendid interior has some fine stained glass, and the square tower is a Washington landmark. *Mt St Alban ☏ 537-6200. Open Mon–Sat, 10–4.30; Sun, 8–4.30.*

Washington Monument The world's tallest masonry structure, designed by Pierre L'Enfant. An elevator takes you to the top. *15th St Constitution Ave. Open daily Apr–Sep.*

White House This elegant porticoed building is the official home of the President. A popular tour takes visitors through five state rooms. Tickets to the more comprehensive "V.I.P." tour can sometimes be obtained through congressional contacts. *1600 Pennsylvania Ave NW ☏ 456-7041. Open Tue–Sat, 10–12.*

Guided tours

Gray Line ☏ 479-5900 has set tours such as "Washington After Dark," but one of the most reasonable ways to view major sights is the *Tourmobile* ☏ 554-7950. These blue-and-white canopied shuttle buses operate continuously, so you can get on or off at any one of the 18 stations and stay as long as you please.

Out of town

Colonial Williamsburg lies 150 miles/240km S of Washington DC in Virginia. Once the capital of the colony of Virginia, it is full of historical interest and has been meticulously restored. Although inevitably somewhat artificial, it successfully captures the atmosphere of 18thC life. *Mt Vernon* lies 16 miles/25km S of the city on the George Washington Parkway in Virginia. A gracious 18thC house overlooking the Potomac, it was the home of George Washington and is still maintained in the style of an old southern plantation. You can also travel there by boat, Mar–Nov, leaving from Pier 4, 6th and Water streets NW ☏ 554-8000.

Spectator sports

Baseball Washington does not have its own major league team. However, you can watch the Baltimore *Orioles* at Baltimore Stadium ☏ 347-2525.

Basketball The Washington *Bullets* play at the Capital Center, Capital Beltway and Central Ave, Landover, Maryland ☏ 350-3900.

Football The *Redskins* are based at the Robert F Kennedy Stadium ☏ 546-2222. Tickets are best obtained through trade associations.

Horse racing For thoroughbred racing, *Laurel Race Course*, Laurel, Maryland ☏ 725-0400, about 18 miles/28km away.

Ice hockey The Washington *Capitols* play at the Capital Center ☏ 350-3500.

Keeping fit

Health clubs *JW Marriott Hotel*, 1331 Pennsylvania Ave NW ☏ 393-2000; *Washington Squash and Nautilus Club*, 1220 20 St NW ☏ 659-9570; *Watergate Health Club*, 2650 Virginia Ave NW ☏ 298-4460; *Westin Fitness Center*, 2401 M St NW ☏ 457-5070.

Bicycling Washington's wide boulevards are ideal for cyclists. For rentals, *Big Wheel Bikes*, 1004 Vermont Ave NW ☏ 638-3301.

Boating The calm Potomac River is especially suitable for canoes or sailboats. *Thompsons Boat Center*, Virginia Ave at Rock Creek Pkwy NW ☏ 333-4861, rents canoes, sailboats and bicycles.

Golf *Rock Creek* course, 16th and Rittenhouse NW ☏ 723-9832, is open to the public. *East Potomac Park* ☏ 863-9007 has both 18-hole and 9-hole courses. The Maryland and

Virginia suburbs have many courses.
Horseback riding *Rock Creek Park* has 14 miles/22km of wooded trails. For information on rentals, horses and instruction, contact *Rock Creek Park Horse Center*, Military and Glover roads NW ☎ 362-0117.
Jogging A favorite jogging course is the *Mall*, from the Lincoln Memorial to the Capitol.
Tennis *Rock Creek Tennis Stadium*, ☎ 723-2669 and *East Potomac Park* ☎ 554-5962; reservations must be made in person.

Local resources

Business services

All of the concierges at the hotels can find you almost any service you may need. Alternatives are *Codus Corporation* ☎ 347-4947 or *Courtesy Associates* ☎ 337-1855.
Photocopying *City Duplicating Service* ☎ 296-0700; *Beaver Press* ☎ 347-6400.
Secretarial *Joan Masters and Sons* ☎ 842-3737; *Courtesy Associates* ☎ 347-5900.
Translators *International Volunteer Information Service*, Language Bank ☎ 783-6540; *Berlitz Language Center* ☎ 331-1160; *Interpreters Bureau* (used by State Dept) ☎ 296-1346.

Communications

Local delivery *Metro* ☎ 387-8200; *All State Messenger Service* ☎ 841-9000; *Messenger Express* ☎ 347-7333.
Long-distance delivery *Federal Express* ☎ 953-3333; *DHL Worldwide* ☎ 296-6950.
Post office Main branch ☎ 523-2323, Massachusetts Ave and N Capitol St.

Convention/exhibition centers

District of Columbia Armory, 2001 E Capitol St ☎ 547-9077; *Washington, Convention and Visitors' Association*, 1575 1 St NW ☎ 789-7000; *Washington DC Convention Center*, 900 9th St NW ☎ 789-1600;

Emergencies

Hospitals *Georgetown University*, 3800 Reservoir Rd NW ☎ 625-7171; *George Washington Medical Center*, 901 23rd St NW ☎ 676-6000; *Columbia Hospital for Women*, 24th and L St NW ☎ 293-6500; *Children's Hospital*, 111 Michigan Ave NW ☎ 745-5000.
Pharmacies *Peoples' Drug Store*, 14th and Thomas Circle ☎ 628-0720; also has locations throughout the city.

Information sources

Business information *Chamber of Commerce*, 1341 G St NW ☎ 347-7202.
Local media The *Washington Post* gives good local, national and international coverage. The *Washington Times* is not so well thought of. The monthly *Regardie's* magazine provides an incisive feature-oriented business commentary while the *Washingtonian* (also monthly) is very helpful for local information. *Dossier* specializes in the latest gossip.
Tourist information *Washington DC Government Office*, 613 G St ☎ 727-1000, gives general information. The most centrally located tourist office is between 14th and 15th streets on Pennsylvania Ave NW ☎ 789-7000. Open 9–5, daily in summer, Mon–Sat the rest of the year. The *Washington Convention and Visitors' Association*, 1575 I St NW ☎ 789-7000, provides brochures on hotels and sightseeing.

Thank-yous

Florists *The Flower Designers*, 3301 New Mexico Ave NW ☎ 966-3400; *David Ladd & Co*, 1622 Wisconsin Ave NW ☎ 337-0413; and *Flowers-Design by David Ellsworth*, 2015 Florida Ave NW ☎ 328-1666.
Gift baskets *Sutton Place Gourmet* ☎ 363-5800, on New Mexico Avenue, can deliver a basket of almost any kind of food. Also *Sutton Place Gift Gallery Ltd* ☎ 966-8228 and *Essentially Chocolate* ☎ 387-6994.

BALTIMORE

Area code ☏ 301

Just 30 miles/48km N of the USA's capital city, Baltimore once had the reputation for being a dirty port and industrial city. Today, although still a major maritime and industrial center, it is a revitalized and rather sophisticated modern city. The Inner Harbor has been redeveloped, yet its port still has 43 miles/69km of waterfront. It is there that Baltimore takes in ores, bananas and automobiles, and where it sends out grain, iron, coal and steel. It is the headquarters of one of the world's biggest spice processors – McCormack; US&G Insurance and Crown Central Petroleum have their national headquarters here as well. General Motors, Martin Marietta, Procter & Gamble, and Black and Decker all have major plants in Baltimore and are important to the city's economy. But the growth industry is biotechnology, based at the Johns Hopkins Medical Center. Baltimore is by no means a tourist town, but the business visitor is likely to be impressed by the scale of energetic renovation that is still going on.

Arriving

Baltimore Washington International Airport

(See WASHINGTON)

City link *Taxi* The center of Baltimore is just 15min from the airport by taxi; 20min during rush hour. The fare should run approximately $12.
Rail There is a daily Amtrak service to Washington and Philadelphia and other East Coast connections ☏ (800) 872-7245. Local commuter rail service is provided by MARC ☏ (800) 325-7245. A free shuttle bus service operates between the airport terminal and the rail station.
Limousine BWI LIM Service ☏ 441-2345 provides an excellent alternative to a cab – a limo/van service to major Baltimore hotels for about $10.
Car rental Five firms are located at BWI: Avis ☏ 859-1680; Budget ☏ 859-0850; Dollar ☏ 859-8950; Hertz ☏ 859-3600; and National ☏ 859-8860.

Getting around

Walking The best way to get around downtown Baltimore is to walk. Driving is manageable, though not really necessary as the area is relatively small and there are skywalks from hotels to buildings.
Driving Parking is available at the Inner Harbor and downtown areas. For car rental information, see *City link*.
Taxi Cabs are generally reliable and can be hailed in the street at any time. If you want to phone ahead, however, try *Diamond* ☏ 947-3333, *Yellow Cab* ☏ 685-1212, *BWI Airport Cab* ☏ 859-1100 or *Sun* ☏ 235-0300.
Limousine *Carey Limo* ☏ 233-7400.
Trolley *Baltimore Trolley Works* is part of the city transportation service. The trolleys run at 7min intervals and stop about every two blocks along the Inner Harbor and Charles Street. Services operate Sun–Thu, 11–10, Fri–Sat, 11–11 ☏ 396-4259. Trolleys are also available for rent.
Bus For routes and times of the *MTA* bus service ☏ 539-5000.
Subway For information on *Metrorail* ☏ 659-2700.

Area by area

Downtown The architecture of Baltimore combines the 20thC in the Charles Center-Inner Harbor area, the 19thC at Mt Vernon Place, and the 18thC at Fells Point. Charles

■ **HOTELS**
- **A** Admiral Fell Inn
- **B** Belvedere
- **C** Cross Keys Inn
- **D** Hyatt Regency
- **E** Peabody Court
- **F** Sheraton Inner Harbor
- **G** Tremont
- **H** Society Hill
- **I** Society Hill Government House
- **J** Tremont Plaza

● **RESTAURANTS**
- La Brasserie (Hotel E)
- Conservatory (Hotel E)
- 8 East (Hotel G)
- **A** Haussner's
- John Eager Howard Room (Hotel B)
- **B** Prime Rib
- **C** Tio Pepe
- Trellis Garden (Hotel D)

◆ **BUILDINGS AND SIGHTS**
- **A** City Hall
- **B** World Trade Center
- **C** Aquarium
- **D** B & O Railway Museum
- **E** Harborplace
- **F** Maryland Science Center and Planetarium
- **G** US Frigate Constitution
- **H** Walter Art Gallery
- **I** Charles Center

Center, the city's main business district, was the first stage in the downtown renaissance; its 33-acre complex has hotels, office buildings, apartments and restaurants. S from the Center is the Baltimore Convention Center. At the waterfront, Harborplace's two pavilions contain more than 100 smart shops, boutiques and restaurants. Nearby are the World Trade Center, with its 27th-floor observation level, the National Aquarium and the Maryland Science Center. N of Charles Center is Mt Vernon Place, established in the early 1800s as the city's most prestigious residential district. The four-block area surrounding the 160ft Washington Monument has fashionable Victorian townhouses inhabited by many of the city's top executives. E from Inner Harbor, at the end of Broadway Street, lies Fells Point. Established in the mid-18thC, this once thriving maritime community is being extensively redeveloped.

Other areas For urban living, many executives choose Federal Hill, a neighborhood of renovated row houses, Mt Vernon and Rowland Park. Fashionable suburban areas are Towson, Timonium and Cockeysville.

Hotels

With the revitalization of downtown Baltimore, major hotel chains such as Marriott, Omni, Hilton, Hyatt and Sheraton have built modern, business-oriented hotels to serve the Convention Center and the Inner Harbor. There are also some recently renovated smaller hotels which might be more suitable for a longer stay, especially if you prefer the comfort of a private apartment-like suite.

Admiral Fell Inn **$$$**
888 S Broadway 21231 ☏ 522-7377 • 37 rooms, 1 restaurant, 1 bar
This small colonial inn at Fells Point is in fact three restored historic townhouses converted into a single hotel. Each room is handsomely decorated, and most have canopied beds. Service is efficient, the staff pleasant. There is a hot tub on the roof, and an attractive pub in the basement. A free van service takes guests anywhere in the city. Health club nearby • 1 meeting room.

Belvedere **$$**
Charles and Chase St 21202 ☏ 332-1000 TX 8745801 • 131 rooms, 48 suites, 3 restaurants, 4 bars, 1 coffee shop
Restoration of Baltimore's grandest hotel began in 1976. Most rooms have full-service kitchens, and the hotel specializes in catering for meetings of 10 to 200. It has a distinguished restaurant, the John Eager Howard Room (see *Restaurants*), as well as the Owl Bar, where you can get a hearty meal in a more casual setting. The stylish lounge on the 13th floor has a splendid view. Beauty and barber shop, gift shops • sauna, pool, whirlpool, racquetball courts, health club • 12 meeting rooms.

Cross Keys Inn **$$$**
5100 Falls Rd 21210 ☏ 532-6900 • 148 rooms, 6 suites, 1 restaurant, 1 bar, 1 coffee shop
Just a 10min drive from downtown, the Cross Keys is quiet, almost suburban in atmosphere. It is situated next to the Cross Keys Village Square, which has a bank, specialty shops and boutiques. The contemporary rooms have private patios; some have steam baths. It is undoubtedly a good choice if you have business in the area, or in the nearby suburbs. Barber, hairdresser • health club nearby, tennis • 10 meeting rooms.

Hyatt Regency **$$$**
300 Light St, Inner Harbor 21202 ☏ 528-1234 TX 87577 • 415 rooms, 25 suites, 3 restaurants, 2 bars, 1 coffee shop
This is Baltimore's top convention hotel, connected by steel walkways to the Convention Center and Harbor Place. The lobby is very Hyatt, with glass elevators, greenery-filled atrium, a piano bar and a casual restaurant, Cascades. On the third level, the Trellis Garden (see *Restaurants*) is more sophisticated. The Regency Club rooms are in the care of a private concierge. Health enthusiasts can enjoy an outdoor recreation deck with pool, jogging track, and three tennis courts. Gift shop, beauty salon • health club • 19 meeting rooms.

Peabody Court **$$$$**
612 Cathedral St 21201 ☏ 727-7101 TX 292126 • 104 rooms, 30 suites, 2 restaurants
Baltimore's closest equivalent to a luxury European hotel is the Peabody Court at Mt Vernon Square. The rooms have an early-19thC European décor, with imported Directoire-style furniture. It has two fine restaurants:

the Conservatory and the slightly more casual La Brasserie (see *Restaurants*). Arrangements with nearby health club • 8 meeting rooms.

Sheraton Inner Harbor **$$$$**
300 S Charles St 21201 ☎ 962-8300 • 333 rooms, 1 restaurant, 1 bar
Specifically a business hotel, the Sheraton is well-equipped for meetings, and a skybridge links it to the Convention Center. The spacious modern lobby has an adjoining lounge. McHenry's offers American cuisine in a relaxed atmosphere; the two-tiered, glittery Impulse bar serves light snacks. Pool, sauna, spa • 11 meeting rooms.

Tremont **$$$**
8 E Pleasant St 21202 ☎ 576-1200 • 59 suites, 1 restaurant, 1 bar
A former apartment building, the all-suite Tremont is a favorite with sport and theater celebrities, who enjoy its privacy and the Downtown Athletic Club facilities available to guests. Corporate suites have a fully equipped kitchen and dining area; executive suites have kitchen, living room, dining room and separate bedroom with two queen-size beds. The celebrated 8 East (see *Restaurants*) is its French restaurant. Pool, sauna • 10 meeting rooms.

OTHER HOTELS

Society Hill ($$) *58 W Biddle St 21201 ☎ 837-3630.*
Society Hill Government House ($$$) *1125 N Calvert St 21202 ☎ 752-7722.*
Tremont Plaza ($$$) *222 St Paul Pl 21202 ☎ 727-2222.*

Clubs

The *Maryland Club*, established in 1896, is the old Baltimore all-male club into which the men of the city's "first families" are born. It serves lunch and dinner, but has no guest rooms. The *Merchants Club*, a refurbished c.1905 building, and the *Center Club* are much used by local people. *The Engineers Society of Baltimore*, whose membership is about 40% engineers, is another favorite dining spot for the local business community.

Restaurants

It comes as no surprise that good seafood, especially Maryland crab, is abundant in Baltimore. But the city's revitalization has widened the variety of good restaurants available, and you can now choose from a range extending from the Conservatory's elegant European atmosphere to the bazaar-like cafés of the Inner Harbor and the ethnic eating places of Little Italy. Baltimore is a city which sees a lot of business conducted over lunch and dinner.

La Brasserie **$$$**
Peabody Court Hotel, 612 Cathedral St ☎ 727-7101 • AE CB DC MC V
Versatile and new, La Brasserie nevertheless achieves something of a 19thC London gentlemen's club atmosphere. Prices are reasonable for very good Continental food; the desserts are fabulous. A good choice for a business lunch.

Conservatory **$$$$$**
Peabody Court Hotel, 612 Cathedral St ☎ 625-1300 • AE CB DC MC V • jacket required • reservations essential
Sophisticated, glass-enclosed and affording a breathtaking view of Baltimore, the Conservatory is one of the city's best restaurants; certainly it ranks as the most expensive. There is a chic bar where you can begin with cocktails before moving on to the superb French cuisine. The $45 *prix fixe* dinner is first-class. Good for celebrating a successful deal.

8 East $$$
Tremont Hotel, 8 E Pleasant St
☎ *576-1200* • AE MC V • *jacket required*
In addition to receiving an American Institute of Architecture award for its Art Deco design, this recent arrival was selected by *Gentlemen's Quarterly* as one of the 50 best new restaurants in the USA. It is small and French, and a great favorite of local senior executives.

Haussner's $$
3226-44 Eastern Ave ☎ *327-8365*
• *closed Sun, Mon* • AE CB DC MC V
• *no reservations*
Despite the cafeteria-style drinking glasses and wall decorations, this time-honored restaurant has long been a favorite of tourists and locals alike. The hearty, varied menu offers German specialties.

John Eager Howard Room $$$
Belvedere Hotel, 1 E Charles St
☎ *547-8220* • AE CB DC MC V
Evocative of the Federal period, with a 1780 portrait of the Revolution hero John Eager Howard hanging over a big stone fireplace, this restaurant has traditionally been the center stage for Maryland society. Gracious service complements the Continental cuisine.

Prime Rib $$$$
1101 N Calvert St ☎ *539-1804* • *D only* • AE CB DC MC V • *jacket required*
The cosmopolitan atmosphere, white tablecloths, candlelight and attentive waiters are an attraction in themselves. But its steaks and, of course, prime ribs are the main reasons for the Prime Rib's popularity with visiting celebrities and the local elite.

Tio Pepe $$$$
10 E Franklin St ☎ *539-4675* • *closed major holidays* • AE MC V
• *reservations essential*
This popular Spanish restaurant in a townhouse basement specializes in excellent regional dishes. It is always crowded, so be sure to make a reservation.

Trellis Garden $$$
Hyatt Regency, 300 Light St
☎ *528-1234* • *D only* • AE CB DC MC V
Overlooking a man-made lake within the Hyatt, this sophisticated restaurant offers dining in an open-air atmosphere with abundant greenery. Continental cuisine is prepared tableside. A good choice for business entertaining.

Harborplace and Little Italy
At the Harborplace complex there are more than a dozen restaurants and cafés, as well as gourmet food shops. With its traditional marketplace atmosphere, the Harborplace is a great place to stroll, shop, dine, snack, sip and browse by the Bay.

Little Italy lies just two blocks E – an old established neighborhood, rich in cultural heritage, with such Italian favorites as *Sabatino's*, Fawn St ☎ 727-9414; *Marconi's*, 106 W Saratoga St ☎ 752-9286; and *Chipparelli's*, 237 S High St ☎ 837-0309.

Bars

Bars are not generally the place for business in Baltimore, but if you want somewhere to have a drink and a conversation, try the *Admiral Fell Inn Pub*, 328 S Broadway, Fells Point ☎ 522-7377; or *8 East Lounge* at the Tremont, 8 E Pleasant St ☎ 576-1200. The hotel bars and nightclubs, strictly for socializing, include *Impulse*, at the Sheraton Harbor, 300 S Charles St ☎ 539-1425; *Martingue's*, 328 Calvert St ☎ 727-7877; *Skylights*, in the Hyatt Regency, 300 Light St ☎ 528-1234; and *Thirteenth Floor* in the Belvedere, Charles and Chase St ☎ 547-8220.

Entertainment

Baltimore entertainment ranges from a night at the opera to the wide-ranging festivals of the Inner Harbor. For a complete listing of what's happening and when ☏ 837-4636. *Baltimore Good Time* is available from the Office of Promotion and Tourism. *Baltimore Box Office* is at the end of Pier 4 at the Inner Harbor ☏ 576-9333.

Music Founded in 1857, and reputedly the oldest music school in America, the *Peabody Conservatory of Music* ☏ 659-8100 not only sponsors musical programs but also has a wonderful library. The *Lynn Opera House* ☏ 625-1400, at Mt Royal and Cathedral streets, is another fine old building – a perfect setting for the Baltimore Opera and large musical productions. The Baltimore Symphony has its season in the *Meyerhoff Symphony Hall*, Cathedral St ☏ 783-8110. The *Civic Center*, 201 W Baltimore St ☏ 347-2020, stages everything from opera to rock.

Theater Stage productions are at the *Morris A Mechanic Theater*, Hopkins Plaza, Baltimore and Charles St ☏ 625-1400, and the *Center Stage*, Calvert St ☏ 332-0033. The Inner Harbor provides all sorts of entertainment from tall ships and waterfront demonstrations to music festivals. In warm weather *Pier Six*, a 2,000-seat open-air pavilion, is a good concert spot.

Shopping

Shopping in Baltimore today is not very different from what it was 200 years ago at the *Lexington Market*, 400 W Lexington St. All sorts of goods are sold in more than 100 stalls and shops. *Antique Row* is in the 700 and 800 blocks of N Howard Street, the 200 block of W Read Street and 300 block of N Charles Street. Fells Point has the *Broadway Market* and many surrounding quaint shops. But the major downtown shopping area is Inner Harbor. *Harborplace* has a fine collection of shops in two buildings – Pratt Street and Light Street pavilions – offering everything from fine clothing and gourmet foods to handmade gifts from all over the world. *Hutzler's* department store is at the Convention Center Mall on Howard Street.

Sightseeing

To get a panoramic view of Baltimore, start at the *Top of the World*, World Trade Center, Pratt St ☏ 837-4515, which overlooks the city and its port.

Aquarium This internationally known aquarium has 5,000 different species of marine life. *Pier 3, Pratt St ☏ 576-3810. Open daily 10–5.*

B & O Railroad Museum *Pratt and Poppleton ☏ 237-2387. Open 10–4.*

Harborplace See *Shopping. Pratt and Light ☏ 332-4191.*

Maryland Science Center and Planetarium *601 Light St ☏ 685-5225. Open 10–5.*

US Frigate Constitution An enjoyable visit for nautical buffs. *Inner Harbor, Constitution Dock ☏ 539-1797. Open daily, 6–6.*

Walters Art Gallery Interesting and eclectic art collection, ranging from Greek artifacts to 20thC paintings. *Charles and Center ☏ 547-2787. Open 11–5, Tue–Sat.*

Guided tours

About Tours ☏ 592-7770 give walking tours of Inner Harbor and Federal Hill; *Baltimore Patriot* ☏ 685-4288 have 90min harbor cruises; *Clipper City* ☏ 539-6063 do a 3½hr sailing adventure; *Baltimore Rent-A-Tour* ☏ 653-2998; *Diversions* ☏ 486-3604 provides personalized tours, as does *Widening Horizons* ☏ 865-3001.

Spectator sports

Baseball The *Baltimore Orioles* play at Memorial Stadium, 33rd and Elbrise St ☏ 243-9800 or 338-1300.

Horseracing *Pimlico Race Course*, 5201 Park Heights Ave ☏ 542-9450; *Laurel Race Course*, Laurel ☏ 725-0400.

Keeping fit

Health clubs *Downtown Athletic Club*, 210 E Center St ☏ 332-0906, provides indoor swimming pool, aerobics, tanning beds and weight equipment. Open to guests at many of the city's hotels. *David Hill YMCA*, 1609 David Hill Ave ☏ 728-1600, has an indoor pool and exercise room.
Bicycling *Hotline* ☏ 659-1663 gives information on bicycle trails.
Golf *Clifton Park Golf Course* ☏ 243-3500.
Tennis *Downtown Racquet Club*, Belvedere Hotel, Charles and Chase ☏ 332-1000.

Local resources

Business services

The *Baltimore Office of Promotion and Tourism* ☏ 837-4636, the *Greater Baltimore Committee* ☏ 727-2820 and *Bedco* (Baltimore Economic Development Company) ☏ 837-9305 offer a wide range of services.
Photocopying and printing *Day Speedy Printing* ☏ 539-8500, 24hr; *ASCO Duplicating Service* ☏ 727-2726; *A1 Copying* ☏ 752-0303; *HQ Services and Offices* ☏ 659-0055.
Secretarial *HQ Services* ☏ 659-0055 provides secretarial and conference facilities.
Translation *Berlitz* ☏ 752-0767; *Academy of Language* ☏ 685-8383.

Communications

Local delivery *Carl Messenger Service* ☏ 265-5548; *Courier Group* ☏ 995-0252; *Maryland Messenger Service* ☏ 859-3372.
Long-distance delivery *Federal Express* ☏ 760-8750; *DHL Worldwide Courier Express* ☏ 768-3756.
Post office Main office is at 900 E Pratt St ☏ 576-1297, 24hr.
Telex *Western Union* ☏ 837-0232.

Conference/exhibition centers

Baltimore Convention Bureau ☏ 659-7300; *Baltimore Arena and Civic Center* ☏ 347-2010; *Festival Hall* ☏ 659-7000.

Emergencies

Hospital *University Hospital*, 22 S Greene St ☏ 528-6722; for doctor referral ☏ 625-0022.
Pharmacy *Drug Fair*, 17 W Baltimore St ☏ 539-0838.

Information sources

Business information The *Greater Baltimore Committee*, 2 Hopkins Plaza ☏ 727-2820, is the main force behind the city's renovation. Also prominent is *Baltimore Economic Development Corporation* ☏ 837-9305.
Local media The *Baltimore Sun* is a daily; the monthly *Baltimore* magazine is good for forthcoming events. *Harborplace News* ☏ 685-1804 stocks a wide range of domestic and foreign newspapers.

Thank-yous

Florists *Wilson's Harborplace Flower Market* ☏ 685-5565; *Fredrick Reitz*, 1309 W Baltimore St ☏ 685-9071; *Penny Lane* in Baltimore County ☏ 833-7788.
Gift baskets *Balloon Bouquets of Baltimore*, 2116 N Charles St ☏ 727-0909; *Sweet Craft Chocolatier* ☏ 332-0714; *Bayside Fruit and Nut Company* ☏ 332-1050; *Honeycomb* ☏ 752-2365; *Calico Cat* ☏ 962-8844; *Crabtree and Evelyn* ☏ 547-0668.

Planning and Reference

Entry details

Documentation

Visas All travellers to the USA except those from Canada and Mexico require a visa. There are various types. The B-1 visa is specially designed for temporary business visitors. Application forms can be obtained from travel agents, airlines, or the local US embassy or consulate. Processing visa applications can take several weeks, though it is possible to obtain a visa in a few hours through major travel agencies, such as American Express. Business visa applicants will require a valid passport and some kind of proof – a letter from a US contact or their own firm will do – of the business nature of the trip. Most visas are multiple entry with a maximum of six months per stay, issued for an indefinite period, and do not need to be renewed. Have the still valid visa transferred to the current passport. The Immigration authorities have the right to refuse entry even if there is a valid visa. There is a directory of undesirable aliens.

Health requirements Only travellers from countries where diseases such as cholera and yellow fever are widespread require vaccination certificates; check with the US embassy.

Driver's license To drive in the USA, it is sufficient to have a license issued by a country that has signed the 1949 Geneva Motoring Convention. Travellers who do not have such a license must apply for a US license by contacting the department of motor vehicles in the state of entry to the USA. A test is necessary in most states.

Immigration Among others, you are asked the following questions on the forms you need to fill in before entry. Are you carrying more than $5,000? Have you recently been on a farm or ranch? Are you carrying fruit or vegetables?

Customs regulations

Basic duty-free allowances are for one liter of wine or spirits and either 200 cigarettes plus 50 cigars or two kilos of tobacco. Personal gifts totalling up to $100 in value are duty-free, but this can be claimed only once in a six-month period. Some state laws permit less alcohol; check with the embassy or airline.

Prohibitions Entry of meat/meat products, fish, fruit, dairy products, vegetables and plants is restricted. Many such items are banned. Some products are not to be carried across state lines; fruit cannot be taken into California, for example. Visitors carrying medication should bring along a prescription or validating letter from a doctor, in case it is a prohibited drug in the USA, where many items, such as codeine, are available only by prescription.

Climate

The USA has many extremes of climate, from deserts and swamps to subtropical forests and permanent glaciers. Some places freeze for months in the winter and bake in the summer. Tornados are an occasional hazard in the Midwest, hurricanes in Florida and the Gulf of Mexico. In summer, the country is almost universally hot, but San Francisco and Seattle are among the exceptions. The winter traveller visiting different regions has to be prepared for all weathers. Remember that offices, restaurants, shops, hotels and homes are centrally heated and air-conditioned, with the result that in summer you go from very hot outdoor temperatures to over-cool indoors. The reverse is true in winter.

The Northeast is a temperate region, with about 3.5in rainfall a month throughout the year. Winds are rarely heavy, though in New York state and New England winter temperatures can be brought down sharply by winds blowing N and NE through Canada. Summers are warm, sometimes hot, and can be oppressively humid in coastal cities such as New York. Daytime temperatures in New York fall to several degrees below freezing, as low as 25°F/-4°C in winter, and remain in the 80s/about 30°C between June and August. Boston is cooler. Snow falls all over the region in winter.

The Midwest The farther W you travel, the drier it gets. Driest are the plains states, in the shadow of the Rockies, with as little as 20in/50cm rainfall a year. Most rain in the region falls in spring and early summer. Winter is very cold in Northern states, with constant and chilling winds making temperatures as low as 20°F/-7°C commonplace. More southerly cities, such as Kansas City and St Louis, also freeze, with low daytime air temperatures around 40°F/4°C. Spring and autumn – also called fall – both tend to be short and pleasant, and summers are hot throughout the region, with temperatures in the 80s/about 30°C. It is generally a dry heat, but humidity can be high in the Great Lakes area.

South and Southeast Frosts are relatively rare in the Deep South and Southeast, but they are fairly common in border states such as Virginia and Kentucky. Winters in Florida are positively pleasant, with temperatures rarely going much below 70°F/18°C. Summers are always hot – around 90°F/32°C throughout the region in July and August – and are more pleasant inland. Florida and the Gulf of Mexico often have 90% humidity for weeks at a time, with violent storms bringing only temporary relief. The average monthly coastal rainfall can be as much as 8in/20.32cm. The difference is quite marked in Texas, where inland cities such as Dallas and San Antonio have 30–40% less rainfall than Houston.

Far West The region splits into three climatic zones. In the N, Oregon and Washington can be very wet, often with snow on high ground inland. Winters are fairly mild, especially in the coastal cities like Seattle, where it rarely freezes, and summers are warm and dry. Along the Pacific coast from the Canadian border to below San Francisco fogs are common in summer. California and the Rockies are drier and sunnier, with altitude determining the temperature; the Rockies and Sierra can be numbingly cold in winter. Even relatively sheltered Denver has winter temperatures as low as the Northern cities. The coastal plain is very different. It never freezes in Los Angeles or San Francisco; summer temperatures in LA are around 80°F/27°C, and in San Francisco around 70°F/21°C. Inland, Arizona and New Mexico are the driest regions in the USA, consisting mainly of desert with an annual rainfall of less than 10in/25.4cm. There are occasional frosts in winter, but summer temperatures in Phoenix, for example, are generally well over 100°F/38°C.

Alaska The largest state in the Union, with extremely varied topography, Alaska has great climatic diversity. Summer temperatures, however, are generally pleasant – about 75°F/24°C in the largest city, Anchorage. Winters are cold, with temperatures sometimes dropping to –10°F (–23°C). In this part of the state rainfall averages about 25in annually.

Hawaii Despite being situated in the tropical zone, Hawaii has a temperate climate, thanks to cooling trade winds; and the temperature in Honolulu normally ranges between 72°F/22°C and 78°F/26°C. The amount of rainfall varies dramatically throughout the island, with some places receiving about 9in annually and others more than 450in.

Information sources

For general business information about the USA, visitors can contact the commercial department of the US embassy in their own country – or any local association established to promote trade and commerce with the USA. Sources of business information inside the USA include the commercial departments in each state and individual city chambers of commerce. More general, nationwide information can be obtained from the Chamber of Commerce of the United States, 1615 H St NW, Washington DC 20062 ☎ (202) 659-6000, or the Council of State Chambers of Commerce, 122 C St NW, Suite 200, Washington DC 20001 ☎ (202) 484-8103. For general tourist information, the traveller should contact the office of the United States Travel and Tourism Administration (USTTA) in his or her home country. In the USA, information is available from state and city tourist offices.

Holidays

The main vacation months in the USA are June–early September, when the schools take their summer break; many factories close down during August. But more and more incentive fares are being introduced to encourage the spread of vacations through the year. There are also many official national, regional and state holidays. The following holidays are observed in all states unless otherwise indicated.

Jan 1 New Year's Day.
3rd Mon in Jan Martin Luther King Day in most Northern states.
Feb 12 Lincoln's Birthday – in 23 Northern states.
3rd Mon in Feb Washington's Birthday; in some states President's day.
Last Mon in May Memorial Day.
Jul 4 Independence Day.
1st Mon in Sep Labor Day.
2nd Mon in Oct Columbus Day or Pioneer's Day, in 44 states.
Nov 11 Veterans' Day.
Tue after 1st Mon in Nov Election Day, even years only.
4th Thu in Nov Thanksgiving Day.
Dec 25 Christmas Day.

Some fixed-date holidays are celebrated on the nearest Monday; in some states, if any holiday falls on a Sunday the following Monday is automatically a holiday. In addition, many cities have their own holidays – for example, Boston observes St Patrick's Day on *Mar 17*.

In cities with a large Jewish population – notably New York – the observance of the major Jewish holidays may affect the business schedule. The dates of these vary slightly from year to year, and the degree of observance also varies, depending upon whether one is Orthodox, Reform or Conservative (the last two being more liberal). The holidays for 1987 are as follows: Passover (commemorating the Exodus from Egypt), *sundown Apr 13–Apr 21*; Rosh Hashanah (New Year), *sundown Sep 23–Sep 25*; Yom Kippur (the Day of Atonement – the holiest day of the year), *sundown Oct 2–Oct 3*; Chanukah (celebrating the rededication of the Temple in 165 BC), *sundown Dec 15–Dec 23*.

Money

The US dollar is divided into 100 cents (¢). Coins in circulation are the penny (1¢), nickel (5¢), dime (10¢), quarter (25¢), half dollar (50¢), and dollar ($1); the last two are not in common use. It is useful to keep a good supply of nickels, dimes and quarters for public telephones and vending machines. Notes (called bills) in circulation are $1, $5, $10, $20, $50, $100, $500, and $1,000. Again, the last two are very rare. All bills are green and of the same size; large denomination bills may be refused. You should avoid carrying large amounts of cash; credit and charge cards and US$ travellers' checks are the safest and most convenient way to take your money.
Credit and charge cards The major cards are widely accepted throughout the USA in hotels, motels, restaurants, stores and gas stations. Renting a car without a credit or charge card can be very

difficult, and most hotels like you to produce one when you check in. Before you leave for the USA, check that your credit card limit is high enough.

Checks US$ travellers' checks can generally be used as if they were cash, though you may need to produce identification. Banks may refuse to cash foreign denomination travellers' checks from non-affiliated issuers.

Changing money in the USA is more difficult than in, say, Europe – another reason for relying on plastic cards and US$ travellers' checks. Visitors are advised to calculate how much money they may need for porters, taxis, etc, and to carry the necessary cash. It is not a good idea to rely on banks. Relatively few banks and hotels will exchange currencies, and specialist currency exchange offices are rare outside international airports.

Bank opening hours are Mon–Fri, 9–3. Some open late one day a week; a few open Sat morning.

Sales taxes

Sales There is no Federal indirect taxation, but cities and states levy a sales tax – 2–9% – on most transactions; prices displayed do not include sales tax.

Tipping

Hotels Bellhops expect $1 minimum or 50–70¢ per bag; in top-class hotels allow $2 per bag or $5 for several bags. There is no need to tip the elevator operator or desk clerk, but regard $1 as the minimum for the doorman on arrival – more if he provides some special service. Thereafter, when you need a taxi 50¢ would do. Tip the chambermaid $1.50 per night. Leave the money in an envelope marked "For the maid."

Restaurants Allow 15–20% of the bill before tax. Tipping the maître d'hotel is usually officially discouraged, but it is often the only way to get a seat in a crowded restaurant.

Bars For waiter service, allow 15–20% of the bill. A tip is expected even if you are served at the bar.

Taxi Drivers expect around 15%, more in New York.

Other situations At railroad stations and airports, 50–75¢ a bag, minimum $1. Haircut, shave, 15–20%. Restroom attendant 25–50¢.

Getting there

Fierce competition between airlines, particularly on North Atlantic and domestic routes, has made it difficult even for skilled travel agents to keep up to date with the options open to the international traveller visiting the USA. Visitor USA (VUSA) fares (see below) are not available to Americans, and US special fares are not available to foreign travel agents. Therefore, if price is a major consideration, it may be cheaper to fly into a major gateway and take a domestic flight to the final destination. If time is crucial, note that not all "direct" international flights are non-stop. The following cities are major gateways: Atlanta, Boston, Chicago, Dallas/Fort Worth, Detroit, Houston, Los Angeles, Miami, Minneapolis/St Paul, New York (JFK and Newark), St Louis, San Francisco, Seattle and Washington DC.

Getting around

The distances involved usually mean that it is best to fly between major cities, rather than go by road or rail. For some journeys – New York to Washington, for example – train can be quicker and more comfortable.

By air

The domestic air network is extremely comprehensive, and numerous discount and promotional fare schemes make it worthwhile shopping around for a flight. VUSA fares (which must be booked outside the USA) give discounts of up to 40% of the normal fare. Frequent Flyer programs or Mileage Clubs offer upgrades, other benefits such as car rental, hotel discounts, and eventually free flights to regular customers of airlines.

By car

The fastest routes are the multi-lane Interstate highways, indicated on maps and signs by I followed by the number on a shield. They have no traffic lights or cross traffic and only limited access and exit points. US and state highways are similar, but with more entrances and exits and some cross traffic.

Regulations There is a 55mph speed limit on all roads nationwide; built-up areas and school zones have lower limits marked by roadside signs. Other regulations vary from state to state, but some are common to all. Overtaking on the inside is permitted on multi-lane highways, and you are usually allowed to turn right on a red light, if the way is clear – though not in New York city. It is illegal to pass a school bus when it has stopped to pick up or unload children, and to drive while under the influence of alcohol. In some states it is illegal to carry alcoholic drinks in a car, unless they are still sealed. Generally it is illegal to take alcohol across state lines.

Gas stations are numerous, although there may be long distances between them on the interstates. Gasoline is sold by the American gallon, 4/5th of an imperial gallon, equivalent to just under four liters.

Car rental is easy, provided you are over 25, have a valid driving license and a credit or charge card. Rates vary from state to state; Florida's are low, New York's high. Quoted rates do not include collision damage waiver, personal accident insurance or tax. If you want to pick up a car in one place and leave it in another, there is usually a drop-off charge; local companies rarely allow you to do this. Corporate rates are worth investigating, as are fly-drive and other special deals for car rental bookings made outside the USA. Large companies generally cover their staff for insurance. Make sure that you don't give rental companies double profits!

National and international firms with toll-free (800) numbers include
Avis ☎ 331-1212
Budget ☎ 527-0700
Dollar ☎ 421-6868
Hertz ☎ 654-3131
National ☎ 227-7368
Thrifty ☎ 331-4200.

Breakdowns and accidents If the car is rented, there will be a leaflet in the glove compartment describing procedures in the case of accident and breakdown. If you break down on a highway, and there is no phone nearby, pull off the road, raise the hood, attach something white – a handkerchief or scarf, for example – to the driver's door handle and wait for a police highway patrol. Walking along a highway, especially at night, is dangerous, and in some states illegal. Unaccompanied women are advised to stay in the car with the doors locked until help arrives.

Officially, all road accidents must be reported to the police.

By rail

The inter-city Amtrak rail network covers 44 states and about 500 cities. Services are most popular up and down the "Northeast Corridor" between Boston, New York and Washington, and on into Florida, and on the West Coast between Los Angeles and San Francisco. Services in the Midwest are minimal and often require more than one change of train. As a means of seeing the country in comfort, the coast-to-coast lines, with their observation cars, bars and club cars, are unsurpassed. But some of the track is in poor condition, and late running is not unusual.

Reservations can be made at city center stations, at travel agents, at Amtrak offices or by calling the Amtrak toll-free number ☎ (800) 872-7245. Discounts are available on some routes for bookings.

By bus

Greyhound and Trailways are the two major long-distance bus companies covering the Continental US with scheduled services.

Hotels

The immense hotel-building boom experienced in the USA in the past two decades has been led by the needs of the ever-growing army of national and international business travellers. In all major US cities there is now a wide choice of first-rate hotels offering a range of business facilities and services rarely found in European provincial hotels.

Styles Most US hotels are purpose-built, and few date back more than 100 years. The most prestigious places to stay are usually the *grandes dames* or the luxury European-style hotels, which pride themselves on their personalized service, but the big de luxe convention hotels will often be a better choice for the traveller who needs access to a wide range of business facilities and services. For those who do not need to adopt a high profile, a room in a mid-range hotel or even a motel is likely to be perfectly adequate for a short stay: in general, price differences between hotels in a city reflect location and the number of restaurants, bars and so on more than the quality of guest rooms.

Facilities The standard US business hotel room is spacious and has two twin beds or a double bed. (Some chains, such as Holiday Inn provide two double beds, for family use.) All rooms have a private bathroom, a direct-dial telephone (use of which may be charged at above standard rates), a color TV and a desk at which to work. Rooms in de luxe hotels have such extras as refrigerators or mini-bars stocked with drinks, in-room movies or cable channels and as many as three telephones, one by the bed, one by the desk and one in the bathroom. More and more hotels now have rooms, or entire floors, reserved for non-smokers.

All business hotels will provide room service, usually 24hrs, and valet or laundry service (usually same day). They all also have a concierge who will help guests with bookings for shows and sightseeing tours, advise on restaurants and shopping, and deal with special requests; however, the extent of such service varies considerably from one hotel (and city) to another. Express check-out or check-in is advertised by many hotels; check-out can usually be expedited by leaving a blank, signed credit card voucher.

Special "executive" or "club" rooms and executive floors are now a fairly common feature of large business hotels in the USA. What you get for the higher price you pay for executive status varies a lot. It may be top-quality accommodation in a self-contained section of the hotel, which has its own lounge and a comprehensive business center (see below) and is serviced by its own concierge. Or it may amount to little more than a slightly-above-standard room and complimentary breakfast and newspaper.

Business services Any business hotel should be able to arrange photocopying and secretarial/typing help, and audio-visual equipment for use in meeting rooms. The best-equipped hotels offer just about any in-house service you care to think of – word processing, translation, computers, computer modems, teleconferencing, a business reference library and links with electronic news/business/stock market information services. However, some hotels' advertising tends to exaggerate the services they offer; so if you know that you will have specific requirements, it is always best to check with the hotel in advance.

Prices and reservations Prices are almost always quoted per single room, excluding tax. Rates vary enormously from city to city. In New York a room in a top-class hotel costs over $200 a night, and a luxury suite can cost more than $500. Such is the expense of hotel accommodation in Manhattan that it is difficult to find acceptable accommodation for under $120 a night. On the other hand, in cities such as Kansas City, you can stay in the best hotels for not much more than $100 a night. Corporate rates giving substantial discounts are widely available. These don't always have to be negotiated in advance.

Major credit and charge cards – American Express (AE), Carte Blanche (CB), Diners Club (DC), MasterCard/Access (MC) and Visa (V) – are accepted by virtually all business hotels. Expect to be asked to give a card number when making a reservation, especially if you will be checking in after 6pm. You may also be asked for a credit card imprint when you check in. To find out if a hotel has a toll-free (800) reservations number, call the national toll-free information directory ☎ (800) 555-1212.

Hotel groups

Telephone reservations numbers given are toll free (800).
Best Western Marketing group for individually-owned hotels throughout the USA. Standards, styles and clientele vary ☎ 528-1234.
Four Seasons Select group of Canadian-owned luxury hotels (flagship Chicago's Ritz-Carlton) which pride themselves on personalized service ☎ 268-6282.
Helmsley Includes some of New York's most luxurious hotels (flagship the Helmsley Palace), as well as those that used to belong to the Harley group ☎ 223-6800.
Hilton More than 260 hotels throughout the USA, including Hawaii. They include not only large luxury hotels but also smaller first-class inns ☎ 445-8667.
Holiday Inns About 1,500 hotels throughout the USA. Reliable standards; large, modern rooms; cable movies. Staff can be offhand. Special privileges for Priority Club and Inner Club members ☎ 465-4329.
Howard Johnson Some 500 budget hotels, mainly in the East, Southeast and Midwest ☎ 654-2000.
Hyatt About 150 top-class and resort hotels, many with excellent business and/or leisure facilities. Striking architecture and design is a Hyatt feature (although acrophobes should beware the vertiginous glass elevators). Gold Passcard holders get special privileges ☎ 228-9000 (outside Nebraska) ☎ 228 9001 (Nebraska).
Inter-Continental About 10 highly-rated hotels, most on the East Coast. Special privileges (such as room upgrades) for members of Six Continents Club ☎ 327-0200.
Marriott Very large group whose hotels vary widely in size and style. Some city hotels have excellent business facilities ☎ 228-9290.
Omni Over 30 high-quality hotels mainly in cities E of the Mississippi River ☎ 228-2121.
Ramada Over 600 hotels and inns throughout the USA. Reliable but rarely inspiring. Ramada Business Card offers privileges and discounts ☎ 272-6232.
Sheraton Some 300 hotels throughout the USA. Generally high standards but rarely the most prestigious place to stay in town. Privileges and discounts available under Sheraton Executive Travellers' Program ☎ 325-3535.
Stouffer About 30 hotels in major cities (flagship Washington's Mayflower). All are located downtown, and most have special floors with business facilities ☎ 468-3571.
Trusthouse Forte Britain's biggest hotel group used to have a slightly dowdy image, but now owns some of the world's premier hotels, such as the George V in Paris. In the USA it owns the budget Travel Lodge chain, as well as a few first-rate city hotels including New York's Westbury ☎ 223-5672.
Westin De luxe hotels in many major cities. Westin Premiere Club members get special privileges ☎ 228-3000.

Wine vintages

Vintage assessments are an inexact science and always a compromise. The following years are recommended for wines from good growers/properties in the classic areas.

Ready: 78 Ready/light year: *80*
Not ready: 85

Red Bordeaux
Médoc/Graves: 86 85 83 82 81 *80* 79 78 75 70 66 62 61
Pomerol/St Emilion: 86 85 83 82 81 *80* 79 78 75 70 66 62 64 61
Great older vintages: 59 55 53 52 45 28

Sauternes/Barsac
86 85 83 *81 80* 76 75 71 70 67

White Burgundy
85 *84* 83 82 79 78 73

Red Burgundy
85 83 *82* 80 *79* 78 76 71

Northern Rhône
86 85 83 82 80 78 76 72 71

Champagne
85 83 82 79 76 75

Alsace
86 85 83 81 79 76

Rhein/Mosel
85 83 81 76 75 71

Barolo
85 83 82 80 79 78 74

Port
83 80 77 *75* 70 66 63 60

Californian Cabernet Sauvignon
86 85 84 80 78 77 76 74

Californian Chardonnay
86 85 84 80

For top pleasure/value in 1987-8 we recommend: 1978 cru bourgeois red Bordeaux; 1980 cru classé red Bordeaux; 1981 Sauternes; 1982 white Burgundy; 1980 red Burgundy; 1985 cru Beaujolais; 1980 Northern Rhône; 1975 champagne; 1985 Alsace; 1983 Rhein/Mosel; 1980 Barolo; 1966 port; 1980 Californian Cabernet; 1984 Californian Chardonnay.

Recommended hotels
Hotels given full entries in the guide have generally been selected on the basis of being the most comfortable and stylish and the best-equipped for business travellers.

Listed under "Other Hotels" are establishments that do not achieve the standards of their competitors but which offer perfectly adequate accommodation, usually at a lower price than the hotels given full entries.

The price symbols have the following meanings:
$ up to $50
$$ $51–80
$$$ $81–110
$$$$ $111–150
$$$$$ over $150
$$$$$ well over $150

At the time of going to press these reflect the price (excluding tax) for one person occupying a standard room.

Restaurants

The restaurant business in the USA has enjoyed tremendous growth in recent years, both at the top-of-the-range gourmet end of the market and in the fast food sector (see *The Industrial Scene: Food and drink*).

Business dining habits vary from region to region and from city to city. In the major cities you will find a wide range of restaurants, suitable for every level of business entertaining. Inevitably, in smaller cities the choice is not so wide; and the top restaurant in such cities will not generally be on a par with the top restaurants in New York or Chicago, for example. Descriptions of the recommended restaurants in different cities reflect the standard within each particular city and the choice available.

Traditionally, French restaurants serving classic or *nouvelle cuisine* are favored for high-powered business entertaining, but there are many exceptions to this rule. Italian restaurants – the cooking is usually Northern Italian – rank among the best of many cities' restaurants. California cuisine is now as fashionable on the East Coast as it is on the West. Seafood predominates in cities such as San Diego and Miami and rib joints and steak houses operate as businessmen's dining clubs in cities as diverse as New York, Chicago and Kansas City. In addition, there are numerous restaurants serving many other national cuisines: Chinese, Japanese, Vietnamese, Mexican, Creole, Polish and Russian. In general, however, it is best to avoid taking a business colleague to a foreign restaurant – apart from French or Italian – unless you know that he or she enjoys that kind of food.

Reservations It is always sensible to make restaurant reservations at least 24hrs ahead. If you have any special requirements, such as a private booth or a table in a non-smoking area, mention them at the time of phoning.

If you are going to arrive late, warn the restaurant or you may lose your table.

Recommended restaurants

The restaurants given full entries in the guide have been selected with the business traveller especially in mind – as well as for the quality of the food – and are those considered by local people to be the best in the city for working meals and business entertaining. A few are recommended for purely social occasions, including celebrations.

The price symbols used in the guide have the following meanings:
$ up to $15
$$ $16–30
$$$ $31–45
$$$$ $46–60
$$$$$ over $60
$$$$$ well over $60
At the time of going to press they reflect the price of a typical dinner for one, including acceptable wine, tax and service. Prices are often lower for lunch.

Bars

It is important for visitors to recognize the growing US antipathy to mixing alcohol with business – especially during the working day. US bars are generally places to relax and unwind in after working hours.

Every city has its own style of bar, with the emphasis on spirits, cocktails and bottled beers; in some there are imitation English or Irish pubs, and these tend to be mainly for entertainment rather than serious talking. Hotel bars are usually the most suitable places to meet if you want a serious business discussion over a drink. Alternatively, a local business contact may suggest meeting in the bar of his or her club.

Laws governing bar opening hours and the sale of alcohol vary from state to state.

Shopping

Standard shop opening hours are 9.30–6, Mon–Sat, but most stores have one or more late-opening days; some, especially in shopping malls, are open until 8.30 or 9 every weekday. Some are even open on Sunday and in large cities there are supermarkets that never close.

Department stores There are no truly nationwide chains of department stores, but some high-class stores such as Bloomingdale's and Saks Fifth Avenue have branches in many cities. Stores such as Sears Roebuck, JC Penney and Montgomery Ward are more middle-market, with a wide range of products but usually a narrower brand choice.

Shopping malls Every city has its modern shopping malls – usually located in the suburbs or on the periphery. A few are located in the heart of town. These modern devlopments often include leisure, entertainment and restaurant complexes.

Sales tax can be avoided in some states if the goods are to be sent out of the state. It always pays to ask if the shop will mail or ship your purchase direct to your home address. Often it is a matter of balancing the tax saved against the extra shipping charges incurred.

Crime

The United States's reputation for violent crime is due partly to the image presented by its entertainment industry and partly to some genuinely high statistics. States with the highest crime rates are Florida, Arizona, Colorado, California, Nevada, Oregon, and Texas. New York has the highest rate for robbery, followed by California, Florida and Maryland. The 1985 figures produced by the FBI showed the violent crime rates (per 100,000 population) for New York City (metropolitan area), Los Angeles, Chicago, San Francisco and Washington DC to be 1,658, 1,179.5, 1073.2, 792.3 and 640.9 respectively.

As in most countries, common sense and safety-consciousness will prevent your becoming one more statistic. As a precaution against credit card fraud it is wise to remove the carbons after signing a voucher.

In hotels, give valuables to the front desk to keep in a safety deposit box, or – where one is available – put them in the safe in your room.

Keeping safe When walking in any city, keep to the well-populated streets; do not enter deserted areas, especially after dark. In big cities, take a cab at night rather than ride the subway or walk, and call for the cab to collect you rather than go out to look for one. If confronted by someone asking for money, hand it over. Don't resist a robbery, and *never* argue with a gun. It is prudent always to divide any money you are carrying between two wallets. Keep cash and cards separate. Try to avoid looking scared, which can persuade a potential mugger that you are vulnerable and an easy target.

Dealing with the police If you are stopped by a policeman, be courteous and helpful. Emphasize that you are a visitor and that if you have broken the law it was innocently and inadvertently done. Never attempt to pay a fine on the spot – which could be construed as attempted bribery, a serious charge. If you are arrested, you are allowed to make one telephone call. Use it to call your nearest consulate for advice or to contact a friend who can find you a lawyer. Duty lawyers are also available; ask the police for details. You are not required to make any statement to the police.

Embassies

The major foreign embassies are all located in Washington DC (☎ area code 202), but most countries have consulates in other principal cities such as Chicago, New York and San Francisco.

Australia, 1601 Massachusetts Ave NW, Washington DC 20036 ☎ 797-3000.
Austria, 2343 Massachusetts Ave NW Washington DC 20008 ☎ 484-4474.
Belgium, 3330 Garfield St NW, Washington DC 20008 ☎ 333-6900.
Britain, 3100 Massachusetts Ave NW Washington DC 20008 ☎ 462-1340.
Canada, 1746 Massachusetts Ave NW, Washington DC 20036 ☎ 785-1400.
Denmark, 3200 Whitehaven St NW, Washington DC 20008 ☎ 234-4300.
Finland, 3216 New Mexico Ave NW, Washington DC 20016 ☎ 363-2430.
France, 4101 Reservoir Rd, Washington DC 20007 ☎ 944-6000.
Federal Republic of Germany (*West*),

4645 Reservoir Rd NW, Washington DC ☏ 298-4000.
Greece, 2221 Massachusetts Ave NW, Washington DC 20008 ☏ 667-3168.
Ireland, 2234 Massachusetts Ave NW, Washington DC 20008 ☏ 462-3939.
Italy, 1601 Fuller St NW, Washington DC 20009 ☏ 328-5500.
Japan, 2520 Massachusetts Ave NW, Washington DC 20008 ☏ 234-2266.
Netherlands, 4200 Linnean Ave NW, Washington DC 20008 ☏ 244-5300.
New Zealand, 37 Observatory Circle NW, Washington DC 20008, ☏ 328-4800.
Norway, 2720 34th St NW, Washington DC 20008 ☏ 333-6000.
Portugal, 2125 Kalorama Rd NW, Washington DC 20008 ☏ 328-8610.
Spain, 2700 15th St NW, Washington DC 20009 ☏ 265-0190.
Sweden, 600 New Hampshire Ave NW Washington DC 20037 ☏ 298-3500.
Switzerland, 2900 Cathedral Ave NW, Washington DC 20008 ☏ 745-7900.
Yugoslavia, 2410 California St NW, Washington DC 20008 ☏ 462-6566

In addition, there is a *Delegation of the Commission of the European Community*, 2100 M St NW, Washington DC 20037 ☏ 862-9500.

Health care

Health care is a wholly private affair in the USA. It is every individual's responsibility to make sure that he or she is fully insured – US costs are higher than in most countries.

If you fall ill

Pharmacists A wide range of over-the-counter medicines are available for minor ailments. For other drugs you will need a prescription; overseas prescriptions are not usually accepted, but most doctors will, for a fee, write a copy prescription without examination. Most towns have at least one late-opening or 24hr pharmacy, and most pharmacists will give basic medical advice.

Doctors Medical practitioners' standards are high. The cost of any malpractice suit means that doctors will err on the side of overtreatment rather than neglect. Technical expertise and equipment are generally as modern as you will find anywhere in the world. To find a doctor, ask at your hotel reception desk or seek the advice of the concierge. Most doctors in large US cities have one or two specialties, even in general practice. Some small communities may have no doctor at all if there is not enough business to support a practice.

Emergency treatment For the emergency services and an ambulance ☏ 911; if the 911 number is not used where you are dialing from, call the operator. Standards of care in hospitals are high, and ambulance crews and medical emergency services are equipped to begin treatment on the spot.

Dental treatment is similar to medical treatment in both standards and costs. In choosing a dentist, take the advice of local contacts, the hotel desk or the concierge.

Costs Doctors expect immediate payment by non-US residents, but most accept credit cards. A single visit to a doctor will cost a minimum of $20. Asking a doctor to come to your hotel will cost at least $40; bandages and drugs are all extra. Hospital care can cost $1,000 per day.

Your admission to the hospital may be delayed unless you carry some evidence of your ability to pay – such as your certificate of insurance (credit cards are not necessarily acceptable as proof of ability to pay). It is also advisable to carry some evidence if you are allergic to any drugs used in emergencies – such as penicillin – or suffer from a disease requiring special treatment, such as diabetes.

Communications

Using the telephone All US numbers have a three-digit area code and a seven-digit subscriber code. Do not use the area code when calling a number in the same area. Numbers prefixed with 800 are toll-free nationwide. Telephone dials/buttons have letters as well as numbers; and some businesses' numbers spell out their name or some other appropriate word, for ease in remembering it. The dialing tone is a continuous tone that should cease when dialing begins. A slow, repeated tone indicates that the number dialed is ringing. A faster repeated tone, the busy signal, indicates that the number dialed is already in use. A very fast rhythmic tone means that circuits are busy. If there is a continuous, high-pitched tone try re-dialing. If the tone persists, call the operator.

Pay phones are widely available in public and semi-public places: hotel and office lobbies, shops, bars and restaurants, transportation depots, gas stations, subway stations and on streets and highways. Most take nickels, dimes and quarters, but many also accept credit cards, such as Visa and MasterCard, or special telephone credit cards. All public telephones have a small plaque giving full operating instructions.

International calls may be made from pay phones – provided that you have plenty of change. Most hotels have international direct-dial phones in the rooms, but there is often a sizable surcharge for calls made using these phones. Many countries now operate a "direct" service, whereby you dial the international operator in your own country and have a call charged to a home-based credit card. An alternative is to ask the person you are calling to accept the charge (known as a "collect" call).

Useful numbers Operator 0 or 00. You can ring the operator for a wide variety of services. Besides dealing with difficulties in connecting a call, the operator will route you to recorded services such as the time and weather forecast and will provide information on local health and dental services, and so on. For telephone information, dial 411 (if within same area code) or 1-(area code)-555-1212 for numbers in other areas. There is a toll-free international inquiries service ☎ (800) 874-4000.

Telegrams and overseas cablegrams can be sent either from your hotel (for which you will pay an additional handling charge) or from Western Union. A further option within the USA is to send a Mailgram, which is delivered the next day for about half the cost of a telegram.

Telex and fax

Many hotels have a telex machine which can be used to send and receive messages for guests, but such a service is not normally operable by the guest. Independent operators run telex bureaus in the larger cities (see *City-by-city: Local resources*). Purolator (see *City-by-city: Couriers*) collects documents and sends them by fax from office to office.

Mail

The US mail service is reasonably efficient. The size of the country means that not all mail can be guaranteed next-day delivery, but first-class letter mail is usually delivered on the second day after posting. But New York delivery times can be longer. All long-distance internal mail is sent by air, without extra airmail charge. Overnight Expressmail is available at a higher cost.

Post offices are generally open Mon–Fri, 9–5. Some open until 1pm Sat. Most big cities have at least one 24hr office. Stamps can be bought at drugstores, hotels, bus and rail stations, and other locations. There is a small extra charge payable anywhere other than a post office.

Couriers Federal Express is the leading company for both local and long-distance deliveries in the USA. Internally they guarantee delivery by 10.30 on the second day. Quoted delivery times for overseas delivery are also subject to a money-back guarantee. Other nationwide courier services include DHL, for international delivery, and Purolator, for internal and overseas services.

Dialing codes

US area codes

The United States (apart from Alaska and Hawaii – see below) is divided into four time zones: Eastern (E), Central (C), Mountain (M) and Pacific (P), each one hour earlier than the previous one.

City (state)	Time zone	Area code
Atlanta (Georgia)	E	404
Atlantic City (New Jersey)	E	609
Baltimore (Maryland)	E	301
Birmingham (Alabama)	C	205
Boston (Massachusetts)	E	617
Buffalo (New York)	E	716
Charlotte (North Carolina)	E	704
Chicago (Illinois)	C	312
Cincinnati (Ohio)	E	513
Cleveland (Ohio)	E	216
Columbus (Ohio)	E	614
Dallas (Texas)	C	214
Denver (Colorado)	M	303
Detroit (Michigan)	E	313
Fort Lauderdale (Florida)	E	305
Fort Worth (Texas)	C	817
Grand Rapids (Michigan)	E	616
Hartford (Connecticut)	E	203
Houston (Texas)	C	713
Indianapolis (Indiana)	E	317
Jersey City (New Jersey)	E	201
Kansas City (Missouri)	C	816
Los Angeles (California)	P	213
Memphis (Tennessee)	C	901
Miami (Florida)	E	305
Milwaukee (Wisconsin)	C	414
Minneapolis (Minnesota)	C	612
Nashville (Tennessee)	C	615
New Orleans (Louisiana)	C	504
New York (New York)	E	212
Norfolk (Virginia)	E	804
Oklahoma City (Oklahoma)	C	405
Philadelphia (Pennsylvania)	E	215
Pittsburgh (Pennsylvania)	E	412
Portland (Oregon)	P	503
Richmond (Virginia)	E	804
Sacramento (California)	P	916
Salt Lake City (Utah)	M	801
St Louis (Missouri)	C	314
San Antonio (Texas)	C	512
San Diego (California)	P	619
San Francisco (California)	P	415
Seattle (Washington)	P	206
Tampa (Florida)	E	813
Toledo (Ohio)	E	419
Tulsa (Oklahoma)	C	918
Washington DC	E	202

Alaska is 5 hours behind Eastern time.
Hawaii is 5 hours behind Eastern time.

International dialing codes

The time differences given are in relation to Eastern time, + indicating the number of hours later and – the number of hours earlier. All country codes are prefixed by 011.

Area	Country code	Time difference
Argentina	54	(+2)
Australia	61	(+13 ~ −15)
Austria	43	(+6)
Bahamas	1 809	(no difference)
Belgium	32	(+6)
Bermuda	1 809 29	(+1)
Brazil	55	(+0 ~ −2)
Britain	44	(+5)
Canada	1	(zones correspond roughly to US)
Colombia	57	(no difference)
Costa Rica	506	(−1)
Denmark	45	(+6)
Egypt	20	(+7)
Eire	353	(+5)
Finland	358	(+7)
France	33	(+6)
Germany (West)	49	(+6)
Greece	30	(+7)
Guatemala	502	(−1)
Hong Kong	852	(+13)
Hungary	36	(+6)
Iceland	354	(+5)
India	91	(+10½)
Indonesia	62	(+12 ~ −14)
Israel	972	(+7)
Italy	39	(+6)
Jamaica	1 809	(no difference)
Japan	81	(+14)
Korea (South)	82	(+14)
Luxembourg	352	(+6)
Mexico	52	(−1)
Netherlands	31	(+6)
New Zealand	64	(+17)
Norway	47	(+6)
Pakistan	92	(+10)
Panama	507	(no difference)
Peru	51	(no difference)
Philippines	63	(+13)
Portugal	351	(+5)
Saudi Arabia	966	(+8)
Singapore	65	(+13)
Spain	34	(+6)
Sweden	46	(+6)
Switzerland	41	(+6)
Taiwan	886	(+13)
Turkey	90	(+8)
USSR	7	(+8 ~ −16)
Venezuela	58	(+1)

Conversion charts

The metric system is not regularly used in the USA, although it is gradually gaining acceptance; the scientific disciplines, for example, use it exclusively. Increasingly, temperatures are given in Celsius (C – also known as Centigrade) in addition to the more commonly used Fahrenheit (F). Shoe and clothing sizes differ from those used in the UK and Continental Europe. Length is denoted in feet and inches (12 inches = 1 foot; 3 feet = 1 yard = 0.91 meter).

Temperature

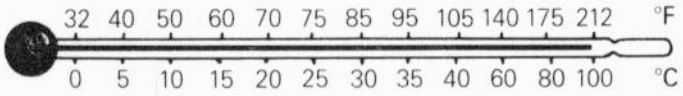

Mass (weight)

kilograms (kg)	kg or lb	pounds (lb)
0.454	=lb **1** kg=	2.205
0.907	**2**	4.409
1.361	**3**	6.614
1.814	**4**	8.819
2.268	**5**	11.023
2.722	**6**	13.228
3.175	**7**	15.432
3.629	**8**	17.637
4.082	**9**	19.842
4.536	**10**	22.046
9.072	**20**	44.092
13.608	**30**	66.139
18.144	**40**	88.185
22.680	**50**	110.231

Length

centimeters (cm)	cm or in	inches (in)
2.54	=in **1** cm=	0.394
5.08	**2**	0.787
7.62	**3**	1.181
10.16	**4**	1.575
12.70	**5**	1.969
15.24	**6**	2.362
17.70	**7**	2.756
20.32	**8**	3.150
22.86	**9**	3.543
25.40	**10**	3.937
50.80	**20**	7.874
76.20	**30**	11.811
101.60	**40**	15.748
127.00	**50**	19.685

Volume

liters (l)	liters or US gallons	US *gallons
3.79	=l **1** gall=	0.26
7.58	**2**	0.52
11.37	**3**	0.78
15.16	**4**	1.04
18.95	**5**	1.30
22.74	**6**	1.56
26.53	**7**	1.82
30.32	**8**	2.08
34.11	**9**	2.34
37.90	**10**	2.60
75.80	**20**	5.20
113.70	**30**	7.80
151.60	**40**	10.40
189.50	**50**	13.00

Distance

kilometers (km)	km or miles	miles
1.609	=mi **1** km=	0.621
3.219	**2**	1.243
4.828	**3**	1.864
6.437	**4**	2.485
8.047	**5**	3.107
9.656	**6**	3.728
11.265	**7**	4.350
12.875	**8**	4.971
14.484	**9**	5.592
16.093	**10**	6.214
32.187	**20**	12.427
48.280	**30**	18.641
64.374	**40**	24.855
80.467	**50**	31.069

* 1 US gallon = 0.83 UK/Imperial gallon
6 US gallons = 5 UK/Imperial gallons

Index

accelerated cost recovery system (ACRS) 62
accidents, car 370
accountancy 75–6; management methods 87
accountants, choosing 75–6
accounting practices 58
acquisitions 59–60
administration, government 41
advertising 79
aerospace industry 30–1, 192, 300, 313
affirmative action 6
AFL-CIO 46, 66
agencies; independent business 52; state 53
agriculture 10–11, 186, 208; biotechnology for 27
aid, foreign 51
AIDS 96
air conditioning, gas 35
Air Express International 55
air travel, internal 369
airports, gateway 369
Akers, John 32, 33
Alaska, climate 367
American Arbitration Association 78
American Bankers Association (ABA) 6, 46, 63
American Bar Association 46
American Export Register 63
American Express 68
American Federation of Labor and Congress of Industrial organizations 46, 66
American Institute of Certified Public Accountants (AICPA) 75–6
American Lawyer Guide to Leading Law Firms, The 77
American Management Consulting Association 63
American Manufacturers' Association 63
American Medical Association 46
American Motors 169
American Stock Exchange (Amex) 73
Amoco 23
Amtrak 19, 53, 370
anti-avoidance of tax measures 62
Anti-Ballistic Missile: ABM system; treaty with USSR (1972) 48
anti-trust legislation 60
anti-dumping duties 80
Antitrust Division of the Department of Justice 53, 63
ANZUS 50
Apple Computer 33
arbitrage 6; arbitrageurs 54
arbitration 78
armed forces 48–9; intelligence units 49
arms control 48
Arnold & Porter 78
arrest, in case of 375
Arthur Andersen 63, 75, 76
Arthur Young & Company 75, 76
Asians 13
AT&T (American Telephone and Telegraph) 22, 34, 162
Atlanta 102–9
attitudes 95–7; to business 82–4
auto industry 169
automation of financial services 68
B'nai B'rith 50
Baker, James 15
Baker & McKenzie 78
Baltimore 359–65
Bank of America 70, 192
Bankers Trust 70
banking 192, 214
banks 69–71; assets 70; opening hours 369
Barron's 91
bars 374
beliefs 95–7
Bell research laboratories 22
Bells, Baby 34
BellSouth 23
Bill of Rights 40
biotechnology 23, 27
birth rate 12
blacks: civil rights 95–6; discrimination 42, 65
Blue Cross health insurance plan 27
Blue Shield health insurance plan 27
board 84–5; presentations to 88
Boardroom Reports 91
Boeing 15, 30, 337
Boesky, Ivan 54
book publishing 39
Boston 110–21
Boston Consulting Group 63
Branch Level Tax 62
breakdown, car 370
Bretton Woods Conference (1944) 6, 17
bribery 90
budget, federal 17, 19
Bureau of the Census 62–3
Bureau of Competition of the Federal Trade Commission 63
bureaucracy 41; power of 45
Burger, Warren 44, 76, 77
bus travel 371
business 52–81; awareness 82–91; framework 56–63; method 87–90
business and government 52–3
business, power in 54–5
business, women in 86–7
Business Week 91
businesses, small 59
Cabinet 41
cable television 39, 79
Canada, trade 14, 15
capital, dependence on foreign 17
capital gains tax 67
car: rental 370; travel by 370
Carnegie, Andrew 21
Carter, President 17, 41, 45, 48
Catholicism, Roman 95
Central Intelligence Agency (CIA) 6, 49
CF Air Freight 55
chairman, of board 84
Chamber of Commerce of the United States 63, 368
chemicals industry 25
Chicago 72, 122–40
Chicago Mercantile Exchange 73
chief executive officers (CEOs) 6, 54, 84–5
chief operating officer (COO) 85
China 51; telephone service 23
Christian Science Monitor 38
Chrysler 21, 28, 29, 169
cinema industry 39
Citibank 70
Citizens for Tax Justice 62
civil rights 42; of blacks 95–6
civil service 41, 44, 45
Civil War 93, 102
class, social 95
Cleveland 141–8
Cleveland clinic 141
clientelism 46
climate 366
closed shops 67
coal 11
college 98
colonists, early 92
Columbus, Christopher 92
commercial banks 68, 69–70
commercial finance firms 71–2
commercial lawyers 77
commercial paper 72
commissions 90
committees, congressional 42, 45

commodities, trade 16; markets 73
communications 375–7
communism, threat of 50–1, 94
companies, top ten, listed 22–3
Compaq 33
competition for industry 20
computer industry 32–3; exports 16
computers, personal (PCs) 22, 32–3; home 83
conglomerates 56
Congress 41–2, 43; power 18, 44
Congressional Budget Office 45
connections, business 55
Constitution (1787) 40, 92, 278; 1920 amendments 93; power under the 43
consumer finance companies 72
consumerism 98
contact, business, making 90
Continental Illinois 69
controlled foreign corporation (CFC) 62
Coopers & Lybrand 76
Corallo, Anthony 55
Cornwallis, General 92
corporate bonds 72
corporation laws, local and state 56–8
corporations 56–8; hierarchies 84–5; power 54; taxes on 61
correspondent banking 69
Council of State Chambers of Commerce 368
Covington & Burling 78
CPAs (certified public accountants) 75
Cravath, Swaine & Moore 78
credit, consumer and financial conglomerates 68
credit cards 368
crime 375; investigation 49; organized 55
crops production, principal (1983) 10
Cuba, illegal immigrants from 13
Customs regulations 366
Dallas 149–57
Declaration of Independence 278
debt, overseas 8
debt markets 72
DEC 54
defense expenditure 8, 19, 48
defense industry 30–1, 46
Defense Intelligence Agency (DIA) 6, 49
deficit, federal 18
deficit, trade 9, 14–15, 20
Deloitte, Haskins & Sells 75, 76
Democrats 18, 40, 47
dental treatment 376
Denver 162–8
deregulation 68
Detroit 169–76
Digital Equipment Corporation (DEC) 32
direct mail advertising 79
Directory of American Firms Operating in Foreign Countries 63
discount stores 36
discrimination: negative 65; positive 42
distribution 81
diversification 21
dividends, tax on 62
doctors 376; charges 376
documentation 366
dollar 17; depreciation 15
dressing for business 90
Drexel 54
drinking 99, 374
driver's license 366; regulations 370
drugs, generic 26–7
DuPont (E.I. du Pont de Nemours) 22–3, 24, 25
Dulles, John Foster 78
Dun and Bradstreet International 63
economic scene 10–11, 18; hegemony 20; relationships 51
Economist 91
EDS 54
education 97–8; expenditure 19
Egypt 51
elderly, discrimination against 66
elections, presidential 40–1
electoral processes 40–1, 42
electricity industry 35
Electronic Data Systems 22
embassies, listed 375–6
emergency treatment 376
employment 64–7; contracts 64–5
energy 11; industries 35
entertainment industry 38–9, 192
entry details 366
environmental lobby, in chemical industry 25
equal opportunities 65–6
equipment leasing 72
equity markets 72
Ernst & Whinney 76
espionage, industrial 88
European Economic Community (EEC) 6, 15; Common Agricultural Policy 80
executive, the 40–1, 44; departments of 41
executive committee 85
Executive Office 41
executive search firms 87
executives: power 84–5; relative insecurity 82; salaries 67, 87
expenditure cuts 19
export enhancement program (EEP) 6, 80
exporting 80
exports key 15–16
Exxon 21, 22, 24
factoring firms 71–2
Fair Labor Standards Act (1938) 65
family 95
farmers: crisis 10–11; lobby 46; ownership 59
fashion: American 238; European 36
fax 377
Federal Bureau of Investigation (FBI) 6, 49
Federal Communications Commission (FCC) 52
Federal Deposit Insurance Corporation (FDIC) 17, 69
Federal Emergency Management Agency (FEMA) 11
federal government 40
Federal Reserve Board 6, 43, 46, 52
Federal Reserve System (Fed) 55, 69
Federal Trade Commission (FTC) 6, 52, 60, 63
federalism 46
feminism 96
fiber optics 34
FiberLan 23
film industry 39
finance: institutions 68; markets 72–3; national 17–19
fishing 11
Florida 12–13
Food and Drug Administration, US (FDA) 26
food exports 16
food industry 37; convenience foods 37; health foods 37; processing 37
Forbes 91
Ford, Henry 169
Ford Motor Company 21, 23, 28, 29, 169, 186
foreign affairs 44
foreign banks 70
foreign corporations, tax on 62
foreign exchange 73
foreign investors 57–8

forestry 11
Fort Worth 158–61
Fortune 91
Fowler, Mark 52
futures market 73
Gallagher Reports 91
gas, natural 11
gas utilities 35
Geneen, Harold 56
General Agreement on Tariffs and Trade (GATT) 6, 15, 51, 80
General Electric 22
General Motors 21, 22, 28, 29, 169, 186, 360
General Tire 21
gifts 90
Gillette 54
Goldman Sachs 71
government 40–2; and business 52–3; intervention 20
government agency securities 72
government securities 72
government services, growth of 43
grain, trade 80
Gramm-Rudman-Hollings budget plan 19
Gramm-Rudman targets 6
Gray, Harry 56
Grenada, invasion of (1983) 49
gross national product (GNP) 18, 20
Group of Five 15
Harvard Business School 86
Hawaii, climate 367
headhunting 87
health: care 376; requirements 366
helicopters 31
Helms, Senator Jesse 47
high technology 21; licenses for export 80
Hispanics 6, 13, 96; discrimination against 66
history 92–4; chronology 94
holidays: Jewish 368; official 368; *see also* vacations
homosexuals 96–7, 319
Honeywell 222
hospitality: business 89; returning 90
hotels 371–3; groups listed 372
House of Representatives 41–2
Houston 177–85
Hughes Aircraft 22, 28; Helicopter 31
IBM (International Business Machines) 22, 32; clones 32–3
illness 376
immigration 13; illegal 13
Immigration, airport 366
Immigration Act (1965) 13
importing 80
imports: key 16; prohibited 366
Inc 91
income, personal 64
income taxes: federal corporate 61; state 61
incorporation 56–7
Independence, Declaration of 92
Indians, American 96
industry and investment 20–1
inflation 8
informality 84, 90, 99
information: business 62–3; sources 367
Institutional Investor 91
insurance companies 68, 73, 74; life 74; medical 27; property 74
intelligence services 49
interest, tax on 62
interest rates 9, 68
Internal Revenue Code (1954) 61
Internal Revenue Service (IRS) 61, 76
international alignments 50–1
Interstate Commerce Commission (ICC) 52
investment 20–1, 54, 55, 73
investment banks 54, 67, 71
Investment Tax Credit 62
invitations 89–90
Iran, arms deal (1986) 9, 45, 49, 50, 51
Israel 50–1, 80
ITT 56
Jamestown 92
Japanese banks 70
Japanese competition 23; motor industry 28, 29
Japanese investment in USA 17
Japanese trade 14, 16; semiconductors 80
Jefferson, Thomas 93
JIT ("just-in-time") parts delivery 28, 81
jobs lost and created 64
Jobs, Steven 32, 33
Johns Hopkins Medical Center 359
Joint Chiefs of Staff (JCS) 49
joint ventures, international 60
journals, business 91
judiciary 42
junk bonds 6, 54–5
Justice Department, Anti-trust Division 53, 63
Kansas City 186–91
Kaufman, Henry 17
Kenyon and Eckhardt 79
King, Martin Luther 102
Kiplinger letters 91
Kissinger, Henry 44
KMG Peat Marwick 75, 76
Korean War 94
labor: force 64; laws 64–6;organizations 46; relations 66–7
Lambert, Burnham 54
Latin America 50; refugees from 13
law 77–8; enforcement agencies, federal 49; firms 77–8
Lawrence Livermore National Laboratory 31
lawyers, training 77
lead 11
legislation, "pork-barrel" 53
legislature 40, 42
leisure 99
letter of engagement, accountant's 76
letter writing 90
Libya 51; bombing raid on (1986) 49
lifestyles 95–7
litigation 77–8; in accountancy 76
living, standard of 8, 20, 36, 98–9
lobbying 45, 343
Lockheed 31
Los Angeles 12, 192–207
Los Angeles Times 38, 91
Lotus: Signal 33
McCann-Erickson Worldwide 79
McDonnell Douglas 16, 30–1
Macintosh computer 33
McKinsey & Company Inc 63, 75
macroeconomic indicators 17
Mafia 55
magazines 38; business 91
mail 377
management: fashions 86; short-sighted 21
management consultancies 63
Manhattan 84
Manhattan Inc 91
manufacturing industries 12, 20; employment in 64; exports 14, 15
Martindale Hubbell Law Directory 56, 77
meals, business 89–90
media 38–9; business 91
medical attention 376
meetings, business 88–9
Memphis 208–13
mergers 56, 59

Merrill Lynch 71
Mexican-Americans 96
Miami 214–21
Middle East 50–1
Midwest 12, 97; climate 367
Midwest Stock Exchange 73
military spending 30
Milken, Michael 54
minerals 11
Minneapolis 222–9
minorities 96
Mississippi River 208, 222, 230, 300
"Mob" *see* Mafia
mobility 95
money, coping with 368–9
money center banks 70
money managers 55
money market fund 71
monoclonal products 27
Montgomery, McCracken, Walker & Rhodes 78
Morgan, Lewis & Bockius 78
Morgan Guaranty 70
Motor Carrier Act (1980) 81
motor industry 28–9; immigrant plants 29
Murdoch, Rupert 58
mutual funds 71
Nader, Ralph 46
NASA (National Aeronautics and Space Administration) 31, 177
NASDAQ (National Association of Securities Dealers Automated Quotation) 73
National Association of Manufacturers 46
National Crime Information Center 49
National Labor Relations Board (NLRB) 52, 65, 67
National Law Journal Directory of the Legal Profession, The 77
National Security Council (NSC) 6, 41, 44, 49
Natural Gas Policy Act (1978) 35
Navy, the 31
NBC 22
New Deal 46, 47, 93
New Orleans 230–7
New York 72, 238–77; business practices 84
New York Futures Exchange 73
New York Stock Exchange (NYSE) 73, 238
New York Times 38, 91
newspapers 38; business 91; national 38
Nicaragua 45, 49, 50, 51
Nightly Business Report 91
Nixon, President 41, 42, 44
North Atlantic Treaty Organization (NATO) 6, 50
Northeast 12, 97; climate 366–7
nuclear deterrent 48
nuclear power industry 35
O'Connor, Sandra Day 44
Office of Management and Budget 18, 41
oil industry 24–5
oil reserves 11
Olsen, Ken 54
Orange County 97
Organization of American States (OAS) 6, 50
Organization for Economic Co-operation and Development (OECD) 6, 51
Pacific Stock Exchange 73
partnerships 59
party politics 47
Paul, Weiss, Rifkind, Wharton & Garrison 78
"Peace Shield" 31
pension funds 73
Pentagon 45
Perelman, Ron 54
Perot, H Ross 54
pharmaceuticals 26–7
pharmacists 376
Philadelphia 278–87
Philadelphia Stock Exchange 73
Philippines 51
Phoenix 288–93
Pickens, T Boone 24
picketing, right of 66
Pittsburgh 294–99
police: dealing with the 99, 375; state and local 49
Political Action Committees 47
political appointments 44
politics 40–51; party 47
pollution 25
population: aging 12; black 13; shifting 12–13
pornography 96
"post-industrial society" 21
poverty level, federal 64, 65
power: breakfast 238; in business 54–5; ladder of 84–5; reins of 43–5
president, company 85
President, the 40–1; power of 43–4
President's men 44
pressure groups 46
Price Waterhouse 75, 76
privatization 53
productivity 21
profits, short-term 59
prohibition 93
proprietorships 59
protectionism 14–15
Protestantism 95
Prudential Insurance 55
public, going 58
public relations 79
public sector 53
public services, contracting out 53
publishing industry 38–9
quotas, import 15, 80
racial discrimination 13, 95–6; positive 42, 96
radio 91
raiders, corporate 54
rail transport 81; travel 370
RCA 22
re-export of technology with US parts banned 80
Reagan, President Ronald 8, 44, 48, 52, 94; dollar policy 17–18; tax 19, 61
"Reaganomics" 8, 14
recession 8
Refugee Act (1980) 13
regional banks 70
regionalism 97
religion 95
Republicans 18, 40, 47
resources 21; human 12–13; natural 10–11
restaurant industries 37
restaurants 373–4
retailing 36
retirement age, mandatory 66
revolutions 51
Rio Treaty 50
road: transport 81; travel 370
Rockefeller, John D 22
Rockwell International 31
Roosevelt, Franklin D 46, 47, 93
Round Table 55
Rules Committee 45
rush-hour congestion 83
S&P Register of Corporations, Directors and Executives 63
Saatchi and Saatchi 79
safety precautions 374
St Louis 300–6
sales tax 369, 375
Salomon Brothers 71
San Antonio 307–12
San Diego 313–18
San Francisco 96, 319–33
Saudi Arabia, competition in petrochemicals 25
Savings and loans associations 70
schools 97–8
Schultz, George 44
Sculley, John 33
Sears Roebuck 23, 68
Seattle 337–42
Secretary of State 44
Securities and Exchange Commission (SEC) 6, 52, 57, 58, 63, 73

securities firms 68, 71
securities law, federal 58
securitization 68
security, national 48–9; pacts 50–1
Senate 41–2, 44
service sector: employment in 64; growth of 21
services, trade in 16
sexes, war of the 96
shareholding 58
Shearman & Sterling 78
Sherman Antitrust Act (1980) 59
shipbuilding industry 31
shopping 374–5
shops, specialty 36
Shuttle Disaster 31
Silicon Valley 87, 97, 334–6
Singer 21
skyscrapers, architecture of 122
slavery, legacy of 95–6
Small Business Administration 53
smoking 86, 99
software industry 32–3
South 97; climate 367
Southeast, climate 367
Southeast Asia Collective Defense Treaty 50
Southeast Asia Treaty Organization (SEATO) 6, 50
Southwest 97
sport 99
"stagflation" 17
Staggers rail deregulation act (1980) 81
Standard Oil of New Jersey *see* Exxon
Standard and Poors Corporation 63
Star Wars *see* Strategic Defense Initiative
state corporations 56–7
state power 46
Statistical Abstract of the United States 63
stock markets 73
stores: department 36, 374; discount 36; stores within 36
Strategic Arms Limitation Talks (SALT) I (1969–72) and II 6, 45, 48
Strategic Arms Reduction Talks (START) 6, 48
Strategic Defense Initiative (Star Wars) 6, 30, 31, 48
strikes 65, 66
subsidies for business 53
Sullivan & Cromwell 78
sunbelt states of the South 12, 53
Supreme Court 42
surveillance, internal 49
Syria 51
Taft-Hartley Act (1947) 65, 66
tariffs 15, 80
taxation 19, 61–2; personal 67; state and federal 62, 67; sales 375
technological revolution 20–1
telecommunications industry 34
telegrams 377
telephone: business by 83, 90; using the 376–7
television: advertising 79; business 91; industry 39
telex 377
tender offer, shares 58
Tennessee Valley Authority (TVA) 53
terrorism 51
Texas 12
thinking, business 86
time zones 100, 378
Thomas Register of American Manufacturers & Thomas Register Catalog File 63
Time 91
tipping 369
Today (NBC) 91
Touche Ross 75, 76
trade, international 8, 14–16, 80; partners 15, 80
Trade Adjustment Assistance 53
trade associations 63, 343
trade publications 91
trading, insider 54, 59
transport 81
travel: to USA 369; within USA 369–71
traveller's checks 368–9
Treasury Regulations 61
trucking 29
Turner, Ted 39
TWA (Trans World Airlines) 186
Union Carbide, 25
unions 20, 66–7
UNITA forces in Angola 51
unitary tax, worldwide 62
United Aircraft Company 56
United Automobile Workers (UAW) 66
United Food and Commercial Workers (UFCW) 66
United Nations Security Council 50
United Technologies (formerly United Aircraft) 56
university education 98
US and Foreign Commercial Service Office of the Department of Commerce 63
US Intelligence Board 49
US Patent and Trademark Office 63
US Postal Service 53
US Securities Exchange Act (1934) 60
US Travel and Tourism Administration (USTTA) 6, 368
USA Today 38
USSR, cold war with 94
USX (US Steel) 21
utilities, public 35
vacations 83–4, 99
vaccinations 366
VAX minicomputer 32
Venture 91
venture capital firms 71
vice presidents 85
video industry 39
Vietnam War 94
Vietnamese refugees 13
Vinson & Elkins 78
vintages 373
visas 366
Volcker, Paul 55
VUSA fares 369
Wachtell, Lipton, Rosen & Katz 78
wage, minimum 65
Wagner Act (1930s) 65
Wall Street 238; collapse (1929) 93
Wall Street Journal 38, 91
Wall Street Week 91
War Powers Act (1973) 49
Ward's Directory of the 55,000 Largest US Corporations 63
Washington DC 343–58
Washington Post 38, 91
WASPS 6
Watchdog Committee 45
Watergate scandal 42, 43
Waxman, Henry A 26
wealth motive 82
weapons: biological 27; nuclear 48
Weinberger, Caspar 19
welfare expenditure 19
West 97; climate 367
"whistle-blowers" 86
wholesale distribution 81
Williams & Connolly 78
withholding tax 61, 62
women: in business 85–6; discrimination against 65–6; rights movement 96
work ethic 83
work and leisure 99
worker involvement 88
working discipline 82–3
working hours 82–3
World War II 94
Worsham, James 30–1
Wozniak, Stephen 32